CW00449890

Praise for *oh baby . . . bii* *motherhood uncensored*

'Fray . . . writes so energetically you can almost hear her . . .
This book is alive'
— *The Press*

'A highly successful, no-holds-barred book on motherhood . . .
The readable and funny, fact-filled result is a remarkable
achievement'
— *North & South*

'The use of everyday language is a relief . . . Her book deals
in an open and honest way with numerous subjects often neglected
in other parenting books'
— *New Idea*

'*Oh Baby* reads like a long, loving chat with a wise aunty . . .
insightful, blunt, compassionate, self-deprecating, affectionate,
funny'
— *New Zealand College of Midwives*

'A force to be reckoned with, Kathy Fray provides a refreshing
and commonsensical approach to modern-day motherhood'
— *Littlies*

'A candid account of what it means to be a mother and doesn't
shrink from telling it like it is . . . a clear-eyed insider's view into
the world of mothering'
— *Air New Zealand magazine*

'Clearly, you are a woman of heart and there are a lot of women
out there who will be blessed to come across you, and your book'
— *Susan Johnson, author*

Fray, Kathy, 1965-
Oh baby . . .: birth, babies and motherhood uncensored / Kathy Fray.
Includes bibliographical references and index.
ISBN 978-1-86941-713-0
1. Childbirth. 2. Motherhood. 3. Babies. 1. Title.
618.2-dc 22

A RANDOM HOUSE BOOK
published by
Random House New Zealand
18 Poland Road, Glenfield, Auckland, New Zealand
www.randomhouse.co.nz

First published 2005. Reprinted 2007 (twice)

ISBN 978 1 86941 713 0

Cover and text design: Sarah Elworthy
Front cover photograph: Gloria-Leigh Logan, Acclaim Images
Author photograph: Christina Hollins, Studio 26
Printed in Australia by Griffin Press

oh baby...

birth, babies & motherhood
uncensored

Kathy Fray

RANDOM HOUSE
NEW ZEALAND

Dedication

Dedicated to all the glorious babies of the world, especially mine.
Dedicated to all the loving husbands of the world, especially mine.
Dedicated to all the selfless mums of the world, especially mine.
Dedicated to all the devoted midwives, obstetricians and
*   paediatricians of the world, especially mine.*
Dedicated to all the supportive girlfriends of the world, especially mine.

I am so blessed!

CONTENTS

Introduction

In any gathering of women there is a camaraderie that exists among those
who have experienced childbirth. It's like a secret handshake or an ultraviolet
mark that only they know distinguishes them as veterans of the same war . . .
A pregnant woman such as yourself is a probationary member of this sorority
. . . And after this forty-week (more or less) probationary period will come
the magic time when you will become a charter member, when you will have
passed the ultimate hazing ritual: DELIVERY.
. . . This sorority of women is full of all sorts of self-congratulation, because
only another mother knows what each of us has gone through to qualify for
membership. Like veterans of war, we show our battle scars like medals:
Caesarean sections, stretch marks, our inability to sneeze without wetting our
pants . . . Secretly we know, we are Earth's real heroes.

Vicki Iovine — *The Girlfriends' Guide To Pregnancy*

Childbirth, babies, motherhood and parenting have become some of the
most frustratingly confusing and hotly contended subjects for us westernised
adults to deal with. In our parents' days it was so much simpler. There were
fewer theories, so policies were more straightforward. But today our lives
exist with the 'smorgasbord buffet' or 'supermarket' syndrome of data
asphyxiation. We have a staggering amount of options to choose from . . .
and so *many* decisions that will need to be made. Nearly every theory will
conflict somewhat with another, or two practices directly oppose each other
— both, of course, always able to prove their case with indisputable evidence!
Aarrrgggghhhh!

As for the physical process of giving birth! Surely for a first-time mother-
to-be it is an enigma how so many contrasting opinions could have been
formed surrounding an event that has already occurred billions of times over.
How on earth is a new mum-to-be expected to know if she is making the
correct 'informed consent' decisions? (Don't you hate that term? Well if you
don't yet, you probably will eventually.)

I liken the child-birthing experience to a complicated labyrinth. Now you know that this maze has a start, you also know it definitely has an end . . . you do know you will eventually be arriving at that exit door of giving birth to your baby. But how fast or slow the journey will be, how easy or difficult it will be, how empowering or demoralising it will feel, and how much assistance you will need along the way . . . The answers are all shrouded in Mystery's cloak — you won't ever know until afterwards. Bugger!

What you can do . . . should do . . . must do . . . is *cheat* by having a really good aerial look over the labyrinth before you start. And that is what the first chapters of this book are committed to . . . helping you through the maze (*'hazing' did you say?*) of giving birth. You *must* understand physiologically the birthing process your body will go through. Knowledge is empowering — ask any second-time mum.

You will also learn soon that a frequent piece of professional advice you will receive is 'Go with your own instinct'. So, in this 'New Age' — when intuition is still only sceptically viewed as the sixth sense — it is ironic that intuition can be given the ultimate responsibility to successfully mother! What if your gut feelings are telling you that you are really unsure you're making the right decisions? That's *tough* to cope with — particularly when you know you are dealing with a little baby's wellbeing.

Who knows if the decisions we make will be right or wrong? All we can really hope for, is that most of what we do is right.

So, why on earth would mothers need yet another book on birth and motherhood? Because this book is NOT written by a midwife, obstetrician, gynaecologist, paediatrician, infancy nurse, child psychologist or any other baby or birth-management scholar. It is written by a *mum*, with ideas from many of her friends who are *mums*, in a language *mums* understand, all from the *mums'* perspective, with loads of tips, insights, stories and recommendations just for *mums*, all strictly out of the trenches of real life experiences. This book is also no official encyclopaedic textbook on birth and babies (*though in my biased opinion it does a great impersonation of one*) — instead it has been written to be like a friend to you.

I am simply a mother — just with a few more births behind me and a few more years experience at mothering. And I am also a mother blessed with a wide circle of wonderful friends who are also all amazing mothers, from whom I've learnt so much. Now, I'm thrilled to pass on to you our collective experience — so you can have the very best mothering times possible. It's time now to pass on some of that lost mother-to-mother wise-woman wisdom.

So for you heavily pregnant first-time mum-to-be, grab yourself a full-cream Grande Macchiato (decaffeinated, of course) with extra foam and chocolate sprinkles, sit in a sinkingly comfortable chair, put your feet up, relax and ENJOY!

Your darling baby is soon to make its dramatic entrance into this confusing world . . . to be lovingly nurtured by you, the baby's feeling-rather-confused mother, and guided with fortitude by his probably even-more-confused father. What a mammoth responsibility we take on! Highs so high you *are* touching Heaven, and lows so low that you *know* you've been in Hell.

Hoist up your Grandma undies, securely fasten your maternity bra, place your breast pads in the upright position, buckle-up those hospital bags, and let the journey begin . . .

But hold on . . . it's disconcerting that no one seems to acknowledge all the weird, bizarre, absurd, disgusting or hilarious things that happen while you're pregnant — instead you are calmly reassured that it's all perfectly normal. It's like there's some unofficial conspiracy or code of silence to let you know only what you need to know at that moment.

Oh heck, so let's first *reflect*, by taking a few indulgent minutes, which you so deserve, and pay great homage to those noble and memorable moments of pregnancy bliss, which are now almost all behind you — YOU'VE DONE SO, SO WELL!

From the moment of her conception my daughter became a magnet for prescription, embroiled in debate: about alcohol units, smoke-free zones and breast versus bottle, about future dairy and gluten allergies, room temperature and sleeping position, about immunisation schedules and vitamins.

Even from before conception, in fact, when I was urged to purge and scrub my body for her future sake, to convert it from inferred hell-hole to temple.

Rachel Cusk — A Life's Work

Remember back to your shocked 'I can't believe I'm pregnant' first trimester? You haven't forgotten the delight already? There was the head-in-the-toilet-bowl 'morning' sickness nausea, caused by your body adjusting to the increased levels of progesterone and oestrogens, which you learnt is not gone by lunchtime and leaves you feeling thoroughly wretched all day; there were those stretched blouse buttons covering up tender and painful busty breasts that became your partner's favourite new toys (*ow*); the constant peeing interruptions to your precious last months of babyless slumber; a new all-time record level of total exhaustion (thanks to the sedative effects of your high progesterone levels). Oh, and we can't forget the nauseous smells; the weird metallic taste in your mouth; and, of course, the insane feeling of losing your mind (well at least some vague control of your now erratically unpredictable emotions).

You have several months of sacrificing the mouth-watering tastes of many of your most favourite delicacies, only to have them replaced with cravings for exotically bizarre culinary combinations. Then you start booking emergency visits to the dentist for temporary fillings (and to double-check those spongy bleeding gums, oh, gingivitis). Then there's the contact-lenses that no longer fit (as pregnancy can change cornea shape); the sinusitis nasal congestion stuffiness and nose-bleeds; constant backache and leg cramps; and rapidly growing but brittle fingernails. But even more intensely weird are the frighteningly vivid dreams, or the insomnia.

Then, the crowning glory of them all . . . pre-eclampsia toxaemia (high blood pressure, and protein in your urine from your kidneys stressing with their filtration rate increase). This is when you are promoted in your pregnancy to the water-retention, 'upholstered body', oedema stage and you are alarmed to find your swollen fingers beginning to grow over your rings, and the top of your puffy feet and swollen ankles spill out over the tops of your shoes like messy cappuccinos (oh, and yes your nose is looking bigger), and maybe you didn't realise, but your vulva is swelling too.

Once the pelvic ligaments soften and relax, you may be perturbed to have a physiotherapist measuring your great mass to issue you with a belly-belt (elasticised maternity corset) to support your pelvic bones. Then in the last weeks with the increasing bulkiness of your abdomen, your centre of gravity totally changes so that with a jumping-bean inside your abdomen and added backache, walking becomes dangerously precarious — especially disembarking escalators when you can no longer see your own feet.

As for your flushed *skin* . . . there's stretch marks, maybe red lines under your belly and blue tracks over your thighs and hips (the massage lotion didn't work for me either), facial pigment changes, darkening freckles and moles, darkened body and facial hair, little red naevi spider-veins appearing on your cheeks, red clammy hands, chafing thighs, and legs with varicose veins from the uterus pressing on blood vessels and impairing blood-flow. There's the half a metre of extra itchy, drive-you-nuts stretching abdomen skin, popped-turkey-timer stick-out belly-button, and hair in places you didn't know it would now permanently grow.

Then your abdomen develops a bizarre vertical line (maybe even hairy) that resembles a road from your pubes to your belly-button. This is called the linea nigra which marks the separation of your recti-abdominal muscles. And did you know your nipples are even starting to grow bifidus lactobacilli (friendly bacteria to later colonise inside your baby's intestines) . . . these are just some of the ravishing things that could happen to you.

You are probably utterly fed up with your limited maternity wardrobe and are longing to wear your jeans again (don't hold your hopes up for that eventuating in under three months). As for your face . . . yes, my pre-existingly round face managed to get even rounder — oh and my neck always disappears.

However we can't forget the interesting internal plumbing issues too, like the squashed-flat bladder with its resulting increased urgent, frequent peeing; the shortness of breath and dyspnoea (laboured difficult breathing); and the wicked indigestion heartburn acid-reflux from the crowded stomach, displaced oesophagus and relaxed sphincter muscle. The high levels of oestrogen are putting more pressure on your gall bladder, but the extra progesterone (responsible for preventing labour during pregnancy) slows down all smooth-muscle movement, leaving residue cholesterol crystals, which are the foundations of gallstones (*oh goody*).

But probably no one warned you in advance, about the sore, aching, stretched ribcage from your abdominal organs pressing against your diaphragm causing your thorax to widen as your ribs flare (or even the occasional fractured rib from a little kicking foot); the aching armpits or shoulders; carpal tunnel syndrome (tingling pins and needles in your hot hands); the dizzy vertigo; the increased burping and farting; the stronger vaginal 'odour', and increased thrush (because of your now sweet glucose-rich vagina). There's the unrecognisable poos (or worse, constipation resulting from the declining peristalsis of the digestive tract), and horror upon horror . . . *haemorrhoids*. I am SO sorry for you if you have endured those indignant anal protrusions, delicately called hanging vines. Equally horrifying, if you earn your piles (or even vulval-vaginal varicose veins) as a memento of delivery — it's OK to scream.

Have you noticed yet that you're also never the perfect pregnancy-sized heffalump? When people ask how pregnant you are (as they touch your belly, which is public property — don't you know?), their reply is always along the lines of either 'Gosh, you're quite compact' or 'Gee, you're quite big'. But no one ever says 'Wow, you're just the perfect size'.

Then 'they' yearn to pass on all their graphic experiences from the war-zones of the delivery suites, combined with copious passionate advice. *Ear-plugs please!*

And all the while, even with abstaining from your usual 'medicinally therapeutic' alcoholic drinks, you've managed to get through nearly the whole ordeal, without the experience curdling the scary but amazing reality

— *that a little tiny human being is growing inside you.* This surely in itself is such a mammoth fact that it should necessitate free weekly visits to a psychiatrist's couch.

Still, raising a bellyful of baby is not *all* bad physically. Far from it. Firstly there's the magical 'mirror look' — you know, silently standing sideways feeling like a Greek Goddess as you admiringly stroke your enormous abdomen . . . There are those daily miraculous and eerie sensations of feeling your baby moving around (even when you're getting the stabbing pains of being kicked in your already bruised ribcage); or feeling your baby hiccupping (in your rectum, I know it's weird) . . . There are your voluptuous (though veiny) blouse-puppets with their enlarged and sexy aubergine-brown darkened areola nipples (and enlarged nodule bumps, all a sign that your breast-tissue milk-sacs are getting ready to produce milk for lactation). These new boobies are something to treasure (you already know they won't look like that forever, but enjoy them while they're such a flattering feature) . . . There's the rapidly growing thick and lustrous shining hair (everywhere) . . . There's the supple glowing clear skin . . . There's the relief of having guilt-free permission to cut out those gruelling gym exercise routines . . . There's the almost socially acceptable joy of ravenously devouring your dinner because pregnancy is the only time in your life you're allowed to look 'fat'.

Thanks to all those extra hormones sex feels more orgasmically erotic than ever before — and during pregnancy, chocolate becomes the recreational drug of choice as its taste turns into something euphoric.

If you're like most of us, during the last months of your pregnancy, you probably make sympathy-seeking comments like:

'I can't breathe, my lungs can't expand.'

'I can't eat any more, I swear my stomach has been pushed up my throat.'

'I can't walk any further, my back aches too much.'

'You have to paint my toenails for me, I can't see them.'

'My feet throb.'

'You need to tie up my boot-laces, I can't reach.'

'The stabbing pains in my sciatic nerve are excruciating!'

'I need antacid intravenously so I can get to sleep!'

'I need a urine catheter so I can sleep for more than 45 minutes in a row!'

'Five pillows are not comfortable enough anymore — I need your pillow as well.'

CONGRATULATIONS, as in this last semester you are completing your Bachelor in Pregnancy Insanity. Now whether enrolled or not, this semester you will be receiving your Masters in Postpartum Dementia. This, writes

Vickie Iovine, is when your partner is thinking, 'Who are you, and what have you done with my wife? . . . But of course, crazy people don't know they're crazy.'

Just as few people tell you all those pregnancy truths, it is the same scenario with childbirth and the first year of motherhood. Friends may say afterwards: 'We didn't dare tell you everything — it would have completely put you off and freaked you out!'

But I don't really believe that, because the more bewildering and perplexing your mothering experiences are, the more it takes away from your mothering enjoyment and satisfaction.

Enlightenment is omnipotent (all-powerful), foresight protects your strength, and insight renews your energy.

So it would be my honour to help you even a little, by passing on to you some of the most valuable women's wisdom I have come across — while hopefully giving you a few giggles at the same time.

You are such an amazing lady as you are about to be, a Mother, and there is NO other job more important on the planet! To quote C.S. Lewis: 'Homemaker is the ultimate career. All other careers exist for one purpose only — to support the ultimate career!'

LOVE and LIGHT
Kathy Fray
xxx

It takes all of nine months for a mother to adapt to the unfolding role of motherhood — you need that time to be able to swallow the enormity of it all.
> Dr William Ferguson, my GP-obstetrician

Points to note

- Some experts may disagree with some of the viewpoints contained in this book; however, all medical information has been critiqued by leading medical professionals — thanks team!
- 'LMC' means the mother-to-be's assigned lead maternity carer (midwife or obstetrician).
- For ease of writing, I often refer to the 'mum', but some information could apply to whoever the principal care giver is.
- For ease of writing, I often refer to the baby as being a boy or a girl, but information applies to both sexes.

- There are a number of traumatic subjects I am specifically not going to attempt to cover in this book, including miscarriage, abortion, still-births, infantile death, premature babies, special-needs babies, SIDS cot-death and widowhood. Within each of these circumstances there are huge variables and it would be insulting to dedicate a couple of paragraphs to any of these tragedies — which require very individual and personalised levels of great wisdom, vast experience and insightful guidance.
- Other topics which could have been included but aren't are multiple-birth babies, adoption, solo-parenting, abusive relationships, blended families, same-sex parenting, grandparent involvement, surrogacy, second babies and sibling rivalry. With these subjects there are just WAY too many 'right' opinions that can be wrong, and 'wrong' opinions that could be right.

Life should NOT be a journey to the grave with the intention of arriving safely in an attractive and well-preserved body, but rather to skid in sideways, chocolate in one hand, wine in the other, body thoroughly used up, totally worn out and screaming "WOO HOO what a ride!"

Author unknown

Special note for Mummies who adopted their baby

If you are one of the unlucky-but-lucky women who have endured the hellish process of adoption, and the ecstatic joy of finally meeting your child, this book is still very much for you too. Admittedly, the information relating to the physical process of childbearing won't apply, but everything else does!

Chapter 1
Being very pregnant!

The amount of oestrogen produced in a [pregnant woman's] single day is equivalent to that generated by a non-pregnant woman's ovaries in three years. In fact, during the course of a single pregnancy, a woman will produce as much oestrogen as a non-pregnant woman could in 150 years.

Dr Miriam Stoppard — *Conception, Pregnancy and Birth*

Wow, your baby will be arriving soon. This is *such* a special time in a woman's life. But what an emotional mix of thrilling excitement, terrifying fear and worrying concerns we all normally feel.

Statistically for about half of you, this was an 'unplanned pregnancy', and that probably created some pretty high anxiety levels, especially in the first weeks, and now again in the last weeks. Then for a good number of you this pregnancy has been more than a nine-month wait, more like a three-year wait, or a four, five, or six-plus year wait for your 'miracle'. So, especially for those of you that had to endure infertility or miscarriages, this is *such* a momentous time in your life!

From Mother Nature's perspective, you are about to accomplish your primary and primal task here on Earth — to *reproduce* (thank goodness we ladies are so much more than that these days). You are about to move onwards (and upwards, and downwards, and sideways) along your life's pathway — being responsible for a helpless human being is both so scary and so elating.

Perhaps you're feeling like you've been pregnant since for ever, or that you are going to be pregnant for ever! Nearly your entire abdominal cavity is now filled with baby, and your baby is rolling around inside your swollen belly putting on a last growth spurt. Your boobies are leaking colostrum, your cervix is softening, and the ligaments and muscles of your pelvis are loosening. Your hormones are going crazy!

Your oestrogens, oestrone and oestradiol, have increased a hundredfold, your oestrogen oestriol has increased about a thousand times. Then of course there are the increases in progesterone, prolactin, oxytocin and more. You are more 'female' than you have ever been before, with a perplexing assortment of emotions . . . you are more weepy, more cranky, feeling more vulnerable, more euphoric, more clingy, more brooding, more nesting, more private, more at peace, more needy, more settled, more introspective and more maternal than your body has ever been before . . . all at the same time!

This increasing of your sensitivity physiologically can also extend to psychic sensory increases (sixth sense, ESP, intuition or instinct, whatever you wish to call it). Trees can appear more radiantly green, flowers more luminous, rainbows more magical, and wondrous things more miraculous. (If you're worried about feeling so sentimental and irrational all at the same time — don't worry, things will return to normal, eventually.)

Feeling forgetful these days? Do you think you accidentally put your short-term memory down the waste-disposal? Feeling like your brain is in a permanent fog? Finding even the most basic concepts hard to comprehend? Well, you are not losing your mind or your grip on reality. This is a very normal side effect of being heavily pregnant — and I have my own theory: it is Mother Nature's way of forcing you to *chill out* — heck all those perplexingly insane and elaborately colourful dreams, night after night, certainly don't help you to feel rested.

But the bad news is that with the arrival of a newborn there also arrives the jet-lag of 'sleep deprivation' — things are going to get worse before they get better. But that's cool! You *will* be able to join in an intellectual conversation again one day — it should be in time for your baby's first birthday. You think I'm kidding!

Preparing mum's mind

It is normal to start 'nesting' late in your pregnancy, when you may be taken over by a sudden instinctive urge to 'put things in order'. That is when without warning you can find yourself obsessively compelled to get the kitset cot put up (even though you know the baby will be in the bassinet for 3–4 months); or you go berko at your partner to finish painting the nursery wardrobe door; or some unknown powerful driving force makes you scrub the oven and tidy out every kitchen cupboard; or after eighteen months of sitting in forgotten piles, you finally just *have* to sort out the photo albums or office paper-war; or you go into a full-house spring-clean mania that has you standing on a chair balanced on the table to wipe the dining-room lampshade. If that's what you're up to now, welcome to the Nutty Nesting

Club — most of us were members.

As part of that psychological need to nest and prepare for your baby, you are likely to be thinking about various questions too. Here are some answers to a few of the most common pregnancy quandaries to help you along . . .

Have I chosen the right LMC (Lead Maternity Carer) for me?

In an ideal situation, by your last trimester, hopefully your LMC is feeling like a 'new best friend' with a great sense of solidarity existing between you — because during childbirth, perhaps more than your pain relief, often even more than your partner, the LMC will be the dominant influence. They'll become the most important person in the world to you, to help you through the ordeal of birth with explanation, reassurance and their supportive presence. And, although you may be just another birth to your LMC, you are likely to remember your LMC for the rest of your life.

My recommendation is to have chosen an LMC who another mother has told you was skilled, experienced and empathetic; who is interested in your birthing preferences; assured in their own conviction of women's prowess and empowerment to give birth; who assures you that they will be happy to help you if you choose to ask for pain relief; and who has informed you and your partner about the possible complications and interventions of childbirth. You need to be feeling that you completely trust your LMC, and that your fears and anxieties have been well addressed.

But, if you have already discovered that you're really not gelling with your LMC, or if you've realised that you plain can't stand them, then be assertive and trade them in for another model. It's not too late, and don't avoid making that move just because you're concerned you might offend them! Your feelings are *way* more important!

I am intrigued about the idea of having a home-birth — would we be safe away from the hospital setting?

Across the worldwide population, around 80 percent of babies are born at home, the great majority without choice. But in westernised countries, based on the assumption that the hospital was the safest place for every woman to give birth, hospitalisation for childbirth became almost universal by the middle of last century. Since then, belief that hospital obstetric intervention could be excessive in low-risk births has drawn political battle lines between opinions of the 'best' birth options: home or hospital, natural or medical, obstetrician or midwife? Without any doubt, there is overwhelming scientific evidence that the less anxious and stressed the mother is feeling at the time, the better are the resulting conditions of the labour, the birth, the baby, the mother, the bonding and the breastfeeding.

For some women, the hospital can seem like a chillingly frightening clinical environment — one full of rules, procedures, uniforms, white coats, stethoscopes and needles. This 'allergy' or 'phobia' towards hospitals can exasperate a woman's fear of the unknown, and add to her feelings of loneliness and uncertainty.

Subsequently, one argument for planned home-births is that they are a more natural, humanised, exhilarating yet calmly peaceful experience; where, with the security of familiar surroundings and all the privacy you require, the woman can feel more in control. There is strong evidence to back this, that birthing at home can often be an emotionally safer private celebration for women by being in a less stressful and more intimate and empowering environment.

Consistently, women say that with planned home-births they experience more satisfaction and enjoyment; with them often reporting to have particularly liked the stress-free feelings and freedom of being completely in control during labour, in their own home, and close to their family. Mothers opting for planned home-births are usually looking forward to higher convenience, better freedom of choice and lower obstetric interference. Some research also shows improved postnatal confidence and better breastfeeding rates.

Research easily demonstrates that fewer drugs are administered to women giving birth at home, primarily because fewer drugs are desired. Mothers who plan home-births tend to have a strong belief in the normalcy of childbirth, and make a conscious choice to embrace natural labour, accepting the birth process as a working process. They may or may not use hydrotherapy for pain relief, and a few will use TENS — see pages 32–34.

Generally home-birthing abolishes the opportunity for instrumental deliveries, though forcep births have been performed in homes in an emergency.

However, women birthing in hospital can be equally motivated towards natural birth, and are not automatically looking to use gas, pethidine or epidurals — but may want to be in a situation where expertise and equipment are readily available should their birth not go well; or they may feel that their domestic situation does not lend itself to giving birth at home.

Research shows that generally home-birthing is most popular with educated middle-class women in their thirties who are giving birth to their second or third child. A distinct advantage with home-birthing is the ability to create a soothing environment with dimmed lights, protected candles, aromatherapy scents, soft music and warmed blankets and towels — though a negative aspect of home-birthing can be the clean-up of childbirth mess (which is bloody).

Many mothers desiring a home-birth tend to familiarise themselves with birthing concepts such as Frederick Leboyer's book *Birth Without Violence*, which includes suggestions such as the birthing room having soft lighting and a lowered noise level; the mother's immediate skin-to-skin contact with her baby; and newborns being bathed in warm water to replicate the nurturing uterus. If you specifically desire and want to strive for your baby to receive such a gentle, reverent arrival, explain this to your LMC, because this can still be achieved in hospital births as well.

Every woman who plans a home-birth is normally realistic about safety issues, and accepts that the hospital can be a lighthouse in a storm. Generally the mother has a good awareness of what is available within the hospital, and her main concern is that any interventions are applied when circumstances clearly indicate the need, rather than enduring 'just in case' interference. If you are planning a home-birth then be aware of some perceived discouragement (the 'Gosh you're brave' comments) — it's wise to be mentally prepared for some negative responses.

Approximately 70–75 percent of first-time mothers with planned home-births, do successfully delivery at home. The other 25–30 percent end up transferring to hospital by car (or occasionally by ambulance) to give birth — about half of these cases are due to failure to progress well in labour, roughly about a third are for rapidly onsetting serious emergencies, and the rest for various other reasons, such as a desire for an epidural.

Although most home-birth mothers can accept hospital outcomes knowing they were appropriate, some research shows that mothers of planned home-births who end up delivering in hospital can sometimes experience high levels of birthing dissatisfaction, typically suffering worse postnatal tearfulness. So, it is very important if you plan a home-birth to create the conscious mindset that still permits the freedom to change your plan, (and the practical preparation of a packed bag) to avoid feeling bitter if you unexpectedly end up in hospital.

Home-birth should be an option for low-risk mothers only — that is women with no known pregnancy problems or envisioned birthing complications identified by her LMC during her antenatal care, for example pre-eclampsia, epilepsy, diabetes, cardiovascular conditions, multiple birth, breech baby or premature birth.

Although childbirth is a natural event, it is always associated with risk, and there is no disputing that emergencies still occur. In many ways, the struggle of childbirth is always cloaked in secrecy. It is impossible to guarantee any birth will be routine, but the home-birth midwife carries essential drugs, IV fluids and full resuscitation equipment should the need arise. For more information you can visit www.homebirth.org.nz, or perhaps read Maggie Banks' book *Homebirth Bound: Mending the Broken Weave*.

Statistically, a consistent eight percent of low-risk pregnancies encounter a potentially life-threatening emergency concerning the mother or baby before, during or after the labour. Emergencies can include the baby in severe distress; umbilical cord prolapse (when the cord falls into the birth canal ahead of the baby); the baby unable to breathe properly after birth (about one in twenty are very slow to start breathing); obstructed delivery such as shoulder dystocia (the baby's shoulders stuck in the birth canal after the head is delivered); mother haemorrhaging (premature separation of the placenta or excessive postnatal bleeding); and some or all of the placenta being retained (not successfully expelled). Due to birthing complications, for an estimated five percent of women, an emergency caesarean section will be a potentially life-saving operation for either themselves or their baby.

These are some of the main unforeseeable reasons why women stopped giving birth at home and started having their babies in large hospitals where, theoretically, these very real (and still common) emergencies could be dealt with quickly and effectively. In large city hospitals there are specialist obstetric, paediatric, anaesthetic and surgical experts, plus the infant intensive-care unit and the blood-bank is usually close at hand.

But, in many small hospitals and even some larger ones they may not have on-site obstetricians, paediatricians and anaesthetists. Small units have to transfer women and babies to a larger base hospital for medical specialists (about 10 percent of births), and sometimes the larger hospitals have to call their specialists in. By no means do all hospitals have blood-banks and neonatal intensive care units, which is why midwives and GP obstetricians are trained to deal with emergencies until specialist input is available.

For most women, a hospital first-birth is their preference, because being surrounded with modern and sophisticated medical apparatus acts as a strong emotional safety-net, making them feel more secure, confident and supported. And, after the birth they generally continue to feel safe in the hospital setting, enjoying help and advice (though sometimes conflicting) from the midwives and nurses.

Current New Zealand funding allows for 48-hours of hospital care after a normal birth, and five days after a caesarean. A downside of the postnatal hospital environment is that the mother can sometimes become dependent upon it (lacking in confidence); or become a little homesick. The upside is that those critical days of rest can be the last respite a new mother has to 'catch her breath' before potentially entering into *years* of a 24–7 workload. (Experienced mothers knowing they're returning home to other children often savour their 'hospital haven'.)

There is absolutely no doubt that birth settings providing lower levels of intervention for low-risk women consistently produce higher levels of satisfaction with the birthing mothers. So, maternity units (birth centres), which are a relatively new third option for birthing and postnatal stays, are growing in popularity. Birth centres usually go to great effort to make the environment homely, informal and un-clinical, while still providing access to some medical emergency technology — though major emergencies are usually 'shipped out' to the nearest large hospital. Birthing centres are perhaps the near-perfect transition between the hospital and home-birth environments.

If you have investigated your options, and have made up your mind that you definitely wish to try to give birth at home, then this is your decision, and no one else's — lawfully, it is also your right.

If you haven't already been on the hospital's maternity tour, do go, even if you're hoping to give birth at home (and bring your birthing partner). It can help to make you feel a little more prepared and less overwhelmed by the intimidating hospital scene — and you also then know where the correct maternity birthing ward entrance is, particularly after-hours. Asking to see the birthing chairs, stools and beanbags can be reassuring too.

Wherever you choose to give birth, do remember that part of your decision on birthing location should also take into account what assistance is then subsequently available to you for those first few critical days of postnatal care. Some women abhor the noise, structure and bland food in hospital, and can feel better supported and more rested at home. Many other women have no issue accepting the routine required to run a large hospital, and treat it like some 'Hi-De-Hi Camp', where you can lie in bed most of the day and have your meals made for you. (If available and affordable, particularly for a first-time mother, having a pre-booked single room all to yourself for your postnatal stay can be invaluable for a restful recovery.)

Childbirth is an immensely personal occasion, and perhaps the most important point is that a woman isn't unduly cajoled into birthing in a location she is not instinctively contented and at peace with. If the place of birth chosen by the mother makes her feel confident and empowered, this is without doubt advantageous to the process of labour.

The main point is, there is no wrong place — there is simply a more-right place for you, and your circumstances.

Apart from my partner and my LMC, do I really need a third labour support person at delivery with us?

Traditionally sisters, mothers, grandmothers and female friends have surrounded women during childbirth, providing tremendous encouraging support. With the move to hospitalised deliveries from the 1920s, this support was taken over by hospital staff.

Half a century later, hospitals realised it is elemental to birthing (emotionally, which directly impacts physiologically) that women receive the support of people they know during labour, so husbands were invited to be present. But, although childbirth can create a magical marital memory, having your partner present who is inexperienced in childbirth still doesn't necessarily provide all that a woman needs during labour.

In some countries, an extra labour support person is employed. She is called a 'Doula', which stems from the Greek word for the most important female slave or woman's servant in an ancient Greek household. These days Doula has come to mean a trained female birth partner, a woman experienced in childbirth who provides continuous support to the mother emotionally, physically and verbally before, during and after delivery, with constant advice, guidance and encouragement. They work alongside the midwife or obstetrician to aid the mother with non-medical nurturing care, and Doulas have consistently been shown to significantly reduce the average length of labours. The same Doula then assists with the early days at home providing emotional support, breastfeeding tips, caring for the newborn and other household tasks. There are only a few professional Doulas available in New Zealand, however some independent midwives have support midwives to provide this role during the birth, which can be very helpful for both the mother and main midwife.

What we all need at childbirth is an intensive, constant and steady one-to-one companionship, devoid of *all* criticism. We require and rely on non-stop attentiveness to our needs, by someone who will not take offence at us being critical or aggressive during the intensive stages. We can need continual physical hands-on assistance (sometimes as little as a hand to squeeze during the contraction peaks); someone providing us with food and drink; a helper offering suggestions of different positions to reduce the discomfort; and constant emotional guidance encouraging us to relax, to help us avoid feeling overwhelmed.

This total loving and undivided attention from *one key person* (other than your LMC) can provide such huge psychological support that it can significantly reduce requests for pain relief (because labour can be less painful). It has also been repeatedly proven to: reduce the average length of

Summary of birth-assistant duties

- Be a 'willing slave', providing a physical and emotional presence of warmth, trust and patience.
- Know the stages of labour (see next chapter).
- Be aware of the intensity of the transition and second stage (she could appear to lose the plot).
- Attempt to improve your physical stamina before the birth (it can be physically gruelling for the assistant as well!).

During birth you will be giving comfort such as:
- Grabbing pillows and blankets for the mother-to-be.
- Rubbing her back.
- Applying hot/cold compresses.
- Giving soothing rhythmic massage. (Some women want touch, others find their skin too sensitive.)
- Cuddling and rocking together.
- Gently stroking her tense neck, shoulders or forehead.
- Physically supporting positions her body tells her to use.
- Continually reminding her to breathe rhythmically (because it is easy for her during contractions, as with any tension or pain, to inadvertently hold her breath and forget to breathe, eventually hypo- or hyperventilating).
- Providing empathetic emotional support with eye-contact (coaching her with steady encouraging reassurance — be her own non-patronising, enthusiastic cheerleader).
- Advocating for her (answer questions, calmly interpret her needs and act on her behalf with staff interaction).
- Backing her 100 percent with her requests for pain relief.
- Providing her with information.
- Helping to reduce her anxieties overall (even down to changing the music and dimming the lights for her).
- Contrary to all of that, sometimes you will need to be completely quiet by ensuring peace in the room, saying nothing and doing nothing, just being there — there can be stages during labour when she'll crave no conversation and no distractions, as her body is insisting she 'inwardly centre'.
- Please see page 53–57 for extra duties if you are the dad-to-be or main support person at home.

labour; reduce the need for episiotomies and operative deliveries; improve the baby's condition; and positively improve the empowerment of the mother's birth experience.

If you choose your partner to be your birth assistant, which is great, then they need to know that during the labour it is their job to give you confidence and physical comfort. Having an adaptable labour support person present is *extremely therapeutic.*

Some men don't think they will cope well with the experience of delivery because of feeling squeamish, or crumbling at seeing someone they love in pain, and so they're nervous about how adequately they can support you. These concerns need to be respected, because it is also possible for a man to be left traumatised by childbirth.

So if you don't feel your partner is equipped to handle being your Doula (or you think he might fall asleep in a chair, or you know he'll constantly be popping out for ciggies), then consider inviting a woman of significance to join the two of you (often it's the woman's own mother, or sister, or an experienced close girlfriend). Whoever you choose, make sure they have at least re-familiarised themselves with the stages of labour in the next chapter, see page 100. Don't avoid making that decision just because you're worried it will offend your partner — your feelings and needs are much more important on this occasion.

Some women also choose to have extra people such as extended family present to share the birth experience. But one piece of advice . . . don't invite anyone who could make you feel at all inhibited, or a person you would be embarrassed to lose your emotional and verbal self-control around.

As a summary, it is imperative to *you* (and enormously advantageous for the physiological process of childbirth) to try to ensure you will have *no* negative energy present at the birth of your baby. In other words, although the raw primal energy of labour has stages that are noisy and anything but peaceful — still strive to *pre*-prepare a comforting birth environment that is calm, serene and tranquil. It really does have an impact.

And by the way, if you want a comprehensive birthing video or photos to be taken, do not expect your main labour support-partner to perform this role as well — they may need to be busy with you. (Ask another person along for that task.)

What will the childbirth be like?

What if I feel inhibited, as if I've got stage fright? I'm scared of making a fool of myself, especially pooing myself, or delivering in some undignified position, screaming too loudly, or doing something else incredibly embarrassing!

We mums who have had hair-raising first deliveries, don't always enjoy hearing of those first-time mums who adored every moment of their sickeningly exhilarating and completely empowering textbook, nine-hour, daytime labour, requiring no pain relief and no stitches and no missed sleep. But then again, we instead can be left with a courageous and impressively brave 'story' — what a warrior, what a heroine!

Now I appreciate that I might be rare, but my attitude in late pregnancy regarding the impending birth was: 'It will be what it will be, and there's nothing I can do about it.' It stopped me worrying about birthing. So, if at all possible, try to take a little of my attitude onboard, by saying to yourself: 'Childbirth will be what it will be, and there's no point worrying about it.' At the same time, remember that what is important is believing in your own body's capability to give birth naturally and unaided.

For the modern self-motivated career woman who is a first-time-mum-to-be, it can be against her mental conditioning to adjust to the concept of moving from the driving seat of her polished successful life, to allowing her body (which, let's face it, she may never have really trusted before to manage itself on its own) the grave responsibility of being in charge of delivering her offspring. This 'fear of letting go' is a *big ask* — but that is what it takes, allowing the inner goddess in you to reveal herself, often for the first time. You can't tame birth!

At the same time, please don't take it to the other extreme: of being so damned determined and fixated with accomplishing an unaided natural birth that you are setting yourself up for miserable disappointment if things don't happen as perfectly as you had visualised and verbalised.

If you are one of those mums-to-be who has been told to expect a big baby, try not to get overly worried about how much more difficult your labour will be, because at the end of the day it's the head circumference and width of the shoulders which are the most relevant, and that does not always relate to a baby's weight (for example, my lightest baby had the largest head).

As for deciding on the birthing position, well, those midwives really have seen hundreds and thousands of births, and it will make no memorable impression on them whatever position your body desires to deliver in.

With our second child's birth, and me still somewhat unaware of the mechanics of the process, I chose to deliver in the popular position of lying on an incline. For the following two and a half years I suffered terribly from the painful tailbone condition called coccydynia (an inflammation in the ligaments around a displaced coccyx) — and I made what I now believe was the mistake of not seeking any physical therapy until months later.

But we had always hoped to have more than two children, so I would sometimes joke that I was happy to go through a third labour just to reposition my tailbone! And it did, thanks to birthing on all fours — it was an almost instant and permanent reprieve from the tiring 24–7 aching butt.

You see, even though birthing on all fours or squatting did somehow repulse me, I can't recommend them enough — they can sometimes be just what the body needs, in comparison to lying on your back at an angle, with all your weight on your bottom, and your legs pushed up to your throat.

As for involuntarily peeing or pooing during the final stage of birth, well it's pretty much impossible to push a baby out without pushing out a bit of poo at the same time, but don't worry, truly, don't give it a second thought, no one else will on the day. Those midwife-nurses, they've seen it all, and heard it all. You scream as long and loud as you like, howl to the moon if you want to. You must not feel inhibited vocally. Time for a little story:

Other mothers often agree with me, that although subsequent babies can have shorter labours, those short sharp labours can be more intense. My first labour went from 9 pm on a Monday night till 4 am on the Wednesday morning, yikes, but it was my first. My second labour was a brilliant 3-hour experience. However, my third was a phenomenally intense two hours. . .

In that third labour, after the final, I would guess, twenty minutes of the first stage's transitional phase during which I was screaming the roof down (my second stage only lasted about a minute or less) . . . well, there I was lying besotted with our new baby, and I could hear the accelerating groans of a woman in the room next door very obviously heading into her transitional phase. I felt so sorry for her having been within earshot of my voice-box (including the occasional profanity), knowing that she still had that ahead of her. And me feeling so relieved, I might add, that I had finished.

It took me a day in hospital to discover which particular mother had been in that delivery suite next to me, and when we caught up I remember saying to her how awful I had felt for her hearing me, knowing what was ahead of her. Her reply was so genuine, 'Heck no, when I heard your baby cry, that spurred me on. I knew I could do it then.' So lovely. The point of the story? Make as much noise as you want, all the other mammals do.

In our great-grandmother's days, and still now in Third World countries, childbirth was and is a dangerous and intrinsically life-threatening occurrence. But we are so lucky to live in a medically advanced country where childbirth has generally become extremely safe. Let us be very grateful!

So, if some parts of your childbirth experience don't end up turning out to be quite as wonderful as you'd hoped, which is not uncommon with birthing your first baby, then that's OK . . . it will all be part of your *story*.

Will my level of fitness (or lack of) hinder birth?

What if I'm not fit at all, and I'm freaking out that I'll fail miserably at this unknown 'test of my endurance'? Or I've always had a really sporty lifestyle, and I've been pretty obsessive about maintaining my fitness levels throughout my pregnancy, but someone told me the other day that being toned is bad for childbirth.

Although aerobic fitness logically provides one with extra physical stamina and endurance for the active stages of labour — certainly physical strength doesn't correlate much with the ease with which a woman births.

Some couch-potato unfit mums dilatate rapidly and seem to spit their babies out. Then some super-fit women's dilatation goes on for what seems like an eternity. And of course vice-versa. Remember, fitness of the body doesn't impact on the functional competence of the uterus. So if you never attended any of those antenatal yoga or antenatal aqua-aerobics classes, and you are now very well aware that you're far from fit, don't cause yourself any extra stress by worrying about it, because it's probably reasonably irrelevant.

However, if you maintained great fitness during your pregnancy, then well done to you, but now STOP. Recent studies are finding correlations between very high levels of physical muscle tone being sometimes problematic in the second stage of childbirth (getting the baby down the birth canal) because enlarged stronger pelvic floor muscles are less 'trampoline-like'. So you really *do* have an excuse to *chill out* now.

Drugs or no drugs, how can I decide?

I'm worried I might be a complete wimp and not be able to cope with any of it! And what about all those theories on how to handle natural childbirth?

In the late nineteenth century, doctors (men) declared childbirth to be perilous, primitive, frightening and outright dangerous — thus requiring their highly specialised medical skills — and that delivery should be left in the hands of the experts (i.e. Don't try this at home). And so began the rapid decline of womanhood's collective inter-generational knowledge on how to give birth — instead we now got delivered.

In the 1940s came the Dr Grantly Dick-Reid (man's) theory that the cause of all childbirth pain was simply fear, a cycle of fear-tension-pain. Then in the 1950s came the Dr Fernand Lamaze (man's) theory that the pain of childbirth can be blocked by using the proper manner of psychoprophylaxis (a self-hypnosis technique using rapid shallow breathing). Then in the mid-1960s came the Robert A. Bradley (man's) theory of prepared birth including the coaching and supportive presence of the husband, and deep belly-breathing throughout each contraction. Then in the 1970s came Dr Frederick Leboyer's (man's) rationale of gentle birthing without violence, theorising that a baby can be coaxed and nudged out (not pushed and pulled), and should arrive with a gentle entry into a peaceful uterine-like environment. Then in the 1980s came Dr Michel Odent's (man's) emphasis on the importance of empowering women to control their own childbirth; and Dr Michael Rosenthal's (man's) holistic stance towards calm and relaxed childbirth.

All these male theories about this exclusively female domain were created to empower women for their birthing experiences. But with each strict (and often idealistic) code of conduct, if the birth ends up very painful, or has myriad interventions — then *she* (the mother) must have done it *wrong*. Oh, what a *failure* she is as a woman. I mean, all those detailed theories written by all those knowledgeable *men* couldn't possibly be wrong, could they? It must have been the woman's fault. How appallingly and atrociously disempowering that can be.

If you want more in-depth and womanly wisdom than this book will provide, then try Sheila Kitzinger's publications. She's rather the British godmother when it comes to natural childbirth and breastfeeding knowledge. If you are a more out-there, alternative person (bit of a hippy at heart) then Ina May Gaskin's *Guide to Childbirth* is a book you may really enjoy. And if you're hungry for the Reality TV of books, then Sandra Grayson's *Childbirth — As It Really Is* or Carol Barbar's *Birth Book* have true-life accounts of individual childbirth experiences.

I remember a friend Kendall (mother of three) saying to me once about how inhumane it is that society no longer expects to have a tooth filled without full pain relief — yet there is still a great expectation for women to deliver babies without pain relief. That is so true.

My second and third childbirths were done naturally without any pain relief and women who manage that can rightfully feel proud. It is no mean feat — in fact submitting to this functional pain is a significant psychological self-discovery. But, oh, it is so irritating when stupid comments get bandied around, like 'Women have been doing it for thousands of years without drugs'. Out of choice? Of course not. That's not technically true anyway. Many Third World countries still use alcohol, narcotic sedation and mood-altering herbal medicines. Anyway, men during wars have had to endure limb amputations without pain relief too. Do you think they would like that practice to continue, just to demonstrate that westernised men are still macho! Complete drivel.

One major reality, however, is that we westernised women are birthing well-nourished *larger* babies these days, without nature increasing the size of our pelvises. So, *please don't* feel that requesting pain relief is in any way indicative of personal weakness. (It's perhaps an indication of your sanity!)

Here is another truth . . . Every labour produces a different level of pain, and not all births are agonising. It depends on so many variables; such as the strength at which the uterus contracts; the position of the baby's head within the pelvis; the amount at which the pelvis has already opened or still needs to widen; and what the baby's shoulders are pushing on. So just because you ask for some pain relief to take the edge off, and your best friend didn't, doesn't mean she was stronger than you, but perhaps her contractions were not as intense as yours. However, during labour, if it is at all possible, see if you can hold out for another quarter of an hour or so before having pain relief administered, because things can change quickly, and you may find you don't need that pain relief so much anymore.

Pharmacological pain relief comes in two forms: **analgesics**, which are general body pain-relievers that take the edge off; and **anaesthetics**, which eliminate all pain to a targeted place on the body. And, as Pat Thomas writes about pain relief in her book *Every Woman's BirthRights*: 'If you ask for it, it should not be denied to you, nor should you be made to feel as if you have failed because you need it.' So let's get on with reviewing the options.

The main pain-relief options available are:

A great birth assistant supporting you during labour

I'm really not kidding! It is absolutely paramount to labour that a woman feels 110 percent *safe* — as it sets up colossal chain reactions mentally (emotionally) that affect her physically (via chemical hormones). So, the positive attention of receiving emotionally loving, one-to-one encouraging support, information, appreciation and understanding can dispel almost all fears and anxieties — resulting in a woman's body producing a higher level of the neuro-hormone endorphins (which specifically assist to block the perception of pain).

Whereas, with a woman who is angry, cold, humiliated or afraid, her body's protective mechanisms produce adrenaline, which quickens her heart-rate, tenses her muscles, intensifies her perception of pain and inhibits her synthesis of oxytocin for productive labour contractions.

Any new experience perceived as dangerous automatically activates our human survival response — producing the 'freeze, flight or fight' reflex. So, eliminating emotional fear and replacing it with loving attention is perhaps *the* most effective pain relief and labour enhancement possible. It can 'kick arse' when it comes to even wanting medical pain relief. This is the most important (and essential) role of your labour support assistant(s) and, of course, midwife (and obstetrician).

Some psychological studies are showing positive correlations between how well informed a mother is about the birthing process (beyond just basic antenatal education classes) and reduced average lengths of labour; and correlations between the decreased levels of pain experienced by mothers receiving excellent birth-assisting attention.

So, reading this book and other books, watching a birthing video, and talking to girlfriends in detail about their childbirth experiences can potentially shorten your own labour time, because your mind becomes more confident to let your body take full control. Childbirth should, ideally, be a satisfying and fulfilling journey, and if you're feeling safe and informed, it is much more possible for you to emotionally 'let go' so your body can feel secure enough to spontaneously work its miracle.

Hydrotherapy — birthing pool (and water birth)

From thundering waterfalls to still pools, water has long been recognised as therapeutic to the human spirit as a symbol of nature's tranquillity and healing peace. Today water therapies abound . . . spas, saunas, aromatherapy baths, flotation tanks, watsu rebirthing, beachside resorts and lake-edge retreats . . . all around us water is a strong relaxant, inducing pampered serenity and mental calm.

So it is not that surprising to have society now accepting that water is also of great benefit for easing the pain of childbirth; and, termed hydrotherapy, it is no longer controversial, radical or foolhardy.

Nearly all water can soothe labour pains — sprayed or splashed, hot or cool, still or moving, hot-water bottles or ice-packs, showers or baths, spas or Jacuzzi whirlpools, hospital birthing pools or hired home-birthing tubs — particularly the weightlessness of being in a really deep bath.

The normal stage to enter a bath or birthpool is not during early labour's latent phase, but after the commencement of active labour (say about 4 cm dilatated). The soothing pain reduction of the warm water, and the pressure release it provides are so effective that a woman can end up staying in the water for most of the labour and, sometimes, for the actual birth.

Disputable theories state that the warm wetness of water aids to dilatate women's cervixes more rapidly — shortening the labour in comparison to women whose cervixes stay 'dry'. Some studies indicate that hydrotherapy can lower blood pressure; there can be less perineal trauma (more relaxed waterlogged perineum tissue has enhanced elasticity); and there can be reduced need for high-tech instrumental intervention.

The full benefits of using water during labour and delivery are still to be fully quantified and qualified by science with assessed hard evidence. As for the baby, science is still having difficulty understanding the mysterious 'diving' reflex babies are born with that prevents them from breathing under water — even with the mouth wide open the top of the lungs is sealed off. (This changes anatomically at around six months.)

Other potential benefits as listed in Dianne Garland's book *Waterbirth* include: increased relaxation, decreased pain, decreased pressure on abdominal muscles and inferior vena cava (main large vein in the lower torso), increased pelvic diameter, increased buoyancy and mobility in the lower-gravity environment, increased contractions, increased endorphin and oxytocin production, increased oxygen and blood supply, improved muscle relaxation and stress alleviation.

To paraphrase Dianne, a water labour potentially benefits the woman to feel more in control by increasing her self-control, self-awareness and consciousness; the secure, warm, private and quiet environment decreases fear and anger; the flotation sensation increases the pain threshold; and the pleasurable, reassuring and serene effect of a waterbirth increases the mother's receptiveness to the baby, and mother-baby interaction; plus the calm and peaceful delivery has a positive effect on a woman's personal satisfaction and perception of her baby's birth. (Beverley Lawrence Beech has also written extensively on waterbirths.)

Complementary new-age therapies (age-old wisdom)

Some women find that using age-old wisdom (now termed new-age) to mentally embrace their symbolic transition into motherhood assists them during the physical transformation of giving birth — since much of it involves gentle holistic and totalistic healing and wellness therapies, which are interested in the balance of body, mind and spirit.

To name but a few: acupressure, acupuncture, affirmations, aromatherapy, Bach flower remedies, chiropractic, homeopathy, mantras, massage, medicinal herbalism, meditation, music, naturopathy, osteopathy, reflexology pressure points, self-hypnosis, shiatsu, touch relaxation therapy, and visualisation. Your LMC may also be able to provide you with a list of the better complementary remedies (and ones to avoid).

TENS machine

This is a 'Trans-cutaneous Electrical Nerve Stimulation' battery-powered machine, which can be booked to hire in advance (from some hospitals and chemists). It has little flat electrodes that you stick on either side of your spine on your lower back (or abdomen or groin) in the first stage of labour.

With every contraction you turn on the handset control (to an adjustable intensity), and it has the ability to 'jam' (interrupt) the pain transmission travelling along the nerve pathways from the uterus and cervix (the pain impulses conducted by the nerve cells are 'blocked' by the electric current). It feels a bit like 'pins and needles', and is also said to stimulate the body's production of pain-relieving substances such as endorphins. You could describe it as an 'electrical back-rub' — since it can be as effective as a decent massage. There are no side effects.

The TENS can be a good distraction mentally too, as 'zapping' the pain gives the mother something active to do. It is great for the latent phase of labour — but can become pretty obsolete in the more advanced active-labour stages.

Entonox machine (gas)

This is a mixture of nitrous oxide (laughing gas) and oxygen, which many mothers use during childbirth. It acts on the brain cells to reduce the perception of pain (it numbs the brain's pain centre), to take the edge off.

This self-administered inhaled analgesic is usually breathed in through a mouth-piece for you to bite on, holding with your teeth — with a valve that opens when you inhale and closes when you exhale. The effect comes on quickly and disappears quickly. Negatively, it can make you feel nauseous, but positively it can make you feel like you're floating. However, there is a trick to making it work most effectively as a pain reliever during labour.

The nitrous oxide takes almost a minute to reach its optimum levels in your bloodstream to dull the contraction pain. So, the labouring mother needs to inhale on the entonox mouthpiece for at least a minute *prior* to the peak of the contraction. If you don't get that timing right, then gas can feel pretty ineffective as a pain reliever during labour. This is where a good labour support person or midwife can be of tremendous assistance by helping guide you through strong, rhythmic breathing.

The potential pain relief that the entonox machine can provide tends to be under-rated because it is not always used most effectively. But nitrous oxide is the closest thing we have to an ideal childbirth pain reliever because it leaves no lasting effects on the mother or baby, and has no adverse effects on the progress of the labour.

Personally, I'm also convinced that the act of biting down with your teeth on something is in itself a great stress releaser too.

Pethidine

This tranquillising analgesic is usually given by intramuscular injection or by IV (intravenous transfusion). Like other narcotics, this morphine derivative depresses the brain's perception of pain (and all other brain functions) so it relaxes you as well.

Pethidine works on the nerve cells in the central nervous system (spinal cord and brain) — so it doesn't remove the pain as such, but alters your brain's perception of pain. It creates a drowsy drunk 'stoned' sensation — but some women don't like its stupefying wooziness, complaining that it made them feel disorientated, as if they'd lost control. Pethidine allows you to still feel your contractions — but they don't hurt nearly as much.

For some women the effect is very good and can last a few hours, and for other women the effect is great for only a few contractions — but a welcomed break.

When pharmaceutical pain relief is criticised for its lingering effects on the newborn, it is the tranquilliser narcotics such as pethidine that are of most concern. If the labouring mother receives pethidine too late (say during the final 1–2 hours) before birth, then the lingering metabolites in the baby's system can create a 'floppy' drowsy unresponsive newborn or a jittery nervous baby; a newborn who may have breathing problems, or breastfeeding difficulties due to reduced sucking. If a newborn is asphyxiated it will be given Narcan (a narcotic antidote) that will instantly reverse the effects of the pethidine — but that is far from ideal. As the duration of childbirth is a very inexact science, this is a drug that LMCs are discriminating about administering, many choosing not to use it at all.

Epidural analgesia

This is a local anaesthetic that causes a nerve block in the spine. It is administered by an anaesthetist who skilfully inserts a hollow needle through the muscles of the mother's back, and then very carefully gets the tip of the needle to lie in the epidural space. A fine catheter tube is then pushed through the hollow needle and the needle is withdrawn, leaving the plastic tube (a cannula) in place. Using a syringe, long-lasting local anaesthetic is pumped through the catheter into the epidural space. The tube is sealed and taped down firmly. The anaesthetic can then be 'topped up' as required. (If the needle punctures the dura [spinal cord covering] by mistake, you can potentially end up getting a complete spinal nerve block, which makes you more heavily anaesthetised and can result in severe headaches lasting up to a week when you are not lying down. The spinal cord extends to only about the waist, so below that there is a reduced risk of damaging the spinal cord.)

There are a number of valid medical reasons why an epidural can be recommended. For example, so that the mother can remain awake for a caesarean birth; to help women with breech babies resist the urge to push prior to full dilatation; for the extra-long hard labour of a posterior positioned baby; for a mother with high blood pressure; or for a woman who is having a long drawn-out first stage to allow her to rest (and sometimes actually sleep) so she will have better stores of reserved energy for the actual birth later.

Epidurals have been routinely administered for childbirth pain relief for some years, and they can be seductively appealing with their potential ability to ensure completely pain-free birth. Some mothers find the numbing feeling (being paralysed) from their waist down (ribs to toes) with their epidural was a marvellous magical miracle, and they believe it to be the most logically sane and humane way to deliver a baby, because in a perfect world, as touted, this creates a painless labour.

But . . . and I'm really sorry to tell you that there are quite a number of 'buts' with epidurals . . . in the real world things don't always work out perfectly — there are risks and there are side effects. About one-third of women still feel some uneven, blotchy pain, or even perhaps more annoyingly, only get partially numbed, say, just on one side. For some women the epidural doesn't take effect properly at all and the pain relief is nonexistent. So, roughly about one in five women who have an epidural seem to end up saying 'Never again.'

Once labour is properly established (at least 5 cm dilatated), an epidural does not dramatically slow down or prolong the first stage of labour. However, epidurals always slow down the second stage of labour, roughly doubling the duration — especially with first births. That is because the pelvic-floor muscles are limp from the anaesthetic, so they can't work as well as they should. Due to this lower muscle tone, the mother is unable to push as effectively to get her baby out. This leads straight on to having much higher chances of needing the intervention of an instrumental forceps delivery or ventouse vacuum extraction (see page 88–89) — and the subsequent increased likelihood of an episiotomy (see page 86–87).

To help avoid needing an assisted instrumental delivery, sometimes the epidural is not topped up so that the anaesthetic can wear off as the woman reaches the end of the first-stage contractions ready for pushing. But, going from no pain into the hefty transitional contractions can be overpowering — especially when the body has not been pumped up over hours with its own morphine-like endorphins. So, this practice has been shown to be of questionable benefit.

Dr Caldeyro-Barcia of the International Federation of Gynaecologists and Obstetricians has said: 'Except for being hanged by the feet, the supine position [lying on the back] is the worst conceivable position for labour and delivery.' Additionally, some childbirth specialists believe that when delivery is in a lying down position with the legs bent upwards, it is difficult for the coccyx bone to tilt back when the baby descends the birth canal, increasing the possibility of being left with tailbone trauma.

Commonly an epidural will cause the cardiovascular complication hypotension (drop in the mother's blood pressure), affecting the oxygen-bearing blood supply to the baby, which would cause fetal respiratory distress. To help prevent hypotension the mother is usually given a saline IV drip — then if her blood pressure drops too significantly, a vasoconstrictor drug such as ephedrine may be given to raise her blood pressure.

These risks associated with an epidural can be exasperated by staying in the supine or semi-reclining position, due to the compression of the abdominal aorta (decreasing supply of fresh oxygenated blood), and the compression of the inferior vena cava (hindering the removal of deoxygenated blood). So lying on alternating sides can assist, especially lying on the right side when weight is not pressing on the heart.

During birth other common epidural side effects can be: uncontrollable shivering, nausea or vomiting, or fever (it can affect your ability to sweat), and, of course, you can be unable to move freely about.

It is a normal part of the epidural process to have a urine catheter inserted up the urethra into the bladder to drain it and prevent it from becoming full. This can cause some degree of trauma to the urinary system, such as temporary partial incontinence (pelvic-floor exercises can help). A urine catheter also increases the chances of a postnatal urinary tract infection.

Other potential longer-term epidural side effects for the mother (commencing 1–2 days after birth and continuing most severely for up to a week) include backaches (a particularly common problem), headaches, neckaches, temporary spinal-nerve damage, slight double-vision, slight deafness, and paralysis or tingling in the hands and legs. Some of these side effects can continue for months in a lesser degree.

So epidurals can be a little of a win-then-lose situation, as women who use them can have less pain during childbirth, but often complain of more pains in the days and weeks afterwards.

Note: It can sometimes take up to an hour or so for an anaesthetist to become available and for the drugs to take full effect. Also, low-dose epidurals can still enable a woman to walk around.

Spinal block anaesthesia (saddle block)
This differs from an epidural in that the medication is injected in one single dose into the cerebrospinal space between two vertebrae in the lower back — so no catheter is left in. It acts almost instantly, eliminating all feeling and most muscle control below the waist, and lasts only a few hours.

A spinal block is usually only ordered late in a labour because a woman can't push very effectively with this. It may be used just before an emergency caesarean, or for a forceps delivery, say when the baby needs turning, or occasionally for a ventouse delivery — giving the option to go immediately on to a caesarean if necessary.

Are there any complementary natural remedies I can take to assist childbirth?

Absolutely. Below is a list of the most commonly recommended therapies.

- With the initial onset of regular, light contractions in latent labour, use a traditional dosage of 1 ml **Blue Cohosh** in some fruit juice every 40 minutes or so, with a *maximum* total of only 6–7 mls. Although a very traditional remedy for assisting the establishment of proper labour, the dosage should be professionally prescribed, as self-prescribing too much can lead to excessive contractions, which could harm the birth outcome. Because of this, question marks exist within modern obstetric medicine as to Blue Cohosh's safety — talk with your LMC.
- For weak contractions take homeopathic **Caulophyllum** every 15 minutes up to six times. (This is the homeopathic version of Blue Cohosh, but has none of the controversial problems of the herbal version.)
- Drink water throughout labour that has a few drops of the Bach flower tincture **Rescue Remedy**. This aids in emotionally calming one's distress in any crisis, startling experience, or exceptionally demanding situation.
- Take **Arnica** (orally) at the onset of initial contractions, at the onset of the second stage, and immediately after the birth in intervalled doses as acute pain and shock symptoms decrease (say quarter-hourly for 1–2 hours, then hourly for 6 hours, then several times a day for 1–2 weeks). Arnica is particularly helpful with bruising and general healing.
- There are also other products available such as Naturo Pharm™'s homeopathic **Birth Aid** (arnica and hypericum).
- **Lavender Pure Essential Oil** is good to use in an aromatherapy diffuser, or lavender incense, for creating a relaxing atmosphere.
- **Clary Sage Pure Essential Oil** (or **Rose**, **Jasmine** or **Ylang Ylang**) are great for massage mixed with a carrier oil (e.g. sweet almond, grapeseed, apricot kernel, safflower or hazelnut) to ease pain. They're good in a hydrotherapy bath too.
- Get knowledgeable about natural birth. Check out the **Pink Kit** available at www.birthingbetter.com.

Who should cut the umbilical cord, and when?

It has become quite a common ritual for the partner to cut the cord — or at least for him to be asked if he would like to. Then comes the question of when the umbilical cord should be severed, which does receive perhaps too much 'bad press' as to what is best for the baby because opinions vary.

Babies are born with a higher blood count than necessary for our air-breathing environment, and receiving any additional blood into their system from the defunct placenta does increase the chance of their postnatal jaundice being more severe.

Some believe that the umbilical cord should not be severed until the baby is breathing independently and the cord has stopped pulsing, as the placenta is still supplying oxygen and iron. Others emphatically dispute that fact, saying that the placenta starts to shear off the wall of the uterus (disconnecting from its blood supply) as soon as the uterus contracts down just as the baby is expelled, making it useless immediately. You may wish to discuss it further with your LMC.

If it's decided that someone other than your LMC is to cut the cord, then it could be nice to warn him or her in advance that cutting the umbilicus is not like slicing a frankfurter! It is tough and fibrous, more like twisted grey gristle.

Sometimes, due to medical emergencies, some of the plans have to be pushed aside as there is no safe option but to prematurely cut the cord — such as when the head is delivered and the cord is wrapped too tightly around the baby's neck for it to be pulled over — then the cord may be cut before the baby has even finished being born.

Do I say 'Yes' or 'No' to the ecbolic (syntometrine/syntocinon) injection/IV after delivery?

One of the most dramatic physiological changes that occurs in pregnancy is the mother's cardiovascular-system blood and water volume and heart output that increases by 25–40 percent to look after the needs of both the mother and fetus. This also provides some protection against blood loss at birth.

When the placenta releases off the uterine wall it leaves a dinner-plate-sized wound with blood vessels pointing straight out, furiously pumping blood — about a pint (500 ml) every minute (or 10 percent of most adults' blood volume) . . . turn a tap on to imagine it. What needs to naturally occur very rapidly is that the uterus has to immediately involute (clamp down) to 'strangle and crush' those blood vessels, so that the blood does not continue pumping out of this massive wound. *An empty and contracted uterus does not bleed.*

Postpartum haemorrhage (excessive bleeding) remains a serious potential complication of childbirth, and is still the leading cause of maternal death in Third World countries. So, to reduce the possibility of postnatal anaemia (excessive blood loss) and the risks associated with blood transfusions, limiting the blood loss at delivery is a very important goal of good modern maternity care.

Currently a bit over three-quarters of New Zealand births have a less than 500 ml blood loss which is an acceptable level; around 10–20 percent of women have a 500–1000 ml blood loss, which will cause some degree of postpartum anaemia; and around 2–6 percent of women have an even greater blood loss, which may be life-threatening.

The key to achieving this is the so-called **active management** of the third stage of labour. This involves giving the mother an injection of an ecbolic (oxytocic uterine stimulant), just as or immediately after the baby is born, combined with traction (tugging) on the umbilical cord to assist rapid expelling of the placenta. Because using this stimulant often results in the placenta being delivered within 5–10 minutes, there is a misbelief that this injection is designed to 'speed up the delivery of the placenta'. Although that is a common side effect, that is *not* its purpose — its main purpose is to aid in the prevention of the debilitating postpartum anaemia caused by excessive blood loss, by ensuring the uterine muscle 'living ligature' fibres contract well and seal the blood vessels by constricting them; the preventable need of heroic actions such as blood transfusions; or the if-all-else-fails step of an immediate hysterectomy (surgical removal of the womb).

However, growing in popularity in some corners is the old-fashioned **expectant physiological** system of 'leave well alone'. No oxytocic drug is given, no clamp is applied to the umbilical cord and the cord is not cut until its pulsing ceases. Instead of the routine practice of clamping the placenta cord, some believe that allowing the blood to continue to flow freely encourages the now purposeless placenta to peel away off the wall of the uterus — since it is believed that a placenta packed full of blood may be less likely to separate, thereby increasing the chances of having a retained placenta. With this natural system, half an hour (or even two hours) later, the mother delivers the placenta, with help from oxytocin naturally stimulated from the new baby suckling, perhaps the mother or her partner massaging her nipples, the aid of gravity from squatting, and great patience.

The argument between the active-management and the expectant-management philosophies, as with so many debates, can be heated, with people

Waterbirth note

Because the active management of delivering the placenta requires the mother to leave the pool or that the pool is drained, the first minutes of interaction between baby and mother may be affected. If opting for the expectant-management system, chances of postpartum haemorrhage are higher.

passionately believing in their own convictions.

Statistically, receiving the ecbolic reduces the chance of serious postpartum haemorrhaging by 60 percent.

At the end of the day, this is one decision only you, the mother, should make for yourself — it's your body.

Do we say 'Yes' or 'No' to the vitamin K injection for our newborn?

It is very common for newborn babies to initially have low levels of vitamin K, which is needed by their liver cells to produce procoagulants (blood-clotting factors) such as prothrombin. It takes a newborn's body usually a little over a week or so to manufacture normal levels, so that means that for those first days newborns are especially vulnerable to VKDB (vitamin K deficiency bleeding) such as excessive bleeding, internally or from the umbilical cord stump or, say, a circumcised penis.

With their naturally slow blood-clotting mechanism from low vitamin K levels, a newborn is also at risk of the potentially life-threatening HDN (haemorrhagic disease of the newborn). Sometimes, even at the most normal of births, the pressures on the baby's head can cause a tiny blood vessel somewhere in the brain to rupture. With a normal blood-clotting mechanism this would be harmless — but if the baby's blood is not clotting as efficiently as it should, without the injection there is a risk of HDN causing permanent brain damage or even death — and it is impossible to accurately predict at birth which babies this may occur in.

So, it is generally not in dispute that extra vitamin K is advisable as a sensible safeguard for all newborns. They are now routinely given an intra-muscular vitamin-K injection at birth — because even breastmilk does not have high quantities of vitamin K.

The injection of vitamin K has caused controversy, including questionable links to leukaemia, though much research has proven it to be very effective. However, some people advocate that vitamin K should be given orally instead — but a problem with that practice is that a newborn is normally spilly, which means that vitamin K given orally has a high chance of being spat or vomited up (it's estimated the efficiency is about halved).

Some others advocate that if a breastfeeding mother eats a diet high in vitamin K (such as alfalfa, green leafy vegetables and meat) then the baby can absorb it through the breastmilk — which is a little ridiculous because by then an infant's brain damage could have already occurred.

Should we invest in umbilical-cord blood-banking?

The average 60–80 ml of blood that can be harvested from your baby's umbilical cord contains millions of miraculous stem cells (which are capable of reproducing all the human body's specialised cells). These amazing stem cells are automatically compatible with a child's own immune system with no risk of rejection. If banked, they could be available years later to facilitate recovery from treatment for a number of diseases such as leukaemia or Hodgkin's disease. The harvested cord blood could also, potentially, have match-compatibility for a parent or sibling — subject to the law allowing it to be used.

Harvesting the cord blood is a simple procedure. Your LMC is supplied with a special hypodermic needle to collect the blood from the cord after the birth. The procedure takes only 2–3 minutes, and obviously there is no pain involved. The cord blood is then couriered to the cord-bank long-term-storage facility where it undergoes a number of processes ensuring the maximum yield of stem cells. The stem cells are then frozen in liquid nitrogen banks.

This is a service that needs to be booked in advance, it currently costs around $2,000 with an ongoing annual fee. Many countries such as America, Britain, France, Germany and Japan have offered this safety-net facility to parents for many years. But it's not cheap — so you will need to make your own very personal decision.

Do we want to take the placenta (afterbirth) home?

Your LMC should ask if you want to take the placenta home. Many parents preserve it in the freezer so that once home it can be buried under a young tree — it makes great fertiliser— or perhaps to mark their baby's baptism or name-giving day. The placenta is revered by many indigenous cultures; burying it under a young tree is an ancient tradition throughout the world. In fact, the placenta (not surprisingly) is very nutritious — which is why most mammalian females eat the placenta after birthing.

In some older human cultures the new mother consumes the placenta — and before you loudly say *yuck*, it is apparently delicious, and is best treated like a piece of liver, say fried, casseroled or turned into pâte! Some believe that with its high levels of zinc, progesterone and oestrogen, eating the placenta would go a very long way to preventing the baby blues and postnatal depression. But for most of us Westernised mums, that idea has a major 'creep factor' attached to it.

Another alternative use for the placenta has been to seek out a doctor of Chinese medicine who can dry it into powder (which can then be put into capsules), since it is said to be a wonderful remedy for future use to help ease the side effects of menopause.

However, modern medical science contradicts those ideas by pointing out that with cooking and digestion, the hormones would cease to be biologically active.

Whatever you decide, just respect that Mother Nature doesn't make rubbish, and that the placenta is a miraculous organ. It belongs to you, and it does not necessarily have to be incinerated with the rest of the hospital garbage.

Do I really need to write down a birth care plan thingy?

Almost every modern book on childbirth instructs you to write down your own birth plan.

But what is it? Well, it's *not* a piece of paper saying you wish to be in first stage labour for a maximum of eight hours, a second stage for no more than thirty minutes, and that you do not wish any pain relief at all!

Birth plans probably began in the 1970s and 1980s when sensible birthing practices battled every day with rigid hospital protocols. But its necessity may be questionable these days — unless you haven't 'got through' to your LMC!

If you do wish to write a birth plan, then it should be written instructions for your LMC as to any adamant decisions you have already made, any opinions or preferences you have, and who you nominate to make decisions on your behalf if, for whatever reason, you are unable to. For example, your LMC needs to be clearly instructed on your decisions regarding the ecbolic-oxytocic and vitamin-K injections, cutting of the umbilical cord, baby's father 'catching' the baby, keeping of the placenta, etc. Your LMC also needs to know of any preferences you have regarding such things as pain relief, fetal monitoring, birthing position, etc. — but don't be inflexible on these subjects, as plans may need to be thrown out the window at the time, especially for a first birth.

No one can ever really plan for what a particular woman's birth will be like — not the midwife, obstetrician, partner or woman herself.

Now, once you are sure that your labour support person, and your LMC both clearly understand your preferences, then you could put a copy into your delivery bag in case, for whatever unforeseen reason, a hospital midwife steps in as your LMC.

My one grave concern with written birth plans is the overly detailed plan, which later becomes a documented disappointment when the mother's childbirth took an entirely different path. So here's my advice, write a birth plan if you want to, but stay as flexible within it as you can — stay open-minded to anticipate the unexpected.

Does birthing vaginally hurt my baby?

Before and during delivery, babies produce in great quantities incredible stress-relieving hormones called catecholamines (e.g. adrenaline and dopamine), which course through their bloodstream. These amazing hormones also give the baby natural protection against oxygen shortages during delivery. Your uterus's contractions push on your baby's bottom inching it downwards, while the walls of the uterus hug it gently (and tightly during each contraction peak).

In fact, the trauma of being squeezed through the birth canal is a key to the success of life, with the incredibly high adrenaline levels assisting to kick-start breathing.

Newborns have two particular built-in reflexes (their 'rooting' and 'stepping' reflexes) that are thought by some to aid with delivery: they wriggle their way forward through the cervix and vagina, while the baby's feet push off from the uterus wall.

A newborn's first cry is not so much a complaint about the childbirth process, but more a rude shock at their new surroundings — the delivery room is probably 15°C colder than your uterus — dimming the lights, and reducing the noise level can be a kind idea.

I'm frightened . . . will my baby be 'normal'?

Most babies are born perfectly normal, but not all. That's just a fact. There is no disguising it. Special-needs babies occur in about three out of every 100 births, with the most common conditions in New Zealand being cerebral palsy and Down's syndrome.

But another of life's ironies is that even when a child is born completely normal, they don't stay perfectly healthy. It is impossible to avoid quickly stepping on to the roller-coaster ride of parental concerns and worries about your child. You'll be worrying about them till your grave, and probably beyond!

But, yes, I know we all yearn to deliver a healthy 'normal' baby, and some of us are lucky enough (because luck is what it is) to receive such God-given *gifts* . . . because that is what they are.

Will my baby love me? Will I be a good mother? Do I have what it takes?

'I don't know how to be a mother . . . I'm not the mothering type . . . I don't feel ready to be a parent!' We all think these thoughts.

Your baby will love you unconditionally for the first couple of years. Then after that they will love you — so long as you find their lost Thomas train or Barbie doll, and give them red jelly instead of the green jelly you made. Then about ten years later they'll probably *hate* you for a time when puberty rears its horns. But truly, babies come pre-programmed ready to love their mums, absolutely and unconditionally.

As for those other two gigantically enormous questions — well, they have been asked billions of times over by women as pregnant as you. And yes, probably most of the time, you will be a wonderful mum — but, sometimes, you might be a horridly crabby mum. And, occasionally, you may even be an utterly vile mother (while you have your own sleep-deprived berko tantrum) — because none of us are perfect.

To quote from the Naish and Roberts book *The Natural Way to Better Birth and Bonding*: 'You should give yourself permission to make your own mistakes. Many parents-to-be are so determined not to make the mistakes their parents made, they lose sight of the best way to deal with a new and different situation. Freeing yourself to make your own mistakes is best achieved by forgiving your own parents theirs. All parents are humans too; there is no such thing as a perfect parent.'

If you were blessed to enjoy a safe and supportive childhood relationship with your own mother, these nurturing skills were implanted deep into your subconscious early in your life. This is certainly a tremendous advantage to enable you to adapt into your new role of motherhood.

However, sometimes a woman's childhood relationship with her mother may have been marred by dysfunction such as neglect, chaos, abuse or abandonment — and sometimes the relationship continues to be horrid into adulthood. In those situations, when it comes to the assumption that all mums naturally possess positive motherhood skills, having been mothered poorly can definitely leave you disadvantaged. You may have never witnessed the pleasures and blessings of motherhood, so you do not have stored in your psyche a sample blueprint of what being a 'good mother' is all about.

But, this does *not* mean that you are unable to be a good mother. Heck no! However it does mean you probably have a greater chance of being more overwhelmed in stressful situations. You should recognise the need to teach yourself more of the fundamental basics to replace those absent positive parental memories. Solutions can include reading books, watching videos, attending parenthood seminars, joining coffee groups, opening up to your doctor, partaking in playcentre courses . . . there's lots of options. But don't try to work it all out at home on your own.

We *all* can go through *tremendous* anxieties during pregnancy (especially the first time), but sometimes not more so than women who have had to endure lengthy and expensive infertility procedures. For those women it can feel as if their yearning to have a baby in some way eliminates their right to whinge sometimes. 'Normal' women can have a moan about how uncomfortable they are in their eighth month of pregnancy, or how sleep-deprived they are with their one-month-old — but somehow women who have 'voluntarily' gone through the (undignified) processes of infertility treatment can be left feeling that they are never allowed to complain — because they should be so jolly happy. That is simply not fair, and with good friends and caring family that is also simply not true. Just because you may have had to work very hard to get pregnant, you are still a fully validated member of the Get-It-Off-Your-Chest Club . . . you do not lose your right to have a bloody good whine-with-a-wine.

But I offer this observation . . . If you're taking the time to read this book, you are obviously keen to be the best mum you can . . . so most likely you will be!

Will my partner be a good dad?

A first-time mum-to-be always wonders what kind of father her partner will be. But remember, he too probably has loads of unanswered questions and anxious thoughts whirling around in his head. Although sometimes it can be difficult to get an accurate grip on quite what our menfolk are concerned about, after some research here's an educated guess.

- Can we as a couple really afford to start this family?
- Will her physical changes be irreversible and irreparable?
- Will her irrational illogical emotions become permanently part of her personality, with her turning into a frumpy grump who never admires me anymore?
- Will she get postnatal depression, and become all needy?
- How can sex ever be as good again?
- Will I panic once she's in labour and embarrassingly lose the plot?
- Will I be able to handle the blood and gore and screaming at delivery without fainting?
- Can I cut the cord without my hands shaking, or me throwing up?
- Will the car engine break down, with a flat tyre, at a nightmare traffic jam, during a storm . . . and I end up having to deliver the baby myself?
- Will being a father mean that I can't be mothered by her anymore?
- Will she blame me for more things, and constantly nag me with insulting unwanted advice about my parenting skills?
- Will she ever accept and trust me with the baby, or will she think I'm

some incompetent father who just isn't good enough for her?
- Will she be a good mother?
- Will she love the baby more than me, and not appreciate and need me anymore?
- Will our baby be normal?
- Will I discover that I don't even like being a father?
- Will my partner die, leaving me a solo dad?

To answer the original question, 'Will my partner be a good Dad?'. . . well the answer to that question, like so many other questions right now, is unknown — you won't be able to know for sure until time passes. But fingers crossed he'll turn out to be just fab!

Now, I do not mean to freak you both out, but this last 'worry' leads us into the possibility of something tragic happening to one or both of you one day, and, as responsible parents, you need to make sure some other things are properly in place now too:
- Diarise to register your new babe under your own medical insurance immediately after birth, before some medical concern rears its ugly head (which could later become a pre-existing condition the medical insurance companies won't ever cover).
- Make sure you both have adequate death and living insurance.
- Make sure you have wills that include provision for children.
- I also strongly suggest you consider organising power of attorney for each other — which enables you to manage your partner's affairs in the event of an unforeseen tragedy.

This is really important stuff, so don't avoid it just because it seems morbid, or a too-grown-up thing to do. Trust me, you will feel much better knowing that it is done.

Will vaginal childbirth mean that sex will never be as satisfying again for me, and him?

After vaginal childbirth, your two pairs of labias (hairy outer and delicate hairless inner flaps) will be extended and are left softer and fleshier from doing their job of stretching out like fans during delivery. Also the entrance to your vagina will remain more yielding (to put it elegantly). As for the obviously well-stretched vagina, and the fear of a tampon falling out when you sneeze (that's rather blunt) — well, regularly doing pelvic-floor exercises after childbirth, although not a complete miracle cure, can greatly assist to tighten things up again (see page 51).

After the intimacy of childbirth, many women later reflect on how improved their sexual confidence becomes. So, trust me when I tell you that there can still be loads of mutual physical pleasure after giving birth — in fact, it can just get better! (More on this subject in later chapters.)

Will we as a couple be happier with a baby, or will a baby ruin everything?

This is a *big* question. Without doubt many couples' relationships flourish after starting a family, because their love towards each other grows so much deeper. However, without doubt, some couples' relationships deteriorate after starting a family — but chances are their relationship was going to deteriorate anyway, with or without children. We *all* would like to look into life's crystal ball to see what is ahead of us on our life's path. But we can't, and that's life.

However, one practical thing that you can have in place is a joint bank account. If you have been living financially independent lives and one of the couple (usually the mum) is about to lose her earning capacity, then *trust me oh new-parents-to-be* when I tell you that, as an investment in positive ongoing marital relations, a fair and mature decision is for mum to have full access to the joint bank account. Organising this in advance could save you both from upset feelings and unpleasant arguments during the exhausting and over-emotional early days of parenting. (Lots more on partner relationships later throughout the book.)

Preparing mum's body

Exercise in preparation for labour

If you are not a gym-junkie and really have not been regularly exercising during your pregnancy, one thing I do *not* want to do is manifest some new worry for your mind to dwell on. Let me assure you millions of women have, and will, give birth highly successfully without having regularly exercised aerobically throughout their pregnancy. So don't stress about it, really. You have enough on your (fuzzy) mind already.

But, if you are starting to have some lack-of-exercise guilt creep into your otherwise nonchalant existence, then there are some exercises that can help strengthen your body ready for labour. There are loads of books and videos out there you can purchase, or borrow from the library. My personal favourites are the yoga-during-pregnancy videos.

One position in particular that can be very helpful to practise as preparation for childbirth is pelvic stretching such as squatting. Some childbirth specialists estimate (though not all agree) that squatting widens the pelvic outlet by around 25 percent and it certainly is one of the most natural positions our body would choose to deliver in. However, due to years of high-heeled shoes and sit-down toilets, many westernised women loose their strength and ankle flexibility to comfortably maintain this position without toppling over. So, practising this position while you are pregnant is very helpful to adjust to your pregnancy 'centre of gravity' while squatting. (Birthing stools are a good compromise, but they do require you to sit on your tailbone, which is a slight disadvantage.)

When and why to give up work

In my mother's day a pregnant woman almost *never* worked — especially once showing. But these days it is commonplace to see a woman eight-and-a-half-months' pregnant rushing around her workplace being irreplaceable.

I am not going to attempt to advocate moral rights and wrongs on this subject. However, I should point out two aspects:

Firstly, try to take as much time off as possible before the due date (ideally 1–2 months at least). This is very important in helping to prevent severe postnatal blues and postnatal depression. This allows your body's circadian biorhythms (internal clock) to adjust to a completely different, quieter pace of life (*especially* if you know you're a bit of an overly organised control-freak). This is also an essential period to allow your psyche the chance to embrace a more relaxed personality, one that is tolerant of monotony — because enjoyment of mothering a newborn and acceptance of monotony go hand-in-hand.

Secondly, particularly beyond 32 weeks, there is great physical stress placed on your joints, spine and muscles; and a massive extra workload placed on your heart, lungs and other vital organs. You should rest whenever possible. Listen to your body! It sends you those messages for valid reasons.

Try not to dismiss your maternal inner needs, even though they may not seem logical.

Preparing the cervix for dilatation

If you're not clear, the cervix is at the top of your vagina — in other words, it's at the bottom of your uterus or womb (same thing).

There are many galenical remedies (medicine composed of herbal or vegetable matter) that have been used since time immemorial (some well over 3000 years) to help with childbirth matters, such as preparing a cervix in the last few weeks leading up to birth and for efficient dilatation. Some remedies appear to be highly effective.

However, modern clinical trials are not available to back up the traditional evidence of these childbirth herbs, chiefly because of lack of funding (as pharmaceutical companies earn their royalty incomes on man-made patentable chemical drugs — not on ingredients found in nature); and because receiving approval for any clinical trials to take place on pregnant women is a major stumbling block.

So, there continues to exist a great divide between the orthodox modern medical practitioners trained in pharmaceutical agents (drugs), and the myriad practitioners of ancient traditional medicine who promote a vast array of natural childbirth remedies.

Taking **raspberry leaf** (tea or tablets), with its alkaloid fragrine, during the last month of pregnancy is strongly believed to be beneficial for toning the uterine muscles to work efficiently during labour.

Some of the other well-known remedies (each performing slightly different late-third-trimester, birthing and postpartum tasks) are black cohosh, black haw, butcher's broom, cramp bark, dong quai, false unicorn root, mugwort, peony and squaw vine. Often only to be consumed in the last month of pregnancy, many of these old-school remedies are also supportive of the mother's endocrine (glandular) system, while containing things like iron for blood and vitality.

But, as with almost everything to do with maternity, there is controversy surrounding the use of any herbal remedies, particularly during pregnancy. It would be advisable to obtain recommendations only from professionals formally trained in alternative medicines, and discuss the options with your LMC, because it is important that they know exactly what you are taking.

Preparing the perineum for stretching

Our modern culture places great significance on the enlarging breasts and growing belly of the pregnant woman, but talks little, if at all, on preconditioning the perineal tissue for the stretching it will be required to do when the baby's head crowns at delivery. (The perineum is the skin and muscle area between the urethra and the anus — the pee-hole and poo-hole.)

It is, however, very commonplace in many older civilisations to massage ointments, creams and oils during pregnancy into this private area, to encourage the perineal skin to become more elastic, to help it not tear during delivery. Although this practice is no longer commonplace advice in our society, it is a part of traditional pregnancy care that you may wish to embrace.

To prepare your perineum for birthing through regular massage is a pretty simple routine: put your thumbs into your vagina, then press downwards and outwards (at the same time) until you feel some slight discomfort, and hold that stretch for a minute or two until you feel the area numbing. Then release the stretch and massage the perineal skin for a couple of minutes with an oil (e.g. wheatgerm, corn, olive, sesame, almond) or cream (e.g. vitamin E, hypericum or calendula).

Pelvic-floor exercises (Kegels)

The pelvic floor is the complex group of levator muscles called the pelvic diaphragm, which act like a slung hammock suspended between the pubic symphysis (pubic bone in front) and the base of the spinal sacrum (the tailbone or coccyx in the back). The stretched pelvic floor supports the internal abdominal organs like a trampoline (intestines, stomach, etc.) and holds in place the pelvic cavity organs such as the uterus, bladder and bowel (rectum). Passing through the pelvic floor are outlets for the urethra, vagina, and anal canal, each with their own individual sphincter muscle rings.

Named after the American gynaecologist Dr A.H. Kegel, these pelvic-floor-muscle exercises are easy to learn, quick to do, and very worthwhile. They are an indisputable therapy for incontinence, and practising them during pregnancy is also said to help reduce pain discomfort after delivery.

Kegels are very simple: Just tighten and pull in your muscles as if you are stopping your pee mid-stream, at the same time as holding in a fart, then visualise those vaginal muscles moving up (3–4 levels) through your pelvis. Hold this squeeze as strongly as you can for 10–30 seconds (if your muscles tremble, you're straining them), keep breathing, then slowly release (repeat a dozen times), even try coughing while you're holding a muscle contraction. Then alternate this with 5–10 short, fast, strong squeeze-and-relax movements. You can even check the strength of your own pelvic floor muscles by inserting two fingers and squeezing.

Note: Doing effective Kegels has nothing to do with tightening your tummy, buttocks or thighs.

The breech (bum-down), transverse (sideways) or posterior (head-down, but back-to-front) baby

If your baby is not lying in the ideal anterior birthing position of head-down, it does not mean you will be forced to endure a caesarean. There are loads of remedies for encouraging a baby to turn before labour commences, including acupuncture, homeopathy, yoga, rentable rocker chairs, and many special exercise positions (old-fashioned, hands-and-knees scrubbing the floor is a good one).

You are going to need to 'teach' your child for many, many years to come, and maybe this is its first lesson. So, do some research, talk to your LMC, get out some library books, surf the internet and become pro-active in discovering ways to encourage your malpositioned baby to turn. The Naish and Roberts book *The Natural Way to Better Birth and Bonding* is a good start.

Note: Home-birthing is not recommended for naturally delivering a baby who is malpositioned, especially if it is transverse or breech — in fact a C-section can be recommended instead.

Breastfeeding school

It's time to go back to school and learn about a new topic that will dominate your life for a while: breastfeeding. Oh, you were just going to learn about it on-the-job half an hour after being in labour for a day? You thought you'd wait till then to have the midwife explain it all to you? *I don't think so!* Not the best plan, Sam!

It really is important for your new job that you ensure you receive some formal instruction on the mechanics of breastfeeding, *before* you need to start doing it. Perhaps you could attend a breastfeeding course with your local lactation consultant, or attend a couple of La Leche League meetings, rent a video, or read a book (especially chapter 4 of this one!). But do something pro-active to learn how to feed your new baby. This is a really important point.

Breastfeeding bits 'n' pieces

You don't need all these things — I'm just telling you about some of what's out there:

Breast shells — these hard plastic marvels protect sore or cracked nipples from further irritation by stopping anything touching your nipples between feeds, and the air circulation helps your skin to heal. They are also great at relieving engorgement discomfort as they collect leaking breastmilk, which can be frozen for use later.

Hydrogel breast pads — More expensive and intended to be worn for 3–7 days (removed for feeding). One pair may be all you need to see you through the sorest first few days.

Nipple shields — these are soft silica nipple covers in the shape of Mexican sombrero hats. These can be useful when babies won't latch on to small or inverted nipples; when the breasts are so engorged that the baby can't latch on; or to protect sore nipples. However, some women who try them end up abhorring them.

Pre-sterilised disposable bottle-bags — great for storing expressed breastmilk in the freezer. As the bags deflate during feeding, the vacuum build-up is said to reduce colic, due to the baby swallowing less air.

Nursing pads for inside your bra — these are designed to stop you leaking through your bra onto your blouse. A favourite are the Pigeon™ brand disposable pads. Once your milk production settles down after a few weeks, you may find washable breast pads are fine most of the time.

U-shaped pillow — designed specifically for breastfeeding, these can be wonderfully supportive for your arms in the early days, as can using a Tri-Pillow to support your back. However, the sooner you become comfortable feeding without pillows (it takes longer after a caesar), the more cruisy life can become, so that you can then conveniently breastfeed at a café with a girlfriend, without feeling as if you need to go home to get perfectly positioned with all those cushions.

Bras — It's best to purchase your non-synthetic maternity bras when you are around eight months pregnant. Do have them professionally fitted by an experienced shop assistant (they should know what enlargement to allow for). I suggest a minimum of two good-quality, well-fitting, firm, cotton maternity bras for the daytime, and one made of softer cotton for night-time. (Breasts can leak milk day and night, so for most mums wearing a maternity bra with pads while sleeping is a necessity — as well as giving comforting support, it prevents milk leaking onto your sheets while you sleep, and helps to prevent breast stretchmarks.)

Preparing dad for your labour of love

Be ready a month before due date

Dear Dad-to-be (or main suport person)
For the male partner the intimacy of witnessing the mother of his child giving birth to his baby can be one of the strongest and most emotionally powerful moments of his life — though some of these 'Men from Mars' aren't so great at expressing their feelings when they're extraordinarily happy. Some men, afterwards, see the mother of their child in a new light, kind of like a heroine — which of course we are! Most of the ball is in the mum's court when it comes to baby production, but there are some things you, the partner, would need sorted *a month in advance of due date.*

Dad-to-be to do list
- As you are likely to be the Contraction-Timing Recorder, understand you need to note the time from the *commencement* of one contraction to the *commencement* of the next contraction — and the duration of each contraction. So do make sure you have, or know where to find, a clock

or watch that has a second hand.

- You need to know where the phone number is for your LMC. Also, understand that when you tell your LMC that contractions are 15 minutes apart and lasting 30 seconds, the LMC might reply, 'Cool, ring me in a couple of hours.' Or, when you tell the LMC that contractions are five minutes apart and lasting one minute and getting stronger, the LMC might reply, 'Get packed up, I'll meet you at the hospital in half an hour.' Or, if you tell the LMC that contractions are three minutes apart and lasting 1¹/₂–2 minutes and are obviously intense, the LMC might yell, 'Get to the hospital, now! And don't stop anywhere en route!'

- Be well aware that it is quite normal for women in the later stages of childbirth, particularly during the transitional phase, to appear *to lose the plot*! This is NOT the time for you to take personal offence at her swearing, glaring, angry eyes, ignoring you, being abrupt, abusive or hypercritical — she is just venting steam and needing to focus inwardly. Try to comprehend, in advance, that a woman in strong labour has *no* energy to waste on being polite or concerning herself with other people's feelings. She loves you and she needs you there.

- When mum-to-be is showing the signs of entering into the transition phase, double-check with the LMC and then, *tell her*, because she's probably lost track by now, and she will need that positive encouraging news. (Refer to the stages of labour in the next chapter, which you MUST READ . . . at least TWICE!)

- Be well forewarned, that if mum-to-be requires a caesarian delivery, she may be unable to drive for a few weeks, lift heavy loads (like the baby carseat and baskets of washing), or stretch (like pegging washing). The immediate recovery period can be as short as 2–3 weeks, but that is not always the case, as some C-sections can be more physically traumatic. Your LMC should advise you both after the birth.

- Please realise that after childbirth, and over the first days, a woman can feel very differently from how she expected to feel regarding the onslaught of well-wishing visitors to the hospital (and at home). So, you need to happily take on the role of bouncer for mum if she has the need, which may mean giving some people polite delay messages until she's ready. Maybe she'll adore all the attention, and hugs and pressies. Just be flexible and helpful so she has the freedom to 'play it by ear'.

- Have the two of you had a discussion yet, before baby arrives, as to *who* will be getting up to attend to (or help with attending to) your new addition during the nights? If you haven't, you'd better talk soon, to avoid unnecessary postnatal feuds. And if mum has a C-section or episiotomy, she may particularly need assistance with pillow placement and refreshments when breastfeeding. Be there for her — looking after your partner is also looking after your baby.

- Make sure you know how to put the baby carseat in the car from *reading the instruction sheet* — and no, we don't want you to just *think* you know. You need to actually know by doing a trial installation to avoid having your partner waiting an unplanned half-hour longer at the hospital because you're running late trying to sort out the rear-facing carseat. Initially, they can be complicated little items — and remember carseats should never be positioned in vehicle seats that have their own collision air-bag.

- Realise, very loudly and clearly, that thanks to Mother Nature's radical postpartum 'hormonal see-saw', mum could be utterly infatuated by your new baby. Because that baby is entirely dependent on her for its nurturing and survival, her body produces a mind-altering hormonal cocktail to help to ensure the new baby dominates all her interests. Know that she *will* come out of the hormonal fog, and she will love you probably more deeply than she did before children. But, for the first little while, Mother Nature forces her to make the baby her top priority and centre of her universe. So Dad, just for a while, give her that space, and don't be jealous of the attention she gives to your tiny helpless infant.

- In case you've forgotten, just as girlfriends can love their baby showers, the guys can enjoy their cigars and 'wetting the baby's head'. So we encourage you (only with your lady's agreement of course, as her wishes preside for the moment) to enjoy an evening of macho camaraderie while mum is in hospital. Just remember to wet the dish-cloth after wetting the baby's head, by cleaning up every little beer-bottle ring on

Summary of Dad-to-do list

- Have a watch with a second hand to time contractions
- Know where the LMC and hospital phone numbers are (key into cellphone if you have one)
- Know the best route to hospital/ birth centre, both in and out of rush-hour traffic
- If you are the birth assistant, read the stages of labour (see next chapter) more than once!
- Be aware of the intensity of the transition and second stage (she could appear to lose the plot)
- After the birth be the bouncer for visitors
- You will need to help with driving, shopping, cooking, ironing, dish-washing and other household chores
- Accept that you will be in the background for a wee while, while the mum and baby bond and discover their routine

the coffee table — *and* don't arrive at the hospital to take your new family home with a hangover. Remember too, mum may not want that particular celebration happening after she gets home.

- Please realise that combining the process of labouring and giving birth, with breastfeeding and all the general stressy tension, mum could *really appreciate* some neck and shoulder massages in the first weeks.

- Very soon down the track, don't be too surprised if you arrive home from work, to have mum burst into tears as you walk through the door. She is probably emotionally exhausted after being sole charge all day with a crying and helpless tiny human who can't tell her what the heck its problem is. If you have always looked forward to immediately unwinding when you get home from work — then that scenario is likely to be on hold for some time. Just be tolerant, patient and compassionate — it will pay big dividends in the end. (Much more on this later in the book.)

Homecoming 'rule' for the dad

Dear Dad-to-be

The hospital homecoming is a REALLY important moment for you as a new dad, and even more so for your partner as a new mum, and, ultimately, for you all as a new *family*.

My personal *plea* to all you partners out there who want to score brownie points with their sore, tired and hormonally charged wives . . . please have that house looking *spotless* when they come home. No dirty dishes on the bench because the dishwasher needs emptying, no overflowing laundry basket because you've been so busy, no 'man-made' crumpled double-bed with wonky duvet, no smelly socks littering the bedroom floor, no fridge that's only got two inches of milk left in the last bottle, no burnt grilling tray from the pizza and cheese toasties you may have been living on, no soggy towels forgotten in the corner of the bathroom floor, and no pantry rubbish-bin overflowing with smelly take-away containers.

Trust me new Dad-to-be when I tell you that there is wisdom on your last evening of postnatal freedom to include the following compulsory check-list: Get most of the dirty laundry washed and at least hanging on the line; wipe down the coffee table, dining table, kitchen benches and bathroom vanity; straighten the couch cushions; use the toilet brush for the purpose it was designed; empty the dishwasher re-filling it only slightly making sure there are no dirty dishes left on the bench; ensure there is loads of milk and a half a cabbage (don't ask why) in the fridge, plus food for the next few days (and spare toilet paper); wipe out any accumulated crud in the kitchen sink; empty all the rubbish bins including re-fitting fresh bag liners; and vacuum at least all the main rooms and hallway.

In the morning, have enough time to make the bed properly and organise a nice nutritious dinner that *you* are going to make that first night (without asking *at all* how to do it, please).

Warning: Chances are the new mum will want to drive *straight home* from hospital (*no* stops on the way) and she will probably want you to stay home with her *all* the rest of that day, and the next. So *be organised* because this is a very special moment, which you don't want turning into a hormonally charged disagreement.

The ongoing unspoken 'rule'

Dear Dad-to-be
Please don't create mess for the new mum to clean up once she's back home!

You know . . . don't leave your plate on the bench when it belongs in the dishwasher, don't leave grundies and stinky socks on the floor when they belong in the washing basket, don't wash your garage dirty hands in the white bathroom sink leaving the bowl dirtier than your hands even were, don't throw your tea-bag in the kitchen sink when you know it goes in the waste disposal — or any other lazy-way-out habits you may have developed.

Because, it may be time for you to *grow up* and stop being quite so mothered yourself. Your partner needs to intensively look after a helpless baby right now, not you! (Hard words perhaps, but they'll only irritate if you know I'm right.)

Preparing for labour

Be ready a month before due date

One of the reasons my babies do well is that everything is ready for them a month before due date. The more prepared you are and the quieter it is in the beginning, the more time you'll have to observe your baby and to get to know him as the individual he is.

Tracy Hogg — *Secrets of the Baby Whisperer*

It is virtually impossible for a Nullipara or Primigravida (medical terms for the first-time mum) to ever really feel prepared for childbirth — because what you're dealing with is a very hard-to-imagine experience. But there are a lot of practical ways in which you can be *organised* for childbirth. (By the way, if you're over 30 years old, medically you're termed an Elderly Primigravida or Geriatric Pregnancy — such confidence building!)

The heavily pregnant emergency kit

- A charged mobile phone with you at all times, with your LMC's contact numbers (and perhaps a second back-up LMC).
- A couple of maxi-maternity sanitary pads and spare large undies in your handbag (in case your waters break in a less than ideal location).
- Plastic sheet (disposable plastic tablecloth or old shower curtain works well) under your sheet in bed (you really do not want a mattress soaked with amniotic fluid left for partner to clean up).
- All household vehicles never on 'E' for empty.
- Cash in the car glove-box for hospital parking.

Great things to have packed in your delivery suite bag

- A copy of your birth plan.
- Playing cards, chess, scrabble or suchlike distractions to take your mind off the initial latent phase of labour.
- A long cotton T-shirt to wear — or use the available hospital gown (if it is the style that does up at the neck and is open down the back, then wear it back to front, as it's easier for monitoring, delivery and breastfeeding).
- A maternity bra and pair of grandma undies for changing into afterwards — high-waisted undies are generally more comfortable, especially after a caesar.
- If you wear contact lenses, the best idea is to pack them into your postnatal bag and wear glasses to delivery instead (you do not want to be trying to find a lost contact in the middle of major contractions).
- A sipper bottle with straw (so you don't need to tip the bottle back to take a drink).
- Blue cohosh, caulophyllum, rescue remedy, arnica and any other natural remedies you've chosen.
- Lipsalve, chapstick or moisturising balm — your lips can get really dry (from the panting).
- Hair-clip or hair-tie if you have long hair.
- Thick warm socks — your feet usually get icy cold during labour.
- Essential oil(s) and aromatherapy diffuser (some hospitals provide electric ones on request because they may not approve of the open flame of a candle).
- Talc or vegetable oil for massage (perhaps fresh wheatgerm oil for the perineum).
- A tennis ball can be useful for massage.
- A hot-water bottle, heating pad, or heatable wheat-bag can be soothing in the lower back.

- A hand-held fan and/or water spray bottle for your labour support person to cool your face.
- A couple of flannels (or cut-up old towel) and a little bucket are great for hot/cold compresses, or to cool your forehead.
- For the mum: light, carbohydrate, wholefood snacks, herbal teas with honey, fruit juice, soup sachets (light broths, not thick creamy soups), crackers, cooked fruit, glucose lollies (e.g. Heards™ barley sugars), or glucose drinks (e.g. Lucozade™).
- For the labour support person(s): snack food, thermos of coffee/tea, bottled/canned energy drinks.
- A portable CD-player or equivalent. Sounds of water (e.g. running stream or the ocean) can be soothing. Personally, I really like having music on during labour, it helps me to relax. (But realise that afterwards you may not like listening to that particular CD again!)
- Togs for your support person(s) so they can hop in the spa bath or shower in case you decide to use hydrotherapy, and you'd like their supportive presence physically.
- Video and camera (high-speed film) — no flash photography on a baby with open eyes, it's awfully mean.
- Perhaps a good-sized mirror to see your baby's head crowning, although maternity hospitals should have these — though you may not be interested at the time!
- If you want to take the placenta home, then perhaps bring a sturdy plastic bag or container with a lid (ice-cream container is good) — although the hospital should provide this.
- Mobile phone and charger (and phone-cards perhaps).
- VIP phone list.
- Little bottles of shampoo and moisturiser, and brush/comb for the shower afterwards.
- A bottle of bubbly and some disposable plastic wine flutes — you will so deserve a toast or two before your milk comes in!

Great things to have packed in your postnatal bag

- Front-opening cotton nighties or pyjamas (though most of us girls prefer to use the drab hospital nighties instead, because initially you're leaking everywhere and every time you mess on a hospital gown you just throw it in the laundry bag and grab a clean one — you're not adding to your own washing pile for when you get home).
- Blouses/tops for during the day that open in the front, and comfy leggings or trackpants. (You don't have to wear 'day' clothes at all during your stay

— you can stay in a nightie all day and night if you want, many women do.)

- Disposable undies (such as Chicco™ or New Beginnings™ panties). They can be a bit tricky to find, but are specifically designed for the early postnatal period — a great idea. Or, alternatively, half a dozen pairs of big old undies you will be happy to throw away.
- Maternity sanitary panty pads (the hospital supply you with some, but you may need more).
- Optionally a postnatal stretchable panty girdle. Modern versions are made of breathable elasticated material. (It used to be very common around the world that a woman would wear a 'binder' after giving birth as a way to restore her abdominal firmness, and because it can feel so wonderfully supportive — but it is one of those 'wise woman' relics of traditional knowledge that have become obsolete.)
- A second (or third) maternity bra.
- Breast pads.
- Breast shells (for looking after sore nipples).
- Your own pillow (if you love your pillow) because most hospital pillows are so stodgy — but cover your pillow with a couple of old pillowcases, as it too will probably get some stray body fluids on it.
- Contact lenses and solutions, and glasses case.
- Spare camera film and phone-cards.
- Pens (they're constantly useful).
- A favourite old mug (hospital cups are so little).
- Magazines and walkman if you have one (to chill out with).
- This book (because it's just so good).
- A pacifier (you *really* might want a dummy for your newborn in the middle of the night, especially in a room shared with other people — and you might need it for the car-ride home too — and no, that doesn't automatically turn your newborn into a dummy-addicted four-year-old).
- Perhaps a few little newborn stretch 'n' grow outfits — often hospitals wrap newborns only in a singlet, nappy and cloth nappy swaddling wraps.
- Unscented wet-wipes (many hospitals don't have them, and they can expect you to dampen a coarse paper-towel — which is not great for wiping sticky meconium poos).
- Lip balm and body moisturiser because the childbirth process can leave you feeling dry all over.
- A bit of lippy and some concealer for the dark circles under your eyes (who wants to be looking like that in all the visitor photos?).
- Homeopathic Hypercal tincture (to put in bathwater; it has wonderful

healing properties).

- Bottle of witch hazel to put on your pad against perineum or caesar stitches once you're no longer allowed the hospital ice pads.
- Homeopathic Arnica to take internally — it has fantastic healing properties. A couple of drops of Arnica — diluted in cooled boiled water and given to your newborn a few times a day — is also an idea if the infant is badly bruised or has other physiological trauma to recover from.
- Earplugs and an eye mask are a good idea to help you get a bit of sleep during the day (and night).
- Your own flannel.
- Extra flannels — can be great to put in the freezer to soothe engorged boobs.
- Fruit juice — you might get a bit bored with water.
- Snacky nibble food — a bit of chocolate can be way up there too.
- A small mirror and a box of tissues can be handy.
- A journal or baby record book, in case you find yourself wanting to write down the story of your baby's arrival, before the passage of time dulls some details.
- Plus the other obvious things like a dressing gown, roomy slippers, toothbrush, toothpaste, soap, shampoo, hairbrush, good deodorant, and hairdryer (remember all those photos that are going to be taken).
- Purse with some coins in it for vending machines.
- Phone list of everyone else to ring beyond the VIPs after delivery — unless your helpful partner will do that at home.
- And don't forget after delivery to swap the mobile phone and charger from the delivery bag to the postnatal bag.
- You also need a separate little bag with your's and baby's going-home things, including comfortable shoes and roomy clothes for you (remember, you'll still be looking 6–7 months' pregnant, and could be feeling rather fragile); and clothes to take baby home in including a nappy, singlet, stretch'n'grow, booties, cardy or jacket, hat, and shawl or baby-wrap. A newborn's little body is not efficient at regulating its temperature yet.

Note: If you are at a birthing centre, many of these things are provided free of charge. So check when you book in. It could save a lot of packing.

Extra preparation for a home-birth

Even if you have no intention of delivering at home, this section is still potentially for you, because a few first-time mothers end up unintentionally delivering at home — most commonly due to an extraordinarily quick labour. (And it occurs more frequently with subsequent births.)

If, however, you have every intention of trying to give birth at home, then it is wise advice to ensure you are well-read on the subjects of home-birth and 'active gentle' birth; and that you have practised ways to diffuse childbirth pain naturally, such as through yoga, meditation and breathing techniques. (Though that is all good advice for any pregnant woman.)

You need great communication between yourself and your LMC who should thoroughly discuss the home-birth procedure with you, and clearly explain to you the extra things you need organised in advance, such as:

- A warm, well-lit room to give birth in.
- Latex sterile gloves.
- Large plastic sheeting as a mattress cover.
- Clean flannels and many clean towels.
- Paper towels, toilet paper and large rubbish bags.
- Couple of large bowls.
- Plastic sandwich bags with crushed ice.
- Lots of pillows, cushions, beanbags, etc. (preferably with removable washable covers).
- Low chairs or stools of various heights for the midwife to adopt different assisting positions.
- Lamp.
- 3–4 birth-pads (refer to your midwife).
- Soft towel or cuddly baby-receiving blanket.
- Set of baby clothes and nappies.
- Thermometer.
- Plenty of maternity sanitary pads (bending some into the curve of your panties and putting them into the freezer in advance can be a great idea).
- Clothes for mother afterwards (e.g. large T-shirt and roomy knickers).
- Clean sheets and pillowslips for after the birth.
- Give advanced thought to room temperature and ventilation (e.g. heating or fan).
- Food for everyone after the birth (plus for midwife and support person during birth).
- Perhaps an extra support person (who is accepting of home-births) to answer the phone, heat hot packs, organise food and drink, etc.
- Child-minder if you have other children.

It can also be a wise idea to have pre-planned in-home postnatal help, particularly to assist with the burdens of housework, and the repetitive interruptions from visitors (as opposed to a hospital's strict visiting hours).

Extra notes on home waterbirth

Portable birthing pools can be hired for home waterbirths, in which case your partner needs to be very willing and able to be actively involved with the responsibilities of everything to do with the pool's organisation, including its assembling, filling, re-filling, emptying, drying and disassembling.

The weight of the full pool needs to be considered with regards to the house structurally (i.e. it may need to be downstairs not upstairs); the pool location should be checked for convenience of filling and emptying; the room needs to be well ventilated with appropriate lighting; it may pay to check the home insurance policy fine-print; electrical equipment in the room should be removed (e.g. stereos, TVs); and plastic 'baby proof' covers should go on electrical sockets (to protect against water and humidity).

Other important equipment includes an aquarium thermometer, plastic sieve or fish-net (to keep the water clear), battery-operated hand-held fan, large towels, flotation aids, battery-operated cassette or CD player, plus waterproof cushions and stools for the midwife.

The partner or support person needs to know it is entirely their responsibility to maintain an ideal 21–22°C air temperature in the room; the pool-water temperature needs to be maintained at 36–38°C (specific to the labouring woman's desires); and the water depth needs to sufficiently cover her lower torso while kneeling, to allow heat to expire through her supported upper torso as she leans on the edge of the bath. It is also really important that you have a 'practice run' of filling and emptying the pool before the birth.

None of the pool responsibility can be part of the midwife's role; her job is to look after the mother-to-be, not the birth pool.

Preparing for baby's homecoming

Be ready a month before due date

Nappy options

Babies need changing about 2000 times in the first 12 months — and 8–12 times daily in the first weeks.

If you'll be using disposables, then cloth nappies make great 'shoulder chuck-up' cloths. With disposable nappies the saying 'you get what you pay for' generally runs true — the vast range of disposable nappy absorbency quality seems to go from hopelessly leaky to extremely full-proof (literally). If you are stocking up beforehand (a good idea because they are not cheap), initially get only a couple of packets of newborn-sized nappies, because some babies grow out of them very quickly.

At some stage the day will arrive when you discover little bits of something jelly-ish in your child's nappy — that is simply some of the nappy absorbency crystals leaking out. Just wipe them off your baby's bottom, and change his nappy.

If you plan to use traditional cloth nappies, then perhaps give yourself a break and use disposables for the first couple of weeks. Or alternatively, before your baby is born, have one month's Home Delivery Nappy Service prepaid (or maybe ask a kind-hearted grandparent to shout you).

With cloth nappies you will need about three dozen (and check out the second-hand option). You would also probably want to use disposable nappy-liners and you will need plastic over-pants — though the humidity they produce can promote nappy-rash. Good alternatives are the Weenies™ or Kushies™ type products of washable reusable nappy-pants.

Using cloth nappies, you will need two nappy buckets with close-fitting lids for soaking (one for wet and one for dirty), so that the pooey ones can be given a hotter wash; plastic snap-on fasteners (or old-fashioned safety-pins); rubber gloves; plastic spatula for scraping poo from nappies; efficient washing machine with a hot-cycle; dryer or washing-line sheltered from rain; bleach for soaking and antibacterial washing powder.

With disposable 'wipes', I suggest you go for the unscented, stronger, thicker cloths. Some mums, though, use wet Chux™ type cloths, which they then rinse, soak and put in the washing machine. And some use cotton balls and water.

Some mothers swear their baby never suffers nappy rash with cloth nappies but does with disposables, and vice versa — each to their own. At the end of the day most mums eventually get hooked on their own individualised nappy system and stick to it.

Baby's bedding options

Baby Moses basket, hanging sling, bassinet, convertible cot or even a drawer on the floor . . . there are heaps of options for the first 3–4 months or so. Then soon comes cot time, which will last $1^{1}/_{2}$–$2^{1}/_{2}$ years.

There are lots of choices to consider when it comes to cots. Infant mattresses need to be reasonably firm (not soft), tight-fitting and, preferably, breathable (not foam). If the bassinet or cot is second-hand, then it is a good idea to buy a new mattress that fits snugly.

Although an infant's bed should not have drafts, it needs to not be stuffy. Personally I'm not a big fan of the cushioned cot bumpers unless they can be tied really tightly to ensure the baby's head can't get stuck under them. But even then they're a favoured home for dust mites, which can cause allergies in some children. Plus, without a cot bumper, air can circulate better and the baby can see into the room, which can be a great source of interest for him/her. But some cot bumpers do look very cute, I know.

Cotton air-cell blankets are marvellous (they have little holes, a bit like crochet). A couple of square-metre cotton or gauze cloths for your newborn's swaddling sleep-wrap are essential. Back-support cushions and abdominal sleep-wraps are also available.

Newborn drawstring nighties (which open at the bottom) are just wonderful for changing nappies in the middle of the night (maybe suggest a friend buys them as a pressie).

If it's winter you may want to get a microwaveable wheat bag, which is great for warming the baby's bed before you put them down. Old empty pillowcases are ideal spit-up cloths over the base-sheet for under the baby's head in the basinet.

From about six months old, I also highly recommend using a BabyOK™ babe-sleeper (see chapter 5, page 227).

The general recommendation to parents is to provide no pillows for the first one to two years — infants don't have much of a neck.

Dr Sprott's anti cot-death recommendations

New Zealander Dr Jim Sprott passionately believes that cot death can be caused by toxic gas poisoning generated from the mattress a baby sleeps on, and he instructs that cot death risks can be virtually eliminated if the baby's mattress and bedding are free from such elements. Dr Sprott's BabySafe bassinet and cot mattress covers are said to eliminate the risk, and are available in baby-care stores at a reasonable cost.

His scientifically researched data includes other recommendations such as not using old mattresses, using only pure woollen or pure cotton over-blankets, and avoiding such things as dry-cot mattress protectors, sheepskin products and duvets. His findings are also supported by some British statistics from the late 1990s, which showed a distinct correlation: the more pre-used (older) a baby's mattress, the higher the incidence of cot death. For more information you can visit his website at www.cotlife2000.co.nz to make your own decision.

Baby's bedroom items

It is desirable in the baby's bedroom to have organised the bassinet (made up with its bedding); a supportive chair with arms and pillows for breastfeeds (a rocking-chair is ideal); a little side-table within reach; a foot-stool can be great; a chest of drawers; and the change table (which should be waist-height). The most basic models of change table are completely adequate, or another inexpensive alternative is to buy a waterproof foam change mat (with raised sides), which can sit on top of a hip-height chest of drawers.

Before baby arrives, get your change table area set up as a work-station with lidded pedal rubbish bin, unscented wet-wipes, nappies and perhaps Curash™ talc all ready to function. If you get given more than one hanging mobile, it's great to have one over the change-table as well as one over the cot.

For night-time feeds and nappy changes, you will want a lamp with a low-wattage bulb (e.g. 15W), or a night-light you can turn on, or a room dimmer switch.

Newborns like their bedroom to be around 18–20°C, and so investing in a thermostatically controlled oil-filled electric heater could be a particularly worthwhile idea.

Do install bedroom smoke-alarms in your room, your baby's room and the rest of the house — and update their batteries twice-annually (at the changes of daylight saving is recommended).

If you have a choice of baby's bedroom location, then a nursery within very close ear-shot of your bed may not be so wonderful; some babies can be incredibly noisy sleepers. Just a little down the hallway can be great — depending on your own preferences.

Note : A lot of people like to have their baby sleeping next to them (in the bassinet) for the first few months. It can be convenient, but you will possibly get less sleep. (See chapter 5.)

Baby bathing items

There are various wonderful 'bath loungers' available for baby to lie on in the bath — even the cheapest towelling or net ones can be fine. You will need soap-free or 5.5pH baby-washing liquid, some little gauze cloth flannels, 2–3 soft towels (the hooded baby ones are cute), unscented vegetable or nut oil for baby massage (I can particularly recommend cold-pressed organic almond oil from a health shop), and maybe a soft baby hairbrush. Novelty bath temperature checkers are also available — 38°C is ideal. The water should be warm but comfortable to your elbow. It's also a good idea to turn all your hot-water thermostats down to the safety recommendation of 50°C to avoid accidental burns.

Another novel alternative to the traditional 'lying down' baby bath, is the midwife-designed Tummy Tub™ (or what I nicknamed my 'baby bath bucket'), which is a particularly useful solution to a shower-only bathroom, and it allows the baby to 'relive the security of the womb'. And for small babies there's always the good old kitchen sink! With our third newborn I even used his older sisters' dolly bath on the kitchen bench.

Daily bathing of babies is unnecessary for newborns — every few days, even once a week is fine (heck, they hardly get dirty). Instead you can wipe their body with a warm, damp, gauze flannel. Some babies hate baths, so sponging them down can ease a lot of stress. But it is also not wrong to bath a baby every day, and it can be a really nice part of their predictable evening routine — especially nice for Dad to do — and a baby can particularly enjoy the magic of bathing or showering with their mum or dad.

First-aid kit

In addition to your general household first-aid kit, relating to your baby you should also have:
  • Baby paracetamol (or infant ibuprofen) for temporary relief of pain and lowering high temperatures.
  • A liquid medicine 'syringe/spoon' dispenser.
  • Little bottle of saline solution (for blocked noses).
  • Digital thermometer (the tympanic ear ones are great if you can stretch your budget that far).
  • Baby sunscreen (try to keep their skin out of strong direct sunlight for the first year).
  • Gripe formula (optional, but recommended).
  • Two newborn dummies (even if you think you won't use them, you might change your mind at 7 pm when you've been trying for the last hour to prepare dinner).
  • Bach flower rescue remedy.
  • Chart of childhood infectious diseases with their symptoms.
  • Infant resuscitation sheet (which you've familiarised yourself with).

Note: It's also sensible to make sure you've got not only a comprehensive first-aid kit at home, but also a small kit in the car, and at anyone else's home where your baby may spend a lot of time.

Going-out items

You will want at least one baby blanket or baby shawl (a great pressie suggestion for a baby shower).

There is a *huge* array of baby capsules and **carseat** options available; some are more expensive initially but can save you money later by converting to a toddler carseat. Investigate all options before making your decision. The carseat will need to face backwards for the first year, and remember no carseats in the front of the car if the vehicle has an airbag.

It's probably not advisable to buy a second-hand carseat, unless you know that it has never been in a vehicle accident. Instead of buying, you can hire carseat pods (with optional trundler-wheels that convert the carseat into a stroller), from Plunket or some baby stores. These usually last only six months. For newborns it's essential to have the snuggly head-support insert too. (There are also neck-cushions available, which are a natty idea.)

With **prams**, **pushchairs** and **strollers** there is a phenomenal variety available, so really do your research when choosing the best version for your lifestyle and pocket. Bear in mind the various pram options for converting into baby-and-toddler double-prams later. And remember, newborns need to lie flat. Look for a large under-basket for shopping storage; reversible handles are a really great idea to avoid sun in Bub's eyes; a removable, washable fabric cover is sensible; large sturdy wheels make them easier to push; sunshades are good; and easy-to-collapse (with one hand) is pretty important too — plus the handles should allow your hands to be at hip height. Second-hand prams can represent great value. Or just wait for the sales and buy the cheapest and lightest model available!

Then there are slings, front-packs, backpacks and side-packs (hip-seats). Front-packs can be great for doing housework or shopping with newborns, and parents often use backpacks for older babies right through to toddlerhood. Side-packs are innovative, but still require one arm around your toddler's waist.

Regarding **baby slings**, I can comment that most (not all) of my friends who have used them say they are great — slings are particularly effective at soothing a baby while trying to do household chores or making dinner. Studies of older societies where infants are constantly carried, are showing how advantageous this can be for infants' neck muscles, alertness visually, back strength and overall contentment — as opposed to western babies who can spend much of their time untouched and horizontal. (Decisions, decisions!)

You'll need a carry-all baby-bag. The good ones can be expensive, so a great pressie idea for a combined gift from friends, or from a generous grandparent. You may wish to avoid the cutesy-pie teddy pictures for something a little more grown-up — even an adult backpack may be an improvement, because it then

Personal observation

Don't leave your newborn permanently strapped in the baby pod when you are out visiting. Take the baby out and lay them flat on their back or tummy on top of their blanket or shawl. They normally prefer it, and it's better for them.

leaves your hands free. The baby-bag will carry the nappies, wipes, spare change of clothes, spare cardy/sweatshirt, hat, baby sunscreen, and infant food.

Note: Plan to limit the amount of car trips you have to do in your first 2–3 weeks at home, as initially it can seem like an incredibly tiring and disruptive effort to get out of the house!

Kitchen and laundry items

If you don't have a clothes dryer, you may want to seriously consider buying one — second-hand even. And if you don't have a microwave and are not 'anti' microwaves, this is also an extremely useful appliance. Clotheshorses are great for drying delicate baby clothing. Drying clothes outside is wonderful because sunshine is a natural bleach and antiseptic.

Stock up in advance on laundry supplies including a stain-removing non-bleach soak or nappy wash (or the old-fashioned quarter-cup of bicarbonate of soda or white vinegar in a bucket, soaking for six hours); some pure-soap (natural) washing detergent for delicate clothes; and some wool and fabric wash conditioner. (For hygiene purposes, initially it can be a good idea to wash baby clothes and nappies separately from your general washing.)

With bottle-feeding (formula or mum's expressed breastmilk), a very useful dishwasher accessory is a little 'cage' to put the lids, nipples and bottle collars in. You may need a **bottle steriliser** — the fanciest ones being electric steamers. But there are also the microwaveable models; the cold-water sterilising solution/tablet option (though some people comment that their baby doesn't like the after-taste); and there's the inexpensive simple old-fashioned method of a saucepan of boiling water (three minutes for teats and dummies, five minutes for bottles). A double-ended bottle-brush is also a must.

Best kinds of baby clothes

This is what my friends and I particularly agree on:
- When choosing singlets, the ones that dome-up at the bottom are great, because they stay in place (don't ride up the back).
- Avoid newborn clothes like T-shirts, sweatshirts or jerseys (that don't un-button) which have to be stretched over a baby's head — babies universally loathe narrow necks being pulled over their heads.
- Avoid clothes with ties and ribbons that can end up in a newborn's mouth.
- Avoid knitted/crocheted cardies that have an open pattern of holes (which a newborn's little fingers can get stuck in).
- Stretch'n'grow one-piece suits with enclosed feet are great, and so cosy.

• The soft natural leather booties (like Bobux™ or Pitter Patters™) although not cheap, last very well and actually stay on a baby's feet. (Good pressie suggestion.)

Note: Remove all the labels and price tags ready for use a month in advance of your due date, from at least all your newborn-size baby clothes. But, keep all your receipts, since a baby grows out of clothes very quickly, and you can swap them for larger sizes if they are unused.

Many mums hand clothes down, and you will probably find that you may be given a lot of things. It is very handy, particularly while they are small, and are growing so quickly.

Sundry extras

• Bouncinettes are very useful with newborns up to 6–7 months, and the most basic models are fine — but there are even battery-operated vibrating bouncinettes available!

• Baby monitors are great for knowing if your baby has woken when you are at the other end of the house — but *not* necessarily for putting on your bedside table next to your eardrum, especially if you are a light sleeper, as you will wake to your baby's cries.

• At supermarkets you can buy small boxes of disposable scented nappy bags. A box of these is great to keep in your baby carry-all bag, so you can conceal a smelly, messy nappy until you can deal with it at home.

• Young babies can enjoy lying under baby-gyms — a couple of different baby-gyms are great items to borrow off girlfriends or buy second-hand.

• One or two blankets or baby texture activity mats are ideal for lying your baby down on, particularly ones with a waterproof backing for the urine that often gets pee'd out during any naked time.

• There are lots of other wonderful items you can consider for when your baby is no longer a newborn, which are covered later in this book.

Preparing for mum's homecoming

Be ready a month before due date

Plan to take some time out immediately following the birth
of your baby . . . Make your bed the centre of the household
— talk, entertain, cuddle, and picnic there.
> Dr Miriam Stoppard — *Conception, Pregnancy and Birth*

Women often forget to think about their *own* postnatal wellness — so below are some ideas to tick off. You MUST organise in advance to look after your own physical wellbeing postnatally, because after your baby arrives you will be biologically programmed to focus on your baby, and ignore your own needs. But, since you are going to be the *most important person on the planet* as far as your baby is concerned, well your little poppet deserves to have you in the *best working order* possible!

Plans for staying healthy and strong, physically and emotionally

Have in your medicine cupboard at home some over-the-counter pain-reliever and anti-inflammatory medication (no aspirin because it thins the blood which can cause heavier bleeding).

After everything your body and mind will need to endure, it is naïve (and almost irresponsible for want of a better description) to plan to do *nothing* for your own healing. It is a cruel form of martyrdom to leave your body and mind to cope without any assistance. *Get real!*

At an absolute minimum, invest now in two months' worth of postnatal multivitamin supplements — there are great ranges available designed specifically for breastfeeding mums. Always check that they include zinc, manganese, evening primrose oil, deep-sea fish oil, magnesium, chromium, iodine and iron.

Pre-buy breastfeeding tops

It can be pretty normal to look about seven months' pregnant in the first week after giving birth, then to look about six months' pregnant in the second or third week, and about five months' pregnant by the fourth or fifth week or so — remember your uterus slowly returns to pre-pregnancy size, it doesn't just spring back like a deflated balloon. Then for the following months it can be quite normal to remain a couple of sizes larger than you were pre-pregnancy (even your pelvic girdle bones are slowly returning to their pre-pregnancy position).

Your pre-pregnancy wardrobe could be utterly inappropriate (plus demoralisingly impossible); and you really won't want to have to wear your pregnancy garb by default because nothing else fits. (While you're at it, how about shoving all the pre-pregnancy clothes out of sight for a while — you really won't need daily reminders of the wardrobe you can no longer fit into, not straight away that's for sure.) So, it's a wise idea to have organised an array of suitably roomy comfortable stretchy clothes for your new job.

There are a growing number of very innovatively-designed and fashionable breastfeeding clothing brands becoming available, such as Mummy Matters™, Lioness™ and Discreet™. So perhaps have a surf on the internet and check out some of the tops there. You certainly are no longer limited to just blouses that button down the front.

I would recommend you have your new motherhood wardrobe sorted well in advance, since it is unlikely you will find yourself wanting to traipse the shops heavily pregnant, or with a newborn. But just remember it'll be better to have clothes a bit baggy, than too tight and unusable.

Get yourself re-aligned

As soon as practical after giving birth (ideally under 6–8 weeks, and not outside three months), it is an ideal time to visit some wonderful, highly recommended, maternity-experienced physio, chiropractor, osteopath or masseuse to professionally 'get things back into place' while your joints and ligaments are still loose and supple, before you get left with a permanently bad back, neck, shoulders or tailbone.

In some countries, this type of treatment is included within standard maternity care, because it is viewed as a cost-cutting investment for the future. So have someone already in mind, and the money put aside for it. It can pay very worthwhile dividends to avoid long-term back, neck, shoulder and posterior problems.

Housework

Newborn babies demand, at least for the first 4–6 weeks, the undivided attention of their mother — nature intends human mothers to become 'enslaved' to their young offspring, as it is the only way to ensure their survival. When a new mother is supported with a peaceful and non-stressful initial first six weeks, she can recover more quickly; the baby can settle more happily; breastfeeding can be accomplished more successfully; and the mother can feel significantly more bonded with her baby.

Until this point in your life, you have accepted that paying for a housekeeper was a luxury you could or couldn't afford. But in today's isolating world, if you cannot have a female relative living with you for the first month or so of motherhood, then you need to pay for such assistance, at least in the form of a housekeeper once or twice a week.

Please don't tell me that you can't afford it — because money is relative. What if I was to guarantee to you, that if you could find the money to *pay* for a month of weekly housecleaner visits, then afterwards you would receive the prize of a stunning four-carat diamond solitaire ring to keep. Could you find the money? Don't be insane — of course you'd find the money. A huge diamond ring, just for the cost of twelve hours housework? Even if you had to borrow the money, work overtime for it, or sell something for it — you would find the money. With the will there's the way.

In the future you will probably be spending extra money on getting the best for your child — paying a premium for better day-care, driving further to get to the better gymnastics coach, paying for some extra private dance lessons at the academy before the exam, investing in a better quality tennis racquet — whatever will make the difference to your child's development, you will do your darndest to afford. So why not invest a bit of money on the relaxed attention your baby can receive for his first six weeks by using a housekeeper! And, have it all paid for before the delivery, so it is not something you need to organise afterwards. Even just for the first four weeks would be really great, during hours that you might go out from the house, so you can return to it vacuumed, dusted, the kitchen tidied and the bathrooms cleaned. Bliss! If the staff at your work are asking you for a farewell gift idea — perhaps prepaid housekeeping could be it.

Another household task you may need to temporarily re-assign, is dog-walking if you usually do that — for at least the first three weeks. Perhaps find a responsible neighbourhood teenager you can pay to do this for you, or it could become hubby's job. (By the way, do realise that some pets can get their noses out of joint with the arrival of a baby, so you may want to have some cat or dog toys stashed at the ready too.)

If your husband is one of those breeds that requires ironed shirts for work and you have been the ironer, perhaps broach the subject in advance as to whether he could be in charge of his own ironing for the first few weeks at least, so it is one less task you need to think about. Or, see if you can have plans jacked up with a friendly local teenager to do your ironing for a little pocket money — or maybe that housecleaner you have booked can iron too.

Pantry reserves

Believe me, *making dinners* quickly becomes a real drag when you've got a brand new baby! You know you need to eat well, but it's been a very long day and you really can't be bothered putting much effort into it. So stock the freezer up in advance with nutritious re-heatable dinners (e.g. shepherd's pie, lasagne, casserole, pizza, pies); bread; veggies; and you can freeze milk and butter too.

Stock the pantry up with quick easy packet and canned meals such as macaroni cheese, pastas, soups, instant mashed potato, canned fruit, cereal, bottled water (if you must insist), fruit juice (you get so thirsty with breastfeeding and can get bored with water), long-life milk (for when you run out of the ordinary stuff, which will happen), and hide some biscuits for when you have visitors. Remember, too, plenty of maternity sanitary pads, toilet paper and pet food.

In other words, try to have things stocked at home in such a way that you will not need to leave the house for the first 3–4 weeks. (Not to say that you may not want to leave the house, it is more a preventative, so that you won't have to leave the house when you're really not feeling like it.) Additionally, signing up for on-line supermarket shopping can be a brilliant idea too.

Eliminate pending household managerial tasks

When a woman has a new baby, often the last thing she wants to be involved with are important decisions or household logistical issues. For example, making a final decision on which kitchen tiles to choose, or which new washing machine to buy, or whether it's best to get the deck waterblasted before or after the house is painted.

So, do try to be rid in advance of all those types of issues, for at least the first six weeks to two months. It can be really hard to make decisions when you're suffering from sleep deprivation.

Join the waiting lists

If there is any possibility that you are planning to return to paid work and will be needing professional childcare, then you'll probably need to get your baby on the waiting lists at several childcare facilities — keeping your choices wide open.

Even if you're planning to be a full-time stay-at-home mum, there are many other enterprises you may still want to join the waiting-lists for, such as the local community crèche, playcentre, toy library, baby-and-mum swimming, baby-and-mum gym, baby-and-mum music and movement, etc. You can always change your mind later.

Preparing for the parental marital relationship

In a recent poll, 40,000 men were asked to identify a woman's ultimate fantasy.
98% of the respondents said that a woman's ultimate fantasy is to have two men at once.
While this has been verified by a recent sociological study,
it appears that most men do not realise that in this fantasy,
one man is cooking and the other is cleaning.

Unknown Joker

How is it possible to completely prepare a couple for the underground atomic implosion that usually occurs in a relationship post-baby? Let's be frank about it — you can't, not really. Just as nothing can truly prepare you for a death, nothing can truly prepare you for a birth. Yes, yes, you already know you'll need to endure tremendous new stresses, tensions, and worries as you adapt to the instant metamorphosis from being a couple of two, into being a family of three. I am not going to attempt to give you the ultimate answers: that's impossible. However, there are certainly aspects of the woman–man relationship that can be worth reviewing, in an attempt to diffuse some of the landmines concealed within the grassy meadows of first-time parenting that you are both about to walk across. Here goes. . .

Dear Dad-to-be

It's no secret that men-folk find we women a mystery with our complicated minds and complex emotions, we know — there are endless jokes bouncing around the planet via email sites that reiterate how confusing men always find women. But, once you know the mechanics of how we tick, you will have a better understanding of our logic . . . we really are not that hard to comprehend. Let me explain.

We women tend to define ourselves by our relationships — not by the results of what we achieve. And we get this sense of self by receiving respect, care and reassurance through our relationships. (We naturally want to offer advice — it's one way we show we care.) We are empowered when we receive compassion and empathy and we are motivated when we are given understanding and validation. We hate being ignored, dismissed and forgotten.

With men, on the other hand, when something is troubling you, it's pretty normal for you to feel a need to back away somewhat, becoming introspective (or what partners will often describe as distant, preoccupied or unresponsive). Your head needs the space to think about your problem and find answers.

But we women, we're just not like that! When something is troubling us, it affects our emotions, and we can feel hopeless and overwhelmed. The cure, though perhaps bizarre to men, is for our hearts to bottom-out. For us, this means being able to experience our feelings, and express our emotions verbally; which enables us to cathartically cleanse ourselves.

At rock bottom we can seem needy and insecure — but we don't need you to fix us! When we want you to fix something, we'll ask you — "Honey, I need you to fix the lid on the rubbish bin" — but when we're bottoming out, all you need to do is listen empathetically, without making 'Mr Fix-It' suggestions. Then pretty soon we float back up towards happiness again.

Another thing — please don't take us literally on everything we say. We embellish and exaggerate — it's our way. For example, if we say 'I'm exhausted, I've got no energy left at all', it actually might mean 'Right now I'm rather tired, and need you to offer to finish dinner and the baby's bath, so I can put my feet up for half an hour. Then I'll be fine again.'

Now that I've explained how bottoming-out first can be an important part of the process of how we women get to feel better again, it is really important for you, as a new dad, to keep this in mind as your partner enters motherhood. There will be times when she appears to be overwhelmed. But that's OK. You need to listen patiently, without getting frustrated. Then, when her 'emotional housekeeping' is over, she will once again be able to see everything that's great about her life . . . and you will be her noble hero.

Dear Mum-to-be
Now I won't go so far as to say that men are more simple to understand than women — but I will say that they are more straightforward. Theirs is a far more black-and-white world — that's why they love us, for our colourfulness. Men have some pretty basic rules:

- When your man is going into his 'cave' (as described in John Gray's book *Men Are From Mars, Women Are From Venus*) just back off and let him do his mulling. Don't keep asking him what the matter is. Just shut up. Give him the space he needs to process his thoughts and ponder, because the more you talk, the longer he'll take.
- Don't offer him advice, or try to force him to talk about it — just leave him alone. All he needs is space and peace right now. Later, he will return from his 'cave' as if nothing happened and nothing is wrong; and this is the right time to talk to him if you need to.
- John Gray's next golden rule is a beauty, because it's so simple. When you want your man to do something, don't start by asking him 'Can you . . .' or 'Could you . . .'. Men unconsciously find that offensive, because it implies they may not be capable of doing the task to your exacting standards. When you need something done, start your sentence with 'Would you . . .', 'Will you . . .' or simply 'I need you to . . .' — to a man, this is far more courteous!

This is important basic information for both sexes to understand about each other — though of course there are loads more resources such as books, courses and counselling available to assist couples with their relationships. (And there's more throughout this book, particularly in chapter 8.)

Now for a final gem of advice from John Gray's book (it's worth having your own copy): One of the nicest things a woman can say to her man is 'it's not your fault'. Three of the nicest things a man can say to his woman are 'Uh-huh', 'Oh' and 'Really'!

Overdue and bored?

*Faith is simply WAITING — as once you've got what you believed
you'd get, you don't need that faith any more. Having true faith
is being happy sitting on the fence waiting.*

Author Unknown

At present a 38–42 week gestation is accepted as 'normal'; before then it is 'pre-term' or premature, and beyond that is 'post-mature' or 'post-term'. About 60–70 percent of first-time mums deliver on or after due date with about half of those delivering after 41 weeks.

When Mother Nature is left alone, about 10–15 percent of labours commence in the 43rd and 44th weeks. However, past 42 weeks there are increased risks of stillbirth, due to problems such as malpresentation and cephalo-pelvic disproportion (when the baby's head and shoulders grow too big), and the skull bones becoming harder. I wonder however if modern medicine is a little overly fixated on establishing 'standard normal parameters' that they can sometimes forget how much things can vary within nature.

I have many friends who have spontaneously gone into labour with generously sized babies a little early, who look down at their newborn and say, 'Well, thank goodness you didn't keep growing for another 3–4 weeks before deciding to join us.' On the other hand, I have one girlfriend who has been induced three times with 42-week pregnancies, who always delivered babies covered in vernix, looking anything but overdue. Their mother commented to me that she believes she actually has a 44-week pregnancy cycle.

Interestingly, her children have a cousin born by elective caesar at 37 weeks, who unexplainably displayed symptoms of being premature. Perhaps she too was really a 44-week pregnancy baby, who was actually delivered seven weeks early. Who knows?

When my LMC suggested inducing me at 41^{1}/$_{2}$ weeks with our first baby, I asked instead to wait until my full, permitted, 42 weeks in the hope that my body would spontaneously go into labour on its own. And gratefully it did. So don't be afraid to wait, and don't feel 'pushed' into being induced unless there is a genuine reason for concern. Also, if your sisters and mother's childbirths were overdue, chances are yours will be too.

Here are some suggestions of things you could be doing while overdue:
- Get cheques written out in advance for pending bills, and get signed up for internet on-line banking and bill-paying services.
- Have all upcoming birthday presents pre-purchased and wrapped.
- Buy blank baby-pressie thank you notes/cards and pre-write some

envelope addresses, including postage.
- Cover a shoebox or similar in baby wrapping-paper to put in the top of your wardrobe, to put all your little babe's mementos in.
- Start a baby memorabilia scrapbook.
- Visit friends and enjoy a peaceful chat over a cuppa.
- Get ready for the hospital by removing your jewellery (including piercings) and nail polish (interferes with finger oxygen-level monitors).
- Spend some hours day-dreaming about your baby. Write your thoughts in a journal. Form a relationship with your soon-to-be-born child.
- Write a letter to your baby all about yourself and its father, your childhoods, your dreams, your hopes for him/her — and seal the letter till babe's eighteenth birthday or suchlike.

Emergency warning signs - call your LMC:

- Vaginal bleeding.
- Sudden, sharp, severe abdominal pains.
- Dizziness (e.g. seeing flashing lights, frontal headaches).
- Swelling that doesn't go down overnight, with sleep.
- Sudden onset of swelling.
- Waters breaking before 37–38 weeks.
- Waters breaking with fluid looking greenish-brown or pinky-red (amniotic liquor should be clear or straw-coloured).
- Reduced fetal movements (at least 10 sets of movements each 24 hours is fine).
- Large amounts of fetal movement, then everything goes very quiet (try drinking icedwater and give bubs an encouraging rub first).
- Labour contractions before 37–38 weeks.
- Severely itchy skin.
- Painful, frequent urination, or urine that is unusually dark, pink, opaque or smelly.

Chapter 2

Organised for delivery . . . yip! Prepared for delivery . . . are you kidding?!

The narration of your baby's birth will become an important part of your motherhood–identity. Almost without exception, they retell the story with a clarity that has the freshness of the original experience.

It doesn't matter if the birth occurred four days, or four years, or four decades earlier, the memory has the same intensity . . . it remains a guiding life narrative marking the road to motherhood.

D. Stern and N. Bruschweiler-Stern — *The Birth of a Mother*

'I'm so excited . . . I'm feeling so apprehensive . . . it's just such an unknown experience . . . shikes . . . this is scary!'

Sounding a bit like what you're thinking? If yes — then you're on track. Nearly all first-time mums (and dads) are incredibly nervous. It's perfectly natural, and perfectly reasonable too!

It should never be denied that in many ways childbirth is the ultimate solitary endurance test — which, by the way, we *all* always pass with high honours, as there is no fail. However, there can also be incredible beauty in giving birth, a sense of accomplishment that surpasses even climbing Everest — but there is so much mystery too. As Tracey W. Gaudet writes in *Consciously Female*, 'If the premenstrual phase of your cycle and PMS are windows to your soul, labour could be said to blow the wall clean away.'

One thing that continues to amaze me is that, just as every baby's fingerprints and footprints are unique, so is every baby's arrival into this world.

> **Note**
>
> Although this chapter describes the hospital birth experience, it is still relevant if a home birth is intended.

Some birth experiences are similar, but no two are ever the same. That is so special! However, that is also very frustrating for a heavily pregnant first-time mum-to-be, as it would be just so much more reassuring to know what you're in for — but you can't be, not even with a pre-booked caesar.

The experience of giving birth to your own baby should ideally be a mentally empowering mastery of the physiological — and a spiritually transforming life event. But in reality that is not always the case for some births.

In this chapter my goal is to lift the veil to this unknown experience so you are left empowered, instead of paralysed with trepidation.

A woman's life-skill of understanding giving birth has, in only a few generations, been almost completely wiped out in our western world. Well gone are the days of the young maiden wiping the perspiration off her married sister's sweaty brow, as she labours through a second birth . . . while their mother vigorously massages her third daughter's back with lavender oil during each contraction to ease the rushing waves of pain . . . while the aunt helps her labouring niece to sip on a special tonic potion . . . all the while at the feet of this labouring mother stands the ever-reassuring presence and infinite generational wisdom of her grandmother who discreetly checks the progress, and tells this, her fourth granddaughter, how very well she is doing as her twelfth great-grandchild inches closer to its birth.

Ironically, in this society of information overload, we, as modern women, are less knowledgeable about the real experience of childbirth than our forebears. For many of us, attending our own child's birth will be the first childbirth we have ever been present at; holding our baby will be the first newborn we've ever got to know closely; and nearly all of our partners (our main birth support person) are even less experienced.

Gone and buried is the intergenerational ancient knowledge and wise-women wisdom many of our great-grandmothers naturally had access to. Fear of childbirth is now rampant when, ironically, *it's never been safer*. But, to be realistic, before we can go forward we need to go back.

The historical reality

The day [in 1917] the ambulance dumped the bloated, beetroot-faced
young woman on us at 11 am we all took turns at observing her case
. . . she died twelve hours later . . . She was admitted to my side
ward and during the day many senior students, and all the resident
staff, tip-toed in frequently to see the clinical picture of the devilish
disease called eclampsia.

*With the least stimulation of light or noise the patient would give
a cry and go into a hideous convulsion and finally relax, cyanosed
and frothing. We followed the standard treatment of the day, but it
availed her little . . . the resident team came in frequently and
learned a life-long lesson that eclampsia kills both the mother and
her unborn babe.*

Doris Gordon — *Backblocks Baby-Doctor*

Historically, infantile death was always an expected tragedy of childbirth, and maternal mortality was a horrific but naturally expected phenomenon too. In the developing world today, women still increase their chances of dying by hundreds of times with every pregnancy they have (about a one in 10–40 chance of dying each time they give birth, dependent on living conditions).

What are the most common reasons for those maternal deaths? Primarily toxaemia (eclampsia with seizures) of the pregnancy; obstructed labours (stuck babies); haemorrhaging (excessive bleeding after childbirth); and septicaemia (infection after childbirth known as puerperal sepsis).

These days the life expectancy of a Western woman is into her eighties (as opposed to fifty-five for an African woman). And for us lucky women in Western society, only one percent of the whole world's pregnancy- and childbirth-related deaths now happen to us. *How lucky we are! How blessed are we!*

Up until the 1700s roughly a third of all babies never lived to see their first birthday, and of those who did, a quarter would not make it to adulthood. So for roughly every three babies a woman gave birth to, she could anticipate seeing only one grow beyond adolescence. During her fertile years she produced an average of six babies and she had a life expectancy around her early forties. Cumulatively, she had almost a 10 percent chance of dying during delivery — so if not her, about one in every ten women she knew died from childbirth. Menopause was not something most women lived long enough to experience.

Male doctors have had an interest in childbirth for thousands of years, but it wasn't until the mid-1700s that 'man-midwives' became formally involved, such as the renowned doctor, William Smellie. He wrote what became a masterpiece of classic obstetric literature, which laid the foundations of modern obstetrics, particularly with his anatomically detailed and accurate illustrations, though early feminists such as Mary Wollstonecraft vehemently disapproved of such male roles. In the mid-1700s, often from the aid of charitable philanthropists, maternity hospitals began to open in Europe primarily to improve childbirth for the poor.

For the next hundred years came the Industrial Revolution, with its dramatic socio-economic changes in technology, inventions, large-scale factories, mechanised production, electricity and the corresponding urbanisation of the agricultural labour-force. But in the 1800s living standards were often truly horrendous, with overcrowded homes, inadequate diet, polluted water and unsanitary sewerage. Children were dying of diarrhoea, whooping cough, bronchitis and pneumonia in unimaginable numbers. In Paris in the early 1800s, at the famous Hôpital des Enfants Trouvés founded by St Vincent de Paul, 70 percent of newborns died in their first year.

By the mid-1800s obstetricians began using anaesthesias such as sulphuric ether. Women began to use doctors more frequently — especially after 1853 when Queen Victoria publicly extolled the miraculous and revolutionary chloroform as a pain-reliever during the birth of her eighth child. Such pioneering (and perilous) medicine was already controversial, with many opponents believing it was sinful to reduce the pain of childbirth by artificial means, and they quoted the Bible's *Genesis* 3:16: 'In sorrow thou shalt bring forth children'.

Obstetricians were paid medical advisers to the upper class, who advocated that because childbirth was consistently problematic it was best treated medically, rather than using traditional midwifery — even though statistics of the day were proving otherwise. Women ceased to 'give birth' — instead they were to 'be delivered'.

Steadily during this period, the percentage of successful forceps deliveries was increasing, as was the growing numbers of caesars with positive outcomes. In the early 1860s Pasteur released his theories on germs, and then two decades later, thanks to Alexander Fleming, the world was given penicillin. So it wasn't until the late 1800s, less than 150 years ago, that medical science finally discovered antisepsis, which made it possible to treat the deadly postnatal puerperal fever. Even with medical advancements and standard-of-living improvements from the mid-1800s till the early 1900s, with roughly one-third of a woman's life spent pregnant or breastfeeding, she still had a 10–25 percent chance of being left with crippling disabilities from giving birth, probably half her children would die as youngsters, and she then had about a one in 200 chance of dying from childbirth. However, the dramatic improvements to society's housing, water, nutrition, sanitation and hygiene eventually lowered childhood deaths from disease — but the average woman still died in her mid-forties.

Not surprisingly, after the First World War hospital births gradually increased, because hospitals were strongly perceived as being the safest option. Mothers wanted access to emergency treatments, as they were less accepting of Acts of God.

In the late 1920s daylight obstetrics became commonplace: by manipulating a woman's labour to within daytime guidelines, including achieving twilight sleep by drugging the mother to oblivion with morphine for pain relief, and the uterine relaxant scopolamine. So many of our own mothers and grandmothers spent great chunks of their labours drugged out of their skull to near unconsciousness — heck, they weren't supposed to move from the recumbent position (lying on their backs) during labour or, even worse, were restrained with their feet in stirrups — being stupefied was the only humane thing to do. But women rarely complained, as the pain relief was effective.

In 1916, Doris Gordon, a headstrong, ambitious 26-year-old, was one of the first two women to graduate from the University Medical School in New Zealand. With a passion for the welfare of women and infants, Doris devoted herself to midwifery and obstetrics, and in 1925 became the first woman in Australasia to gain a fellowship of the Royal College of Surgeons of Edinburgh. Vehemently opposing the state control of pain relief administration, in 1927 she founded the New Zealand Obstetrical Society, and in 1935 Dr Doris Gordon was made an MBE. Dr Gordon became recognised as one of the world's leading obstetricians, and continued to receive many other international accolades.

This fearless advocate relentlessly campaigned the government for improved maternal and infant health services, and as a result of Dr Gordon's efforts, in 1938 New Zealand became the first country in the Commonwealth to fully fund maternity care for all women, including the cost of being attended by their own GP-obstetrician, full midwifery services, access to specialist obstetricians, all medical and anaesthetic care, and a 14-day hospital rest for recovery. She was a godsend to New Zealand women. A decade later, Dr Doris Gordon established the Auckland and Otago University's postgraduate schools of obstetrics and gynaecology. She died in 1956 — and is probably turning in her grave with horror at how eroded those free maternity services have since become.

So by the end of the 1930s most women gave birth in hospital, because this gave them access to extensive medical services and analgesic pain relief such as nitrous oxide and morphine. At the same time, by treating birthing like an operation, in a sterile environment, the number of maternal deaths decreased dramatically.

After the Second World War, Dr Benjamin Spock published *Baby and Child Care*, which became a mothercraft bible, and the world of the 'modern mother' truly began. By the late 1940s, natural births were becoming the exception as the medical establishment's restraints on interfering were lifting; analgesics (such as chloroform, pethidine and Nembutal) and other interventions became part of the normal birth experience. Radical opponents of these methods preached of women's natural 'masochistic pleasure' from 'ecstatic childbirth', which the majority of women understandably rejected as 'safe' painless birth was touted.

Throughout the baby-booming 1950s and 1960s the rates of childbirth mortality improved spectacularly, and the price paid was the homogenised transformation of maternity care services into a 'leave your dignity at the door', clinical, unquestioned and hospital-based machine rampant with conformity, uniformity, rules, hygienic sterility, regulations and unbreakable routines.

By the 1970s home-births were generally no longer seen in New Zealand as a responsible decision; instead all births were to be actively managed. Also, correlations began to be recognised between birthing mothers' levels of fear and anxiety in relation to their hormonal production of adrenaline and oxytocin, so husbands were allowed into the delivery suite in an effort to improve the mindset of the labouring mother. But, in the 1970s and 1980s, most women were still expected during childbirth to pass the reigns of control of their labouring body over to their obstetrician, who was 'God', and spinal epidural analgesia began to be more commonplace. With the fear of death from childbirth no longer dominant, influential psychoanalytical experts began focusing more on numerous theories to explain *how* women should labour.

By late last century, opposition was growing towards obstetrics's 'overused cascade of interventions' (to quote author Sheila Kitzinger). Loads of books (and now websites) preach that obstetrics treats childbirth as a pathological event (like a disease) instead of using a midwifery-based, 'wellness of woman'-centred philosophy, complete with passionate slogans such as Joan Donley's fabulous 'Pizzas are delivered — strong women give birth').

Loud, lobbying 'guardians' continue today to advocate protection of the 'traditional', non-injurious, holistic and non-invasive styles of natural, normal birthing; of a less medicalised and clinically managed atmosphere —where the woman's health can be nourished throughout the birthing process: physically, mentally, emotionally and spiritually. This is, without doubt, a very worthy and highly desirable intention, as yes, childbirth is a natural event.

However, such vehemently forthright opinions (often rampant with sweeping generalisations) create in their wake a distorted and somewhat romanticised image of the past as a 'golden age' of non-interventionist midwives; and that there are no longer any obstetricians who believe in natural births devoid of intervention. This is simply not true.

Childbirth is an event associated with risk, and as mothers we urge modern medicine to employ every precaution to safeguard our wellbeing and that of our babies. Another couple of influencing realities are that today's mothers often deliver larger (better nourished) babies than their ancestors; and when we first give birth our uteruses are usually one to two decades older (so less efficient) than our predecessors' were. So, around 35 percent of mums end up having some intervention during their baby's birth, such as forceps, the ventouse or a caesar, with a higher proportion for first births.

There is a philosophy (among a few ignorant industry heads of maternity care) that it is the 'to posh to push' mothers themselves wanting intervention. What utter baloney! What nearly all mums-to-be hope for is an empowering birth experience, without needing to be some hero who endures torturous levels of pain for her womanly rite of passage. If men had to perform this task, we know they'd hope for exactly the same thing. So, these days some mums request the modern and relatively safe option of epidural pain relief or 'vaginal bypass' elective caesar — 'Well, why not?!' they think.

Today, the technocratic model of maternity care can imitate fertility, stop miscarriages and control labour — but we wouldn't want to be without this knowledge. Perhaps until the cauldron of these disputes stops bubbling, and if you are after a middle-of-the-road approach, it may be best to choose as LMC a midwife who is not anti-obstetrics, or an obstetrician who is pro-natural birth — both have invaluable roles in childbirth.

Medical interventions — obstetric operations

Instead we . . . invented for ourselves a kind of earth-mother hierarchy, feeling ashamed, disappointed or even like failures if we resorted to pain relief or ended up with an emergency caesarean after being cheated of a vaginal delivery.

We turned the experience of birth into our own private movie, casting ourselves in the starring role . . . We do not wish to remember that babies die, strangled in their own cords only minutes from light, nor do we wish to dwell on the fact that women still bleed to death in distant rooms where there is no recourse to drugs designed to stop haemorrhaging . . .

Even if your baby is delivered to you safe and whole, and your own body signs are still vital, you will not escape the faint brush of death's wing.

Susan Johnson — *A Better Woman*

Today we are so insulated against there being any childbirth delivery problems, that we can be ill-prepared for some hard truths. Regardless of whether you hope for a quick painless birth with unrestricted modern medical intervention; or you hope for a magnificent natural birth with no medical intervention; or you are really not that bothered either way because you're prepared to do whatever you have to, to get the task done, with hope that it won't be too horrendous, and your baby arrives safely — you still need information about obstetric interventions.

You see, on average, about one in three births in New Zealand (with a higher proportion of first births), require obstetric intervention — and *so lucky* we are these days to be able to receive such assistance if things go awry.

If your baby's birth doesn't end up being 'normal' and medical intervention is required (without wishing to sound condescending), do try to *be happy* that you had access to medical assistance — because if you were your great-great-aunt or you lived in the Third World the outcome may have been far more traumatic.

My big goal here is *not* to embroil you in the pros and cons of obstetric intervention. (If you want to investigate the subject further there is plenty of conflicting research available.) I believe that it is *not fair* on pregnant women to find themselves surrounded by so many opposing opinions, because somehow at some grotesquely perverted level, it can leave us loaded with guilt if we don't accomplish the 'perfect start' birth — which is *insane*.

So, going against the tide of trends, my goal here is to provide you with many *reassurances* about obstetric interventions. *Not* because I do or don't believe that they are or aren't overused — but because what *you* need to hear at this momentous point in your life is not words of debated controversies, but words of reassuring insightful guidance.

Episiotomy

An episiotomy is the deliberate cutting of the perineal skin and muscle — it can vary in size starting from just a little snip to ease the head as it's crowning; to a larger episiotomy for forceps delivery. With skilled guidance during the delivery (and dependent on your skin's elasticity), an episiotomy should not normally be necessary for a routine birth. An episiotomy increases perineal recovery pain and can make a difference to how the new mother feels for quite a while.

Although some pregnant women cope with the idea of an epidural needle or a caesar incision, there would be very few mums who are relaxed about the idea of receiving an episiotomy. Perhaps all males would have more empathy for their partner's birthing concerns if they knew that to have children, there would be a good chance their penis will be sliced open, and sewn back up, with the medical profession's assurance that it is a common procedure with few complications!

Appropriate reasons for an episiotomy are to speed up delivery when the baby is in distress, and as part of an instrumental vaginal delivery. A local anaesthetic is used and it's normally fairly painless — or it is done without anaesthetic during the crowning of the baby's head as the area is numbed naturally by the skin's nerve endings being stretched flat. The incision is done medio-lateral (on the diagonal) or midline (down the middle), dependent mainly on the LMC's judgement.

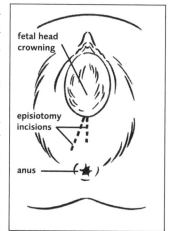

Ask your LMC if they believe routine episiotomies are advisable for natural deliveries to avoid jagged tears; an excessively stretched perineum; enlarged vagina; or loss of muscle tone for sexual satisfaction. If they agree, *change your LMC*, because they are way behind on their medical journal reading. Yes, a small snip can be advantageous, but a longer episiotomy, or being 'sliced from hole to hole' for an instrumental delivery, are practices which should not be performed routinely — too much evidence is starting to accumulate surrounding the negative long-term effects of episiotomies on the pelvic floor muscles.

Interestingly, home-births can have lower rates of episiotomies, but higher rates of a small tear; and because episiotomies are not performed during waterbirths, they too can have higher chances of perineal tears.

Instrumental deliveries

A forceps delivery or ventouse vacuum extraction is usually only used to help the baby out in circumstances of fetal distress or maternal exhaustion. Sometimes the second stage of labour can go on too long and it becomes obvious, even with full dilatation, good contractions and great pushing, that the birth is too challenging and assistance is wise.

Babies find the active pushing phase of labour somewhat stressful, and so the baby's wellbeing can sometimes limit how long a mother can keep pushing unaided when progress is slow.

Other maternal reasons for instrumental intervention include high blood pressure and heart problems, but the most common reason is exhaustion. Difficulty pushing the baby out is most likely to occur with first babies, large babies and especially when epidurals are used.

Perhaps the labour is obstructed by the baby being stuck because it is too large (called disproportion) and is wedged in the pelvic outlet. Or perhaps the baby is not presenting properly, meaning it is lying in an unusual position, and forceps or the ventouse can be used to rotate the baby's head to the correct position, so the mother can then push the baby out herself.

With both types of instrumental deliveries, the normal procedure is for the mother to receive a local or spinal anaesthetic (or have an epidural topped up), and her legs are put in stirrups. Forceps deliveries fail in about one in every 10–50 births (statistics vary greatly). Vacuum extraction fails in about one in every 6–10 births. In those situations the baby is then delivered by caesarean surgery.

Much of the bad press regarding instrumental deliveries, especially forceps, relates to bad outcomes from high-forcep and rotational-forcep deliveries. These days those cases are usually delivered by emergency caesar. The obstetric decision between using low-mid forceps or ventouse comes down to many different issues particular to the situation.

In some cases, instrumental deliveries can increase the perineal pain and pelvic floor damage for the mother after delivery.

Forceps delivery

Versions of forceps have been used for over 350 years — the first hundred years or so in secrecy — so the invention is far from new though, of course, the design of the forceps has obviously been refined over time. Nowadays forcep deliveries are categorised into three types: the reasonably common low, not so common mid, and even rarer high — dependent on how far down the birth canal the baby has managed to progress without intervention.

The forceps are curved to fit the baby's head and mother's pelvis. First one, then the other forcep paddle (they resemble metal salad tongs) is snugly placed along the sides of the baby's head, ideally covering the ears. Their handles are locked together (they are

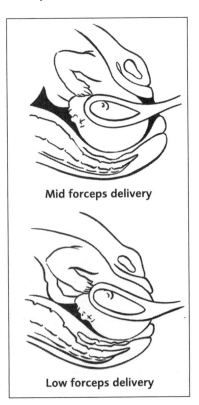

Mid forceps delivery

Low forceps delivery

dove-tailed so they act like a cage that protects the baby's head from pressure in the birth canal), and the baby is pulled as the mother pushes with her contractions. The baby may be born with red marks on its head from the forceps blades, but they disappear soon after delivery.

The ventouse vacuum extractor

This is a flat or cone-shaped cup of synthetic material connected by a tube to a vacuum apparatus. The vacuum cup is placed against the baby's head (an episiotomy may not be required) and a vacuum suction is created — the ventouse cup can even be applied before the cervix is fully dilatated.

The doctor can then move the tubing like a handle aiding with rotating the head to help suck the baby out. (The ventouse can take 10–20 minutes to be positioned, and can leave an obvious, swollen bruise on the baby's head, called a chignon, which will fade in 1–2 weeks.)

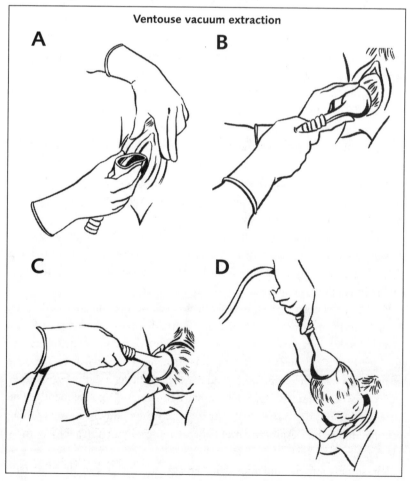

Ventouse vacuum extraction

A B

C D

Caesarean section

A pre-booked caesar operation is called an 'elective' caesarean. An unbooked caesar operation is termed an 'emergency' caesarean — not because the particular situation is necessarily a panicked rush to the operating theatre.

Most new mums don't expect a C-section, however there are a number of valid life-saving reasons why an elective caesar may be the wisest choice. These include escalating pre-eclampsia (immediately cured by the delivery of the baby), a large or breech baby, placenta praevia (see page 92), or the mother being weak and unwell.

Common causes for emergency caesars include placental abruption or abruptio placenta (premature separation off the uterine wall); cord prolapse (when the cord falls into the birth canal ahead of the baby); a malpositioned baby (e.g. breech or transverse); the (some say overly diagnosed) cephalo-pelvic disproportion (when the baby's head is too big to get through the pelvic outlet); and (the rather subjective diagnosis of) fetal distress.

The other (too) common reason to perform a C-section is 'failure to progress in labour'. It is a complicated issue, with advocates and opposers in equal numbers. But C-sections are probably the top unnecessarily performed surgical procedure, and the epidemic increase from single-digit percentages in the 1970s to today's staggering rate has had no corresponding improvement in maternal or infant mortality rates.

So, if you are happy to wait and work with your body to deliver your baby naturally, and your baby is not in distress, then don't opt for a caesar as 'an easy way out' — because it's *not*. Although a C-section is a relatively simple procedure, it is still a fairly major surgical operation that requires a longer period of recuperation than a vaginal delivery.

Medically, caesarians are more dangerous for both the mother and baby. For the mother, there are increased risks of suffering serious haemorrhaging (bleeding excessively), anaemia from blood loss, anaesthesia complications, and other problems common to abdominal surgery.

For the baby born by elective caesar, the lack of a labour means that the baby's body has not produced its normal pre-birth levels of the catecholamine hormones. These help stimulate the baby's lungs to prepare for breathing air, protect the heart and brain against hypoxia, assist the baby to maintain its body temperature, and trigger organs such as the liver, kidney and digestive system to get ready to start functioning independently. The descent through the birth canal prepares the baby's body in a way nothing else can duplicate. Respiratory problems are more common in babies born by elective caesars.

For some mothers undergoing an emergency caesar can detrimentally affect her bonding with the baby due to the 'traumatic' or 'disappointing' birth experience — but, of course, it is much less grief than if her baby had died or was brain damaged. So, if at all possible, C-sections should be reserved only for use when delivering vaginally will be riskier.

When a decision is made during labour to proceed with a C-section, there is usually little mucking around and you are whisked straight into the theatre. There you may be on an operating table which is on such a tilt that you feel like you are about to fall off (which you're not); your arms are strapped out horizontally to your body; and the people (there seems to be a lot of them) are all poised for the 5–15 minutes it takes for your baby to arrive — it's the sewing back up that really takes the time (up to an hour). Getting the baby out can take as little as four minutes in an extreme emergency.

Caesars are usually performed with the mother completely conscious, but numbed below the waist. Some of your pubic hair is shaved, and a narrow catheter tube is inserted through your urethra into your bladder (to drain your urine). If you don't already have an intravenous drip inserted into your hand, you will be given one to keep you hydrated, and finally your abdomen skin will be disinfected.

The surgeon will then make about a 10 cm transverse (horizontal) incision through the skin in the lower part of the abdominal wall called the bikini-line cut (or a vertical incision in very rare extreme emergencies when there is no time to spare). Your abdominal muscles are vertically torn apart (it causes less trauma than cutting them), then incisions are made through the layers of your abdomen wall until the lower uterine wall is revealed and cut. Retractors are inserted to hold all the layers open. If the amniotic sack is still intact, it will bulge through, and the specialist will pop the bag and suck out the fluid (which makes a glug-glug-swoosh sound). The specialist then uses one hand to hold the baby, while using the other hand to push down on the womb. The baby is then lifted out and is officially BORN!

Then the umbilical cord is clamped and cut, the placenta is removed, more suction is used, and then layer by layer you are stitched with absorbable (self-dissolving) sutures (stitches), until your final layer of skin is closed using clamps, staples (metal clips), or non-absorbable suture thread.

This may sound simple, but this is major abdominal surgery, and not something you would generally prefer, because the recovery is a lot longer than delivering vaginally. So although it may sound like a breeze — it's not. It is in no way the easy way out.

If, for whatever reason, your C-section is elective, well probably the biggest shock of that, is adjusting to being pregnant one minute, and just a few minutes later being a mum!

Placenta praevia

If you have this, you will already know all about it. But for you mums who are wondering what it is, placenta praevia is not a disease. It basically means that the site of the placenta in the womb is unusually low and is positioned over the 'os' (covers the mouth) of the cervix opening. This situation definitely requires a C-section delivery, as the placenta is blocking the baby's entrance into the birth canal.

About 15 percent of 16-week scans detect a low-lying placenta, but as the uterus wall enlarges, it is only about 1 in 200–250 pregnancies that result in placenta praevia.

Signs labour is pending

The day of your baby's birth will become the founding event of your new personal calendar. . .

In years to come if someone asks you when you last travelled to California to see your brother, you'll say, 'Let me see, the baby was just walking . . . that would make it 1996.'

D. Stern and N. Bruschweiler-Stern —*The Birth of a Mother*

Softening ligaments

To allow the pelvis to relax and soften ready to open up and deliver the baby, the placenta releases the hormone relaxin to loosen pelvic ligaments. This causes the pubic symphysis (the joint of fibrocartilage that separates the 'fused' pubic bones) to relax, allowing the outlet of the pelvic girdle to widen and become more flexible and stretchable.

The most common subsequent problem in pregnancy relates to the sacroiliac joints of the pelvis causing sciatic nerve pain in the buttocks (usually on just one side), and down the back of the leg — or sometimes pain in the pubic area.

Another downside to the hormone relaxin, is that all ligaments and joints throughout the mother's body relax, so it becomes easy to over-stretch ligaments during exercise, subsequently damaging them. And there can even be an eerie sensation, in the last month or so (though usually not so noticeable in a first pregnancy), as if your pelvic bones are rattling around because everything is so jolly loose. This is when every movement, even walking, can become disconcertingly achy, uncomfortable and outright wobbly.

The lightening (engagement)

For most first-time mums at around the 36th–38th week, their baby's head drops into the brim of the pelvic cavity (the baby engages) and the top of the uterus drops down from the xiphoid process (sternum). This is nicknamed the lightening. For second and subsequent babies, lightening may not occur until you are actually in labour.

With abdominal palpitation examinations, this dropping is measured by descents (e.g. D0, D1, D2, D3 and D4); going from 'D0' when none of the baby's head in the pelvis, to 'D4' when all the head is in the pelvis and can no longer be felt abdominally.

Note: the British system of measuring fetal engagement in fifths is also now common in New Zealand: from 5/5 where all of the head can be felt via abdominal examination (and so the head is not engaged); to 1/5, where only one-fifth of the head can be felt (four-fifths of the head is deeply engaged below the pelvic brim).

With vaginal exams, the descent is measured by stations (e.g. -3, -2, -1, 0, +1, +2 and +3) indicating the position of the very top of the baby's head in relation to the level of the ischial spines of your pelvis; i.e. '-5' when the baby's head first enters the pelvis, and '0' when the head is at the level of the ischial spines.

This engagement (slightly different from the last time you were perhaps engaged) can quickly relieve your previous shortness of breath because of less pressure on your lungs — and, for shorties like me, it can dramatically improve the awful heartburn (indigestion) tolerated for the previous weeks

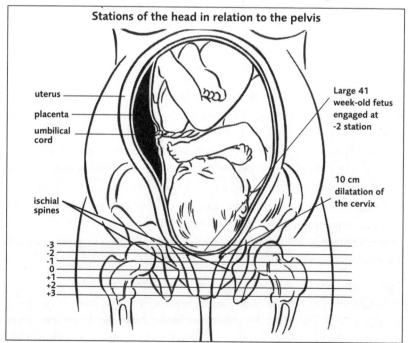

Stations of the head in relation to the pelvis

uterus

placenta

umbilical cord

Large 41 week-old fetus engaged at -2 station

10 cm dilatation of the cervix

ischial spines

-3
-2
-1
0
+1
+2
+3

or months, because your stomach has a bit more room again too.

But, (isn't there always a 'but') there is a price to be paid for that improved comfort . . . and that's the increased pressure on your bladder and groin. Now your new discomforts are increased vaginal discharges (*oh, delightful*); an even shorter time-span between needing to pee (*oh, wonderful*); those uterine practice contractions called Braxton Hicks will probably be felt more frequently and intensely (*oh, goody*); increased pressure on your rectum (*oh, good one*); unpredictable jolts as your baby bounces its head on your pelvic floor (*oh, shikes*); and sometimes even an uncomfortable sensation (*utterly imaginary*) that the bowling ball between your legs (baby's head) is about to fall out (*oh, in our dreams*).

All these new glorious (?) transformations mean that your once graceful model's catwalk style of strutting finally mutates into an inelegant and unrefined gait, nicknamed the tenth-month waddle.

The ripening cervix

The cervix (neck of the uterus) becomes much softer and thinner. A normal unripe cervix feels like the tip of your nose, but a ripe cervix, one well prepared for labour, has a similar texture to lips. This effacing (softening, drawing up and thinning) of the cervix before labour is a very positive sign, and is greatly assisted by the increasing amount of prostaglandins, and of course all those wonderful Braxton Hicks. See page 104 for illustrations of the cervix.

Body shutdown

Within the last day(s) of your body voluntarily going into labour, you may begin to feel a most overwhelming tiredness. Your stools become soft (the body naturally emptying itself); there can be sharp, stabbing pains in places you haven't felt them before; it takes enormous effort to complete any task; and you can become really fed up. You feel like doing absolutely nothing except blobbing out and making a flat spot on the couch. We describe it as a feeling of shutdown. My theory is that your body is trying to force you to rest, before it commences labour. Listen to your body.

Energy intensification

Instead of the body shutdown, or even at the same time, you can begin to feel a sensation of intense energy at a spiritual or ethereal level — as if your aura has been energised to glow particularly brightly. There can be a distinctive change in sensitivity to your inner knowingness too, with heightened senses to smells and sounds. You can find yourself in a mode of super-protective vigilance, wanting to stay close to home — at a mammalian instinctive level you need to shut the world out, in safe, secure readiness.

The show

Normally within about 24 hours of the onset of labour (or frustratingly even up to 2–3 weeks before delivery), many women have one or more 'shows'. This is when you find that your cervix has painlessly dislodged a clear (or pink, blood-tinged) gelatinous mucous plug called the operculum, that looks like a large bit of snot.

Since early in your pregnancy this mucous plug filled and sealed the cervical canal, so it is a great sign to have a show, because it means that the neck of the cervix is already beginning to efface (shorten and thin out). *Cool*! Some believe it is a wise idea to abstain from sex once this mucous plug has dislodged, to avoid possible uterine infection.

If this small show becomes a flood of blood, contact your LMC or the hospital immediately, and they will probably organise an ambulance.

The waters break

Spontaneous rupturing of the amniotic sac (the bag painlessly popping) before the onset of labour only occurs in a small minority of women. Dependent on the position of the baby, it can be a gush or a trickle of odourless fluid. If you are the one in 15–20 that experiences this, then hopefully you won't be standing on a carpeted floor in the middle of a shop as happened to one of my friends. But don't worry, the waters don't run dry — they're constantly replenished.

Due to the risk of potential infection (since the baby's protective sac is no longer sealed), it is usually desirable for the baby to be born within about 24 hours of the membranes rupturing, and sometimes the labour will be induced (brought on) to achieve this. But about 85 percent of women begin early labour spontaneously within about twelve hours and, on average, without induction, deliver within 30 hours. So try to wait the full 24 hours if you can to avoid unnecessary medical inducement. By the way, due to the risk of infection, don't have sex again until after your baby is born.

If the amniotic fluid is brownish-green instead of clear or straw-coloured, contact your LMC and try to put some aside for them to view — this tells your LMC that the baby has already done poos (and the shade will indicate to what extent) — it may mean either the baby is a little stressed, or that he or she is overdue.

For most women the waters will rupture at some stage during birth, and very occasionally a baby is born with the amniotic sac still intact (called 'born in the caul'), which in the old days was a sign of good luck.

Distinguishing false labour (and Braxton Hicks)

Many women experience the relatively painless Braxton Hicks tightenings, which are practice contractions. They are usually 1–2 minutes long and 15–20 minutes apart, but can be sporadic timing-wise (e.g. a nine minute gap, then a 20 minute gap, then a 14 minute gap); so there may or may not be a regular pattern. The contractions don't tend to increase in intensity, and often will weaken if you get up and move around, or stop moving and sit down.

About one in five women experience false labour, which is a bit more than normal Braxton Hicks. False labour contractions may run regularly for a while, without any significant changes in the cervix, then they fizzle out.

Labour, false or otherwise, usually starts with contractions 15–20 minutes apart, or less. But you can always tell if it is real labour — if it goes away, it was false! Women who are particularly busy (e.g. running around after a pre-schooler) can often slip in and out of false labour.

'False' labour is rather a silly name for it, as it is really preparatory labour (it's the uterus rehearsing), and it often occurs before hormones kick off the real labour, which may then start normally a day, or up to a week, later.

When to contact your LMC

Do contact your LMC when *any* signs of labour occur (such as a show, your waters breaking, or any contractions), to help your LMC plan time to be available for you, even at short notice. But be kind and don't ring at 3 a.m. to say your contractions are 20 minutes apart!

Inducing labour

'I'm 41 weeks' pregnant and I want this baby out of me!' If you're thinking that, you're far from the first to complain. Some people are of the opinion that trying to bring your labour on even at full-term is not right. But I certainly remember being full-term, almost completely unable to walk due to excruciating stabbing pains, and feeling *desperate* to get the baby out. So I do sympathise if you're feeling like that too. But this is my theory:

If your uterus and cervix are primed and ready to deliver, one of these age-old remedies might be all your body needs to get things going — I certainly know women who will swear to that.

But, if your uterus or cervix are not finished priming, and are not quite ready to deliver, then probably *none* of these age-old remedies will do anything — I know women who will swear to that too.

Traditional remedies — proven by modern science

- **Your LMC 'sweeps the membranes'**: This is when your LMC inserts their fingers into your vagina to gently stretch and strip away some of the thin membranes to separate them. It's uncomfortable, even painful, but it's probably the most effective method, as it also stimulates production of prostaglandins. With full-term pregnancies after a sweeping of the membranes, women go into labour on average within just a few days.
- **Stimulate your nipples**: This releases oxytocin, which is the uterus-contracting hormone — some people say five minutes of stimulation every quarter hour can produce mild contractions.
- **Make love**: Your partner's semen is a rich source of prostaglandins, and prostaglandins ripen the cervix. Also a woman's orgasm is a cervical contraction, so making love can sometimes produce mild labour uterine contractions.

Traditional remedies — unproven by modern science

- **Do some exercise**: Like mowing the lawns or climbing a hill — I have several girlfriends that this has worked for.
- **Stretch your cervix opening** by sitting in the squatting position.
- **Eat hot spicy food** rich in ginger and cayenne. Having cayenne and ginger present in your lower bowel is understood to stimulate extra circulation to your pelvic area, including the uterus — their laxative action is also thought to be stimulating for delivery.
- Take the homeopathic remedy **Caulophyllum** and/or **Gelsemium** as recommended by a qualified homeopath (and inform your LMC).
- Use **Evening Primrose Oil** on a tampon or put a capsule up your vagina, as this is a natural prostaglandin (check with your LMC).
- **Castor Oil**: Sometimes thought of as a bit of an old wives' tale, this purgative helps empty the bowels. Castor oil has been used for centuries as a trigger on a ripe cervix. How much to take? Some say a couple of tablespoons mixed with a couple of eggs and scrambled can do the trick, others say a tablespoon disguised in orange juice 2–3 times, others say one hit of half a cup of oil in a large glass of orange juice.
- **Enema**: this works in a similar way to castor oil — an empty bowel is said to stimulate a ripe cervix.

- **Visit an acupuncturist**, acupressure practitioner or reflexologist, who specialise in maternity care.
- Herbs **Golden Seal, Juniper, Penny Royal, Schisandra** and/or **Tansy**, and the celloid tissue salt **Potassium Phosphate**, are all traditionally associated with stimulating uterine contractions with a post-term pregnancy (but check with your LMC first). **Black Cohosh** (to ripen the cervix) and **Blue Cohosh** (for a post-mature pregnancy) are also often recommended — but should be taken with caution and only as prescribed by a professionally qualified naturopath. (**Do not self-prescribe Black Cohosh or Blue Cohosh.**)

Medically induced labour — induction

A baby's birth occurring between 38–42 weeks is classed as normal, and although some believe it is more ideal to allow an overdue pregnancy to continue into its 43rd or 44th weeks, at this point statistically the rate of stillbirths increases significantly. That is the main reason to induce an overdue pregnancy.

However, there is an array of other reasons why your LMC may recommend medically kick-starting your labour. For example, pre-eclampsia (toxaemia), diabetes, fetal growth retardation, reduced amniotic fluid volume, reduced fetal movements (ten sets every 24 hours is okay), and if the waters (amniotic sac) have already broken. Induction always requires fetal heart-rate monitoring, and can involve a specialist obstetrician.

Prostaglandins vaginal suppository gel or tablets
Synthetic prostaglandins (or prostin) inserted into the vagina is designed to help ripen (soften and thin) unripe (firm and thick) cervical tissue. It may take 6–24 hours to properly take effect; it may or may not stimulate uterine contractions — but aids to make it more likely that the cervix will dilatate effectively once contractions begin.

Amniotomy (artificial rupture of the membranes)
Amniotomy (ARM) is the rupturing of the waters sac, painless when performed skilfully. This is when the membrane from the bag of amniotic waters is intentionally punctured, so that the forewaters (around 200ml of fluid in front of the baby's head) is released, and the baby's head moves down a little further into the pelvis.

The LMC uses an Amnihook (best described as a long crochet hook) to gently catch the membranes and nick a small hole — you feel a gush of up to about a litre of warm liquid between your legs (depending on the position of the head, which can act like a plug). It can usually only be done if your cervix is already at least 2 cm dilatated. This immediately increases the levels of prostaglandins in the mother's bloodstream (and baby's amniotic fluid), which can stimulate the uterus to contract. If ARM does not succeed in establishing labour, then a Syntocinon drip is almost a certainty.

If already in labour, an amniotomy can help 'move along' a slow dilatation because, with the spongy bag of waters emptied, the baby's head is now pressing harder directly against the mother's cervix, instead of being cushioned by a pillow of water — and this can instruct the uterus to get a move on. This procedure is not called induction, but **augmentation** (boosting) of the existing labour. Usually for most women there is (say within 5–30 minutes) a productive increase of the contraction intensity, and it can help reduce by 1–2 hours the average length of the first stage of labour.

Arguments exist advocating that receiving an ARM is 'wrong', saying that it can make the contractions too strong (in comparison to?); or that Mother Nature designed the bag of waters to act as buffer protection for the baby's head against an undilatated cervix and pelvic bones — but with the waters often breaking naturally, that theory just does not hold water ('scuse the pun).

In reality the amniotic membranes may naturally rupture randomly at any time; before, during or at the very end of labour. It is disputably unlikely that there is any special significance as to when they rupture, naturally or artificially, other than the issue of infection if they remain ruptured for too long.

Pitocin: Syntocinon IV (synthetic oxytocin drip)

Syntocinon (pitocin) is a synthetic hormone designed to mimic oxytocin, which is the hormone driving uterine contractions. Syntocinon is given into the bloodstream (by IV drip) to stimulate uterine contractions when the delivery is being started artificially (called **induction**).

It is also popular to administer this synthetic oxytocin during labour to make the contractions more efficient (called **augmentation**), when things are 'failing to progress', such as moving too slowly from contractions which are too weak; failure of the cervix to dilatate; irregular contractions; and/or a prolonged labour.

However, there are also a multitude of non-medical remedies that can greatly assist to move a sluggish dilatation along, such as the mother changing positions and moving

Important note

If at any time in the hospital at delivery or in the postnatal ward, you are feeling unsure over any matters due to the staff's constant barrage of medical mumbo-jumbo, insist they speak plainly to you — after all it is your body and your baby being discussed.

around; herbal and homeopathic remedies; and many other therapies. A comprehensive reference to many natural options can be found in the Naish and Roberts book *The Natural Way to Better Birth and Bonding*.

Excessive doses of Syntocinon can result in contractions that are often longer, harder, stronger, faster and more frequent; sometimes even violent, double-peaking, overwhelming explosions — increasing your potential need for pain relief. This is not always the case, however, a passionate opposition states that Syntocinon can be the first step in an eventual cascade of medical interventions. This is an overly simplistic analysis, and in fact statistics show that the use of Syntocinon reduces C-section rates: it doesn't cause them.

After a reasonable time, if normal progress isn't occurring, something needs to be done. Before medicalised augmentation, a woman could be in labour for *days* and *days*, becoming (dangerously) weaker and weaker. Mothers and babies can only survive so much time in labour! Ideally, syntocinon is given to women who are *not* progressing when there is a problem, and it can increase chances of a vaginal delivery, compared to giving no assistance. Sometimes the Syntocinon IV fails to induce any contractions at all, or it produces contractions that fail to actually dilatate the cervix. In that case, if the cervix refuses to dilatate, even with the extra boost of synthetic oxytocin, then a C-section is the only option.

Wise Woman advice: Agree to a Syntocinon intravenous infusion if it's the sensible thing to do — but don't agree unless there is a very worthy reason. Give your body as much time as you possibly can to let it work its wondrous miracle. But if Syntocinon is meant to be, then that's fine, and you can usually look forward to a shorter labour. Ask that the IV is not put into your main hand; ask that a generous amount of tubing connects you to the drip-pole bag so that your freedom of movement is not unduly inhibited; and ask that you are not overly monitored with too much cumbersome fetal heart-rate equipment.

Important note

Do not drive yourself to hospital while in labour! If, for whatever reason, your support person, friend or neighbour is unavailable to take you, then call for an ambulance.

Initial overview of the stages of normal labour

The hormone progesterone has been responsible for maintaining the pregnancy by its quietening influence on the uterine muscle. But normally, when the baby is ready, lots of chemical and hormonal activities occur to initiate the production of oxytocin for the labour (oxytocin blocks progesterone).

It is theorised that the baby sends signals to its mother's body to commence labour . . . the fetus increases its copper levels, which causes the placenta to load itself with zinc; fetal cells produce oxytocin that stimulates the placenta to release prostaglandins; the muscle-tissue cells of the uterus form more oxytocin receptors; the placenta produces more oestrogen (days or even hours beforehand); as the light initial contractions begin, then deep inside the mother's brain her hypothalamus signals for more oxytocin to be released from the posterior pituitary gland into her bloodstream to increase the intensity of the contractions . . . and false labour becomes true labour. At the same time, the baby's body prepares itself by beginning to produce catecholamines (stress-reducing hormones).

The first stage of labour: cervix effacement and dilatation

The quiet or latent phase

This period is when your contractions slowly stretch out and shorten your cervix (muscular opening at the bottom of the uterus) until this muscle tissue is drawn up the sides of the lower part of the uterus walls flush against the bottom of your womb. This is called cervical effacement, and it leaves only a thin layer of cervical tissue that will need to dilatate (open up). This is the beginning of creating the birthing canal.

At the same time, during this stretching and shortening of your cervix, the uterine contractions will slowly begin to open the cervix wider and wider (called cervical dilatation). The latent phase of the initial thinning of the cervix (effacement) and first 3–5 cm of dilatation *very generally* takes a first-time mum's uterus *about* half a day — but heck, it varies a lot and many first-birth wombs can take anywhere between one to 24 hours (or more) to complete this initial phase (see page 103 for more details).

The pain during this latent phase is usually reasonably tolerable for most women, and some women occasionally manage to sleep. Most women don't need to be in hospital during the latent phase of labour.

So long as the mother and baby are fine, there should ideally be no time limit set for the latent phase of labour.

The active labour phase

When the effacement (cervical thinning) is complete, usually somewhere between 3–5 cm dilatated, there is a distinctive increase in the strength and intensity of the contractions. This is the time when many women start to request pain relief (hydrotherapy and massage are great too) as the contractions can become intense.

The onset of this active phase (defined by the progressive dilatation of the cervix) until full dilatation at the end of the transition phase, can average around 11–15+ hours for a first-time mum — though of course it varies enormously (see page 109 for more details).

Some women find their skin becoming incredibly sensitive during strong labour and prefer to strip naked, other women feel more comfortable wearing a big T-shirt or hospital gown. But either way, let's face it, the knickers will be coming off!

The transition or advanced active phase

This occurs towards the end of the cervical dilatation (somewhere between 8–10 cm), and this is the final stage before delivery. This is the part often depicted on TV as the 'This is too much, I can't cope!' stage, when some woman acts in a state of delirium. The reality is that for most deliveries, it is the worst part of childbirth!

Transition can be a stormy and challenging hour or less; when gaps between the forceful contractions may not even be a minute long; when your body confuses your mind by thinking that relaxing might harm your insides; and you are likely to get irritable (significant understatement). But trust me when I tell you, it will all shrink into an insignificance when that wee babe arrives! (See page 112 for more details.)

At the end of the first stage of labour, the 'birth canal' is fully formed.

The second stage of labour: expulsion

The mother's abdominal muscles work with her uterine contractions to expulsively push the baby past the pelvic bones, then down and out the birth canal.

Most new mums-to-be assume that this is the worst stage of labour, but many of us later comment that by then you've got past the worst stage (the transition dilatation phase). This second stage of labour can be a tremendously exciting time, because you know you're on the home straight. Somewhere within the next few minutes to a couple of hours (usually averaging about 1–1½ hours for a first-birth uterus), while you're hot, panting and sweaty, your baby's head will crown (start to emerge), and be born, usually facing downwards. The baby spontaneously turns sideways for its shoulders to be delivered and, finally, you will meet your new baby in person. (See page 115 for more details.)

The third stage of labour: delivering the placenta

The third stage consists of lighter contractions for delivering the placenta.

This usually occurs about 5 minutes to 2 hours after the birth of the baby (see page 121 for more details).

Some also refer to a *fourth stage of labour*, which is the momentous first 1–2 hours after delivery of the afterbirth, when the mother may receive some stitches — and both the mother and baby can relax and delight in each other's company, preferably in a tranquil, dimly lit environment. For those precious couple of hours, mothers (and fathers) usually completely forget about the rest of the world entirely! (See page 122 for more details.)

Now let's go into more detail . . .

The first stage of labour — cervix dilatation

In preparing women for labour, I make it a point to explain that although books and classes generally put the emphasis on technique, in fact it's all in the moment, a matter of letting one's physical intelligence respond to the overwhelming energy of the process.

In short, they don't 'do' birth, birth 'does' them, and the key to gaining control is often to lose it.

Elizabeth Davis — *Women's Intuition*

The quiet or latent phase

Oh, this is just *so exciting!* After waiting so long (ten moons as some cultures refer to it), you are in established early labour — probably along the lines of 15–30–60-second strong menstruation-like crampy tightenings (they get longer), every 20–15–10–5 minutes (they get more frequent). You have now commenced the quiet or latent phase. Yee ha! Now, *make yourself a hot sweet drink.* I'm not joking; it's a very good thing to do. (A herbal tea with honey could be perfect.) And some paracetemol (never asprin) is also fine.

It is wise to try to conserve your energy during this phase, because you don't know how far away your next sleep will be. In other words, try to resist urges to do last-minute cleaning in your home. (In the 'big picture' house tidiness is not important, you conserving your valuable energy for childbirth is tremendously important.) Don't be perturbed at this early stage if you feel a bit spewy and/or have some diarrhoea-ish poos — that can be absolutely normal. Your body is preparing itself by doing some last-minute spring-cleaning (emptying).

Many childbirth gurus say that during this initial quiet phase, it is extremely advantageous to stay upright, usually by walking around (or sitting, kneeling or squatting) — being vertical allows the baby's weight, via

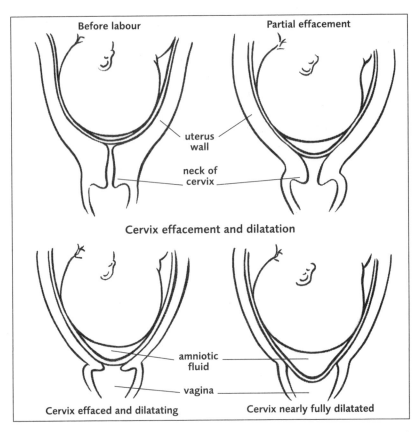

Before labour

Partial effacement

uterus wall

neck of cervix

Cervix effacement and dilatation

amniotic fluid

vagina

Cervix effaced and dilatating

Cervix nearly fully dilatated

gravity, to push against your cervix, improving the effectiveness and regularity of the contractions. You can also sit on a Swiss ball, rolling your hips. However, perhaps better advice is to just rest, relax and take it easy — because hormones are in charge of this phase, and it will happen even if you stand on your head!

You see, although maternity professionals do realise a woman staying upright can shorten the length of labour in comparison to a woman lying down, that is not necessarily a reason to make an exhausted mother pace around at 3 am when she may be in labour all the next day and night! So, save your energy for being more mobile in the active phase, if that is what you feel like doing.

During this latent phase it is also sensible to eat light carbohydrate snacks like crackers or toast; thin soups are good; drink plenty of water, diluted fruit juice and warm drinks to prevent dehydration (which would slow down your labour); suck glucose lollies or sip glucose drinks; and rest when you can. Minimise the Yang foods of raw vegetables and dairy products. And. . . **empty your bladder at least every hour.**

It can be quite normal for there to be periods when labour slows down with reduced contraction activity. This is not necessarily a sign of an incompetent cervix or that you need your labour medically accelerated. It can be an opportunity for your body (and uterus) to have a little rest . . . maybe it feels it needs one. *Wonderful*. But, if you feel your contractions are not strong enough, try squatting.

As your contractions gradually increase in intensity, your abdomen will feel like it is being squeezed by a thick band, like bad period cramps. Some great positions at this stage are rocking, doing belly-dancer circles with your hips, leaning forward while sitting backwards on a chair, and standing while leaning forward onto a wall.

You will need to also start submitting to and *breathing through* the contractions — don't fight them. Take a cleansing deep breath at the commencement of each contraction; take quick deep breaths during the contraction peak; and make a big sighing breath out at the end of each contraction. This deep-belly and rapid breathing also helps to increase your body's production of the pain-killing hormones, endorphins.

Breathing well is important to help you stay centred, and it is *extremely important* to *try hard* to stay *mentally relaxed*, chatty and unstressed — basically in good spirits. If you're anxious, that tension produces adrenaline, which slows labour and makes all pain more painful. I know you'll have a massive mix of excitement and trepidation, but try to chill out. Good advice? *Very!*

You will probably be heading towards the hospital when contractions are about five minutes apart and/or about a minute long — but this will ultimately be guided by your LMC. If you are in any doubt as to when you or your partner should ring, don't worry yourselves . . . just make the phone call and let your LMC do the worrying — that's their job.

Finally, oh man, oh gosh, far out, it's time to get into the car to drive to the hospital, oh wow, flipping heck, freaking out . . . this is IT!

The delivery suite reception should have been told by your LMC of your pending arrival. At the reception check-in desk, the admissions staff should already have your file, and they would usually usher you into

Here's a quick story ...

When I was pregnant with my first, a dear friend of mine, Lisa, who already had a toddler, said to me, 'Kathy, I know everyone's told you all their horror stories about their deliveries, but you know what, when you do finally arrive at that hospital, it is just so special! Because you know that you are about to meet your baby, who you will be bringing home. It really is exciting!' I never forgot Lisa saying that (obviously) — do take her words on board.

your own room fairly expediently. But I should warn you, that occasionally all the delivery suites may be in use, in which case you will be placed wherever they can find you a space — but you should have your own room well before you are up to the birthing stage. Turn your mobiles off now!

Once admitted, some medical assessments are usually performed. The nurse or midwife takes your baseline blood pressure, temperature, and a midstream urine sample to test for the presence of proteins, ketones, blood and glucose to ensure your kidneys are not stressed or in a diabetic state. Probably your LMC will examine your vagina to see how dilatated you are. (These assessments may be re-checked every few hours during your labour.)

Your abdomen will usually also be strapped up to a CTG (cardiotocogram). These are two trace monitors with elastic straps, which are wrapped around your belly for about 20–30 minutes. One strap holds the tocodynamometer, which is a pressure gauge that measures the strength and timing frequency of your contractions; and the other strap holds the ultrasound transducer that monitors your baby's heartbeat. (Don't panic if your baby's heartbeat pattern becomes erratic — it is probably just the transducer losing contact momentarily.) The CTG is done at admissions to find the occasional unsuspected 'clapped out' placenta with a severely stressed fetus.

Personally, I have always really enjoyed being linked to the CTG on arrival, as it seems to make the whole surreal situation seem more real and positively thrilling. It gives a continuous printout of the fetal heartbeat and graphic curves of the contraction surges. You can have the audio volume up so that you can hear your baby's heart beating, which is reassuringly hypnotic; and you can even see your next contraction starting before you begin to feel it. All such a buzz!

If your contractions reduce in intensity once you get to hospital, this is quite normal — all mammals' labours can slow down (or even temporarily stop) if they feel unsafe — it's the sympathetic nervous system's fight-or-flight reflex to produce stress coping catecholamines such as adrenaline. As you get used to your new surroundings, and feel emotionally safe again, then your body will stop producing adrenaline, and will return to focusing on the oxytocic process of labour. (Climbing stairs can sometimes be a good way to remedy a halted or slowed labour.)

During each contraction, because the placenta's bloodflow decreases for a few seconds, it can be normal for the baby's heart-rate to dip (depending on the stage of labour), then return to normal after the contraction. But if the baby's heart-rate is slow to return to its base-line, then this is usually interpreted as a signal that the baby has some 'distress'.

In this situation your LMC may feel it is wise to use EFM (Electronic Fetal

Monitoring) to continuously monitor your precious baby's vital signs, by keeping you strapped to the CTG. If your waters are broken and you are at least 2 cm dilatated, then instead of the CTG, your LMC may suggest that an FSE (fetal scalp electrode) internal monitor is used. This is a tiny spiral wire coil or S-shaped hook electrode which is inserted up your vagina and through your opening cervix, and attached (by piercing) to the skin of your baby's scalp. (However, FSEs are only used if the abdominal transducer is having trouble accurately picking up the fetal heartbeat, especially in advanced labour.)

Some questions are asked as to how much discomfort a scalp monitor causes to a baby, and newborns afterwards can develop a little rash or, more rarely, a small abscess or little bald spot. (Yes, it must hurt — newborns feel pain before they are born.) But it may be the better of two evils — at the end of the day it is used to ensure the infant's welfare, while allowing the mother to be mobile, which is highly advantageous for the natural progress of labour, and advantageous to baby's condition at birth.

Many people are anti-EFM, and certainly in some hospital settings there are levels of 'over-monitoring', when expectant watchfulness using skill and rational thought is replaced by diagnoses made from reading computer print-outs. There needs to be a *reason* for continuous EFM because 'false positive' abnormalities will increase the intervention rate.

However, if everything is considered low risk, monitoring every 15 minutes or so should be fine, so long as the labour continues to be low risk. Because the strap-on monitors restrict your mobility, feel free to ask if it is possible to receive intermittent monitoring (auscultation) by Sonicaid doppler (the sonic wave ultrasound monitor you've probably experienced during your pregnancy); or with the old-fashioned Pinard funundascope (ear trumpet).

For administering pain relief, or to keep you hydrated using normal saline or plasmalyte, your hand may be fitted with an IV (intravenous drip). But this should only be done with your full consent. (A woman can get quite dehydrated in labour, which seems to impair uterine activity.) Any IV should be placed in the arm or hand that you use the least, and fitted with a long connecting tube to give you as much physical freedom as possible. These are the sorts of things it can be difficult (or impossible) for you to talk about at the time, but your support person should advocate and oversee on your behalf.

Getting back to what is going on in your abdomen . . .

Each contraction usually increases to a peak, subsides and disappears. The overall intensity of your contractions should gradually advance — although the level of intensity for individual contractions can go up and down slightly from one to the next.

Feeling waves of contraction pain across the very bottom of your abdomen (just above your pubes) is a particularly good sign that the cervix is opening. The other very common pain position is in the lower back. Nine out of 10 women experience some backache during labour, particularly when the baby's head is pressing against the mother's sacrum (bottom of the spine).

Being instructed (or volunteering) to lie in the supine or recumbent position (on your back) is now clearly understood to be less than ideal because it interferes with the bloodflow to the uterus and placenta — however, some in maternity care still encourage it. Even the semi-recumbent position (on a 40° angle) reduces the effectiveness of the contractions, can increase the pain, and may affect blood circulation. If you want to lie down, then lateral (on your side) and right-side lying can be best.

It is also normal odds that about one in 10 (or more) babies lies in the back-to-front posterior position, with its back facing the mother's spine. This produces what is called a backache labour. Most of the time the baby eventually rotates the 180° needed to change to the anterior position of its own accord, enabling the labour to progress normally.

Unfortunately, in labour it can sometimes be possible to have massive contractions without any real dilatation progress. This can be caused by a kind of uncoordinated uterine muscle action. Some advocate that crouching (say in a bath for comfort) may help move things along. Although that can help with the second stage, its value is questionable in the first stage, and crouching can be exhausting. Perhaps the best action is patience, and giving Mother Nature more time, without rushing her.

If your waters have not yet broken, then the idea of the LMC rupturing them for you may be suggested as a way to speed up your labour.

In roughly 15–20 percent of women (particularly with an overdue baby) when the amniotic fluid is released (the waters break), some amount of meconium (newborn poo) is present, which is a sign of fetal compromise. The LMC will not want the rest of the delivery to be too slow. If labouring in a birth pool, the tub will need to be emptied, cleaned and refilled.

If the amniotic fluid is stained greenish-brown (indicating **meconium**), *and* the EFM reports a poor heart-rate, the LMC will become concerned over the baby's wellbeing. The LMC is likely to recommend continuous monitoring of the baby's heartbeat — which rules out labouring in water. The stained fluid also warns the LMC that it may be necessary to suction out the baby's nose, throat and lung airways after its head is born (often before the shoulders are out) to assist the baby's respiration and to avoid infantile pneumonia (if the baby has inhaled the meconium into its lungs). This procedure is under review, however, due to irritation to the baby. A little

Things that may help backache in labour:

- Your support person applying hot and cold packs to your lower back (e.g. hot-water bottle, heating pad, flannels or frozen peas).
- Your support person massaging or putting firm pressure (say heel of their hand) on the centre or sides of your lower back or top of your buttocks (you'll know where you need it at the time, and it could constantly change).
- Your support person having their hands on your hips and using their thumbs to give your hips circular massage, or pressing into the centre of each buttocks. Working these pressure points can significantly ease the pain.
- Some labouring mums prefer to sit on their own knuckles under each butt cheek.
- A hot shower with the spray directed on your lower back can feel good.
- Kneeling on all fours with your legs wide apart and rocking your pelvis, especially in a bath.
- Kneeling on all fours with your bottom sticking up in the air and your head resting down on a pillow.

(Both of these latter positions use gravity to drop the baby away from your back and sacrum, which eases the pain, and encourages a posterior baby to turn.)

oxygen may also be needed to help the baby establish a regular breathing pattern after birth.

If cervical dilatation is not progressing, your clear waters have ruptured, and patience to wait for Mother Nature is growing thin, administering Syntocinon (usually by IV drip) is generally the next recommended step. Sometimes, however, synthetic oxytocin can over-accelerate the labour, making the contractions too intense (see page 99). This overdose effect can be stopped immediately by adjusting the IV drip.

If you can be happy and patient with Mother Nature's pace, and your baby is not stressed, trust in the natural speed and progress of your cervix's dilatation. This is not a race, and there is no deadline. This is *not* a process that should be unnecessarily rushed, hurried or sped up!

The active labour phase

As labour progresses into the active phase, the length of the regular and rhythmic wave-like contractions will increase to say 60 to 90 seconds long;

and the interval between the start of each contraction reduces down to 5–4–3–2 minutes.

Onset of the active labour phase is generally unmistakable, because the uterine contractions become a lot stronger and more frequent — this usually occurs when the uterus is around 4–5 cm dilatated. There's an old saying, 'If you can talk, then you're not in active labour!'

The top of your uterus is pushing on your baby's bottom with strong force, pressing the head against your cervix to assist it to dilatate. With each tightening you may be able to observe in amazement a clear outline of your baby under your skin — the round bump of the bottom and curve of the spine of your seeing, hearing and feeling new baby.

This is serious labour now. If you allow your mind to feel trapped with immobilising anxiety, it hinders your labour, that's a fact. So perhaps the hardest part mentally is to relinquish control of your body, and lose self-consciousness. Your mind needs to give that control over to your body — and that can be a very big ask.

Is it hard? You bet ya. How long does take? A few hours, say *about* half a day, is a very rough average for a first-delivery uterus, sometimes quicker.

Will you handle it? If you mean by screaming, moaning and grunting (like most of us do), then yes you will handle it.

Is it really that tough? Oh yes, but you will get through it. In fact, chances are you will decide, in time, to voluntarily do it again.

Is it really worth it? Oh my God, yes, when your very own brand new baby arrives into the world, you will be utterly convinced every second of pain was a cheap price to pay. Trust us.

But back to this first delivery . . .

In *active labour*, you will want your support person to help get rid of the world's distractions. You need an environment that is as mentally relaxing as possible. For example, your support person could now:

- Pull the curtains across if the room has daylight windows and dim the room's artificial lighting if possible. (The pupils of your eyes may become very dilatated in active labour, so having the lighting dim can feel good.)
- Put on some relaxing music.
- Put relaxing aromatherapy oil in a diffuser.
- Tone-down or halt the casual, chatty conversation that kept you relaxed in the earlier stage — now you need to enter your own inner, peaceful space.
- Remind you (as you are likely to forget) to **empty your bladder at least**

every hour — a full bladder can anatomically get in the way of your labour advancing.

This active phase is when women traditionally request pharmaceutical pain relief (see pages 34–37). I am certainly *not* against receiving pain relief *at all*. However, having experienced a first birth with pain relief, and two subsequent births without, I can tell you that there are specific ways to manage and diffuse the pain so it can be more tolerable. As the saying goes: 'Express pain, don't repress it.'

Ways to handle active labour contractions:

Relaxation is vital — it's time to centre

I know it sounds like a hard thing to ask of you, but try to keep your mind still, and get your whole inner-self involved, so you can try to centre and bring peace to your emotions. Relaxation is vital for labour — close your eyes with each contraction, centre inwardly and try to eliminate your emotional tensions and anxieties. Sheila Kitzinger explained it beautifully: 'Contractions themselves are not painful, but the tightening and stretching they cause, is painful.' So, the more intense contractions are, the more effectively your cervix is expanding. It's like trying hard to develop an attitude of: 'Wow that was a really good strong contraction.'

Breathe into and through the pain

The empowering ability of good breathing techniques can't be over-emphasised because it gives you the sensation of being in control of your body. Start each contraction with a deliberate exhale out, so you can then take a strong breath into your lungs. Keep breathing deeply and slowly, and as the contraction fades away, blow through your lips a long strong slow sighing breath out. It's good stuff. This way you're working with your uterus — and it helps to avoid accidentally hyperventilating. It may sound corny but try hard to breathe through the centre of the pain to let it go. Your body wants your mind to get intensively absorbed with this 'functional pain-with-a-purpose'. Get excited that things are really starting to happen now. The big ask of a woman in labour is that she truly realises she is an active participant as the birth-giver — not a passive patient being taken over by some biological force.

Coaching with your breathing

In labour we often need to be reminded to avoid contracting muscles other than those we have to. We may also need to hear someone reminding us to breathe. Without realising, we can hold our breath and end up feeling faint. Your support person should be primed for helping you through the active labour phase by gently saying things like 'Relax your shoulders', 'Breathe', 'Unclench your hands', 'Breathe', 'Relax your eyes', 'Breathe', 'Relax your jaw', 'Breathe', 'Uncurl your toes', 'Breathe'.

Numerous positions
Adopt *whatever* position feels the best at that time. Go with your impulses as they arise through your labour. I strongly encourage you to walk, stand upright, move around, squat, sit reclined forward, kneel on a pillow with your head in your partner's lap, squat on a birthing stool, lunge on all fours, pull on the furniture, drape off your partner's shoulders, lie over a beanbag or lean wrong-way-round on a chair. But try to avoid lying down on your back — though lying sideways is fine if you're tiring. Try to use gravity to increase the pressure on your cervix — doing so shortens labour times. Don't be surprised if, over time, you need to change into 7 or 8 different positions. Just give in and allow your body's most basic instincts to lead you! Trust that your body knows the best position for you to be in at that particular moment — it knows what it needs you to do.

Time to make noise
Don't try to hold back or try to control your vocal involvement . . . scream, grunt, howl, moan or groan — whatever it is that you want to do! It really is OK to let go of your vocal inhibitions!

Hydrotherapy
Active labour is an ideal time to start to use hydrotherapy, e.g. shower, bath, spa or birthing pool (see page 32).

The transition (or 'advanced active') phase

The last 15–60 minutes of the first stage of labour is the *transition phase*, which most women think is actually the most painful part of the entire delivery process. This usually starts at about 8 cm dilatated and it is when tumultuous contractions are relentlessly intensifying into sharp peaks. It can seem as if there is hardly a pause between them, and you can feel you have barely enough time to breathe. (With subsequent births the transition phase can sometimes be over very quickly, in just a handful of contractions.)

The build-up from the active to this advanced active phase can be quite sudden — it can make you feel unexpectedly and vulnerably out of control — from your partner's position, you seem to be exuding toxic poison! This really is typically the hardest part of the labour. This is when you may think that you can't do it, you aren't coping, you can't continue — and you may just want to quit and go home!

Apart from being 8–10 cm dilatated, there are other very specific physical signs that may occur indicating to your attendants that you have moved into the transition phase. They are:

- Feeling very restless and agitated.
- Feeling hot then cold then hot again.
- Flushed cheeks and shining eyes.
- Hiccups or burping.
- Icy-cold legs, uncontrollable trembling leg-shakes, or leg-cramps.
- Feeling as if you want to vomit, or perhaps vomiting.
- Feeling as if the biggest poo in your life is about to rip you in half.
- Feeling as if you want to push, before you're fully dilatated.

A mother's mind at this stage in the labour is *scrambled* — she can be under almost a spell of intense feelings — she can be irrational, even delirious and hysterical. It can be virtually impossible for a first-time mother to realise, for

Ways to handle the transitional phase contractions:

- Focus utterly inwardly to centre yourself — shut everything else out.
- When you are in the thick of it, intentionally relax completely between contractions into your own inner world — just flop down into a complete heap to save every kilojoule of energy in preparation for the next contraction.
- Do *whatever* feels best for you to diffuse the intensity, disassociate and release it — panting, blowing, rocking, stamping your feet, banging, thrashing your fists and chanting, or whatever! This is a positive pain not a pointless pain.
- It all sounds peachy in theory (and scary) I know, but you can find help from controlled breathing, counting breaths, breathing alternatively through your mouth then through your nose. It's important to try to avoid hyperventilating as it can make you feel spaced out and anxious.
- Give your body complete permission to forget all the ridiculous dainty, lady-like breathing theories if all your body wants you to do is groan the growling moans of a lioness cubbing, or scream louder than your best-ever orgasm. In fact moaning and groaning increases your body's production of those pain-relieving endorphins, so don't be scared of wailing, roaring or grunting. This is the no-holds-barred-on-volume stage now — and, there should be no 'noise control officer' on your team!

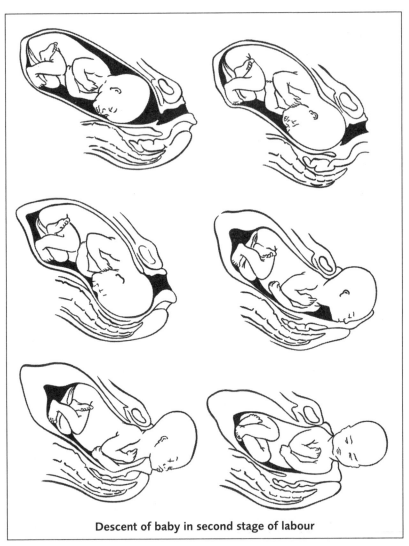

Descent of baby in second stage of labour

herself that she is in this final transition phase of the first stage of labour. For her there may be no clear end in sight, and this can be chillingly frightening.

What she needs is to be reassured very convincingly, 'You are now in the transition phase, you'll be OK again soon. You are not about to tear in half or explode. You've done so well! The worst is almost over!' Then turn the music up, turn the lights down and *stop* any distracting conversation.

The transitional contractions will demand every ounce of concentration and determination you have. You've done so, SO well! Your uterus has almost finished stretching your cervix open . . . just hang in there, it's not long to go now. All you must do is try really hard to relax and focus your mind on your opening cervix — you cannot do anything actively to help your baby out until your cervix is fully dilatated.

Your body's own narcotic endorphins pulse through your system trying hard to allow you to return to a primitive biological state of losing your inhibitions, so you can follow your most basic instincts. For this all-consuming time, there are only two people existing on the planet — you and your baby! You will be drawing on your own deepest inner power, with which *all* women are inherently gifted.

Note: Before you are fully dilatated, you may feel a spontaneous desire to push or bear down. If you are not yet fully dilatated, you will be told to resist this urge, to avoid damaging the cervix by causing it to swell or tear. Resisting that urge to push is very hard to do — but can be *critical*. Taking deep slow breaths can help. Another alternative is the three-count breathing of blow-blow-pant, blow-blow-pant or in reverse pant-pant-blow, pant-pant-blow.

Once the cervix is fully dilatated, the curved passage (birth canal) has now been formed — and your baby's head is free of the constricting cervical opening. If your partner has a peep, he may be able to see the colour of your baby's hair.

The second stage of labour — birthing the baby

The second stage of labour is the time from full, 10 cm dilatation of the cervix until your baby arrives into the big wide world.

The Malaysians have a tradition to mark onset of the second stage of labour. The mother's hair, which has been tied back during the first stage to keep her cool, is let loose. I think that is a beautiful little ritual, signalling to the mother that the worst is over, and she is now on the home straight.

Remember, empty your bladder at least every hour.

Sometimes after full dilatation, but before your body starts to spontaneously receive the expulsive urge to push, there is an in-between period (called the phase of descent), during which the baby descends further into the pelvis to put pressure on the pelvic floor. It is important not to waste energy pushing during this phase, while you are not having the spontaneous natural urges to assist you.

For some deliveries there may be quite a lull in the intensity of contractions before the onset of the second stage, especially if it's been a long transitional phase. If this does happen, enjoy the rest; it is a gift of renewal refreshment straight from Mother Nature herself. This lull can last for 20–60 minutes. Have a shower, walk around, and rock your pelvis in circles. (The pushing reflex is not triggered until the baby's head reaches the pelvic floor.) Often, changing positions can be helpful to move things along.

Sometimes in this situation medical professionals call for oxytocin to get things happening, or simply instruct the woman that it is time to push even though she doesn't feel like doing so. In this predicament you may want to assert yourself and ask for more time (providing the baby is not in distress).

For many other deliveries, there is no pause at all, and the uterus goes straight from stretching contractions to the (quite different) expulsion contractions of the second stage.

Finally, with your cervix fully dilatated, your body is overwhelmed and taken over by tremendous, irresistible, expulsive urges to *push*. The work of this active phase of pushing is achieved by a tidal-wave combination of your involuntary uterine muscle contractions and your own voluntary (but impossible-to-resist) bearing down efforts, using the muscles of your abdomen, chest and uterus all at the same time.

The desire to push is an unbelievably strong instinct you will be almost powerless to resist. Many women, with the subsidence of the painful transitional contractions, and with the commencement of this second stage, find their body and soul completely re-energised, as if infused with renewed strength.

With each uterine contraction lasting 5–6 seconds, there is an incredible and irresistible urge for you to push continuously (if possible, 3–4 short, good pushes are best). With each effort your baby's head steadily descends closer to the outside world, then retreats a little between contractions. It is normal for the LMC to check your baby's heart rate after each contraction.

Often, if the baby's head is pressing on the rectum's nerve pressure-receptors rather than right on the perineum, you can have an alarming feeling, as if you are bursting to expel the biggest poo in your life — but that's no poo, that's your baby knocking at the other door! Keep your mouth loose . . . laugh . . . sing . . . scream 'I love you!'. . . and *breathe* that head out! You will not break in two!

You will be working hard at this point. This is when your pulse will rise and you'll be sweating. Many women feel that this stage is the best phase as they experience the overwhelming satisfaction of really participating, by pushing their baby down their birth canal. At the same time, the baby is often an active participant, with his feet pushing against the top of the uterus — wanting to be born.

Once into this second stage you may feel a great, mounting excitement, as every cell in your body starts to tingle with intense urgency and the thrilling passion of birth.

Ways to handle labour's second stage:

Breathing

There are a few breathing techniques taught for this bearing-down second stage of labour. Your LMC and support person will need to remind you of your breathing options, because it's really hard to remember them at the time. (Even give it a bit of a whirl before delivery so you've got an idea of what it feels like.) There's the taking one deep breath in for one hard push, as you hold the breath — but that can pop cheek blood vessels and strain eyeballs (not so attractive afterwards). There's the taking one deep breath in, and bearing down as you exhale. Then there's my personal preference of holding a few breaths each time, while you push a few times for a few seconds with each breath. This latter technique allows you during contractions to breath in air, and breath out slow steady grunts. Another good idea (which your support person will need to remind you of) is to try not to relax instantaneously after each contraction push. Instead, give out a couple of deep slow breaths — it can help the baby's position recede less at the end of each contraction.

Groans and moans

Somewhat surprisingly, a lot of moaning and screaming at this point can be disadvantageous because it diffuses pressure away from the pushing effort. If progress is a problem, and maximum effort is needed, then it can be better to hold the breath in, because noise can release it.

Labour support person

There are a lot of ways your labour support person can provide really practical help at this stage: supporting you with pillows (and their own body in various positions); coaching you to push; talking you through your breathing; massaging your back; mopping your brow; and spraying your face with cooling water. They can also place hot (or cold) flannels on your stretching perineal skin, as this can really relieve the stinging and helps you to relax that area, which is important. And, your support person can be checking that your soon-to-be-born babe will arrive into a place that is warm, quiet and not too brightly lit.

Delivery positions

For the second stage contractions and actual delivery, just be in *whatever position* feels best. Although rather undignified, birthing on all fours is a strong favourite — as too are all the upright positions such as squatting, standing and kneeling. All these positions use gravity and don't put pressure on your bottom. Standing allows you to swing your pelvis in different positions; being on all fours allows the baby to drop away from your spine which can make it easier to rotate after delivering the head; squatting or semi-squatting positions help to put more pressure on the pelvic floor (as does sitting on a birthing stool, which is less exhausting). Also, psychologically, being upright can make you feel more in control.

Feel for your baby, look for your baby
Put your hand(s) on to your perineal skin so you can feel your own baby inching out to meet you, it also helps you to relax the perineum, and gives you a good indication of the very real progress of your awesomely precious cargo. And/or have your support person hold a good-sized mirror up, if you want, so you can see your emerging baby's head — it can give added incentive for the last few pushes to get your baby out.

The crowning

Crowning can take a few minutes or just seconds.

You will feel a burning-stinging sensation as, finally, your baby's head doesn't slip back between contractions — this is your baby's head tightly stretching your perineal skin tissue as it crowns — it's emerging from your vagina. Stretching the perineal skin so thin naturally anaesthetises it. That is why if the perineum tears or is cut during crowning, often a mother feels only a sense of relief, not pain.

During this thinning your LMC is very likely to tell you to STOP PUSHING, which can be bloody difficult, but you need to go limp and just *pant, pant, pant* to allow a little time for the final stretching of the perineum.

It is very important these precious minutes are not rushed, to avoid an unnecessary episiotomy or other damage to the perineal tissue, muscle and nerve endings. So long as there are no oxygen supply concerns for your baby, your body should be allowed to take its time. Going with a sudden expulsive urge to push at this point can cause an unnecessarily large perineal tear.

Now, my very precious friend, you are highly likely to push out some poo just before you push out your baby's head, but no one else cares, so don't you. It's normal, it's just nature making room. Birthing is messy.

We know it's frightening, and yes you are fantastically brave — but your body is doing exactly what it has been custom-designed to do.

Your LMC will be watching carefully, and giving coaching instructions to you to push . . . and not to push . . . then . . . in one momentous contraction . . . the head pops through the vulval opening of the perineum, and . . .

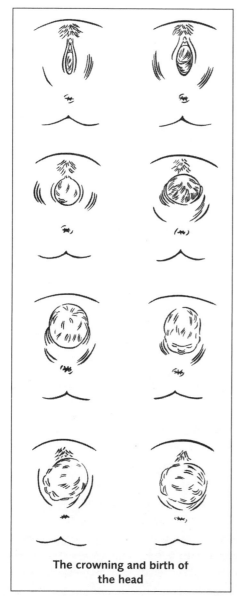

The crowning and birth of the head

Your baby's head is now born!

You will be instructed to stop pushing and *pant, pant, pant.* Your contractions may pause — as Mother Nature (perhaps with a hand from your LMC) then rotates your baby sideways, and the umbilical cord position around your baby's neck is checked. (About 20 percent of babies have one or more loops of umbilical cord around their necks, which is usually loose enough to be pulled over their head — in rare cases when the cord is pulled tight, it may be clamped and cut immediately.)

Then, usually in the next 1–2 contractions, the shoulders slide out with a gush of amniotic water, and the rest of your baby rapidly slithers out, your LMC, your partner or you reaching to receive your slippery baby.

Your baby is born!

Rapturous relief . . . tears of joy . . . collapsed exhaustion . . . screams of ecstasy . . . silent euphoria . . . almost without doubt the most intense moment of your life!

Within the first seconds the baby is given a brief stimulating rub-down; it takes its first gasp of air to inflate its lungs for the first time popping them open like little parachutes; the umbilical cord is often clamped; the first apgar score is recorded (see page 130); and your baby may be given a little helping whiff of some oxygen. Then the about 50 cm-long, 2 cm-thick, grey, tough umbilical cord is sometimes cut (perhaps by the new dad). Or, some mums are given their baby before any of this, cord intact, to be cuddled right from the beginning. If there is nothing of concern with the baby, then there is no reason for delay.

If your baby needs a breathing tube down his airway, he would be placed on a special table complete with heat lamp. (If there are any concerns about your baby, a paediatrician is contacted.) At the all-clear the baby is usually swaddled to keep it warm, and given to you, his *Mum* (what a sweet, sweet word), so you can cuddle your wee bub closely.

After taking its first gasp of air, an amazing chain reaction of miraculous biological upheavals are begun inside your newborn's body within 1–2 minutes. Inflating its lungs causes pressure changes in its whole circulatory system, so that blood floods into the lungs and liver, and the heart's four chambers are triggered. It is thought the increased pressure in these organs then collapses the defunct umbilical blood vessels that bypassed those organs, and these now redundant blood vessels will eventually waste away.

Hearing your baby's first cries can feel like a moment frozen in time. It rouses stirring maternal passions deep inside your body's every cell, feelings difficult to explain in any book . . . like a cold-sweat second of instant awareness that crystallises the reality that the wriggling, kicking, mythical baby inside your belly is truly its own little person, with its own voice.

'Oh my God! I've made a whole new person!' Then this miniature human being may be rested on your tummy — no longer inside your belly, but now outside your belly! The task is done — a circle is closed.

It's time to say '*Hello*' and greet your new darling baby.

You smile from the depths of your soul, while looking through your babe's eyes as windows into the depths of its soul. Feel free to open up any swaddling blanket so you can hold your baby skin-to-skin (it's what your baby wants too).

We mothers make first contact with our new baby in an almost universally instinctive and subconscious pattern: tears of joy roll down our cheeks as we kiss our newborn, breathing in the essence of their scent like a magical elixir, we examine their tiny feet and hands with our fingertips, then caress their entire body with the palms of our hands, and we talk to them — all the while staring deeply into our newborn's eyes.

You will never forget the maternal empowerment of this timeless moment. Touch your baby, stroke your baby, and hold your baby to your skin.

Your baby too is instinctively captivated by your moving and speaking face. Deep, old-soul eyes look back at you as if to say, 'So that's what you look like . . . I've heard your voice for the past five months . . . you look amazing . . . Mummy, you're beautiful.'

Nothing can truly prepare you for *that* moment of mutual wondrous awe.

All those months of pregnancy, and all those hours of labour suddenly become an insignificant cost.

He was wet and dark and I knew him at once and held him to me
and cried. I cried like the river I was, with all my banks broken and
all my silt and sludge washed away. My eyes wept salty tears and
my vagina wept salty blood . . . I cried on and on, washing myself
and our new son clean, weeping my own small river into the great
sea of existence . . .
Giving birth brings a woman the closest she will ever come to the
tender heart of life. Life and death will be right in the room with
you, you will feel life's breath upon your face and know the throb of
life's blood. You will sense for a moment the meaning of existence,
how fragile the membrane is between life and death, and then the
curtains will close again on life's mystery and you will be left with
only the vaguest dream.

Susan Johnson — *A Better Woman*

The third stage of labour — birthing the placenta and membranes

The third stage of labour is the interval from delivery of the baby until the delivery of the afterbirth (placenta and membranes), and control of bleeding. (Note: this chapter describes a managed third stage; for details on the physiological third stage see pages 39–41.)

With active management of the third stage, immediately at the time of the birth an ecbolic (oxytocin) is normally given to the mother by thigh injection (or via an existing IV), which is administered to specifically aid in the prevention of serious haemorrhaging with excessive blood loss (see page 39).

As the placenta separates and releases from the uterine wall lining, the uterus needs to involute quickly to ensure that the blood vessels supplying the placenta are quickly compressed so they rapidly clamp down to prevent the woman suffering a high blood loss (resulting in anaemia, from which it can take weeks to recover).

It can be normal for the uterus to rest for a little time after a baby is delivered. Then contractions (much lighter) will begin again, as the uterus contracts down to be just big enough to contain the placenta. With the LMC or midwife putting pressure on your tummy and gently tugging the cut umbilical cord, the placenta is eventually expelled. This can take anything from just a few minutes to up to 30 minutes. (If it takes too long, the risk of haemorrhaging increases.)

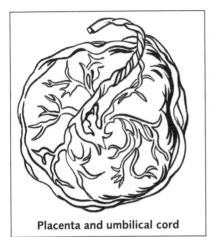

Placenta and umbilical cord

As my dear friend, Ali, reminded me, when you push that placenta out (which by the way without bones is nothing in comparison to a baby) there is a definite whole-body sensation of closure. It's like every tissue in your body knows, all at the same time, that the internal task of creating your baby, has now finished. It's a lovely, kind of euphoric feeling, like every cell in your body is having a tiny little orgasm all at the same time. Glorious!

The placenta (which resembles a 3 cm-thick, 15–20 cm-diameter piece of raw liver), will be examined to ensure it is complete. Most first-time mums are very interested to see what this remarkable organ looks like, particularly knowing it has had the roles of respiratory, excretory and nutrition-delivery systems, acting as your baby's lungs, kidneys, liver and intestines for so many months.

Weighing about half a kilo, the placental 'mother's side' is irregular, rough, spongy, bluish-red and meat-like — this was the side attached to the wall of the uterus. The 'baby's side' has the umbilical cord attached with the main vessels spreading outwards (some say it resembles a tree of life). This side also has a membrane covering it, which makes it white, shiny, glossy and smooth. You will be asked if you would like to take the placenta home.

Sometimes the placenta does not all come away and usually with an epidural or spinal block, the doctor will use his hand to perform an internal manual removal (scraping the placenta off the wall of the uterus).

It is not unusual for women to feel a bit shaky and cold after delivery. In fact, sometimes a woman can have quite profound shaking after completing this final stage of birth, which is mainly because your little 'heater' has been delivered, and your body shivers to increase your core temperature.

The fourth stage of labour — the dawn of bonding

To the world you are one person, but to this one person you are the world.

Author Unknown

After the placenta and amniotic sac are expelled, your blood pressure, pulse and temperature will again be checked. Your fundus (top of the womb), perineum and birth canal will be inspected, and the perineum repaired with stitches, if necessary, under local anaesthesia (often within the first quarter-hour). It is important that anything but the tiniest tear is sutured immediately — before the skin tissue swells. The suturing from a full episiotomy can take up to an hour as your layers of muscle and skin are carefully aligned. Around this time the baby is weighed and labelled.

Then with yours (and your baby's) senses at an amazingly heightened level (like nothing you've experienced before), together you can begin to get to know each other intimately . . . skin to skin contact at this stage is highly recommended for you both.

Some brand new babies look a bit traumatised (which is pretty under-standable) and other babies can look incredibly contented, peaceful, responsive and wide awake. Due to the level of catecholamines, adrenaline and noradrenaline in a newborn's system after a natural birth (twenty times higher than in an adult), they can initially be extremely alert.

Don't at this point allow the system to rush you. You and your partner now need to be unhurried, so that in a peaceful and private environment you can start to fall in love with your new baby (bonding is a slowly unfolding process). You need to be given the space to enjoy this incredibly special moment in your lives, in an atmosphere of relaxed, quiet, intimate togetherness — when you can begin to imagine who your baby resembles, and breathe in that magnetic scent of a brand new baby.

After the placenta was expelled, your progesterone and oestrogen levels dropped, and together with the hormone prolactin taking over, your breasts produce your baby's first feed. This colostrum milk will line your baby's new stomach with an antibody-rich protective barrier against invading bacteria.

Your baby is born equipped to instinctively seek the smell of your naked breasts. In fact, if left on your abdomen, within the first hour your newborn will, without any help, do a 'squirmy-crawl' (using its pushing reflex) up your body towards your breasts, and latch on, perfectly. But this reflex is gone within just a few hours.

So, when you and your baby are ready, ideally within that first hour, and with assistance from the midwife, you will normally give your baby its first breastfeed (just 7–10 ml), which is an amazingly special moment. But, don't feel you have to hurry your baby to feed. First, it needs to feel secure, and then it will instinctively start the rooting reflex, and the nurse-midwife/ LMC will know your baby is ready. That first feed can also greatly assist to create a blueprint of how to suckle in the baby's mind.

Afterwards you will usually be offered some refreshments (something like a hot drink and toast), which you will be ready for — and it's time to make phone calls to spread the thrilling news! (Hospitals generally do not provide a phone in the room.)

It is imperative the three of you, as a new family, are given a good 1–2 hours of alone-time. If necessary, ask the hospital staff to leave you for some privacy (though the top of your womb will be periodically re-checked). This is your time as a glowing, tired, new mother, to hold your baby and experience delirious self-pride and bottomless love.

For those of you able to stand, you can now have the most delicious shower (even though it's freaking you out what a Niagara Falls of bloody liquid seems to be pouring out of you) — but *oh* that shower can feel *so good* (though strangely lonely too, as you realise you are truly alone again for the first time in nine months).

While you're in the shower, your partner could create his own magical and memorable bonding moment, by maybe removing his own shirt and cuddling your baby to his chest so your wee darling can feel his warmth, smell his skin and hear his heartbeat.

Finally, you and your baby, the new *two of you* will be ready to move into the postnatal ward. The new dad can take your delivery bag out to the car, and bring in your postnatal bag. (Don't forget to keep the camera and mobile with you.)

And by the way, new dad, there is usually no need for you to rush off home. If you can stay, wait at least until the new mum is well settled into the postnatal ward.

One to two hours after birth, once fed, cleaned, warm, swaddled and feeling safe and protected, a brand new (exhausted) baby usually then falls into a very deep sleep. *Sigh!*

Go now, my dear friend, and rest too.

Rest the euphoric rest only a new mother can ever experience.

Gaze with heavy eyelids at your sleepy gift.

Let the waves of amazement and wonder wash over and cleanse you with their spray.

For right now, *you* are truly a Goddess!

Chapter 3

And baby makes three . . . oh my gosh — we're parents!

In the sheltered simplicity of the first days after a baby is born,
one sees again the magical closed circle — the miraculous sense
of two people existing only for each other.
Anne Morrow Lindbergh — *Gift From the Sea*

Wow, so you really are a mother now. You're no longer part of a couple, you're part of your *own* new family. That's an overpowering reality to grasp!

After your marathon childbirth experience, and meeting your little miracle for the first time, you are transferred to the postnatal ward in a euphoric foggy adrenaline-buzzing haze of unforgettable, yet fuzzy, clarity. (They wheel you in on a bed, or you may walk.)

Almost immediately, the dawning of a new age for you, as a woman, can begin to engulf the raw essence of your soul, as you begin to comprehend the startling, new responsibility (from which there is no escape) that you are now shouldering for the rest of your days ... *Motherhood.*

Shit!

Did you pack the super-glue for bonding, honey?

The emotional Velcro 'bonding theory' first appeared in the mid-1970s, and by the 1980s 'bonding' had become an accepted maternity term; after which the process became analysed and scrutinised to the point of creating another term — 'poor bonding'.

There are hundreds of factors, physical and emotional, which influence the mother–baby 'bonding' process. Lots of new mums do not always experience the 'instantly-in-mother-love' emotions.

Certainly, there are correlations between how good or traumatic a birth is and how smoothly bonding occurs. For some mums with a new baby, there are feelings of bondage well before there are feelings of bonding.

So for many women, particularly in the first 2–3 days, their dominant feeling is a kind of weird, distant, blank indifference towards their baby and motherhood as they slowly begin to come to terms with the enormity of it all, and go over in their mind their experience of childbirth. That is a very normal reaction.

Bonding is a gradually unfolding experience that can take hours, days, weeks or months to evolve, like a flower opening its petals — some studies have shown that almost half of women don't love their newborns straight away.

But most new mums (and dads) worry about whether they're feeling adequately bonded with their new baby, as if bonding is some super-glue that gushes out of a mother at childbirth, instantly sticking together the new mother and her newborn in some wondrous connection. You may be wondering why yours is not the love-at-first-sight experience you were imagining it would be, but often it's just not like that. *Welcome to the new world of worrying about your child!*

For lactation a mother's body secretes a hormone called prolactin, which is thought by some to help bring on those baby bonding feelings, stimulating a mother's connection with her baby, making her more in sync with her newborn through increased maternal sensitivity (instincts). In a way, this makes a load of sense — how do other mammals know how to mother their young if not by instinct? So, it would be logical that the human babies' mothers too are provided with maternal instincts at a biological level.

But if, deep inside, you are already feeling anxiety or guilt over your indifference and lack of bonded feelings with your brand new charge (a total stranger, let's face it), then realise that you are not abnormal in any way. Many new mums experience feelings towards their newborn that are like a pendulum swinging from tense exhilaration to nervous despair.

There is a substantial amount of literature available designed to enhance your skill at bonding effectively with your baby — and a lot of it, from an idealistic Mother Nature perspective, is quite correct. But some of it can feel like propaganda. It is possible to be beautifully bonded to your baby without following any particular theory — and it is possible to feel completely unbonded after following every theory ever invented.

Perhaps the most useful bonding tools are calm, blissful moments of getting to know each other, such as sitting quietly, chatting face to face up close, or holding your baby skin to skin on your chest, or watching your baby sleeping, breathing, and her expressions.

Bonding is like childbirth: each journey takes its own unique path. It's not like a switch that gets flicked on. Simply, one day you realise you know what your baby needs; or you miss your baby dreadfully when he's with a babysitter; or you experience milk letdown at the same time your baby across town cries to her nana for a feed; or you have a beautiful and vivid dream of your baby when he's older; or you find it hard to remember life without your wee bub; or you just know, intuitively, that there is some psychic connection between you both.

This is the day that you finally realise this little person has squirmed his way deep inside your soul, and that you would give your life for your wee babe … and by then, trust me friend, you are well and truly bonded!

First impressions don't count

Subject to any side effects of pain-relief wearing off, newborns can be amazingly wide awake and alert for the first hour or so (that is, before falling into a deep sleep). One big reason why parents can find it difficult to feel immediately bonded is that their baby looks so different (outright ugly sometimes) from what they had expected. You see, during a pregnancy it is quite normal to create a picture of what your dream-baby may look like. Then when it arrives, oh heck, it can be so different.

Unless you're properly aware of the general appearance of a newborn, there are quite a number of common, but potentially startling and disconcerting, strange features that are, usually, of no concern at all. Here's a list containing most of these.

- Babies are initially wet with mucous and blood and perhaps have some greeny-black meconium poo on them.
- Generally, babies born early or at due date are smeared in a creamy, white, greasy, waxy paste called **vernix caseosa**. It protected baby's skin from becoming prune-like while living underwater for nine months. Perhaps it also aids with a more slippery delivery. In many older cultures, instead of washing off this vernix coating, it is massaged into the baby's smooth buttery skin at its first massage. (This is now happening more frequently here too, as it is a great moisture barrier for skin creases.)
- Overdue babies will often have an overcooked look — their hands and feet appearing especially wrinkled, and the skin perhaps peeling from

being immersed in water for so long.

- Some babies can look like an alien, or wrinkly old person — but they uncrumple after a few days.
- Newborn skin is a violet-blue colour until they have breathed oxygen and pinked up, then they can stay ruddy for the first month.
- Newborn skin is very thin, so blood vessels can easily be seen through it — but as they grow, even within the first month, their skin will become thicker, with more fat deposited under the skin's tissue, so it won't be so see-through.
- Babies' arms are short, their hands closed tight, their thighs are chubby and their heart beats rapidly (about 110–160 beats per minute).
- Babies' legs are short — their head and trunk are 1½ times longer than their legs. (By ten years of age legs are about half the body's height.)
- All newborn's spines are a C-shaped arch — but as the baby gets older and begins to raise its head, then begins to walk, the adult S-shaped spine will develop.
- All newborns have bloated-looking tummies and bowed, almost frog-like legs with feet that turn inwards. This gradually changes over their first couple of years.
- Newborns' faces are shaped by Mother Nature to suckle comfortably, including a receding chin, squashed snub (boxer's) nose and wide mouth. Their skull cranium is huge in comparison to the size of their tiny face — in fact their head is about a quarter the length of their entire body (whereas it's about half that in adults).
- It's not uncommon for their little face to have a bit of bruising too, looking swollen with puffy eyes and eyelids.
- Babies' initial hair colour can bear little resemblance to their final shade, and their first hair often falls out — or later may be worn off to bald areas from spending so much time sleeping.
- Yellowish-white pimple spots or pustules called milia (sebaceous gland hyperplasia) are common over a baby's nose or cheeks. These are just accumulations inside immature, enlarged, blocked sweat glands, and the spots usually disappear within the first month.
- Babies can have scratches from their own long, blue fingernails (The nails soon change to the normal pink colour.)
- All newborns' genitals (testicles with boys and labia with girls) are usually quite enlarged and even hugely swollen (thanks to the mother's high hormone levels) — you didn't just give birth to an extraordinarily well-endowed little man.
- Dusky-blue, purpled legs, feet, hands and/or mouth (called cyanosis),

and mottled skin are common — and for some time after birth. Sometimes a newborn can be 'two-tone' (nicknamed a 'harlequin baby') because his circulation is not yet sending his blood evenly around his body, so one whole side can be a different hue. Or, the baby may have red and white blotches, or alternating patches of pink and white skin. Their blood circulation does eventually sort itself out.

- Vasomotor instability can occur during crying. The newborn's skin can be mottled, and the hands and feet may look bluish — that's normal too.

- Some babies can have quite a bit of dark body hair (called **lanugo**) commonly across the shoulders, forehead and temples — which can be a bit freaky. But don't worry; your genes have not produced prehistoric man. This is quite normal, and it usually falls out or rubs off in the first month.

- Most babies (especially Caucasian) are born with dull slate-bluish-grey coloured eyes, which usually change 6–9 months later. There may even be some tiny, broken, red blood vessels in the whites of their eyes — these will disappear within a couple of weeks.

- Some babies are born with cone heads, which look very strange — so don't be surprised if your little newborn's forehead is flat and sloping back, because the skull bones have slid to slightly overlap, moulding themselves into an egg or spearhead shape. Within a day or so the malleable skull bones will return to their normal positions.

- Some babies have a soggy swelling (or large blister) over part (often a side) of their head from the pushing on the dilatating ring of the cervix (which is called a **caput succedaneum**). It does not affect their brain, is harmless, and it will gradually go, sometimes within just a couple of days.

- Appearing a few hours after birth and increasing in size over the first day or so, about one percent of babies develop one or two blood-filled spongy circles on their heads caused by a ruptured blood vessel during delivery (called a **cephalohaematoma**). But don't worry: your baby isn't injured. This haematoma requires no treatment, it takes on a crater shape as it heals, and can take from 1–6 months to go away.

- Occasionally, a baby's collarbone or arm can be fractured during delivery, which is obviously upsetting — but the good news is that fractures in new babies mend very quickly since their bones are still ossifying (cementing).

- Some babies are born with **club feet**. This is caused by contraction of the tendons or muscles on the inside of their legs. It is corrected by splinting, massage and exercises organised by a specialist.

- Occasionally, babies can be born with little blisters or scars on the thumb or hand from suckling in the uterus.

- There are many kinds of **birthmarks** that can adorn our little newborns — in fact about one in 10 babies has at least one birthmark. Below are some of the more common marks:
  - Melanocytic naevi birthmarks look like brown or black moles. They do become proportionally smaller over time — but may be removed when the child is older for cosmetic purposes.
  - Salmon patches are common little pinky-reddish-purply flat patches of skin, which are blood capillaries under the surface of the skin. They are usually seen at the nape of the neck, nicknamed stork-bite marks; butterfly-shaped marks above the bridge of the nose between the eyebrows, nicknamed angel's kiss; and/or on eyelids. They usually disappear before the first birthday, except marks in the neck area, which can become permanent. (You can usually tell if they will go away, by gently pressing on the skin — if it bleaches and the mark fades, then it will eventually go away.)
  - Mongolian blue spots are dark, slate-blue pigmented birthmarks, commonly at the base of the spine, around the tailbone or on the tummy or legs of dark-skinned babies (seen more commonly on African, Indian, Asian, Polynesian and Southern European-

The apgar tests

One minute and five minutes after a baby is born, a rapid medical assessment observation is made. The newborn receives a score of 0, 1 or 2 on five very basic life processes. These are:
- A: Appearance (skin colour — how blue the extremities are)
- P: Pulse (heart-rate)
- G: Grimacing (reflex crying response to vigorous stimuli, e.g. rubbing)
- A: Activity (muscle tone, involuntary unco-ordinated movements)
- R: Respiration (depth of breathing effort)

A score of 7 to 10 indicates great overall condition. A score of 4 to 6 is considered fair (OK but not optimal) and probably the air passages may need to be cleared and a little extra oxygen given. A score of 3 or less requires more intensive care.

It is usual that the first score is lower than the second (10 is rare for a first score), but the more important measurement is the second score at 5 minutes when most newborns get a score of 7 or above. If the second apgar score is still low, checks will be redone every 5 minutes until it is 7 or 8.

Mediterranean babies). These birthmarks look very like bruises, and sometimes the family needs reassurance that nobody dropped the baby. But they are harmless and most fade in the first year or so.

— Port wine stains are large, flat, dark-red or purple, permanent birthmarks on the baby's skin, most often on the face or neck. These can be a significant cosmetic (and self-esteem) problem — and laser therapy while the child is a pre-schooler is an option some parents later choose.

• The average Westernised newborn weighs 3.2–3.3 kg (7–7½ lb) — but anything between 2.5 kg (5 lb 8 oz) and 4.5 kg (9 lb 12 oz) is still regarded as normal. The average newborn length is 50–51 cm — but anything between 47 cm and 53 cm is normal.

• The average newborn head circumference is 35 cm, but anything between 33 and 37 cm is normal.

• At birth a full-term baby has already grown to almost one-third of its adult height.

Other early checks

There are a series of other medical checks that your LMC will perform on your newborn soon after birth, including:

• Height and head measurements.
• Weight.
• In boys, that both testes are descended (if not, they will be expected to descend within the first year).
• That the anus is formed properly.
• Listening to the heartbeat.
• That the upper palate is complete and not cleft (incompletely developed).
• Hip dislocation.
• Tummy checked that the liver and spleen are the right size.
• State of the skull bones.
• Talipes (club foot).

Your postnatal hospital stay

If your baby arrives during the middle of the night, somehow there's an expectation you will get some sleep but, personally, I never have — I was always too full of adrenaline. If you are capable of sleep, then it's the best thing for you now. And if you are feeling completely limp with exhaustion from the effort of childbirth, and *far* from feeling on some massive high then that is *absolutely fine* too, because your high will kick in, just give it time.

It is eye-opening to see how medical policies have changed so dramatically in such a short period of time. The visionary New Zealand backblocks baby-doctor, Doris Gordon, fought hard in the 1930s for the right of every new mother to be provided with the sanctuary of fourteen days' free rest within a hospital after giving birth.

However, it is true that mothers back then were also forced to have complete bedrest for at least one week, including bedpans and other inappropriate, humbling, hospital routines. The authoritarian medical experts of the day were convinced that getting up before the seventh day would result in a prolapsed uterus or fallen womb — despite strong evidence to the contrary in less-developed countries. This was also the period when babies were separated and isolated from their mothers, being housed in the nursery (except for feeding). Fantastic scheme for mothers to rest — *yes*. Fantastic scheme for instilling bonding — *no*.

Today the health system has swung the pendulum too far back the other way. The average hospital stay is now only around 1–2 days, often even requiring buckling an hours-old, vulnerable baby and fragile mother into a car to transfer from the delivery hospital to the postnatal centre. This is monstrous. And two days is simply not a realistic period to ensure a new mother is going home recovered, confident and competent! (Women are permitted longer stays for clinical reasons such as a C-section, breastfeeding difficulties, or rural isolation.)

Mothers are sometimes six to a room including babies (or worse, eight), which can make sleeping at night virtually impossible (especially for light sleepers). And to top it off, many maternity hospital wards don't even have a nursery at all any more, which makes it tricky to feel relaxed about taking a lengthy bath or an unhurried visit to the toilet. Where available, midwife-run community birth-centres may provide a superior environment of post-natal care.

In nearly all non-Westernised cultures, mothers are cherished, treasured and intensively protected in this fragile time. Forty days of healing rest and recuperation is common in many traditional cultures. Instead, our 'advanced' system encourages the vulnerable mother and baby to return home even before the milk has arrived! And then society wonders why too many new mothers are later readmitted to hospital, due to various postnatal diagnosable and undiagnosable complications and problems. It is a hideous situation, which I sincerely hope will have been improved by the time our girls are mothers — but I won't get started on that topic!

Commonly for the first few days of life all a baby seems to do is sleep —

they are recuperating from the shock of their tiring arrival. But if your newborn is fed and not settling, and it is night-time, then my advice is to assert yourself and ask one of the nurse-midwives to remove your baby from your room so you can sleep more soundly, until your baby is due for its next feed. Perhaps suggest any roomies do the same too if that is what it takes to ensure you can all get some desperately needed sleep, instead of allowing your babies to take turns to keep everybody awake. Most nurse-midwives are lovely and will be helpful. Occasionally such a request might annoy some battle-axe, but be insistent and do what's right for you; because for your baby's sake, your rapid, restful recovery is of paramount importance now.

Apart from the obvious areas you expected to be sore, there can be some other real surprises: puffy bulging eyes, sore eye sockets and pink eyes (from the pressure of pushing); broken capillaries on your cheeks (from the pressure of pushing); blotchy face or blue bruises on your face or chest (from small blood vessels rupturing); dry chapped lips and sore throat (from panting); aching thighs (from being pushed up to your armpits or a long time spent squatting); sore shoulders (from tensing your neck muscles during contractions); sore armpits (squashed brachial artery); tingling hands (carpal-tunnel pinched nerves); general backache (from a sore spine); and often a bruised, dislocated, fractured or even broken coccyx (very sore arse). Plus your mind can be disgusted at just how bloody and messy childbirth is ... and your psyche can feel a weird 'abdominal' emptiness.

Then of course there is the marshmallow, spongy, podgy, cottage-cheese abdomen that still looks a good six-months pregnant, and the water-retented round face, swollen ankles, and puffy feet and hands. Don't worry, soon all that retained water will be leaked, sweated and peed out of you.

You also smell different. Lochia (the normal discharge from the vagina after childbirth) is pungently sweet, and breastmilk is sweet-smelling too. With these combined you now have a new personal scent. (Please don't go overboard covering it up with excessive perfume — newborns are very sensitive to odours.)

My friends often complain of the many different opinions received from staff as a result of shift changes at the hospital, especially when it comes to breastfeeding techniques. It can feel like that, but the funny thing is that once you are an experienced mum, you realise that those wonderful nurse-midwives are all (pretty much) giving the same advice. (It would all become clear if you could stay for 1–1½ weeks, but you can't.)

Getting back to your little miracle . . . Oh newborns smell so fantastic, especially over the top of their heads . . . I'm not sure why, but they do.

I know, you're perhaps high on adrenaline and infatuation — I still get besotted seeing any newborn baby. You may find yourself glued to watching your precious babe as they sleep . . . in euphoric awe that such a godsend is truly yours. Oh God, that is scary! When your baby eventually wakes up again, only occasionally opening their eyes at first, staring back at you in a locked gaze on that first day or two, there seems a soul a thousand times wiser than yourself — a soul as old as Time itself — a soul who is staring deeply into your heart with its own wondrous curiosity. This is your own little miracle.

Everyone deserves some miracles in their life, and you then realise, truly realise, that their arrival has been a personal miracle in your life.

Even as you're feeling so petrified, so apprehensive, and maybe secretly thinking, 'Take it back, I'm not ready, it's too little, this is way too much responsibility for me, I'm still a kid myself' — well, friend, we all felt that way too. We all understand.

General advice for your maternity stay

- Take your time, during those first few days, to observe your new little bundle. Get to know your baby.
- Acknowledge and accept the reality that you are fatigued and need rest!
- Your newborn baby is not as fragile as you think; they're remarkably unbreakable and more resilient than they look. Don't be nervous to touch your baby, you won't bruise her, in fact your firm touch makes her feel relaxed — she has been used to physically feeling secure all her life. The one major golden rule is always to support her oversized head and weak neck.
- In hospital you should be offered paracetamol four-hourly for general pain and discomfort — so, if the staff are busy and have forgotten you, do ask for it.
- If you are having trouble falling to sleep, then ask for a sedative.
- I know that hospital meals are unappetising and far from restaurant standard, but do enjoy having meals made for you.
- It is not natural for Westernised women to allow themselves to be mothered — but for these few days, you really should.
- If you find your mind reliving over and over your birth experience, listen to your urges and write down your baby's birth story — it's a very cathartic thing to do.
- RELAX.

The lochia (vaginal discharge)

Your body needs to heal a large wound inside your uterus, so it is very important you avoid being too energetic, and instead get plenty of rest. It is normal after having a baby (including caesars) to bleed for 2–8 weeks — surprisingly large amounts at first (needing to replace a maternity sanitary pad every 2–3 hours for the first 24–48 hours). Your healing uterus is discharging the lochia, which is a mixture of blood from where the placenta was attached, and the crumbling endometrium lining of the uterus.

Straight after delivery your uterus, which took 40 weeks to grow to the size of a beach-ball, begins involuting (shrinking back). Post-delivery it weighs about a kilo and feels like a firm, round, bulge in your tummy. Two weeks later it weighs about 350 g, and by 6–8 weeks after childbirth it has returned back to normal (the size of an orange), weighing about 100 grams.

For the first 2–5 days or so, the lochia mostly consists of bright red blood, and sometimes blood clots, which to the untrained eye look like lumps of liver. Put aside any large blood clots (say the size of a golf ball or an egg) for your LMC to check, as they may occasionally include bits of placenta, which would be of significant concern.

For the next 5–10 days the lochia reduces in quantity and is then a pinky, rusty-red, brownish colour. After that it changes to yellowish-white or clear.

It can be normal to have a surge of blood after breastfeeding or after walking, but the bleeding should not be excessive.

If the lochia blood suddenly starts heavy gushing (say filling 1–2 sanitary pads in 30–60 minutes) then stay off your feet as much as possible and arrange to see a doctor or your LMC immediately. This could be a secondary haemorrhage, which occurs to 0.5 percent of women within the early weeks after childbirth, and should be treated seriously.

Sanitary pads are recommended for the first six weeks. You'll start with the thick doorstop maternity pads, and progress down to regular pads. As the cervix is still partially open while discharging lochia, tampons (and sex) are not recommended. There is a risk of uterine infection while your placental wound heals (about six weeks).

Postnatal pee

Your first post-delivery pee can seem to take ages to come out. But it's nothing to be worried about, just relax and sit there patiently. This is because of swollen tissue around the bladder and urethral opening (from the baby's head squashing it against your pubic bone during dissension); plus it can lack tone due to the relaxing pregnancy hormones still in your system; and if a catheter was inserted there could be some urethral inflammation.

After the first day you may find you need to urinate very frequently for the next few days. This is your body eliminating all that now-surplus fluid between cell tissue, which was caused by the high levels of pregnancy oestrogen. In fact your urine output can double for a few days.

Postnatal poos and potential constipation

Your poor derrière can be very achy after giving birth, from all the pressure in that general vicinity. Additionally, to avoid premature labour, pregnancy progesterone slowed all your body's smooth muscle functions, including the intestines. So, after having a baby, the movement of faeces through your relaxed bowels is still slow, plus the digestive tract muscles are stretched and potentially traumatised from bruising. Additionally, if you are not consuming adequate water to replenish your production of breastmilk — you could quite quickly become constipated.

Be sure not to take any paracetamol that is combined with codeine, because that too can be constipating — and that is definitely not a problem you want to add to. Do everything in your power to avoid constipation, including drinking loads of water, and consuming only moderate amounts of dairy products, chocolate and white-flour products. Instead, eat lots of raw fruit, raw vegetables and other roughage — the cellulose cell-wall in plant fibre is indigestible to humans, but our colon needs it as a bulking agent to form defecatable faeces (not constipative hard rocks). Wholegrain bread, muesli, oat cereals, beans, brown rice, dried figs, dried prunes, prune juice, kiwifruit and bran muffins are traditional anti-constipation favourites; extra ginger and vitamin C are also beneficial; and a glass of apple cider or hot prune juice with dinner is great too for sluggish digestion.

Don't hesitate to ask the hospital staff for a mild laxative if trouble is brewing with constipation (it is very common after childbirth) — they'll be happy to supply you with a stool-softening suppository, such as glycerine.

Walking is also very beneficial to help a sluggish elimination system get moving. Other good old remedies include aloe vera juice, flaxseed oil, acidophilus yoghurt, slippery elm powder, homeopathic Nux Vomica, ginger tea, or taking a natural, mild, bulking laxative like the soluble fibre psyllium, or fibre granules such as Normacol™, or extra dietary fibre drinks such as Metamucil™. Whatever you do, keep doing it for a good week after the problem has waned.

Recovering from haemorrhoids (piles)

About two-thirds of us experience the loathsome war wound of haemorrhoids in pregnancy, during birth or within a day or so of delivery. Haemorrhoids are swollen veins (herniated tissue) that feel like tender lumps around the anus ranging in size from a pea, to a grape, to a walnut and in severe cases to a plum. They develop rapidly and can be extremely painful. *So foul!*

In late pregnancy, your enlarged uterus presses weight on the blood vessels in your anal area that circulates the blood from that area back to your heart, and that pressure can dilate the veins in the rectum, triggering haemorrhoids. Straining to push out poos while pregnant can cause them, and the straining at childbirth sometimes means you have delivered not just a baby, and a placenta, but also some piles! *Gross.*

Usually once the pressure on that ever-so-personal area has returned to normal, and with proper care, the haemorrhoids shrink away. However, an estimated 5 percent of mothers suffer with lifetime haemorrhoid problems.

The best way to get rid of haemorrhoids is to avoid constipation and straining. Keep the fluid intake up and eat plenty of fruit, vegies and roughage. In more severe cases, a proctologist may cut the haemorrhoid open to remove the blood clot; or shrink them by injecting a concentrated hypotonic salt solution; or freeze them by injecting with liquid nitrogen; or cauterise the blood vessels. With very severe cases they will do a 'haemorrhoidectomy' under general anaesthetic, where they cut around the pile and remove it.

All in all, this is definitely a time for sitting ever so carefully on a donut-shaped pillow. And you have my sincerest and deepest sympathy, sweet undeserving friend!

Remedies that help haemorrhoids include:

- Saltwater baths (1^1/$_2$–2 cups of salt for a bathtub).
- Sitz baths (sitting in the hottest water you can stand) for 20–30 minutes 2–3 times a day.
- Oral anti-inflammatories.
- Over-the-counter haemorrhoid creams.
- Prescription cortisone creams.
- Specialist proctologist prescription medications.
- Gauze pads soaked in witch hazel.
- Acupuncture.
- Aloe vera gel is also a curative.
- Arnica tablets aid with all healing.
- Homeopathic tissue salt calcium flouride tablets.
- Hamamelis Virginiana (homeopathic tincture of witch hazel).

Recovering from a stretched cervix and vagina; forceps or ventouse delivery; episiotomy; stretched, torn or grazed labial skin; perineal tears or stitching

Welcome to the wounded shuffle-walk of the post-delivery ward.

In the first 24 hours you will usually be offered frozen ice-packs to put on your perineum to numb the area and help to prevent swelling.

Soaking in a hot bath in the first 24 hours is not recommended as it can increase perineal swelling and also could increase the risk of infection. But, by the second day you will be encouraged to soak in warm baths: the warmth increases the blood flow, which aids in healing, and generally feels wonderful. (Put some Hypercal or Cyprus tincture in the bath too — great healers — and maybe some relaxing chamomile or lavender pure essential oil.)

Your stretched cervix (doorway to the womb) still has to close up and become tight and narrow again. As for the well-stretched vagina, that will take 3–4 weeks to return to almost its old size, but that's where those good old pelvic-floor exercises over the following 2–3 months will help enormously (see chapter 6, page 245).

Sometimes initially it can be difficult to find a comfortable sitting position, especially for breastfeeding. You can take paracetamol for the 'discomfort'. Isn't that the most under-rated word in modern medicine!

With stitches (especially a full episiotomy), your first post-delivery poo (usually around 1–3 days later) is scary, because you're worried pushing will rip your sutures, and you can't see to gauge what's going on down there. Personally, I recommend waiting until you have (what my husband in sick humour describes as a 'turtle-head' stool), so things can just, well, how do I put it nicely, plop out without too much effort — or a little self-administered, manual extraction can help give relief in the first couple of days too. Another good idea is to hold a pad on your stitches and push upwards, while you bear down.

Gauze soaked in witch hazel or aloe vera gel and placed on your sanitary pad is great. Both are healing agents and pain relievers. Also soothing is using a detachable showerhead to spray the area, or straddling over a bidet. And remember to keep taking your arnica several times a day to promote healing.

The pain of an episiotomy tends to get worse before it gets better because skin swelling makes the stitches tighter. Most stitches dissolve or are removed after 5–6 days. Most pain from a small episiotomy should be gone after say 10 days, or 2–3 weeks for larger episiotomies — and all discomfort should be gone within 4–6 weeks. The perineal area is packed full of blood vessels that make the skin tissue well nourished, so it is an area that traditionally heals rapidly.

Although your urine is sterile, vigilant hygiene is still a must, so lots of warm baths and showers — and it's a popular practice to dry that tender area with a hairdryer instead of patting it dry. Urine is acidic so it will sting raw skin — you can try standing a little over the loo instead of sitting, so that the pee has less chance of touching your sutures — or squirting warm water (perhaps with a few drops of Hypercal in it) over your vaginal opening and perineum at the same time as peeing.

Recovering from a caesarean

Your recovery from a caesarean depends on the reason why the caesar was performed — whether it was after a long labour which then required an emergency caesar, or if it was a pre-scheduled elective caesar.

If you have been through an arduous labour before the caesar, then the recovery will usually be slower because your body and mind are exhausted — especially if you endured the episiotomy of an attempted instrumental vaginal delivery.

The caesar surgery itself can vary: some operations take longer, some can require a larger incision, and sometimes forceps are used. But, even the most straightforward of caesars can be roughly equivalent to recovering from a reasonably serious car-accident.

Immediately after a caesar, when you are in the recovery room for a period of time, the midwife assigned to you will assist you with your baby's first breastfeed. She will also be carefully monitoring that you are recovering as you should be (e.g. checking your blood pressure, temperature, ensuring that feeling is returning to your lower body). Once all is going well, you will be moved into the postnatal ward with your new baby.

For the first 6–24+ hours (dependent on your surgery and individual recovery) you may still be connected to a catheter, drip and strong pain relief (often using a morphine-based analgesic with a self-administered pump-button, impossible-to-overdose system). The pain relief individual patients require for caesars can vary greatly. A urine catheter is used until you feel able to be up and about to take yourself to the toilet.

Holding a pillow against your tummy will help all getting-up and getting-down movements (and coughing, sneezing or laughing). You may remain connected to the drip with pain relief into the second day, dependent on how your recovery is progressing.

You will feel as if you can't do anything on your own at all — but within even as little as six hours the nurse-midwife will be encouraging you to go for a short stroll around the ward, to avoid thrombosis (see page 144) and speed recovery. You'll be bent over at your waist to start with, probably feeling like your abdomen is going to split open, but it won't.

Note: There will be a lot of bleeding from your vagina during the first walks, caused by the blood that had pooled in your pelvic region.

Day two to day seven is the most painful period, though there can be some level of discomfort for 1–2 months. Walking is very beneficial for recovering from all abdominal surgery, and the quicker you are up on your feet again, the quicker the recovery time (exercise improves the blood circulation and healing, and also helps stimulate your intestines and bladder back into working efficiently).

Some women can suffer with severe tummy-gas pains, due partly to the anaesthesia slowing down the intestines. The herb valerian, and peppermint tea can help the discomfort and assist to expel the wind. The antibiotics automatically given to you via the IV in surgery can make you and your baby more vulnerable to yeast infections — vaginal, nipple, or baby's mouth or bottom. A C-section can also slow down the arrival of breastmilk — so frequent breastfeeding is a particularly important stimulant.

Any abdominal surgery can also cause sharp pain under the ribs (due to air pockets trapped in the abdomen from the surgery), or sore shoulders (due to those air pockets pressing the diaphragm on to the phrenic nerve). Occasionally some women have a skin reaction to the morphine pain relief, such as itchy eruptions, for which the nurse-midwife can supply a soothing lotion.

Here's the part that caesar mums loathe — many hospitals have a policy that you can't eat until you have farted. (That is to ensure that your bowels, etc. are functioning post-surgery). How long it takes your body to pass wind is somewhere between 12–36 hours. 'Heaven forbid,' I hear you saying. 'I'll be starving,' you cry. Yup, you will be very hungry by then. Some hospitals allow you to eat light, easily digested food such as crackers or clear soup straight away. But it is not usual to be discharged from hospital until you have done poos. Then high-fibre drinks can assist the whole process, since constipation problems are common.

Breastfeeding is a challenge after a caesar for the first few hours and days, because it's harder to find a comfortable position, but a nurse-midwife can help you initially by handing the baby to you. At the beginning, probably the most successful position will be you and your baby lying on your sides in bed (see page 167).

For at least the first day, you will need to buzz the call-button for a nurse-midwife whenever you need to pick up your baby. Then once you're up and about, sitting in an armchair holding your wee baby in the American-football position will probably work best for breastfeeding — always with loads of pillow-support in those first days. Uterine-involution after-pain contractions during breastfeeding can also be especially painful after a caesar.

(See chapter 4, page 156 for more information on breastfeeding.)

Expect to stay in hospital for 3–5 days depending on how everything is going, and you'll probably need to wear large grandma panties (or even loose boxer shorts) so nothing is pressing on the C-section incision.

Be warned, on the day your stitches get removed, it is not at all unreasonable to want to cry. It is rational to be upset from seeing a raw surgical incision in your belly.

The homeopathic remedies Staphysagria (for healing recovery) and Raphanus (to ease digestion) are both helpful with caesar recovery, as is the herb comfrey, and valerian tea — and arnica is extremely beneficial with all healing processes. Paracetamol is, of course, a good pain reliever — and an over-the-counter anti-inflammatory is also sometimes useful once you're home.

Once back home, you will have to take things reasonably easy. Your LMC may instruct you for the first few weeks not to lift heavy weights (e.g. lifting your baby in the baby capsule carseat into the car, or carrying the washing basket, or bags of supermarket shopping); to avoid strong stretching (e.g. vacuuming and hanging washing on the line); to avoid walking up and down too many stairs; and to be careful getting up from lying or sitting.

You should also vigilantly watch out for a bacterial infection at the wound site with its symptomatic fever, wound redness, swelling tenderness, or oozing pus. If you experience any of these symptoms, see your LMC or doctor immediately.

Driving a car is also often not recommended for a few weeks because of the danger of your internal and/or external wounds tearing if you have to suddenly apply the clutch or brake in an emergency. Your LMC will advise time periods for you dependent on your individual recovery. (It may also pay to check with your vehicle insurance company as to when you are insured to drive post-caesar — some company policies have specific regulations.)

The caesar scar can, in time, become quite itchy and sensitive (even with burning sensations) — calendula cream can help. Generally, your scar will gradually heal over weeks and months, fade to pink and, within 1–2 years, will probably become a silvery line.

If the unexpected process of having had your baby delivered by caesar is causing you to feel robbed or cheated or disappointed that you did not experience a vaginal delivery, then that's not an unexpected reaction. But after you get over the initial unplanned shock of being sliced open, hopefully, in time, you'll feel happy and grateful that such a safe option was so readily available to you, and your heart will go out to that woman in the Third World country, who had the same complications on the same day as you, but

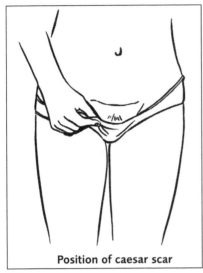
Position of caesar scar

lost her baby. As my dear friend, Tracey, said to me, 'If it wasn't for a cacsar, I probably wouldn't be here and neither would my son — so I have never had a problem in that field!'

Remember, too, the good news — most of you who didn't deliver vaginally have one part of your anatomy, the designer-vagina, remaining in pristine condition — so lucky you! For many women, knowing that they're still intact down there is a huge relief for which they're eternally grateful. If you have to remind yourself of what you've missed out on, just go back to page 137.

Can you give birth vaginally next time if you want to? About 70 percent of C-section women do, and they're termed VBACs (vaginal birth after caesar) — but after two caesars, then usually not. However, there are exceptions, as each pregnancy and childbirth is different. Your LMC would talk to you about your particular chances of birthing naturally — the choice to try is normally yours, and there can be few physiological reasons why you can't. Recommended reading includes Dr Bruce Flamm's book *Birth After Cesarean*, the website www.birthrites.org and the pamphlet 'Care of Women with Breech Presentation or Previous Caesarean Birth' by the NZ Guidelines Group — available from www.nzgg.org.nz.

Mother's little helpers (Part 1)

Always double-check with your LMC or naturopath before taking naturopathic remedies

Gotu kola (Indian Pennywort)
Gotu kola is one of Indian (Ayurvedic) medicine's primary rejuvenative herbs (nicknamed food for the brain); and in China it was recorded 2000 years ago as a herbal medicine. In India, Gotu kola can be called Brahmi because it brings knowledge of Brahman.

Besides improving brain function (such as memory), Gotu kola also has positive effects to aid the circulatory system, improving blood flow and strengthening arteries, veins and capillaries (described traditionally as a blood purifier). In addition, it improves digestion disorders, strengthens the immune system and fortifies the nervous system. Gotu kola is also renowned for its superb skin-healing qualities.

So, altogether it has become a favoured traditional gynaecological herb for mothers recovering from perineal tears, episiotomies and vulval lesions. Also, due to its beneficial effects on inactive patients confined to bed, it's great for women after C-sections.

False unicorn root

False unicorn root was traditionally a miscarriage preventative and morning-sickness nausea remedy with Native American women. Over time, countless women have used false unicorn root as a powerful uterine and ovarian tonic for disorders of the female reproductive system, assisting to normalise organ function. It can also help with menstrual and uterine problems such as afterbirth contractions, menstrual cramping, heavy bleeding at menopause, and has a reputation of increasing women's fertility — maybe not a big selling point right at this moment.

Chaste tree berries (*Vitex agnus-castus*)

This is a very old Mediterranean medicinal shrub often featured in Greek mythology and even mentioned by Hippocrates. It is traditionally used to treat menstrual-cycle complaints (particularly PMS), female hormonal imbalances, and as a post-pregnancy support.

At the base of the brain is the hypothalamus, and hanging by a 'stalk' below it is the grape-sized master gland, the pituitary. The hypothalamus triggers the pituitary to release the ovary stimulating hormones known as FSH (follicle stimulating hormone) and LH (luteinising hormone), which in turn stimulate the ovary to produce oestrogens and progesterone. It is this relationship, the pituitary–hypothalamic axis, which it is believed *Vitex agnus-castus* positively affects, by decreasing FSH (lowering oestrogens) and increasing LH (increasing progesterone); thus improving and normalising the oestrogen–progesterone ratio.

Also known as monk's pepper, *Vitex agnus-castus* does not provide rapid results; it is best used long-term because its benefits develop slowly.

Shatavari (*Asparagus racemosus*)

This Indian herb (in Sanskrit named 'Shatamuli') is the most important tonic used in Ayurvedic medicine for treating female reproductive-system health disorders. This Hindi word translates to 'she who possesses a hundred husbands', which is referring to its rejuvenating effects upon the reproductive organs.

Shatavari is used traditionally to improve the quantity and quality of breastmilk, to enhance feelings of love, for sexual debility, increased fertility, healing inflamed tissue, and to improve the body's own healing power. This is a soothing and calming tonic.

More recovery issues

Recovering from anaesthetics and analgesics

Nausea, vomiting and digestion problems can all be normal side effects of anaesthesias. Also, many people believe analgesics and anaesthetics, such as an epidural, spinal block, or general anaesthetic, cause a lot of damage from free radicals, increasing your need for antioxidant nutrition. So, it could be a wise idea to take supplements of zinc, selenium, and vitamins A, C and E for the first 1–2 months postpartum. Some people also like to take a liver-detoxifier remedy after such medication — but that may not be appropriate with breastfeeding — check with the manufacturer's instructions.

Some women who have epidurals suffer soreness in the lower back where the catheter was inserted. Evidence is also mounting regarding longer-term side effects from an epidural in the months after birth, including backaches, headaches, migraines, tingling hands or feet, and even neuralgia (burning or stabbing nerve pain). So if you did have an epidural, it could be particularly worthwhile to visit a chiropractor, osteopath or similar once you're home, to assist in ensuring a smoother recovery.

Thrombosis

After delivery the body naturally produces coagulants to prevent haemorrhaging, but this can also make liquid blood become more solid, especially in places where blood pools (called thrombosis). Superficial thrombosis can cause haemorrhoids to swell and become more painful after childbirth. Varicose veins can also become inflamed, tender, hot and red (called superficial phlebitis). They are commonly treated with medication, rest and elastic stockings, and are not a serious condition.

However, blood pooling in an immobilised patient, especially in the legs, creates the risk of a blood-clot forming, such as with deep vein thrombosis, which is why you are encouraged to walk about. The symptoms of a blood-clot in a leg vein are a tightening or swelling in the leg, ankle or foot, which may be painful to walk on. This is a very serious condition requiring urgent medical attention.

In a leg vein the blood-clot can become dislodged and travel, risking obstructing blood flow and causing tissue to die. If a clot reaches the heart it could cause a myocardial infarction (death to some of the coronary heart muscle), or if it travels to the lungs it could cause a pulmonary embolism (a block in the pulmonary artery preventing blood from the heart entering the lungs).

Zits, night-sweats, cold and hot flushes

Why fresh pimples? Well that's just hormones, of course. And if you find yourself heavily perspiring, waking up from night-sweats (sometimes so profuse you need to change the sheets) or suffering from cold and hot flushes (even together at the same time), be warned that it is just another way of Mother Nature helping to reduce all your extra water from pregnancy. It is triggered by the dramatic decline in pregnancy hormones. (Some women can continue to suffer from night-sweats for months.)

Prolapsed uterus (fallen womb)

The uterus should normally lie in a tipped-forward position within your pelvic cavity, but occasionally it can be displaced from childbirth so that it is lying directly above the vagina, which then creates the risk of the womb falling down into the vagina. Eeeekk!

So, if you ever feel your cervix sagging down low in your vagina, or even see it poking out of your vagina, although it obviously would be rather frightening, try not to panic. Just lie down immediately with pillows under your bottom to elevate your pelvis, and call your LMC straight away so they can manually reposition your uterus. You will need to stay in bed for a few days afterwards with household assistance to look after your newborn — and a few hundred pelvic-floor exercises every day will be strongly advised. In the very unlikely situation that your doctor declares a hysterectomy is necessary — definitely seek a second medical opinion!

Anal fissure

An anal fissure is a small tear in the skin lining the rectum's anal canal (anus) that occurs with about one in 10 women as a consequence of childbirth (or to men and women from other causes such as constipation).

With an anal fissure you can feel a sharp, stinging or burning pain during and after a bowel movement (like passing glass while pooing), because when the sphincter muscle rings expand, it stretches the fissure open. Sometimes fissures can itch, bleed lightly, or have a yellowish discharge — maybe a spot of red blood on the toilet paper.

Most anal fissures heal spontaneously after a few days or 2–3 weeks. Assisting treatments include soaking in a shallow, hot bath for 15–20 minutes several times a day; having a saline bath (cup of salt in the bath water); increasing dietary fibre (e.g. cereal, fresh fruit, vegetables); taking a stool bulking agent (stool softener); drinking 6–8 glasses of water a day; and using moist tissues instead of dry toilet paper. Zinc oxide cream, hydrocortisone ointment, and applying talc (talcum powder) can also soothe the wound — as can other prescribed treatments such as suppositories containing local anaesthetic.

Sometimes, minor day-surgery such as a sphincterotomy is needed when a deeper fissure is not healing successfully. A small cut is made in the anal sphincter muscle above the tear, to stop it going into spasm. But, thankfully, for most women an anal fissure is not of major concern.

Obstetric fistula

Without access to modern medical assistance and C-sections, about one in 12–20 (dependant on birthing care) women suffer prolonged difficulty in childbirth with an obstructed labour (say five days of childbirth labour), commonly resulting in a stillborn baby.

Due to the prolonged obstructed labour, blood supply can be cut off to the bladder, rectum or vagina which causes some of the tissue to die. This results, for tens of thousands of women worldwide each year, in a torn hole (fistula) through which urine and/or faeces can pass uncontrollably.

In the Westernised world, obstetric fistulas are now quite rare, but in the developing world, they remain a common trauma from unassisted labours, affecting an estimated 5 percent of women globally. The resulting incontinence usually causes women profound emotional trauma with a loss of social status and dignity. They are often abandoned by their husbands, and shamed as stinking, leaking, social outcasts.

There are a few dedicated volunteer doctors and wonderful nurses running charity hospitals that are working hard to provide these disadvantaged women with free or inexpensive corrective surgery, particularly in Africa. (Great charities to donate to if you're able.)

Your baby's postnatal hospital stay

General care for your baby

Dressing bub

In utero the fetus is totally dependent on its mother via the placenta to maintain its temperature, so at birth a newborn's ability to regulate its own temperature is poor. Additionally, with lower levels of fat stored under the skin's dermis, a baby can lose its heat several times faster than an adult. So, it is important a newborn is protected from becoming cold.

However, most newborns seem to hate being naked, or having their nappy changed. So if your little babe is crying its wee heart out when you change him, then that's normal, you're not doing anything wrong.

Bathing bub

The hospital midwife or your LMC should show you in person how to bath your newborn baby. In the early days many babies loathe being given a bath, so if they're screaming, it's nothing you're doing wrong. Once at home they don't seem to have so much aversion to having a bath (or shower) with Mum or Dad — and that can be really lovely.

When cleaning your baby, do make sure you get into all the wrinkles — as those crevices can accumulate gunk. Do dry all those creases and wrinkles really well too. And no cotton buds up their nose or in the ears.

Little boys' penises need a good flannelly wash with water — never attempt to retract the foreskin, because in babies it is adherent to the penis glans and not supposed to retract. It will not do so until they are about 3–6 years of age. (Remember, the orifice of a little girl's vagina does not need douching either.)

Umbilical cord stump hygiene

You do not need to give any special treatment to your baby's cord stump. It may weep or bleed, but this is not harmful (it doesn't hurt your baby, as the cord itself had no feeling). Just wash away any residue with a damp cotton bud at bath-time or change-time.

It is not necessary to use surgical alcohol or witch hazel on this wound, as these prevent the good bacteria from digesting the dead cells, hindering cord separation. Your LMC or a hospital midwife will remove the cord clamp usually a couple of days after delivery.

The stump then turns black, dries up and falls off in about 5–10 days — and your baby's belly-button will be revealed to you for the first time — and at that moment you will truly appreciate that your own belly-button's shape had nothing to do with your mother's obstetrician's ability at tying knots! After the stump falls off, your baby's umbilicus (belly-button) could be slightly open for a few days.

It is normal for the stump to become a little smelly, but if it begins actively bleeding, or gets infected (the navel is red, hot, oozing pus or smelling bad) then you should quickly see your LMC or a doctor.

Nail trimming

Babies are frequently born with incredibly long fingernails, so you will need to trim them pronto, because with their flailing arms, the nails can be lethal weapons on themselves (e.g. scratching their cornea).

Some mums use nail clippers, some use nail scissors, some use special baby nail cutters, some use an emery nail-file board, and then there's nature's original system of mum gently chewing her baby's nails down. It doesn't really matter how you do it, but just get the job done, and it can often be easier doing it when the baby is asleep.

Newborns' vision, smell and hearing

From the sixteenth week in utero, your fetus became sensitive to light, and by 32 weeks had the same ability to see as a full-term baby. But it is normal for a newborn to gaze around in a foggy way for the first month, even cross-eyed — it makes you wonder if they're seeing anything! In reality a newborn has clearish sight for only a short distance, contrast is poor, and beyond half a metre is blurry.

Within seconds of birth, the baby's brain is already forming networks to remember his mother's scent and the unique smell of her breastmilk. Just remember that babies are very sensitive to odours, so avoid heavy perfumes, strongly scented deodorants and smelly room deodorisers.

Hearing is a baby's most finely developed sense at birth, and a newborn can recognise his mother's voice in a crowd.

Moro startle reflex

When your LMC examines your newborn, while lying baby on its back, they lift the head slightly before letting it quickly drop a few inches to startle the baby. Babies respond by throwing out their limbs, almost straightening their legs and arms, as if to catch something, in a sort of embrace. This shows that they are moving all their limbs in an equal, normal way.

You may also see your newborn's startle reflex triggered by a sudden movement or loud noise.

Other primitive reflexes

As well as the Moro reflex newborn babies are also initially equipped with other reflexes. These include:
- A rooting reflex (when their cheek is touched, they turn their face towards that side and open their mouth).
- A sucking reflex (when their mouth palate is touched).
- A survival reflex (turning their head to get more air if their mouth and nose are covered).
- A stepping reflex: when they are held in a standing position and their feet touch a hard surface, they look as if they're trying to walk. (No, you haven't given birth to a baby who already knows how to walk.)

- The recently discovered 'diving' reflex that stops a baby breathing underwater for the first six months, even with its mouth wide open.
- The magical grasp reflex: when you touch the palms of their hands or the soles of their feet, their fingers or toes close over. (One wonders if perhaps, when a tiny hand grasps onto the finger of an adult, this reflex is designed to capture the hearts of its parents.)

Such primitive reflexes will diminish and eventually disappear over the first 3–9 months, as other more grown-up involuntary responses start to emerge (e.g. jerking their hand or foot back from something that is painful).

Baby's first poos

Within 48 hours of birth, your baby should produce its first dirty nappy, and for the first 1–2 days a new baby's poo can range from something like black tar to dark green sludge. This is called **meconium** and it is the amniotic fluid debris (e.g. bile and mucous), which had accumulated in its intestine before birth. It's pretty sticky stuff and looks so freaky, but it is odourless. (Careful: it stains clothing.) Then, as the digestive system gets used to functioning, they go to a transitional brown, batter-like poo, on to golden-yellow poos by the fourth or fifth day.

It's not unusual for a newborn to have more than a dozen dirty nappies a day (including perhaps some weird looking loose, green and watery poos), but a minimum of 3–4 poos per day for the first 5–7 days is good. Then a small group of newborns change from this pattern to having one bowel motion every 6–10 days — but it is not constipation if when the poo arrives it is soft. Still, if you are concerned you may want to see your LMC or doctor to have it checked out.

Note: A poo in a very young baby can be equivalent to a brown patch the size of a large coin, or about a teaspoon of mush.

Baby's first pee

Within 24 hours your baby should produce its first wet nappy, and a newborn's first pee can stain a nappy red or dark pink because of the urates (uric acid salts) it contains.

If your wee newborn has not urinated by 36 hours, tell your LMC or a nurse-midwife. If you are finding it difficult to see in a disposable nappy if your baby has peed, then placing a tissue between their bottom and the nappy can be a good trick. After that, a minimum of six pees per day for the first 5–7 days is good.

Neonatal physiological jaundice

Jaundice is very common in newborns — in fact almost all babies briefly become at least a little jaundiced (this is when they have a tan or orange-pink skin tone). It most commonly develops after the second day, peaking between the third to fifth day, and disappearing after a week to 10 days.

Babies at birth have a red blood count that is about 25 percent higher than normal due to the low-oxygen environment of the womb, so when these red blood cells pass their use-by date, they are broken down, and one of the components that remains is a yellowish pigment called bilirubin. This builds up in the baby's bloodstream because the liver, whose job it is to extract excess bilirubin, is not fully functioning in the first days of a newborn life, producing a yellow discolouration to a baby's skin tissue and eyes.

Sunlight helps to break down some of the bilirubin in their skin, reducing the workload on the liver. So it can be helpful to put your baby near a window, uncovering them a little so the *indirect* sunlight can reach their torso and limbs.

A heavier dose of jaundice (e.g. when the palms or soles are yellow too, or if the baby is unwell in any way) can be helped with phototherapy treatment (sleeping them under ultraviolet light), as this produces a photochemical breakdown of bilirubin into substances that are then passed out in the urine. Another high-tech form of phototherapy is a blanket filled with fibre-optic wands emitting light, which is wrapped around the baby and turned on.

Jaundiced babies can become sleepy, but need plenty of breastfeeding to cope with excreting the bilirubin, so it's probably a good idea to feed a jaundiced newborn every couple of hours, even if it means rousing them.

Complementary remedies that are traditionally accepted as assisting with jaundice, is for the breastfeeding mother to take liver-boosting herbal remedies herself such as St Mary's thistle, dandelion root, or schisandra.

Pathological jaundice

If jaundice appears within the first 24 hours of birth, becomes excessively severe, or lasts longer than normal, it could indicate the presence of an underlying problem such as a metabolic or structural liver dysfunction, bacterial or viral infection, or mother–infant blood incompatibility. If you're not in hospital you need to see a doctor straight away, as pathological jaundice can have serious consequences. If the bilirubin levels become very high this can cause irreversible brain damage, a condition called kernicterus.

Breastmilk jaundice

Occasionally new babies can develop jaundice on say the fifth to tenth day, peaking during the second or third week. This is breastmilk jaundice, which is when hormones in the mother's milk inhibit the baby's production of enzymes to breakdown and excrete bilirubin, and it can last for several weeks, or even up to a couple of months.

Because breastmilk jaundice is a diagnosis made only after more rare or serious underlying causes of jaundice are ruled out, you should refer this to your LMC or doctor.

Coughs, snuffles, sneezes, grunts, rattles and hiccups

Newborns can cough and sneeze and snuffle quite a bit really, as their little system clears out the fluid they have been breathing for the last nine months. (Pity you can't teach them to blow their noses.) And a baby's sleeping face has many expressions — grunting scowls, lip-smacking smiles, murmuring jerks and squirming puckers.

Babies who, in the womb, may have breathed meconium into their lungs can sound especially rattly, which is disturbing to a new mum. The homeopathic drops Nux Vomica, diluted in cooled, boiled water and given orally, are good to help a newborn with this.

Bright lights can make a newborn sneeze because it stimulates the nerves of their nose as well as their eyes. Hiccupping is very common in all babies, especially after a feed. Newborns also seem to breathe very lightly, initially, but their breathing gets stronger every day.

Twitches and jerks

Another bizarre thing to see in your wee newborn are startled jumps, twitching and jerking in their sleep, or their whole body startling when you pick them up — but it's all normal. These muscle spasms are called myoclonic jerks.

Newborns sleep very solidly, especially during the REM (Rapid Eye Movement) stage, where they appear to be stirring, with lots of wee fussing noises, little jerky movements, and strange facial expressions.

Clicky hips

Your wee babe will be regularly checked for a congenital dislocation of the hip. It is rare but, if undiagnosed, can lead to a permanent limp and lifelong arthritis in the affected hip joint.

If your baby's hips are a bit clicky, and/or the legs' skin creases below their bottom are not symmetrical, then at about four months your bub will probably be X-rayed and checked by an orthopaedic surgeon.

If a baby has a clunky hip, or the hip is dislocating (when the ball at the head of the thighbone does not fit snugly into the hip socket of the pelvic girdle), then this is treated seriously, and these babies are usually put into a special harness splint for 3–4 months. (This condition is more common in girls.)

Guthrie heel-prick test

Around 2–5 days after birth, a hospital nurse (or midwife in your home), will prick your newborn's heel and squeeze out a little blood onto a blotting-paper like card. This newborn screening is done to test for seven metabolic disorders (such as cystic fibrosis), some of which if undiagnosed can result in permanent severe retardation, but if discovered very early are usually treatable. (A midwife will be happy to explain in more detail.) Most newborns do, understandably, get pretty upset at having this done, and nursing them afterwards can help calm them. A little Hypercal lotion on the heel afterwards can ease things.

My baby's getting boobies

Often newborns (girls and boys) can develop enlarged breasts (called neonatal mastitis) peaking at about day 4 when their nipples can even leak a little (nicknamed witch's milk). It usually takes a couple of weeks for this to go away, but sometimes it can take months for the swelling to completely subside, and it can be lopsided.

Little-girl newborns can even have a miniature period of a little bloody discharge from their vagina (called pseudo-menstruation), which is just some cells from their tiny womb lining.

Both conditions are normal.

Diarrhoea and vomiting

It is unusual for a breastfed newborn to have digestive problems. But if your newborn is vomiting up all feeds over say a six-hour period and has loose watery or green poos, you should speak with a doctor quickly. A new baby's digestive system is very vulnerable to gastrointestinal infections, and vomiting is often a sign of general infection (e.g. urinary infection). This is very serious in newborns.

The maternity 'baby blues'

OK, it's about three to four days (or within the first week) after the initial thrillingly euphoric (or outright traumatic) arrival of your little bub. Probably with some drugs in your system, tender stitches and perhaps some anaemia, this extreme-sport fear-factor ordeal is normally immediately followed by an elated, excited, laughing couple of days. Then comes the onslaught of sleep deprivation, childbirth-disappointment thoughts, sore nipples, breastfeeding difficulties, sore boobs from your milk coming in, partner worries, non-stop well-meaning visitors, and the all-encompassing, exhausting, raw, emotional turmoil of the whole anxious upheaval. This is all normal, but *this does not cause the baby blues.*

When the placenta's hormone factory was shut down at delivery, a drastic plunging and reshuffling of hormone levels occurred in your body. Oestrogen levels that were as much as 1000 percent higher than normal nose-dived drastically, and progesterone levels (which had been acting as a natural anti-depressant) crashed to just 5 percent of what they had been for the last nine months. You are, so to speak, on a 'cold-turkey' drug withdrawal from high levels of natural opiates (endorphins) and other hormones, while enduring a new staggering hormonally driven cocktail of emotions. Or, as Dr Miriam Stoppard describes it, 'The withdrawal of the huge amounts of pregnancy hormones is like the withdrawal of a life-force'. *This is what causes the baby blues.*

A little further down the track, there's another earthquake aftershock as your progesterone levels dwindle down to zero (*oh, man*) and the oestrogen levels halve again. In such circumstances, it is not unreasonable that most women can find it a little hard to adjust (big understatement) without the situation creating unstable emotions and affecting your mental processes. *Hell yeah!* The rug has been pulled out from under your feet, you feel fragile and weak, and you are weeping buckets — as everything seems wrong.

At the same time, you are beginning to come to grips with some of the processes of mothering a newborn, so you may be starting to feel just a little more self-sufficient and independent. However, physiologically this is all quite a violent shock to the brain's hypothalamus (chemical message supervisory centre) — and your body may need to wait up to two months for your pair of previously inactive almond-sized ovaries to crank back up to their normal hormone-production levels, in place of the placenta that had taken over producing your oestrogen and progesterone for half of the last year.

So, nearly every new mother will experience some level of the baby blues (and it can vary from one birth to the next).

Does the list on the following page sum it up for you? That's all normal! Women who escape this rough period are in the minority. Author Tracy

Symptoms of the baby blues

- Bursting into tears. Fragile emotional weepiness, for seemingly minor or 'no real' reasons.
- Sudden mood swings. Feeling deliriously happy, but decidedly lousy and inadequate, all at the same time.
- Being hypersensitive to criticism, or being anxious about your ability to mother a baby (the can't-cope feeling of a self-confidence crisis).
- A mixture of low spirits, vulnerability, discouragement, numbness or irritability.
- Indecisiveness and poor concentration (slow cognitive functions).
- Feeling unbonded with your baby.
- Insomnia, restless sleep or headaches (feeling physically exhausted, but unable to sleep).

Hogg aptly describes it as a 'tsunami wave drowning out your sanity and sense of wellbeing'.

This is all the post-pregnancy medical condition nicknamed the baby blues and it affects about 75–80 percent of new mums. Such feelings are biologically beyond your control! So don't add self-loathing and guilt to the pile too.

Also, just these few days after birth, you are beginning to comprehend the irreversible extent to which your previously predictable world has been permanently turned upside down. So, there can be unexpected emotions — such as feeling a grief for the death of the old you, and the loss of your carefree youthfulness, because 24-7 responsibilities are now yours forever more.

In the nineteenth century the baby blues were known as 'milk fever' because it coincides with the beginning of one's milk production. But please, you are not going crazy, this is mostly hormonal, and it is temporary — so don't consume yourself worrying. Think of it as just a really bad case of PMS.

Although the experience does feel distressing, all you really need is supportive reassurance and, perhaps, some Bach flower Rescue Remedy a few times a day would be helpful too. Some experts advocate eating less sugary foods, and more potassium-rich foods (such as bananas and tomatoes).

Baby blues has nothing to do with postnatal depression — unless it is abnormally severe (see page 367 for details on this). Typically the condition is reasonably mild and short lived, from just a few crazy hours to a few overcast days, with the commonest worst peak being days 4–6. It should have subsided significantly by day 10, and be resolved completely by day 14. And three months later you will be scratching your head to recall exactly what those baby blues felt like. But in the meantime, this is certainly a good time for your partner to wear his thickest skin!

If you suffer badly with a severe experience of the baby blues (say finding bub almost impossible to manage), make sure your LMC and doctor know, because this can be a biological trigger for postnatal depression.

If your baby blues don't kick in until day 10–14, or persist past two weeks, talk immediately to your LMC or doctor — because this is not the baby blues, and could be something more complex such as postnatal depression, or worse postnatal psychosis. (See pages 265, 367 and 374 for more details.)

Warning: Instead of suffering the baby blues, some women have the 'baby pinks' when they are over-coping and illogically on top of the world (being way too capable and peachy) . . . She's at the supermarket the day after giving birth, having sex within the first week, not eating properly, having difficulty sleeping, or refusing to rest enough. This should be carefully watched, because it can be a trigger for a pending depressive imbalance.

Time to face the music

It is time to go home and face your new life, your new role, and your new label. You are now a *mother*!

If you feel like you couldn't possibly really be a mother, and that your baby is just a newborn you're babysitting for a while, then I reckon that's a pretty normal feeling too — because let's face it, the whole experience is surreal.

One last piece of advice: don't expect to be able to leave the hosptial quickly. The hospital needs to issue you with your maternal- and infant-discharge paperwork, and with busy staff these formalities can sometimes take all morning. So, I suggest you start to get ready to go mid-morning, have another lingering bath, enjoy another hour of lying down with no washing to do, even take advantage of grabbing lunch there too before you leave. And don't forget to remove your baby's name card out of their bassinet to put in his memento box.

CONGRATULATIONS new Mum, you have done it, you've got through it, and now . . . let the real journey begin!!

You do not become a different person once you have had a baby; it is just that all the colours of your personality may become more vivid.
  Sheila Kitzinger — *The Complete Book of Pregnancy and Childbirth*

Chapter 4

Starting breast or bottle feeding

Give yourself forty days of not expecting too much. Of course, everyone (Dad included) wants breastfeeding to go smoothly immediately, so after two or three days, you or your partner might become impatient and concerned. But to really get comfortable and to breastfeed correctly, it often takes longer.

Tracy Hogg — *Secrets of the Baby Whisperer*

Oh heck, did you have glorious visions of being the Madonna and child? Oh how sweet — so did many of us. But the real truth is that we nearly all hoped that: 'Maybe ours will be the baby that suckles perfectly on bosoms that lovingly nourish him, with little or no pain for me the mother.' And you know what, that has pretty much happened for a lucky few of my friends, but it's not the norm.

Although breastfeeding is a simple process, it can also be an extremely challenging experience. The hard reality is that the majority of first-time mothers experience some breastfeeding difficulties; plus about 20 percent of new mums have particularly difficult pain with sore nipples. Retrospectively, many new mums reflect that they should have sought more one-on-one guidance when learning to breastfeed.

You see, it can take many, many days for a mother to learn the art of teaching her baby to latch and suckle properly, during which time it can feel to a new mother like a very lonely struggle, which it is. We can't remove our boobs and strap them onto our partners, no matter how much we'd like to be relieved of the burden of making breastfeeding work.

Eventually, once the mother is feeling sussed, then it can still take days or weeks for the baby to fully understand what they need to do. On top of that, about one in 10 babies is plain uninterested, sleepy or both. So, it can easily be a month until your newborn will latch on perfectly, first time every time, without causing you any discomfort. Then it can be a further couple of weeks after that until you begin to sense a synchronicity between you, your baby and breastfeeding. But major essentials for a lactating mum's success are the Three R's: being *Relaxed, Rested* and *Ravenous*.

You didn't expect the birth to be a breeze, and that's behind you now. I suggest putting breastfeeding into that same kind of category i.e. it's not necessarily easy, in fact you have about a two-in-three chance of experiencing initial difficulties with breastfeeding, but . . . it is worth persevering.

And is it really worth it? Without hesitation, I would have to say 'Definitely YES, YES, YES'!

Breastmilk is easily digestible and nutritionally perfect for your baby, it's portable and practical, it requires no pre-mixing or heating, it's virtually free, and, after a little while, requires almost no paraphernalia — and, with your memory-chip malfunctioning, the other major bonus is, you can never forget to take it with you. Breastfeeding is more than just providing human milk — it is a lifestyle.

Breastmilk, unlike formula, adapts itself to your baby's individual needs. For example, both our girls were born in winter, but our son was born in spring. I remember being so surprised at how different the milk I expressed for him looked — it was much runnier than the girls' milk. And then it dawned on me, it was now the height of summer, and he required more thirst-quenching milk than the girls had needed. Fully breastfed babies do not need to drink water — even in the hottest weather.

Breastmilk can vary significantly in its appearance, sometimes it's white and creamy, sometimes yellowish and thin, sometimes even bluish-clear. It's all perfectly normal! Mother Nature is amazing at customising to her babies' needs.

Scientists studying mothers who tandem breastfeed both a newborn and toddler, find that the breasts produce two different kinds of milk for the two children, including colostrum for the newborn. And with premature babies, miraculously the breasts produce milk even higher in growth hormones, nitrogen and protein.

Breastfeeding also provides numerous physiological and psychological benefits over formula-feeding, to both your baby and yourself. *If you can just persist long enough* to make breastfeeding all finally gel, it is also the laziest way to feed your baby too.

There is, without doubt, something very magical, mystical and mythical (even spiritual) about breastfeeding your baby ... and that's the indescribable Goddess sensation ... seeing your body nourishing your babe, as you supply your infant with every protein chain, glucose sugar, lipid fat and water molecule in its entire body. It is a powerfully proud and humbling experience, witnessing your life give life!

Although the journey can be hell, the end results can be heavenly!

World War III: breastmilk versus formula

But it isn't just the baby's stomach that is nourished at the breast ...
baby is fed emotionally ... Breastfeeding is like a self-sufficient
health-care system, a two-way process helping not only the baby but
the mother too.
           Carol Dunham and the Body Shop Team — *Mamatoto*

The debate of breast versus bottle is of course not really World War III, but it can certainly feel like it when heavyweights such as the World Health Organisation (WHO) and UNICEF lobby the indisputable scientific benefits of the 'Breast is Best' mantra.

The level of missionary zeal from some breastfeeding activists — 'lactivists' — can seem overwhelmingly condemning to those who do not conform to their idealistic policy of a minimum of two years' lactation.

Certainly babies are drinking, pooing, peeing, metabolising, growing machines. So, of course, the more nutritionally perfect nourishment the baby receives, the more optimally perfect development the baby can experience. However, there can be numerous circumstances where bottle-feeding may be the best decision.

Perhaps you adopted your baby. Perhaps your milk-ducts have been injured from an accident, or removed by surgery. Perhaps you have a glandular hormonal deficiency, or a chronic disease such as cancer, and must take medicine that would contaminate your milk. Perhaps your baby is lactose intolerant and is actually allergic to your milk. Or, perhaps your nipples are traumatised, so you're expressing your breastmilk and feeding your baby from the bottle for a time.

Receiving poignant reminders that in the past babies didn't usually survive unless their mothers succeeded with breastfeeding are uncalled for these days. We're not living in the past, and we have access to highly nutritious infant formula and state-of-the-art medicine. We also have a whole new set of problems to contend with, such as fitting breastfeeding in with career obligations.

This book, although needing to be frank and unbiased in its information, also strives not to judge. So, if for whatever reason your baby is not exclusively breastfed, then that is your own business.

Women who bottle-feed their babies soon become well aware of society's judgemental attitudes. But if you are able to successfully breastfeed, *please don't* become another person who looks down her nose at the bottle-feeding mother. Just give her a genuinely friendly smile instead . . . you could make her day!

This is not scoffing at the Breast is Best policy, but simply saying that mothers whose babies consume formula should not consume guilt — because *a formula-fed baby with a guilt-fed mother is just a disaster waiting to happen*!

So, if you're reading this book; you're treasuring the closeness of feeds; you're adoringly attending to your baby's endless needs; and you're feeding your baby formula; then you are absolutely, categorically, still being a *great* mother to your thriving baby!

These days, many maternity hospitals have ratified the WHO–UNICEF baby-friendly hospital policies with the aim of protecting women's rights by smoothing the way for breastfeeding in an encouraging, cocooned environment. However, these policies have been interpreted and adopted in varying degrees, with a strong influence from individual hospital maternity department heads.

Of all these WHO–UNICEF directives, it is the very last point that seems

The WHO–UNICEF breastfeeding guidelines:

- A written breastfeeding policy communicated to staff, with staff trained to implement it.
- Pregnant women informed of breastfeeding benefits and management.
- Mothers helped to initiate breastfeeding within half-an-hour of childbirth.
- Mothers shown how to breastfeed, and encouraged to breastfeed on demand.
- Mothers shown how to maintain lactation if they are separated from their infant.
- Mothers and infants allowed to be together (rooming-in) 24 hours a day.
- Infants given no artificial teats or pacifiers.
- Newborns given no food or drink other than breastmilk — unless medically indicated.

to generate the most controversy — though it's not the whole issue. From a New Zealand viewpoint, this debate can be divided into two main areas of concern: firstly, topping up a newborn with formula during the first days before the mother's milk comes in; and secondly, the side effects of long-term partial or total formula feeding. Let me explain.

Topping up newborns

It is normal for babies to lose about 5 percent of their body weight (200–250 g or about half a pound), in the first few days of colostrum feeds until the mother's full milk comes in — even up to a 10 percent weight-loss can be OK.

For most babies, supplementing their initial feeds with formula until the mother's full milk comes in is not usually considered. But, it can be discussed if there are medical indicators such as if the baby has a low birth-weight, sunken fontanelle, is unusually unsettled, extremely lethargic or obviously hungry. A very sleepy newborn is of particular concern because this can be a sign of an untreated infection (e.g. urinary tract infection or meningitis), or a sign of being underfed (conserving energy).

The primary paediatric medical concern and reason for recommending a formula top-up is not to prevent the newborn from loosing too much weight, but to ensure adequate and safe blood-sugar levels are maintained to avoid the newborn becoming hypoglycaemic, or dehydrated.

Some Birth Centre advocates zealously talk of the serious consequences of feeding a newborn 'just one bottle', such as increasing the likelihood of allergies, bowel infection and diarrhoea. Other hospitals take an overly casual approach, stemming from antiquated advice, of too-frequently topping up newborns unnecessarily. It is true that supplementing human milk sources with the likes of cows' milk and goats' milk goes back thousands of years.

All in all, it is a very contentious issue, and it is important you are fully informed. But be aware that, when you are given 'informed choice', you may also be asked to give 'informed consent'.

Perhaps the best advice this book can give is to listen to your own mothering instincts. If a nurse-midwife is suggesting a formula top-up and you feel it is unnecessary, then insist it not be done. If a nurse-midwife is disapproving of a formula top-up and you feel it is necessary, then insist it be done. This is your baby, and your intuition will usually be right — every baby is different.

Partial or total formula feeding

It is ironic that only 50 years (or so) ago, many believed breastfeeding to be primitive and old-fashioned. But breast is best these days, and natural, we know! However, breastfeeding is not always the bed of roses some breast-is-best activists like to make it out to be, which unless you are well prepared can leaving you feeling like a defective mother.

Even when latch-on is a breeze, breastfeeding isn't without its negative sides — it can be very taxing. Your body requires a substantial amount of energy to manufacture milk, which can be draining — and certainly exclusive breastfeeding can be an exhausting 24–7 lifestyle (but parenting is a 24–7 lifestyle commitment).

In New Zealand maternity statistics for the first 2–6 weeks state that about 65 percent of mothers are primarily breastfeeding their baby; approximately 20 percent are fully feeding formula; and the rest are giving a mixture of breast and formula. By 3–4 months of age, about 55 percent of mothers are fully breastfeeding; around 30 percent are fully formula-feeding; and the rest are giving a mixture. By 4–7 months, only about 25 percent of mothers are still fully breastfeeding; around 40 percent are formula-feeding; and the rest are giving the mix. These are some of the best breastfeeding statistics in the world.

However, and here's the big BUT, the more science gains a fuller understanding of the perfect uniqueness of human milk, the more it realises how tremendously important exclusive breastfeeding is for an infant. Human milk is the ideal nutrition to support the optimal growth and development of human babies for the first six months after birth. To flippantly say 'Oh, he'll be OK on formula!' is now understood to be a rather ignorant remark. For extensive details on some of the medical benefits of breastmilk, see Appendix D at the end of this book, page 468, or visit the website www.lalecheleague.org.

It is also of relevance to lay out the (disputable) biological benefits of breastfeeding to the mother:

- Lessened lochia bleeding discharge, and more rapid uterus involution (returning to pre-pregnancy size).
- Earlier return to pre-pregnancy weight.
- Nature (theoretically at least) will not allow a mammalian mother to come to harm from feeding her newborn, so, to partially relieve sleep deprivation, the lactating mother's body increases production of the hormone serotonin, facilitating a quicker and deeper level of sleep. This allows for more restful sleep in shorter intervals.
- Breastfeeding for even two months shows significant improvements in the mother's systemic and emotional health with lower levels of anxiety and muscular tension, and improved wound healing.
- Exclusive breastfeeding on-demand, day and *night*, provides 98 percent-effective contraception for six months through amenorrhoea (absence of menstruation). (See page 304.)
- Continuing research is finding correlations between breastfeeding and reduced rates of cancers, including breast, ovarian, endometrial, oesophageal, thyroid and uterine cancer.
- Reduced household expenditure from cost of formula, reduced levels of work absenteeism and lost income for parents due to childhood illnesses in the future mean significant economic benefits.

Note: At a biological level, babies need calm and serenity for feeding, especially in the first 2–3 weeks — it is also their soul food. So, it is important to acknowledge this joint experience while feeding by making a conscious commitment to give your baby your undivided attention during all feeds in those first weeks — as an investment in the mother–baby bond, and in the baby's physiological and emotional development.

It is, perhaps, of no real surprise that the baby's en-face direct gaze (ideal visual focusing measurement) is the exact distance from the mother's bent arm to the mother's eyes, because feeding — in the early weeks especially — is a hugely important experience for the baby with the establishing of its mother–newborn social and bonding relationship.

It really can be a simple decision: make peaceful unhurried feed times your top daily priority.

In the very early days

*Do you want to try putting her to the breast? the midwife enquires
... The word 'natural' appears in a sort of cartoon bubble in my
head. I do not, it is true, feel entirely natural. I feel as though
somebody is sucking my breast in public.*

Rachel Cusk — *A Life's Work*

The hormone alchemy

What glorious hormonal alchemy the female body produces to create milk
for breastfeeding!

When the placenta released from your uterine wall, it triggered the
hormone production necessary for breastfeeding. Now, when your baby

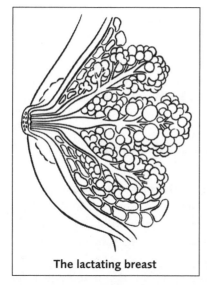

The lactating breast

suckles, it stimulates the nerve endings
of your nipple areolae, and they send a
message to the hypothalamus. The
hypothalamus then instructs your
anterior pituitary gland to secrete
prolactin (that is basically new to your
body), which instructs the breasts
(mammary glands) to produce milk
secretion in each breast's 15–25 lobes
(grape-like alveoli lobule clusters) that
contain the milk-producing alveolar
glands.

The hypothalamus also sends instructions for the release of the hormone
oxytocin (stored in the posterior
pituitary gland). The oxytocin triggers
the milk ejection 'let-down reflex' by contracting the network of muscle walls
surrounding the lobes to squeeze the milk-sacs, ejecting the milk into the
lactiferous ducts that flow to the nipple.

This all feels like a tingling, buzzing sensation inside your boobs as the
milk is forced from the mammary alveolar glands into the lactiferous milk-
ducts, which are then emptied as the milk is finally delivered to your nipple
openings. The rush of oxytocin-rich blood also warms your breasts, and you
can actually feel them getting hotter. You really are now, without doubt, a
portable dairy factory!

In the early days of breastfeeding, when you hear your baby smack her lips
or when you even just think about feeding your baby, it can activate this

milk-ejection let-down reflex. This can also easily occur when your baby is crying — or even other people's babies are crying, (including those on TV). But, when a new mother is anxious, angry, upset, tense, worried or stressed — before or during breastfeeding — the oxytocin let-down can be interrupted by the body's adrenal gland production of catecholamines (e.g. adrenaline), which hinders or halts the milk-ejection let-down reflex.

That's why it is important to try to create a calm, relaxing atmosphere for each and every feed of a newborn (e.g. turn your mobile off in the hospital, and continue at home by taking the phone off the hook).

For these efforts you will be well rewarded, as oxytocin promotes feelings of happiness and contentment in you and your baby. *Sigh*!

The other good news is that within a few weeks your hormones will be less temperamental, and your milk flow will be less influenced by your emotions — or babies crying on TV!

The brand-new colostrum-fed baby

Your breasts feed your newborn colostrum for the first 30–70 hours, which is part of Mother Nature's way of gently allowing your wee baby's stomach and bowels to get used to performing their functions. Don't be surprised if some early feeds are returned to you with additional mucous — it was in their stomach at birth.

The rich, sweet and yellow, watery colostrum is easily digested and provides little, but sufficient, calorie value, while supplying lots of protein, vitamins, trace minerals, milk sugar, and a huge amount of immune-boosting anti-infection antibodies (immunoglobulins). Colostrum also protects the baby's gastrointestines by lining the alimentary canal with a coating on the gut walls; it also acts as a gentle laxative helping the baby to poo out the meconium, and helps to reduce jaundice.

There are loads of different theories about the best system for breastfeeding newborns in the first days before the full-milk arrives. Without doubt, the more people whose opinion you seek, the more varying replies you will receive.

Below are my own personal recommendations, which are backed up by numerous books by some of the experts:
- For the first 24 hours expect to feed your baby for about 5–10 minutes each side whenever he wants it (say 2–5 hourly). Be very vigilant to ensure correct latch-on during this first day. Day-one newborns can be very sleepy, though this typically changes on day two.
- For the second 24 hours expect to feed your baby for about 10–15 minutes each side every couple of hours or so. (The feed times are getting

longer, because your baby is getting stronger and more experienced.)
- For the third day expect to feed your baby for about 15–20 minutes each side every 2–3 hours.
- By the fourth day your milk will probably have come in, and you can begin feeding, for about 40 minutes, every 3 hours or so, switching breasts each time — so yes, that's about 5–6 hours a day!

The fundamentals of feeding and burping

In the past, their [a new mother's] mothers and grandmothers, who had the time and patience to accompany them through hours of nursing, taught new mothers. Today, this responsibility falls to a member of a hospital staff or a lactation consultant, who may be pressed for time.

Brown and Dowd-Struck — *The Post-Pregnancy Handbook*

Universal signs a newborn is hungry

There certainly exists classic body language in all babies to try to tell their grown-up that they're hungry. These signs are listed below (but babies don't necessarily show *all* these 'signs'):
- Baby showing increased activity or alertness, maybe rapid eye movements.
- Baby purses his lips or does lip-smacking.
- Baby sticks his tongue out to the sides.
- Baby tries to suck his finger or hand, or rams his fist into his mouth.
- Baby turns his head from side to side, or arches his back while stretching his neck backwards with his mouth open.
- A late indicator feeding cue that baby is very hungry (try to avoid because it can be harder to feed): baby makes small cough-cough sounds (like trying to clear the throat); or baby cries with a demanding rhythm (e.g. *aaah*-pause-*aaah*-pause-*aaah*).

Note: A non-newborn sucking his thumb, hand or tongue within 2–3 hours of a feed is usually just self-soothing, and may want a pacifier. It does not *automatically* mean they're hungry.

Getting the basic breastfeeding technique right

It is helpful that a newborn is correctly taught how to latch on properly for its very first feeds — because it creates a strong blueprint within the baby's subconscious (which is highly beneficial to your nipples). So, for the welfare of your wee infant (and your pain threshold), you as the new mum need to actively seek assistance with this, and that can feel uncomfortably weird . . . having some woman (hospital nurse-midwife) grabbing your (previously ever-so-personal) breast, and manoeuvring your pinched nipple into your baby's mouth, like it's some large bath plug being shoved into the plug-hole. For many of us, that is the first time in our lives another woman has ever grabbed our titties, let alone it being someone who is treating them like appendages that no longer belong to us.

That midwifery style of teaching a new mother how to breastfeed is an old-school technique. The advice received from multiple nurse-midwives can feel like a contradictory mish-mash of ideas, so current acceptable practice is a hands-off technique. This allows the mother to accomplish successful breastfeeding themselves, with guidance and help from the midwife.

So here's the basic breastfeeding technique:
Pour yourself a large glass of water to drink before, or to have within reach during or after every feed. There are pleasant naturopathic lactational herbal teas available that encourage your body and mind to relax, such as chamomile, catnip, hops or lemon balm. Having a soothing cup of tea before beginning breastfeeding can be a great idea.

Before sitting down, go to the toilet, then rotate your shoulders in circles to pre-release any tensions, take the phone off the hook, put a 'Come Back Later' or 'Let Yourself In' note on the front door, perhaps put on some relaxing music, and plonk yourself down in a comfortable chair, knowing that unless the house is on fire you won't be getting up again for a good half-hour. Ideally you need to know you will be free from all interruptions, free of all clothing restrictions, and free of all time limitations. Get your back well supported, get your butt really comfortable, don't be leaning back or hunching forward, and have your arms well propped up too (with pillows or chair armrests, or both).

When you're ready, and you're in a quiet atmosphere away from distractions, and mentally as relaxed as possible, then position your baby sideways with his *tummy* against your *tummy*, almost level with your breast, with Bub's head higher than its bottom, and your arm supporting its neck and shoulders. Bub's nose should be in line with your nipple; and his chin, chest and knees should face your breast — not the ceiling. Remember: 'nose to hose'.

Newborns come equipped with an instinctive reaction called the rooting reflex, which is a primitive survival skill originating deep within the brain stem. To see it in action, hold your breast with your nipple stroking Bub's cheek and brushing onto his bottom lip — this encourages a newborn to open its mouth. And when he opens his mouth as wide as a yawn (like a baby

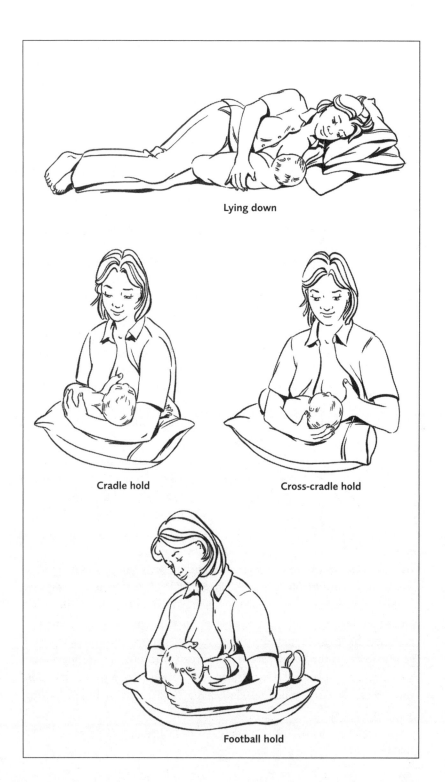

Lying down

Cradle hold

Cross-cradle hold

Football hold

bird), then quickly and firmly bring your baby's mouth over the coloured part of your breast. *Bring your baby to your breast — do NOT bring the breast to the baby*, because this creates a poor latch-on. (A few women may need to 'pinch' their breast behind the nipple to help it stand out and become a more easily grasped mouthful.) Your nipple and a good 2 cm of breast tissue below it are inside the baby's mouth.

Latching on

Now suckling, Bub's top and bottom lips should be flanged right back, like a fish, to create a suction seal (against your breast their lips look like the right side of the letter 'K').

The area around your nipple (the areola) is soft with bumpy oil-producing nodules (called Montgomery's tubercles), which lubricate and protect the nipple skin, and enable a good latch-on (without it, the baby's lips would 'slide' off smooth breast skin). Your entire nipple and most of the coloured areola area should be in baby's mouth, with his chin on your breast — not centred like a 'bulls-eye' though, you will be able to see some of the top of your areola. (The very tip end of your nipple will end up almost at the very back of your baby's mouth.)

Now, use your arm to bring your wee baby's body snugly towards you so you're very comfortably close — *again, DON'T lean your body forward towards the baby, bring the baby to you.* The tip of your baby's nose will usually touch your breast (or sometimes seem smothered in boob). If you think Bub can't possibly breathe unmuffled with all that titty up his nose, then push gently down on the fleshy part of your breast with one or two fingers (not the coloured nipple area). Or another good idea is to cup your hand under your breast, or put a rolled-up cloth-nappy underneath it before feeding, which gives boob-lift.

It can be normal in the early days to feel some pain just at the start of each feed.

You should now see a strong steady muscular wriggling movement on the bony area at the top of Bub's jawbone just by the temple/ear/jaw-hinge. This shows your baby is suckling correctly and, fingers crossed, you will see and hear him swallow every 1–5 sucks, (infant suckling is a very different process from an adult sucking on a straw). You may feel like bubbly wine is flowing through your breasts.

Once everything's perfect, *drop your shoulders and relax*!

But, if you're not seeing those signs, and Bub's cheeks are dimpled or hollow; or Bub is making a tongue clicking sound; or your breasts are feeling or looking misshapen; or your nipples are flattened or creased after feeding; or you are feeling real pain throughout the feeding — then these are all strong indicators that Bub is poorly positioned, (or part-way through a feed a good latch-on has deteriorated). It will eventually frustrate your baby, as your milk won't be flowing properly. You'll probably end up being gummed, which can cause significant nipple damage.

So if latch-on is not correct, you now need to be an assertive parent. Even though it is likely to annoy your wee bub, you need to re-position your baby to get him latched correctly. Remember, you are the parent, and you know best (not baby). The most popular ways to release the suction of a baby's lips on a boobie, are to:

- Insert your little finger into the corner of Bub's mouth to release the suction.
- Put your finger right up to Bub's mouth against your breast and press down on his chin.

Don't ever yank baby off — you'll damage your nipples.

Once latch-on is working well, sit back, flick on some daytime soap or a talk show and chill out. Oh sorry, you swore you were never going to do that! Stop being too disciplined, put down that latest parenting magazine homework reading . . . you're not going to get addicted to daytime TV (well not really, not too much, probably). Whatever you do, *relax*!

After the feed is finished; pay some attention to your upper back by looking upwards to the ceiling; give your spine a restorative stretch arching your back; lift up your arms above your head and rotate them in their shoulder sockets; rotate your neck; and even give your neck and shoulders a rub.

Early feeding points to note

- The hours between feeds are counted from the beginning of one feeding session, to the beginning of the next.
- A newborn can take a good 45 minutes to feed, dependent on their individual strength and personality and your milk flow, but it shouldn't take

longer. If it does, something's not right.

- Don't be surprised when your milk squirts out your nipple like a sprinkler from several holes, or like a shower rose spraying out myriad holes — breastmilk doesn't come out of just one hole. It also smells vaguely like tin, a sort of metallic odour.

- It is useful, worthy old wisdom to put 1–2 drops of your antiseptic-rich colostrum milk into your baby's eyes in those first couple of days to protect against infections. It doesn't sting the baby at all.

- It can help in the early days of erratic feeds and sleep deprivation, to write down the details of your baby's feeds, e.g. right 25 minutes and left 10 minutes. Because it means that you don't need to rely on a sieve-like mind to remember those details for the next feed . . . many a mum has wondered 'Which boob's turn first this time?'.

- It is understood that a newborn's intestines take about a hundred days to create competent protection against bacterial micro-organisms, and that the digestion of human breastmilk creates an intestinal environment for a baby designed to kill harmful bacteria and promote growth of good bacteria (e.g. lactobacilli). So, as previously explained, any substance other than human breastmilk (which provides the antibodies) can potentially provoke an allergic reaction, such as gastric problems.

- A baby's suckling reflex is almost more like a chomping action, and it can be very strong. Newborns also have the swallowing reflex (which they learnt in utero) and a gagging reflex (splutter coughs) to clear the breathing passages if they swallow too much.

- Babies, especially newborns, don't feed continuously. They feed in bursts and only gulp every few sucks. Along the lines of suck-suck-suck-suck-swallow-suck-suck-pause-suck-suck-swallow-pause-pause-suck-suck-suck-swallow-suck-suck-pause-suck . . . see the pattern? There is none, it's random. So when they pause, don't think you need to re-latch — Bub is just having a little rest. It's an exhausting aerobic work-out for a baby. As babies get older, they often like to pause mid-feed to enjoy a sociable smile or two!

- Some babies seem to be born ferociously hungry, and others are less interested. Everything varies in nature.

- When your baby dozes off during a feed, you need to gently wake Bub to re-start the sucking reflex. Don't assume it means Bub has had a full feed and now needs to go to bed! Your baby could have just had a cute little hit of oxytocin and is now very relaxed. So talk to your baby, remove her booties and rub or tickle her feet, jiggle your arm that's holding her, tug lightly on her earlobes, wipe a damp cloth over her forehead, change her nappy — in other words do something gentle to arouse Bub to kick-start her back into sucking.

- Babies are supposed to feel the caring touch of being caressed as they suckle, and some believe these positive feelings help to release the hormone insulin within their bodies. This is required for the calories of milk to be absorbed.

- As an infant's stomach begins to digest milk protein, it produces large amounts of the digestive enzyme, rennin, which converts infant milk into something resembling curdy, sour milk. So if your baby spits up a curdy substance, don't think your milk has somehow badly curdled or soured in its tummy — the milk is just partly digested.

- Solely breastfed babies' stools are not an unpleasant odour but actually have a sweet smell; they are an orangey-yellow-tan colour (nicknamed Karitane yellow); they may be quite watery or have the consistency of grainy cottage cheese, mustard or puréed pumpkin. Breastfed babies' poo has no 'offensive scent' as the babies' intestines break down every human milk protein to the very last amino-acid molecule.

- It is very normal, especially in the early days, that when you are breastfeeding your newborn, your other boobie starts leaking too. (If this continues beyond 2–3 weeks you may be producing too much milk which can be a problem for you and your baby — reducing breastmilk production is covered later in this chapter; see page 184.)

- Surprisingly, the size of a woman's breasts has no effect on their ability to make milk, or the quantity they produce.

- If you have what are called inverted or retracted, flat nipples (ones that don't stick out), this is usually more of a problem in just the first week or so while establishing breastfeeding, as your nipples are being moulded by your babe's suckling. Stimulating your nipples yourself to become firm before feeding can help. Nipple shields may (or may not) help — as can advice from a positive, encouraging midwife or lactation consultant — but it *absolutely* is possible to successfully breastfeed with inverted or flat nipples.

Universal signs the baby has wind and needs burping

Babies can swallow air when feeding and this accumulates as a bubble of air in their stomachs. This is a natural and normal occurrence. (Wind that is not burped upwards will eventually be farted downwards.)

In many older cultures around the world it is not normal for there to be such an incessant need to burp their babies. But we, in the West, have developed our own ritualised cultural phenomenon of generating a burp out of our babies before and/or midway through and/or after feeding.

Your baby actually uses very distinct body language to tell you they are uncomfortable with wind, and would appreciate some help to get rid of it — though of course they may not display all the signs:

- Baby curls his tongue upwards.
- Baby seems to scream, but he makes no sound.
- Baby gasps or pants.
- Baby makes high-pitched wailing shrills.
- Baby may hold his breath between screams.
- Baby makes screwed-up faces, resembling a cross between smiling and pain, maybe rolling his eyes.
- Baby's body tenses or becomes rigid.
- Baby's arms may slightly shake, or make jerky movements.
- Baby may squirm on his bottom, or pull his legs up to his chest.

Getting the basic burping techniques right

Techniques for winding babies (or 'bubbling' as Dr Spock used to call it) are a subject that has endless options, recommendations and theories. But there is no magical answer for all babies. It is a predicament solved by great patience and trial and error. Here is a selection of old favourites to choose from:

- Hold Bub over your shoulder with legs straight down and rub upwards, or gently pat Bub on the back (but don't go overboard with patting too vigorously).
- With Bub lying on his back, pull his legs up gently in a cycling motion.
- Lay Bub on his tummy across your forearm rubbing the back (so your supporting arm is putting light pressure on Bub's abdomen).
- Rub Bub's tummy in a backward 'C' (which traces the colon).
- Sit Bub straight-upright sideways in your lap, slightly leaning forward, supporting Bub's head under the chin with your other hand, then rub their back in light anti-clockwise circles (which traces the colon), or rub upwards.
- Lie Bub down flat and then stand Bub up a few times (to move the bubble of air up to the top of his stomach).

Burping points to note

- Always have a chuck cloth (cloth nappies are great) over your shoulder or under your baby's chin, as burps often include a little regurgitated milk — this is called possetting. (Soda water can help neutralise regurgitated milk if it gets on delicate fabrics.)
- You do not have to burp a baby halfway through the feed unless your

little Bub shows signs of having wind.

- Don't feel as if you have to burp Bub straight after finishing feeding — it is optional! A 5–10 minute wait with him sitting on your lap facing you while you 'talk' to each other, can sometimes make it easy to get rid of pesky wind — because during that time he may self-burp.
- If after 5 minutes of trying to burp your baby, nothing has popped up to say 'Hello', then so long as Bub is not uncomfortable, forget about it.
- Babies' tummies can really bulge after a good feed — that's normal.
- If your baby is often spitting-up after his feeds and is fussing (or even crying) after feeds, he may actually be over-fed. (So check that you're not misinterpreting some tired or overstimulated signs as hunger signs.) An overfed baby's tummy can make gurgling sounds.
- Sometimes a baby falls asleep or pulls off during a feed because air is making Bub feel full. Sit Bub up for burping and perhaps remove any booties or socks, as coldish feet can help keep a baby awake to finish his feed.
- A lot of partners can often be great yielders of stubborn baby-burps — I don't know why, maybe it's that male, single-focused-goal approach instead of our feminine multi-tasking.

What goes down may not stay down

Possetting

This is a baby spilling milk with wind at the end of a feed as a sort of drool. It is nothing to worry about — it's the baby version of a barfy burp. Possetting usually starts to sort itself out by six months of age, and is gone before their first birthday.

Regurgitation

This is when a baby throws-up in an effortless spasm a larger-than-spilly amount of milk — it can look like the whole contents of Bub's stomach (but isn't really). 'Spilly babies' (or what our grandmothers named 'happy spitters') are not

How to know your baby is getting enough breastmilk

Perhaps the most important thing is to feel reassured that your baby is well fed from breasts that are producing the perfect amount of milk.

If your baby is having at least 8 breast-feeds every 24 hours, is obviously swallowing during the feeds and seems happily satisfied after the feeds, then these are strong indicators that everything is fine. Other positive signs that a new-born is adequately fed are that he's doing at least four poos a day; that by about the fifth day there's no more meconium poo; that he's doing at least half-a-dozen pees a day; that he is back to his birth weight within say 10 days; and from then on gaining around 100–200 g per week.

bothered by their regurgitation, or who it lands on. These babies usually have normal weight gains — they are just huge creators of laundry (and full-time bib wearers).

Regurgitation usually occurs when the mum's milk supply is very fast, or the baby has drunk too much, or because he has a bubble of air in his tummy, or all three. Don't worry if this happens occasionally, but if it's persistent then contact your LMC, doctor or a lactation consultant.

If the vomit is greeny-yellow (contains bile); or is bloodstained; or the regurgitation is more like forceful projectile vomiting (which flies quite a few metres at great velocity, see page 264); then you should contact your LMC or doctor.

Mum's body: a nightmare of torture? A miracle of nature!

Engorgement: say 'Hi' to the biggest boobs you've ever had

Normally around the second, third or fourth day postpartum a mum's milk comes in, and for most ladies it is a very distinct sensation. (Sometimes engorgement can be slower — up to a week — particularly after a caesar, which makes it important for C-section mothers to very frequently feed their newborn to stimulate milk production.)

Engorgement can start with a slight fever (which can last for up to a day), and strong tingling in your breasts as they get warmer (like they're itchy on the inside), then within as little as a couple of hours, or much longer, your boobs can become shiny-looking, firm, tight, full and hot, maybe with the nipples stretched flat . . . and so huge — sometimes they double in size!

For a new mother, these massive veiny appendages can, for the first time in her life, feel like lead-heavy painful attachments. I swear my hooters always looked so similar to rock-hard, over-inflated balloons that if you pricked them they'd fly around the room.

The peak of true engorgement (over-full production of milk) usually lasts about 24–36 hours, and what a very uncomfortable day or so it can be — plus, during this time, the initial let-down at feeds can be painful.

Engorgement ends as soon as your milk production settles down and adjusts itself to meet your baby's demands. Feeding your baby during engorgement teaches your body how much milk your breasts need to be making. It is then normal for breasts to decrease in size at about one week after childbirth (and then commonly again at around six weeks) — so don't be surprised when they stop feeling so firm. It does not mean you are no longer producing enough milk — you are more likely to be producing the perfect amount of milk. By the way, not every woman experiences uncomfortable engorgement!

Here are some ideas to ease engorgement

- Stand in a warm shower with the spray landing on your boobies.
- Soak in a warm bath with the water covering your aching titties — if the bath is deep enough.
- Apply an ice or heat pack (e.g. hot-water bottle), or wrap your breasts in a hot, wet, cloth nappy.
- Fill the bathroom vanity sink with warm water, and give your titties a miniature bath.
- Manually express a little milk between feeds.
- You may need to express a little off your enormously swollen boobs before feeds to soften the areola area so your baby can latch on better.
- Give your giant hooters massaging strokes while you feed.
- Wear supportive and professionally fitted cotton bras, 24–7.
- Do shoulder overarm circles every couple of hours with your arms.
- Ask someone to give you a relaxing neck and upper back massage before feeds.
- Avoid using a baby sling or suchlike that crosses the breast or compresses the nipple.
- Take homeopathic Phytolacca (pokeweed root) — a couple of drops every couple of hours.
- Apply a poultice ointment (pasty putty) made from pokeweed root, comfrey or parsley.
- Apply a cold compress with the essential oils rose or lavender.
- Place a fridge-chilled (raw) cabbage leaf over each breast inside your bra, and change it every 1–2 hours once it goes limp — science still can't explain exactly why cabbage leaves are so soothing (though there is some [over]concern about cabbage leaves potentially detrimentally reducing milk-flow after engorgement).
- Wrap your breasts in a hot or cold towel with a compress inside of grated or mashed ginger root, and/or raw mashed potatoes. (Blimmin' heck, I hear you thinking, this motherhood life is just too weird sometimes — so true).
- Use a cold pack after feeds for comfort and to decrease swelling.
- Put newborn disposable nappies in the freezer and wear as a cold pack (cover with a cloth). They fit around the boobies very well.
- Rest — every 2–2$^{1}/_{2}$ hours at least — and eat well.

- Drink a lot of liquid — drinking less water does not prevent engorgement, and drinking lots of water doesn't make engorgement worse.

Pigging out

After several pregnant months of being unable to squeeze in full meals, now you can truly relish eating again. They say it is common for the appetite of a breastfeeding mother to increase 'slightly'. Personally, I would have described it more along the lines of developing a voracious hunger! . . . My tummy would rumble so much at 3 am or 4 am, I just had to make some toast and a milky hot drink to get back to sleep . . . Or, after quickly devouring my own dinner, I would find myself staring at my husband's plate to see what food he might have left over . . . so hungry! By the way, you need even more protein while breastfeeding than during pregnancy.

In the first week your breasts produce colostrum and experience engorgement; in the second week your breasts go into a transitional phase of producing kilojoule-rich milk, which has particularly high levels of fat and lactose (milk sugar). The mother's super-hungry phase usually passes after those first couple of weeks, as your breasts settle down to produce mature milk. But things can remain erratic for another month or so, as your hypothalamus fully establishes the delicate balance between milk supply and demand.

So, let your appetite go with the flow for the first few weeks. I always used the philosophy, that 'If I'm hungry, I'm not producing my best milk, and that's not what's best for our baby — so I should eat.'

The milkman's arrived . . . milkwoman!

With mature milk, at the beginning of the feed your baby receives the thirst quenching low-calorie protein-rich **fore-milk**. This fore-milk has two parts: for the first few minutes it is a watery fast-flowing sweet mineral-salt-rich, thirst-quenching milk (consistency of trim milk), which is rich in the relaxing hormone oxytocin, carbohydrates and high levels of lactose (milk sugar). Then arrives the main high-protein fattier milk (consistency of regular milk).

Then towards the end of the breastfeed starts the thick and creamy, fat-rich, protein-rich tummy-filling high-calorie nourishing **hind-milk** (consistency of runny cream). This signals to the baby that the meal is finishing, he is now full, and can soon release his suckle.

When your wee baby finishes and pulls off the first breast, then offer the other breast, but accept that there is a good chance it will be turned down, because baby is what we nickname 'milk drunk' (a very cute look indeed).

Your baby has now enjoyed his soup, main and dessert.

But, if you switch breasts too fast, instead giving Bub say 10 minutes each side, then Bub has only been served two soups, a small main, and no dessert. Poor baby! The high amounts of lactose sugar in all that fore-milk, can also irritate Bub's digestive system, creating an irritable and distended (swollen) tummy; maybe with green poo, and frequent noisy machine-gun poo. Chances are, Bub will be hungry again too in no time at all, which then creates a vicious cycle.

You see, once your milk has arrived, just one breast per feed can be perfect — depending on your baby and your breasts — so don't feel your baby is not getting adequate milk because he refuses the second boob. It is also very healthy for your breasts to be sucked dry, as it reduces chances of getting a blocked duct, mastitis or a breast abscess.

In the early days, *after* your milk comes in, a rough guideline with a newborn is not to breastfeed less than two hourly (this teaches a newborn to snack, missing the rich hind-milk), but no less frequently than 3–4 hourly — so about 8–12 feeds in every 24 hours. Some sleepy newborns may need to be woken after four hours for their feeds.

Chafed, cracked, blistered or bleeding nipples

No amount of your partner's bedroom foreplay can ever prepare your virginal nipples for a newborn vigorously (or ferociously) sucking on them for 6–8 hours a day — but breastfeeding should not be extremely painful.

It is normal for your nipples to be somewhat damaged in the first days, but if it persists then there's a 95 percent chance your baby has not yet been taught the correct way to latch-on. Most likely your nipple is not deep enough inside your baby's mouth. But please don't give up breastfeeding yet — it's just time to seek guidance.

If your baby seems to keep forgetting how to latch-on (more common, ironically, with boys), well they've probably lost their focus because they're very hungry. They will need to calm down and slow down, but you can't tell them that!

I don't understand what is still going wrong

It can be possible to be doing nothing incorrectly, yet breastfeeding is not successful due to undiagnosed maternal factors or infant anatomy affecting things. Below is a list of causes for breastfeeding problems other than incorrect latch-on:

• Insignificant last stage of breast tissue development maturing by the 12th

10 steps to help cure SNS (Sore Nipple Syndrome):

- Step 1: Check your breastfeeding technique with someone of unquestionable experience (midwife, hospital lactation consultant, La Leche League, or carefully chosen girlfriend who has successfully breastfed 2–3 children).
- Step 2: Make sure you've got the other basics correct too, e.g. only removing baby off your breasts by inserting your little finger into the corner of the mouth to release the suction first. Don't wash your breasts with soap (this removes your skin's natural oils). Don't rub nipples dry, just pat them. Don't think you need to wash your nipples between feeds either!
- Step 3: Have your LMC or doctor check in case there is another undiagnosed medical reason why your nipples are so sore. Such as: your nipples have a yeast infection [see page 186]; the cracked, scabby nipples are colonised with your own skin bacteria and need an antibiotic cream; your nipples have eczema; your nipple arteries are having Raynaud's spasms (after the baby finishes, nipples turn white, then blue, then red); or perhaps your baby is tongue-tied [see page 180] and is damaging your nipples.
- Step 4: Use breast shells — these are fantastic little inventions. They're hard plastic covers that fit over your sore nipples, so that nothing but air touches them between feeds. Sterilised breast shells can also collect leaking breastmilk, which can then be frozen for use later.
- Step 5: Before feeding take paracetamol, use a warm compress to assist the let-down reflex, rub your sore nipple with an ice-cube (to numb it somewhat), and offer your less painful nipple first. (If your baby swallows a little blood from your nipples it doesn't harm her.)
- Step 6: Allow your nipples to air-dry with your milk and baby's saliva still on them as both are anti-infective and act as natural healing agents —leave the flaps open on your maternity bra if possible.
- Step 7: Go topless — oh man what I sight, I know. But giving your nipples half an hour a day of indirect sunshine can do great things (it's true) — and just hope that the meter reader doesn't turn up at that particular moment.
- Step 8: Ensure you are taking a daily vitamin and mineral supplement designed for lactating mothers (deficient levels of zinc, vitamin C and vitamin E, for example, affect your skin's ability to heal).
- Step 9: Some experts recommend avoiding all ointments and oils, because the areola Montgomery glands secrete enough natural oils to

maintain nipple elasticity. Yet, there are a lot of potions and ointments in the marketplace for sore nipples. Some of the most popular remedies are vitamin A, pure lanolin, glycerine, sorbolene, vitamin E capsule liquid, aloe vera, olive oil, hypericum, calendula, and the combination of the last two, hypercal. I really can't strongly advocate one remedy over another, as every mother can swear by a different ointment. It is trial and error, but perhaps first try the remedies with 'natural' ingredients rather than hydrocortisone — and if you can visibly see the medication on your nipples, then you've applied too much (remember, it's also going in your baby's mouth). In the same way that dry cracked lips are made worse by constant wetting and drying, and need a very good quality moisturiser to help break that cycle; so too the nipples can need a top quality moisturiser treatment to allow healing and avoid infection.

- Step 10: Use nipple shields when feeding your baby (the latex silica covers that look like a Mexican sombrero hat). They work well for some mums' sore nipples, but others find they make things more difficult.

to 16th week of pregnancy — the breasts need to enlarge during pregnancy as an indicator that they can produce milk.

- Anatomy of the breast, e.g. previous breast reduction, breast enlargement, or trauma to the breast tissue.
- Configuration of the nipples (non-protractile inverted nipples can sometimes affect breastfeeding); overly firm breast tissue (e.g. engorgement); or small baby combined with big nipples.
- Caesar — there is an associated risk with C-section births of delayed milk production (and epidurals can also slightly delay milk production).
- Wet breast pads or synthetic bras.
- History of infertility and/or assisted conception — higher statistical risk of breastfeeding problems, because lactation involves hormones that may have contributed to the infertility problem in the first place.
- Retained placental fragments, or maternal uterine infection (puerperal sepsis) — both can delay the production of mature milk (see pages 249–50).
- Maternal illness (e.g. cold, flu); physical exhaustion and extreme tiredness; depression; and/or unsupportive partner.
- Maternal thyroid dysfunction (see page 251).
- A minor anatomical abnormality (e.g. Ankyloglossia, or tongue-tie, see page 180).
- Baby with a disinterested sleepy disposition — more likely to be male.
- Baby develops oral aversion (e.g. a baby who was born with meconium

aspiration and receives, vigorous, deep oral suction at birth or intubation now dislikes things put in its mouth).

- Baby with unusually shaped mouth or cleft pallet (malformed roof of the mouth), neurological or genetic problem (e.g. Downs), poor muscle tone, or extreme prematurity.
- Contraception hormones can interfere with a good milk supply if started before the supply is well established (see page 304).
- Maternal psychological factors such as a history of sexual abuse creating a 'dislike' or rejection of breastfeeding.

Ankyloglossia or short fraenulum (tongue-tie)

Under everyone's tongue is a fold of membrane called the fraenulum (or fraenum by dentists) that connects the tongue to the floor of the mouth. Almost 2–4+ percent of newborns are born with a short or tight fold of fraenulum membrane that extends further forward than normal, which can dramatically restrict the movement of the tongue. This is known as partial or full ankyloglossia, or 'tongue-tie'. (Try talking while keeping your tongue stuck flat behind your bottom teeth, and you'll understand.)

Ankyloglossia is more common in boys, and being tongue-tied can cause long-term problems with mastication (chewing), swallowing (chewed food), speech (lisp), orthodontics (dental) and mandibular (lower jaw) abnormalities, plus potential psychological issues (from being ridiculed and the like).

In a newborn, ankyloglossia can often interfere with breastfeeding success. Breastfeeding problems arise with one in five babies who are tongue-tied. The problem more dramatically affects first-time mums — because the hypothalamus of experienced mothers' brains has a more autonomic (involuntary) biological response to suckling.

The simple solution: Fraenotomy (fraenulectomy or tongue-tie division surgery)

This is a minor surgical procedure, where the infant is swaddled to keep it immobile, then the releasing of the membrane is done by a 'snipping' of the fraenulum using a pair of sterile iris (blunt-ended) scissors. It is a safe, simple and effective procedure. In infants, this is an almost bloodless procedure and no local anaesthesia is required. Often almost straight away the mother can feel improvements to the breastfeeding, with the suckle being stronger, smoother and significantly more comfortable.

Through all our high-tech medical advancements, somehow this old-school procedure (which used to be commonly performed by midwives at birth) is no longer standard practice. The concerning and frustrating aspect for parents is that there are only a minority of GPs who are confident to perform this 'instant fix' — though it should really be part of standard midwifery care. It may take determined parental persistence to find the right person willing to do this minor surgery.

Organisations such as UNICEF, with their 'baby friendly' initiatives, are trying to enlighten the medical community. For more information, pictures and descriptions, a great reference is the website by renowned dentist Brian Palmer at www.brianpalmerdds.com.

Other red flag signs that a baby may have ankyloglossia:
- Painful, ineffective, inefficient or prolonged feedings due to baby's difficulty to latch-on with a good seal for suckling.
- Baby's inability to sustain the latch (slipping and sliding off the breast).
- Mother's nipple trauma (flushed and inflamed with blisters, cracks, bleeding or infection), due to the baby 'gumming' at the breast: the lower jaw gum-pad compresses the breast, instead of it being separated and cushioned by the thickness of the tongue.
- The excruciating unrelenting nipple pain during feeding creating an inability for the mother's milk let-down reflex to occur proficiently.
- Baby unable to lift his tethered square-ish tongue (lack of elasticity, as too attached); or lifting tongue makes it change to a V-shape (instead of staying round or square).
- Baby unable to stick his tongue out over his lower gums and lips (decreased elasticity to its length).
- Baby's tongue unable to touch the roof of its mouth, when the mouth is open.
- Dissatisfied, irritated, frustrated baby; 'head-banging'; arching away or waving its arms during feeds.
- Baby suckling for a short time, getting fed up, fatigued, falling asleep, and waking an hour later hungry — baby seems to feed almost continuously.
- Baby gaining weight slowly, perhaps 'failing to thrive'.
- Baby unusually sleepy (poor feeding, so conserving energy).
- Mother having repetitive plugged ducts or mastitis breast infections due to incomplete breast drainage (baby not emptying the breast).

My nipples are still in excruciating pain

'I have tried all the recommendations, and I am still in real pain at every breastfeed. I'm about to give up on the whole damn idea!'

The purpose of our body being equipped with nerve endings in our cutaneous (skin) tissue, is for them to register pain, so that our body can tell our brain: 'Stop doing what the heck you are doing because it's harming me!' (That's why the umbilical cord doesn't feel pain: because it needs to be cut.)

So, when you have reached your own personal threshold of 'discomfort' (as some breastfeeding devotees prefer to conservatively describe it), my controversial advice is to listen to the pleading of your body and give your nipples some time off to heal.

Also, it is very difficult to relax an in-pain adrenaline-pumped body, to enable the oxytocin milk let-down to successfully occur — well, not when you are enduring the searing pain of someone sucking on a bleeding, cracked and blistered part of your more delicate anatomy — plus your baby can end up stressed and tense from its frustration at trying to feed on a breast which is not generously releasing its milk. And that creates a vicious cycle.

I am definitely NOT suggesting you give up breastfeeding! No, just express a few feeds and give baby 'bottled you' or 'spoon-fed you' for 1–3 days. I know, lots of experts will fervently disagree with me, but it's what your body is pleading for you to do. This system, of giving one's nipples a little vacation, has worked for me in the first week with all my (highly successfully) breastfed babes — and I believe was simply listening to my body.

If that is all it will take to get you over the worst hump, and prevent you mutinying by committing breastfeeding hara-kiri, *go, Girl*.

My theory is that many mothers who give up breastfeeding earlier than they had hoped, do so because of the pressure from inanely high expectations to grin and bear the pain. To me this can be very cruel and torturous 'Breastapo' propaganda. A little temporary understanding and flexible relief may be all that is needed to get those very sore nipples back on the road to recovery and full functioning.

The elusive perfect lactating diet

Oh heck, this is a bit of a mini-hot-potato subject, and so there are loads of books written on what a mother should (and should not) eat while breastfeeding, and this book won't bother to be another one. But, as a rather large generalisation:

- Great food for lactating mums are natural, organic foods free of herbicides, pesticides, colourings and additives, e.g. brown rice, oats, leafy greens, red vegetables, orange vegetables, avocados, nuts, seaweed, vegetable juices and garlic. (Avoid parsley and sage, which can inhibit lactation.)

- Great herbal supplements for lactation include blessed thistle, marshmallow, squaw vine and catnip. There are also herbal tea blends created especially for breastfeeding mums. Particularly good food lists are found in the Naish and Roberts book *The Natural Way to Better Breastfeeding*.

However, at the end of the day, so long as you are not malnourished or binge eating, your breastmilk will consistently be highly nutritious.

Increasing breastmilk production

Many women think they have too little milk for their baby — but genuine cases are really quite rare.

What is more frequent is milk under-supply caused by outside contributing factors. These include a lack of the one-to-one, calm, guiding assistance needed for correct latch-on, and stress making it impossible to relax the body long enough to turn off its fight-or-flight hormone response of epinephrine (adrenaline) and norepinephrine (noradrenaline) so that the milk let-down can occur.

However, for those women who are committed to persevering — but their breasts are struggling to produce adequate milk — apart from congratulating you on your dedication, there are a number of practical ideas that may assist.

Renowned British midwife, Sheila Kitzinger, recommends a 'Twenty-four-hour Peak Production Plan' of putting the baby to your breast every time he stirs over a 24-hour period, and at least every 2½ hours (waking him if necessary, but not at night). This seems to work particularly well in the first six weeks.

Red flags that your baby may not be getting enough to eat:

- Baby continues to lose weight after day five.
- Baby is below birth weight at two weeks of age.
- Baby is gaining less than 120 g per week after the first week, or less than 500 g per month.
- Baby has less than six pees a day (or less than five heavy-ish disposable nappies).
- Baby has pee that is yellow and strong smelling.
- Baby has infrequent dry, hard, green poo.
- Baby has a worried-looking face.
- Baby is not alert, active and reasonably content for some periods each day.
- Baby is unusually lethargic and sleepy.
- Baby has a weak cry.
- Baby is obviously unhappy and dissatisfied after breastfeeding and is restless and fussy.

These can mean that breastfeeding needs professional attention and that, for the time being, the baby probably needs 10 unrushed breastfeeds every 24 hours, including through the night.

But probably the best recommendation to increase milk production, as explained by the American midwife Ina May Gaskin in her book *Spiritual Midwifery*, is realising that you need to slow your pace of life, increase the number of feeding sessions, eat well, drink vast amounts of water daily, and get plenty of sleep.

There are also health shop remedies that many women swear by for effectively improving milk production (and the baby's satisfaction level with the milk) such as raspberry leaf, blessed thistle, marshmallow, borage and various homeopathic remedies. Plus alfalfa (sprouts or tea) is known to be beneficial to increasing milk flow production, as is the Ayurvedic herb shatavari (see page 143). By the way, drinking milk does not increase milk production (remember, dairy cows don't drink milk).

If simple measures don't seem to be working, you could consult your LMC, lactation consultant, La Leche League or doctor, as the prescribed medication domperidone may also be effective to increase milk supply.

Interestingly, with commitment it is possible for a woman who has completely stopped breastfeeding to re-lactate — that is, to stimulate her breasts over several weeks to produce milk again. Even adoptive mothers, not just ones who have previously breastfed, may be able to produce some breastmilk with medication and support from an experienced lactation consultant.

Red flags that your breasts may be overproducing milk:

- Your baby gets very uncomfortable, cries incessantly, is windy and has frequent green poo (maybe with mucous).
- When you breastfeed on one side, the other boob leaks a lot of milk (beyond the first few weeks).
- When your baby pulls off your nipple, your milk squirts some distance.
- During feeding you hear a 'milk hitting the bottom' tummy sound.
- The baby can swallow a lot of air as well as milk with the fast rush of milk, which makes the baby think it's full.
- The baby can be in pain because feeding is stimulating pooing.
- The baby can 'head-bang' during feeds, arching its back, and pulling off the breast to protect its airway, dragging the nipple with it, then may refuse to feed.

Reducing breastmilk production

Some women's breasts over-produce milk, creating a let-down volume that is too great for their baby's needs and capabilities – hence the saying, 'I had milk for Africa!' This phenomena commonly occurs at between three and six weeks, but some women's breasts can remain over-producing for longer (more so after giving birth to second and subsequent babies).

From the baby's perspective it can be like trying to drink gushing water from a garden hose. Women who over-produce do not necessarily have babies that suffer discomfort; some can cope with high-volume feeds without apparent distress. But often the situation can be misinterpreted as the baby having reflux, or the mother's breasts not producing enough milk.

One particularly sensible idea is to sit on a backwards incline when feeding, to use gravity's help to slow the fast flow. Other ideas are to drink a little sage or jasmine tea; eat some parsley (e.g. tabbouleh); and perhaps the low-dose contraceptive mini-pill could help (due to the progesterone). In some cases a low-dose oestrogen-containing pill for a few days can also reduce the oversupply problem.

Afterpains

During a woman's entire life she feels her uterus contract: during her period cycle they're called menstrual cramps; during her pregnancy they're called Braxton Hicks; during labour they're official contractions; and when it's during breastfeeding they're called afterpains (or subinvolution). So as you can guess, afterpains during the early days of breastfeeding, feel like contractions or period pains.

The oxytocin your body receives to trigger the milk let-down also causes the uterus to contract, helping it to shrink back efficiently, which is Mother Nature's beneficial way of helping your uterus to return to its pre-pregnancy size (of a fist), and subsequently reduce your lochia discharge.

Afterpains can be much stronger (even quite severe) with second and subsequent babies, because the uterus has to work harder to involute itself down to its unpregnant size. Paracetamol and heat packs (e.g. hot-water bottle) can be useful because, heck, they can hurt. Herbal teas of motherwort, false unicorn and shepherd's purse can also help.

Be wary of any bright-red bleeding restarting (after lochia bleeding has settled), with crampy abdominal pain; this could mean infection or retained placental fragments (see page 249).

Oxytocin overload

Are you beginning to ask yourself 'Why am I falling asleep almost every time I'm breastfeeding?' Or alternatively, 'I am finding breastfeeding sexually stimulating — am I some weird sicko?'

Oh sweetie, you're just having a little 'oxytocin overdose' — your body is releasing lots of this love hormone. Sometimes it relaxes you so much you wake up to find your little babe is still suckling away — and other times you can feel quite orgasmic (literally).

Think of this as a well-deserved bonus direct from Mother Nature herself. Lucky you!

Hives and headaches

If you experience a body-rash like hives from breastfeeding, you could be having a very rare allergic reaction to the extra oxytocin in your body and may need antihistamines. Seek professional advice.

If you are getting headaches during or straight after breastfeeding, this could be something to do with your pituitary gland's release of the hormones oxytocin and prolactin, or is more likely to be neck-tension from poor breastfeeding positioning. Again, seek professional advice.

Yeast infection: mother and baby thrush

Nicknamed thrush, Candida albicans (previously called monilia) is caused by a dimorphic organism — meaning that it can exist in two distinctly different forms — changing from a non-invasive yeast-like form, into an invasive tangled fungal mass of feeding and growing threads with root-like extensions. That is why thrush is also known as a yeast infection.

Before having a baby most women would have experienced, at some stage, the drive-you-insane itchiness of vaginal thrush — but with motherhood can come a whole new version.

For the mother, this common fungal infection can cause the breast nipple and areola to become inflamed, red, shiny, painful and cracked, with perhaps itching or a searing, burning, 'glass inside the breast' sensation during and after feeds. Chances are your baby will also get thrush (or maybe the baby gave it to you). For the baby, **oral thrush** looks like white patches of milk curd on the tongue or on the inside of the cheeks, which cannot be wiped or rubbed off (sometimes a baby's whole tongue goes white) and the baby may develop a nappy rash of red spots, a fever, or diarrhoea.

In either case, it is important to seek treatment, to avoid the localised candida becoming systemic (affecting the whole body internally).

A pharmaceutical remedy for the baby and nipples can be to use antifungal medication (such as Daktarin™ oral gel or topical Nystatin™ liquid), or antibiotics. Unfortunately, antibiotics also kill off the beneficial bacteria that normally suppress candida, so that can cause a win-then-lose scenario.

Old-fashioned treatments are painting baby's mouth with a well-diluted mixture of the natural fungicide gentian violet a couple of times a day (though some now claim it is carcinogenic); washing your nipples with vinegar (and rinsing them) before and after feeds; and after feeding giving your babe some sterile water with a couple of drops of vinegar in it. (Because vinegar is acidic, thrush can't grow.) Recolonisation of the mother's own beneficial lactobacilli bacteria is also a very sensible idea too, through eating acidophilus and bifidus yoghurt. Another worthwhile move is to eliminate all sugars and refined carbohydrates from your diet while you're both recovering from thrush — this starves the fungus.

There are also homeopathic treatments that mother and baby can take including Baptisia and Naturopharm's Thrushmed™.

Blocked duct

A blocked (or plugged or clogged) duct is caused by milk congealing in a milk-secreting duct, and shows itself as a pinkish-red flushed-looking patch on your breast with a tender concrete-like lump; or an area that is particularly painful during the milk let-down; or a white spot on the nipple with milk under the skin. It commonly occurs from engorgement, a too-tight bra, blocked nipple opening, breasts that are not being fully emptied at feeds, or a duct that has become kinked. (Don't forget to periodically lift your boobies up in front of a mirror to check underneath for red patches.)

To avoid a blocked duct progressing on to become a breast infection, it is imperative you slow your life down (to give your body time to heal); and that the breast gets sucked completely dry as soon as possible, using a breast pump if necessary; and continue to favour that side with lengthy frequent feeding until the red patch disappears.

During feeding it is also a good idea to rub around the lump, stroking towards the nipple, as if trying to knead it out. Giving your breasts a rest from feeding is the worst thing to do. Do also contact your LMC or doctor. A number of people swear by the homeopathic treatment phytollaca.

Mastitis breast infection

Usually originating from a blocked duct (because warm milk standing in your breasts too long is an ideal culture for bacteria), or from infection entering through a cracked nipple, mastitis is an inflammation of the mammary gland tissue that makes you feel like you're getting the flu (fever, chills, body-aches, headaches, shakes, unusual tiredness, nausea or vomiting); plus the breast area can become red, swollen, hot, painful, with a burning throbbing feeling, and/or there can be streaks of reddened lines across the breast.

Mastitis is particularly common 10–28 days after childbirth in about one in 10 mothers (usually first-timers). To avoid mastitis progressing to a breast abcess, it requires the immediate medical attention of prescribed antibiotics (contact your LMC or doctor), and perhaps anti-inflammatory or analgesic pain-relieving medication; bed-rest for at least 24 hours (or maybe a few days); perhaps soothing hot/cold compresses on the breast; increased fluids (to help flush the toxins); and a nutritious diet to assist the stressed and depressed immune system.

You definitely don't stop breastfeeding because the breast needs to be regularly emptied to help heal the infection — every 2–2½ hours is ideal. By the way, mastitis does not get passed on to your baby and it does not affect the milk, just the breast tissue.

As with all infections, it is always a good idea to boost your immune system at the same time with the likes of vitamin C. (Mastitis is a common problem with dairy cows too. Oh delightful, now we really do have udders!)

Note:

A simple blocked duct can, within hours, turn into mastitis, which within a day can become a breast abscess. Don't procrastinate about getting your breasts checked if you think you could possibly have one of the above problems. *A breast abscess is no joke!*

Breast abscess

This is the nightmare stage that develops after untreated mastitis — a pocket of pus develops inside the breast tissue that causes severe throbbing pain. It usually requires a surgical incision to lance and drain the abscess. This is a foul thing to have to go through, and avoidable.

With the appropriate surgeon doing the appropriate procedure, you do not have to stop breastfeeding.

Advice overload and conflicting opinions: too many 'experts'!

Bub's finally got the hang of it now . . .

Once your milk supply is 'in', your baby is latching well and everything is going swimmingly, then you can within just days expect the 2–3-hourly feeds to stretch out to 3–4-hourly feeds — which are more efficient and far less taxing on a breastfeeding mother (so about 6–8 feeds a day).

Once your baby is around 5.5 kg (12 lbs) you may find that your little baby, who now has a much larger stomach, may completely empty one breast and want more — and that's great, that's what the other side is for.

Also, once a baby has the hang of breastfeeding, often their sucking can become a ferocious, frenzied, spluttering bluster at the beginning of each feed, gulping down the thirst-quenching fore-milk; which then changes to longer harder sucks as Bub enjoys the higher-protein, thicker hind-milk.

Breastfeeding needs and deserves your full attention and concentration. It is an important time for developmental interaction because, as the baby grows, there can be increasing amounts of communication. To paraphrase from Naish and Roberts' *The Natural Way To Better Breastfeeding*, do give your baby time to nurse: breastfeeding will increasingly be marked by pauses and non-verbal interactions that distract from suckling — the baby plays with your clothes, strokes your skin, plays with your other nipple, looks around and gazes at you. But take the time to foster these delightful moments — they are the beginnings of social interactions. So, when it's possible, try to choose a private and quiet place to breastfeed.

La Leche League International

In America in the 1950s, breastfeeding rates had dropped close to 20 percent, and out of great concern and seeking comradeship, the La Leche League was formed at a church picnic. ('La Leche' is Spanish for 'the milk' — it would have been socially unacceptable at that time to use the words breast or breastfeeding.) In 1964 they changed their name to La Leche League International, as they were starting to open branches overseas, including New Zealand.

Probably the most famous book produced by LLLI is *The Womanly Art of Breastfeeding*. LLLI's mission statement is:

To help mothers worldwide to breastfeed through mother-to-mother support, encouragement, information and education; and to promote a better understanding of breastfeeding as an important element in the healthy development of the baby and mother.

Joining the pro-breastfeeding environment of La Leche League meetings may not be for everyone, but some mums really enjoy it. However, for *any* mother needing breastfeeding assistance, LLLI has very good resources, including: peer counselling (mothers trained to provide in-person and telephone breastfeeding information and support within their local community); newsletters; and a website www.lalecheleague.org/LLLNZ/

So what the heck is 'normal' anyhow?

- Expect babies under two months old to feed for about 30–40 minutes. As they get older and stronger, they get more efficient. So an average 2–3 month-old feeds for about 20–30 minutes, and a 3–6 month-old for about 15–20 minutes. However, that can vary significantly from one baby to the next.

- Once babies have got the hang of breastfeeding and have grown a little older, they can often empty a breast in 15 minutes or less, so a complete feed could take as little as 10–30 minutes. It is not that uncommon for babies who are a few months old to be able to 'suck Mum dry' within 5–10 minutes a side.

- Plan to teach your baby to mellow out for feed-times. Babies can have trouble feeding well if they are wound up, due to their shallow breathing and tensed tummy — they also swallow more air, which usually results in a bellyache. So try not to teach your baby that the solution to her cries is for you to ram your nipple into her screaming mouth — aim for feeds to be soothing. (Plus if your baby's cries upset you, then that can hinder your milk let-down, which makes her scream even more.) Breastfeeding in an old-fashioned rocking chair with a footstool can be very therapeutic for both mother and baby.

- Because breastmilk is body temperature, you don't always know you're leaking until you look down at your top in the middle of the supermarket to see a humiliating wet patch on your blouse. If you can feel the milk let-down occurring before you want it to, one trick is to push your breast upwards on the nipple with your fist.

- Some experts say that about 80 percent of the baby's feed is consumed in their first 5–10 minutes of suckling — other experts say up to 90 percent is consumed in just the first five minutes. All babies (and all breasts for that matter) are different!

- By three-months old (to due date) you can expect your baby to be averaging just 5–6 feeds a day — but never less than four.

- Constipation in breastfed babies is rare, as mothers' milk is Mother Nature's perfection. But if it does happen, increasing the amount of fruit mum eats can assist.

- During the first few weeks, some babies develop little pads that look like blisters on the lips, from sucking. These are nothing to worry about and will disappear of their own accord.

- For the first three months, a newborn increases weight by an average of less than an ounce a day or around 100–200 g (4–8 oz) per week — but this varies a lot, so don't be concerned if your health professional isn't. Some mothers have petite babies (like me and lots of my friends) and some mothers have big babies (like lots of my friends). A typical baby doubles its birth-weight by around four months, and triples it by about 12 months. Relative to their body weight, babies consume 2–3 times the calories a day of an obese person!

- Lactating mothers require around an extra 2700 kj (400 calories) a day to produce a litre of breastmilk. If the mother is not eating red meat, she is also advised to take a supplement to provide good levels of vitamin B12, calcium, iron and vitamin D. An acceptable maximum dieting weight-loss for a lactating mother per week is 500 g (half a kilo). If you are concerned, Weight Watchers and some other diet regimes have specialised lactation programs. Or just accept your motherly figure with loving respect for the time being.

- Before you go to bed at night, it can be a nice idea to have a thermos of hot drink ready to sip on while you're feeding your babe during the wee hours of the night.

- If your one-month-old is breastfeeding for an hour or more each time, then after the first 45 minutes, Bub is probably no longer swallowing, but sucking to pacify herself (with breastfeeding if you pay close attention, you can *feel* the difference; you won't feel the same pulling sucks). One suggestion is to detach Bub from the breast, and perhaps provide a pacifier for her to unwind (see page 193).

- Breastfed babies tend to be leaner than formula-fed babies, especially in the second half of the first year (partially because breastmilk causes less water retention in babies). Don't be concerned if your friend's formula-fed or solids-fed baby is looking more bonny (larger) — that's quite normal.

- Babies can't poo and suck at the same time, so if your baby stops sucking while he's feeding, and begins to grunt, he's probably filling his nappy.

- Without warning a normally great-feeding 2–5 month old may start to refuse the breast by screaming and/or pulling off your boobs. This might be caused by a change in your milk flavour due to menstruation, ovulation, contraception or pregnancy(!); or it could be baby's impatience to wait for the milk let-down; or it could just be your baby growing up and becoming more aware of distractions making them nosy and curious. If you can persevere through these stages, things usually come right again.

- It's a good idea to wait an hour after exercising before breastfeeding, as the lactic acid your body produces during exercise can give baby a tummy ache.

- Sometimes your wee bub will sleep right through a feed. If it's during the day, it could be wise to wake them up to avoid your baby getting its daytime and night-time mixed up. If Bub sleeps through a feed at night, wonderful, just express off a little if you need to ease that bursting boob sensation, but otherwise just realise your baby is growing up.

- Breastmilk is a non-static, living, dynamic fluid that takes on the flavours of the mother's diet (unlike formula that always tastes the same). Some research has shown that children who have been breastfed will more easily accept a wider variety of food tastes (subject to their personality as well). So, the longer you breastfeed, then in theory the more accepting your toddler will be to varying flavours (particularly, say, if you have a preference for strongly flavoured ethnic foods).

- It is very common at around nine months for babies to lose interest in breastfeeding by becoming more thirst-quenching snack-breastfeeders (as solid food becomes more prevalent). In fact, all three of our babies self-weaned at around 9–10 months of age (oh, poor rejected me). Babies at this age can also be more sociable when feeding, such as stopping feeding to look around with a big smile on their dial, while your embarrassed and shy nipple is flashed for the world to admire. This is the stage when you may need to feed in quiet distraction-free environments, to maintain some level of productive suckling and wishful modesty.

- Breastfeeding can help an infant's response to vaccines by assisting to avoid negative reactions through the boosting of the baby's immune system.

- If you are prescribed antibiotics, it may pay to give yourself and your baby some acidophilus-bifidus yoghurt to avoid digestion upsets from the antibiotics destroying their friendly gut lactobacilli flora.

Growth spurts

Babies commonly get hungrier for a few days (preparing for growth spurts) around 6–10 days, 3–4 weeks, 6–7 weeks, 12–13 weeks and six months, when they can almost double the length of their breastfeeds to 'teach' your breasts to increase their milk production.

On-demand feeding versus scheduled feeding

Phew-ee . . . this subject is a really smelly can-of-worms. One of those 'You're damned if you do and you're damned if you don't' topics.

On-demand feeding works on the premise that babies should receive food whenever they desire it, and that they are too little to be regulated by a clock. So, whenever they signal they are hungry, they should receive food. This is a baby-led methodology to feeding — things are on the baby's terms — because only the baby knows when they're hungry. A good reference book for this can be Naish and Roberts' *The Natural Way To Better Breastfeeding*.

The 'anti' demand-feeding experts feel that because it is too easy to misinterpret many of the baby's other cries as hunger, this is encouraging the baby to snack-feed 10–12 times a day. This could result in the baby failing to thrive and enjoy good long sleeps, because it hasn't filled its tummy with the thicker hind milk. So life for the mother and household can become chaotically unpredictable, with the parents feeling as if they have 'no life'.

Scheduled feeding has a reputation of employing a regimented inflexible routine of clock-watching to predetermine the time of each feed. This system was made famous in the 1990s with Gary Ezzo's *BabyWise* book, in which he encourages the 'PDF' system (Parent-Directed Feeding). This did, and still does, generate controversy (much of which hugely exaggerates Ezzo's quite 'flexible' feeding ideas). However, hospital nurseries used scheduled feeding techniques on babies a long time before Gary Ezzo wrote his book. Many feel that an infant fed regularly like this, due to their subsequently stable digestive metabolism, will demand more milk . . . so is better able to thrive.

But of course the 'anti' schedule-feeding experts can produce statistics to show that fed-on-demand babies gain more weight than those fed at timed intervals.

And vice-versa.

This decision will be a very personal part of your own parenting methodology. Perhaps no one philosophy is 100 percent wrong, just as it is probably not 100 percent right! But there does exist a middle-ground in this debate too . . . one of feeding your baby when it demands it, while still encouraging the baby to drink a full-feed.

Many say, and I do agree, that it is imperative for establishing good *sleeping* habits, that a baby learns how to feed to *fill* their tummies. That is how a baby receives the important fattier hind-milk — instead of just the thirst-quenching watery fore-milk. Many experts also agree that regularly feeding a baby less than two hourly, is not teaching them to feed — its teaching them to snack.

If you do return your baby to the breast within two hours of the commencement of the last feed, it can be a good idea to put Bub back onto the same breast first, to ensure he finishes receiving all of the fatty hind-milk, which will satisfy him more.

Pacifiers and thumb sucking

All humans enjoy spending time relaxing and unwinding. Maybe for you it's a cup of tea and the morning paper; or a sauna and shower after an aerobics class; or a coffee and magazine in the afternoon sun. Maybe it's a wine and cigarette on the deck after dinner; or a good book and a hot chocolate in bed. And for babies, in their extremely limited capacity, their comfort activity is *sucking*.

Mother Nature provides human babies with a powerful self-soothing, self-calming reflex (sucking), and babies can be seen on ultrasound sucking their thumb or hand in utero. Sucking stimulates the relaxing hormone oxytocin in their little bodies, which sets off reflexes that slow their heartbeats and improve their digestion.

So whether you like the idea or not, sucking is just what babies do, especially in the first 3–4 months. Babies can even suck their mouth in their sleep! You see, sucking is not just for filling their tummy, it's also for relaxing and comforting them.

If your baby did not discover its thumb in utero, then, like mums have done for thousands of years, you could perhaps teach your baby to find its thumb (or fingers); or you may want to help your baby by giving it something to suck on — and in this modern world it's called a pacifier (or a dummy).

'Dummy' is an awful word, but it's one that's stuck. Calling it a pacifier is more applicable, because that is what it is — though I love author Mara Lee's name for it: the 'Bubba-Plugger'.

Some mothers prefer not to offer a pacifier, which can sometimes result in their own nipples becoming a human pacifier. In fact, many experts for numerous reasons believe pacifiers are diabolical. And many other experts for numerous reasons believe pacifiers perform an important and very natural role, and that the anti-dummy opinions are simply extremist twaddle. Perhaps a particularly worthy piece of advice is not to start using a pacifier until the baby is doing well with its breastfeeding suckling.

But as a large generalisation, I have found that most mothers are not anti-pacifiers as such — but are more anti the images of a three-year-old still sucking on a dummy, or a five-year-old who still sucks their thumb.

Another large generalisation is that if you have a baby who enjoys sucking his little thumb, then it is possible to teach a toddler that this pleasure is for bedtime only (we managed it, and so have lots of other parents). Then again, some parents have tried really hard, and found it an impossible habit to break.

At the end of the day, whether you decide to use a pacifier or not, you will be influenced by a range of factors — with perhaps the most dominant factor being the frequency of the eardrum-shattering, mind-bending crescendo shrills of infant crying you are exposed to.

So if you don't end up using a pacifier on this baby, don't be too judgemental of others, as you may change your mind with a second baby.

Alcohol and medications while breastfeeding

Some experts preach that breastfeeding mothers should have no alcohol at all. But after no alcohol during the pregnancy, requesting no alcohol during lactation can be equivalent to asking a mother to abstain from all alcohol for up to three years per child — and some of us, who are just too sinfully human, can't do that! Peronally, when it came to Saturday nights, my gauge used to be, 'If I'm sober enough to legally drive, then I'm sober enough to breastfeed'.

An interesting point for you to note is that breastmilk contains the same alcohol content as your bloodstream. As Anne Enight writes in her book *Making Babies*, '[Alcohol] is reabsorbed into your bloodstream as you sober up. Two hours after a glass of wine, you might as well have been drinking water . . . If your baby sleeps for twelve hours, then you can drink your head off for the first three of them and, when morning comes, you might feel poisoned, but you will not be poisonous.' However, Anne also reminds us that 'the children of women who drink daily show no difference in cognitive development at one year, but they do show a small but significant delay in motor development'.

With regard to general pharmaceutical medicines, many medications will state that they are not recommended for consumption by a pregnant or breastfeeding mother, which seems a reasonable precaution. *However*, with pregnancy and motherhood, that virtuous policy of being unable to consume any pharmaceutical medicine whatsoever for two to three years per child — almost no relief for all coughs, colds, flus, hayfever, headaches, migraines, backache, etc. — may start to wear a little thin, especially when you're enduring your fourth cold in three months, and all you want to do is stop those aching chills so you can get some housework done, get rid of the throbbing headache so you can think straight, and unblock your snotty nose so you can have a solid sleep!

The primary reason so many physicians advocate avoiding medications during lactation is not because they are likely to be harmful to your baby, but because full clinical testing has not been undertaken — it is not always ethical to test medication on breastfed infants. However, by using a knowledge of lactation pharmacology the risk level of the theoretical maximum dose a baby may receive can be assessed. This will determine the possible effect on a breastfed infant from a drug taken by the baby's mother.

Many exceptions exist but, as a general rule, it is far less than one percent of the maternal dose of a drug that will ultimately find its way into breastmilk. The mechanics of drugs entering breastmilk is mainly by passive diffusion (i.e. molecules crossing from the mother's blood capillary walls through the alveolar cell linings) into the milk buds. During the first 10 days after childbirth, large gaps exist between the breast cells positively enhancing access for immuno-globulins and lymphocytes to enter the milk, but this also means it is easier for medications to enter the breastmilk. After that time, the cells swell and the intracellular gaps lessen — so for the first two weeks, more medications are able to enter the milk.

On the cutting edge of this complex subject, and creator of disputably the most complete reference on drugs during breastfeeding, is Dr Thomas Hale's lactational pharmacology manual titled *Medications and Mothers' Milk*. The big no-no drugs in conjunction with breastfeeding are chemotherapy or radioactive treatments, but with regards to general pharmaceutical medications, to quote Dr Hale: 'Most medications have few side effects to breastfeeding infants because the dose transfer via milk is almost always too low to be clinically relevant, or it is poorly absorbed by the infant.' With very few exceptions, breastmilk with a tiny amount of medication is safer for a baby than formula — with almost all medications, breastfeeding can continue.

So, rather than taking the less desirable option of the 'pump and dump' system (expressing to throw away your breastmilk, and replacing it with formula) or, even worse, giving up breastfeeding altogether, become better informed about what medications are safe to consume. Some are safer than others.

The general golden rules on taking medications during lactation are primarily:

- Choose short-acting medications (i.e. medications that need to be taken several times a day rather than once daily or 12-hourly doses).
- Consume medication immediately before or after a breastfeed, to enable their peak to occur between breastfeeds.
- Avoid all drugs that affect brain function (e.g. sedatives).
- Take no recreational or illegal drugs, as they can stay in the infant's system for weeks, wreaking havoc.
- Try to avoid non-prescribed medications in the first two weeks of breastfeeding.

See appendix E, page 470 for a list of medications.

Disclaimer: This book is NOT confirming that use of any medication is 100 percent safe. It is ultimately the reader's responsibility. The author can accept no liable responsibility.

Bottle time?

Fifty years ago mothers were not snubbed for bottlefeeding their babies, but today there is a tremendously unsupportive environment for women (and babies for that matter), who choose (or have no choice but) to bottlefeed.

So I respect Mara Lee's advice in *Baby's First Year for Dummies*: 'If, at whatever time or for whatever reason, you decide breastfeeding isn't for you, stand by your choice and banish any guilty feelings that swing your way. Breastfeeding doesn't automatically make you a better mother — looking after you and your baby's best interests does.'

Guidebooks on infant bottlefeeding are a rare find in any library. However, one is *Bottle Babies: A New Zealand Guide to Guilt-free Bottle Feeding* by Adelia Ferguson.

Nipple confusion: fiction or fact?

Oh, fact or fiction surrounding 'nipple confusion' is another hornet's nest of fiercely opposing opinions . . .

I believe giving this condition the name of nipple 'confusion' is actually rather confusing in itself, because it tends to imply that the baby develops confusion between the bottle and breast. What it more accurately means is that a baby develops a *preference* for bottle over breast (or vice-versa). So, it could be more applicable to re-name the issue nipple preference or nipple refusal, rather than nipple confusion.

In breastfeeding the baby places its tongue beneath the nipple, and when she stops her pumping-sucks, the milk stops flowing. Whereas, in bottle-feeding the baby places the tongue in front of the nipple, and controls the milk flow by placing her tongue over the hole.

Many 'experts' fervently believe that it is unrealistic to expect a baby to be able to switch back and forth between the two systems, and that pacifiers add to their 'confusion'. There is also no doubt that infants can sometimes develop a strong preference to the breast or the bottle; or to one breast in particular; or to one specific kind of bottle teat.

So the real question is **'Can you teach a baby to happily accept both breast and bottle?'**

To this question, I can say an emphatic 'Yes', because I have accomplished it with all of our children, and know lots of other mothers who have too. So, yes, it is definitely feasible. Now I am *not* advocating that doing so is the best thing to do, nor guaranteeing that it will work successfully with your baby.

I strongly advise getting the breastfeeding technique established first, before introducing the bottle. (For example, in neonatal intensive care units, they will often tube-feed a baby in preference to bottle-feeding, if the baby still isn't yet successfully breastfeeding.)

Steps to teach a baby to accept both breast and bottle

So you desire to do this, or have to do this due to outside commitments? Can you and your baby manage it? I don't know.

At the end of the day it will be your very individual situation that will determine whether you solely breastfeed or solely bottle-feed or strive to use a combination of both. What I can do is explain to you the systems, theories and steps I can recommend.

- Once breastfeeding is successfully established, introduce the bottle, preferably within the second week after birth (don't wait the six weeks some 'experts' advocate). 'Baby Whisperer' Tracy Hogg also believes, like me, that after three weeks of age, trying to switch a baby between breast and bottle can become increasingly difficult (though certainly not impossible) — and that the window of opportunity has usually diminished beyond six weeks of age.
- Initially, replace the baby's hungriest feed (usually first thing in the morning) with expressed milk, say 2–3 times a week — no more at the beginning or the baby could begin to prefer the bottle which is less work for him.
- Constantly vary the type of bottle and teat used (say, have three quite different kinds) to ensure the baby stays flexible and adaptable.
- In the third to fourth week, begin to rotate what time of day the occasional breastfeed is replaced by the bottle, a few times a week.
- After six months, if you choose to, start to introduce formula instead of expressed breastmilk. Again, start with Bub's hungriest first feed in the morning and breastmilk diluted with formula to ease Bub into the taste.

That's it! A very simple method.

Mother Nature looks after her precious newborn babies, and equips them with a primal survival instinct for attempting to suckle on almost anything put in their mouth . . . your finger, your breast, a silicone pacifier, a rubber teat — anything that vaguely resembles a nipple, natural or man-made.

Introduced properly, babies can have an incredible ability to adapt to alternating food sources — they can be as flexible as you teach them to be.

Consistency with bottle-use

Question: My baby was taking both breast and bottle, but I slackened with the bottle and didn't give her one for three weeks — and now she's turning

The advantages of a flexible feeder:

- Sore, blistered and bleeding nipples can have a rest to recover from ferocious sucking.
- Mother can continue to feed her baby breastmilk regardless of the situations.
- Mother can have greater personal freedom, and is not always the critical factor as to whether baby is hungry or not.
- Other people, e.g. baby's father, also have the opportunity to enjoy feeding the baby.
- It is possible to 'cluster feed', topping the baby up full to the brim before going down for the overnight sleep — even though the breasts can be at their lightest at that time of the day.
- Dad can give the 10 pm feed, so that Mum can go to bed at 9 pm and still get eight hours' sleep including a 3 am breastfeed.
- Parents can enjoy going out to social events or attend to business meetings, with lessened babysitting worries.
- Parental life, in general, becomes more flexible.
- Weaning the baby off breastfeeding can be more seamless.
- In a genuine emergency, when mother cannot be there for her baby, the baby can still be fed.

The disadvantages and risks:

- You risk the possibility of creating teat preference in the baby, because milk from a bottle flows faster than a breast. (Some experts advocate using a training cup instead of a bottle, but that is not practical with young babies, and spoon feeding is very tedious.)
- Your baby may receive formula earlier than if it had been fully breastfed.

her nose up at it. *What do I do?*

Believe it or not I made the same mistake myself with all three of our children — always because breastfeeding was just so jolly convenient. (You would think I would have learnt the first time — and at least after the second time!)

With my first baby, I contacted our local Plunket Family Centre in a panic. They gave some very solid advice: I needed to realise that my baby was perfectly capable of drinking from a bottle — she was just choosing not to. It was really a battle of wills.

So at her next morning feed (being the hungriest one) I offered her the bottle, which she refused. But I kept offering it as the only option and, within two hours, she gobbled it down happily.

When I was slack about keeping up the occasional bottle-feed with our other children, I had to go through that same process. Our second child held out for six hours, and our third baby objected for three hours.

Expressing and freezing breastmilk

It can be a useful skill to familiarise yourself with how to hand-express your own breastmilk — especially to trigger the let-down reflex. It is best learnt in person, so ask your LMC, Plunket nurse or La Leche League to demonstrate.

There are a large selection of breast-pumps available, from a basic manual (hand-operated) model to quite high-tech manual models; to battery-powered pumps; to efficient electric pumps; to hospital-style double-boob machines. It can also be possible to hire breast-pumps from local baby stores or chemists — or buy expensive models second-hand.

Does it feel weird having your breasts pumped? For sure! But 99 percent of the weirdness is in the head, not the titty. The titty is just doing what comes naturally.

If your breasts are over-producing milk, then you will probably be freezing plenty of leftovers. But what if your breasts seem to supply just the exact amount so there are no leftovers, and you want to start to accumulate frozen breastmilk?

Well, you need to think outside the square. For example, use a breast-pump for an extra 5–10 minutes a side after each breastfeed to really suck them dry; or add in an extra, pumped breastfeed once a day to increase your milk production. Whatever you do, just realise that you are training your breasts to produce extra milk, and this can take a few days to accomplish.

Expressed milk should be refrigerated or frozen straight away. Expressed milk can be at the back of a cold fridge for about two days — but it will need shaking, as it separates into layers.

Breastmilk can be frozen for up to 3–4 months. Thaw frozen milk by placing the sealed container in a bowl of warm water for half an hour, or slowly thaw in the fridge. Thawed milk can be stored in the fridge for only a day. Never re-freeze milk, and always discard any leftover, reheated milk.

To freeze expressed milk in an ice-cube tray, you could put the tray through a cycle in the bottle-steriliser. Or if the ice-cube tray won't fit, another idea is to dribble 2–3 teaspoons of water over the tray and put it inside a brand new plastic freezer bag (rolls of freezer bags come already sterile); then with the bag open, put them both in the microwave and nuke the tray to steam it sterile. After expressing, fill the tray with the breastmilk, freeze it inside the same plastic bag, and once frozen empty the cubes into the plastic bag, remove the ice-cube tray, and write the date on the freezer bag. (You can also buy disposable, sterile plastic bottle-liners to express into and freeze instead of using ice-cube trays.)

Bottle-feeding hints

- There are different hole sizes at the top of bottle teats: newborn (0–3 months), medium flow (3–6 months) and fast flow (6–18 months).
- If you can't decide which brand or shape of bottle nipple to buy, pick the teat that most closely resembles your own nipples, perhaps the long latex version rather than silicone — there are also 'breast-bottles' designed to simulate breastfeeding with a bosom-like shape. But don't buy all the same style of bottles and teats — have a bit of variety to ensure that your baby stays flexible as it gets older to accept different bottles.
- Sterilising baby bottles (and breast-pump equipment) properly is really important to help ensure young babies avoid gastrointestinal infection, which can be serious. The question of what kind of sterilising equipment to opt for can be confusing as there's a lot of variety.
- How many months is it necessary to sterilise your baby's bottles for? I'd suggest until Bub starts putting everything in her mouth to teethe on. After that, a good rinse with a bottle brush and full dishwasher cycle is adequate.
- Bottle bags are cute thermal containers available for storing warmed milk bottles when you're going out. There are also electric bottle warmers available, including some that operate using a car cigarette-lighter.
- To test that milk is heated correctly, just splash a few drops onto your sensitive wrist skin, and it should feel neither warm nor cold. Then unscrew the baby bottle cap very slightly (to allow air to flow).
- Hold the bottle at an angle for baby so that the teat is always full of milk (which helps stop your baby swallowing air with the feed).
- As a big generalisation, baby girls can be happy to attempt to start to hold their own bottle, with your help, from as young as four months old, whereas baby boys tend to prefer you to hold it for longer. Interesting!

Milk and microwaves

In almost every baby-care book, it is advocated to stand the bottle in warm water to heat it and to *never ever* use a microwave to heat babies' milk bottles, because they heat the liquid unevenly (creating hot spots) potentially scalding your baby's mouth and oesophagus; because microwaves change the molecular structure of food nutrients; because high temperatures can destroy breastmilk antibacterials; and because microwaves use micro-waves.

Yet I know of many, many mothers who *do* use their microwave for heating milk — certainly the majority of modern mothers are doing so.

So what's going on here? Why are so few doing what they're told? Why are so many mums being so naughty?

Now I agree that a good chunk of our brain power seems to have evaporated, but perhaps us mums do have enough brain-power left to be capable of *shaking* the bottle adequately *after* using a microwave to heat it, to successfully ensure the liquid's heat is distributed evenly.

So I will be really rebellious (and realistic) by saying that you probably will end up getting to know exactly how many seconds it takes in your microwave to heat formula, and you can learn how to expertly shake the bottle so the heat is distributed evenly. *BUT*, try to avoid heating breastmilk in the microwave, and *do be careful* if using other people's microwaves, as they can vary in power.

Question marks over cows' milk formulas

My husband and I are both 1960s babies. His old Plunket book and my mother's old Dr Spock book are fascinating to read in terms of how much knowledge we have gained in only one generation. Then, some mothers of 'modern' bottle-fed babies were instructed to mix a 'formula' (where the word originates from) of cows' milk, boiled water, brown sugar, perhaps some fluoride, and maybe barley added for hungrier babies. *Cripes!* By today's standard, that's a pretty horrific concoction to feed a newborn, but just those few decades ago it was the pinnacle of good mothering.

Today, apart from traditional cows' milk baby-formulas, there are also soy milk and goats' milk formulas, and all three are constantly suffering from on-going debates as to which is most suitable for babies as a replacement to human milk. If your baby is not 100 percent breastmilk-fed, then this is yet another decision you will need to make based on conflicting information.

For example, regarding cows' milk formula, supposedly up to 15 percent of New Zealand's dairy herds are infected with Johne's disease, which some scientists believe can cause Crohn's disease in humans — in New Zealand there are about 2000–3000 new cases of Crohn's disease each year, and research is beginning to question whether pasteurisation is adequate.

If your infant is not breastfed and is suffering from any of the following problems, you may like to try swapping them from cows' milk formula to a goats' milk formula: eczema; asthma; recurrent diarrhoea; repeated vomiting; persistent colic; recurrent bronchitis; or constant rhinorrhea (runny nose).

Promoters of goats' milk products explain that both the fat and protein globules of goats' milk are closer in size to human breastmilk, and so are more easily digested by infants than cows' milk. (But the same is true of civilisations where goats' milk is the 'main' milk: allergic reactions can be improved by switching to cows' milk.)

Like almost everything these days, goats' milk and goats' milk formula are both subject to some bad press. Straight goats' milk should not be used in place of breastmilk, as it is very low in folate and missing adequate amounts of essential fats, vitamins and minerals that are contained in breastmilk.

Some parents avoid all dairy completely for their children, and use a soy milk formula instead. But serious health concerns have also been raised about the high plant isoflavone (oestrogen-affecting) levels in soy milk, soy-based infant formulas, and soy baby foods — and the effect these hormones may have on the body's development through childhood, particularly regarding fertility. So many experts are now recommending avoiding all soy products completely within a baby's first two years — though China has been using soy as their main milk for thousands of years, and certainly haven't suffered infertility issues.

Another alternative, growing in popularity for toddlers (particularly for children with asthma or eczema), is rice milk, and it is quite yummy. But as it is a little low in fat, some experts recommend adding a teaspoon of flaxseed oil with each bottle.

At the end of the day, which formula, if any, you choose will be determined by a number of factors probably including price, friends' recommendations, availability, and your baby's preferences.

Formula-feeding points to note

- Within just 2–3 weeks of birth, a formula-fed baby can be down to just 5–6 feeds daily (less than a breastfed baby, because formula takes longer to digest).
- Formula-fed babies' stools have a pooey odour, they're a little curdy (a bit solidish), and are pale brown.
- If a formula-fed baby is a little constipated (common after a changeover from breastmilk), then it probably means the baby needs more fluid, so you could try giving some cooled, boiled water or diluted prune juice. If that doesn't work, then you need to seek further advice.
- It is said that formula is typically digested by babies at a rate of about 30 ml per hour, so, for example, to see a baby through a six-hour sleep, he will need at least 180+ ml.
- You can boil the kettle once, first thing in the morning, and pour the

water into the bottles. It can then remain on the kitchen bench at room temperature all day, ready for mixing with formula.

- It used to be commonplace to mix the whole day's formula bottles up in one hit. However, the milk used in powdered formula is only pasteurised (not sterilised, as that would remove nutrients). To prevent potentially contaminating bacteria incubating, it is recommended that you prepare powdered formula immediately before feeding. (Powdered formula cans should be covered, kept in a clean dry place, and used within four weeks of opening the tin.)
- Practise at home adding just the right amount of boiling water to a pre-mixed concentrate of formula, to get it just right for baby's taste. (Asking a waitress at a café or restaurant for some boiling water can be a lot easier than asking them to heat your baby's bottle, which they never get right).

To a woman who longs to keep breastfeeding her baby, breastmilk represents pure evidence. It is evidence of love, of nurture, of the physical skill of the human body to provide everything a newborn child needs to survive.

Susan Johnson — *A Better Woman*

Chapter 5

I beg you, wee darling, please go to sleep and stay asleep . . . I need the rest!

*What a good many people don't realise is that **babies need parents'** **direction** to establish proper sleep habits. In fact, the reason so-called sleep problems are common is because so many parents don't realise that **they**, not their babies, must control bedtime ... Sleep is a learned process that is initiated and reinforced by parents. Hence, they have to **teach** their babies how to get to sleep.*

Tracy Hogg — *Secrets of the Baby Whisperer*

When heavily pregnant with your first baby, you may sometimes have felt a little swamped with people's remarks regarding the pending sleep deprivation that was going to beset you once your baby was born . . . 'You should appreciate your peaceful night's sleep, dear, while you can!' 'You'll be falling asleep at 8 o'clock out of sheer exhaustion, you know — no more late nights for you for a long while'.

Oh, and wasn't it foul! All that condescending, patronising, killjoy advice — with the most awful part being that you knew it was probably quite true. Unless, of course, you ordered your cuddly cooing baby with the customised, luxury accessory of being born a great sleeper — oh no, did you forget to tick that box?

Let's face it, probably the most challenging part of being a new parent (primarily a new mother) is the reality that it can be a jolly long time until you are able to relish eight hours of uninterrupted sleep again. As Kaz Cooke writes in *Kid-Wrangling*, 'The sleeping habits of a newborn baby are perfectly logical and sensible — unless you're not a newborn baby, in which case they're completely and utterly insane.'

It can be pretty normal for new parents to lose about two hours of sleep per night for the first couple of months, and an hour a night for the rest of the first year. Yikes! And for some parents it can be much worse — primarily dependent on how well the parents have taught their baby good sleep habits.

Sleep deprivation rates as the most challenging difficulty for the majority of new mothers (numbers two and three are usually breastfeeding problems or marital relationship adjustments).

I need to warn you that the tone of this chapter is a little different from the rest of the book. Its advice is more succinct and less flexible — some might even say it's bossier and more dictatorial. However, there is a very important reason why — *the side effects of parental (and infant) sleep deprivation are SO monstrous, insidious and harmful!*

As Christopher Green says in his book *Toddler Taming*, 'Sleep deprivation is a form of torture, and parents who chronically lack sleep become a little deranged, which is not good for their children'! And Marc Weissbluth writes in *Happy Sleep Habits, Happy Child*, 'There is growing evidence that good night-sleepers make smarter children.'

Extreme sleep deprivation is nothing less than an abominable monster, and it can be the largest contributor to family stress, marital discord and maternal depression. But it's also a spirit-breaking burden that can often, retrospectively, have been preventable. One fact: lack of sleep kills a human quicker than lack of food!

As adults, our sleep cycles are about 90 minutes long: they begin with about half-an-hour of shallow sleep; then about 50 minutes of deep sleep when the brain activity slows down, and bodily repairs are carried out; then a very valuable 10 minutes of REM (rapid eye movement) sleep, which is a bombardment of activity in the brain, while the body is paralysed (to prevent us acting out our dreams) as our brain sorts out its filing cabinets.

However, when you are awoken from an uncompleted sleep cycle, and then go back to sleep, the cycle starts again from the beginning. So, it is very possible to be having say four two-hour naps over a 24 hour period — but to still be drastically REM-sleep-deprived, which plays havoc on your brain functions, trashes your memory and leaves you feeling in a permanent fog like jet-lag. The brain's circadian biorhythms, which synchronises the body's 24-hour cycle to trigger the pineal gland's night-time secretion of the sleep hormone melatonin . . . well, it goes all up the wazoo! You can't think straight, you're unable to concentrate, you feel despondent — you can even be an unsafe driver!

Depriving human beings of REM sleep has been recognised for a very long time as an effective form of *torture*. Your body goes completely out of equilibrium! The stress of sleep deprivation prompts the adrenal glands to produce the stress-coping hormone cortisol — but the body is not meant to have long-term high levels of cortisol. Among other side effects, it makes you crave carbohydrates (starches and sugars) for their instant energy, stuffs up your digestion and mucks up the immune system making the body more susceptible to disease — so you become unwell, which adds even more load to your already oppressive burdens.

The challenge for parents successfully teaching their babies how to sleep through the night is a very old and perplexing quandary. In the last century, however, this dilemma has on occasion mutated into a *very fiery* subject indeed . . . full of theories and fads. There are now *so* many infant experts, and so many sleep scientists (often with conflicting theories), and so many intensely devout and unswervingly held opinions.

For me, it became a personal mission to teach our new babies positive sleeping patterns, enabling them to sleep soundly through the night as expediently as possible — to assist their wee brains to develop unhindered, and to eliminate my own sleep deprivation enabling me to be a more energised mother. Our babies consistently slept through the night (10–12 pm until 6–7 am) by 5–6 weeks of age to due date, and hopefully there will be no significant reason why your precious bundle can't do the same.

This chapter's infant sleep philosophies will be disagreeable to some of you . . . almost at some deep soul-level you could find adopting the following infant sleep theories utterly objectionable. And you know what? That's OK. The world would be a dull and boring place if we all thought the same way and had the same ideas.

However, if you intend to assist your baby to sleep through the night as soon as possible, then this chapter could be for you!

Here is a *fundamental point* that many new parents do not realise, usually just because nobody has bothered to mention it to them: most young babies don't know how to go to sleep without a noisy moving uterus, so it is one of your first *jobs* as parents to *teach* your baby *how* to go to sleep outside the womb.

So, in this chapter I will provide you with the best advice I can, from my heart to yours, in the most (hopefully) easy-to-understand way; and

Note:

The underlying theme of this chapter is: one of the best things for you, your baby and your household is to do what it takes to give your baby the ability to go to sleep unaided. Babies are happier and healthier when they have been taught solid sleep habits . . . and so are the parents!

what I'm going to explain is an amalgamated merging of infant sleep theories from many philosophies, blended into one sensible, practical and logical plan. It gives detailed explanations of my infant sleep philosophies, which are a blend of some of the most tested, tried and true strategies; with extremist ideologies mellowed.

To help simplify things, I have summarised teaching babies to be good sleepers as: **12 Golden Rules** and **12 Magical Secrets** and **20 Do's and Don'ts**.

A baby who doesn't sleep well won't have the neurological resources she needs to function efficiently. She's likely to become cranky and uncoordinated. She won't attend well to her mum's breast or to a bottle. She won't have the energy she needs to explore her world. And, worst of all, being overtired will actually ruin her sleep. That's because bad sleep habits are self-perpetuating. Some babies get so overtired that they can't physically wind down or drop off. They finally fall asleep only when they are totally exhausted. It's painful to see an infant so wired and upset that she literally has to scream herself to sleep in order to block out the world. What's even worse is that when she finally does sleep, it's fitful and abbreviated, sometimes no more than twenty minutes, so she's cranky practically all the time . . . bad sleep habits are learned.

Tracy Hogg — *Secrets of the Baby Whisperer*

The amount of sleep babies need

Newborn to one month old:
About 16–20 hours in every 24 (say 6–8 sleeps of 2–3 hours) — then by 3–4 weeks-old (to due date), one 5–6 hour sleep at night (e.g. 10 pm–4 am).

2–3 months old:
About 15–18 hours in every 24, with about half of that at night (e.g. 7–8 hours overnight by 7–9 weeks, and 9–11 hours by 3–4 months). The rest are three day-sleeps (say about 1^1/2–3 hours each).

4–6 months old:
About 15–17 hours in every 24, with about two-thirds of that at night (say 10–12 hours overnight by 16–24 weeks (e.g. 8 pm–6 am), and the rest are 2–3 day-sleeps (each say 2–2^1/2 hours long).

6–8 months old:
About 14–16 hours in every 24, with about 10–12 hours of that overnight (say 8 pm–6 am), and the rest are a morning and an afternoon day-sleep (each say 1^1/2–2^1/2 hours long).

9–12 months old:
About 14–15 hours in every 24, with about 11–12 hours of that overnight

(say 7 pm–6 am), and the rest are two short day-sleeps (say 1½–2 hours) or one long (say 3–4 hours) day-sleep.

12–18 months old:

About 13–15 hours including one day-sleep ending by 3–4 pm (so say 10–12 hours overnight). The day-sleep is usually finally dropped between the ages of 2–4 years.

Note: At 28–32 weeks' gestation a fetus is already experiencing REM sleep. As a newborn this active REM sleep (including its normally accompanying less regular breathing, increased heart-rate and twitching limbs) is the most dominant part of a wee baby's sleep pattern (say 50 percent).

By the time a baby is just 3–4 months old their sleep style is maturing, and so the quieter quiescence (non-REM) sleep becomes more dominant (with its deep even breathing, lying still, and occasional startle jerk).

SIDS (sudden infant death syndrome)/cot-death:

The general preventatives for this tragedy, affecting mainly under 6–8 month-olds, and primarily 2–4 month-olds, are:
- For the first six months, sleep baby on its back, never on its front — and only on its side with an abdominal sleep-wrap, a support pillow or rolled-up cloth nappy to make it *impossible* for the baby to accidentally roll onto its tummy (though some experts are against side-sleeping, and others warn of flat-head syndrome caused by back sleeping).
- No co-sleeping with a drunk or stoned parent, or with a parent who smells smoky.
- Use a firm mattress — no soft mattresses or waterbeds (and preferably a new mattress for each new baby).
- Avoid everything that enables baby's neck to curve forward, bringing the chin in towards the chest (such as a pillow). This pushes the tongue into the pharynx and narrows the upper airway. Try to have the spine straight. So, take a sleeping baby out of its car seat as soon as practicable.
- Use light cotton/woolen air-cell blankets — no heavy blankets, loose covers, pillows, or soft toys near the baby's head.
- Using pacifiers is not unsafe (some research shows they may provide some protection).
- Keep baby in a smoke-free home.
- Don't allow the baby to get too hot.
- Breastfeeding provides antibody protection against infection, but its benefits protecting against cot death are vague.
- Use a Dr Sprott BabySafe mattress or mattress cover (see page 65).

The First Magical Secret:

It is one of your first jobs as parents to teach your baby HOW to go to sleep and stay asleep because most babies don't know how.

It is very normal for a brand new baby, after their first hour or so of being so beautifully alert, to sleep for pretty much the following 24 hours (except for feeds) out of sheer exhaustion. A day-two baby can seem to do nothing but feed every couple of hours, which stimulates the breast tissue to prepare for milk production. That's a common pattern in newborns.

Then, once recovered from the exhaustion of their birth (and often just around the same stage that you're leaving hospital and experiencing engorgement), your wee baby starts to become its own little person and begins to show its personality (see Tracy Hogg's definitions in chapter 6, page 271).

This is why new parents once home, so often end up scratching their heads: 'But our baby was so settled in hospital. What are we doing wrong?' *Welcome to the complex world of parenting!*

Newborns arrive in this world having previously enjoyed complete control over when they nodded off to sleep (in the womb), and this sleep was always done in a constantly moving, always touching and tremendously noisy environment. So it is ironic that, as new parents, we presume our babies can naturally sleep soundly in a perfectly still bassinet during the peacefulness of night-time — when you think about it, it's the opposite of what your wee baby has been living in for months.

You could try to recreate the womb atmosphere with sound, touch and movement, but then for how many months or years do you want to be stuck with those rituals! At the end of the day, enduring a baby who is a bad sleeper can have enormously detrimental repercussions on the mother, the marriage, the baby's wellbeing and the household.

> **GOLDEN RULE NUMBER 1:**
> Begin establishing a constant routine, ideally from day one.

The Second Magical Secret:

Babies love predictability. Structure in their little life is extremely calming, reassuring and comforting to them. It makes them feel secure — it's their soul food.

Many theories abound as to what age (if ever) is biologically most suitable to introduce a structured sleep pattern into a child's life. Some experts say three months, some experts say six months, and a number of others (myself included) say *straight away*. (Note: If your baby is no longer a newborn, then it may be well and truly time to start — it just might be a slightly bumpier ride to begin with.)

There are some particularly loud beliefs that the brains of babies less than six months of age are unable to pattern their sleep to a 24-hour day, which is bizarre information. Thousands of infant nurses, midwives, nannies and mothers like myself know that ideology can be proved wrong over and over.

Babies at only a few weeks (or even days) old are often capable of learning to habitually enjoy their longest sleep during the darkness and stillness of night-time.

And this *predictability gives the baby a sense of calm*. Which brings us quickly on to the next golden rule.

> ## GOLDEN RULE NUMBER 2:
> The constant routine should be: sleeptime then feedtime then playtime then sleeptime.

The *extremely common* mistake, which many new parents make, is that they do things in the reversed order of playtime, then feedtime, then sleeptime.

This is WRONG! Because . . .

Your baby should wake up because she's hungry (*not go to bed because she's full*). Upon waking, your well-rested and hungry baby can then feed properly. After feeding, your baby can then play happily because she is fed and well rested. Once your wee baby tells you she's tired again (through her very clear language of tired signs) — then it's back to bed to let the cycle begin again.

It's that simple!

The two exceptions

- It is normal for babies to have extra feeds late afternoon and early evening before going to bed at night-time. This cluster-feeding is designed to tank them up for their longest sleep.
- Infant feeds during the night have no playtime period, including the 5 am feeds. (Our household policy was, if it's still dark, it's still night-time!)

With a brand new baby, you can think of the complete sleep-feed-play cycle occurring about every 3–4 hours: the feeding part takes about 25–40 minutes; the play-awake time takes about 45–60 minutes (yes, that's all). So, just one-and-a-half hours or thereabouts after baby wakes, it's time to be back in bed again.

During the first three months, the baby will become a stronger, more efficient sucker, so the playtime will increase as the feedtime (and sleeptime) reduces.

Within even the first week you want to expect their little routine to start to shape into something *very roughly* like this:

7 am	wake, feed, then play
8.30 am	down to sleep
10.30 am	wake, feed, then play
12 noon	down to sleep
1.30 pm	wake, feed, then play
3.30 pm	down to sleep
5 pm	wake, feed, then play
6 pm	extra feed and bath
7 pm	extra feed, and down to sleep
11 pm	wake, feed, down to sleep
3 am	wake, feed, down to sleep

It can be significantly easier to work your life around a baby who has been taught to have predictable habits, rather than working around a baby who has no routine. Plus the routine does *not* have to be strictly adhered to. It is, as I once heard beautifully described, 'organisation which can accommodate chaos'.

Some mothers find it easier *on themselves* to have their baby strictly routined, and other mums (like me) prefer to have *loads* of flexibility.

With just one baby a full-time mother can have pretty reasonable control over an infant's schedule. With a baby and an older toddler, it can be a bit trickier. But certainly with a pre-schooler, toddler and a new baby (take it from me) it does get a little challenging to maintain baby day-sleep routines, as you're constantly dealing with the other children's schedules, activities and noise — but don't fret, as by the third baby you are feeling a *lot* more confident with what you're doing, and you've learnt how *very flexible* babies can be when their life revolves around a *constant routine*.

The Third Magical Secret:

Daytime affects Night-time: teaching a baby how to sleep through the **night** *is totally dependent on how well you are teaching them to sleep during the* **day**.

Baby experts often say, 'The more sleep a baby has, the more it wants' and that can be very true indeed. Well-slept babies are healthier, have better growth, and are far less irritable during their awake periods. That's an indisputable fact.

Voice of a baby, if only he could talk:

'When I was in Mummy's tummy, I could sleep any time I wanted to. It was always dark and warm and safe and cosy. Mummy's heartbeat was so soothing, and her movement lulled me to sleep. In fact, when she lay down really still at night, then that would often wake me up.

But now that I've arrived, it's so frustrating. I try so hard to tell Mummy when I'm tired and need to go to bed. I screw up my face, I whine and grizzle, I clench my fists and make jerky movements. That's all I'm able to do so far. And what does she do? She tries to feed me another drink, or worse, shows me an interesting toy. Yeah I know, both are kind of good for a little while, but by then I'm really tired.

Young babies who don't day-sleep but do sleep through the night, are doing it by default. In other words they sleep out of sheer exhaustion — not because they're naturally a good night-time sleeper, or because you've successfully taught them how to go to sleep on their own. Once older and less exhausted at night, sleep-resistant problems are likely to occur, because the infant hasn't learnt how to fall asleep without the aid of extreme fatigue.

Finally after I've been waiting for ages, crying and getting annoyed, Mummy works out that I must be tired. Phew! I've been trying to tell her for over an hour now — it's like she can't hear me. But now I'm so over-tired and over-stimulated, it's hard for me to relax.

So once in bed I like to cry for a while, it's soothing for me, because I can shut everything out and it makes my body produce relaxing hormones so I can calm down. But heck Mummy won't even let me do that on my own. She's in and out, and in and out of my bedroom, rocking me, patting me — OH JUST GIVE ME SOME PEACE PLEASE! But not too quiet thanks, some vacuuming or the radio or some other humdrum sound is great. Background noise lets me zone-out. I've grown up with lots of noise in Mummy's tummy you see.

Another thing that bothers me is that I'd really like to be wrapped up for my sleeps, nice and tight, so I can feel cosy like I used to be inside Mummy's tummy. But my Mummy doesn't do that, so I end up sprawled out on my back with my arms up high, it's awful — and I don't know how to make my arms come back down. And doesn't she know that I still can't control my startle-reflex yet, so my arms or legs end up accidentally waking me up, or worse my fingernails scratch my face. It's so annoying. I hate it when that happens, it makes me cry — then she comes in and gets me up, but once again I haven't even finished sleeping. I feel so tired nearly all the time, and that makes me cranky. It's just so frustrating. All I can do is cry.

Quite often I wake up after I've been sleeping for not even an hour. I can't help it, it just happens, my brain is still learning how to stay asleep for longer. But then Mummy thinks I've finished my rest, and I haven't. I need to go back to sleep, that's why I'm crying, so I can go back to sleep again. But oh no ... here she comes! She's going to get me out of bed again! Oh heck! Oh no, not more food again!

When your little baby was a fetus in utero, she could doze off to sleep at the perfect moment, any time she wanted to. There was nothing much to look at, and nothing much to do, so whenever Bub was slightly tired, she would snooze. But now she is relying on a pair of highly inexperienced first-time parents, who perhaps have not yet learnt the Baby Language of Tired Signs, to be able to work out when it is her 'right' sleep-time . . . and many new parents *get it wrong*.

Plunket advocates that the biggest reason babies won't sleep is that they are *overstimulated* and *overtired*. New parents need to *learn* how to observe and understand their unsettled crying baby, because there are specific 'perfect windows of time' to put a newborn down to sleep, but these windows are very easy for the untrained eye to miss!

Naturally, understanding the communication of small babies seems challenging. However, once you've learnt how to tune in to your baby's need for sleep, you and your baby can enjoy each other even more. That sounds rather 'peachy' . . . but it's true.

After a newborn wakes up

STAGE 1: Feedtime
Once you have finished feeding baby, it's a sensible time to then check their nappy, and clothing comfort (need another layer? need less layers?).

STAGE 2: Playtime

Now it is Happy Time — this is baby's awake-activity period: lying on a play-mat under a baby-gym, in the bouncinette looking out a window, having a chat on Mummy's knee, going for a stroll in the pram, being cuddled by a visitor, etc. *Your wee baby is relaxed, is looking around, and his hands are unclenched.*

STAGE 3: The Tired Signs

Now watch carefully for baby's Tired Signs, remembering that every baby doesn't display them all, because they each have their own personality:

- Body becomes tense.
- Jerky arm and leg movements (young babies) or become less co-ordinated (older infants falling, stumbling, bumbling).
- Fists clenching.
- Facial contortions (frowns, grimacing).
- Cranky grumpy fussing noises, e.g. grizzling, whining, grunting.
- Moves head from side to side.
- Sucking fists.
- Big blinks.
- Burying head into your chest.
- A nasal-sounding wailing cry that builds in intensity.
- A first yawn.

The Fourth Magical Secret:

Tired babies fall asleep easily. Overtired or overstimulated babies take longer to settle.

GOLDEN RULE NUMBER 4:
Quick! Use this window of time! Put baby to sleep *NOW*, while Bub is *tired*, not a few minutes later when Bub is *overtired*.

At this point many novice parents often misinterpret their young baby's tired signs, thinking instead that their babe is bored (so they offer a distraction, like a different toy or change in view); or parents think that their baby is hungry (so they offer another feed). Another popular idea is to pass the baby to someone else — but newborns can find it very tiring and unsettling to be passed from mum to dad to relative to friend and back.

These are all just temporary distractions, which cumulatively make the baby overstimulated and overtired (and potentially overfed) — so they take longer to settle later when you eventually put them to bed.

Universal overtired or overstimulated signs of babies

Newborns can go from tired to overtired (lovingly named midget meltdown) within *just a few minutes!* If your newborn is displaying any of the following signs, she is probably overtired or overstimulated:

- A fixed-focused spaced-out stare (this wide-eyed look is often mistaken for alertness, but actually means they're very tired indeed).
- Flailing arms, kicking legs.
- Second and subsequent yawns.
- Short wailing cries with short breaths in-between, escalating to long hard red-in-the-face crying. This crying is saying 'I'm way overstimulated, I've had enough, I'm overtired, I'm trying to block everything out now'.
- Baby may seem angry. (Babies who seem angry all the time could be tired all the time due to their constant lack of sleep.)
- Turning away from light or people (if they have head control).
- Losing eye contact.
- Jitteriness of the lower jaw, turning pale around the mouth.
- Red, bloodshot eyes.
- Eyes slowly shutting and springing open again.
- Nodding off and jolting awake.
- Squirming when picked up and turning in towards your body.
- Stiff body, arching their back leaning backwards.
- Rubbing their eyes or cheeks, pulling their ears or scratching their face (not seen in newborns).

The Fifth Magical Secret:

Wee babies live only on instincts and reflexes. The better day-sleeper you teach your baby to be, then the better night-sleeper they will automatically become.

GOLDEN RULE NUMBER 5:
Always put baby down to sleep *awake.*

Every single time your wee bub is put down to sleep, she *must* be *awake* — even if you have to slightly wake up an already asleep baby. But *always* put your babe down to sleep *awake.*

Otherwise if your baby wakes up shortly afterwards, which babies often do, then she doesn't know how she got there or how to go back to sleep on her own without your help again.

This is probably *the* biggest cause of a baby's day-sleeps being way too short, and a huge factor with night-waking too.

The Sixth Magical Secret:

Babies who are unable to go to sleep unaided, are unable to learn to sleep right through the night!

GOLDEN RULE NUMBER 6:
Teach your baby how to fall asleep by herself, as that is how, when she wakes in the middle of the night, she will be able to fall back to sleep on her own.

Putting Baby to Sleep: Step 1

Newborns should always be put to bed swaddled (wrapped) until 3–6 months of age (until they begin to unwrap themselves). So wrap them up all cosy, like a parcel, using a one-metre square sheet of cotton or gauze material as a sleep-wrap.

You see, before birth, babies have already developed memories of touch. That is why when they are wrapped up in a swaddling cloth it makes them feel secure — it replicates how they felt in the womb. It also helps prevent their startle-reflex from waking them up and stops them accidentally scratching themselves. Additionally, a baby's brain hasn't yet finished perfecting its paralysing effects during sleep (that prevent us physically acting out our dreams). So, for the first year or so, infant sleep can have a lot of movement.

GOLDEN RULE NUMBER 7:
Babies should always be put to bed swaddled. It makes them feel snug and secure.

Swaddling Guidelines:

When swaddled, newborns have just their heads poking out. Place their arms crossed over their chest and immobilised, as they don't yet know these scary appendages belong to them, let alone how to have any control over them.

At around 6–7 weeks of age (to due date), you could swaddle them tightly enough to keep their flailing arms and legs contained, but they may like their hands up on their chest near their chin (hands exposed near their face).

By about 3–4 months old, you can swaddle them with the option of one arm left out, so they can find their thumb or fingers if you want.

By 6 months of age my recommendation is to have promoted them into their cot and be using a BabyOK™ babe-sleeper (Refer Twelfth Magical Secret, see page 227).

The Seventh Magical Secret:

Give baby a bedtime routine. Newborns don't understand what you say, but they can understand what you do.

Putting Baby to Bed: Step 2

Have a ritualised order of events during the day and at night because routines are very soothing for babies. They get great comfort in predictability. So, create your own unique routine, especially for the evening bedtime. Maybe something like bath-time, massage, dressing, last feed, a lullaby (vary the songs), swaddling, tucking into bed, kissing good night, lights out, then some catchphrase like 'Bye, Bye — Love You', and the door closes. *Always the same routine every night* — but not always necessarily the same person (sometimes Dad, sometimes Mum, sometimes Nana — vary it). Such a routine is *very portable* for you to use in other people's houses, and for babysitters to use too.

During the day, use a shorter routine. For example, pull the curtains, sing a lullaby, swaddle, tuck into bed, kiss good-bye, and close the door. Again, it's *extremely portable* so it can easily be used at friends' houses during the day.

The Eighth Magical Secret:

Don't make the household quiet for sleeptime, instead add some noise.

Putting Baby to Bed: Step 3

If the house is quiet, add some droning noise (e.g. put a radio outside baby's bedroom door). Babies sleep deeply and are relatively immune to sounds, so long as they're not encouraged to expect peaceful quiet — it can even be possible to vacuum under their cot while they're sleeping!

But do, however, shield your baby from sudden loud noises — don't leave their bedroom window open when your husband is planning to use the weed-eater or chainsaw!

Maintaining your wee baby's natural ability to sleep through noise helps to ensure that, as they get older, they become a toddler who is a noise-tolerant sleeper. Teach a baby to sleep solidly, and that's what they'll be capable of doing.

AIR-RAID WARNING!

Get to your nearest bomb shelter immediately. Incendiaries from hostile anti-baby-crying protesters about to commence!

(These are harsh words, and not everyone finds it easy to allow their baby to do this — there is no easy answer for these parents.)

Putting Baby to Bed: Step 4

The following strategy is vehemently opposed in some quarters, and critically acclaimed in many other sectors — it is your parental decision to make.

When you leave the bedroom, my recommendation is that you have no specific intention of returning, not until after Bub has finished the sleep you know she needs.

Take note those readers with anti controlled-crying philosophies. *Please* do not misinterpret the recommendation: this is not a cruel, traumatic or heartless instruction that a parent shouldn't ever re-enter the baby's bedroom before she has slept. This is simply a recommendation that it is not the parent's *intention* to do so.

You see, a baby's brain is little and inexperienced. So it can be *confusing* for a small baby to have someone coming back into their bedroom who picks them up, cuddles them, then puts them back down again for sleep — such mixed signals . . . The baby thinks 'Am I getting up now, or going to sleep now? I don't understand. You're confusing me. You're overstimulating me. Now I'm overtired!'

Some controlled-crying experts recommend popping back in to check on your baby after some minutes of crying; to give them brief, settling controlled comforting, sometimes termed checking or visiting. But that theory can have a tendency to fail, because the baby assumes you are there to rescue him, and subsequently when you leave again, he can really crank up the crying. It can become ear-popping, crystal-cracking, blood-curdling screaming — simply because you were giving confusing signals.

You see, it should take 2–20 minutes for newborns to fall asleep. If you walk in before they are asleep then most babies' reaction is: 'Oh yes, I like you, I want you to stay' which sounds like 'Waaa Waaa Waaa'.

Very quickly too, little babies grow into bigger babies, who learn that 'All I have to do is to keep crying, and eventually she will get me back up. Works every time!'

Sometimes a little baby will cry because you put her down to bed a bit too late. She's now a little overtired, so will vent her frustrations by crying.

Sometimes a little baby will cry because you put her down to bed a bit too early. She's not quite completely tired-out enough yet, so will expend the last of her energy by crying.

And sometimes a little baby will cry incessantly because you completely missed the boat. He is now very overtired and wound up like a cuckoo clock, and will scream his little lungs out for half an hour plus, until he has finally unwound enough to go to sleep — which is absolutely awful. (A few drops of the Bach flower Rescue Remedy can sometimes help, and it is completely safe for babies.)

Among other purposes, crying is the way babies *shut-off* and *block-out* external stimulation — which is why babies cry when they're overtired and/or overstimulated.

Please don't beat yourself up about it, and don't think your baby is suffering or you are breaking her spirit. Just leave her to find the right moment to fall sleep — so long as you're not putting baby to bed overtired every time, as that would be cruel.

This system, as taught by many infant sleep experts, is simply using the process of *not interfering* with your wee Bub as they learn how to go to sleep unaided outside the womb.

Crying also assists a baby to unwind because it stimulates production of the relaxing happiness hormones into their bloodstream.

As Bub's crying becomes more intense, it is normal for a baby to become a little red in the face and even perspire a bit. (Older babies can cry in bed until they become hysterical, which is revolting, and another reason why it is so important to start teaching them from very young how to go to sleep. It avoids preventable problems developing later down the track).

Please don't get distressed and fill yourself with self-guilt when your baby cries after you put her down to bed — just allow her to self-settle. The crying will usually crescendo into about three high-pitched wailing peaks (baby-language for 'I'm exhausted'), before the crying begins to reduce in intensity.

Babies crying themselves to sleep also have a predictable crying pattern: as they are getting ready to fall asleep, the *length of crying gets shorter*, and the *pauses of silence between cries gets longer*.

Something roughly a bit like this:
10 minutes crying, then 10 seconds silence, then
5 minutes crying, then 15 seconds silence, then
3 minutes crying, then 1 minute silence, then
1 minute crying, then 2 minutes silence, then
20 seconds crying, then 1 minute fidgeting, then
they *plummet* to sleep (unlike adults who *drift* to sleep)

Important note to all fathers:

On numerous occasions I have seen girlfriends try so hard to teach their little babies how to learn good sleep-routine habits, only to have Dad ruin the whole process by being 'unable to stand the baby's cries anymore' (usually just when Bub is almost asleep), and in goes Dad to get the baby up. Let me point four things out to you, sweet Papa-bear:

- Firstly, your entire household will be 100 percent happier once your baby is taught to sleep through the night.
- Secondly, it is biologically much tougher on the mother to hear her baby cry; it surges her hormones, so don't for one second think that it is easier on her.
- Thirdly a well-slept baby is not only happier but also healthier (and some experts say brainier too).
- And finally, we thought you were a tough, macho guy — heck, deal with it like a man.

Putting Baby to Sleep: Step 5

Now that Bub is in bed, well, it is Mum's Time! Whose time? Your time! It's now time to do whatever you want to do, while your baby is enjoying its sleep.

Have a long shower, slowly sip a cuppa, prepare yourself a nice lunch, do a crossword, sort out the washing if you must, read a book, tidy the house if it's annoying you, paint your nails, have a long girl-chat on the phone, catch up on your emails, prepare dinner, or even go to sleep yourself — but do something personally rewarding (something that makes you feel like you've got something successfully accomplished — even if it's just fulfilling an aching necessity to do *nothing*).

Two Important Points:

- While your baby is still waking through the night, you *must* use some of their day-sleep time each day for you to day-kip, especially in the afternoons during the first six weeks. Take the phone off the hook and go and lie down! (Remember your body still needs its own rest to heal the massive wound on the placental wall of your uterus, to recover from the childbirth marathon, and to produce breastmilk.)
- If you can't ignore the housework, at least ring a friend so you can yack while you deal with mundane things like making beds, washing dishes, sorting laundry, tidying the lounge and peeling spuds. I do it all the time! (An electrician told me once how bad the cordless-phone radiation is on

your brain — oh man, I'm in deep doo-doo now.)

GOLDEN RULE NUMBER 9:
No sleep props and no sleep aids: don't teach your baby that they can't go to sleep unaided.

That's right . . . NO dummying to sleep, NO rocking to sleep, NO patting to sleep, NO carrying to sleep, NO feeding to sleep, NO driving to sleep, NO night-lights, NO special sleepy music, NO heavy fabric blackout curtain or dark roller-blind, NO bed-vibrator . . .

NO INDUCEMENTS FOR NORMAL SLEEP — otherwise you are going to create an insecure baby who is addictively dependent on some outside influence giving them the OK to sleep — a sleep-aid junkie. Then your baby is lacking even the most basic fundamental human right — *to go to sleep on its own.*

Babies are *completely capable* of sleeping without props. It is simply the parent who mistakenly thinks their baby needs help.

Too quickly this one-week-old that appears to need to be fed, or rocked with its dummy to sleep, can turn into a ten-month-old who refuses day-sleeps and demands an hour of your time every night to lull it to sleep with tranquillising sleep-props.

This is *not* saying that there will never be occasions when your child will need (and deserves) loving assistance to lull it to la-la land due to an unusual outside influence — like a bad cold, or a noisy neighbour's party, or a plane flight, or a special event which forced your sweet babe to become unavoidably overtired. But that is very different from instilling sleep dysfunctions that become the norm.

The Tenth Magical Secret:

If a baby can't fall asleep on their own at 8 pm, then they sure as heck can't fall asleep on their own at 4 am either.

Putting Baby to Bed: Step 6

Babies often wake and whimper during a sleep period for no apparent reason, but left alone they can go back to sleep. This is the end of one sleep cycle (about every 30–60 minutes), before the next cycle commences.

Day-sleeps for example, are made up of say 2–6 sleep cycles before Bub will have properly finished sleeping. So if your little bub starts fussing, don't rush in to intervene too quickly (especially within the first hour of going down for a day-sleep).

> **GOLDEN RULE NUMBER 10:**
> *Avoid accidental parenting. Start as you mean to go on. Don't start something new unless you want it to become a permanent routine ritual.*

That's right, don't start any new habit without expecting your baby to become rapidly addicted to it. So always start as you mean to go on!

Are you happy to cuddle and walk around with your four-kilo baby to help her sleep? . . . You'd better be happy to still be doing that when she weighs ten kilos. Are you happy to rock your month-old for ten minutes to induce him to go to sleep? . . . You'd better be happy to be rocking him for an hour when he's 12 months old. Are you happy to lie down and cuddle your three month old to sleep on your chest? . . . You'd better be happy to go back in at 4 am to do the same thing again, and still potentially be cuddling her to sleep when she's two years old.

For some parents these are intentionally part of their attachment parenting ideology — and in those cases there is nothing necessarily wrong with their decisions. However that is not the style of parenting this chapter supports. As Tracy Hogg states, 'Independence is not neglect.'

Some experts recommend parents being freely prepared to use any sleep inducements only until the baby is about six months of age. On this particular point I, and many other experts, *vehemently disagree* (and that's OK, we're allowed to).

In our logic, if you wait until six months of age to start to remove sleep-aid inducements like rocking or feeding to sleep that your wee baby has already learnt to associate with sleep, they can then have traumatic difficulties falling asleep. My personal philosophy is that it can be much tougher on a seven-month old than a seven-day old to be left for the first time to go to sleep unaided.

Let me give you some real-life examples . . .
- A five-month-old with a cold, who has been sleeping through the night for the past two months, cries out at 3 am because of her blocked nose. She's offered a bottle for solace to calm her down, and two months later she's still crying out at 3 am every night for that yummy bottle.

- A grumpy, teething ten-month-old will only go back to sleep at 4 am if he is allowed into Mummy and Daddy's bed. Eighteen months later his parents wake every morning to find a third little person has joined them in their bed, and they're expecting another baby next month.
- A one-year-old has always gone to bed with his dummy at night, and Mum has always come in to find it when he loses it — several times a night. He has no intention of giving it up, his screaming is an effective deterrent to that fanciful idea. At three years of age, he still cries out in the middle of the night for Mum to find his lost dummy, and in a zombie-robot-like state she continues — several times every night — to get out of bed to retrieve it for him.
- A mum finds the only way for her little girl to have an afternoon sleep is to drive around so she nods off in the carseat. Sometimes it takes ten minutes, other times half an hour; and then she crosses her fingers that her little baby doesn't wake up once home when she turns the engine off. Often she just leaves the station wagon idling in the carport.

All parents, at some time or another, resort to the ever-popular, wing-it philosophy of accidental parenting. Sometimes, desperate novice parents have come up with some extraordinarily novel ideas to entice their baby to sleep, such as attaching a vibrating electric toothbrush wrapped in a cloth nappy to the cot! — or removing the baby-seat from the car, sitting it on top of a humming clothes dryer, and belting the baby in for her afternoon siesta — those vibrations will generally guarantee a baby falls asleep!

If you start using sleep props from week 1, you can almost guarantee problems will clearly emerge as early as 6–8 weeks, when you discover that your wee baby is already heavily addicted to a particular sleep prop.

It can rapidly all become a vicious cycle of parents finding it harder and harder to remove the dummy, music, rocking or feeding-to-sleep from the routine of their two-month-old, then their five-month-old, then their 10-month-old, then their one-year-old, and then their two-year-old.

Now, too, the parents have endured a couple of years of broken sleeps. As crazy as it sounds, this is not an unusual extreme. It's really common! All too quickly that two-year-old grows into a sleep-resistant, stubborn toddler, and then into an always-stays-up-late, obstinate pre-schooler. It can all become exponentially harder and harder to break these bad habits.

If young children never get *taught* to break their fighting-sleep routine, it can take years for them to self-cure (if ever) — or they start primary school and finally might sleep solidly through the night due to sheer exhaustion. So too the parents unless they have another younger child who has also been allowed to become sleep-resistant).

All these little nightmares are an awful price that loving, well-meaning and attentive parents may pay for not starting out as they need to go on.

As Tracy Hogg so accurately writes about bad-sleeping babies: 'You need to understand what's going on here and take responsibility for the bad habits you fostered. Then the hard part: Have the conviction and perseverance to help your baby learn a new and better way ... Your baby isn't doing anything wilful or spiteful ... You can untrain your baby ... Changing habits takes time.'

Pacifiers and rocking

I am not advocating that one should never use dummies or that babies shouldn't be rocked! I am simply recommending that you do not use such tools to entice a baby to sleep. All babies love to be rocked, and of course touch and movement are essential to their brain stimulation and development. But don't create a baby who is addicted to movement in order to induce sleep.

A pacifier can be invaluable for ensuring peace (and sanity) during times when you can emotionally benefit from it (e.g. while at the supermarket, eating your dinner, doing errands, etc.) and for babies under four months of age, sucking is an inherently instinctive relaxant (see also page 193).

Co-sleeping

Historically, co-sleeping has been commonplace due to economic necessity, but in the mid-1970s books, such as Hugh Jolly's *Book of Child Care*, reintroduced the idea. These days some parents embrace the idea of a family bed by making a conscious decision to adopt the co-sleeping philosophy — and there is nothing necessarily wrong with that when it is their joint preference.

In fact, when a mother and baby co-sleep, it is said to be possible for the mother and baby's sleep-awake patterns to synchronise, with breastfeeding being done in a far less aroused state.

Authors Dr William and Martha Sears are famous American paediatricians who strongly advocate co-sleeping. However many parents detest the idea of needing to co-sleep for months, or years, with their children. And difficulties can arise when another child comes along. Neither philosophy, of co-sleeping or not co-sleeping, is categorically wrong. Parenting styles should be proudly individualistic.

The Eleventh Magical Secret:

Don't instil in your baby an addiction for her own bed. Babies learn to be as flexible as you teach them to be.

Right from the start, vary your baby's sleep locations at least once or twice a week — especially if you want to continue any kind of reasonable social life. Put them down in your bed for a day-sleep, put the port-a-cot up in the lounge overnight, use the spare blow-up mattress, give them a pram day-sleep, etc. . . . be inventive. Vary things so that they will be able to go down to bed whenever they're due, wherever they are.

My husband can sleep almost anywhere. You could put him in a freezing tent with his feet sticking out, the wind blowing and rain dripping on his head, and he'd still be able to sleep! To me, that's amazing as I am a lifelong insomniac — how else do you think I fitted in writing this book? So I wanted to ensure our children were given his 'gift' of being able to sleep wherever, and what a fabulous gift it is. But that gift is returned to us too — because we can enjoy a good social life, rarely needing babysitters. Great-sleeping children aren't luck — they are the result of strategy.

I've been quite obsessive with our children on this point. (Every parent usually obsesses about something.) From tiny babies I have ensured our kids stayed super-flexible with their sleep habits — sometimes nicknaming them my flexi-babies.

We have always taken our kids out all over the place on the weekends, and they love Saturday nights. We're nearly *always* up to something, even if it's just to a friend's house for dinner and cards. It's no big deal to our children to go to sleep on a blow-up mattress, or to top-and-tail in a bed with a friend — that's cool and exciting to them. And once put to bed, they know they are expected to go to sleep.

So try not to let your wee babe become an own-bed addict! It's an awful insecurity for one so young.

Also, I know all little bubs love soft cuddly things, and that's beautifully cute. But please don't *encourage* your baby to fall in love with one particular toy or blankie for bedtime, because soon they can't go to sleep without it. Again that's encouraging insecurities in wee children, who are far too young to have any insecurities! I know it seems adorable at the beginning, but it's not amusing when you've misplaced the essential item; or you're at a friend's place and forgot to bring it; or it's become so drooled on it's verging on being a health-hazard. There's nothing wrong with toddlers going to bed with some soft-toy friends, but just not the same critically essential toy every single night, that's all.

GOLDEN RULE NUMBER 11:
At night, fill them to the brim, creating the turkey-dinner sensation.

Remember how, on Christmas Day, after a massive lunch-time feast of roast turkey all everyone wants to do is rest — that's your objective here, every evening. Your goal is to give baby the turkey-dinner feeling. Physiologically, a full stomach makes you feel tired. Your body wants you to be inactive so it can concentrate on digestion.

By following all the guidelines in this chapter, you should expect your baby to be sleeping through the night (7–8 hours straight) somewhere between 3 and 9 weeks after due date.

If at three months of age your baby is still not achieving this, and you know you have taught your baby well how to fall asleep, then perhaps the issue is that an empty tummy is waking your baby. Here are a few ideas on how to deal with this:

- Express off some of your fat-rich milk each morning to top baby up with late at night.
- Lactating mums can try **blessed thistle** capsules or tea (available at health shops). It is said to thicken the milk. It also commonly makes the baby less 'windy'. If blessed thistle doesn't do the trick, then the mother could also try the herbal supplement marshmallow and/or a calcium supplement and/or lecithin, which all traditionally help the baby find the milk more satisfying.
- Controversially, you may like to make your breastfed baby's last night feed a formula feed instead of breast. (Please, breast-is-best advocates, don't fiercely object to that suggestion.) Certainly breastmilk is the priority — but equally important for the baby's development are solid sleeps and the prevention of extreme maternal sleep-deprivation.
- If your baby is already formula-fed, then perhaps it may be time for the thicker 'for hungry babies' product for the last feed in the evening.

Note: Have a gap of at least 20 minutes between the final feed and final bedtime, so that the baby doesn't learn to associate feeding with sleep.

The Twelfth Magical Secret:

Use a BabyOK™ Babe-Sleeper: the best infant 'sleep-secure' ever designed.

At 3–6 months of age, your bub will probably begin unravelling their swaddling sleep-wrap, and the bassinet will be getting too small. It's time to move them into the cot, and I personally recommend to immediately start using a BabyOK™ Babe-Sleeper. I am particularly familiar with this product because, with my wonderful mum, I helped create it. So in our biased opinion and looking through our rose-coloured glasses, we certainly believe that it is nothing less than the best thing since sliced bread, as the saying goes.

(For information and testimonials, refer www.babyokproducts.com.)

What is a BabyOK™ Babe-Sleeper and how does it work?

- A 100 percent cotton sleep-bag attached with patent-pending stitching to its own special 100 percent cotton base-sheet.
- It is designed to fit 6–30 month old infants (or as early as three months for exceptionally physically active, larger babies).
- It allows a baby to very comfortably role from back-to-side and side-to-tummy (but helps inhibit a very young baby from rolling onto its tummy).
- It allows an infant to sit up after finishing sleeping (but it's virtually impossible for a toddler to stand up, climb out or fall out of the cot).
- It makes it challenging for the infant to push its blankets off — and even if it succeeds, baby still has an extra layer on to protect from the cold.
- Being 100 percent cotton, it is designed for year-round use so it is totally suitable even on the hottest of days.
- It is portable and fits all cot sizes, all port-a-cots and standard single beds — and with a little ingenuity can also be used on a double bed. It can replace a port-a-cot if a single bed is available.
- It replaces both top and bottom cot sheets.
- It is reinforced for durability.

> **GOLDEN RULE NUMBER 12:**
> Changing bad baby habits takes three days.

For some people, reading this chapter will come a little later than ideal, and you may already be aware that your wee baby has developed quite a number of sleep issues which need resolving — sooner rather than later.

Baby Whisperer author, Tracy Hogg, outlines the series of steps required to reverse bad habits, and this includes taking small steps to solve one problem at a time. So if, for example, it is normal for you to lie down with your seven-month-old baby till she goes to sleep, with lullaby music on, a dummy in her mouth and, a night-light on, and she still wakes up again twice more through the night, requiring the same or a similar ritual to get back to sleep — you need to be removing each sleep-aid prop one at a time. It would be too traumatic for your little babe to change everything all at once. Things need to be addressed in three-day increments.

Perhaps you even need to remind yourself that you are the parent; you are in charge; and you know what's best for you, your baby and your household. Bite the bullet and get the task done. Your seven-month-old is too young to be in charge.

But be warned: you need to expect a little going backwards before things start to move forward. Some habits die hard. This is when your level of commitment to your plan (especially on the second night) will be tested. You need to face the reality that you created these bad habits, out of good intentions I know, but only you can 'encourage' the bad habits to fade away, and this process will probably test the fortitude of your mental and emotional endurance.

So if, for example, your ten-month-old is still waking at 2 am every night, sitting up and screaming in his cot waiting for you to move him into your bed or for you to give him a bottle — then don't be surprised if he sits up dozens of times the first night after you lie him back down to tuck him in. Then expect regression. On the second night he could sit up more times. But usually by the third night the bad habit will dramatically reduce. On the fourth, fifth and sixth nights, you're bound to hear the stirring of his 2 am internal alarm clock but he will probably be pretty receptive to the knowledge that he now needs to go back to sleep.

Remember this is *only* a test of wills. Any thoughts of 'He won't let me put him down awake' or 'She hates her cot' or 'He's scared of the dark' or 'She's afraid to be on her own' are insecurities you have accidentally created. Accept that fact. Take responsibility for your well-intentioned errors of judgement. And just move on. They're hardly going to be the only parenting mistakes you'll make!

The twenty 'do's' and 'don'ts'

1. DO realise that when we as adults sleep overnight, we are not in one solid sleep that entire time. Our sleep actually occurs in about 90 minute cycles, but we have learnt to barely notice the moments between cycles. A baby's sleep cycles are only around 30–60 minutes.
2. DON'T rush in when you hear your baby stirring less than an hour after you put your baby down during the day, just because it sounds like she's finished her sleep — she's only finished a sleep cycle. Hearing a little whimper does not mean you need to rescue her. Stop interfering — just leave her alone and undisturbed to continue into the next sleep-cycle.
3. DO remember, temperament aside, if your baby is always waking up cranky during day sleeps, then chances are you may be getting him up as he stirs between cycles, not when he has actually finished sleeping.
4. DON'T let a young baby sleep for longer than 3–4 hours each sleep during the daytime, otherwise they are bound to get their daytime and night-time confused, e.g. having a six-hour sleep during the day, and a three-hour sleep at night.
5. DO realise you actually have to train a baby's circadian biorhythms to

know the difference between day and night. It does not occur naturally — in fact, most babies seem to be born with their day-night clock back-to-front. But even within just the first week it can be successfully reversed.

6. DON'T be startled if your baby sleeps with its eyes partially open, even during REM sleep. Freaky, but normal.

7. DO ensure your baby is especially snugly warm in bed for the first month or so. After that they need say one extra layer of clothing or one extra layer of bedding than you would use on yourself (e.g. a BabyOK™ babe-sleeper).

8. DO set a focused goal of having your baby well entrenched in good sleep habits by, at most, the age of three months, for a very specific reason: from then on your baby may begin teething (big time). If she is already a poor sleeper, the news ain't great, because teething will go on until she's 2^{1}/$_{2}$–3 years old. (Forgetting for the moment the many times she will be unwell with a blocked nose or sore throat or ear infection or nappy rash — or all five together!)

9. DO realise that night-lights can be a wonderful way to teach children to be scared of the dark. Also, some research is now showing links between night-sleeps in early childhood in a room with night-lights and short-sightedness later in life. But night-lights are useful to turn on as middle-of-the-night lights to give a newborn a feed. They are also great in the hallway at night for toilet-trained children, and grown ups!

10. DO use a baby monitor when you are out of ear-shot to know when your sleeping baby has woken — but you do not have to have the monitor on your bedside table. Many newborns can be very noisy sleepers, and if you are a light sleeper, you really don't need to hear every groan, grizzle, whine, snort, burp, startle, sneeze, hiccup and fart your baby makes — you need your sleep too. Unless you are a very heavy sleeper, you *will* instinctively wake to your baby's cry.

11. DO have a routine at your baby's first morning wake-up that is at a respectable hour (the sun up at least, and nothing less than a '6' at the beginning of the time). Let your wee baby know that this is definitely the get-up time. A gentle, friendly, happy greeting along the lines of: 'Good morning, sweet-pea! How are you today? Did you have some nice dreams? It's time to get up now, you must be hungry.' Be enthusiastic. Be smiling. It teaches your baby that the night-time sleep is finished.

12. DO be calm, quiet and very boring when your baby wakes up during the night-time for feeds — and don't excessively change your baby's nappies during the middle of the night (say for poos not for pees if you're

using quality absorbent disposable nappies).

13. DO NOT make the bassinet or cot an overly stimulating environment with loads of mobiles, toys, activities etc. Yes there should be a few things of interest to look at, but not heaps of stimulating toys. It should be a serene restful environment. You want to teach baby that the cot is for going to sleep in.

14. DO discourage your infant from waking loudly too early, by putting some toys in her cot (while she's asleep, before you go to bed) as surprises for her to play with when she wakes. You may gain an hour's sleep in the mornings because your little sunshine is happily playing.

15. DO sleep your baby on her back for the first six months as a cot-death preventative. To avoid creating a flat-headed baby, you can alternate the sleeping position of a young baby's head between the back side, left side and right side. To avoid the baby developing a flat head, some parents opt to lie the infant on its side, using a rolled-up cloth nappy down their back, little wedge-shaped triangular sleep-support cushion, or abdominal sleep-wrap to support their spine, which can seem a great idea. Frustratingly, because of the risk of an infant rolling onto their tummy at under six months of age, lying a young infant on his side makes him twice as likely to suffer from SIDS (Sudden Infant Death Syndrome). A baby sleeping on her front is *five times* as likely to have SIDS than an infant sleeping on her back. In reality, some young babies are just such energetic wriggly squirmers, you can find it virtually impossible to keep your under-six-month-old off her tummy in the cot, because she is a bit of an 'early developer' with her physical co-ordination. In which case, using an abdominal sleep-wrap product can be a sensible decision.

16. DO NOT resort to offering middle-of-the-night feeds once your baby has slept through the night. It is way too easy for parents to have an infant successfully sleeping through the night, just to up-turn everything by offering a 'wee-hour comfort-feed' through teething, illness or similar — and very quickly they've re-created a baby hooked again on the middle-of-the-night snack.

17. DO realise that even little babies who have already been taught to sleep through the night, will still occasionally wake up screaming (perhaps they have just had a bad dream). An effective 'quick-fix' remedy, is to give babe 3–4 drops of Bach flower Rescue Remedy (to calm their emotions), re-tuck baby, re-kiss them goodnight, and re-say 'Night, night'. You can also expect other unsettled changes such as when starting to eat solids, or starting to be mobile, or growth spurts, to cause some

sleep disruptions — but none are reasons to introduce sleep inducement props.

18. DO know some babies abhor sleeping in a dirty nappy (which is frustrating for parents when they produce poos one hour into what should be a three-hour day-sleep). Sometimes by repeating your rituals they will go back to sleep. Other times they may have had just enough sleep to convince themselves they've finished their sleep. You will simply need to try to give them an extra hour at their next sleep.

19. DON'T routinely let your wee baby fall asleep in a place that is not specifically intentioned for sleeping (e.g. in a bouncinette), as it is sending them mixed signals. It's going to happen occasionally, and that's fine . . . you leave your baby in the bouncer while you have a shower, and come out to find your little poppet is fast asleep. That's OK. But wake baby a little before you put them down to sleep properly in their bed. Your baby will probably cry a bit, but that's OK too, they'll soon nod off again, fingers crossed.

20. DO NOT freak out at the very occasional use of a sedative on children, when you just know it is the wise and sensible thing to do (e.g. their little nose is blocked up with a horrid cold, and the boy next door is practising on his drums) but sedation shouldn't be used routinely as a sleep inducement solution. (If you do that, it's the equivalent of teaching your child to become addicted to sleeping tablets.)

Conclusion

Infant sleeping is a very touchy subject. I know that just as there may be many experts who say 'Well done, Kathy, I wholeheartedly agree', there will probably be just as many experts who, for whatever reasons, feel my recommendations are simply 'horrific advice'.

We all want our children to learn how to go to sleep unaided and on their own — without it taking years to achieve. My husband and I are proud to have three children who have been successfully taught to be great sleepers, and this chapter explains how we accomplished it. But it's not really 'magic' at all, and it's far from being any kind of 'secret'.

However, at the end of the day, *you* are your baby's parent. And only you should make the decisions as to what is best for your baby. If you are not utterly comfortable with these recommendations, then do your own research. There's plenty of information out there. You too may be able to teach your child how to become an equally awesome sleeper, using an entirely different strategy.

So do what is right, in your heart, for you, your baby and your family. I have confidence in yourself, in your own instincts and convictions — listen to your own inner wisdom.

Whatever your decision, there will be some expert's theory that backs you up. Richard Ferber, Robin Barker, Rosey Cummings, Gina Ford, Brian Symon and Marc Weissbluth are some of the more well-known writers on this topic.

But there is one thing that nearly all the experts can agree on, and that is that teaching your baby to become a good sleeper is *one of the most satisfying and directly rewarding things a parent can do.*

At the end of the day, I simply wish you true happiness and pure pleasure in your role of parenting!

I knew I was awake because I was standing upright. I craved sleep in the most intense physical way, as if my whole being was thirsty for it. Never in my whole life had I known an exhaustion so complete that it seemed to reach the lining of my bones . . .

After one hundred and eighty-five nights of waking three, four and five times a night I considered myself conquered . . . Everything we had used to get him to sleep until now, all the advice we had been given about rocking, the use of a dummy, the singing of lullabies, the reduction of visual stimulation, every single prop we had ever used had to go.

Susan Johnson — *A Better Woman*

Chapter 6
The fourth trimester

In many cultures the mother must be reintroduced into the community, for she has become a new person ... We in the West have mostly given up our ancient rituals of introduction; might this explain why women in our culture often experience the return to society as an anticlimax? With no ceremonies to mark the occasion, there's no way of expressing the transformations that have taken place. On the surface, the world hasn't changed; and yet to the mother, everything feels different.

Carol Dunham and the Body Shop Team — *Mamatoto*

When you were last at home you were a couple — but now you're a family! What a surreal, almost delusional, experience it is. It's some crazy kaleidoscope mix of floating on clouds and running over hot coals, as the overpowering reality and overwhelming anxiety sets in. You are now forever ultimately responsible 24-7 for your newborn baby's life. *Shikes!*

With or without the mysterious bonding having occurred, nearly all new mums have their heart-strings stretched so tight it is as if they have been catapulted into space, circled Mars, and are returning back down to Earth on some crash course trajectory.

You may be so in love with your baby! You thought you knew what love was, but not like this, this is a whole new level of devotion and besotted enrapture you didn't know existed in the universe, except perhaps in Heaven. How is it that no one ever told you it was this intense? (They did, you just couldn't comprehend it back then.) Ina May Gaskin describes in *Spiritual Midwifery*, 'Brand new babies are gorgeous. Being with a new baby, giving the baby your whole attention feels like giving your soul a drink of fresh pure water.' Surely, part of a helpless baby's survival skills involves placing his mother under an irresistible spell — like a puppet-master pulling the strings of his marionette — manipulating and dominating her body and mind. Unconditional love is biological — it perpetuates our species.

As you know, for many of our mothers or grandmothers, the stay in maternity hospital was for a whole (now amazing) two weeks. The very real advantage of this was that when a mother finally got home, she was physically recovered from the trauma of giving birth — and she was mentally and emotionally recovered from the hormonal plunges. The new mother was well past engorgement; her baby had been latching on to the breasts perfectly for at least a week; the baby blues were long gone; and the hospital system had already taught her baby the routine of sleep-feed-awake-sleep. The new mother was significantly better equipped for her new role at home on her own. My own mother still recounts how wonderfully cosseted such a length of hospital stay left her feeling — she reminisces that after the eighth day, every extra day's stay in hospital was worth a week's recovery at home.

Thirty (or so) years ago resolute women were hell-bent on eradicating the intimidating and overbearing, Draconian practices that were part of those 'old school' health services — and this lobbying action produced some immensely positive results. However, since then, government funding for maternity care has been ever so slowly eroded, to the point now that most mothers are home from hospital within just two days, and are even offered incentives to not stay in hospital at all. *(Which is an absolute atrocity, but I won't get myself started on that subject!)* I remember a dear friend and midwife once commenting to me that probably the most 'natural' environment for a new mother would be shifting to a commune for the first few months, where experienced mothers would surround her, pamper her and her baby, while providing her with tremendous support. But, instead, our society expects a new mother to cope at home on her own, for years!

So, even though you've probably never changed a nappy before yesterday, the mothercraft skills you will need for caring for your baby are to be learned on the job. Even the most seemingly straightforward tasks can seem complicated in the early days. But in time, you really are going to be fine.

Welcome to the six-week or 40-day *Fourth and Final Trimester* of pregnancy, the end of a 300-day journey since conception!

Welcome home, Mum

Walking through your front door for the first time with your precious darling newborn has got to rate as one of the most fantastically wonderful, but frighteningly spooky, moments of a woman's life. Out loud you might be saying 'Welcome home, Baby', but in your mind you're thinking 'Now what?' That's very normal. As Mara Lee writes in *Baby's First Year for Dummies*,

'You're smart, you're capable, you can hold down a responsible job, but do you know what to do with your baby as soon as you get him home? . . . Arriving home with a newborn is known to transform the most logical and confident person into an indecisive wreck.'

It is commonplace for a newborn to have a honeymoon (birthing recovery) period of sleeping a lot for the first few days. Then after that, for the first time, their true personality begins to be revealed around the third or fourth day. This can be when your 'love at first sight' reaction of 'milky timelessness' might start to feel like it was more of a hormone-induced infatuation, because you're now dealing with a 'relentlessly demanding enigmatic bundle of joyful and joyless stress'. *But that's normal, you're fine . . . you're right on track.*

In the early days at home you could feel appalled that at 2 pm you are still bleary-eyed, unshowered, in your dressing gown, and feeling like you're stuck on a macabre merry-go-round of feeding and changing, feeding and changing. You may feel claustrophobically entangled by the washing piling up, the unmade beds, the bombsite kitchen and the chaotic lounge. Then your mind wonders why you're feeling hunger pangs, before realising you've forgotten to eat lunch . . . or you wonder why your teeth are so furry, then realise you haven't brushed them yet that day . . . or your partner rings at 5.30 pm to say he's leaving work and casually asks what's for tea, and you realise nothing even remotely resembling a dinner is yet in the pipeline. *But that's normal, you're fine . . . you're on track.*

During the day an endless, fumbling, clumsy and hormone-cocktail altered-state can shroud you in some crushing feelings of inadequacy, as if you're being preposterously slovenly. Both useless and used, you find your days don't belong to you anymore; the divisions defining the beginning, middle and end of your day no longer exist. You are starting to learn too, that new mothers don't usually end their day with a satisfying feeling that it's been a job well done, well not in the way you may have been used to, because the work never finishes. *That's still normal, you're still fine . . . and you're still on track.*

There can be some really crazy things going on in your compost-heap brain that keep making your 'emotional temperature' go up and down — you are on a fierce concoction of mind-altering hormones (some call it maternal preoccupation madness) which is all quite normal. It can feel like you've been on such a party high after delivery, that what you've now got is a wicked hangover of uncomfortable stitches, sleep deprivation, a foggy memory of the past few days, and worries about things you didn't anticipate worrying about — all resulting in some major mood swings, which in themselves also irk you because that's not how you think you ought to feel. *Believe it or not, that is normal, you are fine . . . and you are right on track.*

On top of all of that, standing naked in front of a mirror can feel psychopathically depressing — the cottage-cheese tummy, the horrifically saggy thighs, the swollen breasts, blistered nipples, your still rounded face, thick fingers and puffy feet — it all looks irreparable. You are leaking milk, blood, urine, sweat and tears! But amazingly, nearly all of this is self-repairing. *It's all very normal, it's all fine . . . you're on track still.*

I suggest starting motherhood with the attitude that you are not anticipating being able to get your day organised at all in the very early weeks — then everything you *do* manage to get done is a great bonus! Here's a new Golden Rule for this fourth trimester: *Only do things that make you happy.* This life is so new to both you and your baby. So rid yourself of any expectations of being the confident superhuman Supermum straight away — instead, embrace being extraordinarily ordinary! Take the phone off the hook if it's causing you stress, ignore secondary household chores and if any impending visitors are thoughtful enough to offer to bring your dinner with them, then reply 'Yes please!' Make the mental decision *not* to overwork. *Just relax, it'll make you feel more normal, everything is fine . . . you're on track.*

You're knackered, and exhaustion can switch off any person's happy mode. Perhaps you're irked because you already detest wearing the 'kangaroo care' earth-mother baby-sling all day — you thought you'd love it, but you're already loathing it! Or perhaps you find your mind daydreaming about some wonderful nanny coming to take over? Are you feeling crippling embarrassment and shame deep inside, because sometimes you find yourself wondering if you even did the right thing by deciding to become a mother? Such guilt-laden self-recrimination! In fact your conscious mind seems to have mutated into a jumbled screw-up, littered with guilt, guilt and more guilt! *That is so normal, you are still fine . . . and still right on track!*

Welcome to the fourth and final trimester.

So much to do, so little time but — lie down with your feet elevated

Midwife and writer Sheila Kitzinger puts it so well: 'The birth was great! But looking after a baby twenty-four hours a day seven days a week is hard labour.' So true.

However, after nine months of pregnancy and giving birth, it is really important, in the first six weeks, to try to spend more time lying down than standing up — and sit as much as you can too, to avoid standing. Rest is paramount. And when you lie down, try having your feet raised higher than your head — it's a very good position to recoup in. Know too that several short strolls are significantly more advisable than one long walk. Carrying anything heavier than your baby is also not a great idea.

This is wise advice for the first three to six months postpartum. Apart from your healing uterus (and other body parts), after childbirth your body is also ultra-sensitive to your blood's insulin levels, which can result in making you feel weak, with reduced energy. Listen to your healing body. If you don't, you'll probably get a headache or migraine . . . or even sicker.

With our first baby I started early contractions on the Monday night, and had no sleep that night. We went into hospital the next day, and at 9 pm on the Tuesday night my waters were broken to move things along (which they certainly did). Then in just three hours, by midnight, I was fully dilatated, and ready to start pushing. Joy of joys I thought we were on the home straight. After four hours of pushing, I resigned myself to the reality that I was not able to get my now transverse baby out without help, and at 4 am on the Wednesday morning, she was born by forceps delivery.

By the time we were settled into the postnatal ward it was mid-Wednesday morning. There was absolutely no possibility of sleep during that day in my shared room with all the crying babies, talking mothers, laughing visitors, nurses and midwives coming and going, and coming and going.

Finally on the Wednesday night, after having been awake since Monday morning and having been in latent labour for 24 hours, and active labour for 7–8 hours, and recovering from a spinal block and full episiotomy, it was now dark, the curtains were pulled across, it was quiet and it was officially time to sleep . . . until the first baby in our room woke . . . back to sleep again . . . oh, awake again, it's my baby's turn, she won't settle, time to pace up and down the ward aisle so my roomies can sleep . . . back to sleep again . . . woken up again (the sun's coming up, oh God, save me). And the next couple of nights, at that particular hospital, were no improvement.

So when I arrived home on the Saturday at lunchtime, just in time for the baby blues and engorgement, I had enjoyed (?) the gigantic total of 20 hours' sleep in six days, and still had a very tender fanny and excruciatingly sore nipples. So can you guess what happened by the next night? I got *sick* . . . sick with a bad cold.

Almost two years later, a month after our *second* daughter was born, with a 23-month-old also in tow, I came down with full-blown influenza (that's right, not a cold, but the genuine, think-you're-dying flu), and was bedridden — oh except for mothering a toddler and a newborn of course. That's when motherhood is no bed of roses — more like a garbage heap of prickles and thorns — a definite low-point on the When-Motherhood-Sucks-The-Most rating-scale.

With my third baby, I went into labour late on a Friday night, giving birth within two hours (it can be done with a third) in the wee hours of the Saturday morning, and came home from the hospital on the Sunday. My husband took the Monday off work (the joys of self-employment) to take the girls to gymnastics in the morning; my mum took the girls to pre-school and crèche on Tuesday morning; and by 9.30 the next morning I was breast-feeding my newborn at one daughter's toddler ballet class after having dropped the other daughter off to pre-school. Quite ridiculous really.

Six weeks later I didn't feel as if a bus had backed over me: I felt as if a *train* had driven over me with 20 carriages. I would have been so much wiser to have asked someone else to take my four year old to pre-school, and have since realised that it is not essential a 2½ year old attends all her ballet lessons!

I can give you endless other stories from many girlfriends, as to the myriad illnesses they endured with a newborn, primarily because they were so bloody worn out. Heed what Vicki Iovine wrote in her *Girlfriend's Guide to Surviving the First Year of Motherhood*: 'Don't stand when you can sit, don't sit when you can lie down and don't stay awake when you can sleep . . . If you don't get some rest, you stand a very good chance of getting sick.'

Author Tracy Hogg advocates new mums send themselves to bed from 2–5 pm every day or, if they can't manage that, to take at least three one-hour naps every day during the first six weeks, for rejuvenating rest (not chatting on the phone or writing thank-you notes). 'You can't give 100 percent if you're only operating with 50 percent of the sleep that you need. Even if you have help, even if you don't feel tired, you have this huge wound inside you. If you don't get enough rest, I guarantee that six weeks later you'll feel as if a bus hit you. However don't let me be the one to say I told you so.'

Regardless of how many days you stay in hospital, probably by the second, third or fourth day at *home*, it is normal to arrive at an all-time low.

Answerphone

It's a great idea to change your answerphone message so it can eliminate 'unnecessary' calls — 'Hi, thanks for ringing Jack and Jill. Jill's busy with our new son Joey at the moment, or having a rest (midwife's orders). Joey was born on the 17th weighing 7½ lbs. We're all doing great, and we'd love to catch up with you soon. Please ring back later, in the mornings is best. Cheers.'

Visitors

I know that you may have heard advice regarding post-birth visitors such as: don't fret about how tidy your house is; limit the visitor's length of stay; ask them to prepare their own tea or coffee; or never wake a sleeping baby for a visitor to hold. And this is all really great forthright advice.

But I also know that, depending on the visitor and the relationship you have with them, sometimes being so frank could make you far more uncomfortable than tolerating Aunty Mildred loudly cooing at your son as she sips on her third cup of tea.

Remember, young babies can be very flexible, so try to go with the flow, and try to lose any new-mother intensity that has crept inside you. Just chill out and relax, there is no hurry. Receiving visitors at home as a new mother can be some very proud moments you'll remember for the rest of your life . . . enjoy them!

'Placenta brain' — postpartum dementia and amnesia

I remember my dear friend Tracey exclaiming to me once, 'I'm sure I delivered half my brain with the placenta!' But as she had her first baby a year before me, it took me a year to truly understand what she meant.

If you thought your memory had deteriorated in your last trimester before having your baby — let me tell you, it can be major 'space cadet' brain-obliterated time now. Thanks to those massive biochemical transformations you can find yourself in a naturally altered state. It's Mother Nature's way of forcing you to concentrate on one thing: your baby. It's also your cue to simplify your life — if you can't remember what you were supposed to do that day, well you won't be stressing out about it, will you!

I remember, as a new mother, freaking out into an instant cold-sweat when I realised I hadn't felt my baby kick all day — because I'd forgotten that I'd already given birth. I also remember Tracey ringing me with great excitement one day when her second child was crawling, saying 'It's back! I've got my brain back again!' And it can be like that . . . one day, you realise the fog has lifted.

Every new mother will experience her postnatal absentmindedness in a slightly different out-to-lunch way. How is it that I, once a high-pressure executive, am able to forget something as critical as needing to buy more nappies or more milk (or worse, more petrol) while I'm out?

I learnt, for me anyway, that it was a silly idea to try to fill my head with lots of important lists because, often as not, I'd forget. One of my solutions was to write everything down in my appointment calendar. It does scare me a little, the number of probably quite important things I've completely forgotten over time (to even write down that is), but as I can't remember what they are — well, *bugger*.

Another thing that I found worked, for my sieve of a brain, was never to go to the shops without a written list. Otherwise I could park the car, know for sure that there were three different things I went to buy, but two of them have utterly vanished. And . . . *always* put the car keys down in the *same place* at home.

Another thing I lost, especially after the birth of our third baby, was a huge portion of my adult vocabulary. I distinctly remember a family gathering when our third baby was 2½ months old — if I hadn't met me before, I am sure I would have felt sorry for that poor little housewife who was struggling to join in with the most ordinary of general conversations: 'She's nice but a bit thick' I would have thought.

It is like being lost inside a cloud, unable to comprehend why everyone else seems to be on a different planet. It's as if they're talking a foreign language, and when you try to communicate with them you can never retrieve the words you want from your memory bank, and you can't remember a big chunk of the local lingo anymore . . . especially nouns!

I am truly in awe of women who successfully manage to go back to work-mode quickly after giving birth. My formerly razor-sharp brain is only now starting to return to something close to its pre-pregnancy capability. And it seems from all the girlfriends I have asked, that so long as there are young children in the house, your brain's sharp-focus lens remains misplaced, and sometimes it's lost for good.

I also remember (between pregnancies when my cognitive abilities and short-term memory were partially functional again), hearing of a newspaper article in which British (I think, but can't remember) researchers had made the astounding discovery that a woman's brain temporarily shrinks about 3 percent of its volume from about her last trimester, through to when the newborn is around 6–9 months old (eek) — so for those of you still unable to add, that totals almost a year!

Advice overload pending! Don't compare — don't despair

You are now likely, even more than in pregnancy, to receive an onslaught of people's well-meaning, but unsolicited *advice* (which by the way, continues for *years*). It will vary from old-fashioned out-dated practices, to academic theory, to nit-picking criticising, to the fervour of 'born-again evangelical' parenting 'experts'.

I agree wholeheartedly with what Dr Christopher Green wrote in *Babies!*, 'The very best care you can give is to love, enjoy and have fun with your children and then do what feels right and works for you. If this does not happen to coincide with what other people tell you, then just ignore them . . . When the going gets tough, advice should only be accepted from friends and family who offer to roll up their sleeves and help.'

It can be a wise idea to have a simple pre-planned tactic to deal with the common frustration of unwanted advice. Tracy Hogg suggests a standard reply such as 'Wow, that's really interesting — it sounds like it really worked for your family' while in your head you're saying 'I'm going to do it my way'.

Or you could try the technique my charming friend Anna uses when she receives unwanted advice, with her standard reply 'A-ha, mmmmm, yip, mmmm' (while saying to herself 'Stuff that idea').

Isolation — I'm so flippin' lonely

After your busy stay in hospital, followed by the whirlwind barrage of visitors at home, you can suddenly feel as if the isolation is suffocating you, drowning you, devouring you, utterly destroying your confidence and shredding your identity. This can be especially true for a previously respected, independently minded, successful career woman who perhaps worked up to the last hours before delivery.

Your new tiny 'boss' can be overwhelming you with his demands. He can seem to treat you like a cross between an unpaid nanny and a slave, and give you no positive feedback for all those sacrifices you are making — you have to wait a month or two for just one teeny-weeny maybe-smile!

I remember someone saying to me when I was overdue with my first baby 'They're easier in than out' and sometimes with a newborn you can find yourself wishing to return to the haven and simplicity of being pregnant, a kind of longing to rub that bellyful of baby again while enjoying a leisurely shower.

While pregnant you may have often been the centre of attention. In a way, pregnancy gave you some extra (perhaps even glamourous) status. You also had pampering prenatal attention medically, and at delivery you were the centre of the universe. But since the birth it seems everyone — medical staff, family, friends, your partner — seems way more interested in the baby than you. So little attention — right when you need it the most.

So, in the second or third week of motherhood you may be feeling totally isolated, cooped up at home, and abandoned by society . . . and so awfully ordinary.

If you have been feeling this way, then know you are not alone, truly. Most modern mums have some feelings like this at the start. But the hard reality is that only you can remedy this.

Here are some therapeutic self-help fixes for those first few weeks:

- Rest more, afternoon siestas at least — make shut-eye a priority until you are feeling human again. Tired mums are ratty mums.
- To avoid the 'crazy out-of-control' feelings triggered by transient hypoglycaemia (low blood sugar), eat some protein and complex carbohydrates every 3–4 hours, e.g. grains, fruit, veggies and legumes (peas, beans).
- Ring a friend or invite a friend over for a sanity-saving conversation (experienced mothers only).
- Get the pram or front-pack out and enjoy a 15–20 minute stroll. Enjoy the fresh air in a wide-open space.
- Join a mums' coffee group through Plunket or Parents Centre or similar. Or organise your first antenatal class reunion with the other new mums and mums-to-be and start a regular coffee group. This can be a great way to casually but effectively discuss many of the common concerns mother-hood brings.
- Book in to attend a new parenting course through the hospital or Parents Centre or similar.
- Book to spend the day at your local Plunket Family Centre watching their mothering videos, and being pampered with pots of tea and fresh muffins.
- Drop your baby off to a girlfriend so you can do a few errands peacefully and relish some shopping-alone-time.
- Do some babysitting-swapping, shopping or swimming with a girlfriend — go out together and take turns at watching the kids.
- Put your baby into a gym crèche for an hour or so and go for a sauna and spa to recharge your batteries (forget the work-out for now).
- Once you are up in the morning, get yourself dressed *as soon as you can* (not in any clothes that require ironing of course), and put on a bit of lippy and a squirt of perfume *before* starting any dishes or washing or housework — before a shower even, if necessary — it will make you feel much less bedraggled. Your entire morning can feel a lot more productive, and you will have a much more positive day.
- Accept that most of the feelings that you can't cope with a weekend social-life are psychological. Newborns can be amazingly portable. But *don't* feel pressured — move life along at your own new (slower) pace.

There are lots of ways to improve your mindset, so if you don't like feeling isolated you *do* need to remedy the problem *yourself*. Recognise that you are being driven to your limit before you reach a total meltdown — even if it's telling a close friend, your mum, LMC or Plunket that you need some help to remedy the problem. Getting out of the house once a day does particularly great things to help lift the spirits and to normalise your new life.

It is common for women to feel that with gaining a baby they have lost their personal identity. But you have not lost your identity — you simply have a new identity. Were you previously a high-flying power-woman thriving in a prestigious career? Oh man, you really could be in trouble now . . . 'How hard can it be?' you'd thought. But now, something the weight of a few blocks of cheese has turned your super-organised life into utter disarray — and it seems to be getting worse! Young (20-something) mums can have an easier time adjusting to going with the flow of mothering a newborn than power mums.

The aspect that can be hardest to swallow is that this new identity of motherhood doesn't seem to have the same level of grandeur attached to it — because almost any female can become a mother without any kind of career commitment or tertiary degree. It is a self-esteem–ego issue.

Only you can eventually come to terms with your new self-image, and realise that the sole-charge responsibilities created by your promotion to motherhood are the most important work roles on the planet. You *will* eventually receive dividends, as your babies grow to become wonderful children — there is a business term for this: 'delayed gratification'.

Know that taking care of yourself is taking care of your baby

In the first chapter, I mentioned the importance of making preparations for looking after *yourself* postpartum. When the human body endures ongoing physical pain it can incite debilitating asthenia (a fatigue that makes the body feel weak, thus forcing it to rest for healing).

Have you organised those rejuvenating remedies yet? Or have you forgotten, been too busy, haven't got around to it yet? Important things to do now for your own rapid physical recovery include:

- Taking a daily comprehensive multivitamin and mineral supplement designed for lactating mothers — and having low coffee and tea intake, because they neutralise some nutrients.
- Visiting an osteopath, chiropractor, physiotherapist or masseuse who is experienced in maternity care in the first 6–8 weeks postpartum, to put things back into place. This is especially important if you have been left with a sore tail-bone or backache, which can be extremely debilitating. Help avoid the permanent wrinkles of a furrowed brow:

get your body sorted.

- There are also many herbal formulations, herbal teas and flower-essence remedies which can be hugely beneficial. (An excellent reference for this is the Naish and Roberts book *The Natural Way to Better Birth and Bonding*, and see pages 142, 377 and 393 of this book.)

Pelvic floor exercises (Kegels)

During pregnancy, hormones caused the pelvic-floor muscles to relax, then during delivery they were rigidly stretched and received rather a battering.

In the distant past it used to be relatively common for the delivering doctor to sew an extra stitch in the perineum, appallingly nicknamed the husband's knot, to combat a slackened pelvic floor and restore the vaginal opening to a virginal size (improving the husband's sexual pleasure). But this violation did not remedy a weak pelvic floor, and in fact could cause lifelong discomfort or sexual pain for the woman.

Known as Kegels, 'elevators' or 'exercises for the Yoni' (the Sanskrit word for the sacred temple we call the vagina), pelvic-floor exercises are the correct postpartum remedy to prevent: urinary sphincter incontinence (such as peeing when you cough, sneeze, jump or jog); urinary frequency (having to pee a lot); flaccidity (weakened vaginal muscles affecting sexual enjoyment, or your tampon falling out); and to tone up the anal sphincter muscle (to make you your old self at pooing). (See page 51 for exercise instructions.)

After childbirth, the delicate sensitivity within your genitals can feel numbed, and physiologically it actually is for a while. Within say 7–10 days of childbirth it is a very wise idea, even if your vaginal delivery ended in a caesar, to re-start your pelvic-floor exercises — the increased blood supply to the area through exercise is also very beneficial for healing.

If, three weeks after childbirth, you can stop your urine flow mid-stream (but don't do this too regularly because it can damage your bladder), or hold a Kegels contraction for 3–4 seconds, then you're on track and doing really well. It can easily take several months to restore things to their former strength.

But no other serious exercise workouts please until you know your pelvic floor is well recovered. In fact it is certainly profound advice to do pelvic-floor exercises for 5–10 minutes every day for the rest of your life. These days I try to remember to do one every time I open the fridge, and every time I'm stopped at a red light. No one ever knew — till now. Copy my habit or come up with your own system.

Your husband will appreciate it (and you will too) because when those particular muscles are toned, you will enjoy more responsive, vivid and pleasurable orgasms!

Body-toning exercise and diet time, right?

For the first week or two after childbirth the only exercises you should be doing are cleansing breaths (in through the nose, out through the mouth); Kegels (pelvic-floor toning); gentle walking; and rotating your ankles. *That's all!*

In fact with all those hormonally softened ligaments, there is a massive pile of medical evidence confirming that it is not a wise idea to start back on any *serious* exercise regime within the *first three months* postpartum — and absolutely *no* using exercise equipment such as weight-training or serious aerobic activity within the first six weeks.

This is one time in your life when you need to *stop* thinking about toning your own body (and those addictive endorphin hits) — just for a short time. If your personal gym instructor is telling you it's fine to be straight back into your tough exercise regimes postnatally, perhaps it may pay to seek a second professional opinion. Gentle exercising such as walking and swimming is preferable.

As for dieting, it can be rather pointless in the first three months, because during pregnancy your digestive tract became far more absorbent than it usually is (which is partly why pregnant women are always hungry); and it takes several months after birth for it to return to normal. So, no serious dieting for the first months, *especially* if you're breastfeeding.

I know how those women's magazines are rife with celebrities who are praised for regaining their former figures within months of birth, or condemned for taking too long. But that is not as nature intended. Know in your heart that you are being more sensible, more level-headed and a stronger woman by allowing Mother Nature to take her time — instead of letting social expectations decide what is best for you and your body.

Split abdomen muscles (diastasis recti)

Sometimes in the second half of pregnancy or during delivery, the left and right rectus abdominis (front abdominal) muscles which are normally joined by a fibrous strip, after stretching from their normal, say, 33-cm to about 50-cm length, can painlessly (and unpreventably) separate like a zip down the middle — in other words your tummy's 'eight-pack' is now two 4-packs!

To check for diastasis recti, 4–7 days after delivery (your LMC should be checking as well), lie on your back with your knees bent and feet flat on the floor. Tuck your chin towards your chest, and slowly lift your head (and shoulders slightly) pressing your lower back into the floor. Now, place your fingertips in the middle of your abdomen just above your belly-button. If you

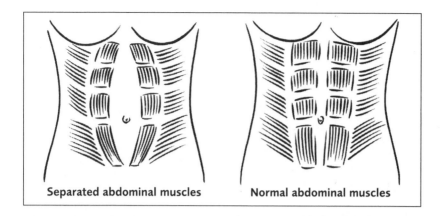

Separated abdominal muscles   **Normal abdominal muscles**

feel a soft pulpy gap between the muscles of more than two fingers width, then you probably have split recti muscles.

The following gentle exercise is designed to correct this over a couple of weeks: Lie down on the floor on your back with your knees bent. Cross your arms over your tummy. Breathe in, and then slowly breathe out raising your head slightly off the floor. At the same time use your hands to *pull* the two recti abdominal muscles towards each other. This encourages the recti back together.

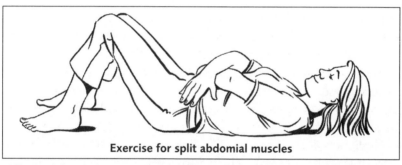

Exercise for split abdomial muscles

During the time your recti are split, exercise may need to be professionally modified (and definitely no sit-ups). If the condition persists past a couple of months postpartum, or if the gap widens, then see your doctor; occasionally surgery may be necessary to mend the muscles.

Vaginal thrush yeast infection (Candida albicans)

Few women would experience having a baby, and not also know first-hand the displeasure of the itching, burning and cottage-cheese curd-like discharge caused by vaginal thrush. However, thrush does not like an acidic environment, so an old-fashioned remedy is to douche two to four times a day for about a week with diluted cider vinegar (1:5 solution).

Aloe vera gel is a soothing ointment for sore vagina lips, or the gel on a peeled aloe vera leaf inserted as a vaginal suppository is great to combat against vaginal yeast infections. The other option of course, if the thrush is causing you major unnecessary stress, is an antifungal thrush treatment prescription from your doctor, or the oral capsules available from pharmacies.

When suffering with thrush, it also pays to reduce your refined sugar intake, eat a generous quantity of unsweetened live-culture yoghurt (e.g. acidophilus, bifidobacteria or probiotics) — and remember to wear cotton undies, not nylon. (See page 186 for maternal nipple and infant oral thrush yeast infections.)

Dysuria: difficult or painful frequent urination

During pregnancy the uterus squashes the ureters (slender 30–35 cm tubes from kidneys to bladder), causing distensions (swelling) of the upper urinary tract and impairing draining. This predisposes the kidneys to infection. Add to the equation the physical strain of birthing; a distended (stretched) bladder and urethral sphincters (rings of muscle that keep the urethra closed); a bruised urethra tube; perhaps use of a catheter up the urethra during delivery; general tiredness and less resistant immune defence system, and — hey presto — you could be lining yourself up for a urinary tract, urethra or bladder infection, such as cystitis or urethritis.

If you start getting painful abdominal aches or a lower backache (maybe just on one side) and perhaps headaches; or have red, murky, cloudy, dark-coloured or blood-tinged urine; painful burning stinging urine; or you are frequently wanting to urgently pee perhaps with little result; and perhaps experience a rise in temperature, then it's time to touch base with your LMC or doctor, quickly.

Alkalinising drinks such as Ural™, Citravescent™ and Uriclense™ can be of great benefit. Drinking cranberry juice is also excellent as a remedy and preventative.

A phenomenal one-quarter of the body's total blood supply passes through the kidneys every minute to maintain the purity and chemical balance of circulating blood. So don't be slack on treating cystitis (bladder infection): if left untreated it can lead to the far more serious pyelitis or pyelonephritis (inflamed kidney bacterial infection).

Postpartum anaemia

A good chunk of women are already anaemic by the end of their pregnancy, and if you suffered a higher-than-average blood loss at delivery (say more than 500 ml) you are probably anaemic, with low iron stores and lowered resistance to infection.

Symptoms of postpartum anaemia are: feeling weak, fatigued, excessively tired, impatient, listless or constantly irritable. If anaemia is severe you may look pale and ashen, notice heart palpitations (irregular rapid beats), be breathless, or feel faint when you get to your feet. If in doubt, you can have your iron levels checked by a blood-test. If treatment is required, a follow-up check to see that the treatment goal has been achieved will be needed.

There is quite a lot you can do for yourself, such as taking a ferrous gluconate iron supplement. Another good idea is to take an iron supplement with vitamin C (to aid assimilation). Other popular iron options include blackstrap molasses, Floradix™ and Ferrograd-C™. Folate (folic acid) with a complex vitamin B supplement (especially B12) can also be helpful; and reducing caffeine and tannin consumption (e.g. tea and coffee), because they inhibit iron absorption. Another important thing to do (and sometimes it's the hardest) is *rest*.

Apart from those pro-active actions, a diet rich in iron is a sensible idea, the richest source being lean red meat. Other iron-rich foods include seaweed, spinach, avocados, all dark green vegetables, prunes, apricots, other dried fruit, beans, nuts, peas, lentils, wholemeal bread, egg yolk and alfalfa sprouts. The homeopathic remedy China is also a traditional complementary remedy.

All in all, it is a time to ask for extra help around the home to ease your workload — I know, for some of you independent, self-sufficient women, it goes against your customary 'work ethic', but you're in a new job now and still in a convalescing condition.

Puerperal sepsis (Postpartum uterine infection)

If your bleeding is still heavy after 10 days, bleeding becomes heavier, or it changes back to bright red, this indicates the placental wound is not healing properly, and you need to talk with your LMC or doctor promptly. There is always a small risk of secondary haemorrhaging occurring even some weeks after delivery, especially if there was a retained fragment of the placenta, and/or if an infection develops in the lining of the uterus.

A high temperature, cold sweats, shivering, acute stomach pains (tenderness often just on one side), lower back pains and/or unpleasantly foul-smelling lochia are all strong signs that small remnants of the placenta remain in the uterus and/or there is a uterine infection. This is a serious problem that requires medical attention, including antibiotics. (If there are the same symptoms without uterine pain, this could indicate a general infection, such as within suturing.) Either way, see your LMC or doctor straight away.

Before antibiotics this serious post-delivery uterine infection was known as Childbed Fever or Puerperal Fever, and it was a leading cause of female deaths right up until World War II.

If you do require antibiotics, it is always a sensible idea to consume acidophilus and bifidus yoghurt at the same time and afterwards, to help to maintain the body's natural, intestinal, bacterial flora.

D and C time?

Occasionally for a few women small pieces of placenta or amniotic sac membrane may have been, unknowingly, left inside the uterus. If they don't get discharged naturally within the first couple of days after delivery (usually as part of a blood clot), they are highly likely to cause haemorrhaging or infection, which before modern medicine was usually fatal. Today one remedy is a D and C (dilatation and curettage).

This is a surgical procedure (performed under general anaesthetic). The surgeon expands your cervix opening with an instrument called a dilatator, then the uterine lining is scraped to remove tissue with a curette (scoop- or spoon-shaped surgical instrument). It's not the most pleasant of processes, but it can act as an almost 'instant' cure.

Coccydynia (tailbone pain)

The coccyx (or tailbone) is the last 3–5 (usually 4) spinal vertebrae fused together to form a bony triangular point. Apart from injuring the tailbone from falling on your bottom, childbirth is the next most common cause of coccydynia (pain in the tailbone).

Dependent on the damage, pain can vary, especially when sitting, from slight discomfort to a constant chronic pain not dissimilar to being impaled on an arrow! It can sometimes take a long time to come right, but usually it eventually does — at least to a point of being tolerable.

When the pain is severe or persistent, sustained relief may be provided from a corticosteroid injection(s) — cortisone as a numbing agent, and the steroid as an anti-inflammatory to allow more rapid healing.

Some experts and patients swear that manipulation or mobilisation (e.g. massage, stretching, ultrasound therapy or anal repositioning of the tailbone) does not help, and can even hinder recovery. Other experts and patients swear by receiving relief through the likes of a chiropractor or osteopath.

In rare, extreme, situations, there is the surgical treatment of a coccygectomy (removal of the coccyx tailbone). The operation is a relatively simple one, particularly as there are no major nerve roots in that region of the spine. However, full recovery can take many months, there are infection risks due to the surgery being so close to the anal rectum, and there are question marks as to how much being without a tailbone affects the pelvic floor — but most patients find the pain is eventually substantially reduced or completely eliminated after surgery.

Postpartum hyperthyroidism (thyroiditis) and postpartum hypothyroidism (myxoedema)

The thyroid gland controls the body's metabolism: primarily the rate at which every cell in the body maintains its heat and receives its continuous supply of chemical energy to power its activities (e.g. burning glucose).

Sometimes the thyroid can become under-active in the year following childbirth (called postpartum hypothyroidism). It can be difficult to diagnose and it is often dismissed as normal maternal tiredness, because the symptoms of this slowed metabolism are physical sluggishness and mental dullness. Other signs can include a puffy face, forgetfulness, low body temperature, dry skin, weight gain, poor muscle tone (weakness, aching), exhaustion and fatigue. Sometimes it is mistakenly treated as postnatal depression. However, a blood test provides a quick diagnosis.

For about three-quarters of sufferers the replacement hormone thyroxine will be needed for only a short time, until the mother's own glandular production normalises. For the other quarter of sufferers, blood tests will indicate that they may require thyroxine for life. But either way, the treatment is positively life enhancing, as it helps the body to restore itself to a healthy balanced state, making childcare and life in general much easier (and it does not affect breastfeeding).

Sometimes the thyroid may initially become overactive (called hyperthyroidism). Symptoms can include a firm, swollen, tender neck, tremors, heart palpitations (strong heartbeats you feel), a sharp loss of weight, feeling hot, nervous, agitated and a general inability to sleep or relax. Symptoms then change to a slowed metabolic rate resulting in mental and physical sluggishness, as for hypothyroidism.

Note: Without iodine the thyroid cannot function effectively and people develop an enlarged thyroid named goitre. To combat this most salt in the West is now iodised, so goitres have become rare in the developed world.

Postpartum zinc deficiency

When a person's body is deficient in zinc it can show itself in their behaviour — they may become irritable, aggressive and angry, hyperactive and/or depressed. Other symptoms of zinc deficiency are a reduced sensitivity to taste, acne pimples and slow skin healing. Treatment of zinc deficiency can take months to recover from, or may require life-long remedies.

However, too much zinc can be as bad as too little zinc — so around 15–50 mg daily is usually the recommended dose. Zinc can positively assist to lower oestrogen levels while increasing progesterone, and help to improve the immune system and build strong bones.

Zinc-rich foods include ginger, potatoes, garlic, carrots, whole grains, mushrooms, beans, seafood, meat and green vegetables such as broccoli, watercress and spinach.

A particularly great source of information on the importance of adequate zinc levels in new mothers can be found in the Naish and Roberts *The Natural Way* series of books and their *In The Zone* diet plan.

To paraphrase Naish and Roberts: zinc is involved in over 200 enzyme systems in the body and has extremely important functions in the period immediately following birth, and during the whole period of breastfeeding. Adequate zinc levels battle postnatal depression, protect against cracked nipples, promote contented babies and are fundamentally important for the glandular secretions involved with instinctual maternal behaviour.

Your spine commands respect

It is up to you to treat your back with great respect, particularly during the first two to three months after childbirth — to avoid being left with a life-long problem. Your back is very vulnerable while it recovers from the lower-back strains caused by the frontal weight of pregnancy; the ligament-relaxing pregnancy hormones; the physiological experience of giving birth; and the abdomen weakened from caesarean surgery.

So lift weights, especially your baby, by bending at the knees — 'cause that baby will just grow heavier. Don't use your back like a crane.

The two-month whammy

It is quite common for mums to have another major energy crash at about 8–10 weeks after birth, so watch out for the 'bus that backs around the corner to mow you down'. Sometimes you can see it coming, but most times you've been run down before you know it, and you aren't quite sure what hit you.

This is a physical manifestation of your accumulated lack of sleep — but it can affect you emotionally because you are mentally fragile and vulnerable. Ration how you're choosing to spend your energy reserves, and learn to respect that they are limited. Sweet precious girlfriend, things *do* get better.

(This topic is covered in great detail later in the book.)

Summing it all up!

Try not to freak out too much about the whole physiological postpartum package. You may be starting to question whether your body will ever be the same; you may be wondering if those baggy maternity undies will ever stop feeling more comfortable than your pre-pregnancy G-strings, or if your feet will ever comfortably fit your pre-pregnancy shoes again. If you are breastfeeding, you might be starting to count down to the time when you can again eat and drink whatever you want again.

Sorry, your body won't ever be exactly the same as pre-motherhood, but it can return to a normal enough state for you to probably consider having another baby in the future. Hard to imagine right now? Lots of us do it, more than twice too. *You will be fine*, just give it time.

Welcome home to the witching hour, Dad

Dear New Dad

Across the entire planet around 4.30–6.30 pm, it seems nearly all households with babies, toddlers or small children find that things go a bit crazy. Babies' senses become overloaded and they get irritable, clingy and want extra feeds. Toddlers go crazy. Pre-schoolers have berko meltdowns. And young schoolchildren plain lose the plot. Once the first baby arrives, and with siblings usually following, this Hell Hour can continue for years. *So please be aware that after having a baby, arriving home from work may not be a peaceful event for you for quite some time.*

Arsenic hour is also the time of day when Mum is at the end of her tether, and needs help because she's now overwhelmingly tired. She feels as if she's achieved almost nothing all day, and is crabby and frazzled by trying to get dinner and bathtime organised while wearing a blouse wet with baby spew.

So, New Dad, please *accept* that for some time to come you won't be the centre of attention when you arrive home, and instead support your partner in the joint venture — your family.

The big plus for you is that in the not too distant future you *will* be the centre of attention when you arrive home, as your little one starts yelling out excitedly 'Daddy's home! Daddy's home!' and it will ALL have been so worth it.

Every aspect of a marital relationship goes through a rugged metamorphosis after the birth of a first child — more on this in chapter 8. But for the meantime, author Tracy Hogg beautifully explains what most new parents want the other to understand:

SHE WANTS HIM TO KNOW: how much the delivery hurt; how tired she is; how overwhelming breastfeeding is; how much breastfeeding hurts; that she's crying or yelling because she's hormonal, not because of him; and that she can't explain why she's crying.

HE WANTS HER TO KNOW: criticising everything he does doesn't help; that the baby isn't made out of china and won't break; that he's doing his best; that it hurts him when she dismisses his ideas about the baby; that he's feeling more pressure now to provide for his new family; and that he's depressed and overwhelmed, too.

Dear new Dad, here are some great things you can do to help
- Tell her you love her, and show her you love her.
- Listen without having a solution (support her without comment).
- Don't take 'No' for an answer when she says she doesn't want your help, do chores without being asked (e.g. shopping, cleaning, laundry, vacuuming).
- Generously give her the time and space to come to terms with her new life, she has good reasons not to feel like her usual self.
- Don't try to fix her problems (just ride them out).
- Don't be a patronising cheerleader.
- Don't stand over her with criticisms.
- Don't wonder aloud where things are kept (pay more attention or use your noggin).
- Don't phone from the supermarket with questions (just work it out for yourself)!

> **Note:**
>
> No rough-play yet, Dad, with a small baby — it can unintentionally cause brain-damage equivalent to shaking a baby. Your baby will love rough-play when he/she's a one-year-old toddler, not before.

Welcome home, darling Baby

Happily, what is needed is not any special or expensive equipment or endeavour. Talking, singing and reading to children, encouraging and endorsing their emerging skills, caressing, cuddling and playing with them are some of the ingredients required to build their brains. … Of all this flood of sensory experiences, positive physical touch is the most vital.

Learning is, quite obviously, founded on memory … It is the depth and power of human memory that has allowed humans to dominate all other species.

Dr Robin Fancourt — *Brainy Babies*

It is thought by scientists that the babies of prehistoric man developed in the womb for more like a year before being born. However, combining the increasing human brain size, and the effects that walking upright had on the pelvis, babies needed to be born earlier. So the human baby is one of the most helpless and defenceless of baby mammals — in many ways it has to finish its gestation outside its mother's womb.

In a few months time, when you have seen what a tremendous developmental difference there is between a brand new full-term baby with its downy head, and a robust three-month-old infant with its smooth head movements and responding smile, you too will probably agree that human babies are born 'too early'.

Did you know that the adult brain requires 20 percent of our body's total oxygen and calorie supply, but in babies it is an astronomical 50 percent? As so well explained in Dr Robin Fancourt's book *Brainy Babies,* a newborn's brain is quite spectacular as it is already two-thirds the size of an adult's, and it already contains almost all the neuron cells it will ever have: one hundred billion brain cells, with their axons wrapped by 10 times as many myelin cells that nurture and protect them like 'the bubble-wrapping of a parcel'. But, unlike the newborn's other organs, the majority of their brain cells are still immature, i.e. most of their brain's neurons are not as yet performing their ultimate functions, as they are not yet fully myelinated or connected to communicate with other brain cells.

Through the baby's daily sensory experiences, their neurons gain phenomenal growths of randomly linked pathways and networks. The average eight-month-old has already created 500 million brain-cell connections, and by age two a toddler has 1000 trillion connections. This is twice as many as adults have, and their brains are twice as active. At age three, the pre-schooler has a brain $2^1/2$ times as active as an adult's, and their brain will remain at this level until they are around 10 years old.

Then, gradual pruning of these pathways occurs with so that, by late adolescence, the brain's ability to adapt has declined, but its power to display particular talents has increased. By age 18 the child has reached the adult level of 500 million connections.

General development

What is 'normal'?
'Normal' is a cycle in the washing machine!

Author Unknown

Human development starts from the head down (e.g. babies can see and hear before they can stand); and from the centre of the body outwards (e.g. they can control arms before controlling fingers). And all those glorious milestones like smiling, sitting-up, crawling, walking, first words and teeth are truly exciting.

At the end of this book is a General Development Guide (Appendix A, page 452), that runs through the weeks and months of the first two years or so. It is a list of what you can *generally* expect your baby to be doing as she grows, along with some play ideas and other comments.

However, many infants will excel in certain areas and be slower in other areas. This is not a sign of their intelligence — but it certainly may be a sign of their personality, interests and natural talents.

Please do not be alarmed if your baby does not do all the things listed within each time-line — a genius often likes to focus more on certain things!

There are lots of books available listing guidelines on infant development, however, few of them ever make mention of a baby's cranky periods, which can very regularly occur just before major neurological (brain) growth developments. These are included in Appendix A (pages 452–464).

Be wary of the Green-Eyed Monster

All babies develop in their own unique way, and you may be surprised by some of the subtle (and not so subtle) comments other parents make! 'Your six-month-old Juliet isn't sitting-up on her own yet? Oh my Romeo could do it perfectly at five months old' . . . 'Your fourteen-month-old Jack isn't walking yet? That's a bit slow I think, I know my Jill was walking well before her first birthday'. (It can almost make you feel like you have the only normal child around, because everyone else's is so jolly advanced!) As one mum is quoted as saying in the *Little Treasures* pregnancy and birth magazine: 'Don't worry about other people's comments — if it's not a problem to you, it's not a problem.'

So be aware that some parents can't seem to help themselves from sounding like outright skites — as if their baby is cleverer than yours because of their superior parenting skills!

Why all these exaggerations? We're all just so jolly proud of our babes! The bugger is that some parents will talk of their child in that vain way for the rest of their lives, and we need to learn to ignore such fanciful exhibitionists.

It isn't a race! Achieving milestones is not a competition — there is no deadline.

There are lots of bewildering things that can go on with a very young baby, so listed below to give you peace of mind are some of the more common issues to contend with.

Baby pees and poos

Newborn bladders are very small and their kidneys are unable to concentrate urine for the first couple of months, so in the earliest days young babies can wee up to 30+ times a day. But soon, in the next few weeks, you should expect about 6–12 wet nappies each 24 hours (virtually a nappy change every feed). Frequent wet nappies are normal once the breastmilk is in, and are a good measure of hydration. Infant urine should not be dark, bright yellow, or have a strong smell, because that probably means your baby is dehydrated, which should be treated seriously. (See section on dehydration, page 263.)

After the very early days of newborn meconium-poos, a young breastfed baby may produce 4–8 orangey-yellow poos a day for the rest of their first 1–3 months. It can be quite normal for a breastfed baby's pooing frequency to vary substantially — from nearly every breastfeed, to just once every 1–10 days (if the poo is soft, then the baby doesn't have constipation). It is normal for a bottle-fed baby to have brown smelly poos 1–2 times a day.

With all babies, the occasional 'green' stool (moss-green, or resembling guacamole) is OK too, so long as it's not accompanied by vomiting. However, small, hard, dry poos or consistently green poos can all be strong signs of dehydration. (In case you're wondering 'Why green?', the alkaline liver bile stored in the gallbladder that gets secreted into the small intestine is green.)

By three months, pooing once every 1–2 days is normal for a breastfed baby. Then, by toddler age, a poo once or twice a day is normal — usually huge stinkaroos.

It is normal for babies to vocalise some noises when doing poos (as they haven't yet learnt the social etiquette of not grunting). But if you feel your baby is excessively straining to poo then your wee baby may have a spastic or tight anal sphincter muscle, which it's best to talk to your LMC or doctor about.

Overdressed versus underdressed

Until a newborn is a few weeks old or around 3.5 kgs (8 lbs), whichever is the later, a baby is very vulnerable to rapidly losing heat — so, for example, a newborn should always have booties, a hat, a shawl and perhaps mittens when going out. Try to avoid taking a wee newborn out in the wind — it's really not great for him — but, if it's unavoidable, make sure a hat covers your baby's ears.

After those early weeks with increased fat stores under their skin and around their organs, a baby's body has a slightly better ability to maintain body heat; but not until he is over six months old and is an actively mobile toddler creating lots of muscular body heat, should he be dressed in the same number of layers of clothing as you. A good rule of thumb is to dress your babe in one more layer than you are wearing (e.g. if your arms need sleeves, then your baby also needs a cardy). And babies should always have their feet covered unless it is hot weather.

However, it is more imperative to not *overdress* a baby, because allowing them to overheat is dangerous (being too hot is far more serious for an infant than being too cold). The reality is that it is OK for an infant's hands and feet to be a little cool, so long as their 'core' (torso) temperature is maintained. If you're not sure, feel your baby's neck or back or tummy — it should feel comfortably cosy.

Conjunctivitis: pink-eye (sticky eyes)

It can be common for an infant to have a watery eye, which may be caused by a tear duct that has not fully opened. However, conjunctivitis is also very common in babies because their tiny tear-ducts can block with infection. Conjunctivitis reveals itself as a baby's eye gunked up with yellow discharges that go crusty, and although not serious it is contagious, even from one eye to the other.

The modern remedy is antibiotic drops or ointment. A great homeopathic remedy is oral Hepar-Sulph. Also, a few drops of Mum's breastmilk in baby's eyes is a great idea — it contains natural antibacterial substances, and is totally non-irritating.

Nappy rashes: ammonia dermatitis and Candida albicans

The topic of nappy rash can be a bit of a hornet's nest due to the vast array of remedies available! But normally, if the rash is shiny, red and flat, it is probably a case of **ammonia dermatitis** burns. As a general consensus from my girlfriends and myself, Curash™ baby talc powder or a dust of cornflour is great to sprinkle on where a bit of redness has appeared. Zinc oxide and castor oil is a good protective barrier cream — but don't use it all the time, just overnight, as necessary.

If the nappy rash has turned into red bumpy pimples (or perhaps even with water blister pustules) it is probably the fungal infection **Candida albicans** or **thrush,** which initially thrives in the warm moist skin creases then spreads outwards, creating a red, raw rash. Calendula cream, Hypercal cream, aloe vera gel, health shop antifungal agents and Daktozin™ can be effective on this angry nappy rash.

If using cloth nappies, avoid using harsh detergents or ammonias by washing in a mild soap. And avoid using plastic-lined disposable nappies or plastic over-pants, as these make for a rather sweaty environment.

Weleda™ nappy rash lotion and Naturo Pharm™ Nappymed relief ointment are also useful in both situations.

My personal plea to you is to try the more natural treatments, including homeopathy, before getting into the prescription-only steroid-type medications. But one of the very best and cheapest cures for nappy rash is at least half-an-hour a day of naked time!

Other baby skin things

Often newborns can have **peeling skin** in the first or second week — this is very common particularly on the hands, feet and tummy, especially with overdue babies.

There's the very common seborrhoea called **cradle cap** (also known as scurfy scalp), which is caused by an overactivity of the sebaceous oil glands. It starts as pink, raised patches of skin on the scalp that become a yellow-brown crust resembling a dry, scaly eczema — not pretty at all. You can massage the scalp with a vegetable oil, or baby moisturiser, leaving it for a few hours until shampooing at bath time and then rubbing it with a soft baby hairbrush — or leave the oil in overnight, then comb or gently pick the dry skin off the next day. Or an old-fashioned remedy is a paste of 2 tsp bicarbonate soda and 1 tsp water rubbed on, left for five minutes and washed off with baby shampoo.

Seborrhoeic **dermatitis** can occur in the creases under the neck or top of the legs or under the arms — or as a red rash on the face. It usually starts to improve at a month old, and is normally gone by a year old — although a good homeopath could probably eradicate it sooner. Certainly it could be wise to avoid the cortisone-like steroid medications as your first option.

Erythema toxicum, nicknamed **hormone pimples**, are the very common tiny, red, pinhead, flat pimples that usually join in clusters, arriving at around 2–4 weeks of age predominantly on the face, and most are gone by about eight weeks. Some babies develop a rash over their entire body that resembles small pimples with red rims, and it can fluctuate over different parts of their body. In severe cases, you can definitely cancel the baby photo competition entry!

Dry skin can also be a problem (rough chapped cheeks are particularly common). Some say to treat this after bathing with a glycerine-sorbolene cream. Another recommendation is to massage the dry skin with a cold-pressed oil — but whatever you do, don't wash baby with regular soap.

All these little external imperfections are quite normal. With our babies I always conferred with our homeopath, and she could often supply me with an inexpensive remedy which would usually produce miraculous and rapid cures, based on the holistic philosophy that each condition is an outward sign of a small constitutional imbalance in the baby's equilibrium.

Baby massage

Baby massage is not some trendy new idea, but is an expression of love which has been a routine part of infant care all over the world for generations, and in some of the most ancient of civilisations. Babies are exquisitely sensitive to touch, and love through touch is a language they can comprehend. For example, in neonatal hospital units medical staff are now aware of how healing touch-therapy can be, and how developmentally hindering touch-deprivation is.

Infant massage helps strengthen and regulate circulatory, respiratory and digestive systems, and it can help relieve constipation, gas and colic. It is also a powerful form of relaxing healing that can soothe an infant's stress (and subsequently lower their body's secretion of cortisone), which calms them.

Once the umbilical stump has fallen off, after bathing, a baby often enjoys 2–3 minutes of massage (which is fantastic for their development), and within several weeks this could extend up to 15–20 minutes (crying or squirming means they've had enough).

Massage is best done in a nice warm room with the baby lying on a cosy towel. Nut oils are particularly gentle on babies' skin (e.g. cold-pressed almond oil), especially if combined with a little aloe vera gel or a few drops of lavender essential oil — avoid the petroleum-based baby oils. It can be nice to warm up your hands and the oil by rubbing your palms together first.

If you don't have an instinct for massaging Bub, speak to your LMC, attend a course, or grab a book or video from the local library (such as *Baby Massage* by Heath and Bainbridge) — or just close your eyes and let your heart guide you.

Fontanelles

Fontanelles are where a newborn's skull bones have not yet fused their sutures (meshed joins), which allows their skull to be compressed during birth, and to continue growing during their infancy. These cranial 'soft spots' are not painful or particularly dangerous to touch, as the brain is still protected by the meninges' tough, leathery, fibrous covering, but the baby's pulse can be felt through them.

Newborns have several fontanelles. The most well known is in the middle on the top of the head, towards the front, known as the anterior fontanelle or bregma. It is diamond-shaped (say 2–2½ cm wide by 3–4 cm long), and will gradually reduce in size until it is completely closed, usually at about 16–18 months of age, and ossified (turned to bone) by 22–24 months.

Another soft spot up high at the back of the skull, the posterior fontanelle or lambda, is much smaller in size,

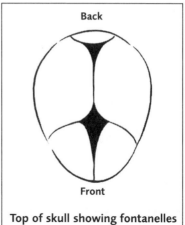

Top of skull showing fontanelles

triangular in shape, and closes by 6–8 weeks of age. Plus there is a small pair of mastoid fontanelles, one behind each ear, and a pair of anterolateral fontanelles on the sides of the skull behind the eyes.

IMPORTANT FONTANELLE INFORMATION
- If the top fontanelle is *sunken* and your baby is unwell, has refused a couple of feeds and/or has been vomiting — then see your LMC or doctor.
- If the top fontanelle is *firmly raised* and your baby is extremely irritable and/or is crying a high-pitched wail — then see your LMC or doctor.
- If your baby is happy, growing and well, then usually a sunken or raised fontanelle means nothing, but feel free to check with your LMC or doctor.

Baby with a little cold and runny nose

Many babies are born with very rattly sounding breathing (especially caesar babes who haven't been squeezed through the birth canal, and babies that have inhaled meconium in utero). With such tiny nasal passages even a weeny bit of snotty mucous can sound very snorty.

All babies are born with the ability to both breath through their nose and swallow from a good suction — in fact, initially they can only breathe through their noses. Trying to feed a baby with a blocked nose can get them quite upset, unhappy and all in a tizz, because then they can't suck and breathe at the same time.

There are a few pre-feeding solutions you can try to help alleviate the predicament. Firstly, put 2–3 drops of saline solution into each nostril to help loosen and dry things up. (Saline is obtainable from a chemist, or you can dissolve 1/4 tsp plain salt in a cup of cooled, boiled water.) Secondly put a few drops of breastmilk into baby's nostrils; or thirdly gently suction out the mucous with a rubber bulb syringe.

For a more persistent blocked nose, squirt a buffered hypertonic saline solution into the nostrils to help 'pull' the fluid out of the swollen membranes of a congested nose. (Buffered hypertonic saline: 1/2 tsp plain salt and 1/4 tsp baking soda dissolved in a cup of cooled, boiled water.) Babies usually abhor all four remedies, but they do usually help. If that still doesn't solve the problem, and it's turning into a bigger problem, you could try an infant decongestant and see your LMC or doctor (and perhaps a homeopath).

When putting babies to bed, remember too the old-fashioned remedy of putting the head-end legs of the bassinet on telephone books to give it height, so that their bed is on a little slope. That can help prevent the nose from blocking so badly, so that your babe is more comfortable.

It is normal and positive for an infant with a little virus to sleep more (but not *all* day). It can be quite normal for an infant with a virus to lose their appetite too — but give them as much breastmilk as they will take or if formula-fed, perhaps a commercially prepared baby rehydration-electrolyte solution.

It can be quite common too for babies to have runny noses through a lot of the winter months. This can often be just an over-production of mucous.

Echinacea and vitamin C, consumed by the mother, work through the breastmilk to help the baby's immune system fight a cold.

Strawberry birthmarks (haemangiomas)

Within the first few days or weeks after birth, some babies can develop a tiny red dot birthmark that gradually increases in size over the first 6–12 months to perhaps a 2.5 cm, bright-red bumpy-lump.

Strawberry birthmarks can be very upsetting for some parents, especially when it is combined with cruel and hurtful comments from ignorant people. But the great majority of these raised red or purplish marks do slowly reduce over years (or quite spontaneously disappear), and have usually completely gone by the child's fifth to 10th birthday.

Umbilical hernia

After the cord drops off some babies can develop an umbilical hernia, which is harmless, and will usually right itself in the first year — and some babies just have a sticky-out belly-button.

However, if a balloon-like swelling appears, see your LMC or doctor. Otherwise, most children's belly-buttons look quite normal given time.

Fevers

It is rare for a newborn (under three months of age) to have a fever, and fevers in newborns can be very serious. If your newborn has a temperature of 38°C or higher, give him infant paracetamol, and see your LMC, doctor or the A&E immediately.

Diarrhoea, vomiting, gastroenteritis and dehydration

Diarrhoea is usually caused by toxic bacteria irritating the colon: the food residue rushes through the large intestine (to get rid of it quicker) without the body having enough time to absorb all the water content — thus creating watery poo. **Gastroenteritis** (inflammation of the stomach and intestines) is uncommon in totally breastfed babies. Its symptoms are vomiting, diarrhoea, tummy cramps, loss of appetite, and smelly poo maybe with mucous or blood in it.

Both conditions are very concerning in a young baby because they can quickly cause serious dehydration.

The symptoms of **dehydration** include: dry skin, a dry tongue and mouth, lacking tears, looking withdrawn, dull sunken eyes, a sunken fontanelle, refusing feeds, irritability, lethargy and/or being unresponsive. When the body is dehydrated (e.g. through diarrhoea, **vomiting**, sweating, blood loss) it increases the kidney's reabsorption of water resulting in little and dark, concentrated urine; the body loses essential minerals called electrolytes, and this imbalance can seriously impair other bodily functions.

Infantile dehydration is dangerous, and especially serious in wee babies — so don't treat it lightly. See your LMC, doctor or A&E at once. They'll probably prescribe a commercially prepared electrolyte-rehydration drink, plus possibly hospitalisation for observation.

Otitis media (middle-ear infections)

Middle-ear infections (called otitis media) are reasonably common in littlies (more so between six months and two years of age). They often can't tell you where it is hurting, although it is pretty obvious if they're old enough to pull or rub their ears, or if there is discharge from their ears. Other symptoms can be a high temperature, diarrhoea and crying for no apparent reason.

Some believe that because Westernised babies spend so much time horizontal they are particularly susceptible to bacteria from their eustachian tubes entering the middle ear (the tubes run between the back of the throat and the middle ear).

The traditional modern treatment is antibiotics. However, this methodology is under increasing scrutiny because antibiotics can seriously weaken the natural immune system resulting in the body becoming even more susceptible to the same or similar infection the next time it encounters it.

There is now a trend to let the child's own defence system fight the infection unaided (but with infant paracetamol given for the pain) — and a burst eardrum, although undesirable, is usually not a major problem, and most heal completely.

There are a vast range of alternative medicines available from a homeopath, naturopath or chemist to assist your babe's immune system to function as efficiently as possible; for example, Naturo Pharm's Earmed Relief™ (and see pages 358–363).

Projectile vomiting

This is when, after feeding, the milk is violently propelled a couple of metres (even vomited out the nose). Typically appearing at 2–6 weeks of age, and more common in boys, this may be pyloric stenosis, which is a narrowing (mechanical obstruction) of the pylorus passage outlet from the stomach to the small intestine due to pyloric muscular enlargement.

The baby can also subsequently suffer from dehydration and constipation. In serious cases a relatively simple operation to widen the pylorus can fix the problem.

Warning:

Don't pay attention to others' dismissive comments if your instincts are telling you there's something really wrong with your baby!

Reasons to visit the doctor

- A 0–4-week-old with a fever of 38°C or over. Give infant paracetamol, undress layers of clothing, and seek urgent medical advice.
- A 1–3-month-old with a fever of 38°C or over. Give infant paracetamol, undress layers of clothing, and seek prompt medical advice.
- An over-three-month-old with a fever of 38°C half an hour after having paracetamol, or with continually high temperatures for more than a day.
- Troubled, difficult breathing (call an ambulance).
- Convulsions, seizure fits (call an ambulance with a newborn).
- Hard to arouse, unresponsive, lethargic, droopy, floppy, or apathetic.
- Crying and listless for no apparent reason.
- Breathing with grunting or wheeziness (possible asthma).
- Loud, dry or wheezy cough.
- Pale ashen complexion.

- Irritable with swollen abdomen or severe abdominal tummy pain.
- Dehydration (e.g. dry lips, mouth lacking saliva, dark urine, sunken fontanelle, sunken eyes, lack of tears).
- Poos that are consistently green coloured (the occasional green poo is fine).
- Poos with blood or pus-like mucous in them.
- Bad-smelling poo from a breastfed baby (it should smell sweet).
- Diarrhoea lasting longer than eight hours.
- Diarrhoea with vomiting.
- Refusing several feeds in a row.
- Is upset by his head, neck or ears.
- Abnormally low temperature (e.g. 34–36°C).
- Runny nose with a fever and/or persistent cough.
- Runny nose and looking sick and lethargic.
- Runny nose and sleeping a lot more than usual.
- Unusual rash, or strange lump.
- Cradle cap that spreads or gets infected.
- Yellow or green vomit (containing bile) or blood-stained vomit.
- Vomiting for over four hours.
- One eye that doesn't change position.
- Or anything else you're feeling concerned about — it's natural and normal as a first-time mum to feel a little anxiety ridden — you're not being neutic, and there's no need to apologise to the medical staff for wasting their time.

NOTE: Do not give infants aspirin (or disprin) due to its potential side effects on blood clotting. For pain relief and fever relief, use paracetamol or ibuprofen designed for children.

Postnatal psychosis (PNP) part 1

Every time I close the door on reality it comes in through the windows.

Author Unknown

Postnatal psychosis, also known as postpartum psychotic depression, is a frightening, devastating and explosive mental illness. Officially it affects about 2–3 women in every 1000 births. It is a complete break with reality, where the mother has become entirely out of touch.

The vast majority of PNP occurs within the first two weeks after childbirth. This is when, thanks to an endorphin overload, progesterone reduction, and radical oestrogen drop (and probably other triggers), there is a classic 10–14–day 'meltdown' from the overactivity in the signal pathways that affect the neurotransmitters (such as dopamine, which is also linked with schizophrenia and other mental illnesses).

When correctly diagnosed at the earliest signs, and immediately treated with anti-psychotic, mood-stabilising medication such as lithium, this illness does not need to be a big issue (though breastfeeding usually isn't continued in conjunction with lithium). Mothers with this severe psychiatric disturbance can then feel significantly improved within days, can be feeling much better within 2–3 weeks, and functioning quite normally again within a few months.

But, if the mother is left undiagnosed (even for days) she will begin to unravel mentally in a downward spiral, becoming increasingly unwell, commonly resulting in her being placed in a psychiatric hospital for days, weeks or months.

Unlike mild depressions, the horrid side of psychosis is that typically *the sufferer is completely unaware they are extremely unwell,* because she can (falsely) be feeling great! In fact, a woman with PNP can temporarily appear quite well (actually *too* well) . . . but then she will become deeply mentally ill with clinical depression. She may not necessarily be feeling 'down'.

The frightening reality is that *every single day* the woman is left undiagnosed, the recovery time can be increased by months! So this is where the knowledgeable awareness of friends and family becomes extremely critical.

Very normal women living in very normal circumstances who experienced a smooth pregnancy and/or childbirth, can suffer PNP — primarily due to severe post-pregnancy hormonal and biological changes and imbalances — in other words *all* women are potential candidates. However, it does seem to occur more commonly (as a very large generalisation) in women:

- Who are older first-time mothers.
- Who approach motherhood as a new career move.
- Who read and read, and plan and plan during the pregnancy about child-birth and motherhood.
- Who have 'Superwoman Syndrome' during the pregnancy, e.g. working furiously at the gym while maintaining an important career role.
- Who have a C-section delivery (post-operative psychosis).
- Who are tackling their whole new image with a self-imposed perfectionist standard of successful motherhood — associating it with looking good, maintaining a tidy house, and coping infallibly with their new role

— even though no one has *told* them they must include managing to bake cakes and bottle preserves in their now scrambled days!
- Who have a family or personal history of mental illness.
- Or, *none of the above.*

Symptoms of PNP

By about a week post delivery (after the baby blues should be over), PNP can begin with symptoms very similar to postnatal depression (see page 367) but with emotional *highs* added in. The symptoms of PNP can vary from person to person, but always follows this pattern:
- Difficulty with concentration and co-ordination.
- Changing moods swinging from elevated to irritable.
- Restlessness, insomnia, horrendous nightmares, a decreased need for, or fear of, sleep.
- Immense fatigue — or endless energy.
- An inability to feel pain (e.g. caesar stitches).
- Overactive, overenthusiastic, excessively cheerful behaviour.
- Feeling overly capable (like Superwoman), excited and elated.
- Rushing from one task to another.
- Bossy and demanding — angry and aggressive if annoyed.
- Agitated and suspicious.
- Organising grandiose ideas and schemes (e.g. for business money-making, or excessive spending).
- Obsessing over things (e.g. lists) or having obsessive thoughts.
- Hyperactive with racing thoughts and increased brain function (e.g. improved maths skill).
- Distressing, delusional, false beliefs (e.g. that people are trying to harm her).
- Sensation of improved ESP or sixth sense (increased intuition, astral travelling, talking with God, reading minds).
- Uncontrollable urge to talk a lot — and quickly.
- Strange ideas and bizarre delusions.
- Severely altered or disturbed, frantic, hysterical reactions.
- Overwhelming hopelessness, or embarrassment, or feelings of inadequacy.
- Obsessive religious beliefs (e.g. believing her baby is the Messiah).
- Blowing out of proportion any pre-existing phobias or fears (e.g. heights, sharp objects, insects, animals).
- The brakes completely fail on her emotional response controls.
- Experiences hypersensitivity to outside stimuli, or false senses (e.g. touch, taste, smell, temperature — being different to reality).

- Abnormal perceptions (e.g. blurred vision; sees abnormal things like ghouls, angels, or animated objects; or hears imaginary things such as delusional voices commanding her to do profound things).

If left untreated this runaway train called PNP will always de-rail by rapidly developing into severe depression symptoms such as panic attacks, frightening hallucinations and paranoia, which collectively result in a new mother's brain rapidly becoming bipolar and disjointed from all reality. For example, she may believe that the TV or radio is talking directly to her, or she could be suicidal; or she could be hostile to her baby, the baby's father, friends or family.

She is *completely unaware* she is behaving abnormally, and she will have little (if any) control over her behaviour. She has lost the ability to think and act normally due to the brain's chemical imbalances taking place. Though not her fault, until properly medicated, this woman is no longer capable of being responsible for the welfare of any person — including her baby and herself.

Mood stabilising medication (and psychotherapy) is always required for this serious illness — the condition does not pass of its own accord — and admission to hospital is often necessary.

Once commencing the long process of recovering, the sufferer will need immense support to come to terms with the stigma of what has just happened to her. When we all hope for perfect motherhood, those that end up receiving the unlucky, one-in-500 booby-prize of developing this dreadful illness, need and deserve an immense amount of non-judgemental emotional empathy.

Tremendous practical support is also needed by the family to cope with the horrific situation (of the temporarily motherless newborn and partnerless father). The father will also need emotional support for the traumatic grief and (utterly unanticipated) upheaval he is going through as a temporary solo-dad.

Although it takes time, a full recovery is possible . . . but if the woman has to be institutionalised, she can be left with some very deep wounds.

A woman who has experienced PNP has about a 20–25 percent chance of it recurring during, or after, subsequent pregnancies. More information is available at www.pnpsupport.org.nz.

A month down the track

In settled agricultural societies families are large and there's always
an experienced woman — relative or midwife — to stay with a

*new mother and baby and care for them . . . [Today] a link is
missing in the chain by which the tried and tested cultural lore of
childcare is passed down. Modern mothers make up for it by
exchanging tips with friends, and even with strangers in baby
magazine columns.*
Carol Dunham and the Body Shop Team — Mamatoto

New baby courses

These can feel like 'sweet-as-sugar' courses, but I can say that I know a lot
of women who have made the effort to attend them (me included, and it is
an effort) — and the great majority feel it was time well spent. This is
probably because 4–6 weeks into raising a baby, most new mothers start
feeling primed and ready to take in any new information they can to deal
with their challenging little bundle. So, make the effort to attend. Hopefully,
you too will reflect that it was worthwhile.

Coffee groups

Coffee groups are one topic where almost any selection of experienced mums
will provide you with a variety of opinions.

'It was foul — we tried getting together a few times — but they were all
just so house-wifey — majorly not my scene' . . . 'It was so therapeutic —
like attending free counselling without paying for a psychiatrist' . . . 'The
competitiveness between that judgemental gaggle of know-all mothers was
awful — each subtly trying to prove their baby was smarter than the next, as
they out-baked and out-tidied each other, each mother proving she was
more in control of her life, while living in her superior house' . . . 'That group
of mums formed such a close relationship, a sanctuary where I could bleat on
for half an hour about the drama of trying to buy new bras while Junior
wouldn't stop screaming' . . . 'They were all such virtuous stay-at-home
"Muffia" mothers and I had gone back to work — I felt awkward and bored
with their dull conversation' . . . 'Before being a mother, I'd always preferred
the company of men, but now I have learnt to value the strong sisterhood bond
of solidarity those amazing ladies give each other' . . . 'I'd find myself tidying
the house at the expense of my hungry, dirty baby just to show how well I
was coping — it took months for me to realise I had nothing to prove to those
women' . . . 'A bunch of us antenatal-class mums who went back to work,
started meeting for lunch every second Thursday, and it still is one of my high
points each fortnight' . . . 'A couple of the mothers were so aloof and strongly
opinionated with their judgemental remarks, it was horrid — then finally me
and the other three mums decided to leave those two to it, and created our own

sort of mini-group — years later the four of us are still really great friends'.

It seems that coffee groups either work brilliantly well or fail miserably — with not a lot of ground in-between. Primarily, they work superbly when the mothers 'gel' — and over years these women often end up becoming some of one's closest and dearest friends. Or they fail miserably because the friendships simply don't 'gel'.

If you try a coffee group that doesn't work for you, please don't give up on the idea completely — try a different coffee group, or create one of your own — because when it does 'gel', they can be a phenomenal source of mothering education and emotional support — a camaraderie of true understanding and genuine sympathetic appreciation of how challenging the role of being a mum can be. Statistics show that 90 percent of Kiwi mums who give coffee groups a go find they're 'quite good' or 'wonderful'.

Coffee groups can eradicate your 'I'm-the-only-one-feeling-this-way syndrome', and can make you feel like an interesting adult again. In fact, it is normal for female friendships to often take on quite a new dimension once you're a mother. Coffee groups can start out as a little social luxury, but turn into some psychological necessity, as they become a wonderful sounding board for all motherhood issues. As author Robin Lim writes, 'Women are women's best and most available resource', and as author John Gray writes, 'When a woman's wave crashes and her partner is in his cave, it is essential that she have other sources of support.'

Personally I've been involved in numerous coffee groups over the years, and often they have evolved into Friday afternoon wine groups and ladies' night out groups and couples' restaurant dining groups and family pot-luck dinner groups and even ladies' childless weekends-away groups. I have made many close friends over the years — one fabulous couple from our original antenatal class became such dear friends that they are our son's godparents.

Making the effort to have coffee groups as part of my life has repaid me with massive rewards — and, of course, many of those friends' children have become some of our children's closest friends, so the kids have loved it too.

Highly recommended reading: *Secrets of the Baby Whisperer*

Author Tracy Hogg is blessed with an extraordinary intuition for how babies tick — in my humble opinion it is *really* worth buying your own copy of her first book, *Secrets of the Baby Whisperer*.

To me her wisdom is plain common sense, beautifully disguised as pure genius! Tracy explains that, in her experience, infants generally fit into one of five broad temperamental types, and she provides fabulous instructions for understanding and dealing with the type of baby you have. Here's a tiny overview of the repertoire of behaviours:

ANGEL BABY — The kind of baby every first-time mother expects to have. Just as good as gold with a mild, amenable disposition, who seems almost eternally happy, and wakes up coo-ing.

TEXTBOOK BABY — A predictable easy-to-handle, no surprises, baby you can easily mould — one who wakes up with a little fussing 'Hello? Is anyone there?' fidget.

TOUCHY BABY — This baby is ultra-sensitive, sucks a lot, adores structure and predictability, is fragile with surprises, prone to meltdowns, and wakes up crying.

SPIRITED BABY — The active, high-energy, fidgety baby who already knows what it likes and won't hesitate to tell you — has a mind of his own. Wakes up with fussing squirming coughs, which quickly progress to all-out crying and flailing.

GRUMPY BABY — This baby is like an 'old soul' who is cranky to be back in the world — intense and disagreeable, but likes consistency. It's impossible to coax a just-woken-up smile out of this one.

Very sadly, in November 2004 Tracy Hogg lost her battle with melanoma. But her legacy lives on, in her other books Secrets of the Baby Whisperer for Toddlers *and* The Baby Whisperer Solves All Your Problems; *and her TV series. Thank you, Tracy, for your outstanding wisdom and contribution to motherhood literature. The world misses you.*

Chapter 7

You've slept, fed, burped and you're dry . . . why are you *still* crying?

In fact, from the time that babies are about four weeks old until they reach the 12-week mark, most babies tend to get pretty crabby for no apparent reason at least once every day . . . Expect to have a bad patch each day ... and possibly one bad day each week. And, if it doesn't happen, rejoice!

Mara Lee — *Baby's First Year for Dummies*

Have you ever thought about how innocent, 'helpless', human creatures manage to get fed, clothed, cuddled, warmed and talked to? By crying! Then all their needs are met. And all people, especially women, are inherently born with some level of parental instincts, but certainly a lifetime of previously ignoring one's own intuition can leave you with a deeply eroded faith in your own natural hunches — especially when a six-week old pooing and spewing drinking-machine, won't stop crying . . . and crying . . . and crying.

Sometimes a screaming bundle of misery with seemingly nothing wrong can make you want to scream too, 'What the heck is wrong with you my red-faced squawker?'

Hearing your baby crying inconsolably for extended periods of time doesn't just give you a throbbing headache, it also gives you a massive heartache. Your stomach ties into knots, while your fractured and fragile self-confidence can get crushed into sharp painful splinters, which then puncture any remaining self-esteem.

As a new mother you can feel that you are required to learn some foreign (baby) language composed of sounds and body movements — and *you are*. Author Tracy Hogg warns, 'Your baby will lose her ability to tell you what she wants if you don't learn to tune in to what her different cries mean. They'll all start to merge into one big "pay attention!" cry.'

The 1–2 hours a day of normal newborn crying often gradually increases, till at about six to eight weeks of age, an average baby can cry 3–4 hours out of 24. So, please don't be too upset when they seem to be doing a lot of crying for no obvious reason. (The true cause is often only known by your baby and God!) As Tracy Hogg also points out, 'One of the most damaging misconceptions I hear: crying baby equals bad parenting' — it doesn't!

Interestingly, quite a number of studies have shown that strategies such as trying to never let your baby scream or carrying a baby in a sling for hours each day can make little impact on the amount some babies fuss — some babies are just very fussy difficult babies no matter *what* their mother does.

A really important point to understand when your baby cries is that you are not necessarily doing anything *wrong*. You do not automatically understand your baby less than some other mother, just because your baby cries more.

The good news is that most babies' crying begins to reduce, so that by three months of age, a wee baby is crying for about an hour each day. But as a big generalisation, a couple of hours of crying a day is still totally normal.

Responding to her baby's cries is what a mother is biologically programmed to do. In fact, amazing biochemical changes which take place within a mother's body in response to her infant's cries force her to pick up her baby — Mother Nature has ways of trying to guarantee that her babies will not be ignored.

Try not to be *embarrassed* about your baby crying, *it's what babies do.* That's like being embarrassed that your child is talking. A baby crying is simply a baby talking. (By the way, babies don't normally produce tears until they are two months old.)

Try not to fret when you can't respond immediately — so long as you can usually get to them before complete meltdown occurs — remember if this was your second or third child he might have to wait for attention.

Also, try hard to chill out and *relax* your attitude towards your baby's cries. There are probably millions of other babies crying right now all around the world!

Theories about why babies cry

When parents don't stop to really listen and learn how to distinguish different cries, those cries, which numerous studies on crying have proven ARE differentiated at birth, in time actually BECOME indistinguishable. In other words, when a baby is not responded to at

all or if every cry is 'answered' with food, Baby learns that it doesn't
matter how she cries — it always results in the same outcome.
Eventually, she gives up and all her cries WILL sound the same.
                    Tracy Hogg — *Secrets of the Baby Whisperer*

If your baby is 'crying all day', then there is a high possibility, you may have inadvertently missed his cues and he is overfed, fatigued and/or overstimulated.

Babies' cries NEVER mean (*so don't misinterpret them as*) 'I'm scared of the dark', 'I hate my bed', 'I'm being naughty', 'You've caused me misery' or 'I don't like you'!

In chapter 4, we described the body language that accompanies the 'I'm hungry', 'My tummy aches, I need burping', 'I'm overfed', 'I'm hungry because I'm not suckling properly', and 'I want to suckle my pacifier' cries.

In chapter 5, we described the body language typifying the cries of 'I'm tired', 'I'm overtired', 'My brain is in sensory overload because of all the people or noise or lights', 'I'm tired and need to sleep but I can't seem to' and 'My body's floppy and jerky so I want to be snugly wrapped'.

Commonly there are also cries for 'I've finished sleeping and want to get up now', 'I'm hot', 'I'm cold', 'I'm uncomfortable and want a different position', 'Wow — that was scary', 'This place is too noisy', 'I want to be held and comforted', 'I need a predictable routine', 'My nappy's wet', 'My nappy's dirty', and 'Eeek — my bottom's squeezing something out'.

Then after the initial newborn period, with neurological maturing, there are the cries that can quickly creep up on an unsuspecting mother, including 'I'm lonely and need a cuddle', 'I miss my mummy', 'I'm in an angry, furious or annoyed mood', 'I'm in a grizzly, cranky and grumpy mood', 'You're upset — and that makes me upset too — are you OK?', and 'There's nothing wrong with me — I was just checking you're still here'. Babies can also cry more when their mother smells smoky, and when lactating mothers drink too much caffeine or alcohol, or medication alters the flavour of her milk.

Some 'high-need' fussy-by-nature babies are trickier to soothe than others (say about 40 percent are easy, 40 percent are not so easy, and 20 percent are outright difficult). So, the amount a baby cries is also strongly influenced by his *temperament* or *personality*.

Your role is to get behind the eyes of your child, to become the leading authority and biggest expert on the planet of *your* child.

Now, apart from the specific 'I'm bored', 'I'm sick', 'I'm teething', 'I have reflux', 'I have a milk-protein allergy', 'I am lactose intolerant' and 'I have colic' cries, which will be explained in this chapter, there are other theories as to why babies will inexplicably cry over lengthy periods of time for no obvious reason. Some theories currently in circulation follow:

The tension-release theory

Apart from being a means to ensure a baby's survival needs are met, crying can also be a mechanism to diffuse tension. Emotional tears are chemically different from tears caused by something irritating the eye. They contain more stress hormones — it's as if crying is biologically an effort to rid the body of unwanted stress. Crying also stimulates production of the mood-elevating and pain-relieving endorphin hormones.

So, crying can be a way of releasing emotional and physical pain. In fact, crying can go on long after a physical pain has ended, because the process of crying can help discharge the emotional pain. That goes a long way to explaining why we all sometimes 'feel so much better after a good cry'.

The zinc theory

It is theorised that a zinc-deficient baby can cry inconsolably, be very difficult to soothe, and be agitated and jittery. That is another reason why it can be a wise idea for breastfeeding mothers to take a vitamin and mineral supplement designed for lactating mothers, and eat foods rich in zinc.

The Van De Rijt and Plooij theory

When I was pregnant with our first child, I was very fortunate to be given a book written by Hetty Van De Rijt and Frans Plooij titled *Why They Cry*. It gives a fantastic explanation of the neurological developments in a child's first year. I strongly recommend getting hold of your own copy — it is packed full of great information.

As a basic overview, their ground-breaking research found that, in relation to a baby's due date, and caused primarily by the massive neurological developmental changes within the brain, all babies seem to go through inexplicably cranky-clingy-crying periods at around the same time: 5 weeks, 8 weeks, 12 weeks, 19 weeks, 26 weeks, 37 weeks, 46 weeks, 55 weeks, 64 weeks and 75 weeks. *(The onset may vary by a week or two, but you can be pretty sure of their arrival.)*

During those transitions, parents can easily misinterpret what is happening, and can end up concerned that their 'usually placid, happy baby' is crying more, is wanting to be held more, wants more or fewer feeds — and is generally 'just not being themselves'. Then, a few days into this, often the mother trots off to the doctor who checks the baby over to find nothing seemingly wrong — then a couple of days later, the baby returns to normal and the parents breathe a sigh of relief, but are left scratching their heads in confused wonder.

The fabulous thing about reading *Why They Cry* is that being forewarned to expect these cranky-clingy times means that when they do happen, you know exactly what you are dealing with. Knowledge is power.

The Harvey Karp theory

Californian paediatrician to the 'stars', Dr Harvey Karp, and his book *The Happiest Baby On The Block* are receiving more and more recognition and praise. Dr Karp believes that new babies can experience fourth trimester issues (as if Mother Nature delivers human babies a little earlier than is ideal).

These are babies who have difficulty adjusting due to the number of stimuli outside their mother's body, and react by crying and crying.

So, Dr Karp recommends that by trying to 'recreate' the womb atmosphere, it can be possible to alleviate some, if not all, of a baby's crying or colicky symptoms. He advocates using the 'Five S's': Swaddling; the Side-to-stomach lying positions; Shushing sounds (white noise); Swinging (motion); and Sucking (bottle, breast, pacifier or thumb).

The birth trauma theory

There is the fringe topic of birth trauma, which asks 'Why is it that at a subconscious level, our modern society seems to dismiss the concept of infantile birth trauma?' (As if a baby doesn't begin to feel pain or fear until *after* their arrival?)

We appreciate that mothers can be traumatised by childbirth, and that infants can be traumatised by many other situations. To theorise that a newborn can be traumatised by its own delivery is not outside the realms of logical possibilities. More interesting reading on this subject can be found in Aletha Solter's book *The Aware Baby*.

The Saint Pelagius theory

There is the really 'out there' theory taught by the fourth-century Celtic missionary, Saint Pelagius, who hypothesised that when newborns arrive straight from Heaven (where all is divinely perfect), the imperfect reality of the lower Earth plane leaves them feeling disillusioned and so, of course they cry — they are homesick for paradise. At the time, the Church condemned Saint Pelagius as a heretic, because since the downfall of Adam and Eve, babies do not come straight from Heaven, and they inherently have the trait of 'human wickedness'.

At the end of the day, all parents, even those with the most angelic of babies, encounter perplexing times of endless crying.

And for those of you who receive miserable, angry, fussy or 'high-needs' babies — you can spend even more time searching for solutions. But, let's get started on some of the common reasons infants cry.

The sick baby

When a baby cries, there is always the possibility they are unwell. Below are the most obvious signs all may not be okay:

- A prolonged cry that sounds whiny, nasal and low pitched.
- A weak sounding cry.
- 38°+C temperature (e.g. urinary tract infection).
- Vomiting.
- Seizures.
- Diarrhoea.
- Limpness.
- Rash (e.g. allergies, dermatitis).
- Pale or blue-tinged skin and feeling cold to the touch.
- Coughing.
- Wheezy breathing.
- Hitting or pulling at their ears (earache).
- Attempting then refusing feeds.
- See page 264 for a more detailed list.

The teething baby

Did you know some babies are born with teeth? My great-uncle was born with two! On the other hand, some infants don't get their first teeth until after their first birthday. Babies vary tremendously as to when, and in what order, the little 'pearls' arrive in their mouth. But as a big generalisation:

Estimated arrival time of baby teeth
- Bottom two front incisors (biting teeth) by 6 months.
- Top two front incisors by 7 months.
- Two more pairs of incisors, top and bottom, by 8–12 months.
- Four back molars (grinding teeth) at 10–14 months.
- Four canines (pointed teeth) at 16–20 months.
- Four more back molars at 24–30 months.

A total of twenty baby teeth!

The term teething does not just mean when a tooth is cutting through the gum, but also when the teeth are moving towards the gums.

If your baby is not co-operating to let you have a good look inside its mouth, you can always do the 'clink test': gently tap a teaspoon on their gums to hear if there is a new pearly white.

Symptoms of teething
- Crying, irritable, grizzly, cranky, clingy, fretful, sooky.
- Mild fever (say 37.5°C–37.9°C).
- Trouble sleeping, waking up crying.
- Very 'mouthy' — desperate to chew and gnaw on things.
- Lots of chewing on fingers in their mouth.
- Producing more saliva and dribbling more than usual (which can cause a rash on the chin, or chafing from continual dummy use).
- One or both cheeks bright red, occasional spot on face.
- Stools looser or runnier than usual (not diarrhoea).
- Nappy rash.
- Rejecting milk or meals.
- Gums tender and swollen (where a tooth is about to cut through).
- Tugging their ears (but teething does not cause ear infections).

Possible remedies for teething
- Chilled teething rings.
- Infant paracetamol or infant ibuprofen for the pain (especially for sleeping).
- A barley drink can help neutralise the acidity of a baby's saliva.
- Homeopathic chamomilla.
- Other homeopathic remedies such as Weleda™'s Baby Teething Powder and Naturo Pharm™'s Teethmed Relief.
- Chemists sell teething gels to rub on the gums (e.g. Bonjela™) — especially useful before bedtime.
- Teething toys for your little babe to relish slobbering all over.
- Eliminate starchy foods from their diet.
- Homeopathic aconite is very effective with counteracting the one red-cheek scenario.
- Great teething food ideas include frozen bananas (peel and wrap in cling-film to freeze), dried bananas (buy at health shops), pieces of peeled apple wrapped in gauze-cloth to gnaw on, cold celery sticks, and freezing the wet corner of a flannel to chew on. (But always be very careful to avoid baby choking on small pieces of food.)

The bored baby

The baby is not crying because you are a bad mother . . .
The baby is crying because the baby is a baby.
Kaz Cooke — Kid-Wrangling

It can actually be fairly easy to interpret that your baby is bored, fed up and wanting some stimulation. They normally cry a whiny whimpering moan, or an annoyed roaring cry. They turn away from an object, or play with their fingers — and the crying ends abruptly when the baby is picked up. This is your cue to give them a change of scenery (and often also a change of position).

Babies can find pretty simple things quite fascinating: lying on their tummies with one or two toys within reach; or lying on their backs under a baby gym; or reclined on a baby bouncer looking out the window; there are lots of options! Many other ideas are listed at the end of this chapter, (see page 290, Mysterious-crying solutions).

The lactose-intolerant baby

Lactose intolerance (also known as lactase deficiency) is sensitivity to the carbohydrate content in milk from mammals — in other words, an intolerance or inability to efficiently break down the sugar lactose.

It is rare for children to be truly lactose intolerant, especially Caucasian or European children — so this has tended to be an over-diagnosed condition. However, it is estimated that over half of all babies experience some small degree (for say 1–2 weeks) of lactase deficiency at some stage within their first five months.

To break down lactose, the baby's digestive system provides the enzyme lactase, but if it doesn't, or if there is not enough lactase, fermentation in the large bowel (colon) eventually breaks down the lactose. However, that bacterial fermentation causes side effects.

Symptoms of lactose intolerance
- Watery acidic diarrhoea (poo can even be frothy).
- Swollen, bloated abdomen.
- Excessive farting.
- Stomach cramping, pain that causes crying.
- General irritability.
- A rumbling stomach.

Note: Lactose intolerance does not cause vomiting.

Common causes of lactose intolerance

- A baby does not produce lactase — extremely rare except in Scandinavia. This is a low-weight, dehydrated and very unwell baby.
- A baby produces levels of lactase that are lower than normal — this is rare in Caucasians and Europeans, but more common in darker-skinned races around the world. It commonly occurs after weaning, and before the age of six.
- A baby who is low in iron can have difficulty with lactose digestion.
- Antibiotics or a parasitic infection (e.g. Giardia) can temporarily reduce the baby's lactase levels.
- An episode of gastroenteritis (serious vomiting or diarrhoea) can cause an infant's lactase levels to drop for 1–8 weeks.

Possible remedies for lactose intolerance

- A mother's diet will not affect her breastmilk's consistent levels of lactose. But, it is important to ensure the baby gets all the hind-milk because the fat content aids with the digestion (in other words, make sure the first breast is empty before offering the other breast).
- Delay weaning: breastmilk contains lactase enzymes that help the infant's digestion.
- Space breastfeeds out to at least three-hourly, to avoid the baby snack-feeding on fore-milk.
- With formula-fed babies, swap to a lactose-free formula.
- Try lactase drops.
- Once off breast or formula, full-fat milk is better than low-fat varieties. Avoid food containing skim-milk powders.
- Heated milk foods such as custard, milk puddings and warm milk tend to be more tolerable than cold or non-cooked dairy products.
- Fermented dairy products such as cheeses, butter and yoghurt are usually reasonably well tolerated; and the Swiss cheeses Gruyère and Emmental are lactose-free.

The milk-protein-allergic baby (cow's-milk allergy)

This is an allergic response (more aptly described as an 'oversensitive intolerance') to proteins commonly found in cows' milk; the immune system has an abnormal reaction because it thinks the protein is a threat and goes into attack-mode. It is the commonest allergy in young children (roughly about one in 20) — and is called cows' milk protein allergy (CMPA). Fortunately, most infants outgrow this allergy, usually between three months and three years of age (and almost half in time for ice-creams at their first birthday).

Both formula-fed and breastfed babies can be allergic (although chances are significantly lowered in breastfed babes) — formula-fed babies allergic to the cows' milk proteins in the formula, and breastfed babies from the dairy products consumed by their mother. Symptoms can show between three-quarters of an hour (rapid onset) to more than 20 hours after ingestion. Although there is no treatment as such, symptoms can be controlled.

Symptoms of milk-protein allergy

Symptoms can appear within the first months of life, or first month of being fed formula.

- As with all allergies, the body's defence system produces histamines to make the blood vessels dilatate and capillaries secrete, which can cause an itchy bumpy skin rash (hives), eczema or dermatitis.
- Loose poo (diarrhoea), possibly containing blood.
- Mucosa membranes produce extra mucous, which can make baby wheezy and congested with constant sniffles or continual clear runny nose.
- Abdominal cramping pains.
- Irritable colicky crying.
- Vomiting.
- Consistent constipation.
- Nappy rash.
- Nausea or behavioural changes.
- Sudden and extremely serious anaphylactic reaction including face, mouth and tongue swelling, making it difficult to breathe. (This is very rare.)

Possible remedies for milk-protein allergy

- Avoid introducing formula within the first three months, and continue breastfeeding for as long as possible, ideally for at least six months.
- If breastfeeding, remove all dairy products from your own diet, and any other foods that are allergenic.
- If formula-feeding, change to a goats' milk formula or hydrolysed hypoallergenic formula, or soy-based formula (but many infants are also allergic to this). It is trial and error.
- Try antihistamine medications (natural or pharmaceutical).
- Make the baby's diet dairy-free once it is on solids (but a cows' milk protein allergy usually means an infant can still eat beef).
- Put a hot-water bottle or heated wheat bag wrapped in a handtowel or cloth nappy, on baby's tummy.
- Offer a relaxing pacifier for baby to suckle on to aid digestion.
- Consider having baby's constitution analysed by a classical homeopath.
- Consider having baby's wellbeing checked by a naturopath.

• Half or more of CMPA infants go on to develop other hyposensitivity intolerances such as allergies to soy, eggs, peanuts, citrus fruit and/or inhaled allergens such as pollen.

The reflux baby

Gastro-oesophageal reflux (GOR) is the baby equivalent of heartburn and also goes by the names of acid reflex and acid indigestion. The immature valve (lower oesophageal sphincter) at the top of your baby's stomach, which is supposed to stop contents moving back up the oesophagus from the stomach, is unreliable (not as tight as normal), and acid-containing food from the stomach regurgitates back into the oesophagus. It is a painful condition. Some experts estimate that about two-thirds of all babies have some degree of GOR (especially in the first 2–3 months when the valve is loose), and other experts quote one-third to half of all babies.

GOR often peaks at around four months, then begins subsiding from around seven months, and is usually outgrown by nine to 12 months (though some toddlers can continue to have reflux problems into their childhood and even adulthood).

However, when symptoms are more severe and interfere with the baby's growth, development, respiration and/or could cause serious damage such as ulceration, then the condition is identified as a disease (going from GOR to GORD).

Symptoms of gastro-oesophageal reflux

Symptoms emerge at 2–4 weeks of age.
• Baby is vomiting, sometimes projectile vomits like a volcano, even out their nostrils. (If there are bloody flecks in the vomit, this should be treated seriously as evidence of GORD.)
• Erratic feeding pattern (refusing to feed because of associating feeding with pain, or wanting to constantly feed to neutralise stomach acids with the antacid effects of the milk).
• Latches on to feed, then shortly afterwards turns head away, arching neck or back, even tossing head from side to side.
• Fussing or in pain after eating (even up to an hour afterwards).
• Baby is comfortable when upright, but wails when laid down. (This can also be a symptom of colic.)
• Drools excessively.
• May be a restless sleeper, being woken by bursts of pain.
• Has wet hiccups or wet burps.
• Makes choking, gagging, throaty noises; may have sour breath or recurring wheezing or coughing episodes (from the stomach contents

entering the back of babe's throat or his lungs).
- Constant swallowing.
- Often seems to suffer from respiratory problems (such as colds, chest infections, wheezing and/or sleep apnoea).
- Poor weight gain.

Note: An overfed baby can commonly be misinterpreted as a baby with reflux (see page 184).

Possible remedies for gastro-oesophageal reflux

You will need to have lots of bibs, towels and a reliable washing machine — though not all reflux babies regularly regurgitate.

- Breastfeeding is strongly preferred over formula, because breastmilk is a natural antacid, is more rapidly digested, is more intestine-friendly and produces softer poos.
- If breastfeeding, take lactation herbs to thicken your breastmilk; if formula-feeding, swap to a thickened formula.
- If formula-feeding, the teat hole should permit milk droplets to flow at a too-fast-to-count-the-drips rate, but not 'pour' out.
- Because swallowing air aggravates reflux, burping during and after feeds can make good sense — infant winding drops may also help.
- Give smaller more frequent feeds of say half as much, twice as often — but, to avoid instilling negative snacking habits, don't encourage feeds less than two hourly.
- Eliminate all starchy foods in the diet if on solids.
- Allow half an hour of quiet time after feeds.
- Use infant antacid barrier drops such as Gaviscon™ or Mylanta™.
- Position baby semi-upright during the day, including during feeds, so that gravity can assist to keep the food down — especially after feeding. (Lying flat on the back can be very aggravating to reflux.)
- Elevate the head-end of baby's bed on an angle (about 30°) and sleep baby on his *left side* so that the gastric inlet is higher than the outlet. (Using an abdominal sleep-wrap or baby back-support pillow may also be helpful to stop the baby sliding.)
- Avoid leaving baby sitting forward with a curved spine for long periods (such as hunched in a carseat or in a pushchair).
- Avoid treating baby with decongestants (which dry their mucous production).
- Warmth on baby's tummy can assist, e.g. a hot-water bottle or heat-pack wrapped in a cloth nappy.
- Gentle tummy massage may help.
- A pacifier to suckle on may help digestion, as it triggers oxytocin

production and stimulates saliva production which can ease reflux irritation. (The down-side is that the baby could end up swallowing more air.)

- Consider having baby checked by a neonatal cranial osteopath.
- Consider having baby's constitution analysed by a classical homeopath.
- Consider having baby's wellbeing checked by a naturopath.
- Don't encourage baby to become too 'bonny' — obesity can aggravate reflux.
- In severe cases, try a prescription-only infant acid-blocker (e.g. Losec™ or Zantac™) at night-time (to reduce stomach-acid production).
- In severe cases, request a prescription-only, prokinetic motility medicine (such as Prepulsid, Metoclopramide or Cisapride) to increase the muscle tone of the lower oesophageal sphincter muscle.
- Because crying increases intra-abdominal pressure, it is not possible for a reflux baby to 'cry out' an attack of GOR.
- Babies with GORD are high-needs babies requiring intensive parental care. Attachment parenting (such as the mother wearing a baby sling) may be beneficial.
- Reflux at four months old is a valid excuse to get on with feeding rapidly digestible solid foods, which stay down more easily than liquid.
- Most babies show significant improvements once they can maintain an upright posture (e.g. sitting and standing).
- See a doctor or specialist if you are worried.

The colicky baby

Just as people might say, 'Oh I had a bit of a bad flu last week', when all they had was a cold — the same thing is true of parents saying, 'Oh our baby had a bit of bad colic yesterday', when it just had some stubborn wind that was difficult to bring up. Most babies have an unsettled period every day, often it's the late afternoon to early evening. To add to the confusion there are other genuine medical conditions that can initially appear to be colic, such as a milk-protein allergy, a lactose intolerance or gastro-oesophageal reflux.

Colic is not a disease — it is a temporary physical disorder. Some experts estimate that about 20–25 percent of babies can suffer a little from colic, but that only about 10 percent of those (i.e. one in 40–50 babies) are considered severe cases. Other experts estimate that about one in 20 babies suffer from full-blown colic. But either way, it is reasonably common.

The strange reality is that colicky babies do not fail to thrive. Despite all their hours of crying, babies with colic are otherwise healthy and happy. In fact, they are often a picture of good health, with a strong sucking reflex and good appetite — they may have an above average weight gain.

Professionals still don't have a conclusive answer, or solution, to colic — it is an incompletely understood phenomenon. Statistically, it is more prevalent in first-born Caucasian babies from mothers in their thirties, but nobody really knows what colic is and what causes it — it's one of the mysteries of Mother Nature. There are of course a number of theories as to the most possible causes of colic:

Theories about causes of colic

- The baby swallows air causing heartburn and gas pains; and/or inadequate burping, causing gas to be trapped between intestinal contractions resulting in excessively stretched segments of intestine.
- Immaturity of the baby's digestive system with inefficient peristalsis (wavelike movement that progresses food along the alimentary canal), e.g. intestinal muscle spasms causing abdominal cramps, spasmodic colon or under-active gastrointestinal tract.
- Adjusting to the stimuli outside the mother's womb causes the baby to be tensed with stress.
- Physiological problems, e.g. insufficient friendly gut flora, or imbalances in intestinal enzymes, hormones or serotonin metabolites.
- General overfeeding, e.g. 1–2 hourly.
- An 'overactive' breastmilk let-down reflex provides too much milk too quickly, making the baby fuss.
- Feeding only on the lactose-rich fore-milk, or swapping breasts during feeding before the baby has received all the fat-rich hind-milk, results in symptoms of lactose-intolerant crying — even though the baby is not actually lactose intolerant — and misdiagnosed as colic.
- Gastro-oesophageal reflux, milk allergies and other intolerances mimicking colic.
- Anxious or tense infant from stress in the home.
- Undiagnosed maternal depression. (Depression may upset the mother's understanding of her baby's signs and symptoms, and she may later realise she had a normal crying baby — depression messes with your mind!)
- A larger than average baby who demands food.
- Feeding baby when it is cold (so its tummy is tensed).
- Mother whose diet is too rich in simple carbohydrates and too low in quality protein, or needs nutritional supplements.
- Numerous lists of culprit foods that it is recommended a breastfeeding mother should avoid, including: wheat (especially refined carbohydrates), yeast, sugar, chocolate, coffee, tea, eggs, peanuts, cows' milk

and dairy products, beef, chicken, pork, beans and curry spices. Plus: colourings, preservatives, soy, vitamin supplements, alcohol, liquorice, some fruits or too much fruit (particularly citrus, strawberries, plums, peaches, pineapple, grapes, dried fruit). Also lots of vegetables (especially raw), including: onion, cabbage, turnips, celery, peppers, watercress, leeks, garlic, cauliflower, Brussels sprouts, broccoli, turnips, radish and beans. *Blimmin' heck — there's not a load of options left.*

- MOST REALISTIC CAUSE OF COLIC: Parents and baby have *bad luck!* Try to accept that your baby has awkward biological rhythms, and that this is just part of your journey along the parenting path, and know that this phase will come to an end!

Note: Changing a breastfed baby to formula is usually *not* the solution.

Symptoms of colic

- Starts at one, two, three or four weeks of age.
- Prolonged bitter crying, irritability, restlessness and writhing 'climbing' movements.
- Baby is comfortable when upright, but wails when laid down — but not always a symptom.
- Loud, intense, continuous and ear-piercing cries that typically go on for 3–4 hours, for no apparent reason.
- Sudden, shrill, high-pitched shrieks for prolonged periods of the day and/or night.
- Inconsolable despite your efforts to cuddle and soothe — baby doesn't want to be held.
- Attacks usually occur around the same time each day, becoming predictable (commonly late afternoons and early evenings).
- Baby draws its knees (legs) well up to the stomach as if in great abdominal pain from an acute tummy-ache — or sticks legs out rigidly straight with an arched back.
- Taut tummy — a hard and swollen belly, which can have grumbling sounds.
- Flailing arms and/or clenched fists.
- Obvious distress with a look of misery — baby is clearly in agony.
- Red in the face, which may become pale and blue around the mouth if the attack is long or severe.
- Cold hands and feet.
- May spit up occasionally.
- Crying episodes can sometimes start or end with the baby sobbing, shaking, farting or doing poos.
- Colic gets worse over the early weeks before it gets better.

- Colic is usually outgrown by 3–5 months (but occasionally takes up to a year).
- You feel overwhelmingly wretched from seeing your baby so miserable.

Possible remedies for colic for baby

A heap of trial and error is involved!

- Burp baby.
- Remove baby from an overstimulating environment.
- Check that you are not fiddling with your baby while feeding (e.g. playing with her toes or rubbing her arm). Your baby's language is touch, and to her your 'chatting' may be overstimulating, exciting, distracting, and making her tummy uptight.
- A pacifier to suckle may help digestion, as it triggers oxytocin production. The down-side is that the baby could end up swallowing more air.
- Allow the baby some frustration from crying, in the hope that it stimulates endorphins.
- Feed your baby when your breasts aren't engorged (express a little off if necessary), and feed when the baby is not ravenously hungry.
- Feed in a calm, relaxed atmosphere away from loud music and bright lights (though that is good advice for all babies).
- If the baby is formula fed, swap formula to a brand designed for colicky babies (hypoallergenic), and swap the bottle and teat to a style designed for colicky babies, such as Chicco™'s anti-colic bottle or Avent™'s disposable bottle bags and anti-colic teats.
- Use Dr Harvey Karp's 'Five S's'. (See page 276.)
- Warmth can be soothing, so lie baby on a hot-water bottle or heated wheat-bag wrapped in a hand-towel or cloth nappy. Or, fill a little zip-lock plastic bag with warm water and place it on baby's tummy under their nappy. Or, lie baby face down on your lap with a warm hot-water bottle under their belly.
- Massage can be soothing: rub the tummy clockwise, rub the back anti-clockwise (both following the direction of the large intestine's colon); do bicycling motions with baby's legs, give a foot massage.
- Try naturopathic and homeopathic remedies such as Weleda™'s Baby Colic Powder and Naturo Pharm™'s Colimed Relief.
- Try every brand of infant winding drops.
- Try gripe water. Traditionally it contains fennel, and perhaps ginger or dill, and baking soda — but it can also be full of fructose sugar. Variations of gripe waters have been used by mothers for almost 300 years to improve a baby's digestion and relieve colicky crying. (It's available in most supermarkets.)

- A little acidophilus and bifidus yoghurt may help baby's digestion — it is also good for the breastfeeding mother to consume.
- Antispasmodic prescription-only medicine (e.g. Merbentyl).
- Breastfeeding mother can take essential-fatty-acid supplements, or give a formula-fed baby a teaspoon of Efamol™ daily.
- Avoid feeding baby starchy food.
- Small amounts of the following essential oils taken internally by baby are said to potentially relieve colic: dill weed seed, caraway seed, cinnamon bark, clove bud and cardamom seed.
- Breastfeeding mothers can try natural teas such as catnip, fennel seed, peppermint, liquorice, chamomile, ginger, mothers milk and/or lactagogue; and add rosemary to your diet — all reputably have good tonic effects on a baby.
- Consider having baby checked by a neonatal cranial osteopath.
- Consider having baby's constitution analysed by a classical homeopath.
- Consider having baby's wellbeing checked by a naturopath.
- Consider having baby visit an acupuncturist who treats babies.
- Try hard not to repress crying with over-the-counter sedatives, except occasionally for night-time sleeps (ensuring it doesn't become habitual, otherwise it's like an adult becoming addicted to sleeping tablets).
- Be prepared to try all the crying solutions at the end of this chapter, see page 290.
- In extreme desperation only, take baby for a car-ride to help them fall asleep.

Possible remedies for parents

Remember it's no one's fault! Accept that this high-needs baby makes you a high-needs parent!

- Keep saying to yourself 'This is not forever, colic does end, life will get better, this is a phase that will pass'.
- Get out of the house at least once a day for a change of scene and some fresh air.
- Get earplugs (screaming next to your ear can be painful).
- Consider yourself, your needs and your sleep as a priority too.
- Ignore ignorant criticisms and questioning, sideways looks.
- Have a shower to drown out the noise and relax a little.
- Listen to relaxing music on headphones while you get jobs done around the house.
- Try to focus your mind on other matters — let the baby cry in his bassinet if necessary, so you can take a short break over a cup of coffee and magazine (with earplugs or Walkman).

- When your baby is sleeping, ring a friend to have a good moan and a therapeutic cry, and to receive some reassuring understanding.
- Alleviate the feelings of isolation that colic can create, by joining a colic-parent-support coffee group, or by joining an internet colic-parent chat-room.
- Release your feelings by starting to write a personal journal.
- Arrange for family or a friend to babysit so you and your partner can go out for dinner — even if it's just a breather of pizza on a picnic bench.
- If you're worried about what the neighbours might be thinking, knock on their doors and explain that your baby has colic. They'll probably be very sympathetic.
- Ask for practical help from family, friends and professionals, realising that you also need to receive positive encouragement.
- Take turns with your partner, alternating each night as to who is at home to deal with that mind-numbing period. You, as mum, need a break to get away from the screaming (not just a break to make dinner) and away from the house on your own. Go for a walk, go to a yoga class, stroll along the beach, have a sauna or spa at the gym, go for a jog — give yourself, for the sake of your sanity and ability to effectively parent (and to avoid a total meltdown), some time away from the gut-wrenching brain-curdling howls.
- Try hard to not resent the situation — don't compare, so you don't despair.
- Know that your baby's colic screams are NOT caused by bad parenting!

Parents of high-needs babies

Parents of a baby with genuine colic, reflux (especially GORD), lactose intolerance or a milk-protein allergy deserve everybody's full-blown sympathy, understanding and immense respect. They have been handed what can be a dreadfully miserable and exhausting, crappy sentence — it often causes emotionally stressful anxiety. It's like torture, as if knives are constantly being driven into their hearts as they fail to console their shrieking, rigid baby.

Combined with extreme sleep-deprivation, a high-needs baby can really pump up their parents' heart-rate and blood pressure through helplessness and frustration at being unable to ease their baby's suffering. It can utterly demoralise, overwhelm and, ultimately, defeat even the most previously competent of parents, turning their lives into a bleak darkness of crushed confidence. It can cause significant marital tension — especially if the dad is able to 'escape' to his job.

The mother can have feelings of self-doubt, failure, rejection, resentment, incompetence, worthlessness, helplessness, loneliness, isolation, frustration and she may even feel as if she is being punished. Combining all that with sleep deprivation and the muscle strain from holding a baby for long periods of time; headaches, nausea and exhaustion can soon set in. It has been reported that 70 percent of parents of babies with colic have dark fantasies at some stage: imagining giving their baby away, or committing infanticide (killing their baby).

The point is, dear, sweet, precious parents-of-a-high-needs-baby, don't let the acidity of guilt decompose the remnants of confidence you have. Your baby *will* outgrow this condition (reflux or colic), and it is not your fault. If you can feel your exhausted and emotionally drained self going psychopathically crazed inside, and you are getting close to your own personal breaking point: talk to your GP, who may suggest an antidepressant. Don't be ashamed; don't be too proud to say that you feel like you can't take it anymore! Look after your own emotions first, so you are then better equipped to look after your baby. And know that high-needs babies do not turn out to be more difficult children, or adults.

Be a wonderful friend

If you are a good friend of a mother with a high-needs baby, one of the best ways you can help is to insist on regularly relieving her of her screaming bundle for a few hours each week.

Mysterious-crying solutions

When a woman has a child she enters the institution of Motherhood, which binds her to her children with cords woven from her own compassion, and makes her a target for the incompetence, selfishness, neglect and posturing of others.

Aminatta Forna — *Mother of all Myths*

One thing that becomes crystal clear regarding methods of helping babies to stop crying, is 'one size doesn't fit all': *all babies are different!* Man, that's a huge understatement.

Finding successful ways to encourage babies to stop crying is probably the biggest trial-and-error experiment that has ever existed — because it has been going on since the dawn of man, is still going on, and is likely to continue to go on for all eternity!

Be prepared for wastage — because you'll waste time, and energy, and positivity, and probably money. Be prepared for disappointments too — you will need great tolerance and patience. And be prepared for unwanted advice. But . . . you'll also experience miraculous joy from attaining momentous and triumphant victories — as you witness the wailing, seething monster transform back into your cooing, beloved and contented wee cherub. This job satisfaction is better described as ecstatic rapture!

Swaddling

Wrapping a baby like a burrito provides them with the same kind of continuous support and touching they received in utero. (See page 217).

White noise

When thousands of random, unrelated sound-frequency tones are combined together at equal power, it is called white noise.

White noise masks or drowns out other sounds and is understood to settle the brain into the meditative alpha state. White-noise machines and white-noise CDs are available, which can be very soothing to babies. Or, try one of your appliances: turn on a fan; turn on or play a recorded tape of your hairdryer or vacuum cleaner; and tune a radio between stations.

Sound CDs and tapes

Lots of CDs and cassette tapes have been created especially for soothing babies. They feature: slushing sounds (to imitate the continual bloodflow and whooshing heartbeat sounds heard in the womb); rhythmic sounds, e.g. baroque music, Mozart, Vivaldi, classical guitar, classical flute, massage music and lullabies; or environmental sounds, e.g. waterfalls and ocean waves. Babies also like to hear recordings of their own mother singing lullabies (even badly); a medley tape of some of your favourite, soothing tunes you listened to while pregnant; or recordings of their own cries.

Other monotonous sounds

Babies enjoy zoning out to many boring, droning, sounds such as a loudly ticking clock, running or dripping water, bathroom extractor, metronome (suggest setting at 60 beats), dishwasher, washing machine, dryer, air-conditioner, or the radio on an easy-listening station.

Visual hypnotisers

Babies also enjoy zoning out by watching a monotonous movement, such as children or pets playing outside, waves on a beach, cars zooming past, running water, a fish aquarium, revolving ceiling fan, a clock's swinging pendulum, chandeliers, swaying wind shadows, leaves fluttering on a tree, curtains being blown by the wind, water flowing from a shower, a metronome, a fire, mum on an exercise machine.

Delightful sights

Babies enjoy pleasurable sights such as pictures of smiling faces, pet animals, a flower to see and smell, or (a big favourite) looking at a mirror. There are also infant videos and DVDs (e.g. 'Baby Einstein'), which are good in moderation — a quick video while you have a shower perhaps. But of course babies need sights that are interactive, such as a real person, for their social development.

Movement

Babies love all kinds of gentle movement. These include battery-operated indoor baby swings, car-rides, getting outside for a stroll in the pram or in a baby front-pack, rolling baby over a beach-ball or large exercise ball, gentle trampoline-bouncing, rocking, jigging, vibrating bouncinettes and of course comfort sucking on a pacifier.

Warm fuzzies

Your baby will enjoy doing things with you, such as being cradled in a baby sling; you talking to him while gently patting his back or bottom; snuggling while nuzzling into your neck; lying on your chest skin-to-skin with his ear listening to your heartbeat; enjoying a warm bath together (infused with lavender oil); singing, humming, murmuring and cooing (such as lullabies with gentle movement); baby massage with lavender oil diluted in a massage carrier oil (such as almond); dancing with baby on your hip (e.g. swinging, dipping, rocking, waltzing, tango, bounces, twirls). And why do we so often automatically hold our babies on the left-side of our chest — perhaps intuitively so the baby can hear our heartbeat.

Phantom cries

I used to imagine I heard the phone or the doorbell ringing when I was in the shower, now I hear phantom baby cries.
Jennifer Ismail, freelance writer

One of the bizarre side effects of hearing your baby cry is that it seems to leave some echoing blueprint within your subconscious, so that you can begin to hear very audible cries from your out-of-sight baby (who isn't actually crying).

When our eldest was three months old, I can distinctly remember attending a child's birthday party on a week day (now I was *really* a mother). I commented to the birthday girl's mum, one of my oldest and dearest friends Lisa, that I could swear I could hear my daughter's cries from the bedroom. 'Oh they're just phantom cries,' she casually commented, 'That's when you think you can hear your baby crying, but they're not — don't worry, you're not going mad.' I was greatly relieved to hear that, bearing in mind I'd been hearing phantom cries for almost three months by then.

This is how the body reacts when a baby keeps screaming and screaming: the heart of the mother begins to pound harder, thrashing about in its cage of bones, squirting out blood. The temples throb and the spit on your tongue and between your teeth dries up.

Sweat springs up in the palms of your hands and the soles of your feet, and every instinct in your body tells you to escape; but you cannot run. You will hear screams in the shower and in your dreams, you will hear screams through the very lining of your head.

Susan Johnson — *A Better Woman*

Chapter 8

Three's a crowd?
Three's a family!

When our grandmothers and mothers gave birth . . .

Fewer women worked outside the home and women probably had fewer professional aspirations. Most importantly, they were less well informed (psychology is a recent science), asked fewer questions about their children's emotional development, and usually worried much less than we do about the way in which they were bringing up their children.

In contrast, mothers today are more concerned, tenser, and much more sensitive to criticisms from a society that seems to tolerate only 'perfect' mothers.

Sylvia Brown and Mary Dowd Struck — *The Post-Pregnancy Handbook*

The couples I saw around me were in good marriages. But the new parents were brittle ... The women were wiped out from baby care and whatever other work they were doing. They looked at the conflicting expectations of motherhood and the workplace, of their feminism and their marriages, and thought: Nothing I do is enough.

The men, too, were tired — they worked all day and came home to have a baby thrust at them. They looked at their father's lives and saw that expectations upon their own lives had doubled, and thought: Nothing I do is enough.

Naomi Wolf — *Misconceptions*

Wow, massive dynamic changes have occurred in your household! It's one thing to live alone together as a couple, and then invite a flatmate to join you. It's a totally different dimension when the third person is a screaming, pooing, vomiting bundle of demands, who can't even *tell* you what their problem is . . . well, that is introducing your household to a whole new world

. . . and it can be like an apocalyptic bomb going off!

In the early 1970s the usual age for childbearing was the early twenties, but now it is the early thirties, with about a third of births in the late thirties and a good chunk in the early forties too. Instead of the postmodern era's 2.5 children, the average is now less than two children per family in New Zealand. These days women are often putting off their first baby until they reach that career goal, finish the house extension, pay off the sporty red cabriolet, climb Machu Picchu, lose 8 kg or clean out the linen cupboard!

Fruitful fertility is often no longer a source of pride — it can just create problems. Motherhood is no longer valued as a kind of maturity zenith. Instead, achieving social status and finding sexual fulfilment are now accepted in society as 'making it'.

Additionally, we now tend to pre-plan and advance-organise to avoid unexpected problems, repeating edifying adages like 'You make your own luck'. Combining that philosophy with the fact that motherhood is now avoidable, and some womanly rights have been almost completely eliminated from society — whinging about the drawbacks and disadvantages of the motherhood role is barely tolerated. It is an insane situation, which is why making friendships with other (sympathetic) mothers can feel so cathartic.

We are an untraditional and revolutionary style of mother today — something this planet has seen little of before. Prior to starting families we may have been a respected, successful, travelled, accomplished, proven, prosperous, autonomous, intrinsically individual woman — expert in being self-assured, self-confident, self-contained, self-controlled, self-determined, self-disciplined and self-sufficient, with self-respect, self-worth and high self-esteem. We may also have been too self-absorbed and self-centred, suffering from self-blame, self-destructiveness, self-importance and self-consciousness. Who made us so damned important to ourselves?

If you as a couple had your own 'anal' draft plans as to what your household life would be like once 'baby made three' . . . chances are, they've ended up in file 13 (the rubbish). If that is the case and your lifestyle priorities have had to be scrapped (at least temporarily) — what now?

Your exclusive coupledom has come to an abrupt end. It was not so hard to juggle two balls but now, learning to juggle three, you're always dropping one on the ground. *Who's been landing face first in your household the most?*

This chapter is filled with my biased and experienced-based ideas as to how we (and many of our friends and family) have maintained positive marital relationships while jointly loving a third tiny being, and while managing to avoid suffocating pangs of loss of self. I know there are probably thousands of books, websites and courses on this subject — containing 'expert' opinions that directly conflict with each other. This is because, statistically, there is about a 50–50 chance of new parents' relationships deteriorating over time, or stabilising and improving over time.

I remember attending a course for parents of toddlers, where the lady tutoring the 'marital relationship' session was a 'formally and professionally trained expert', who was also a solo mother with an underlying attitude of 'If it's not working, drop him and get out'. The couples attending, all new parents, surmised that perhaps she wasn't the most suitable teacher on the subject of maintaining successful marital relations!

Let's face it, *no* couple's relationship is perfect, but Mark and I can say we have a perfectly imperfect relationship. In fact, from my observations, couples that seem perfect usually aren't; and couples that seem imperfect can often be a great team.

Anyway, I could not write this book without dedicating a chapter to this tricky subject!

Child-centred versus parent-centred parenting

The 'core' relationship in a family is that between a husband and wife. Put that relationship first, and children will instinctively know they are in a 'safe' place and will feel secure — and the parents will still be each other's best friend when the children have grown up and left home.

My mum

Some experts believe that, when adults make the conscious decision to become parents, the child-centred parenting method of always considering the child's own preferences first, with all-giving, free-flowing love, can be a joy for the parents to participate in. They can bestow their unlimited affection on their child, successfully satisfying all his or her needs with harmonious parent-baby synchronicity. And, the opposite, authoritarian system of someone deciding what is best for a child for his or her first eighteen years, the same experts believe, produces misery for everyone involved. It creates numerous behavioural problems, and suggests that an idea such as disciplined sleep routines incites child abuse, and that all smacking legitimises violence. *'Interesting concept'* you say. Further reading on the child-centred approach can be found in many books, including from authors Penelope Leach, James Levine, Jan Hunt, and William and Martha Sears.

Some other experts believe that efficiently managed, regulated routines with a tough-love discipline approach of teaching morals (such as teaching a toddler not to touch the stereo instead of utterly kid-proofing the house) are parenting with foresight. That parents have the experience to teach an inexperienced child the limits of acceptable behaviour, thereby guiding them into life with encouragement and correction in order to instil integrity. They see within the opposite system an abdication of parental authority and responsibility, resulting in a reduction in the significance of the parents' relationship, and overly-indulged and manipulative monsters being in charge of their parents. *'Interesting concept'* you say. Further reading on this approach can be found in many books, including by authors Michele Borba, John Rosemond and Gary Ezzo.

In my formally untrained opinion it appears to me that when both parents jointly make a unanimous decision to adopt a particular style, then either system has the ability to work well with extremely positive outcomes.

But there is no system that is suitable for everybody — and different beliefs within society provide a perfectly natural, healthy and necessary diversity. What gets under my skin is the ferocious anger and extremist zeal with which quite a number of experts seek to advocate their beliefs, by trading irrational exaggerations and personal insults with their opponents via the media — fighting like scatty little children.

What also deeply saddens me is seeing couples' relationships turning to custard because the two parents are using opposing systems. For example, the new mother (thanks particularly to all those hormones) adopts an all-encompassing child-centred all-baby-all-the-time approach — while the husband assumed they would be maintaining a somewhat parent-centred ideology. Now he feels like the redundant third-wheel.

Oh, sounds like you two? Did you forget to talk about that before the baby arrived? Hmmm.

So, what did my husband and I choose to do? Well, we were a couple living a full and fulfilling life for a decade before having our children . . . time flies when you're having fun. When a baby became part of our marriage, I am of the (controversial) opinion, that the most important person in my life was still my husband. (Don't misinterpret that to suggest I fed my husband his dinner ahead of our hungry baby. Use common sense, please!)

If you are of the opinion that your baby is a higher priority than your partner, then that might be right for you, and that too is also a controversial opinion. But, we wanted to protect our marriage first. There is a saying 'Great marriages make great parents' and that has been our goal.

Mum, let your man be joint managing director

Perhaps the most common mistake any new mother can make is to become so fiercely protective of her new charge, which she only wants the best for, that she forgets that second-best is still fine.

Think back: when is your earliest childhood memory? Probably at around four years of age. So you know what that means? All your baby-perfectionism is never going to be remembered by your little darling. And here's the scary thing, your big darling (the dad) can find it hard to forget all your martyrdom and baby-perfectionism, and your unrealistic expectations for him to be the perfect father.

Please, unless it is potentially life-threatening, *don't criticise* your baby's dad when he's trying to parent. Guys generally are not at all confident to start with. They're well aware you're having heaps more practice than they are, and if you want them to continue to help you, just tell them that every dad-duty they're doing is wonderful! Otherwise, they will quickly learn that the grief isn't worth the effort of trying to help. (Heck, their dads didn't have to do all that 'woman's work' — so why should they, just to end up getting shrilled at.)

So, if your man puts the nappy on so loosely that it's about to fall down, don't worry about it. What's the worst thing that will happen — you'll need to wash one extra baby outfit . . . What if he is holding the bottle incorrectly and your wee babe is fussing? Don't interfere, he will probably soon say 'Baby can't be hungry' — to which you can reply 'Maybe not, Hun, I'll give it another go a bit later' . . . What if he dresses Bub in the most embarrassingly bizarre combination of clothes that you're left wondering how you could have ever married a man with such a lack of taste? Well, bite your tongue, and say 'Oh great, you got Babe dressed.'

But this coin has two sides. So, when he manages to get it right, then *tell* him so. 'Thanks so much, Hun, for dressing her so smartly, she looks really cute' . . . 'Thanks so much for dealing with that major pooey nappy, it's amazing what can exit out of Junior' . . . 'Thanks so much for giving Bub her apple-custard, there's less mess on her face than when I do it' . . . because like all humans, he too responds to praise.

I remember one afternoon I babysat for a close girlfriend so she could go out. When her sweet (macho) hubby arrived home from work — a man who has been a dear friend since before my twenty-first — their youngest daughter needed her clothes changed, and he insisted he would get the task done. Quite a few minutes later, I thought I'd better just check how things were going, to find him trying to put her singlet on feet-first. It was such a funny sight, I almost wet my pants (sorry, Shane!), but I just said, 'You know, I find those singlets are a bit easier to get on if I put their head in first', to which he replied something like 'Oh OK, I'll try it.'

Men can be so gorgeous. Don't take that beauty away from them with your reflex-action, snapping perfectionism, when your baby is *fine*! Try not to be an over-possessive new mum by criticising and re-doing your partner's less-than-perfect efforts — he's had less practice (and perhaps paid less attention, we know).

Don't teach your husband how to be helpless. Mums hate to feel as if they're nagging their husbands, and dads loathe coming home to a boss who's barking commands. One of the best pieces of advice I've read was, 'Divide up the jobs and stay out of each other's territory.' Men love concrete tasks, so when he comes home each evening, have your independent, pre-designated roles. It is easier to both know who does what and each get on with it — without criticising the other!

Often it's something like Dad does the bath and baby massage while Mum makes dinner. Then Dad does the burping and lullaby while Mum cleans up dinner. I know that's very stereotypical, and truly you do it any way that works for you, but that's the point . . . Find the roles that work for you, and leave each other in their sole-charge positions.

As for the night-watch, well Dr Christopher Green (and obviously he's a man) observed that new dads can generally tolerate cold food, unwashed clothes and reduced attention. But when they're deprived of sleep, they fall apart. While that may be bluntly honest, it will certainly get up a lot of women's noses.

My husband has never ever gotten up in the middle of the night to any of our children — he sleeps so soundly it was never worth my effort to try to wake him up. But just as a crying baby rarely woke him, his early alarm clock rarely wakes me. I am very aware that many wives (and jealous husbands) will think this is appalling, and in a way it is (sorry, Honey). But he is a foreman on building sites, and I wanted his head as well-slept and clear-brained as possible, before he goes walking across scaffolding like a monkey, or using power tools with cut-your-fingers-off blades. I willingly took the night-wakes on as my job.

That worked for us, but there is *no reason* why that should have to work in your household, especially if you know you fall apart with anything under 8–9 hours' sleep.

Remember, at the end of the day, most men want to be securely happy in a solid relationship with a loving wife and adoring children. A new mother has countless opportunities to turn their partner's dream into a complete nightmare. Almost every woman is inherently born with the ability to bitch — the nag-gene. But try hard, really, really hard, not to bitch at your man about his fatherhood skills or parenting ideas. If you really must get it off your chest, save it for your diary or an understanding girlfriend.

The squalid bomb-site

You trawl the house for washing the whole time and feel like your life is being sucked up by the hoover.

Kate Figes — *Life After Birth*

I hate housework! You make the beds, you do the dishes — and six months later you have to start all over again.

Joan Rivers, comedian

My mother tells the story of one unforgettable winter's day she spent indoors with her first-born — my sister Helen — as a nine-month-old. Mum decided, with typical mothering ingenuity, to tie the playpen to the hinges of the kitchen cupboards to safely keep it in one place, while she got on with baking, dressmaking and drying the nappies over a heater.

Later that evening, when my father walked into that 3 x 5 metre kitchen-dining room after a stressful day and working late at the office, he was not only greeted by my mother's smile — but also by the kitchen bench covered in unwashed baking dishes, a vast pile of unfolded nappies, dressmaking material scraps and pattern paper covering most of the floor, toys scattered everywhere thanks to my sister throwing them out of the play-pen after mum would throw them in, and the play-pen still tied to the kitchen cupboard. Collectively, not a pretty picture. Mum recalls to this day the pained look on Dad's face, and vowed to herself to never inflict such a homecoming on him again.

Even while writing this book, for some time I relaxed from my normally level 6–7 (quite tidy) house, down to a deteriorated level 3–4 (chaotic mess throughout the entire house), when I made the conscious decision to ignore the mess to get on with writing. And my dear sweet husband finally got the courage up to, ever so delicately, broach the subject by asking, 'Hun, are you OK at the moment?' To which I replied, 'Sure, what do you mean, have I been cranky or something?' 'No, no, it's nothing, you've been fine.' 'Well what is it then? Come on, tell me, what's concerning you?' 'It's just, well, it's just . . . the *house*!' I laughed so hard. The poor sweetie had thought he might be on thin ice.

You know our menfolk don't like too much chaos. Even though we can work around it, because we're focusing on something else, but those guys do look forward to coming home to their refuge. They yearn to come home to a happy contented wife, who loves her role, and enjoys putting a nice simple dinner on the table. It's their soul food.

I remember a friend, Sandra, telling me once that she decided to not put anything away for a whole day — not one toy or dish or towel — and not to make any beds or fold any washing or wipe up any mess. Instead, she just had fun enjoying her kids all day. When her husband returned home that night, of course the reaction was, 'Wow what happened here today?' to which she replied something like, 'Nothing unusual — I just didn't tidy up today.' It proved a point, and he no longer wondered what she did!

But of course there is another side to this coin, and that is the mum who becomes so territorial and fastidious with her domain that when her caveman arrives home, he and his belongings can be made to feel more like pieces of clutter that are creating unwanted mess — that's not welcoming.

Lets face it, if mums aren't able to maintain a house in a reasonable state of relative tidiness, their menfolk can really find it depressing. But if we do maintain the house in a reasonable state of relative tidiness, then we can feel unappreciated and that's depressing.

So one answer to the riddle . . . try to tidy things up a bit before your caveman comes in from his hard day of hunting; but every so often let things run amuck. Take a break from gathering up the mess, so he doesn't forget what it is that you do. Then both the Hunter and the Gatherer are happy!

Sex? Maybe . . .

At the recommended time, we try a bit of sex. It's a wasteland down there. Women are awful liars. I do not think of all the women who gave birth in pain any more, I think of all the women who conceived in pain; the Irish families with eleven months between one child and the next.

Anne Enright — *Making Babies*

Lots of new mums after giving birth think 'Sex? Sex! I don't know that I'm ever having sex again — please, just leave my body alone. My body's been tenanted for most of the past year, and this landlord needs some solitude for a while. You're not to bring that thing anywhere near my insides — well not till I maybe want another child.'

The medically recommended period of sexual abstinence is six weeks or so after delivery, due to the possibility of uterine infection. But often it's not until your baby's two to three months old that you will realise you may not have had a delectable cuddle (let alone climactic snog) for a very long time, and the subject of resuscitating life in your boudoir enters your consciousness (or maybe you start receiving hints from your he-man).

It is usual at the six-week postnatal check for your GP or LMC to remind you that it may be time to be considering the need for contraception again — oh yes, some women do have two babies born in the same calendar year, and I don't mean twins. (I have one girlfriend who was thoroughly enjoying sex again just a couple of weeks after a full episiotomy. Eeek!) My advice to you on this so-very-personal topic is that if you aren't feeling like sex, just know that *you are not frigid* or unusual at all, you're quite normal in fact.

Points to note for first postnatal sex:

- No sex while there is still lochia bleeding.
- No sex before an episiotomy or caesar scar has fully healed.
- About two out of three women initially find sex 'uncomfortable'.
- If you had an episiotomy, then you have a particularly high chance that first sex postpartum will be somewhat painful — but the same discomfort should not go on for months. (See Dyspareunia, page 303.)
- Due to the oxytocin released in your bloodstream from love-making, in the first weeks your boobs may leak milk, and you may feel uterus involution contractions afterwards.
- If your perineum is sore afterwards, a cold witch-hazel compress will probably feel pretty good.
- Especially if you're breastfeeding, due to the drop in oestrogen, you are going to need lubrication (because it's normal to be dry), so have some lubricant such as KY Jelly™ or even some olive oil ready for the big reunion.

Sex-life after birthing life? No, thank you!

Mother Nature can interfere with a woman's libido for up to two years post childbirth, in an attempt to try to prevent the female from becoming impregnated again too soon.

Also, if the mother's body is low in some vitamins or minerals (e.g. folic acid from anaemia) then that will affect the sexual-pleasure centre of the brain, by making a woman feel disinterested.

Additionally, one of our body's basic survival mechanisms is to hinder sexual arousal when we are angry, anxious, cold, fearful, hungry, in pain, sad or tired. So here's the point that many new dads don't get (and many couples don't have a clue about either) . . .

When a new mum is feeling overwhelmed, ugly, exhausted and unloved — she usually loses the natural desire to 'mate' because in Nature these are far from suitable circumstances for conception. When she's a milking machine at one end, frankly she may have no inclination to perform her 'conjugal duties' at the other!

And after childbirth, there can also be a delicate but profound change in how the new mum perceives her partner — she can find his attractiveness subtly influenced by how he performs as a father, more than by his performance as a partner.

If her husband willingly helps with chores, adoringly enjoys nurturing their child, displays that he's a good dad, happily shares the parenting load, lovingly pays her caring attention, and maintains close bonds with her emotionally — *hey presto*, just like magic, she may find him sexually attractive — because in Nature these are suitable circumstances for conception.

There is a subtle, unconscious link between a man's enthusiasm for being a dad and assisting domestically and a woman's sexual enthusiasm, even though a lot of women and most men are probably unaware of this correlation. Naomi Wolf highlights these studies in *Misconceptions*, as outlined in John Gottman and Nan Silver's book *The Seven Principles for Making Marriage Work*.

When you are finally ready to move on from a cuddle, and want to rock each other's world again, then it can be very nice to return to the pleasure of having sex-for-just-two again (instead of that three's-a-crowd sex when your baby was kicking). But I must remind you girls (and boys) that sex can also make for leaking titties, with milk even shooting out during orgasm!

As for positions, well in the early days the classic man-on-top can be uncomfortable after childbirth — it can be much better to go for the woman-on-top. By the way, did you realise that the clitoris is the only organ in the human body that has pleasure as its single function? And, as highlighted by Eve Ensler in *The Vagina Monologues*, it has twice as many sensitive nerve endings as a penis!

Dyspareunia — painful sex

As many as one in five women can experience dyspareunia (acute pain during sex), that is not gradually decreasing three-plus months after giving birth. Or, for example, they may find the seam in jeans impossibly uncomfortable.

If you are one of that 20 percent of women, you should discuss it with your LMC or doctor even at just six weeks after childbirth, and have the sore area looked at — it's a condition that may need to be sorted out medically, and can almost always be fixed.

It could be problems such as a stitch not removed (or absorbed); or a neuroma (lump of tangled nerve tissue at the episiotomy scar); or a granuloma (lump of inflamed skin tissue); or vaginismus (sudden painful contractions of the vaginal muscles in spasm response to touch). Ongoing painful sex doesn't need to be tolerated!

Breastfeeding: the natural contraceptive?

It's a common joke that birth control in the postnatal period is mostly achieved through 'baby interruptus'.
   Naish and Roberts — *The Natural Way To Better Breastfeeding*

It is reasonably common for a fully lactating mother to take 6–12 months before their menstruation returns, often coinciding with the baby's increasing appetite for solid food; or within a couple of months after weaning. So it is quite true that breastfeeding is a natural birth control — but its effectiveness can vary from one woman to another depending on many contributing factors. For example, with our first baby I had no periods for 11 months; with our second baby I had lochia for a month and a first period two weeks later; and with our third child, I can't remember — bit of postnatal amnesia I reckon.

If total abstinence is not a happening thing, and if you definitely do not want to fall pregnant straight away, then it is sensible to rely on some form of birth-control method other than just breastfeeding, because some women do give birth again within twelve months. Remember, that just as soon as your ovary follicles secrete the right levels of oestrogen again, and before you menstruate your first postnatal period, *you may ovulate*.

And when that first postpartum period does arrive, it can be particularly heavy. The homeopathic remedy China can help, as can the naturopathic remedies of sage tea, evening primrose oil and chaste tree berry.

Barrier birth-control methods include the likes of condoms, spermicides (e.g. foam), and diaphragms. (Note: If you used a diaphragm before childbirth, you're very likely to need to be re-fitted for a new size.)

There is the IUD (intrauterine device) that is inserted into the uterus through the cervix and prevents the implantation of a fertilised egg on the interior wall of the womb. IUDs are most successfully used by women who have previously given birth, and can often provide a trouble-free form of contraception, with the IUD simply needing to be replaced every few years. Some IUDs (e.g. Mirena®) secrete mood-stabilising progesterone — but that may interfere with breastmilk production.

There is the world's most-used form of contraception, 'the pill' — one of the most widely used drugs on the planet. The pill tricks the hypothalamic-pituitary control system by lulling it to sleep because it thinks the woman is pregnant. She has no ovarian follicle eggs maturing so her ovulation ceases, which also results in a reduced menstrual flow. Commonly, breastfeeding mums are offered the mini-pill (progesterone only, no oestrogen) as it is less likely to interfere with the lactation hormone prolactin. However, any hormonal contraception can upset the fine balance that can be required to produce perfect amounts of breastmilk.

For the sake of breastfeeding, some experts strongly advocate avoiding all hormonal contraception including injectable contraception (e.g. Depo-Provera®), and implants (e.g. Norplant®) ideally until the baby is six months of age, or at least until a good milk supply is well established. For your information, some research is suggesting that prolonged use of Depo-Provera® is causing an irreversible loss of bone density.

There are, of course, the usually permanent birth-control methods of male vasectomy (a simple operation that cuts the ducts running between the testes and penis); or female tubal ligation (that clamps the fallopian tubes running between the ovaries and uterus). The female operation is major surgery, so it is one that some women pre-plan to include with a C-section.

The three main types of natural birth-control are, firstly, coitus interruptus, which is withdrawing the penis just before ejaculation, but this is not a greatly reliable method as those little boys are designed for long-distance swimming!

Secondly, there is the natural-family-planning, fertility-awareness 'rhythm method' of the woman knowing when she is ovulating and fertile because, even without breastfeeding, a woman is only fertile about 30 days a year. This method involves the woman accurately recording her temperature daily to know when it lowers slightly just prior to ovulation, and rises slightly just after ovulation, and noting the changes in consistency of her vaginal mucous (which becomes sticky and then clear and stringy like egg-white during the fertile period). However, breastfeeding disrupts these signs and symptoms.

Thirdly, there is LAM or the lactational amenorrhoea (absence of menstrual periods) method. It is well known that breastfeeding suppresses a woman's fertility — however, what many women don't realise is that if they can tick 'Yes to all' in the list below, then they have a less than two percent chance of falling pregnant:

- Mother's period hasn't returned.
- Baby is less than six months old.
- Mother is breastfeeding on demand during the day (minimum of 4-hourly).
- Mother is breastfeeding on demand during the night (minimum of 6-hourly).
- Baby is receiving no other feeds (liquids or solids).

Contraception and birth control methods are an intensely personal decision — so it's a matter of finding the right one for your needs . . . or getting on with giving your baby a brother or sister!

B.C. — A.D. (before children — after delivery)

Every pre-child couple has their own unique habits, their own quirky routines, and although things may need to be somewhat tweaked, don't allow yourselves to lose what was your joint identity.

It can be really hard to find the time to be a couple because you can no longer be so free and easy (losing spontaneity is a parental cost), but I can't encourage you enough to make every effort as a couple to continue to be a couple . . . continue doing whatever it is that you used to really enjoy.

Such as watching old sci-fi videos on Friday nights cuddled on the couch with a king-size bar of chocolate; or having Sunday brunch at your favourite café; or enjoying a wine on the deck after dinner; or going on bush-walks together; or completing the crossword together over coffee; or having breakfast in bed on Saturday mornings with a good book; or meeting your friends at the local pub on Thursdays after work. Whatever it was that was special to you two, maintain it, don't lose it. Yes it will take more effort to get out of the house, but persevere, and soon that effort will become easier. Young babies can be extremely portable if you allow them to be!

For us personally, a must is to socialise on the weekends, usually on Saturday nights, even if it is just friends coming over for a BBQ. As a mother I have almost obsessively ensured that my weekends feel like weekends — I had seen too many mothers before me disappear off the social circuit due to 'parenting commitments'.

We have *taught* our children to easily go to sleep wherever, and over the years they've slept in some really crazy places while we've been out. And our kids thrive on it too, they're wonderfully well-socialised, independent little individuals.

Another one of my personal favourite times to socialise these days is on

Friday afternoons with girlfriends and a few wines. I find it a great way to chill out for the start of the weekend.

I remember once trying to invite a couple over for dinner who had two children aged four and five-and-a-half. I started by suggesting that us mums could get together on the Friday afternoon with the kids, and the dads could join us later with a takeaway dinner. But that was turned down: 'Oh not on Fridays, it's the end of the week and the kids are tired.' How about a Saturday night? I suggested. We could give the kids something simple to eat, throw them down to bed, and have a few laughs ourselves over the dinner table. But that was politely turned down: 'Oh we'd have to be gone by 7 o'clock because the children won't go to sleep in someone else's house.' So, I suggested perhaps they came over on a Sunday afternoon, as we could let all the kids have a play, and then have an early dinner all together. But that too was politely turned down: 'Oh no we have to be home on Sunday nights as the children need some quieter time and an early night with Monday being the next day.' *Good grief.* So, of course, I gave up.

Had they as a couple cut out nearly all their socialising for the past five years? And for how many more years did they plan to forego their weekend evenings? Parents need adult company too.

Parenting versus partnering: so who does she really love the most?

For the baby's biological survival, Mother Nature provides new mums with her strongest hormonal cocktail, to ensure the new mother stays preoccupied with making the new baby her number-one priority! Mother Nature is not about to rely on the ram, bull or stallion to stick around.

Although human beings generally desire to live monogamously in a family unit if at all possible — some new dads' noses can get out of joint because they start getting *jealous* of the naturally strong bond between the mum and baby. He's thinking, 'So now that she has a baby, I feel like just a sperm donor. Who does she love the most? That helpless incontinent vomiting squawker, or me?' (When the mum asks herself that question, it usually has no right answer.) But you know what, to maintain your family, a more important question is . . . Who does your partner think you love most?

Most women have to deal with a male partner who is trying to embrace all his scary new responsibilities too, like now being the main household provider. He's trying to get it all right, but may be repeatedly boxed with a left-hand jab (or hit out of the ring completely) from just *trying* to get it right. So try not to take your own self-doubts out on your imperfect partner.

Just as we need to feel as if we are the most important person in the world to our partners, our partners need to feel that they are the most needed person in the world to us. In the same breath, it is also time for the man of the household to grow up.

> The most important thing a father can do for his children is to love their mother.

But women hear me roar: No woman should ever stick around for a second to endure being bashed or battered (physically or mentally) to maintain a relationship with her children's father. Absolutely, categorically, NO.

She's/he's really pissed me off this time

As a couple, try to make a concerted effort not to have Majors over Minors. In other words, try hard not to have some awful argument over something really trivial . . . I know you didn't want your baby to have a bottle in the late afternoon because it would fill her up before dinner, but it's happened, oh well, no one's died . . . I know you asked him to grab the nappies before you went out, and he forgot, but you can buy a packet at the petrol station . . . I know you think you didn't deserve her yelling at you that loudly for forgetting the milk on your way home, but remember, she only had five hours' sleep last night, and she's tired!

Whatever you do, when you are annoyed at something your partner does or does not do, don't criticise him with hostile contempt — so no derogatory comments about his character, no sarcasm, no sneering, no personal put-downs, no regurgitating past disappointments — and no defensive stone-walling on your part by refusing to talk. Express your honest feelings in a respectful way. Don't sulk, hold grudges, make bitchy or jerkish comments — in other words, don't act like children!

And . . . try hard to *never* go to sleep at night with an unresolved argument. That's just so foul, and you won't have time to deal with it the next morning, or the next early evening, and by then the whole thing's gone on for 24 hours. Always sort things out before you go to sleep. If it's unresolvable, even just agree to disagree — because time will probably resolve it.

But my life has deteriorated so much

My life as a mother had become just what I feared. My delight in our child was absolute. At the same time, I experienced a tightening of the world's circumference; I was chained to the couch, nursing; I was stunned with fatigue; I was a vast primate of flesh — none of the weight gained in pregnancy had 'melted away'.

Naomi Wolf — *Misconceptions*

For some of you, the ideas I have given so far in this chapter make sense, but you have been rocked to the core! You may be feeling so trapped in such a deep dingy hole of epic mothering commitment, that it feels too difficult to climb up the ladder of life, to get yourself back to ground level — the ball and chain attached to your foot are too heavy. A lot of us have felt that way in the aftermath of childbirth, but rarely admit it.

You get so tired, so scared, so sad and so dammed pissed off that you don't have enough energy left for the effort needed to climb out. Most days you don't even have a reason to get dressed, let alone entertain!

After the brief new-mother interlude of feeling like a star, you realise through the labour of childbirth, that you have been teleported into full adulthood. But, somehow, your partner's transformation is going to be more gradual — and on some unexplainable level, you resent him for that.

You didn't marry your husband for him to be the breadwinner and head of the household. You married him because he was your best friend, and you wanted to spend the rest of your life with your best friend. But somehow now, as he subconsciously applies the new aftershave scent 'Master', your relationship seems irreconcilably feudal.

So where has that friendship vanished? It's as if it has completely evaporated. He seems to have become some defensive and evasive saboteur. You have lost so much, but it feels appalling to allow yourself to grieve for your old life, so you're left aching with a grief that you've not yet come to terms with.

You've lost the confident, vibrant, competent, self-reliant, multi-dimensional, independent you.

You've lost the slim (well, slimmer!) body you felt good being inside of, the body you may have sweated hours and hours to achieve, and in under one year it has become the worst body you've ever had in your entire life. You know that has impacted on your sexual identity, and you're utterly fed up with hearing how pelvic-floor exercises are such a damn cure-all.

You've lost your financial worth and status in the hierarchy of 'success' — and now you miss all those old ego-reinforcing experiences that you didn't think you needed.

You've lost all privacy and personal freedom, and time to just do what you want to do at that moment, be it breakfast in bed, a soak in a bath, a flick through the newspaper with a perfect coffee, trying on a skirt in a shop, having a long chat on the phone, popping quickly into the dairy, or watching your favourite TV programme without fear of interruption. In fact, you have lost almost all control over every second of your life and you're never alone, yet you used to have full control over your entire day. You've lost the right to eat a leisurely dinner, stay up late, to come and go as you please, to daydream, or even to have a flippin' weekend off work. You've lost all rights to please yourself, forever.

You thought motherhood would be fun, interlaced with precious moments of tranquil peace — but you sure ain't having that much fun, and there's almost no peace. So you often find yourself envying your partner's free and independent lifestyle — resenting his game of golf or touch rugby or squash on a Wednesday night, or his work's Friday afternoon Happy Hour drinks that he continues to enjoy.

You've become aware, too, that you've somehow lost your position of being a little girl, you've moved up a generation. You're forever a woman now — and a boring one at that. You're even feeling shame at your resentment towards your tiny screamer, for taking your time away from enjoying the company of your partner, alone.

You've lost your inner sense of control. Your raw emotions are undiluted, and you can't push the stop button on your mind's video of the haunting birth. Frankly, you feel as if you have lost your whole identity in one massive, annihilating explosion. It's been blown into a million insignificant fragments. You had your identity right up until arriving at the delivery suite — you were that appealingly pregnant lady with that nice hairstyle and those fashionable clothes doing that interesting career.

And now too, probably worst of all, you may feel as if you have lost your best friend. He finds refuge in his work then he comes home, gives you a peck on the cheek, lavishes attention on your baby (which you so love to see) but gives you, the person, almost no attention, or at least never the right attention.

He rarely seems to think to do anything more around the house than that which you've asked him to do, and he hardly ever caringly asks how he can be of help to you. In fact, he never seems to ask enough about how you're coping. You know he doesn't really want to talk deeply with you to hear about how depressed you feel — and you feel too pitiful to tell him even if he did ask.

You miss the two of you being together in your old coupleness. You know that he's taken on the head of the household role, maybe he thinks his job now is to just bring home the cash, and take out the trash — because clearly it is your job to be the childcarer — you're so much more 'natural' at it than him, of course (not).

You know, too, in your heart, that professionally your goals, dreams and aspirations will always be of lesser importance now. All that conscientious dedication or overtime without pay — was it all for nothing?

You're so bloody lonely and alienated, you feel such anger and despair, you feel dowdy on the outside and heinous on the inside. You've lost the old you, and you detest the new you.

Everyone tells you how in love you will become with your own children, *and you are utterly committed* to your baby: you know now you would die for your child. But you're lost inside some cavernous emotional darkness. Deep inside, you are withering from a slow, painful, aching agony.

My dear sweet friend, you're *not* alone.

What can you do about it? Nothing . . . And everything . . .

And the first thing to do is to come to terms with accepting the predicament.

You have lost the old you, and you are now feeling paralysed by the new you. And, only you can work through and get past your sense of personal loss. How do you do that? One day at a time, one step at a time.

The self-help list for the life-sucks syndrome

I'm so dull now that my personality even bores myself!
Alison, my girlfriend (mother of two pre-schoolers)

Here is a list of practical suggestions and restorative tonics to help you to start coming to terms with your new life, to create a new normality, as you re-invent and fall in love with yourself all over again.

But, try not to get even more tired from reading this list. Instead think of it as shelves in a supermarket from which you will pick ingredients to improve the taste, texture and palatability of your life.

- Make rest a priority in your day, because tiredness makes everything more difficult to cope with. Go to bed earlier. If you've got itchy burning sore eyes, blurry vision, chills, waves of fatigue, slowed reflexes, anxiety, lethargy, irritability, inability to concentrate and you rarely smile or laugh anymore, realise that these can all be signs of extreme sleep-deprivation.
- Make improving your diet a priority too. You need to eat well. Eat little but often (even six meals a day while breastfeeding). Get good-quality foods into your body, especially high-protein snacks (that fight fatigue and depression). Drink loads of water, and cut back on excess salt — even eliminate caffeine and sugar if you can. (They create a blood-sugar imbalance.) Oats (such as muesli or porridge) can be a great tonic for the nerves. Teas such as Siberian ginseng or Withania (Indian ginseng) benefit your adrenal glands and your levels of energy intensity.
- If you know you are constantly emotionally or physically stressed, your

blood glucose levels are probably suffering, and you may be (unintentionally or subconsciously) running your life on adrenaline (along with its subsequent cravings for high-starch, high-sugar and high-fat foods). Realise it, and try to make the intentional and conscious decision to *stop* it — eating better and resting more is the right start. Another side effect of all that adrenaline and cortisol pumping through your veins, is the suppression of your immune system, which makes you more vulnerable to becoming sick. I know your first thought is probably to ignore your own needs for the time being, but please don't deprive yourself — remember, depriving you is depriving your baby of the best you.

- If you are getting cracks in the corners of your mouth, mouth sores, are feeling irritable, fatigued or emotionally unstable, these signs are usually indications that you are particularly low on vitamin B.
- Take a comprehensive daily maternity multivitamin and trace mineral supplement, because you need the wellbeing those nutrients will provide your body and mind, especially folic acid, potassium, manganese, zinc and omega-3.
- *Teach your baby to sleep through the night* — if you can sleep solidly at night, you will be much less irritable. Stop making excuses as to why your particular baby won't sleep through the night, and finally realise that it can be done (and the sooner the better) otherwise none of the rest of these suggestions will probably work, because you'll be too darn tired! (Go back to the basics of chapter 5, pages 205–233.)
- Delay any majors in your life if possible, such as redecorating, renovations or shifting house. If there are things in your everyday environment that are stressful, try to rid yourself of them — *not counting the baby, that is!* If you've got some old issues or unfinished business stressing you out, take charge of whatever it is and deal with it. Doing so will stop you feeling so out of control.
- Realise you may need to begin to *teach* yourself to *enjoy* again, to crack a smile on that frowning dial, and smiling with your eyes again too. Seek to purposefully locate (and use) your sense of humour — we all deserve to be happy.
- Have a blood test to check your iron levels and thyroid activity.
- Visit an osteopath to check that your lower back and sacrum (pelvis posterior) have not been slightly displaced from childbirth, as this can impact on the emotional brain, the 'limbic system', affecting your instinctual reflexes, emotional drive, and moods such as pleasure.
- Have a repairs-and-maintenance service visit with your naturopath *and* homeopath — homeopathy and naturopathy work brilliantly together.

Homeopathic tinctures and naturopathic herbs can provide great healing. Bach flower remedies and pure essential oil aromatherapy can also be very beneficial.

- Try to disregard pressure from other peoples' expectations of you as a mother and ignore criticisms and unwanted advice.
- Lower the expectations you place on yourself, realising second-best is still just fine — your baby will never remember! Reduce your need for control, so you can chill out and go-with-the-flow of your new career. Avoid being the tormenting taskmaster to yourself, and forget the misguided ideals of being the Supermum who has everything perfect (your house and you particularly) . . . instead *enjoy* and *cuddle* your baby, and just *be* in the moment. Motherhood *can* be delightfully spontaneous!
- If one of your Supermum ambitions was to use only cloth nappies and now you're resenting how labour-intensive they can be, why not join the majority of modern mums and try disposables? Lowering standards of perfection can be so freeing! If your main deterrent against changing is the fact that you'd told the world you would never use disposables, well it's time the world met the new liberated you — a woman empowered with the ability to change her mind! (Changing your mind is something you'll do often on the whole journey of parenthood.)
- If a couple of months have passed since the birth of your baby, and you're still feeling disappointment, bitterness or anger about how imperfectly the delivery went, then admit it, cathartically write your story down in a journal, and mentally hand it over to the universe (i.e. God, life, fate), making the conscious decision to get on with your new life. Don't let those insidious, festering emotions permanently anaesthetise and stain your new mothering memories.
- If some of that birth-experience disappointment stems back to thoughts that, for whatever reason(s), you should have been better prepared, or feel somehow that you didn't assert enough control over the birthing process, then accept that new wisdom with humbleness and dignity, know you've learnt from it, let it go, and move on.
- Realise with *welcoming acceptance* that your life has changed forever — and how exciting is that! Realise too, that you don't need to conform to any stereotypical role of being a mother — choose to be different, to be a proud individual, radical even, but choose to be a person with her own completely unique mothering style.
- If it stops you feeling irked, then make it your first priority, every day, to get yourself showered and dressed with a little make-up on before 9 am — even before the dishes, before the washing, before the tidying, before

your breakfast if necessary — just decide your appearance is the *first* household task, and remind yourself you are not being selfish. (Your baby does not need to be asleep for you to have a shower — lying on a rug or in a bouncinette watching you is just fine.) As author Robin Lim says, 'Water often washes away much more than dirt. It can wash away stress and loosen stuck tears'.

- Or, if it stops you feeling irked, then slob till the afternoon in your grungy pyjamas, to emphasise to yourself that this is your time of recovery and rest.
- If you're really peeved about something or someone, go and thump a pillow. Think of it as your equivalent to a punch-bag at the gym. Release your pent up annoyance on a pillow, it can feel so therapeutic.
- If you haven't yet, then start to massage your baby — soothing your baby nourishes your own soul because it can almost instantaneously improve the mum-baby bond. If you feel as if you're floundering with your baby massage technique, then attend a course, hire a video, read a book, or surf the net, but get pro-active and teach yourself how to do infant massage. (See page 260.)
- Get outside of the house at least once a day, every day, and the earlier the better, newborns are very portable — even just a five-minute stroll (not hike) with the pushchair around the block; or lying on a picnic rug reading a great book; or sitting under a tree with your eyes closed; or having a latte and yummy muffin outside at a café while browsing a magazine; or a sunset meander along the beach. Getting outdoors, especially for a half-hour walk, is mentally refreshing and emotionally uplifting. Another particularly healing thing to do is planting and weeding flowers or vegetables — it is a grounding activity that envelops you in Mother Earth's restorative energy.
- Give yourself at least a 20–30 minute lunch break every day, where you zone-out from mothering. Read a glossy magazine, do a crossword, watch *Oprah* or *Dr Phil*, even get secretly addicted to *East Enders* if you want to. It really doesn't matter. Just give yourself that half-hour of carefree time each lunchtime, regardless of everything else you should be doing. It's so refreshing!
- Avoid continual isolation. Have some friends over for a cuppa, even every day if that's what you want; or have lengthy chats on the phone; or relax with friends sharing a bottle of wine (in moderation, as alcohol is actually a depressant). Hearing other mothers whinge can be very normalising.
- Be cheerful. Be kind. It's that old swings-and-roundabouts universal law

of reaping what you sow, and getting what you give.

- If you don't already have an inspiring, encouraging friend who has similar philosophies to yours, then find one. Keep circulating socially until you find that 'sister' to buddy-up with. Close friends can provide amazing support.

- Join a coffee group for new mothers . . . start your own or ring Plunket, or Parents Centre or the local Community Centre — but find a group of new mothers to join with, because it can be an incredibly supportive and empathetic environment. And teach yourself to be a good conversationalist too — which means listening twice as much as you talk.

- Don't add to the walls of secret conspiracy about how much motherhood comes naturally to you by talking the breezy garbage that your life is wonderful and everything is fine. Instead, knock down those walls by admitting how stressful, mundane and sometimes overwhelming the exhausting hard work of motherhood and being ordinary is. Tell the truth!

- If you've got what you feel is a silly question you need answered, ring the parent-help lines, e.g. Plunket. That's what they're there for. They won't think your question is silly and they won't think you're stupid. They've heard it all before, and they can provide you with instant support.

- If you are still reeling at how difficult it is now to fit in with your childless friends, that's quite common. You may be worlds apart for now — that's logical and to be expected. True friends never really leave — but they too could be feeling awkward (especially any childless girlfriends who are suffering through the desperate craving of infertility).

- Remember the activities you used to enjoy, and *do* them! Some mothers become so adept at turning themselves into pious martyrs.

- Find a fragment of time every day — heck even sixty seconds — to relax your body with some deep breathing and a few neck rolls. Meditation, especially guided (when you listen to a recorded voice) can be a wonderful way to eliminate negative feelings, and discover positive ones.

- Squeeze in a little mild exercise — at least 10 minutes every day — working up to the ideal minimum of say half-an-hour of vigorous exercise 4–5 times a week. For now, dance to a few of your favourite songs (or your baby's favourites); or do some slow stretching; or workout at home to an exercise video/DVD. Or try to get to a few classes a week that include guided-relaxation, meditation-type techniques, such as yoga, tai chi or pilates — or go for a swim or a jog. And, no, your two-month-old baby is not too young to be in a gym crèche for 1–2 hours.

Get some exercise-induced endorphins (happy chemicals) back into your famished system.

- If possible, keep one room in your home sane, i.e. maintain one room in your house that is free of baby-clutter and always stays tidy, so it can be your baby-free refuge sometimes.
- In the early–mid afternoon do most of the preparation for an easy, nutritious dinner — so you're not attempting to spend an uninterrupted 45 minutes in the kitchen during the arsenic hour. (When you make dinners, you can double the amount to freeze for another evening.)
- Do a surface tidy-up in the late afternoons — run around for 10–15 minutes putting things away. Regaining some sense of orderliness can be a great remedy to giving you the feeling of being so much more in control. (And it is also encouraging to have at least this one visible indicator that you got something done during the day!)
- Stop treating your partner like an emotional spittoon — hocking up all your negative emotions and spitting them in his face. Appreciate that he too is enduring the challenge of finding his way 'home' to your new lives. When your partner comes home, try saying in a happy tone 'Hi, Hun! How was work?' (this is *his* soul food). Resist launching full throttle into unloading a negative summary of your day. That may seem unreasonable because huge parts of you want to empty your overflowing whinge bin, and you want him to fully comprehend how busy and stressed you have been, and just how hard you really *do* work. We mums understand. But, that is as if he has opened the door to have a pie thrown at his face. So be positive, accept his one-word replies, give him some time to adjust to the 'home' environment, then the time will come when it's right for you to say something like, 'I need you to listen for a while, so I can tell you about my day'.
- If you have a partner, don't make the mistake of setting yourself up with the martyrdom of being the essential person to do things for the baby, like the bath, or massage or settling. Get your partner involved, and allow him to make mistakes without correction. Who says your way is the only way?
- Book emergency babysitting for a rejuvenating night out in the next few days, just the two of you, even if it's just fish and chips in the park — but invest time in being alone together outside the house.
- Book a regular 'date' with each other alone ('date-night' as they nickname it in America). Preferably weekly, or fortnightly is OK, but monthly at an absolute minimum. Maybe jogging together; playing sport together; entrée and dessert at your favourite restaurant; a beer and a few games of billiards in a local bar; falling asleep as your head rests on hubby's

tummy-pillow under an old oak tree in the park ... But just *knowing* you will see each other alone once a week when you are an unencumbered couple who can please yourselves, is an extremely beneficial ritualistic tonic for a couple's relationship.

• Join or start a babysitting club (where payment is with hours not money). Or alternatively, swap babysitting with friends.

• *Pamper* yourself, *mother* yourself — don't underestimate the psychological benefits of being kind to yourself at least once a day — it is not vanity to reinforce your worth to yourself. *Allow* others to do that for you too — if they offer help, accept it.

• Book a weekly time, say Sunday nights, when you have 1–2 hours in the bathroom by yourself. Put a facial mask on and wallow in a steamy bath with candles and aromatherapy oils (especially rose, jasmine and chamomile). Wax your legs, shave your underarms, pluck your eyebrows, condition-treatment your hair, paint your nails, read a great book, meditate — whatever is your soul food. Explain to your partner, assert yourself if necessary, that this is *your time*, and unless the house is on fire or someone is dying, under no circumstances are you to be interrupted.

• Come to the realisation that you deserve an attractive yet practical work wardrobe and comfortable shoes. Stop making your pre-motherhood weekend-only clothes last you a full week. (For you shopaholics out there, this probably is not an issue. But, for others of us, it can become an internal battle to convince ourselves that owning a pleasant array of casual, comfortable and vaguely fashionable clothes for motherhood can be just as important, psychologically, as previously possessing the appropriate executive wardrobe of tailored suits, quality high heels and colour-co-ordinated handbag.)

• Chill out! Don't be so rigidly inflexible. Let some of the balls you're juggling drop. Stop trying to please (and be liked by) everyone. Draw the line on some responsibilities, give some responsibilities away — it will free you emotionally. Just say 'No' more often — hold back that selfless side. Know what is absolutely important to you, and put your own needs first.

• Stop being so damn essential — 'I couldn't go out with the girls last Thursday night, as baby wasn't settling'; 'I just couldn't bring myself to leave baby with a babysitter he didn't know for us to go to that party, so I told hubby to go without me'; 'I couldn't go to dinner at the restaurant that night as baby had a little cold and babysitting could have been too disruptive on his sleep pattern'. Stop the martyring excuses.

• If you can afford it, get a monthly massage, and take on a weekly or fortnightly house cleaner.

• Make a conscious effort to find the time to create your own special moment to treasure with your baby every day — remember, that is what life really is all about.

Unpaid work versus paid work

When I dropped him off for the first time he clung to me, crying, and I had to peel him off before I could close the door behind me … tears welled in my eyes and I thought of my mother's disapproval of women who had children at the last minute as a kind of modern life accessory, only to dump them later on someone else to look after.

Susan Johnson — *A Better Woman*

The deep-pile nanny, the nanny who exists to cushion the impact of parenthood, was, I discovered, the preserve of the wealthy. All other forms of childcare appeared to operate on the principles of a public callbox. You push coins into the slot. When your money runs out you are abruptly and unceremoniously cut off.

Rachel Cusk — *A Life's Work*

To work, or not to work: that is the question . . . but if you psychoanalysed the 'answer', its personality would be described as a deranged, confused, bewildered lost soul. There is no right or wrong response, only what is best for you.

Yet, hasn't society done an astoundingly stupendous job of telling women what they need to do to be a perfect mother? Collectively, it's an insulting slap in the face.

We're not stupid, you know.

Historically, women have always worked while raising their children. That's a fact. The credo that mothers should not abandon their children for paid work, but should stay home with their offspring, only became possible in the 1950s and 1960s — which was the brief window in time between two world wars, and the feminist fight for contraception and equal pay. But pretty much since then, and nearly always before then, the idea of full-time motherhood was simply a whimsical notion — the difference these days, is that most paid work can't be done with your children present.

Time for a brief history lesson . . .

Throughout most of history, the purpose of marriage was procreation, and the purpose of children was to provide family income, security for old age, and social status. Infants were collectively raised by the extended family, until they could contribute financially — be it as shepherd boy, chimney sweep, milking the cows, or in industry doing jobs that required small hands.

Children could not be cosseted through their childhood — they simply went from infanthood to working.

By going back not even a couple of centuries, we find that for most mothers on the planet (except the wealthy), life was always about *survival*. Having enough food for your half-dozen children was the priority — not whether each child had a socially well-adjusted personality! Also, because contraception wasn't an option, it was not unusual for a *grandmother* to give birth to her last child in her forties. As Kate Figes writes, 'Motherhood was linked to child-bearing rather than child-rearing.'

In the mid–late 1700s the first books started to appear that introduced to the wealthier upper-class the idea that motherhood should be delightfully satisfying; that mothers had ethical responsibilities to raise their children to be moral Christians; and that this noble duty required emotional responsibility and devoted commitment. *That was it; the first woeful seeds were sewn of men defining mothercraft.* Mothers began to feel guilt.

So began the barrage of books that bombard us today. The opinions, theories, principles, norms and guidelines: Rousseau, Balzac, Buchan, Combe, Watson, Holt, Truby King, Bowlby, Freud, Piaget, Dick-Reid, Spock, Rogers, Jung, Winnicott, Brazleton, Jolly, Odent, Bettelheim, Ferber, Belsky, Klaus and Kennel . . . all of these men leading lights in the cult of 'good motherhood', contributing so much doctrine.

During the Victorian era, it became a widespread practice to give infants patented medicinal remedies to quieten their cries from hunger, teething and illness — *that* was being a good mother. Opium was legal, and so plentiful ranges of patented infant tonics were commonplace, all of which contained opium, morphine or laudanum (opium dissolved in alcohol).

At that time, even if not in paid employment outside the home, the mother (unless she was upper class) had to work incredibly hard. She physically slaved from dawn to dusk with the washing, scrubbing, sewing and cooking. How on earth could that middle-class mother (let alone the very poor mother) truly devote hours of her time to the pleasure of her children? It was impossible, and 'unnecessary'!

But alas, as science and society was defining the essence of a 'good' mother, then all mothers were supposedly to blame for their own problematic urchins . . . it became accepted that mothers (never fathers) were capable of *jeopardising* the wellbeing of their own children. Oh the *guilt*, such *guilt*.

In the first half of the twentieth century, Western women became a crucial labour force in two world wars. Then finally, for the sake of the unemployed war heroes, fashion returned to dresses with small waists and full skirts, as society resurrected the philosophies that a woman's place was in the home.

Heck, and by now her house had an electric oven, washing machine, refrigerator, fitted carpets, vacuum cleaner, electric sewing machine, electric iron, flushing toilet, isolation, loneliness, stress, anxiety, suburban neurosis, phenobarbital, librium, benzodiazepine, and the most popular of them all, the dainty yellow valium pill known as Mother's Little Helper.

In the 1960s as the celebrated baby-boom children (those cherished by their devoted stay-at-home mums) were growing into adults, the world was forced to change, with their peace, love, hippydom, anti-war and anti-spanking manifestos. But there was unforeseen fallout to come from the 1970s feminist liberation movement.

You see, before 'Equal Pay for Equal Work' was voiced, it was commonly accepted that men always received a higher salary for the same work, as society expected them to pay for all courting (dating) costs; the engagement ring (usually a month's wage); to be the main contributor to buying a first home; and as soon as the wife was pregnant, pay for all home and household expenses for many years to come, if not for the rest of his working life.

So, by the 1980s, as the cost of living relative to wages rose, mothers had to return to the workforce in droves, because their husbands could now only cover about half of a household's outgoings. At the same time, the workplace culture could no longer accomodate the disturbances of children — in fact, not much of modern society is geared for the needs of children and mothers. Finding a well-designed infant feeding room in a shopping mall is still rare.

In the 1990s, in some communities, there emerged the belief that mothers relying on their partner's income were, not only disadvantaging their children, but ignoring their own potentiality. *The last nail was driven into the coffin — mothers can never get it right.*

However, also during that last quarter of the twentieth century, after 4000 years of social oppression, Western women were finally beginning to reclaim their (original) matriarchal positions within society, while they were 'fulfilling their potential' with fantastic, wonderful, stimulating and often highly qualified careers.

So now modern, educated mothers of the new millennium are left with the always perplexing, enigmatic, problematic and virtually unsolvable conundrum, of whether to choose the guilt of working, or the guilt of not working. And if finances dictate there is no option but to work, then there's the guilt of not having the choice of your first-preferred guilt. It's so absurd, that it's sadly comical. What makes combining a family and career easier: being born a man!

In Naomi Wolf's book *Misconceptions*, she insightfully describes modern society's expectation of the machine mum, who is able to work at top capacity up to the due date; takes one to three months off to deliver, nurture and bond; finds top-notch childcare; and returns to work to express her breastmilk in the ladies' toilet. If she successfully manages to negotiate reduced work hours, that package usually includes no reduction in workload, but a reduction in salary. While she is made to feel privileged to have been given such flexibility, it is made crystal clear that she can't be considered for promotion until she returns to full-time work.

This then melds with her heart-wrenching guilt at leaving her infant to be mothered by his 'other mummy', the au pair; or the massive shame she feels every time her child is a little off-colour and is still required to attend the crèche; and the guilt-inducing writings about the daycare 'parental death' experience and resulting 'emotionally aggressive non-compliant behaviour caused from poor infant-parent attachment' typical of a pre-schooler whose mother has worked in his first year, or works full-time. (Pre-school play used to be about painting, play-dough, slides and swings — but now it's a social science with goals and analysed reviews.)

But — lest we forget — stay-at-home mums are more vulnerable to depression, and depressed mothers are not the best mothers!

And then there's the self-employed mum who crams her work at home into the moments when her baby is sleeping, and after her baby is in bed at night. Then, as the child gets older, mum pacifies her with crayons, biscuits, pots of dairy-food, or another video — or by regretfully yelling out, 'Mummy's trying to work — I need some PEACE!'

To quote Kate Figes in *Life After Birth*: 'Working mothers can just about manage to juggle work, motherhood and their relationship provided that nothing else happens.'

The sacrifice

It is currently fashionable to subscribe to the view that women have achieved equality with men . . .[but] it is merely a veneer of equality which hides a significant fault-line. At home, precious little has actually changed . . . it is the mother who is expected to make the necessary sacrifices to fulfil obligations . . . what perpetuates this imbalance is the mystique of motherhood: the idea that the mother's role is unique, biological and irreplaceable . . . Motherhood is the largest single remaining obstacle to women achieving equality in contemporary, post-modern society. The problem is not children, having children or the love and care of children, but the framing of Motherhood and the endurance of the myths that surround it.
Aminatta Forna — Mother of all Myths

These days, when we take on the role of motherhood, the majority of us sacrifice 'fulfilling our own full potential' in almost every other avenue of our lives — it's not too dissimilar to the highly talented businessman who gives his career up to run a charitable trust close to his heart for a very basic income; or a top plastic surgeon who leaves his lucrative practice to dedicate himself to helping victims of war in a Third World country.

Perhaps you could have been the top real-estate salesperson in your town if only you could have committed more time; perhaps you could have discovered the cure for a disease if you hadn't put your career in microbiology on hold; perhaps you could have been the best CEO one corporation ever had if you'd continued up their corporate ladder; perhaps you could have become a world-renowned artist if you'd been able to stay in France for ten more years picking grapes. Or, perhaps, you *will* reach the pinnacle of your career, but forever wonder how much better a mother you might have been if you'd just stayed home.

Being a mum takes unimaginable commitment, energy and time. For most of us, this means we live with the knowledge that we will probably never be able to 'fulfil our full potential' in loads of other areas of life. The price feels vaguely acceptable, as we do the most important job on the planet, and we do it so bloody well. However, there will be times when people will treat you in a way that you know would simply not have happened if your life had continued on its old path, and that will irk you.

This is not to say that motherhood cannot be great — it is more to acknowledge that you could also have achieved greatness (and greater respect within society) in other ways too.

Motherhood means you become someone else, and that's a sacrifice. We are expected to embrace every aspect of this experience in a way that it is no sacrifice at all, and sometimes it isn't . . . as we discover new areas of greatness and fulfilment of our new potential that we didn't even know we had in us.

Certainly, producing no monetary income and having no outside job title can make many mums feel as if they're drifting, lost on the ocean of life. And needing to ask one's partner for money can feel uncomfortably demeaning. For many, being financially dependent can create feelings of great powerlessness. Studies have found that women who work outside the home (paid or unpaid) are less vulnerable to depression — because it's important to have a life that extends beyond the (prison) walls of the house.

Many women enjoy returning to the workforce, seeing it as a mentally stimulating opportunity to use their brains again; wear dryclean-only clothes again; talk socially or intellectually with mature adults again; enjoy a break from boring, menial domesticity; feel pride and satisfaction at earning money again — it can be an energising and refreshing rediscovery of our old selves, providing renewed self-esteem from a few hours of taking responsibility for a job, and getting it done.

This can be a very happy scenario, so long as she is not partnered with someone who keeps reminding her of her childcare and other associated expenses. And/or a husband who, since the birth, seems to have somehow gained more than his previous 50-percent share of clout in the partnership, so the newly self-appointed macho head-of-the-household decrees that the woman's job is to stay at home. As the joke goes: A foolish husband says to his wife, 'Honey, you stick to the washin', ironin', cookin' and scrubbin'. No wife of mine is gonna work!'.

For many other mothers, giving up paid work to be a kept women is almost pure bliss. Such as, the business tycooness who happily gives up the Armani suits, Prada accessories, two hours each day in traffic jams and pretentious, business breakfast-meetings; or the overworked secretary who joyfully hands in her letter of resignation to be rid of her chauvinistic, egotistic, arsehole boss. They're relishing blobbing out in a real world complete with shopping carts, pushchair, baby front-pack, and the most precious five-kilo bundle of joy on the whole planet! Suddenly life can, for once, become more spontaneous, instead of needing to be so time-managed.

This may be a woman who, although she has the ability to contribute financially to the family finances, actually loathes the idea of leaving her child to return to work. So, together, she and her partner agree that for her happiness (and subsequently the family's happiness), that being anything other than a full-time mother is an intolerable idea.

A stay-at-home mum can be a pretty happy camper — so long as she is not partnered with a man who cannot stomach any further reductions in their present or future lifestyle; a man who believes full-time motherhood is an intolerable luxury; and that the baby needs to fit into the gaps of their life. Or the type of man who decrees, from his new head-of-the-household role that, out of economic necessity, she must put their child into daycare and return to the workforce, with even less time for herself, and for sleep.

But for nearly all women who give up work for most of the pre-school years, it can become extremely difficult (if not virtually impossible) to return to their career at the same level of confidence, prestige, income and seniority — most likely, they will need to work back up to that position, and some women's careers never really bounce back.

Frankly, it can be an impossible dilemma of heartache, psychologically and financially, often resulting as a lose-lose situation without a solution — only compromises. Author Jane Sellman is renowned for saying, 'The phrase "working mother" is redundant'; and feminist journalist Gloria Steinem has said, 'I am yet to hear a man ask for advice on how to combine marriage and a career'.

For some, motherhood, immediately or eventually, gives a sort of noble, indispensable and quintessential status — they *are* The Home. They find they revel in their identity of being fundamentally essential to several people; it feels good and gives them pride. And so it should.

For a seemingly growing number of mums, after the intensive baby years, motherhood can open doors into rooms of fabulous and self-rewarding adventures they would never have dreamt of entering before having children. Often, out of an initial desire, say to produce income while continuing to be available to their children, mothers unveil talents they simply never knew they had; or they discover interests in subjects that now fascinate them.

Caring less about their old set of priorities — as the maturing soul knows now how inconsequential some of those values were — makes these changes possible. Motherhood, after a while, can allow you to become freer — freer to attempt something and fail without it demoralising you — because that still makes you more contented, than never having risked trying.

Motherhood can be a doorway into the Bohemian state of living; to your own sense of values, seeking inner authenticity; and standing up for your own unique way to live — the embryonic beginnings of learning to trust life's unknown journeys.

It's the banking clerk who becomes a beauty therapist; it's the sales executive who discovers she makes wonderful pottery; it's those little cottage industries popping up everywhere we turn; it's the nurse who becomes an interior designer; it's the flight attendant who becomes a landscaper; it's the woman attending university for the first time in her life; it's the bookkeeper who becomes a midwife; it's the travel consultant who becomes a writer!

I remember discussing with a friend Sue how we mothers are in many ways longing for the simplicity of our own mothers' and grandmothers' lives. We conceded that we adore our automatic washing machines and our dishwashers — and our dryers and microwaves are pretty great too. But that's where it can end.

It also amazes me how often on TV reality series, when families revert to an early colonial lifestyle, the common theme the participants continually comment on is how refreshing it is to enjoy such a simple life — even not having to choose between 59 different types of fruit juice, 46 different types of shampoo, 18 different washing powders, and 27 different kinds of loo paper when you're doing the grocery shopping.

In a way, our generation is becoming a society of city dwellers longing for the countryside. My husband is a builder-foreman who specialises in the construction of eco-natural houses. And almost every time I explain that to someone, the reply is consistently along the lines of, 'Oh I'd love to have a house like that.' I believe many of our generation long to stop working so hard to earn enough money to achieve 'financial security' (whatever pot of gold at the end of the rainbow that really is), and to stop spoiling their materially over-indulged kids; and wish instead that they just had more time to talk and play with their children. Remember, playing with Mum and Dad is soul food for infants and children.

If you would like to work from home, but are struggling to find a workable solution, then there is another way to be a paid stay-at-home mum, and that is to be a childcarer. A good place to start when considering this option is to talk with some of the professional home-childcare operators such as Barnardos, Amanda's, Porse and Jemma's. Many mothers do this work during their own children's pre-school years, and continue once their children are at school, as it allows them to be home for their children after school, during school holidays and when their children are sick.

I remember too, pre-children, being on a work trip inspecting hotels in Fiji. Many Fijians continue to live in traditional villages and, while waiting for a boat transfer to an island resort, I asked a young Fijian man what work he did. He laughed a deep contented laugh, as he replied, 'Only one in three adults in our village needs to work, our lives are simple. I think you tourists are all mad. You work so hard all year just to come here for two weeks. That's crazy!' Maybe he's right.

Self-sacrifice and self-denial seem integral to motherhood because a child's demands and needs are limitless . . . But there is no such thing as a 'good' mother, only a good-enough mother . . . it is increasingly hard for women to feel as if they are 'good' mothers, when paradoxically they have probably never done a better job.

Kate Figes — *Life After Birth*

Chapter 9

Double-edged swords, cans of worms and hot potatoes!

DOUBLE-EDGED SWORD: Effective or capable of being interpreted in two ways.
CAN OF WORMS: A source of unforeseen and troublesome complexity.
HOT POTATO: A problem that is so controversial or sensitive that those handling it risk unpleasant consequences.
                                                Microsoft Bookshelf Definitions

Not long into your new life as a parent, you will become acutely aware that there are innumerable controversial parenting subjects that trigger intensely debated arguments. You will need to make black and white decisions, based on information that is mostly in shades of grey. Welcome to the worrying world of 'informed parental consent'.

The word 'debate' derives from the old French word de-battre, meaning 'to beat'. Interesting. So, if you end up feeling battered by zealous opinions, perhaps you're on the right track. No, you should be deliberating over a discussion involving opposing points of view, in order to form your final decision. *Oh, I wish it were that easy.*

The word 'argument' derives from old French and Latin words meaning 'to make clear'. So, an argument is a discussion in which disagreement is expressed regarding conflicting points of view, i.e. people using facts, proof and evidence aim to persuade their opponents of the truths or untruths of their argument. *Sounds peachy.*

But in reality, when it comes to parenting issues, these discussions of divided and contradictory opinions often result in anger — especially when these controversies unite large groups of people, and involve our cherished children — vulnerable, defenceless and powerless.

In this chapter, my goal is to provide you with a brief overview of a handful of subjects commonly discussed at mothers' coffee groups. It is *not* my intention to lead you to any specific conclusion, and if you feel this chapter is at all biased towards one side, for that I apologise.

These are all controversial subjects that modern parents are often required to make firm, informed decisions about. To write this book and ignore these subjects (or to provide the information with a definitive answer) is not in the best interests of the mothers and fathers who will read this book.

Some questions never really have *one* 'right' answer.

So in conclusion . . . GOOD LUCK!

The question of circumcision

This topic is an extremely private, individual and personal decision.

Some believe circumcision to be more hygienic. Some believe the glands at the top of the penis are supposed to always be protected by the foreskin. Some believe it is important for little boys to resemble their dad. Some believe it is more important for little boys to resemble most of the other little boys in a school changing room. Some believe a circumcised penis is aesthetically better looking. Some believe an uncircumcised penis is more sensitive and enjoys enhanced sexual pleasure. Some believe circumcision is essential for cultural or religious reasons.

Through most of the twentieth century in the Western world, the removal of the penis foreskin has been performed very routinely without much question — 30 years ago nearly all boys were circumcised at a few days old *without anaesthetic!* With no pain relief during this acutely painful amputation, their subsequent coma-like sleep was a shock reaction to an extremely physiologically traumatic event, and the resulting cortisol stress-hormone levels.

With the emergence of more free-thinking adults the pendulum has now definitely swung in the other direction, to a more common view of circumcision as a dismantling of Mother Nature's perfect design. These days in New Zealand it is more common for boys not to be circumcised.

Circumcision is now, generally, an elective surgery using local anaesthetic. It is usually performed when the boy is a few weeks old, with the parents paying the cost. And like all surgeries it has risks, including excessive bleeding, and infection. (The penis may occasionally be damaged irreparably.) Sometimes circumcision is clinically necessary due to a ballooning foreskin when the boy pees, and phimosis (when the opening of the foreskin is too narrow, preventing it from being drawn back).

At the end of the day, it is an extremely personal decision, and one that deserves the non-judgemental respect of other peoples' values.

The question of fluoride

The topic of fluoride being added to drinking water to prevent tooth decay is a very hot potato. Many revered scientists are disputing flouride's effectiveness, and many countries around the world have now banned the adding of fluoride to municipal water supplies.

New Zealand Health Department records show a steady decline in childhood tooth decay for the decades from 1930 to 1990. However, there was not a noticeable drop in the cavity rate in the years after fluoridation was introduced in the 1960s.

Although fluoride received topically (e.g. externally through direct contact with the tooth, say via toothpaste) helps prevent tooth decay, flouride that is ingested (introduced internally and systemically into the bloodstream, say through drinking water) does not hinder tooth decay, and is highly likely to cause harmful side effects. Fluoride, although not as poisonous as arsenic, is corrosive, more toxic than lead, and anything but benign.

The element fluorine is the most negatively charged and most chemically active of all elements on Earth. This means its atomic particle valence shells search for the strongest molecular bond, which means it can wreak havoc with everything in its path, creating even more toxic molecular combinations. That is why industry loves it, from etching computer chips to polishing aluminium, to being a common key ingredient in insecticides and rat poison — by the 1930s, disposal of polluting industrial-fluoride waste had become an expensive nightmare. At the same time, funded by top fluoride-emitters such as ALCOA (Aluminium Company of America), 'new research' emerged claiming the harmless dental benefits of consuming diluted fluoride. With the help of public-relations guru, Edward Bernays (the man who made smoking respectable for women), Americans and the rest of the Westernised world were encouraged to embrace fluoridated water, fluoride tablets and fluoride toothpaste. Now the industrial fluoride was no longer toxic waste — it was a profitable new product line!

There are vast amounts of information from scientists, doctors, Nobel Prize winners in medicine and chemistry, dentists, environmentalists, researchers and many countries' governments, all opposing the use of fluoride in drinking water. It is true the tooth surface can become harder, but the tooth itself can become more brittle. Evidence is also accumulating of correlations between levels of fluoride in water supplies and problems with asthma, eczema, chronic fatigue, lower IQ and learning disabilities, lethargy, depression, fluorosis (mottling of tooth enamel), serious fluorosis (major bone deformation disorder where ligaments calcify), and other bone disorders (e.g. osteoporosis, bone fractures, arthritis).

If you are on tank water, you can supplement your children's topical fluoride intake simply by using fluoridated toothpaste, while teaching the child to spit out (not swallow) the toothpaste. (But no fluoride in the first six months and no childhood sodium fluoride supplements — perhaps calcium fluoride tablets, if you must.)

If you are on a town water supply where fluoride is already added to your drinking water, you may want to consider drinking distilled spring water, using a reverse-osmosis water-filter or water distillation unit, or buying bottled water, and taking antioxidant supplements.

To help make your mind up, you might have to do your own investigative research.

The question of immunisation

Granted, information is empowering . . . Regretfully, many parents today are victims of information overload . . . Worse still, their own common sense has been drowned out by other people's ideas.
Tracy Hogg — *Secrets of the Baby Whisperer*

Immunisation and vaccination of infants require the fully informed consent of the parent or guardian, free of coercion. However, this is the biggest can of worms and the most hotly contended topic of all . . . SO many *passionate* opinions, for and against.

The 'pro' lobby says all the negative hype is pure fear mongering that uses scientific information selectively with great bias. The 'anti' lobby insists all vaccines are like playing Russian roulette and quote dramatic statistics and horrific stories. It is *way too scary* for this book to offer you a definitive answer. You need to do your own investigations to make up your own mind and decide for yourself.

In New Zealand the improved living conditions from the late 1800s to the mid-1900s (such as sanitation, hygiene, water, housing and nutrition) reduced childhood diseases by a staggering 98 percent. Then as science continued to advance, vaccines started to become commonplace in the late 1950s and early 1960s, in an effort to save children from diseases which caused particularly nasty suffering, permanent disablement or death. But even from the first smallpox vaccine a century ago, New Zealand has always had a strong anti-immunisation voice.

In many ways, although included under the umbrella of modern medicine, vaccines are not really a medicine as such. They actively and artificially expose the lymphatic immune system to pathogens (micro-organisms that produce disease, such as bacteria and viruses), in order for the body to manufacture the disease antibodies and subsequent immunological memory. The purpose of vaccinations is to induce protection by changing a person's immune system from vulnerable to protected. Some vaccines provide lifetime protection, some provide a limited time of protection — and science can never guarantee protection levels for each individual because every person's immune system is unique, some responding more or less effectively than others.

Vaccines are like insurance policies: the vaccine is an insurance policy that has been designed to provide good chances of protection; an insurance policy that may or may not ever need to be put to use; and an insurance policy that may or may not provide the required cover.

To understand how vaccinations are designed to work, it is necessary to have a basic understanding of how the body's defence process, known as the lymphatic immune system, functions. To appreciate the motivation for science to have created vaccines, it is necessary to have an understanding of what each disease entails. To comprehend the controversy that has always surrounded vaccinations, it is necessary to realise this is a very complex topic and one that many feel society has been indoctrinated into believing is completely safe and effective, without thorough-enough investigative research.

Here the goal is to introduce you to the debate and provide you with an outline of the science behind diseases and their vaccines (which can be difficult to locate in layman's terms). Then, armed with that knowledge, you will be better equipped to investigate the plethora of 'anti-' and 'pro-' immunisation information if you choose to.

As a baby grows inside its mother's womb, it is provided directly from the mother via the placenta with massive amounts of immune-protecting antibodies. So, yes, the stronger the mother's immune system is, then the stronger the infant's inherited immunity will be.

While the fetus grows, its own immune system learns to remember all its own body molecules as Itself (which is why, for example transplanted organs are rejected without medication).

Once a baby is born (with the exception of extremely premature babies), the baby's body immediately recognises it is no longer inside the sterile environment of the womb, and kick-starts its lifelong task of protecting itself from the germs it is now covered in — as even in the cleanest of postnatal environments, all babies are covered in germs.

The infant's inherited immune system is passive and provides no long-term immunological memory, and so it slowly wanes over the months after birth as the baby begins to develop its own active immunological memories. (Breastfeeding continually boosts and stimulates an infant's passive immune system in their first year — however the bulk of its initial immunity is inherited during the final trimester in the womb.)

Now, to explain medical science's perspective on vaccines . . .

Every protein antigen (e.g. a germ) has a different 'shape', and the body's immune-system leucocytic white blood cells (called lymphocytes) work on a 'key and lock' system. That is, they have the ability to locate just the right lymphocyte key to lock each antigen (micro-organism, such as a germ molecule) — to inactivate the antigen, rendering it harmless and thus 'switching on' a new antibody (immunoglobulin).

Once such antigen-binding occurs, the lymphatic immune system now has a memory of this foreign substance and its corresponding antibody, and the immune system then clones its own army of identical antigen-specific cells — thus creating a stronger and faster response to the same germ with any future encounters. The body's immune system cannot distinguish between an antigen being introduced naturally from the environment, or artificially via a vaccine — it is simply one of the thousands of antigens it is dealing with at any one time.

The earliest vaccines were whole-cell — that is they contained the complete dead organisms of the disease, requiring the body to produce say 60+ different kinds of antibodies. However, with advances in science over the last 20–30 years providing better understanding of the immune system, current New Zealand childhood vaccines often only provide just the crucial key-lock 'piece' of the disease organism, thus requiring the body to produce say just a couple of types of antibodies to be protected against the entire disease organism. From the immune system's perspective, it recognises this one crucial piece as looking identical to the complete disease organism, and so it reacts as if it was the actual disease.

To put this in some perspective, the current DTaP-IPV vaccine (diphtheria, tetanus, pertussis and polio) has less than a dozen pieces; the HibHepB (haemophilus influenzae B and hepatitis B) vaccine has three pieces, and the MeNZB (meningococcal B) has only one single antigen. In contrast a sore throat from streptococcal has at least 60 different antigens that the immune system needs to respond to and bind with.

So, modern multiple vaccines can be less 'work' for the body's immune system than even the common sore throat — and the modern style of multiple vaccines prevents the infant becoming a pin-cushion. (Many vaccines are repeated during infancy to ensure enough antibodies are generated for longer-term and more thorough protection.)

The anti-immunisation view insists medical science is still grappling with fully understanding the newborn and childhood immune system. They quote research that finds some antigen-specific antibodies simply indicate that the immune system has come into contact with a specific antigen, without showing a crystal-clear correlation between the number of antibodies and the level of protection gained against, say, whooping cough. And they highlight 'copious evidence' of vaccines causing the likes of autoimmune diseases, allergies, asthma, cancers, diabetes, arthritis and cot death.

There is also great controversy surrounding the international medical advisory boards and their recommendations of vaccination levels, which have continued to increase greatly over the past 50 years. However, in New Zealand the standard infant and childhood vaccinations endorsed by the New Zealand Government, are decided by our drug licensing board MedSafe. Its purpose is to work independently of the pharmaceutical companies in an effort to cautiously ensure that New Zealand recommendations are unbiased. (New Zealand's recommendations are more conservative than those of some Westernised countries.)

In 1991 Mike Godfrey (doctor of nutritional medicine and environmental health) surveyed Kiwis, receiving over a thousand replies to his questionnaire. He found that approximately two-thirds of the children were immunised and approximately one-third were not. In the immunised children, higher percentages were listed for autism, epilepsy, the alimentary canal condition Crohn's disease, tonsillitis, ADHD, grommets (from recurring ear infections), asthma and eczema. However, because the questionnaire response was voluntary, it created an emotive 'unscientific' environment where parents of sickly children could be more motivated to reply than parents of healthy children.

In the USA, the VICP (national Vaccine Injury Compensation Program) has been set up, and it has reportedly paid out many millions of dollars to families who have blamed immunisations for ill-health conditions — including asthma, eczema, autism, multiple sclerosis (nervous system disease), Crohn's disease, various autoimmune diseases (destruction of the body's tissues by its own immune response), and cot-death. This compensation has occurred at the same time as science believing it is accumulating massive amounts of evidence to contradict all such claims — but in the litigation-rich culture of the USA, sometimes paying out can be cheaper than arguing the point.

Here, New Zealand GPs must fully promote all officially recommended vaccinations using government-sanctioned literature, or they lose their government immunisation funding. So, undoubtedly this too is not an atmosphere conducive to parents receiving unbiased opinion and all the information relevant to making a truly 'informed consent decision free of any coercion'.

All in all, it's a hornet's nest of a topic.

Now let's look at the individual diseases and the vaccines recommended by MedSafe:

Free vaccinations

Pertussis (whooping cough)

Whooping cough is highly infectious and characterised by its insidious three months of violent dog-bark coughing generated from thick mucous phlegm and a runny nose. Complications of whooping cough include otitis media (ear infection), pneumonia (inflammation of the lungs), vomiting, apnoea (temporarily not breathing) causing cyanosis (bluish colouring of skin due to inadequate oxygen in the blood); and in extreme cases lung damage, brain damage, convulsions and death. Mortality rates are highest in the under one-year-olds, especially in the first few months of life. Beyond three years of age death rates are very low.

Some statistics suggest that 70 percent of whooping cough cases are vaccinated, which could be quite true because the disease memory from the vaccine wanes over time. However, it is also said that generally the vaccinated children experience a milder dose of whooping cough, which is as medical science meant it to be (though the evidence of that is under question). Certainly, newborns under two months are the most vulnerable to this disease, as even if they have had the vaccine it may not work in time.

Diphtheria

This is a serious disease that is often fatal, which young children are more vulnerable to. It primarily inflames the membranes of the upper respiratory tract and pharynx, with a growth in the throat that can lead to suffocation. Diphtheria also produces a powerful toxin that damages the myocardium heart muscle (causing serious heart problems), the peripheral nervous system (causing paralysis), the kidneys (reducing urine flow creating renal failure), other organ damage, and commonly death (more than one in 20). Protection through scheduled vaccines is around 90 percent.

Tetanus

Tetanus spores (micro-organisms) enter the body through a wound, even just a trivial cut, and then irreversibly bind to the central nervous system (shutting down the brain and spinal cord). Its toxins cause weakness, stiffness, cramps, difficulty in chewing and swallowing, breathing difficulties, rigid muscles, very painful muscle spasms, convulsions and commonly death (about one in 10). Protection through scheduled vaccines is close to 100 percent.

For your interest: when people receive a tetanus injection *after* being wounded (e.g. an adult whose tetanus immunity has probably expired), then it is a tetanus immunoglobin antibody jab (not antigens), which has a long list of possible side effects, but none perhaps as fatal as death!

Polio (poliomyelitis or infant paralysis)

Although polio has almost been eradicated from the planet, it is highly infectious and, characteristically, a disease of children. It is easily imported into New Zealand by international travellers. Polio irreparably damages the central nervous system causing fever, vomiting and muscle stiffness, creating permanent crippling paralysis of the legs to half its victims, and death to about five percent.

Since the vaccine was introduced in New Zealand 40 years ago, only a handful of cases of polio have occurred here, the most recent in 1998 when an unimmunised mother contracted polio from the faeces of her baby after its immunisation. Because of that case, the old vaccine of oral drops has been replaced with a non-live polio vaccine that is now part of a multi-vaccine injection.

Hib (Haemophilus influenzae type B)

Contrary to the sound of its medical name, Hib has nothing to do with the flu virus as it is a bacteria. Hib causes meningitis (inflammation of the membranes that cover the brain), pneumonia, epiglottitis (suffocating swelling of the throat obstructing breathing), septic arthritis (infection in joints), bacteraemia (bacteria in the blood), cellulitis (skin infections), empyema (pus around the lungs), and permanent deafness, brain damage or death.

Before 1994 when the vaccine was introduced, Hib was the most common cause of the life-threatening bacterial meningitis in children under five (especially 6–11 month olds) with approximately 150 cases a year of meningitis and epiglottitis. Since the vaccine was introduced, there are now just 3–4 cases a year of these seriously ill children, probably one of which is from a fully vaccinated infant (due to its immune system, for whatever reason, being less effective). Protection through scheduled immunisations is almost 100 percent.

Hepatitis B

In 1985 it was found that 15 percent of New Zealand children had previous hepatitis B infection experience. Subsequently the neonatal immunisation was introduced in 1987–88, and after the three doses about 95 percent of people develop protection.

When babies or children contract hepatitis B they are much more likely (than adults) to end up as long-term carriers of the disease (able to pass it on through blood or sex); and it leaves them with a high risk (about one in four) of later developing liver disease or liver cancer (even many decades later), and causing liver-related symptoms such as jaundice, nausea, lack of appetite and general feelings of unwellness. Children not vaccinated for hepatitis B are more likely to require childhood liver transplants, and hepatitis B causes more vaccine-preventable deaths (usually from liver cancer) in New Zealand than any other virus except influenza.

Hepatitis B vaccine is also given to newborns who are in high-risk situations (e.g. when the mother or someone in the household has hepatitis B). A similar policy applies to newborns known to be exposed to increased risks of contracting **tuberculosis**.

There are particular concerns regarding low birth-weight premature infants receiving the hepatitis B vaccine at under six weeks or under 2 kg, and in that situation all the pros and cons should definitely be thoroughly discussed.

MMR (mumps, measles and rubella)

This is a 'live' vaccine, however the cells of the virus organisms have been heavily modified to no longer be pathogenic (capable of causing the disease). But, the immune system does not recognise that the cell is no longer pathogenic and creates the required antibodies.

The MMR vaccine cannot be given under 15 months because it is ineffective due to infants' inherited immunity. Later, MMR is said to give lifetime protection to 90 percent of recipients. The booster at four years is to catch the 10 percent whose immune systems failed to create antibodies with the first exposure at 15 months.

However, if your child has a blood test any time after the 15-month injection, you could ask that the immunity for mumps, measles and rubella is also tested to decide whether the booster shot is necessary.

Originally, the booster shot was given at 11 years. However, after New Zealand's 1997 measles epidemic (over 2000 cases) this second vaccine was brought forward to four years to prevent future epidemics. (Controversially, a supposed 40 percent of the cases of measles in New Zealand's 1984–5 epidemic was in vaccinated children.)

In 1998 a British gastroenterologist, Dr Andrew Wakefield, was the leading author in a paper that suggested there might be a relationship between the MMR vaccine and neurological brain disorders such as autism, or the alimentary canal condition, Crohn's disease. The report stated that it did not prove a link; it only suggested the theoretical possibility of one. But the stakes of such implications are high, and so the report received immense media attention complete with the usual, exaggerated, propaganda-style speculative journalism — and so another seed of parental anxiety was sown.

Autistic children can often develop quite normally until say 12–24 months when disability traits start to show in the child's reasoning, communication and social interaction. The true cause of autism is unknown, however it has generally been accepted that autism is a genetic, fetal-brain-development defect (though most biomedical research on autism to date has focused only on genetics). It is also generally accepted by science that children do not 'catch' autism, but that it certainly can be the result of a pregnant mother having German measles; or alternatively a child after suffering from encephalitis (brain inflammation) can display autistic-like behaviour.

Dr Wakefield's investigations have been swarming with controversies. There has been criticism of his lack of basic scientific practices; the co-researchers of the report now strongly disassociate themselves from his idea of a link; the majority of medical colleges and journals remain unconvinced; plus, it has since come to light, he was paid £50,000 for 'research' by parents planning legal action that MMR had harmed their children.

Since then, the pro-vaccine medical community state they have done exhaustive epidemiological (study of disease) investigations on any such link, and now fervently believe they have put to rest all such concerns, with indisputably strong evidence that no such correlation exists.

But, massive controversy continues. For example, due to immune-system abnormalities being found in individuals with neurological damage, some medical scientists believe the cause of autism to be a far more complex synchronisation of the nervous, immune and endocrine (gland) systems, with some children having a predisposed frailness for autoimmune derailment from vaccine toxification, which jeopardises their inherent weakness. These arguments gain momentum when celebrities such as John Travolta and Kelly Preston give their support to TAAP (The Autism Autoimmunity Project), alongside an impressive list of respected university doctors.

So, while there continues to be no firm agreement between experts, parents need to make a decision.

Measles

This is a highly infectious disease that spreads quickly — it's pretty much 100 percent contagious. After initial unwellness (fever, cough, irritability, exhaustion, conjunctivitis), the measles' freckly, spotty rash usually starts on the face and spreads over the entire body. Common complications include otitis media (ear infection), diarrhoea, and croup (obstructed airways with barking cough).

There are also many other rare, though severe, complications that can occur — including death. In fact around the world measles is the most common vaccine-preventable cause of child deaths, especially in the under-fours.

Children not immunised against measles have a one in 25 chance of the disease developing into pneumonia; and a one in 2000 chance of it developing into encephalitis (inflammation of the brain), with a subsequent high risk of brain damage.

However, the chances of getting serious complications and dying from measles are much higher than this in developing countries where children are poorly nourished.

Children immunised against measles have a medically known one in one million chance of developing encephalitis from the immunisation — hence the vaccine must not be given to children with compromised immune systems as a result of rare immune disorders or chemotherapy.

Mumps

Mumps used to be a commonly anticipated childhood disease before the vaccine. It is traditionally associated with a swelling around the ears (big puffed-out cheeks due to an infection of the salivary glands); and painful swelling of post-puberty male gonads; plus there are numerous other potential complications. The traditional concern with young men and mumps was the risk of sterility, however, it can also cause permanent deafness in both sexes.

Mumps is one of the most common causes of viral meningitis (brain membrane inflammation) and viral encephalitis (brain tissue inflammation) in unimmunised children under 15 months of age. Between 1970 and 1991 there were epidemics of mumps every 3–4 years in New Zealand with over 2000 hospital admissions. Since the MMR vaccine was introduced in 1992 there have been no further epidemics.

Rubella (German measles)

Rubella is a mild disease of swollen glands and joint pains, with a rash that primarily affects young children over the head and neck. Rubella becomes gravely serious when a mother contracts the disease in the early stages of pregnancy, which results in a 90 percent chance of severe birth defects in the fetus.

Rubella immunisations used to be given to 11-year-old girls, but this failed to stop the disease circulating. Now it is included with measles and mumps and given to both sexes — to protect females during future pregnancies, and to protect females from male carriers.

Meningococcal B

New Zealand has had an epidemic of one particular strain of this disease which has caused about 90 percent of all meningococcal B disease, and 80 percent of all meningococcal disease overall. Meningococcal B commonly causes meningitis (bacterial inflammation of the brain's meninges membranes) and septicaemia (bacterial destruction of body tissue and toxins in the blood causing blood poisoning). The initial symptoms may (or may not) include nausea, vomiting, headaches and often a rash caused by ruptured blood vessels (flat dark red/purple spots or freckly spots). The rash must be taken very seriously, especially in the under-fives.

With the sudden onset of the infectious meningococcal rash, even with hospitalisation, other serious complications can occur within hours including disseminated intravascular coagulation (overstimulation of the blood-clotting mechanism resulting in spontaneous bleeding), shock (low blood-pressure associated with circulatory collapse), and symptoms of meningitis such as intense headache, fever, loss of appetite, intolerance to light and sound, rigid muscles, especially neck, and even convulsions, vomiting and delirium. Meningococcal B can also cause arthritis, myocarditis (inflamed heart muscle), pericarditis (inflammation of the heart's membrane sac) and pneumonia (lung inflammation).

The vaccine MeNZB, based on similar overseas vaccines for epidemic strains, has been developed from a single protein antigen (one 'key-lock' piece) specifically for the New Zealand strain. Time will tell if it needs to stay on the New Zealand immunisation schedule permanently.

Dependent on an individual's immune system, one MeNZB vaccine has at least a 75 percent effectiveness rating. So children receive a course of three injections four to six weeks apart — with protection expected to last for a few years.

Optional extra vaccines

Meningococcal C

This is an expensive optional vaccine but one worth considering. The disease is very nasty and similar to Meningococcal B with flu-like symptoms that worsen within hours, including muscular pain, fever, a stiff neck, and aversion to bright lights. The disease then develops a serious red or purple rash, and can quickly become fatal. There is not currently an epidemic strain of this disease in New Zealand, but it could be accidentally imported.

Pneumococcal disease (Streptococcus pneumoniae)

This is also an expensive vaccine, but one worth considering. Streptococcus pneumoniae is the most common cause of otitis media (middle ear infection) in children, and also commonly causes sinusitis (inflamed sinuses), pneumonia, and even death from pneumonia. It can also cause meningitis, bacteraemia, endocarditis (inflammation of the heart's inner lining), occasionally affects the peritoneal cavity (covering on abdominal organs) and the fallopian tubes (which run between the ovaries and the uterus).

The risk of pneumococcal disease is higher in infants and children under five years. However, because of how T-cells function within the body, the vaccine is not very effective if given in the first two years. Once administered it gives 70–80 percent protection.

Varicella (chickenpox)

Chickenpox begins with a freckly spotty rash that turns into small blisters over the entire body, even including the inside of the mouth and inside the vagina. As the blisters dry they become itchy. The number of blisters can vary from just a few, to hundreds.

Chickenpox in childhood is generally mild and not usually of concern, except regarding the sores healing without becoming septic from bacterial infection. However, every person who has ever had chickenpox has the potential to later (usually over 40 years of age) experience a sporadic reactivation of the virus, known as herpes zoster (shingles), which is nasty and debilitating.

Tip
If you have already had your first baby, and have never had chickenpox, then as a woman who myself experienced very nasty adult chickenpox (while pregnant), you may want to consider an adult vaccination, as there are also risks to the fetus.

If a person has not experienced chickenpox in childhood, then a vaccine could be well worthwhile, as chickenpox in adolescence or adulthood can be far more serious than in childhood, and can include complications such as cerebellitis (inflammation of the cerebellum or hind-brain), meningitis, transverse myelitis (inflammation of spinal cord tissue causing paralysis), pneumonia, and thrombocytopaenia (reduction in blood platelets causing many other concerns).

Like most vaccinations, varicella is said to give protection for a limited number of years, however more recent data is suggesting it is even longer lasting.

What can you do if you do choose to immunise?

Suggestions below are given by some experts as recommendations — this book is neither formally endorsing nor dismissing them. The decision is up to you.

- Give children vitamin A after receiving the pertussis (whooping cough) and measles vaccines.
- Give children a good dose of vitamin C before and after receiving any vaccine.
- Except for very premature babies (say 28 weeks or 1 kg), vaccines should be administered by gestational age (birth date) not chronological age (due date) — as that relates to how long their immune system has been functioning outside the sterile womb.
- If the baby is ill or sickly, delay vaccines until they are healthy — with the exception of the vaccine that includes whooping cough (pertussis) because this is such a nasty disease for a wee baby to experience.
- If the baby has a fever (say a temperature 38°C or over), delay vaccination as this could be a sign that their immune system is already particularly busy fighting an infection.
- If you prefer, ask that injections be split up leaving a gap of a month or so between vaccines.
- Visit a professional homeopath for tinctures to give the baby before and after vaccinations, to reduce the severity of any adverse reactions.
- If your family has a history of immunological problems (e.g. allergies, previous vaccine reactions) or neurological problems (e.g. epilepsy, convulsions), then be particularly thorough in your investigative research, to ensure your decision is well informed.
- Remember that if afterwards your baby has a little redness, pain or swelling at the injection site; is grizzly, irritable, or drowsy; and/or has a mild fever (say 37.5°–38°C), these are usually positive indications that his immune system is responding to the vaccine as it is meant to.
- After the MMR vaccine an uncontagious rash and high fever (say 39.5°C) may occur — 5–10 days later. You can administer infant paracetamol or infant ibuprofen.
- As a pro-active parent, ask to receive the vaccine-packaging insert so you can recognise adverse reactions if they occur. And do officially report any vaccine reaction in writing to CARM (the Centre for Adverse Reaction Monitoring, Freepost no.112002, PO Box 913, Dunedin), so it can be added to the statistics — even if you're not sure the problem is directly related to the vaccine. Remember to include the vaccine batch number (refer the infant's *Well Child* immunisation book).

Some things to be aware of

It is not compulsory in New Zealand for GPs or hospitals to notify officials of the adverse reactions their patients encounter from immunisations administered, so there is a strong belief in some quarters that vaccine reactions are grossly under-reported in this country. The interesting point to note is that in other countries, where the reporting of adverse reactions is compulsory, statistically fewer reports are made. So, in some distorted way, our voluntary system seems to produce more information.

In reality there is not one methodology for a vaccine trial that can cover all possible aspects of the long-term outcome concerns relating to immunisations. Science, instead, has to use a range of methods to investigate any hypothesis and look for long-term consequences, such as 'cohort follow-up', 'case control' and 'retrospective analysis'. One particularly useful source of information for vaccine safety research is the massive health-care organisations' databases in the USA, where children's full medical and vaccination histories can be quickly accessed to provide data on any proposed link with a disease.

The anti-immunisation stance emphatically believes that the vast majority of the above-listed childhood diseases are usually reasonably mild in developed countries, and that experiencing such diseases serves to strengthen children's immune systems and provide lasting immunity. That philosophy is reasonably indisputable.

However, what is in dispute is the belief that unvaccinated children are generally healthier children. Science and the medical profession are, of course, adamant that extensive and more than adequate research testing is always done before the introduction of a vaccine. However, some parent groups continue to have great concerns because they believe no adequate long-term safety studies have been completed that compare the health of unvaccinated children against vaccinated — and that existing tests are often too short or too small.

Adding to this discussion, it is a reality that some parents who don't vaccinate their child can be more vigilant with everything else that enters their children's bodies, including encouraging organic produce and holistic medicines, while discouraging junk food and pharmaceuticals. So, it would make sense that, at a fundamental systemic level, those children could be healthier, with a stronger resilience to disease.

Another past concern was that the heavy metal mercury (thiomersal) was used as a preservative within vaccine solutions. This has now been removed from all childhood vaccinations used in New Zealand.

There are also concerns voiced about aluminium hydroxide, used in some vaccines to enhance the immune response so that the vaccine effect will be stronger. In high doses the aluminium can be neuro-toxic (toxic to the brain). But aluminium hydroxide is the most common metallic element on earth; it has widespread use in human tissue, and is found in breastmilk and infant-milk formulas. In fact, the amount of this aluminium contained in a vaccine is only equivalent to the same amount consumed in a day's worth of baby formula (dependent on the age of the baby).

There are also concerns in some quarters about immunisations that are administered before the baby's blood-brain barrier has matured. Some say around three months of age is safer — though that is conjecture and not a magical date physiologically speaking.

Capilliaries within the brain create the least permeable, most discriminating filter in our entire body, the 'blood-brain barrier'. It prevents many damaging substances and harmful molecules circulating in the blood from entering the brain's cerebrospinal extra-cellular fluid, thus protecting brain tissue. Molecules that can get through it include respiratory gases, alcohol, nicotine and anaesthetic drugs.

Undoubtedly young babies are more vulnerable to some diseases due to the higher risk of pathogens crossing their blood-brain barrier more easily than in older children (e.g. some forms of meningitis). On the other hand, the vaccine antigens given to young babies in New Zealand are not live and, hence, only stimulate the immune system to create a memory, but cannot cause the disease. So the disagreement continues.

For information on the anti-immunisation argument, there are a lot of pro-active contacts including the Immunisation Awareness Society (www.ias.org.nz). They have published a book, *Investigate before you Vaccinate: Making an Informed Decision about vaccination in New Zealand*.

For information on the pro-immunisation argument, you can access literature and advice from your GP or the Immunisation Advisory Centre (0800 IMMUNE), or get hold of the New Zealand Ministry of Health's *Immunisation Handbook*.

The question of organic food

Humans are born into their historical situations and find something to stand for. They form a union with another human being who also has found some purpose. The children born to this union then reconcile these two positions by pursuing a higher synthesis . . .
Our children take our level of vibration (knowledge) and raise it even higher. This is how we, as humans, continue evolution.
James Redfield — *The Celestine Prophecy*

The type of food human beings have always eaten — until 50–60 years ago — is now fashionably named organic or biodynamic food — meaning it is grown without synthetic fertilisers, insecticides, herbicides, post-harvest fungicides, growth promoting hormones or antibiotic growth promoters. And processed organic food is made without artificial colourings, flavour enhancers, preservatives or other synthetic additives, and contains no genetically modified or irradiated ingredients (food zapped with large doses of ionising radiation to sterilise it).

With the globalisation and inter-connectedness of our planet, and mankind's ongoing interference with nature and the environment, we are becoming even more vulnerable to infectious diseases.

The topic of organic food is a can of worms because some of the people who are 'very pro' can, inadvertently, come across as evangelistic, back-to-nature ideologists with a reactionary, alarmist stance. But more and more it is becoming commonly accepted that the colouring-rich ice-cream, chemically filled biscuits and highly processed chippies being fed to children are affecting their behaviour, health and ability to learn. Heck, even the animals in our zoos are fed organic food. Great reading on this topic can be found in Sue Kedgley's *Eating Safely in a Toxic World*.

Asthma, eczema and hyperactivity

Asthma rates have doubled in New Zealand in the past couple of decades (25 percent of New Zealand children now suffer from asthma) and 10 percent of New Zealand children suffer from eczema. There are strong feelings in some quarters that this may largely be diet related, but the establishment continues to downplay any links between additives and allergies.

Interestingly, in holistic medicine such as homeopathy, the 'sister' conditions of asthma and eczema are not treated as actual diseases, but instead they are considered to be the side effects caused by some other more constitutionally related imbalance.

It is now understood that sulphite preservatives can trigger asthma attacks in a good chunk of asthmatics. In one American survey done in the 1990s, medical doctors and experts recommended a ban on the use of sulphites in all foods. Asthmatics especially may be wise to consider choosing foods labelled 'no preservatives' and 'no artificial/synthetic antioxidants'.

Presently 10 percent of New Zealand children are also hyperactive, and it is already well recognised that colourings, caffeine (such as in energy drinks and some soft drinks) and sugar, all provoke hyperactivity even in children not formally labelled hyperactive.

Pesticides

What's happening to our clean, green fruit and veggies? Pesticides are not really that big an issue are they?

Did you realise that a lot of the beautiful-looking fruit and some vegetables in our supermarkets are sprayed with wax to improve their appearance — just visit an organic produce shop and you will see what apples naturally can look like. (Washing does not remove the wax coating.) Apples can be sprayed with various chemicals 15–20 times before harvest.

New Zealand growers purchase around 4000 tonnes of pesticide-active ingredients every year, with around 400 kg of pesticides being used for every square kilometre of pasture and cropland. Washing and peeling removes some pesticide residues, but many are systemic (they penetrate into the cell structure of the plant). Additionally, after picking, some produce is also drenched in fungicides.

Innumerable studies have linked pesticides to cancer (from exposure to insecticides). Breads and cereals can also contain high levels of pesticides due to the insecticides used on wheat. Quite a number of pesticides used in New Zealand are internationally considered 'probable' human carcinogens, and even more are thought of as 'possible' human carcinogens. (Carcinogens are substances that are found to cause cancer.)

It is difficult to prove cause and effects of pesticides on reproductive abnormalities, but a number of studies are showing an association with birth defects. Evidence is also accumulating that some industrial chemicals and pesticides interfere with the human endocrine (hormone-gland) system.

Monkeys exposed to continuous low levels of dioxins have developed endometriosis, which is a common disease of the reproductive system among New Zealand women. And roughly 70,000 chemicals in use around the world have not yet been tested for their effects on the human endocrine-gland system.

There are correlations beginning to be drawn between pesticides and the nervous system (memory, alertness, attention, concentration). Also hundreds of studies have shown that pesticides, even in small doses, can be toxic to the lymphatic immune system, making us more susceptible to disease.

Many researchers also suggest pesticides and heavy metals are causing the dramatically diminishing male sperm counts — reduced by up to 50 percent over the past 50 years. Supporting this, studies show that men who eat only organic produce have higher sperm counts. It's all rather frightening.

Growth hormones

What about all the growth hormone stuff in our meat that people keep talking about?

On the whole New Zealand meat is much less contaminated with pesticides than our fruits and vegetables — but there are, instead, antibiotics and synthetic growth hormones (including testosterone and progesterone, which alter the animal's oestrogen).

Did you know that more than half the world's supply of antibiotics is used on farm animals? And a large proportion of these antibiotics are growth promotants (called feed enhancers) that are fed to animals specifically to make them grow faster, rather than to treat disease — that way the animals put on weight more quickly while eating less food — and the meat industry can truthfully state that their animals are not fed 'growth hormones'.

This reminds me of one Saturday when I was organising the main meal for a dinner party. In one of my older recipe books the ingredients list called for '500 g chicken or 4 x single boneless chicken breasts'. I asked my husband to pick up two double or four single boneless chicken breasts on his way home. When he plonked the chicken on the kitchen bench, it weighed a phenomenal 1.5 kg — that's a *tripling* in the weight of an average chicken breast!

Thirty years ago, chickens took about two months to grow to marketable size, now they take less than half that time. And, yes, New Zealand chickens may not be getting fed hormones, but they are getting fed copious amounts of antibiotic growth promotants on a daily basis. And, for your interest, eating lean meat is best because persistent pesticides concentrate in fatty tissue.

In just the last 15–20 years, the average age of New Zealand girls' first periods has changed from 12–14yrs to 8–11yrs. It is strongly suggested this relates to diet (i.e. improved nutrition and the chemicals and hormones found in modern food).

You see, at birth females are born with all the eggs for their lifetime of ovulation, although our fertile years have a limited time-span. Logically, if our daughters are generally starting their periods 3–4 years earlier than we did, then they are also strongly likely to have the onset of menopause 3–4 years earlier too. Girls under ten are way too young to have to deal with the side effects and responsibilities of menstruation! And our girls in their late thirties are way too young to be entering menopause! It's such an awful and unnatural imbalance.

Did you also know that apparently the average New Zealand woman's bra size has increased in the last few decades from a 12B to a 12D/14C. As a nation, our women are menstruating earlier and becoming larger breasted. These evolutionary changes would normally have taken Mother Nature thousands of years to achieve.

Scientists are also warning that the practice of continuously feeding antibiotics to animals is producing strains of antibiotic-resistant bacteria that can easily be passed onto humans. The New Zealand Veterinary Association says nature's resistance to antibiotics (and other animal treatments such as anthelmintics used to control worms) is developing so rapidly it is outstripping scientists' ability to develop new products.

But organic food is so expensive!

Many consumers are now looking at eating organic food as an investment in their long-term health, because of the questionable effects of consuming residue chemicals and pesticides. But organic food can seem incredibly expensive — but it isn't really, it's simply that producing food *inorganically* has *reduced* the overall cost of food production. (When I was little, eating roast chicken was an expensive treat — now it's a cheap dinner you can buy at the service station.)

I'm not going to venture into the topic of the biotechnology revolution (or as others call it 'biowarfare') surrounding genetically engineered and modified food, such as fish genes into fruits, and chicken genes into fish. But I will admit to having anti-GE bumper stickers on the back window of my car — I believe that assuming it is a straight-forward idea to introduce genetically engineered food into the human body is potentially a naïve stance.

The immature brain, digestive system, nervous system, immune system, kidneys and liver that children have makes them far more vulnerable and sensitive than adults to most chemical substances (particularly toxins). So when introducing solids, we decided to feed our children mostly organic baby foods.

Now that they are older, and with organic food being so much dearer than non-organic food, we've tried to give our children a lot of their *staple* foods as organic — with the 'frilly' bits being conventional. For example, I'll use organic bread, but the butter and honey will be non-organic. Plus, I try to supply my children with only organic fruit.

In motherhood, your life is spent trusting in the unknowable.
Author unknown

Chapter 10

Big miracles for our little miracles

The old expression 'The buck stops here' takes on a new meaning for mothers. Twenty-four hours of every day you are the ultimate decision maker concerning your baby's life . . . It's akin to being a CEO, a policeman on duty, or a physician on call. All eyes turn to the person in authority and expect that person to know what to do. When the baby cries in the middle of the night or breaks out in a rash or spits up its lunch, all eyes will turn to you.

D. Stern and N. Bruschweiler-Stern — *The Birth of a Mother*

Today, there is one parenting topic that reeks with the stench of tumultuous contention — and that is *How To Cure your Sick Child*.

Although GPs provide modern society's first place to look for a cure, they are of course not mankind's *traditional* source of healing. In evolutionary terms, modern paediatrics is a very young medical science — yet its scientifically based wisdom has without question dramatically and positively influenced millions of lives!

However, with increased questioning of the medical profession, a growing number of parents are asking serious questions about the 'pharmacological war' waged upon their wee darlings.

Soon after entering the world of parenthood, you will notice that some parents only ever take their child to the local GP; whereas some other parents will try almost any alternative, to avoid taking their child to the GP. So what is going on here? Why is there so much faith in, and so little faith in, modern medicine?

Lee Carroll writes in *The Indigo Children*, 'Today's weirdness is often tomorrow's science.' How true. Look, for example, at yoga, hypnotherapy, chiropractics, osteopathy, iridology, acupuncture, reflexology, aromatherapy, shiatsu-acupressure or detoxification. Until relatively recently, all these healing therapies used to be considered by the Western mainstream as eccentric, freaky, hippyish bullshit. But now they are topics commonly chatted about by executives during lunchtime in the boardroom — and even government health departments and medical health insurance companies are needing to accept that there are viable and effective complementary and alternative therapies beyond Westernised medicine's existing understanding of the science of healing.

Just look at some of the many other New Age (old age) healing therapies becoming more accepted these days, such as India's 5000-year-old Ayurvedic healing, enzymatics, bioenergetics, electromagnotherapy, phytotherapy, reiki, Chinese moxibustion, prolotherapy, qigong, polarity therapy, oligotherapy, auricular therapy, microcosm energy, muscuoloskeletality, oxygenation, orthomolecularity, kinesiology, feldenkrais, maharishi vedic, aura soma, Bowen therapy, neuro-link bio-feedback, chelation, the Alexander technique, mandalas, chakra alignment, macrobiotics, trepanation . . . the list really does go on.

Scientists are being forced to look beyond their old knowledge of, say, the benefits of vitamin and mineral supplements, to grasp a fuller understanding of the molecular interactions of high-quality nourishment in compounds: for example, the new appreciation that antioxidants neutralise damaging free radicals.

There is an almost infinite knowledge of nutrition and healing that science is yet to comprehend, such as phytonutrients (the active ingredients in herbal medicines); and nutriceuticals (the phytochemicals found in natural foods) that are functional, bioactive chemical compounds with health-promoting, medicinal or disease-prevention properties. They are found in whole foods, such as unrefined fruits, vegetables, beans, nuts, grains and seeds.

The more medical science learns, the more it realises it doesn't understand! Almost 2500 years ago the Greek philosopher Plato said, 'This is the great error of our day in the treatment of the human being, that the physicians separate the soul from the body'.

When will medicine learn! When measurable indisputable proof is the main faith, what happens to the intuitive and holistic therapies that are outside the realms of medical science's 'tape measures and scales'? Does modern medicine take the 'prudent' sceptical attitude of 'provide us with the scientific evidence before we will believe you'? *Oh, let us pray not!* Let us hope that the most open scientific minds lead medicine into the realms of the incomprehensible magical cures and miraculous remedies. Modern medicine doesn't know it all, so why pretend that it does?

Life becomes just a little bit more confusing to us non-scientists as to what the heck we should be consuming, and in what forms, and quantities.

In this chapter we enter into one of my personal pet-peeve topics. In an attempt to assist you, this chapter features introductions to a few of the current most popular alternative and complementary healing therapies. At the same time as being 'pro' complementary therapies, I am also 'pro' modern medicine — let's be real, most premature babies, for example, wouldn't survive without antibiotics.

Antibiotics, unquestionably, play a vital role in modern medicine, and in fact have revolutionised human life-spans. However, along with a growing number of GPs, I am anti the over-prescription of Western medications such as antibiotics for general day-to-day childhood illness.

Libraries and the internet are brimming with information outlining concerns regarding over-prescription of antibiotics and the cumulative side effects — and, of course, the global side effect is the (re)emergence of infectious diseases. To explain in layman's terms: medical science is unable to develop new types of antibiotics and antiviral drugs fast enough to compete with mutated new strains of bacteria and viruses.

It is a medical time-bomb that started ticking when antibiotics were first prescribed — a bomb that has already exploded with the arrival of early 'super-bugs', survivable only by humans with *experienced, robust immune systems.*

Anatomy and physiology

A wise man is he who knows he knows not.

Socrates, Greek philosopher

As your infant grows, I recommend you learn more about how such things as vitamins, minerals, herbal nutrients and nature's oils can positively affect your child's state of wellness — and with the explosion of the internet, it has become much easier to do so.

While your child is growing up, you can choose to embrace learning about their (and your) anatomy (structure) and physiology (function). Then, as your precious child experiences illness and disease, you could take personal responsibility by becoming knowledgeably aware of their condition, and current research and contributing factors that may have been overlooked. Making simple lifestyle modifications can often affect the severity of many conditions.

I am not suggesting parents try to qualify themselves as doctors by completing their own internet-surfing medical 'degree'! I am simply stating that knowledge is empowering.

For example, grasp an understanding of:

- The cardiovascular system (e.g. heart, blood vessels, blood pressure, pulmonary and systemic circulation).
- The respiratory system (e.g. trachea, bronchus, lungs, nose, pharynx, larynx, bronchitis, asthma, sinusitis and resuscitation).
- The nervous system (e.g. central, peripheral, neurons, brain, spinal cord, reflexes, neurotransmitters and concussion).
- The endocrine system (e.g. pituitary, adrenals, pineal, thymus, thyroid, gonads, hormones, growth, metabolism and diabetes).
- The musculoskeletal systems (e.g. bones, marrow, skeletal muscles, tendons, ligaments, cartilage and bone fractures).
- The digestive gastrointestinal system (e.g. saliva, oesophagus, stomach, pancreas, liver, gall bladder, intestines, appendix, rectum, anus, heartburn, vomiting, constipation and diarrhoea).
- The urinary renal system (e.g. kidneys, bladder, UTIs and dehydration).
- The lymphatic and immune system (e.g. tonsils, thymus, spleen, lymph nodes, pus, immune defences, tonsilitis, allergies and inflammation).
- The integumentary system (e.g. skin, hair, sweat and oil glands, and nails).
- The reproductive system (e.g. mammaries, penis, scrotum, testes, ovaries, uterus, vagina).
- The special anatomy and physiology of the eyes, ears, mouth, nose and blood (e.g. vision, hearing, balance, taste and smell).

Allopathic medicine versus Vis medicatrix naturae

We are standing on the brink of a global crisis in infectious diseases. No country is safe … Some bacteria are resistant to as many as 10 different drugs … In the race for supremacy, microbes are sprinting ahead [of mankind] … Many of the most powerful antibiotics have been rendered impotent.

World Health Organisation Report, 1996

Allopathic means modern medicine. The mainstream medical profession uses evidence-based research, such as double-blind trials, as its model for best practice. The public's previously unquestioned reliance on modern medicine is diminishing, and questions are being asked about alternative therapies and complementary remedies.

Vis medicatrix naturae translates as 'the healing power of nature'. Generally this means benefiting from nature to strengthen and support the body, while gently stimulating it to self-heal using its own curative forces. And this is the strategy behind almost all alternative healing-therapies, which focus not just on maintaining total health, but on treating the symptoms of illness as manifestations of the body trying to correct an underlying imbalance.

Allopathic (modern) medicine defines alternative medicine by its own criteria, as therapies that have not been shown in a 'randomised controlled manner' (via clinical trials) to be deemed *safe* and *effective*.

But this is where things become unstuck, because modern medical science is still in its infancy in terms of understanding the complexities of Mother Nature, and in many instances it is still a long way from having the right technology to scientifically measure and explain the mechanics of how many alternative therapies work. Time and time again throughout history, science has known that something works, but not *why* it works. Eventually technology catches up so that scientists (and subsequently the human race), can understand *how* something works.

Modern medicine creates therapies that are designed to work effectively for the masses; whereas many alternative medicines address the individual (i.e. every patient is inherently unique). This is the main difference.

Homeopathy, for example, can easily diagnose 50 different kinds of cough, each needing a different vibrational tincture remedy, available in half-a-dozen different levels of dose. And osteopathy, as another example, is a difficult five-year degree (heck, nursing and midwifery are only three years), which requires the practitioner to use intuition as a diagnostic aid to detect intangible, immeasurable variations.

If, for example, we were to apply modern medicine's principles to the subject of God, well, there would be no God — his healing presence has not been *indisputably* proven to be safe and effective by randomised, controlled, double-blind clinical research. But humans continue to pray to their God(s) for improved health, and medical miracles credited to God continue to occur!

Time and time again, I have seen parents place *all* their faith in modern (pharmaceutical) medicine. Then after a couple of years and thirty or so doctors' visits, including specialists, without significant improvement — out of desperation they try something alternative. They visit one or two alternative medical practitioners without any radical improvement, and give up on all complementary medicines. Then they return for the 31st visit to their local doctor, giving the GP another opportunity to fail. I just don't get it.

A frustrating aspect of many modern medications is their commonly designed function to *reduce symptoms*, or *suppress symptoms* by 'taking over' a body's curative abilities. You know . . . tummy ache, take an analgesic . . . blocked nose, take a decongestant . . . sneezing and itching, take an antihistamine . . . eczema, use steroid cream . . . ear infections or glue ear, get grommets . . . tonsillitis, have a tonsillectomy . . . baby with urinary tract problems, take antibiotics for a year. It's frightening.

This results in a person's immune system failing to develop, through normal exposure, into what should become a naturally robust defence mechanism. How can you tell? Epidemic proportions of Westernised children experience recurring bronchitis, tonsillitis, middle-ear infections, glue ear, eczema, asthma, urinary tract infections, and the list goes on.

The intention of alternative healing initially is to reduce symptoms (with remedies that can often act similarly to conventional modern treatments in many respects). But, alternative therapies then focus their full attention on searching for the *cause* of the condition.

In many ways, alternative therapies don't so much intend to provide medicinal cures, but rather to provide wellness on a holistic (all body) level. This can be a very different approach from Western allopathic medicine. The public need to be educated to understand that most modern medical treatments are designed to help the patient live with the symptoms by reducing or lessening them — rarely by actually curing the problem.

I see three problems:

1. There are too few GPs with formal training in alternative medicinal therapies.
2. Impatient parents want instant cures. (Parents feel powerless.)
3. The New Zealand health system still doesn't formally acknowledge the time-proven effectiveness of many ancient medical remedies, so GPs are unable to write prescriptions for alternatives, even if they wanted to. (The New Zealand government is particularly outdated in comparison to many other developed countries with their policy of largely ignoring medical practices currently accepted overseas as mainstream, such as homeopathy and naturopathy.)

Behind the scenes is the commercial reality that pharmaceutical corporations are only able to patent (and thus receive their income from) man-made medicines. So profits (and therefore research funds) can be much lower when developing medicines found in nature — except when patenting synthesised copies of natural cures, such as codeine and morphine (copied from opium poppies); aspirin (copied from white willow bark); penicillin (copied from mould); and lifesaving digoxin heart-failure medicine (copied from the foxglove plant).

Before having children, my husband was hugely cynical of any medicine even slightly 'out there'. Just a few years later, I heard him explaining to dinner-party guests that he now felt, 'Instead of remedies such as homeopathy being called alternative medicine, the medical options would more correctly be re-named *ancient traditional medicines* and the *modern alternatives.*' Why are Mark and I now such strong believers in traditional medicines? To put it bluntly . . . because, prescribed properly, the stuff works so bloody well!

Some time in the future, all these different healing wisdoms, modern and ancient, will eventually combine, I'm sure, into some stupendous, miraculous and universal holistic (all body) medical therapy — but certainly not in our lifetime! In the meantime, you need to make confusing decisions on behalf of your precious children as to what healing therapies they will receive.

Naturopathy and homeopathy

Minds are like parachutes; they only function when open.
Sir James Dewar, Inventor

Naturopathy uses healing powers from Mother Nature (natural substances such as herbs and minerals). Some believe that God created the Earth with the perfect cure for every disease — it is just a matter of discovering them all. If this philosophy is true (which none of us can dispute for sure until we knock on the Pearly Gates and ask Him), then naturopathy, with its reverence to nature, goes a *long* way towards unearthing vast amounts of natural remedies for 'dis-ease' as it is more correctly pronounced.

Homeopathy is a natural, pharmaceutical science which uses infinitesimal micro-doses of a vast array of ingredients selected from plants, mineral sources and other natural substances, transformed into vibrational tinctures, which are used to enhance the body's natural healing processes. In other words, the remedies stimulate the body's own defence and immune system to 'kick-start' defending and healing itself.

It's great to combine the herbs and dietary supplements of naturopathy to promote wellness physiologically, with the tinctures of homeopathy to promote mental and emotional wellness. With knowledgeable practitioners, these therapies together create an enriching and uplifting healing partnership.

The tricky part of homeopathy is to successfully find the precisely correct homeopathic medicine to treat each individual's unique pattern of symptoms. Then, the amazing (and still not completely understood) truth is that these minute doses *only* have an effect on the person if it is the *correct remedy*. If a wrong remedy is given, then *nothing* happens. Bizarre! This reality also makes it impossible to overdose on homeopathic medicine — however, it is possible to overuse remedies.

Self-prescription of homeopathic remedies is fine for relieving acute symptoms (rapid onset, severe, brief duration). However, homeopathic remedies should not be used for chronic symptoms (long-term, ongoing, slow-changing) — unless prescribed by a homeopathic practitioner.

The commonly used, most basic homeopathic remedies are inexpensively available at chemists and health shops for use internally (mouth drops, mouth sprays and sugar-tablets) and externally (creams, gels, oils, ointments and lotions). Some names that may already be familiar to you include arnica, aconite, belladonna, calendula, chamomilla, hepar-sulph, hypericum, nux vomica, pulsatilla, and rhus tox. Plus there's a great array of pre-mixed combinations to aid with particular types of conditions. Stronger doses and a much wider range of remedies are available through a homeopathic practitioner. With homeopathic treatments it is always important to avoid taking them with, or exposing them to mint, eucalyptus, caffeine, cigarettes and camphor, which can neutralise the remedies.

Naturopathy and homeopathy both work on a holistic and individual approach . . . meaning that the correct remedy can only be diagnosed by looking at the whole person — never just at one individual symptom.

When the strong immune system of a child raised homeopathically and naturopathically combines with the perfect natural healing remedy, the results can be instant, or very fast.

In other words, the illness still goes through its various stages, *but* they will all occur *much faster* — it's as if an experienced, robust immune system speeds up recovery. So for our children, for example, it is quite normal for a 'five-day virus' to last one day; or for nappy rash to disappear by the next nappy change; or for a 'two-weeks in bed influenza' to last just 3–4 days; or for them to be completely recovered from the likes of tonsillitis or bronchiolitis within just 1–2 days — sometimes things linger a bit longer, but that's unusual.

So how do children's immune systems develop into a strong, robust and rapidly effective defence mechanism? Very easily — *by getting used*!

Promoting a robust immune defence system

Every time parents *routinely* feed their child medications such as antibiotics, they weaken that child's immune system, resulting in a child that is more and more susceptible to the illness they are treating (and similar illnesses). That is why there is increasing concern sounding around the planet — we are *weakening* our children, dramatically.

If your child's immune defence system is already far from 'virginal' and has received the likes of antibiotics, antiviral drugs, anaesthetics, and/or steroids, it is still possible to 'turn the clock back'. But, please don't kid yourself that having arnica, rescue remedy and echinacea in your medicine cupboard will transform your child's immune system. It's going to take much more work than that.

The requirement it takes is *commitment* on your part to make the effort, take the time, and invest the money (it's not cheap), into recruiting a classical homeopath and naturopath to begin the (potentially lengthy, dependent on your child's medical history) process, of 'peeling back the layers' (not dissimilar to an onion). Finally your child's inherent constitution (physical and mental) will be revealed. Discovering the root causes of an individual's susceptibility to particular medical conditions eventually enables the practitioners to return a child to a state of optimum-functioning equilibrium and balance (a homeostatic state, as modern medicine terms it).

I have met few parents willing to do what it takes to accomplish this, but I am full of admiration for those that do — especially as it is easier, cheaper, and socially more acceptable to use only prescriptions from your GP.

Thankfully, many GPs are increasingly becoming much more open-minded and enlightened regarding alternatives — slowly but surely, more GPs are opting to be trained in subjects such as homeopathy, naturopathy and iridology — our own GP, for example, is also trained in acupuncture.

With a cleansed lymphatic system, and a homeopathically and naturopathically well-nourished individual constitution, a child's immune defence system can be brought back to its original strength, ready to be further developed by the bacteria and diseases it will encounter.

As my girlfriend Kim, who has the same philosophy as me, once said: 'How can we hope our children's bodies could be capable of fighting the really serious diseases, if they can't even cope with a bit of tonsillitis?' The world is already seeing the devastating havoc super-bugs can create. People with robust immune systems survive, those with weakened immune systems die. Scary, but true.

Summary guide

- Naturopathy and homeopathy can be very effective in helping speed up the body's recovery processes for conditions such as ear infections (usually eradicating the need for grommets, which come with their own set of on-going problems), recurring tonsillitis (often avoiding surgery), anaemia, bites, blisters, broken bones, bronchiolitis, bronchitis, bruises, burns, chickenpox, colds, coughs, croup (barking cough), cuts, diarrhoea, Giardia, glue ear, grazes, hand-foot-and-mouth, Coxsackie's virus, influenza, measles, mumps, scalds, skin boils, sore throats, sprains, stings, thrush, vomiting, and a newborn's recovery from inhaling meconium.

• Naturopathy and homeopathy can almost miraculously improve both the acute symptoms and long-term fight against skin irritations such as eczema and food allergies (in conjunction with diet modification), and childhood asthma with its breathlessness, coughing and wheezing.

• Naturopathy and homeopathy are wondrous at taking the edge off and/or curing colic, convulsions, cradle cap, diabetes, fevers, fits, gastric reflux, gastroenteritis, jaundice, vaccination reactions, infantile pimples (hormone rash), nappy rash, shock, teething, and hundreds of other problems.

• Homeopathy can also be quite miraculous with childhood psychological and emotional issues. A few examples of extreme personality difficulties which can be improved with naturopathy and homeopathy include a tendency towards violence, hyperactivity, aggressive behaviour, bed-wetting issues, habitual stealing, anxiety, restlessness, irrational fears, inferiority complexes, timidity, lack of confidence, low self-esteem, jealousy, rage, lost-the-plot tantrums, ADD, ADHD and more.

Every so often, I can just 'see' a deterioration in the temperament of one or other of our children. It may show in ongoing episodes of losing the plot, not being 'themselves', or seeming to have lost some ability to experience contentment. I know I have an acutely heightened awareness of these subtleties, because I have become very familiar with our children's individual signs of imbalance. At this point, I give them a boost of their constitutional remedy to put their system back into homeostatic equilibrium, and then within a few days they are back to their old more-contented selves again. It is understandable that many parents could simply dismiss such behaviour as the child going through one of their difficult phases, with the behaviour potentially becoming their 'normal' personality trait.

Cranial osteopathy

Any science that considers only the physical
understands only the corpse.

Rudolph Steiner, Austrian philosopher

It is a miracle how human babies' heads have evolved such soft, pliable skull bones that are so perfectly designed to overlap (to reduce the head circumference) as they descend the narrow birth canal.

After a few days these naturally resilient and springy skull plates should return to their normal positions, and the babies' own body healing mechanisms should fix any residual damage or stresses. But like everything in nature, things vary, and for some babies unresolved small skull tensions can remain.

Few births are truly easy for the baby — heck, in Victorian times one in 20 babies died at birth. Perhaps in an 'enlightened' world, a cranial osteopathy check would be standard practice after all lengthy labours (including those resulting in caesars), all forceps deliveries, all ventouse deliveries, and all fast deliveries. Plus, it would be recommended after all other births. But that's not part of the present maternity healthcare process.

So within the first 1–2 weeks after arriving home from hospital, as an investment in their wellness, it can be recommended to take newborn babies to a cranial osteopath to have them checked for any residual misalignment caused from their birth.

To diagnose any problems, the cranial osteopath gently holds the baby's head while feeling for the cranial rhythmic flow of the cerebrospinal fluid (vaguely similar to a heartbeat but much slower) and the osteopath individually checks all the skull-bone suture joins. If they discover any strains, they perform extremely gentle manipulations on the bones (to the untrained eye, it can look as if the osteo is hardly doing anything). The osteo will also do a complete body check including the back, neck, spine, sacrum, pelvis and abdomen. Afterwards it is normal for the baby to seem particularly relaxed, and they'll often spend the afternoon 'sleeping it off'.

Conditions with which cranial osteopathy can particularly help

- Constantly crying screaming babies (from whinging to colic).
- Grumpy, irritable, upset babies.
- Jumpy babies.
- Windy babies.
- Spilly babies (e.g. reflux).
- Feeding difficulties.
- Persistent coughs and colds.
- Conjunctivitis (sticky eyes), ear infections and glue ear.
- Disturbed sleep (e.g. sleeplessness, jitteriness).
- Breathing disorders (e.g. asthma, bronchitis).
- Allergies.
- Colicky babies.
- Hyperactivity.
- Lots more.

It can be quite normal for some people to rave about the results of their alternative-style healing, while others think their results were rubbish (probably mostly dependent on the quality of the practitioner, and/or the level of parental commitment to the process).

But, on the subject of infantile cranial osteopathy, I have experienced unanimous positive feedback from all friends who tried it. Comments vary from 'Yes, it worked quite well really' to 'The improvement was like a spectacular miracle.' Babies tend to respond very well to the subtle corrections of cranial osteopathy, with much quicker results than adults.

After your baby is checked as a newborn, it could be a good wellness investment to have your child re-checked every 2–3 years, and after bad falls.

Cranio-sacral therapists, such as osteopaths, constantly treat older children with left-right brain imbalances too (such as dyslexia, visual dysfunctions, clumsiness and poor co-ordination) — who in those experts' opinion can commonly have obvious birth or head-fall skull trauma.

New trendy old medicines

I give this section the name of 'trendy' not as a disrespect to these wonderful remedies — but because most of these ancient medicines are presently particularly popular, and are all highly recommended for any household's first-aid kit.

Aloe vera

Although aloe plants look similar to cacti, they are members of the lily family, and there are over 200 species of aloe plants growing in arid and tropical countries around the world. The healing properties of the gel inside the leaves of the aloe vera plant were discovered centuries ago, and have been used by many different cultures since ancient Egyptian times. They are easy to grow — it's a great idea to have an aloe vera plant growing in a pot inside or in the garden, as you only need to break off a leaf to use it.

Aloe vera gel has wonderfully restorative effects on skin because it has a pH level almost identical to human skin, and it can also be taken internally. Aloe vera gel is recognised as a good remedy to help soothe and heal minor burns, itchy insect bites, nappy rash, cuts, scratches, and sunburn, and taken internally for colds, ear infections, sore throats, toothaches and asthma attacks. (If you don't have a plant, you can buy the gel.)

Arnica

Probably the best known of all homeopathic remedies, arnica is derived from the herb *Arnica montana* (mountain daisy), and comes in various forms including sprays, drops and tablets for taking internally; and creams and gels for external use. Arnica is globally renowned for its anti-inflammatory healing of bruises, knocks, falls, sprains, strains, sore aching muscles, fractures, pain, swelling, traumatic injuries, concussion, insect bites and stings, nose-bleeds, and is used pre- and post-surgery. (It should not be applied to broken skin.)

Bach flower essences — Rescue Remedy

In 1930 London, surgeon and bacteriologist (and later pathologist) Dr Edward Bach, disgruntled with the practices of modern medicine, abandoned his lucrative London clinic and traditional medical science, to devote the rest of his life to discovering medicinal remedies he was sure could be found in nature.

Over the following six years, Dr Bach discovered 38 flower-essence remedies, which were categorised into seven groups. He found treating the emotive personalities of patients by alleviating their unhappy feelings was a very effective way to unblock the body's natural restorative abilities. Sadly, Dr Bach then died, but by the end of the 1930s Bach flower remedies were being used all over the world.

Probably the most famous Bach flower tincture is called Rescue Remedy, which is a combination of five flower essences. Rescue Remedy has an immediate calming and emotionally stabilising effect in stressful conditions. Around the world people use it for many different situations, e.g. traumatic accidents or emergencies, before public speaking, before tests, for an over-active mind before sleep, and after arguments.

It is completely safe to use in pregnancy, during labour, by breastfeeding mothers and to give to babies. It is useful with an overtired or overstimulated baby, a baby woken by a fright, an upset colicky baby, tantrumming toddler, and an upset child after injury or nightmare.

Calendula

Calendula is a homeopathic remedy derived from the herb *Calendula officinalis* (marigold), which is available in various healing forms, including drops for taking internally, and creams and gels for external use.

Calendula is an antiseptic (kills bacteria) and analgesic (pain-reliever) that is globally renowned for its soothing healing of injured skin;

dry, chapped skin; cuts, abrasions, rashes, blistering and minor burns. It helps stop bleeding and promotes healthy skin texture and tissue repair to reduce scars.

Colloidal silver

Silver has been used for thousands of years as a natural antibiotic healing remedy as it has antibacterial, antiviral and antifungal qualities and germ-fighting attributes. It is a powerful preventative against infections, because it works as a catalyst to disable the oxygen-metabolising enzyme in single-celled bacteria, fungi and viruses.

Colloidal silver is made up of ultra-fine molecules of silver suspended in water — the particles of silver and water are 'bound together'. When taken internally colloidal silver provides tremendously positive effects on the body's immune system; and topically it assists to generate less scar tissue due to its rapid healing qualities. Colloidal silver is non-toxic — except to single-cell micro-organisms such as viruses, fungi and bacteria.

Colloidal silver is reputed to have very positive effects on many conditions, including cell regeneration, acute illnesses, acute toxicity, sinusitis, hay-fever, sore throats, staphylococcus, streptococcus, stomach flu, tonsillitis, all viruses, yeast infections, cuts, abrasions, open wounds, eczema, itches, acne, insect bites, septic infections, colds, flus, burns, allergies, boils, dermatitis, cold sores, parasitic infections, conjunctivitis, glue ear, nappy rash, thrush, bladder infections, problems of digestion, and about 600 other conditions.

It is tasteless, doesn't sting and does not interfere with other medications.

Echinacea

Native to America and known as the purple coneflower, *Echinacea* is harvested for its roots, seeds, flower-heads and juice; and was a main medicinal remedy used by the American Indians. With the arrival of colonial settlers, by the early 1900s echinacea had become the most popular medicinal herb prescribed in America, and within three decades was being exported in great quantities to Europe.

Echinacea is one of Mother Nature's natural antibiotics, and is an excellent remedy to help rid the body of microbial infections. It has traditionally been used for treating insect bites, teeth or gum pains, colds, measles, mumps, bacterial and viral attacks, boils, laryngitis, tonsillitis, nose and sinus problems, septic sores and cuts, streptococcus and staphylococcus. It also has excellent immunity-stimulating properties, plus it 'cleanses' the lymph and blood systems.

Use echinacea when the body is sickly, run-down, or has a sluggish immune system that is having difficulty fighting such conditions as a lingering cold, recurring thrush, and as an alternative to antibiotics. Even the (conservative) WHO reportedly supports the use of echinacea for colds, flus, infections of the respiratory and urinary tracts, poorly healing wounds and chronic ulcerations.

Food of the Gods — ghee

Warm cows' or goats' milk mixed with honey and ghee (clarified butter) is known as Food of the Gods. Breastmilk is sweet and fatty, and this yummy combination in its own way reproduces that nurturing love. It is wonderful to give your upset child or upset self.

To make ghee, heat unsalted butter over a low heat for 10–15 minutes, pour off the liquid and foam into a lidded jar, and discard the sediment at the bottom. Da-dah! You now have a jar of ghee, and it does not need to be refrigerated.

Garlic

Known as the stinking rose or Russian penicillin, the health benefits of garlic have been known for thousands of years, but now science is paying garlic more attention, and research is providing some astonishing results, with garlic's only negative side effects being its taste and odour.

Garlic's chemical properties are complicated . . . diallyl disulphides, ajoenes, dithiins . . . but it is garlic's compound allicin that is perhaps the most famous. When fresh garlic is crushed it releases the garlic enzyme allinase, which rapidly changes the garlic clove's alliin to allicin — but this compound only exists in this state for a few hours (and alters with cooking).

Mixing a little fresh well-crushed raw garlic into infant milk, juice or food, has been shown to display fantastic antifungal and antibiotic powers, and can be used to treat oral thrush, streptococcus, colds, flus, and children whose systems have become antibiotic-resistant. And of course the sulphur-rich components in cooked garlic do provide many general health benefits, including to the cardiovascular and immune systems.

The scientific research for more understanding on garlic continues.

Hypercal/Hyperical

Hypercal is a homeopathic combined remedy of calendula (marigold) and hypericum (St John's wort). It comes in various forms including drops, creams and gel for external use.

Hypercal is globally renowned for its calming healing of skin infection, injured skin, cuts and sores. It helps the skin recover quickly, promoting healthy, rapid healing. (Hypericum is a natural antiseptic and analgesic healing agent which stops bleeding and relieves sharp pains, infection and nerve damage.)

Olive leaf extract

Referred to in the Bible as the 'Tree of Life', the wonderful health benefits of olives and olive oil are well known. However, there is still little general awareness of the very real healing powers available from the tree's leaves. Olive leaf extract has been used since Egyptian times, and started to show up in medical journals from the late 1800s. However, scientists are now discovering that olive leaf extract is one of nature's best broad-spectrum medicines, with compounds that are antimicrobial (fighting disease micro-organisms); antiviral; and antiretroviral (fighting viruses that contain genetic material that integrates with human cells).

So, among other things, modern research has found that olive leaf extract is particularly effective against viruses, bacteria, fungus, yeast infections, and worm parasites; that is aids coronary blood flow — and that even doses several hundred times higher than recommended have no toxic or adverse side effects.

Spirulina

Named for its spiral shape microscopically, spirulina is a remarkable single-celled, blue-green algae plant. Without any doubt, it can be called a 'super-concentrated wonder food' because its nutrient profile is so strong. It is very high in protein; rich in iron (for red blood cells' oxygen transfer, essential for building a strong bodily system); it has great amounts of vitamin B12 (essential for a healthy nervous system); beta carotene (an antioxidant essential for growth, vision and mucous membranes); an array of amino acids (fundamental constituents of the body's protein); fatty acids (fundamental constituents of the body's lipid cell membranes); and even includes rare essential fatty acids (essential for body growth, but cannot be synthesised by the body, i.e. must be ingested), and many more nutrients. Spirulina is a powerful general dietary supplement.

Tea tree oil

In the 1900s carbolic acid was medicine's standard antiseptic bactericide, but in 1923 Dr A. R. Penfold discovered that tea tree oil was considerably stronger. Tea tree oil is now recognised as a very effective antiseptic and antibacterial agent, fungicide and germicide. Used externally and internally, it also promotes tissue regeneration.

Tea tree oil has many uses, including treating burns, thrush, cuts, nappy rash, ear aches, insect bites and stings, pimples, scaly scalp, sinus and bronchial congestion, eczema, splinters and sunburn.

Conclusion

This chapter had the potential to be much longer, because I feel passionate about first treating wellness (instead of just treating sickness). I could easily have gone on and on, in an effort to convince you of the benefits of using the healing power of Mother Nature.

If you think I have already written too much and it has irked you, then I apologise. But for some of you, this information will impact on the rest of your life; and for others, this information will have almost no influence at all.

It is yet another parental decision you will need to make.

Don't let your romantic aversion to science blind you to the Buddha in the computer chip.
Joseph Campbell, *Ten Commandments for Reading Mythology*

Chapter 11

This is more than baby blues . . . I really don't feel right!

One of the worst aspects of being a parent for me is the self-discovery, being face to face with one's secret insanity and brokenness and rage …that way down deep, way past being kind and religious and trying to take care of everyone, I was seething. Now it's close to the surface. I feel it race from my centre up into my arms and down into my hands and it scares the shit out of me.

Anne Lamott — *Operating Instructions*

Your baby is at least a couple of months old now, you know you would die for your precious babe, and perhaps you never knew it was possible to love a person so much — *but* you're feeling decidedly 'unlike you' . . . actually, who the heck are you anymore?

Are you You still, or just Her in the mirror, the one with the mammoth boobs, spewed on baggy shirt, grey bags under pink eyes, wash-and-wear hairstyle, maternity leggings, raggy slippers and a significant number of misplaced brain-cells. Your partner, too, may be beginning to wonder if his previously stunningly beautiful bride is now missing a big chunk of filling in her sandwich!

Here's the thing: nearly all of us have felt like that.

You're not a bad mother because you sometimes feel disappointed, anxious and bedraggled and you resent the baby you love. You're not pathetic just because you fall asleep on the couch during a dinner party. You're not a failure when emotionally you're a mix of Jekyll and Hyde, swinging from adoring motherhood to loathing motherhood. You're not being irrational as you rant and rant, on and on, about marriage worries and money worries and motherhood worries and baby worries — well actually, maybe you are a bit, but that's still OK. It's not unreasonable for you to be angry because no one warned you just what hauntingly intense and agonising torture giving birth can be (they thought they couldn't tell you because you'd be too petrified).

You *are* a normal mother of a baby if: every morning brings compounding jetlag; every lunchtime makes you feel like a cross between a milking machine and a washing machine; and every evening brings some tears. Don't be ashamed to admit to yourself (as you can be your toughest critic) that it is reasonable (and actually a perfectly sane reaction) to need time to adjust to feeling trapped in your new, brutally monotonous and ordinary life, with its grave responsibilities and unprestigious label. Discovering, to your surprise, that you are incapable of bestowing unlimited unconditional love makes you guilty of nothing — it only confirms your humanness.

In our mothers', grandmothers' and great-grandmothers' days, there was more expectation that a woman could be fulfilled by her role of motherhood — and of course that belief was often far from the real truth.

Today, however, the role of mother can be so undervalued (even by fathers) that it is often not even regarded as a real job. Heck, you can apply for a student loan to attend a university course in archaeology or anthropology, but you won't be granted any loans to attend any courses on parenting — as if mothering is a hobby that occupies us between our real work.

Society continues to support the view that when a man is anxious, he's just stressed and, considering his career pressures, that's understandable. But when a mother's anxious, then she's unduly depressed and, considering her workload, that's weak.

On top of that, today's women are repeatedly informed that they *cannot* possibly find complete personal fulfilment just from motherhood — they also need a personal exercise routine (preferably with a personal trainer of course); they need a personal skin beautifying regime, a personally uplifting sex life, personal time-out for meditation, a wardrobe full of personal favourites, a regularly visited personal hairdresser, oh, and don't forget an articulate and interesting personality . . . what a load of codswallop.

I remember attending a child's birthday party on a week day when another mother asked, 'And what do you do?' I was flabbergasted. I'd thought she was one of 'us', but she wasn't, she was from the 'I resumed my life perfectly fine' club. As it happens, at that time I could have replied aloofly, 'Oh I'm the managing director of a travel wholesaler with four branches nationwide that specialises in European accommodation', but I was so irked at her question, I said, 'I'm a mum, of course, can't you tell?'.

These days, if you admit to feeling complete fulfilment through motherhood, you're damned. At the same time, if you admit you can't find complete fulfilment through motherhood, you're also damned. It's a lose-lose situation in the public (and private) arena, which is why so many women suffer in secret. Instead I want to yell it out . . .

You have a mammoth adjustment to go through and the idea that your mothering blues will consist of one teary-eyed day is as unlikely as being able to completely dissociate your mind from the pain of childbirth, or that breastfeeding is always natural and easy.

There is usually an exhausting, painful *grief* a new mother goes through — no matter how good your pregnancy turned out to be, or how thrilling the delivery was, or how beautiful an experience breastfeeding has ended up becoming, or how crazily in love you are with your new baby — it is OK to feel disappointed sometimes (or at your wits' end) with the now permanent role of motherhood; and the self-sacrifice, relentless devotion, and shocking loss of self. Of course, you are eternally grateful to have been blessed with your little miracle and you deeply love your partner, but it is still normal to feel grotty, fat and thoroughly fed-up at times; and to yearn to be able to return to your old life, even if for just a few hours. You're not *bad* to think that way. Heck, this is the one job you can never resign from, and it's unrealistic to expect that you should *like* your work *all* the time.

However, about 15–20 percent of new mothers (though from my observations I believe it's more like 20–25 percent) find that during their normal postpartum adjustment they experience an episode of severe depression, or end up, as Naomi Wolf describes it in *Misconceptions*, 'bottoming out on some weird biochemical feeling of grief'. Like some insidious 'battle fatigue', inwardly you may feel an unrelenting sad hollowness, and be unable to understand why you're feeling like such a moody, irritable, grumbling, crumbling lost-soul that is no longer living, just existing. You're feeling like there's no way out and life is never getting better, optimism is vanishing before your eyes, and is being replaced instead with an intense inability to chill out anymore . . . you're feeling like a pressure-cooker about to implode. You're sick and tired of being sick and tired!

Before childbirth, you'd imagined feeling like the Madonna with Child, but instead now you're thinking, 'If one more bloody person asks "How's the baby?" I'm going to kill them.' It is a sense of guilt-ridden self-blaming outrage that used to be called the Homemaker Syndrome, Housewives' Disease or Suburban Neurosis — or as author Deborah McKinlay named it in *Bosom Buddies*, the 'Black Holes of a Maternal Mental Meltdown'.

Some mums are clever enough to publicly maintain an everything-is-fine persona, while robotically functioning competently. But there may be a chill in the air at home, starting with, as author Jenny Phillips describes in *Mothers Matter Too*, a 'tight-lipped martyrdom or seething resentment'. And these bottled-up feelings of anger, if left unaddressed, can mutate into a self-perpetuating shame and guilt at not feeling happy; because in your heart there is an inexplicable psychodynamic aching darkness, which is not going away. You may be coping with your baby and household tasks, but you are not enjoying *life*!

But here's the thing: unlike the baby blues, even though this is relatively common, it is NOT '*normal*' for a mother to feel these levels of depressing sadness — those feelings are a sign something out-of-kilter needs to be remedied, and quickly.

This is a postnatal stress disorder or postpartum depressive reaction. It is more intense and longer lasting than the baby blues, comes in more than one variety, can start any time during the baby's first year, lasts from a couple of months to years, and it is not possible to shake off the condition — it's like a bad toothache, it requires treatment.

However, during its untreated period, depression's long dark shadow can destroy family relationships, and is also well documented as an impairer of infant development, so it is not something you should treat by using bravado to carry on alone. You're a wise woman to reach out for help.

Postpartum or postnatal depression

Depression functions in the place where people hate both themselves and other people. It attracts complication, paranoia, impossibility, slippages, sneering, and pride. These emotions are ragged and infectious; they happen, not only inside you, but between you and everyone else in the room. The depressive think that they are self-contained, but they never stop leaking misery, banality and hatred.
Anne Enright — *Making Babies*

Referred to as PND (postnatal depression) or PPD (postpartum depression), this condition has varying symptoms and severities, and has been medically misunderstood and under-recognised for a very long time. Until only very recent times, PND was often assumed to be just a feeble-minded mother who is unable to cope with her baby, is critical of her husband, is overly fatigued, has lost interest in herself and/or her baby, panics emotionally, cries too easily and has no real backbone. In other words, such a woman ought psychologically to successfully come to terms with her new role (a 'pull yourself together' culture).

More recently, some have blamed PND on the modern woman 'wanting it all'.

With these harsh, stereotyped explanations, society has made it horrendously difficult for a woman to feel comfortable admitting that she isn't feeling right. Such stigma, such shame! You can get more depressed just considering that you might be a bit depressed!

It is only now, as science begins to understand more of the innumerable intricacies of how the human body functions, particularly brain chemistry, that PND is understood to be an endogenous problem (derived within the body) — and not simply the product of a person of weak character! But, medical science still has no definitive explanation for postnatal depression.

Who is most vulnerable to postnatal depression? It is a fact that any woman who becomes a mother is vulnerable, because statistically the aftermath of pregnancy, birth and motherhood puts a woman's mental health at risk. This is primarily due to the neurological and hormonal changes, combined with the extremely demanding stresses of mothering a young baby, and the 24-7 presence of a baby. The process of experiencing pregnancy, childbirth and motherhood challenges a female at every single level — biologically, psychologically and socially.

The undisputed facts about PND

- PND is defined as a non-psychotic depressive illness of mild to moderate severity. It is not particularly different from other depressions, except for the high level of susceptibility that the process of pregnancy, childbirth and motherhood places on a woman.
- PND is a common problem, yet continues to be frequently undiagnosed, and untreated by the medical profession. Maternal mental morbidity is rife (morbidity means an abnormal pathological state).
- Because, often, admitting to not coping can make a mother feel even more inadequate, women are characteristically reluctant to seek help for their PND problems or symptoms — even though deep inside they want help.
- Women are most vulnerable to PND in the first six weeks to three months after childbirth, nevertheless it can begin any time within the first year.
- This anxiety or mood disorder can last anywhere from a few weeks to a few years (or for a lifetime if never recognised or self-cured).
- Modern studies are confirming direct links between a mother's physical health during birthing recovery and her emotional wellbeing. *Yes, I know that is a particularly obvious correlation!*
- The partner of a depressed mother becomes more likely to also suffer from depression.

- One of the best screening tools to diagnose PND is to complete the ten multichoice questions of the EPDS (Edinburgh Postnatal Depression Scale) — at six weeks, three months and six months after the birth. A score of less than nine means you're fine; 9–12 means borderline possible depression; and 13 or above indicates probable or major depression. (You can find this multichoice questionnaire on the internet.)
- PND is very treatable; the recovery rate with treatment (pharmacological and psycho-social) is high.
- The earlier PND is nipped in the bud, the less psycho-social damage will occur.
- The longer it is left untreated, the longer it may take to recover from.
- An untreated, depressed mother can, unintentionally but significantly damage her children, due to the adversely affected mother-infant relationship: a depressed mother with her blank face and non-interactive mannerisms disengages from her baby's cues, giving fewer positive and more negative responses to her infant; she finds managing a crying baby more difficult; and some depressed mothers can be insensitively rough or even hostile with their baby. Potentially, this has harmful effects on the emotional, cognitive (learning, memory, etc.) development, and social behaviour of the baby short- and long-term, with babies having higher rates of insecure attachment to mother, infant distress and reduced responsiveness.
- However, studies on depressed mothers who *are* diagnosed and receiving treatment clearly show their children to be well-adjusted socially, and generally successful, with fewer learning difficulties.
- One sad side effect of recovering from PND is that afterwards, once back to your 'old self', there can be a guilt over the joyless months you've lost as your baby was growing up, because you can never get those moments back as happy memories. So don't delay asking for help — the sooner the better!

Triggers for PND — primary causes

- The seismic hormonal changes after delivery (particularly the massive drops in progesterone, and oestrogen sensitivity, and their effects on neurotransmitters within the brain).
- Recent adverse life-crisis event(s) (e.g. death of family member or close friend, redundancy, shifting homes, marriage, childbirth) and the effect on inter-personal relationships.
- Being anxious, stressed, insecure or irrational; having pessimistic negative expectations of childbirth, parental burden, or fear of labour; having a 'worrier', unassertive and non-coping vulnerable personality; having pre-

existing lack of self-interest or low self-esteem.

- Severe postnatal 'blues' (very changeable emotions), or extreme postnatal 'pinks' (e.g. difficulty sleeping, not eating properly, not resting enough). (See page 152).
- History of premenstrual tension syndrome.
- Personal or family history of psychiatric disturbance or illness (e.g. anxiety, depression, bipolar disorder, schizophrenia, alcoholism).
- Shocking delivery (e.g. too early, too quick), or traumatic delivery (e.g. pain, feeling of loss of control, powerlessness or fear). Mothers can suffer from post-traumatic stress disorder mimicking and being misdiagnosed as postnatal depression. (See page 374 for details on post-traumatic stress disorder.)
- Low-quality, deficient social-support network (e.g. lacking assistance, isolation, feeling of abandonment, dysfunctional relationship) or lack of a close, confiding relationship that gives emotional and practical support.
- Poor-quality marital relationship (problems with partner, arguing and difficulty talking, relationship in crisis).
- Mother's own dysfunctional childhood (e.g. history of abuse, or ambivalent relationship with mother who was a poor role model).
- Loss of mother at a young age (say before age eleven).
- Infant-related stressors (e.g. premature, sickly, colicky or high-needs baby).
- Extreme tiredness, prolonged exhaustion, fatigue, stress, sleep deprivation.
- Failure to successfully breastfeed.
- Having two or more young children.
- Feeling uneducated or inexperienced, lacking parenting skills (e.g. being an only/youngest child), or being uninformed regarding childbirth, the baby blues and postnatal depression.
- Ongoing backpain, sleep disorder, headaches or migraines.
- Urinary or faecal incontinence (leaking pee or poos).
- Underactive or overactive thyroid dysfunction (mistaken for postnatal depression). (See page 251.)
- Other illness or major health problem that is acute (rapid onset and severe) or chronic (disease of long duration).
- Other major surgery.
- Partner who is depressed.
- Socio-demographic factors (e.g. mother who is single, poor, uneducated, socially disadvantaged, adolescent or an older woman).
- Preoccupation with outside worries (e.g. housing or financial problems).
- Rapid return to work (within first weeks), or having no outside employment

(or being previously unemployed).

- Nutritional deficiencies, such as copper, essential fatty acids, lecithin (a phospholipid), iron (anaemia), vitamin B, vitamin E, essential amino acids and zinc — or low blood pressure.

Possible triggers for PND — secondary causes

- Obstetric events (e.g. disappointing obstetric complications).
- Very early discharge from hospital (say within hours).
- Choosing not to breastfeed, or experiencing breastfeeding difficulties.
- Unsupportive spouse during pregnancy (e.g. not attending antenatal classes).
- Financial hardships (e.g. low household income or unemployment), or low occupational status.
- Ongoing negative family relationship issues (particularly between the new mum and her own mother).
- More coughs, colds or minor illnesses than usual.
- Painful perineum (sore fanny), or caesarean-section pain.
- Constipation or haemorrhoids.
- Other health problems (e.g. mastitis, varicose veins, urinary infections, vaginal infections).
- Pregnancy was unplanned, mother has had multiple pregnancies, or the baby was not the gender hoped for.
- Infertility issues prior to pregnancy.
- Sexual problems (e.g. painful intercourse or lacking desire), or contraception problems.
- Inability to converse fluently in the local language, or being an ethnic minority race.

Symptoms of PND

Number and degree of symptoms varies for every individual.

- Miserable, depressed mood of a deep, unrelenting sadness — like a gut ache, nearly all or all the time (though often worse in the morning).
- Tearfulness, or crying 'all' the time, or the inability to cry even though you need to.
- Feeling immense shame, low self-worth, unrelenting self-guilt or crippling self-reproach (e.g. blaming oneself unnecessarily when things go wrong); or lacking confidence, so feeling like an inadequate failure suffering massive self-doubt.
- Plummeting self-image and self-esteem — feeling miserable, ugly, dowdy, unattractive, uninteresting or unstimulating, or being nervous, anxious,

tense and worried for 'no good reason'.

- Feeling overwhelmed, finding it difficult to cope, like an inability to deal with the baby or routine tasks, things getting on top of you, feeling that the role is too much for you.
- Feeling confused, indecisive, uncertain, lacking concentration, inability to think straight, poor memory, can't make decisions (e.g. having difficulty in planning and organising normal everyday activities).
- Loss of optimism, feeling hopeless, helpless or despondent, and fearing that such feelings will never go away.
- Feeling like you can't express disappointments for fear of seeming 'ungrateful' and ending up utterly embarrassed by your 'pathetic' self.
- Feeling anger or resentment at being trapped in your new life, or feeling devastatingly let-down by your childbirth experience.
- Feeling tired, exhausted, apathetic, lethargic, nauseated and wanting to do absolutely nothing.
- Being irritable and hypersensitive, or finding it difficult to laugh and see the funny side of things any more.
- Feeling like there is no light at the end of the tunnel — maybe losing days, vaguely wandering from one end of the house to the other, trying to remember where to put things or where to find things.
- Finding it hard to look forward to things with enjoyment, avoiding going out.
- Lacking interest, having no interest, or feeling unenthusiastic towards normal activities you used to enjoy.
- Feeling alone and remote, or fearing being alone.
- Feeling or making distance between self and loved ones.
- Fear of contact with other people and/or fear of socialising.
- Sudden impulsive stopping of breastfeeding.
- Lost vocabulary — can't find the right words in conversations.
- Poor appetite and lack of appetite, or can't stop eating (overeating).
- Compulsively obsessing over everyday things, e.g. over-the-top interest in household cleanliness or personal appearance (if not addressed, these obsessions can stay with you for the rest of your life).
- Being uncharacteristically lazy and slack with care about the appearance of the house and/or you personally.
- Fearing being labelled as, or fearing being, a bad mother.
- Worsening tiredness, anxiety and disquiet in the evenings.
- Insomnia, wakeful sleeps, even being so unhappy or 'speedy' there is difficulty in sleeping, or having obsessive concern about lack of sleep. Or, having a chronic desire for sleep (sleeping too much), and finding it

overly hard to get up in the morning.

- Feeling like a cross between someone about to have a nervous breakdown, and just a plain old, nasty person.
- Feeling 'unbonded' or not 'in love' with the baby, and guilt over lack of maternal feelings.
- Perspiring hands and/or palpitations (irregular rapid heartbeat pulses).
- Being overactive and never stopping (it numbs the pain).
- Talking all the time, even when hardly anyone is listening to you — or not talking at all.
- Having no interest in sex, making constant excuses to avoid it (though a low libido can be very normal postpartum) — or becoming obsessed with 'getting off' on sex.
- Increasing self-medication (e.g. alcohol, drugs etc.).
- Blaming yourself and feeling worthless — or regarding yourself as blameless as you are the victim of other people and life (the 'Why me?' syndrome).
- Believing that life events are beyond your control, or that having good things happen is decided by fate and not by your own actions (having no control, feeling out of control), saying things like 'fate', 'God's will', or 'have to'.
- Panic attacks or feeling scared for no good reason.
- Frightening recurring thoughts, or imagining and fearing bizarre disasters.
- Hair loss in patches.
- Having harmful or even violent thoughts towards the baby, which might be overcompensated for by being overly concerned with the baby; or the other extreme of 'infant neglect' to avoid hurting the baby.
- Having suicidal 'wish I were dead' thoughts or plans.
- Unable to feel anything.

Depression is now often understood to be caused by a chemical imbalance in parts of the brain relating to neuro-transmitters, such as serotonin. However, the neuro-chemicals of pleasure and elation that swamp the brain at childbirth, such as dopamine and the endorphins, can certainly mask things for a while.

During the last half of the pregnancy, the placenta takes over the mother's hypothalamus function of triggering the release of her cortisol stress-coping hormones. But, once the placenta is expelled during birth, it can take up to another three months for the mother's hypothalamus to resume maintaining normal cortisol levels, which can result in adrenal exhaustion (and the side effect of depression).

Additionally, sometimes after pregnancy the mother's neuro-hormonal balance does not return to normal, which can specifically result in her neuro-transmitter levels (especially serotonin) not returning to normal. Serotonin is the neuro-transmitter that allows the brain to experience the emotion of happiness. So, a little like iron deficiency makes you feel tired, a lowered serotonin level makes you feel sad — and it is physically impossible to 'psyche yourself' out of that condition.

The serotoninergic system also controls the moods of satisfaction and contentment, and appetite and sleep; norepinephrine controls alertness and energy stimulation; and dopamine moderates social interaction. Neuro-transmitters are, as author Dr Robin Fancourt describes in *Brainy Babies*, 'like a spark in a spark plug': these chemicals aid the passage of electrical impulses in the brain from one neuron (nerve cell) to another.

The body produces neuro-transmitters mainly during sleep in preparation for the next day's 're-uptake'. So, the sleep deprivation of new motherhood can (not surprisingly) hinder normal production.

Post-pregnancy chemical imbalances can persist for months, and can *seriously* impair a mother's enjoyment of life! While depressions generally clear up on their own eventually, some depressed mothers can benefit hugely from modern (or perhaps traditional) medications to reduce the severity of the depressive symptoms and/or assist to shorten the period of the illness, until the body returns to regulating its own (correct) levels of hormones and neuro-transmitters.

There is NO wisdom in hesitating to ask for help. You lose, your partner loses, and your baby loses.

Post-traumatic stress disorder (PTSD)

I don't believe most of the risk factors individually would tip so many women over the edge. But add them up: the low status we assign to mothering; the high value Western cultures place on a girlish figure; the isolation of today's nuclear family; the workplace pressure that sends husbands away from home when their partners need them most; the absence of ritual that would allow the new mother to mourn her lost self; the trauma of Caesarean section or high-intervention birth . . . the surprise should not be how many new mothers are depressed . . . but, rather, how many, in spite of all this, do well.

Naomi Wolf — *Misconceptions*

When *any* person experiences, witnesses or participates in an overwhelming, emotionally traumatic event in their life that causes them to feel painful anguish, severe fright, petrified terror, and/or are in a critically life-threatening situation, PTSD is a *normal* psychological reaction. (In World War I and World War II it was called 'shell shock', then came the term 'battle fatigue syndrome'.) That is why it is now recognised that addressing PTSD is a vital part of recovery for victims or survivors of all traumatic events, such as rape, serious car accidents, armed hostage hold-ups, natural disasters and terrorist bombings. Today the medical profession is geared up for handling the fall-out PTSD victims are likely to experience.

In our mothers' and grandmothers' days, women were more realistically aware that childbirth always involved dangers, and that things often don't go perfectly. By comparison, modern mothers-to-be are usually taught that birth should be a 'normal, natural, beautiful and positive' experience. While that is true for many, all this focus on the (overly romanticised) perfect birth is almost *setting mums up* to feel immense disappointment when their birth experience was far from a majestic occasion.

So there is a grumbling starting to be heard that some existing antenatal classes can be unrealistically rosy and optimistic, and are failing to provide a realistic expectation of what labour can be like, by focusing on textbook births and skipping around common and serious complications.

Although things usually go well at the majority of births, there are a lot of little things which can and do go wrong. For perhaps one in 15 women, delivery can turn into a harrowing, shocking, or even intensely terrifying experience. It may end up being anything but natural or normal. For some women, such traumatic events can leave the psychological scars of PTSD. The effects of PTSD can linger for months or even years — and can also easily be misdiagnosed as the baby blues or postnatal depression.

Most common causes of a 'traumatic delivery'

- Overworked staff who *(unconsciously, I'm sure)* manage in a hurried impersonal manner to make the mother feel as if she has lost all control over the future fate of her *body*, her *baby* and the birth — her instincts and the natural process of childbirth are left ignored, and she may feel like a piece of meat with a baby inside that needs to come out.
- Delivery problems, including lack of empathy, sensitivity, sympathy, emotional support, dignity and no one speaking quietly, calmly and clearly to the labouring mother.
- Invasive, obstetric dire-emergency procedures (life-on-the-line agonising minutes or hours).
- The mother's 'natural childbirth experience' has gone horribly wrong — she fears for her life and/or the life of her baby.

Mothers can also experience PTSD from intensely stressful traumatic pregnancies, and both they and fathers can experience PTSD when their brand new baby's life hangs in the balance, and baby has to be transferred to NICU (neonatal intensive care unit) or SCBU (special care baby unit). Parents may have a desperate, unfulfilled need for explanations.

Specific characteristic symptoms of PTSD:

- **Intrusion**: memories of the trauma recur unexpectedly (like in the middle of washing the dishes), suddenly an episode (called flashbacks) of vivid memories and painful emotions take over the victim.
- **Avoidance**: at first, the person feels numb, has diminished emotions, but can complete their routines mechanically. Then they see-saw between this inability to feel and express emotions, and the flood of emotions during flashbacks. So they will avoid situations or activities that are reminders of the original traumatic event, in an effort to avoid worsening the symptoms. (Say like avoiding driving down the road where the hospital is, or avoiding visiting other new mothers in hospital). There is an underlying inability to resolve their painful feelings, which commonly results in depression.
- **Hyperarousal**: person may become suddenly irritable or explosive, even when not provoked. Everyday stresses can send them over the edge, crying or panicking, when, for example, a TV programme comes on featuring birth. They may have trouble concentrating, may develop insomnia, and may have startled reactions.
- **Self-medication**: in an effort to get rid of the painful flashbacks, loneliness and panic attacks, they may turn to alcohol or drugs.

What therapies help PTSD?

The following can all help: counselling, psychotherapy, a good psychiatrist, sometimes medication, and a support group where someone who knows what it is like will listen to you. In New Zealand, TABS (Trauma And Birth Stress charitable trust) are doing wonderful awareness work to help mums with PTSD. You can find out more on the internet. Start by visiting www.tabs.org.nz.

Postnatal psychosis part 2

Further to the information on psychosis in chapter six (page 265), a second (rarer) version of PNP can start anywhere from three months to two years after childbirth.

Usually it occurs in a mother who has been suffering with undiagnosed postnatal depression or post-traumatic stress disorder, who has also endured an accumulation of other difficult stresses, which have combined to develop into (or 'set her up' for) psychosis. It is almost like a classic psychotic breakdown from the accumulation of stresses, but is usually diagnosed as postnatal psychosis if it occurs within two years of childbirth.

Alternatively, it could be a mother who has been suffering with postnatal psychosis for some time, but has not yet obviously 'crashed and burned'. Instead, her massive adrenaline levels have enabled her to live on with endless energy, resulting in creating her own bipolar lifestyle — such as being Supermum, using psychic rationale, and being emotionally and mentally irrational — an all encompassing agitated turmoil, which can be extremely stressful on a marital relationship.

With long-term medication, this condition is very treatable.

Mother's little helpers (Part 2)

Mother Nature and Father Time are the greatest healers.
Robin Lim — *After the Baby's Birth — A Woman's Way to Wellness*

The brain is the most complicated and mysterious organ in our body, performing an intricately complicated balancing act of immeasurable activities — most hidden from us — and medical science is still researching the roles of hormonal therapies and natural complementary therapies for treating neurological disorders such as postnatal depression disorders.

So, for the meantime perhaps the best advice will be to seek professional help and listen to your intuition in your personal search for your own individual solutions.

The most inexpensive remedy (but sometimes the most difficult to obtain) is genuine non-judgemental encouragement and support from your partner, family and friends. Try, if you can, to seek out people who will be accepting, loving and encouraging, people who will listen to you and give practical help.

Following is a list of additional options to get you started on the road to uplifting your spirits.

Note 1: It is normal to continue to take medication for about six months after recovery, then gradually reduce the dose.

Note 2: If using naturopathic herbs, visit a qualified naturopath rather than self-prescribing.

Counselling, psychotherapy and couples' intervention

Welcome to the world of psycho-social management. Such 'interventions' include talk therapies such as counselling and psychodynamic psycho-therapy. These consistently prove to be of great assistance to maternal mental-health problems. Having a few sessions of supportive listening absent of opinions and advice, and providing an opportunity for the mother to tell her birth story and discuss her anxious concerns, can reduce depression very effectively. Counselling that includes practical advice regarding the lack of support for the mother, and counselling that deals with her feelings of being unable to cope and her general lack of pleasurable experiences, have both been proven to be of great benefit.

Cognitive behaviour therapy with its problem-solving approach, even over the telephone, can be just as effective as some antidepressants. Interpersonal therapy, which focuses on the mother's present and past relationships, and how they relate to her current depression, can also significantly relieve depressive symptoms.

Another great reliever of depression for new parents is to attend some sort of parenting group where everyone shares their reactions to the new experiences of becoming a parent. These sessions can be very cathartic and therapeutic, because they allow new parents, as couples, to realise that most of their issues aren't unique.

St John's Wort (*Hypericum perforatum*)

So named because it annually blooms in Europe by the feast day of Saint John the Baptist, St John's Wort has been known as a medicinal herb for centuries. It has a long, magical and fabled history. For example, around the summer solstice early Christians would soak the plant's flowers in olive oil that would turn blood red (due to the hypericum) to symbolise the blood of martyred John the Baptist, then it would be cast onto bonfires or used to bless crops and to ward off evil spirits.

Also known as the devil's scourge, St John's Wort has been used, predominantly by 'wise women' and midwives for many hundreds of years, to 'chase away the devil of psychotic madness' and other illnesses of the imagination and understanding, such as melancholia and anxiety. Even soldiers in the crusades would drink it with wine to steady their nerves.

This mood-enhancing antidepressant supplement increases the availability of serotonin in the neuron synapses (brain nerve-cell junctions), norepinephrine (which improves alertness and increases energy), and dopamine (which increases the feeling of wellbeing).

Many believe St John's Wort is a legitimate alternative to pharmaceutical antidepressants. In some Westernised countries it is more popularly prescribed than the drugs Zoloft™ and Prozac™. It is also very popular for treating insomnia, mood swings, fatigue, PMS and menopause. As with pharmaceutical antidepressants, the effects of St John's Wort take six weeks to become fully apparent.

Like all alternative or natural remedies, the effectiveness of St John's Wort and its potential interactions with other medications (such as the contraceptive pill) mean that modern medicine always recommends caution.

Ginkgo biloba

Traced back two million years (even before the Ice Age), *Ginkgo biloba* is thought to be the oldest species of tree — one tree can live a thousand years. Today there is a refined mood enhancement supplement that contains GBE (*Ginkgo biloba* extract) and this is a very effective treatment for depression.

This natural antidepressant stabilises cell membranes, inhibiting lipid breakdown and aiding cell use of oxygen and glucose. It is a mental and vascular stimulant, which normalises blood circulation (especially in the brain's hippocampus and striatum), and so protects the brain, liver, eyes and blood vessels.

GBE is used medicinally for a wealth of mental-function problems, including depression (increases neurotransmitter production), mental concentration (gives a clearer mind), and Alzheimer's. It also helps to reverse mental deterioration (such as from strokes). It is often prescribed by doctors in some Western countries, and has almost immediate effects.

Siberian ginseng (*Eleutherococcus senticosus*)

Although Siberian ginseng is not a 'true' panax ginseng, it is a distant relative and shares similar uses. Being a mood enhancement supplement, Siberian ginseng gives marvellous protection against stress.

This natural antidepressant can help to combat depression, insomnia, moodiness, fatigue, poor memory, lack of focus, mental tension, is an immune system booster, improves the balance of the brain's important neuro-transmitters, and increases physical performance and endurance.

Essential amino acids

Your liver manufacturers about 80 percent of the amino acids your body needs — the other 20 percent can only be supplied by diet, and are therefore called 'essential amino acids'. Amino acids are the building blocks of protein chains, and having low levels of certain amino acids can depress a person's moods. For example, low tyrosine or phenylalanine can create abnormal levels of mood-regulating chemicals in the brain such as dopamine. Low levels of SAM-e (S-adenosyl methionine) can imbalance catecholamines, which can depress the mood. Depleted levels of 5-HTP (5-Hydroxytryptophan) affects production levels of the powerful neuro-transmitter serotonin, which affects mood, such as satisfaction and wellbeing. This causes depressed moods including anxiety, insomnia, reduced appetite and lowered libido.

Taking an essential amino acid supplement can be positively mood-enhancing, and it is advantageous if it is combined with vitamin C (ascorbic acid) and vitamin B6.

5-HTP (5-Hydroxytryptophan)

In medicine a 'precursor' is the substance from which another, more biologically active substance is formed. L-tryptophan is the essential amino acid that the body converts into 5-HTP, and 5-HTP is the precursor (intermediate metabolite) of serotonin and the brain's pineal gland melatonin. Serotonin is the main brain neuro-transmitter that controls both mood regulation (combating anxiety and depression) and impulse control (combating aggression and controlling sleep).

Taking 5-HTP supplements can work well as an antidepressant to combat mild-to-moderate depression by increasing the production of serotonin. 5-HTP has also been shown to increase the activity of brain dopamine and adrenal noradrenaline, which help regulate alertness and mood. This results in 5-HTP relieving depression, improving mood, treating anxiety, enhancing sleep quality, improving cognitive abilities, and suppressing the carbohydrate (sugar/starch) cravings typical with depression. Some are heralding 5-HTP as Prozac's 'true alternative'. (5-HTP supplements are derived from seeds of the West African medicinal plant *Griffonia simplicifolia*.)

Note: Do not self-prescribe higher doses of 5-HTP than instructed on packaging, and 5-HTP should not be used in conjunction with a pharmaceutical antidepressant.

Pharmaceutical antidepressant medications

Gone are the days of routinely treating depression with the addictive benzodiazepine-based medications such as valium. Medical science understands so much more now about the human brain's chemical complexities. Yet the more scientists learn about how the brain functions, the more science realises it doesn't yet understand. But there is a whole new generation of pharmaceutical antidepressant medications.

Three points to note:

- Antidepressants generally take six weeks to work fully.
- A side effect of antidepressants can be a reduced libido, simply because of an improved level of contentment!
- If your doctor recommends weaning your baby from breastfeeding during a medicalised recovery from depression, then do seek a second opinion. For many mums with depression, breastfeeding her precious baby may be the only high points of her day, and discontinuing can add to her sense of failure. Plus, it *is* possible to obtain medications that allow breastfeeding to continue safely — especially compared to formula-feeding or the effect of a mother suffering from untreated depression.

SSRIs (selective serotonin re-uptake inhibitors)
SSRIs such as Aropax™, Cipramal™ and Prozac™ block the reabsorption of the neuro-transmitter serotonin by the neuron synapses, thus increasing the availability of serotonin inside the brain, and prolonging its action on the brain. SSRIs have not been proven as harmful during breastfeeding, however, Aropax™ is widely accepted as the best choice for lactating mothers.

TCAs (tricyclic antidepressants)
Tricyclic antidepressant medications such as Elavil, Lentizol and Tofranil affect noradrenaline and serotonin, and have a mild tranquillising action.

MAOIs (monoamine oxidase inhibitors)
MAO (Monoamine oxidase) is an enzyme that is involved in the oxidation reaction of the hormones adrenaline, noradrenaline and the neuro-transmitter serotonin. MAOIs such as Phenelzine and Manerix prevent the activity of the MAO enzyme in brain tissue, therefore affecting mood. This medication shouldn't be taken while breastfeeding.

The master's degree in 'womanly fortitude'

There are billions of tiny lights glowing inside each one of us, and it can feel as if the effort it takes to produce each child is so great that it extinguishes a few of those lights for ever. We can live perfectly well without them, but that does not mean that we do not need time to mourn their loss.

Kate Figes — *Life After Birth*

While pregnant we wonder '*When* will we be back to *normal* again?' — but we don't want to be told the truthful answer: '*Never*'. Motherhood is one of the few truly one-way experiences in life — and we can't completely grasp that until *after* we give birth.

We Western women can escape from almost *everything* else in life: if you don't like your career, you can resign; if you don't like your home, you can move; if you no longer love your husband, you can divorce. (And something else you're now acutely aware of: if your husband no longer enjoys being a father, he can leave!) But, most of us know that, no matter how much we may not enjoy motherhood sometimes, we can't leave; we could never leave our babies.

When you start perusing the shelves of motherhood books at the library or in bookstores, you can be taken aback by the growing number of gorgeous paperback biographical accounts of women's wondrous and torturous odysseys. As mothers we can read these chronicles with immense sympathy and great joy. We blink away spontaneous tears as we recall our own motherhood moments of heavenly pleasure and miserable suffering.

The theory that experiencing the highs and lows of motherhood leaves you emotionally protected against other life tribulations is scarcely a scientific concept. In regards to formally recognised 'mental illnesses' this possibility goes *against* the statistics that depression commonly reoccurs and can be genetic.

But . . . there is something distinctively unique, mentally and emotionally, about one's journey through motherhood. And few women are left without scars, as they hold their stretchmark medals and caesar-incision trophies high on the main stage of life: 'I did it.' 'I got through it.' 'I'm greater now!' In her book *Mothers Matter Too* Jenny Phillips describes it as being immunised against depression recurring in the future.

Some women, a small minority, do manage to cruise through early motherhood without it costing them a complete re-evaluation of what is really important in their life . . . a motherhood experience that doesn't force them to reinvent their personal values and put in perspective what is precious and priceless. But for most of us, sometime in that first year, it will occur . . . just as it's meant to.

And what is it we are left with?

WISDOM . . . Wonderful, invaluable, real-life enlightenment.

The extreme hardships you go through, whatever they are . . . dysfunctional family background, motherlessness, fatherlessness, infertility, unwanted pregnancy, adoption, traumatic birth, special needs child, abusive partner, divorce, partner abandonment, solo-motherhood, sickness, death, financial hardship, physical pain, isolating loneliness, career miseries, unforeseeable catastrophes, the wretched torment of depression . . . and so many other agonising experiences that are always beyond our control.

Such tragedies can force upon you the need to reassess your personal priorities — concerns of status may vanish, fears of others' overrated opinions may disappear, and money may no longer be such a priority.

Tragedies cumulatively inoculate your spirit to cope with future ordeals that will cross your path.

It's then you realise those hardships are a significant part of your journey . . . They're your defining moments.

Dear Lord
So far today, I am doing all right.
I have not gossiped, lost my temper, been greedy, grumpy, nasty,
selfish, or self-indulgent.
I have not whined, complained, cursed, or eaten any chocolate.
I have charged nothing on my credit card.
However, I will be getting out of bed in a minute,
and I think I will really need your help then.
Amen.

Author unknown

Chapter 12

They're only little for such a short time

No, I decided, as Xena reached out and knocked over the glass of juice I had just poured myself, having the perfect home no longer interested me. Of much greater concern were the people who lived in my home, and that was perhaps the most significant life change of all.

Mara Lee — *Staying Mum*

I am only as strong as the coffee I drink, the hairspray I use, and the friends that I have.

Unknown joker

Wow, it has been a mammoth three months or so! You have come a long way along the learning curve of becoming a first-time mother. Motherhood makes you vulnerable, and brings out the pioneering woman in you. Or as another saying goes, 'A woman is like a teabag — you don't know how strong she is until you put her in hot water.'

I read once of a midwife commenting that the *only* time society encourages mothers to look after themselves before their children is on an aeroplane, where they are told that in an emergency they should put their own oxygen mask on first — if you're not breathing, you can't be of much help to your children!

Hopefully, by now things are a little less hectic than they were a few weeks ago for you, and you are probably able to 'predict' your baby's behaviour a lot more. Ideally, you are starting to create your own routines and are able to make plans again.

Heck, maybe now your kitchen bench gets cleared of dishes reasonably regularly; clothes are getting washed and dried within 1–2 days; the house is tolerably tidy; you are experiencing acceptable levels of showering again;

your social life has returned somewhat; you're feeling loads more comfortable in your new role; and you're beginning to feel, dare I say it, somewhat *confident* (yee ha) with your new responsibilities. Great stuff!

Or maybe things aren't going that great for you. Perhaps some outside influences are interfering with your ability to enjoy new motherhood. Perhaps, medically things are not perfect for your little bub (and if that is the case, *please,* consider asking for medical assistance for yourself as well as your baby, because you're helping your baby if you're in the best frame of mind possible).

Or perhaps you're still enduring sleepless nights and are now *so* tired, that every cell in your body is aching, all at the same time. If that is the case, then consider re-reading and actioning chapter 5 (see page 205) to get baby's sleep sorted.

How's life?

When women are depressed, they eat or go shopping.
Men invade another country.

Elayne Boosler, Comedian

Stop the insidious self-blame

Mothers can get incredibly proficient at blaming themselves for so much to do with their baby: 'He didn't have a good morning sleep, because I put him down too late' . . . 'She got all upset trying to crawl, because I dressed her in a skirt' . . . 'He didn't eat a good dinner, because I hadn't heated it quite right' . . . 'She woke up three times last night, because I'd run out of teething gel for her gums' . . .

Just STOP IT!

Any time you hear yourself about to explain why something went wrong by saying 'because I', *stop* yourself straight away. You are doing a *fabulous* job, and your subconscious motherhood ego does *not* need all that negative input.

Nine months in and nine months out

Don't read women's magazines with stories about celebrities who are
the shape of Chupa Chups with gravity-defying bosoms a week after
the birth. They're freaks. Rich, pampered, freaky freakified freaks who
are just a little too on the freaky side. And this is no time to be
concerned about what Elizabeth Hurley did with her arse.

Kaz Cooke — *Kid-Wrangling*

While watching one of our girls at dancing one day, it amused me to look at one of the dance teachers who was very pregnant. Here, this normally taut, trim and toned body had a butt that was getting bigger and bigger, her thighs were enlarging almost before our eyes, her neck was thickening to create that attractive 'wrestler' look, and her normally shapely upper arms were flapping. Even with all that constant dance instruction, she had *no* control over the weight gain. It is nature's way of protecting the species by building up reserves for breastfeeding.

That same week I read tabloid publicity of how a famous celebrity was putting in such 'admirable efforts' to lose weight post-pregnancy — with a little help from the specialist personal postnatal fitness trainer, the personal dietician-nutritionist, the personal chef, the masseuse, the lymphatic drainage treatments for water retention, and the nannies (*of course*) to look after her new baby while she was doing all those bodily 'repairs'!

Even if, before your baby is six months of age, you start working your butt off (*literally*) with exercising (*while polishing your own halo*) . . . or if you have focused your entire attention on mothering (*which by the way has a self-polishing halo*), it's pretty normal to end up with a stubborn four, five, six or seven-plus kilos over and above your pre-pregnancy weight.

There are theories that if no longer breastfeeding, at around nine months postpartum, the mother's body starts to 'let go' of the stored fat, to allow it to be lost through diet and exercise. Before then, for some women, depending on genes and many other contributing factors, trying to lose weight can be a futile uphill battle. Author Vicki Iovine calls it the 'Nine Months Up, Nine Months Down' theory.

By the way it can also take up to a year for your pelvic bones (the ligaments loosened and widened for birth) to return to where they used to be, so you can finally get out of those leggings and comfortably squeeze into your old jeans again — if you didn't give up long ago and are already wearing the *new* jeans.

There are those amazingly lucky ladies — like one acquaintance of mine — who can look fantastic in a miniskirt just one week after a caesar (*unreal but true*). Another friend, Karen, who had her first baby three months before I had my first, found that with breastfeeding the weight just 'fell off her'. She was left with no stretch marks, and was lighter than her pre-pregnancy weight before I even gave birth!

The Super-woman Syndrome

Some women say it *is* possible to 'have it all'. That is, happy, well-adjusted, well-achieving children; a loving, devoted husband; a fulfilling, rewarding career; a clean and tidy, beautiful home; a well-exercised and toned body; the security of financial independence; an exciting social life; a stimulating sex life; and a radiant, porcelain complexion.

Maybe that is eventually achievable — but it sure doesn't usually happen in the first year of motherhood. And it would be rare for a mother to accomplish all that while feeling completely guilt free and truly personally fulfilled. Realise it can be just an enigmatic charade, and while you're so fixated on achieving, you can be missing out on enjoying *today*. (And by the way, getting to 'have it all' actually translates as 'having to do it all'.)

I remember one close friend who was working while one child was at school and being cared for after school, and her other child was in full-time day-care. She worked full time and on some weekends in a senior position in a very stressful high-pressure career. Plus, she was committing to a strict diet regimen; fitting in several exercise classes each week at the gym after work; and she also voiced being annoyed at herself for not having a fuller, weekend social life. For some time, I was really concerned she was about to hit some 'critical overload' point — like a kettle that had been boiling so long it was about to run out of water and blow up. What happened? Her life did explode — her marriage, to be precise. And yet, she thought she was doing everything 'right'.

I know that many of our mothers and grandmothers didn't have dishwashers, automatic washing machines, dryers and self-opening garage doors with internal access. But what they did have was a *far* less complex life — *far* less complicated days and *far* less mothering guilt (if any). They were raising their children in a society with a *far* less intricate matrix of (judgemental) utopian ideals about mothering behaviour and standards.

This ordinary-extraordinary super-mother lifestyle, incorporating the idea that babies need to fit into their mother's world, is a relatively recent fad that hopefully will pass before our own daughters become mothers. And anyway, if you want your daughter to be genuinely happy when she mothers children, *show her how*. Don't try to be Superwoman. You're already are a truly *super* woman!

My baby sure ain't no newborn anymore

In my experience, two things occur when a baby is a few months old. Firstly, you start taking photos of your wee darling sitting propped up with cushions and a big goofy smile on her adorable face. And secondly, you notice a tiny newborn at the supermarket, which makes your baby look gigantic. Yes you do have a baby, but you sure don't have a newborn anymore!

Mum, I'm so bored!

Newborns growing out of newbornhood start to get bored — and this can really sneak up on an unsuspecting mother. There is a great range of 'activities' now available for small babies. Here are some ideas:

- Mobiles hanging over the cot and change table.
- Electric swing-chair (usually battery operated).
- Bath-ring bath-seat from approximately six months old (or at least a non-slip bathmat), so baby can sit up in the bath for playtime with a few toys, e.g. stacker cups, sea creatures and a watering can (almost any plastic containers can be fascinating, including old shampoo bottles and sieves). Adding a few drops of food colouring to the water can also be cool. But remember, *never* leave an infant unsupervised in the bath, even in a bath-ring seat.
- Jolly Jumper™ (use for a maximum of half an hour per day from say five to six months on).
- Exersaucer, which is like an immobile baby-walker. (Statistically, baby-walkers cause more toddler injuries than any other piece of equipment — so be very cautious using one, particularly if your home has ridges between the changes in types of flooring, or stairs. But stationary Exersaucers are great.)
- There are some fabulous, visually fascinating television programmes created specifically for babies and toddlers available on VHS and DVD. And I have to tell you the babes seem to *adore* them. They usually incorporate classical music. So when you need to take a shower, or make dinner, or hang out the washing, or do a little work in the office — you can plant your baby down in front of the TV in their bouncinette or Exersaucer for half an hour — and enjoy a little peace and quiet. They'll enjoy themselves, and it's great brain food. Some of the better-known brands include Baby Einstein™, Brainy Baby™ and Majors For Minors™. Please don't feel guilty for leaving them in front of the TV for a *little* while.

Time for a new carseat

It won't be long before your baby's capsule car-pod will be too small — usually at around six months, or 9 kg, or when their feet reach the end. Time to go shopping again.

The carseat with its harness safety-belt is able to be fitted rear-facing, and it's recommended your baby stays rear-facing until about a year old, or around 12 kg. Then the carseat is turned around to be forward-facing — and

I tell you that can make one very happy toddler, as car drives become so much more interesting for them.

Later, when your child is at about 14–18 kg, you will promote him again to a booster-seat (which is usually just polystyrene covered in material) that uses the normal vehicle diagonal safety-belt. Legally, children are required to use a carseat or booster-seat until the age of five — but up until about 26 kg or 6–7 years old, they are always better off in a booster-seat.

There's such a numerous array of carseat options it pays to have a very good look around before making your final decision. Some toddler carseats go on to double as preschool and school-age booster-seats. And remember, if buying second-hand, only buy when you know the history of the carseat — it's unwise to buy one that has already been in a car-accident, or is more than a decade old.

Note: Recommendations and legislation regarding child carseats are constantly amended — so use this information only as a rough guideline.

Introduce the playpen

I suggest using a playpen as soon as your baby can start to roll over and/or be propped up to sit. With a playpen full of their toys, your little babe can learn to look forward to being placed in this safe environment — they won't see it as a 'jail' — gosh no, it's their 'playground'!

I'm not advocating that babies should spend hours of their day trapped inside a playpen. However, it can provide great flexibility to you — even for simple joys, such as *having a shower*. (And then, when you have more than one child, *you* can sit in the playpen in peace with your coffee and nail polish!)

Toddler-proofing

With crawling infants your house needs to be toddler-proofed to make it safe, but try to avoid developing a tide mark — there should still be some things within their grasp that are 'Uh-uh, no touch, not a toy' items, to enable you to begin to teach your little crawler the difference between right and wrong behaviour. This makes it much easier to visit homes that are not toddler-proofed. Well, that's my theory anyway, and it worked for us.

But I'm not going to preach to you about the ethics of toddler-proofing — or, heck, *how* to toddler-proof your home. Why not? Because I give you that much credit! And as my sweetie-pie dad used to say to us kids with a smile, 'Because you're big enough, and ugly enough, to do it yourself!.' (Plunket provides very good safety guidelines, as does the *Well Child* book.)

Baby sign-language: Mummy, I'm trying to tell you something!

In the late 1970s, sign-language interpreter Joseph Garcia began to notice that the hearing babies of deaf parents, were learning to communicate their desires and wants through sign language at a much younger age than children of hearing parents. Since then much research has been done, and around the world experts are starting to realise that infants (as with chimpanzees) are extremely capable of communicating using sign language much earlier than they're physiologically able to speak — even before their first birthday. Joseph Garcia wrote the (now famous) book *Sign with your Baby*.

Most parents naturally encourage their baby at 6–7 months old to wave bye-bye, and babies are often getting quite good at it by 8–9 months of age. It is exactly the same with baby sign-language — but using really useful communicative words like 'eat', 'milk', 'more', 'tired', 'finished', 'brush teeth', 'cat', 'swing' — unlimited possibilities really. Baby-sign language can become an invaluable two-way communication tool for the next two years, until your toddler is able to talk with some clarity, at about two-and-a-half years of age.

It is so worth teaching your baby to sign, because there are immense benefits from being able to clearly communicate with your baby before he can talk. Also, you speaking the word at the same time can assist tremendously with language development once he is physically capable of talking.

Using baby sign-language can help greatly to avoid some unnecessary tantrums of frustration, because your baby will be much better equipped to communicate his needs to you.

Another great reference book for this is *Baby Signs* by Linda Acredolo and Susan Goodwin. There is also excellent advice available at www.babytalk.co.nz.

Fear of strangers and separation anxiety

At 6–9 months of age babies start to learn that the world is made up of two kinds of people — those they know and those they don't know. And at this developmental stage they can lose their happy, personality-plus disposition, and develop a fear of strangers, and even fears of some people they know.

So don't be surprised when your seven-month-old starts to become a little 'cling-on' (but much cuter than the Star Trek variety). It is normal at this stage for your infant to just want Mum, they love you so much they don't want you out of sight. This can continue until after their first birthday, between 12–18 months. It's best to get them used to the babysitter or crèche before then!

They can get a little clever then too, crying when you leave them somewhere, crying when you get back as if to tell you off, and having a fabulous little time while you're gone. So don't get the guilts, because your infant is learning the lesson that when you leave, you will return.

It can be quite normal for them not to get anxious at Dad leaving for work, as they're already used to that. So if you are being given the DK (Drama King) or DQ (Drama Queen) performance, stay upbeat. Don't you get all teary-eyed too. Treat it as if it's no big deal. Maybe have a goodbye routine, and a hello routine.

Also, often those 'loyalty cries' are not so much saying, 'Don't leave me here, I don't like it' — but 'I want you to stay too, it's so much fun.'

The self-feeding baby

Soon your wee bub may be able to hold her own bottle for feeding, which is a momentous occasion when it begins to occur regularly, as it can suddenly free up *hours* of your time every day! But on a deeper level it is a little saddening, as you realise first hand how very un-newborn your baby now is.

But another cool moment down the track is when you realise your baby can now self-feed their bottle *while you're driving*. That's seriously good multi-tasking!

However, here are two recommended fundamental no-no's you may want to consider when it comes to infants self-feeding their bottle:

- No *lying down flat* to drink from bottles, i.e. a bouncinette seat can be quite a good incline. When babies are lying flat, milk can trickle from the back of their throat into the eustachian tubes, leading to middle-ear infections.
- No bottles in the cot to fall asleep with. Not just because they are an avoidable sleep-aid, but also because the last sip of milk tends to get left in the mouth as the baby falls asleep, which can rapidly create tooth cavities.

Fevers and seizure convulsions

A parent cannot tell with a small baby, that a fever is not something more serious — two big concerns being meningitis and septicaemia. So, as a guideline:

A temperature 38°C or higher (before paracetamol) in an under-six-week-old is an emergency that needs urgent medical attention; and a temperature of 38°C in a six-week- to three-month-old (after paracetamol) also requires prompt medical attention. However, from around three months onwards infants can experience fevers and this is then a very normal part of their immune system development — and often the fever can be gone the next day. (A normal temperature is 36.2–37.5°C.)

Fever is commonly the body's reaction to infection. The body increases its temperature, assisting its defence processes to increase their metabolic rate and inhibit bacterial growth. Shivering (having the 'chills') is an effective way for the body to increase its temperature, because musculo-skeletal activity produces heat. Mild fever also fights infection because the liver and spleen make fewer iron and zinc nutrients available for the bacteria to multiply.

When the body becomes warm and flushed (e.g. having the 'sweats'), this is usually a positive sign that things are improving, because the body is now taking action to lower its fever temperature.

Although it is very wise to ensure your infant's temperature is at a safe level, don't go 'nuts' trying to reduce it to under 37.5–38°C. Simply undress your infant, down to a nappy and singlet and sheet, give them a dose of baby-paracetamol (if they're over 38°C) and perhaps give them a tepid (lukewarm) bath. If after half an hour their temperature is still over 38°C, or if they have a high temperature for more than a day, then you should talk with a doctor.

Naturo Pharm™ make a great homeopathic remedy for babies and children called Fevamed Relief, and the homeopathic remedy Belladonna is also excellent for all fevers.

The main concern of high fevers in young children is the risk of a febrile convulsion (fever fit or seizure), though this does not usually occur in babies less than 6–9 months of age. Temperatures of 39.5°C and higher can 'cook' the brain, scrambling enzymes and other body proteins.

Many in the medical profession advocate that these convulsions cause no harmful long-term effects (apart from freaking the parents out), and certainly some children are constitutionally more susceptible to fitting from fever.

During a febrile convulsion, the infant stiffens and loses consciousness, their whole body can jerk, and their lips may turn blue. There is no known remedy for preventing seizures, and there is no strong link between infant seizures and children later developing epilepsy, as that is a totally different medical condition.

If your child does go into a convulsion, try not to panic *(pretty hard not to, I know)*, place them on a soft surface for the few minutes of the seizure — and rest assured your precious baby will not choke by swallowing his tongue.

If the fit goes on for more than five minutes then your wee babe may need medication to stop the seizure, so it's off to the nearest doctor or hospital. If you know you're too upset to drive them safely yourself, call a neighbour, a friend or an ambulance!

Mother's little helpers (part 3)

How ya feelin' on the inside, honey? Now I know I've preached earlier in this book about making yourself a priority, but just in case you've forgotten — in the devoted busyness and self-sacrificing dedication of it all, and you're feeling somewhat harassed, jaded, irked, knackered or weary — good help can be just a health shop away.

Below are a few body boosters you could consider — remember to always double-check what you're ingesting if you're still breastfeeding:

Korean or Chinese ginseng (*Panax ginseng*)

Derived from the Greek words 'Akos' (cure) and 'Pan' (all), *Panax ginseng* comes close to being the perfect herbal cure-all. It helps to restore the physiological balance of the body's mental and physical capacities — aiding the body to heal itself.

An Asian herb, exalted in mythology, it has been used as a medicine for thousands of years. Its influence is gentle, slow, cumulative and broad.

Panax ginseng is commonly used to boost energy (treat weakness, exhaustion and fatigue); to sharpen the mind (treat loss of concentration); to reduce stress; to boost the immune system (enhance immune responses); to modulate blood pressure; to regulate blood-sugar levels (e.g. diabetes); to strengthen the cardiovascular system (circulation); to raise athletic stamina (including sexually); as an anti-inflammatory; as an antioxidant; and as a supplemental cancer therapy. Even the conservative WHO formally recognises its unique qualities.

The constituents of *Panax ginseng* are remarkably complex and still an unsolved mystery to modern science. (Natural white ginseng is steam-processed to produce the higher-potency red ginseng.)

Evening primrose oil

Evening primrose oil gets its name from its night-blooming wildflowers, and it is a remarkably concentrated source of the EFA (essential fatty acid) Omega 6, called GLA (gamma-linolenic acid). This gives evening primrose oil wonderful healing qualities; it assists the body's hormone production of prostaglandins, and is a natural anti-inflammatory.

Evening primrose oil is particularly helpful to relieve the discomforts of PMS, breast tenderness, menstruation, menstrual cramps, endometriosis-related inflammation, fibrocystic breasts, irritable bowels, carbohydrate cravings, mood swings, anxiety, irritability, headaches and water retention.

It is recommended to take evening primrose oil — say 500 mg twice daily — with or after food, with a multi-mineral-vitamin supplement that includes zinc, vitamin C, magnesium, vitamin E and complex vitamin B. After several months you may also see improvements in your nails, hair and skin.

Flaxseed oil (linseed oil)
Flaxseed oil is rich in EFAs (essential fatty acids) such as omega 3 and omega 6, and is renowned for its benefits to the reproductive, central nervous, immune and circulatory systems — ultimately lowering cholesterol and high blood pressure, and reducing the potential risk of heart disease. It is also good for fatigue and depression.

Flaxseed oil also appears to combat bacteria, funguses and viruses (such as cold sores and shingles). The lignins (a complex plant cell compound) in flaxseed oil appear to positively affect hormone problems, such as stabilising women's oestrogen-progesterone ratio. It is best taken with food — say 1–2 tbsp daily, or as ground flaxseed sprinkled on food.

Damiana (*Turnera diffusa aphrodisiaca*)
Derived from one of the 'Plants of Love', damiana is used as a stress tonic for strengthening the nervous, hormone and reproductive systems. It is also said to have aphrodisiac qualities, which makes it an anti-inhibitor and antidepressant for stimulating the libido of both sexes (supposed to enhance sexual potency for improved lovemaking). *'Mmmm . . . I might be getting ready for that now,' you may be thinking.*

The maternity magical mystery tour: what Mum's left with

I refuse to think of them as chin hairs. I think of them as stray eyebrows.

Janette Barber, Comedy writer

One saggy boob said to the other saggy boob: 'If we don't get some support soon, people will think we're nuts!'

Unknown Joker

Medical science estimates that a woman's body takes a full year to properly recover from being pregnant and giving birth — though evidence is mounting that suggests her body never completely recovers. *Any mother could have told them that!*

More recent research is showing that 60–80 percent of mothers are left with at least one new minor pathological abnormality (e.g. tiredness, backaches, neck problems, shoulder pains, constipation, haemorrhoids, tingling hands or feet, headaches or nausea); and 20–40 percent of mothers are left with a more serious abnormality (e.g. painful perineum, breast problems, tearful depression, high blood pressure, excessive vaginal discharge, abnormal bleeding, frequent urinating, recurring urinary tract infections, migraines, uncontrollable farting, urinary incontinence or faecal incontinence). Other reports indicate that about 30–50 percent of mothers develop a permanent *range* of completely new physical problems after having a baby!

But what about all the other things that everyone seems to have inadvertently forgotten to mention? Apart from long-term tiredness, here's a quick guide to the other main 'highlights':

Boob-droop

I can distinctly recall, at the age of 21, admiring my self-supporting attributes, and thinking to myself how I couldn't imagine them ever being really droopy — they were so jolly perky! How naïve I was.

Many theories abound that if you wear a well-fitted, quality maternity bra that gives good support, day and night, while pregnant and lactating, then your boobies won't change shape. What a load of shite! The fibrous tissue 'sling' that makes up your breasts has no ability to regain its former shape once stretched from engorgement and lactation — that's a fact.

Once pregnant I wasn't obsessed with maintaining my titties' pre-motherhood shape, but I did do all the 'right' things: I had maternity bras professionally fitted at the correct stages; and I supported those twins 24 hours a day for almost a year with each child . . . and they're saggy as heck, but I love them anyway.

My husband's theory is that boobies spend so many hours out of their 'harnesses' during breastfeeding, and that with all that ferocious baby sucking, it's inevitable gravity affects them.

Truly, girls, I really don't care, and neither should you. Push-up bras are great. And even women who never breastfeed eventually suffer from boob-droop.

Welcome too — once breastfeeding is finished — to a new bra-size. But who knows what! Some women say their boobies end up bigger — and many complain they shrivel away so significantly they end up resembling chest pimples. It's a lucky/unlucky dip. And boobs can change again after subsequent babies.

Another permanent and obvious sign that you are a mother is those sexy, enlarged, darkened nipples. They may reduce in size and lighten slightly over time — but they'll never again look like the little pink virginal button nipples that women who haven't been pregnant possess.

The tummy and stretch marks

Oh heck, not sure if I should even go there . . . too depressing! How on earth do those supermodels have babies and return to the catwalk in bikinis? A-ha . . . but what about all those models who have babies that you never see again — that's what happens. They're nearly all like us, half a square metre of extra abdomen skin shrunken into a wrinkly pile of creases; or worse, half a square metre of extra skin left filled with the new, more bountiful you! Bloody heck.

But remember, there are three billion women who don't look like supermodels, especially these days. When our mothers were young mums, models were only 5–10 percent lighter than the average woman (heck, Marilyn Monroe was a size 14) — but today's models are 20–25 percent lighter than the average woman. It's all rather cruel.

How prominently striae (pregnancy stretch marks) adorn your skin can depend on your body's inherent tolerance, or intolerance, of having its skin stretched on your tummy, breasts, thighs, hips and upper arms. Though this is not entirely genetic, genes are a strong influence.

Striae eventually change from reddish-purplish streaks to silvery-white lines, but to tell you that your stretch marks will eventually become 'barely noticeable' would be to mislead most women.

After their nine-month stretch, your tummy muscles will never have that sexy concaved look again (if they ever did), not unless you do thousands of stomach curls.

Then there's also the re-shaped belly-button. A pregnant woman's navel gets stretched pretty much flat, or worse pops out. Some mums can still look cute afterwards with a belly-button ring, but not all.

So, for many mums, being seen in togs isn't easy.

- **Worse-Case Scenario**: You only wear togs where nobody knows you, or with close friends.
- **Best-Case Scenario**: Your bikini bottoms are the hi-top design, because you 'hang over' the top of low-cut bikini bottoms.

Tight shoes

When the placenta produced the hormone relaxin to soften your pelvic ligaments ready for stretching during birth, relaxin loosened all the ligaments in your entire body, including your feet! Not all women are left with permanently bigger feet, but it is very normal to go up a half or full shoe size. That's why so many of your pre-pregnancy shoes may continue to feel uncomfortably tight. This happens predominantly from the first pregnancy, but can recur with subsequent pregnancies. (Yes, that's right, you can start out as a size 7 and eventually end up an 8½.)

My skin's a mess

Increased acne due to fluctuating hormones and the stress of tiredness is, unfortunately, quite normal.

The **chloasma** 'mask of pregnancy' (brown-skin) pigment changes were caused during pregnancy by oestrogen working overtime. They are more common in brunettes and are usually on the face (mostly the forehead, temples, nose, cheeks or neck).

Supposedly these marks eventually fade and disappear within three months of delivery, but some of mine took significantly longer — and the mask of pregnancy can be seen permanently on some mothers' faces. (In reverse, dark-skinned women can develop white patches.) Sunlight and the oral contraceptive pill can maintain the marks, so wear a strong sunblock. However, calendula cream, evening primrose oil and echinacea may help get rid of them.

Pregnancy can also generate blood moles (**cherry angiomas**) and red spots (**star angiomas**). However, if these are visible at your bub's first birthday, you may want to visit a dermatologist who can burn off red spots and blood moles.

If you developed a **linea nigra** from your belly-button to your pubes, it's a good idea not to expose that skin to the sun. It may take three-plus months to fade.

If any of your **moles** changed in size, shape or colour, or you have any new black moles, visit a dermatologist. Maternity hormones make moles more susceptible to developing pre-cancerous cells.

Heck, anything else?

Yes, you may be left with hair growing permanently in places it didn't before (commonly on the face); if you already had **skin tags** (fibroepithelial polyps) then they've probably grown bigger; nails can be more brittle (and white spots on nails mean you're mineral-deficient); and it can take 6–9 months for your eyeball to fit your old contact lenses.

My hair's falling out in clumps

During pregnancy, the high levels of hormones shut down your normal cycle of growing and losing hair, and then your hair can grow into a fuller, shiny, silky mop as it 'stalls' in the growth phase.

So, any time after the birth of your baby (commonly from around the third to sixth months postpartum), masses of hair can fall out, as 9–12 months' worth of hair that should have gradually been shed drops out. But don't worry, you won't go bald; it will stop once you return to your pre-pregnancy mop.

Warn hubby that he will need to unclog the shower drain continually for up to a couple of years — until your hair is its normal weight again. You could also try eating seaweed and more green leafy vegetables, which are said to help stabilise hormone levels.

Often a woman's hair will also permanently change: straight hair can turn curly; curly hair can turn straight; blonde hair can go brown, and brown hair can go blonde. It's anyone's guess.

What about down 'there'?

If you've delivered vaginally, your vagina has been stretched bigger, but it can tighten up again. Yes, your relaxed vagina may now need 'super' tampons instead of 'slims'. But whatever you do, try not to get all precious and upset about it, it's just a fact of life. In fact, more damage can be done to a woman's pelvic-floor muscles by a second pregnancy than a first. *Sorry, you probably didn't want to hear that.*

You've also perhaps now got a natural tendency towards having a lazy bladder. However, doing your Kegels (see page 51) can make a very significant difference, including helping to avoid incontinence due to muscle atrophy during menopause. *Divine — can't wait!*

Another change is that your external genitalia (the vulva's large and small labia lips) have almost doubled in size, and will remain a permanently darkened colour (just as your nipples have).

If you had a forceps or vacuum delivery (especially with an episiotomy), you have higher chances of experiencing perineal pain during sex — but this does not need to be tolerated permanently, you should then seek the advice of an understanding GP or gynaecologist. (If your concerns aren't treated seriously and with compassion, then seek further professional advice until you are looked after with excellence.)

But I'm OK, I had a caesar

Oh no, no, no. If you had a C-section, statistically you have higher chances (than women who deliver vaginally) of developing backache, constipation, depression, tiredness, insomnia and farting.

The body is usually feeling pretty normal again within a couple of months of the birth, but by three months approximately one in three women are still feeling unrecovered from the surgery, and about one in five still have pain at the incision site. It can take up to six months for some women's bodies to recover fully from a C-section (and some veterans say it's more like a year).

Some women say that even long-term, getting up off the floor from being down changing a nappy or from lying on the floor, can be a bit of a mission, especially after multiple caesars.

Even eight or so months after birth, it can be normal for the caesar incision to become itchy and red before it reduces to form its permanent scar. Indirect sunlight can help the scar to heal, as can massaging with vitamin E oil and Hypercal cream — but avoid direct sunlight for about a year.

A year or so down the track there may still not be much feeling in the skin around the scar site. Some women end up having a permanent loss of feeling in their lower abdomen around the incision area.

I can't stop worrying about my baby

If your baby's birth was assisted, you might wonder if and worry that your baby's health problems are related to the delivery. So I just want to tell you that we can all have those sorts of thoughts . . . 'He needs glasses, it must have been the forceps' . . . 'She's got no interest in crawling, I'm sure it's because of her misshapen head from the ventouse vacuum'.

We all go a little mad with the responsibilities of keeping such a vulnerable and defenceless wee human being safe and protected. You're probably noticing by now that you and your intuition are growing an 'on-guard responsory' aerial designed to pick up danger signals at any time! And the bad news is, the worrying never ends.

Once your baby is mobile there'll be countless new opportunities to worry: school will create a whole new set of worries; adolescence is a minefield; and then there's adulthood. I remember my older sister commenting that she had never been so worried about her kids in her entire life as when they first got their driving licences — she knew it was a fact that they were safer if she was driving. We all worry, and that's perfectly fine, natural and beautiful.

But, if your worrying about your baby is making you feel emotionally unstuck, that's not normal. Perhaps you may want to re-read the previous chapter, or talk to your doctor.

New career image

Yes, you have a new career title — but you're already aware of that fact. You are 'the mother of so-and-so'.

However, what may come as a surprise — when you swap your business suit, briefcase and high-heels for casual clothes, a baby-bag and an infant on your hip — is that overnight many men (*and even some women, how dare they — traitors*) treat you with a significantly lower level of professional (and intellectual) respect, as if you really did deliver half your brain with the placenta.

You may have condescending 'Yes, Dears' said to you, and even the irritating line 'Perhaps you should check with your husband'.

Inside, your seething indignation can bubble and boil. 'Don't they know who I am? Well, who I used to be? My presence used to command some respect.' Not any more, Honey, at least, not from the likes of them anyway.

After years of mothering, you'd think I'd be accustomed to it, but I'm not. I remember complaining to my husband, 'I wish you could be in my skin for just a couple of hours — all five-foot-nothing with long hair, flat shoes and breasts — and try taking the family station wagon full of carseats for a mechanical check, with a baby on your hip, just so you can experience first-hand what an idiot they assume you are.'

No more sick leave

Once you are a mother, there are no more holiday leaves or weekends off, let alone sick leave! To quote Anne Morrow Lindbergh, 'By and large, mothers and housewives are the only workers who do not have regular time off. They are the great vacationless class.'

Never again will your lips utter those delectable words, 'I've been in bed the last three days with a bad cold.' Oh . . . how glorious those squandered paid sick days once were, which you never really appreciated at the time.

Instead, there will be all-time lows to being a sick mother — like being eight-months pregnant with a sore throat, runny nose, ear infection, a husband out-of-town for work, and a T.T.T.T. (teething tired tantrumming toddler) playing 'Bet You Can't Catch Me'.

Over the years to come you will probably develop your own long list of times when you were ill, but couldn't allow your body to be — to the point where lying in bed all day with only a cold will be pure, unimaginable luxury.

Speaking 'parentese'

Mother Nature pre-programmes adults (especially women) to change pitch when we speak to infants — we go right into a melody of short, high-pitched sounds, nicknamed 'parentese'.

It does not happen by accident. Research has proven that infants learn more quickly when spoken to in parentese — in comparison to being talked to in a normal adult tone.

Babies are drawn to and truly enjoy listening to people talking to them in parentese — so you're not going crazy.

Heck, what else am I left with?

Here is a list of the other most common subtle (and not so subtle) changes.
- You may be one of the 50 percent of women that have rediscovered their previous energy level 2–6 months postpartum — or you may be one of the 50 percent of women that still suffer from fatigue more than six months after giving birth. (Massive influencing factors being whether you have taught your baby to sleep through the night and your diet.)
- Statistically only a bit over half of mothers are their pre-pregnancy weight by their baby's first birthday — and it takes a full year for the body to rediscover its waistline again.
- The night-sweats, carpal tunnel syndrome (tingling hands) and thoracic outlet syndrome (sore armpits or shoulders) can continue for months — but should all normally be well gone by babe's first birthday.
- If you never used to suffer from PMT, you might start to after having a baby. Or if you used to suffer from PMT, you may no longer suffer from pre-menstrual cramps, which is a major bonus — except then the onset of your period can catch you off-guard.
- You may be the one in ten women who will now periodically suffer from migraines, but never used to before having a child.
- You may be left permanently with easily aggravated back problems — and the years ahead of carrying and lifting young children won't help.
- You may be left with haemorrhoid problems for months, or develop a lifetime susceptibility to those vile eruptions; and/or you could now be susceptible to varicose veins.
- Some 'experts' say to stop jogging after two children, due to the strain on the pelvic floor. But you're the expert on you.
- Maybe the calves on your legs have gone 'skinny' — the fat has just been redistributed. Exercise will help tone things.
- Ongoing bizarre, terrifying and violent dreams are surprisingly common.
- You receive a dentist's bill that stings — if you haven't yet had a dental check-up, then you need to: your baby absorbed a heap of your calcium stores.
- Your cool, sporty-racer shopping-cart car gets swapped for a station wagon or 4x4 SUV.
- White clothing is eliminated from your wardrobe for an indeterminate

period of time — mashed banana leaves stains.

- There's a whole new range of people you are nice to and can enjoy talking to — the type of people you didn't notice before, e.g. other mothers.
- It's near impossible not to smile at another woman's baby.
- You become more organised and efficient — but all the repetitive packing and unpacking becomes a drag. (I was efficient until the third baby in four years, and then it all went to pot!)
- Holidays away won't be easy to pack for, and will never be as relaxing — unless you don't take the kids, but then you worry about the kids. And swimming won't be the same — either one of you is watching the baby, or the baby's in the water with you.
- Violent films just aren't so enjoyable now — and almost every time an actress portrays childbirth on TV you will feel disappointment at their acting skills.
- You now find it gut-wrenching to watch those child orphans and refugees of war on the World Vision CCF-type adverts, because you wish you could sponsor every child on the planet.
- You become more grateful for all your life's blessings.

Things your pelvic-floor exercises have failed to 'cure' that you should not be putting up with

If you have been doing your Kegels every day, and are sure you are doing them correctly, then by three months it would be unusual for you to still be leaking urine, experiencing vaginal farts, or having water continuing to drip out of your vagina after a bath. If you have any of these symptoms, it's time to seek professional help.

This also applies if you are experiencing uncontrollable farting (called flatus incontinence), or if you find there is soiling of poos on your knickers (called faecal incontinence) between going to the toilet.

These are all obvious symptoms that your sphincter muscles are not, for various potential reasons, working properly.

If you are no longer in contact with your LMC, then you should see your family doctor, and he/she will be able to help, or you may be referred to a specialist, such as a gynaecologist, proctologist or urologist.

It might be an embarrassing area to discuss, but these problems are definitely not a 'normal' part of the postnatal experience, and can cause devastating long-term effects. So seek help: they are *definitely* not things you have to put up with, and there are specialists out there who will be able to make a difference. (**Note:** Due to hormones, the pelvic-floor muscles don't regain all their tone until a woman stops breastfeeding.)

Paget's disease of the breast

No doubt you are aware of the importance of performing monthly checks for breast lumps and changes. If, during a monthly breast self-examination, you detect a nipple lump, or you have areola-skin irritation that will not heal and lasts for more than a month, then see your doctor.

Paget's disease is a rare form of breast cancer. An eczema-ish, dermatitis-like, scaly red rash forms on the skin of the nipple (often harmless in appearance); and it perhaps spreads to the areola (darker area of skin around the nipple). This inflamed skin may be crusty, bleeding, or have an oozing discharge; and there may be an itchy or burning sensation.

The majority of women with Paget's disease also have an undetected breast cancer lump.

Treatments include a lumpectomy (surgical removal of the tumour); mastectomy (surgical removal of the breast); radiotherapy (radiation); hormone therapy (e.g. Tamoxifen); and chemotherapy (i.e. cell-destroying cytotoxic drugs).

Intuition — original thought

Before the baby came you may have strived to maintain … rational
control of your life. Maybe your work demanded predictable responses
… With a baby, however, much of your time will be spent in
spontaneous activities, requiring that you reach blindly into your bag
of intuitions and come up with a suitable reaction on the spot.
    D. Stern and N. Bruschweiler-Stern — *The Birth of a Mother*

One essential aspect of lovingly nurturing and respecting yourself, is the intrinsic need to pay significant caring attention to your own intuition. As author Jeanne Elizabeth Blum writes in her book *Woman Heal Thyself*, 'Intuition is your most powerful ally — it can allow you to "tune-in" to yourself, so you can get to know your own needs.'

Our vast reservoir of feminine intuition is, many believe, a blessing given by the universal creator to every woman. However, in the 'white noise' of this modern world, it can be hard — near impossible — to find a pure stillness of mind and body for long enough to be able to tune-in and hear this great helper communicating with us. To make this happen it's best to be in a relaxed state of mind.

Before explaining what intuitive thoughts are, it is necessary to precede this with an explanation of what they are *not*. Intuitive thoughts are not logical, analytical, rational, reasonable, deductive, goal-oriented or time aware. Sometimes they can first appear to be irrelevant, implausible, impossible, daft, crazy or completely insane — and even, occasionally, egotistically absorbed with your own self-importance. But that's only what seems to be, not what is.

Intuition is simply, as Blum describes it, a 'knowing or seeing without apparent effort': it's an instant attraction or an instant aversion; it's nagging thoughts, great hunches, persistent ideas, energetic flashes, precognitive dreams, strong impulses, powerful gut feelings, mind-reading, a déjà vu experience, psychic knowing, or your 'mummy-radar' (which is particularly useful with toddlers). It is a 'not feeling right' or a sense of knowing; it's commonsense, a flying-by-the-seat-of-your-pants, the little voice within, a feeling of calm, or an urgent pull. It's clairvoyance, clairaudience, divine inspiration, an epiphany, inklings, insight, instinct, inspiration, knowingness, the subconscious, spiritual revelation, prophecy, extrasensory perception, premonition, the fifth dimension, or the sixth sense — whatever you want to call it! And another thing about intuition . . . it's *always* right.

But how can you tell when it's real? Very simply: it's when a fast thought enters your mind, and is usually accompanied by an emotional feeling, or tangible manifestation, e.g. an ache in your heart, or butterflies behind your belly-button, or knots in your stomach, or the hairs standing up on the back of your neck or on your arms — you know what I'm talking about. Recognise it, this is your intuition, *screaming*.

Then, when you start to contemplate more on the particular thought, often your conscious, rational mind will kick in, which has the frustrating ability to smother intuition with logic, reason, hesitancy, disbelief, fear and dread.

But, here's the important truth, as described by Blum: *'Each time you acknowledge your intuition, you strengthen it — each time you deny your intuitive function, then you weaken your intuition.'*

An effective way to cultivate your intuition is through turning off your brain's beta waves (which characteristically create alert, rational, sensible, logical, apprehensive, anxious or fearful mindsets); and replacing them with alpha waves (which are rhythmic, smooth, gentle, spontaneous and internally focused) and theta waves (which are deep, meditative, stress-lowering and emotionally uplifting).

The alpha state is the 'thinking of nothing in particular' times when you can have your own 'eureka' moments. Nearly all the great thinkers of history experienced their most wondrous thoughts while in this not-deliberately-thinking alpha state. The theta state increases mental productivity, improves sleep and heightens intuition. To quote Albert Einstein, 'Problems cannot be solved at the same level of awareness that created them.'

The most traditional ways to turn the beta waves down (relax your senses) and turn the alpha and theta waves up (increase your sensitivity), have been through pious practices such as meditation, mantric chants, prayer, worship and chakra yoga to 'evoke the Kundalini' — and many other ancient ascetic transcendent devotions.

If that is all way outside your comfort zone, then that's fine, there are still lots of other ways to rest your mind. Rhythmic activities like swimming, jogging, dancing and walking on the beach or through a tranquil forest can all help. Immersing oneself in writing, listening to music, painting, sculpting, or reading inspiring philosophy or powerful poetry may be your thing. It's simply a matter of finding a way to relax that suits you, which allows you to clear your emotions and balance your equilibrium by allowing your mind to drift. There are also synchronised binaural 'pink sound' CDs such as Hemi-Sync® and Holosync®, to aid with focused states of consciousness.

Then, don't be too surprised if you occasionally experience vivid 'wisdom' dreams that appear to give you a new understanding of the Universe. Some believe it is not your mind envisioning these enriching dreams: it is the Universe lifting the veil on its great wisdom through your dreams. Motherhood melded with intuitive awareness can shift your cosmic position, so to speak.

Eventually, intuition can develop into your own best advisor . . . an inner knowing, a shift of consciousness that has evolved into a powerful resource of foresight and personal enlightenment — an inherent wisdom of understanding, which you can always rely on for perfect guidance, even in the most difficult times. And when answers to questions or solutions to problems aren't appearing, wait with an understanding that the reply will always arrive at exactly the right time.

As Blum writes, 'Listen for the answers in your gut, as your Intuition will silently teach you what you need to do — especially in the role of Motherhood which needs you to rely on yourself to a degree usually never experienced in your life before!'.

One major advantage of listening to your own intuition, is that your Self is given an improved sense of purpose and completeness. In the revolutionary late-1960s, author Malcolm Westcott extensively researched intuition and wrote *Toward a Contemporary Psychology in Intuition*. In this respected book he describes intuitive people.

Characteristics of intuitive people

- Confidence, independence, liberated self-sufficiency.
- Unconventionality, originality, spontaneity and curiousity — even eccentricity. They embrace uncertainty, knowing that the 'daily grind' is

not the only way to 'get ahead'.
- They love all aspects of life — pleasing and disappointing — and enjoy their position in the universe.
- Emotionally involved in the abstract, they deliberately expose themselves to new ideas, stimulating experiences and opportunities for self-expression.
- Understanding that truth is supposition and conjecture, they appreciate there aren't always clear 'right' and 'wrong' decisions.
- Unafraid of exploring uncertainties and absurd notions, and are prepared to ignore facts and logic.
- Comfortable with and able to accept challenges and criticism, they are also able to reject and detach from it, if necessary.
- Willing to change, but are resistant to outside control and direction.
- Foresighted and discerning, they have strong integrity, humanitarian ethics, positive intentions, harmonious purpose and inner poise.
- Being authentic to themselves, they have discarded obsolete rationale. They will not give in for peace, harmony or someone else's affection: they have learnt to say 'no'.

So, please don't push your intuition aside. Many describe it as the only certain road to absolute truth. It can be your direct-dial mobile-phone to the infinite wisdom of your own soul, plus you gain a few friends on your side (such as guides, angels, saints, gods, goddesses, the universal creator, Jesus, Mary, Allah, Vishnu, Buddha, Mohammad, Confucius, Granddad Pat, Great Aunty Nell) . . . it's all there for your unlimited access if you heed your intuition, take note of what it instructs you to do, be mindful of what it's telling you . . . and learn to trust it.

If this introduction to intuitive and original thought has been inspiring to you, personally, there are many avenues for further exploration — the library is a good place to start.

And know too, it can take (and can be meant to take) a lifetime to get it right! We are all works in progress.

When we talk to God, we're praying. When God talks to us, we're schitzophrenic.

Lily Tomlin, Actress

Chapter 13
Starting solid foods

Just as a 'good' eating baby can make a new parent feel wonderfully competent, a 'trouble' eating baby can make even the most competent new parent feel like a failure.

Author Unknown

Starting your baby on solid food is a special and momentous (and messy) occasion in their development. It's so exciting to place those first weenie spoonfuls into that little mouth. And when you know it's your last baby, it can even feel kind of sad too — they grow up *so* quickly.

Some babies take to solids so rapidly that they'll quickly make it known to you what your new role should be: constantly shovelling bowls of mash into their gaping mouths. Fussy babies can be quite the opposite, and instead will live their whole lives with a petite and picky appetite.

Of course, like every baby-related topic, there are loads of opinions as to the best ways to introduce solids. And, of course, there are *many* conflicting recommendations too. In this chapter I'm going to tell you what I (and some of my friends) decided to do. With this and all the other ideas you've received, you can develop a system customised to your baby, you, your family, your lifestyle and your philosophies.

Time to go shopping again!

You're going to need some 'equipment' to make the transition into eating solids practical. Time to go shopping again. Take a friend and stop for a muffin — you deserve a large mochaccino.

Highchairs

Gosh, there are endless options for highchair styles these days, from the old-fashioned wooden style that seem almost doll-sized (but aren't), to the enormous (and sometimes initially too big for littlies) plastic versions with numerous adjustments. Then there are the gravity-defying, bench-hanging, trayless models — and so on. Where do you start? How do you decide what's best?

My friend Tracey said, 'Get one with a small tray, 'cause then they can make less mess.' That was enough to persuade me to buy an old-fashioned highchair. Perhaps my best advice is: buy whichever one is on sale; or whichever one seems the best value second-hand; or whichever one has pushed your must-have button.

Another well-priced option is the fabric 'everywhere' chair, which hooks over most dining-room chairs, keeping your baby securely seated. It is substantially easier to carry, in your bulging baby-bag, than carrying the plastic portable highchair plus your bulging baby-bag.

Sometimes highchairs can be seen primarily as a way to keep a messy, sticky toddler restricted at a convenient height for you to shovel in spoonfuls of nutritious mush — and that is absolutely correct. However, from six months onwards, a highchair also serves as a hugely important tool for introducing a toddler to the social occasion of eating within the family. That's where a highchair is invaluable!

As soon as all our children were able to sit up they sat next to the dining table and joined us for the family dinner — including our family rituals of no toys at the dinner table; ignoring the phone; everyone sharing their day's high-points and low-points (if any); first child finished chooses the fruit; and no one leaves until everyone's finished. On most nights of the week, we strive to make dinner in our house a buzzy family occasion.

I appreciate that some parents find it easier to feed their children at 5 pm, and feed the adults at 8 pm after the kids are in bed. But my gut feeling is that those children are missing out on important social interaction.

One final reflective comment I will add is that we hummed and hawed over buying one of the portable plastic dining-chair booster-seats that double as a portable highchair with attachable tray. And I must concede that it has been an extremely well-used piece of equipment, primarily as a booster seat so that from about 18 months our babies could properly sit with us at the dining table for meals.

Feeding accessories

- Invest in a couple of the soft-tip, soft-bite, silicone-type feeding-spoons — they do work so much better on littlies than metal teaspoons, because they don't hurt teething gums and are perfect for wiping around messy mouths.

- I found the tie-on bibs too fiddly and time-consuming, and the velcro variety too easy for my darlings to pull off. My all-time favourites are the stretchy-hole-straight-over-the-head design. (Don't get plastic-backed bibs, because they can suffocate children.)
- A plastic splat-mat for the inevitable spills is a sensible idea, and essential if your highchair has to sit over carpet.
- Food processors are fantastic for making large quantities of your own fresh baby-mush — but another great gadget to convert small amounts of adult leftovers into baby food is an electric hand-blender or stick-mixer (with high-sided container).
- To make bulk baby-food, steam the veggies or fruit, then mush them up in the blender or food-processor, and freeze the food in ice-cube trays. Muffin trays are good for this also. Once the portions are frozen, pop them out and transfer the frozen lumps into empty ice-cream containers and store in the freezer. Then you can provide almost unlimited combinations and concoctions at meal times. Pretty much everything but bananas and avocados freeze — and remember not to add any salt, pepper, sugar, oil, fat or chilli to infant food.
- Once your darling demands her own spoon, the bowls with a suction-base are wonderful to help keep the dish stuck to the highchair tray.

Ptyalin: why babies should not be fed starch

It is pretty normal these days to start a baby on some solids at around 4–6 months. But *don't* feel rushed at four months to get them onto solids, as breastmilk (or formula) on its own is *fine* for two more months, and by then a baby also has better head control. However, if your baby is large (say over 8 kg or 18 lb) and obviously a ravenous feeder, then you *may* want to get started on solids as early as four months.

When you do get started it can be a *messy* experience, because your baby has to *teach* her tongue some new tricks that can be difficult to master — so a rather essential parental tool during this stage is *a sense of humour!*

Thanks to their 'extrusion tongue-thrust reflex' of pushing their tongue forward (which is usually lost at around six months of age), without meaning to, babies usually push the food out with their tongue at first, as they don't yet know how to eat (they only know how to suckle). So give your baby at least a month of trying solids before you begin to worry about their inability to properly consume food!

In this book, my best intentions have been to create for you a very open-minded middle-of-the-road approach, free of 'radical ideologies'. *However*, I must concede there are three topics that are personal pet peeves of mine, on which my opinions are extremely strong, and those are:

1. That all babies need to be *taught* how to sleep through the night, and can be (chapter 5, page 205).
2. That natural holistic and complementary medicines should be embraced by parents (chapter 10, page 347).
3. That farinaceous foods (carbohydrate-rich, starchy foods, e.g. rice, breads, pasta, corn, potatoes, porridge, cereals, toast, biscuits, cakes, tapioca) are the *worst* foods to feed young babies!

I will explain . . .

For almost 200 years, medical science has understood that the amylase enzyme 'ptyalin' (pronounced ty-u-lin) contained within our saliva is a critical chemical involved in beginning the body's digestive processes to break starch down into sugars, *and* science knows that infants do not produce normal levels of ptyalin until they have a mouth full of teeth.

With ptyalin missing from your baby's saliva, two problematic bodily reactions often occur after you feed your baby starch (e.g. baby rice, baby cereals, baby porridge, mashed potatoes, bread rusks, crackers):

• The indigestible starch 'ferments', and this can potentially cause numerous digestive disorders.
• Mucous 'thickens' and can potentially cause ear, nose and throat problems.

Perhaps this is a plausible partial explanation for the epidemic levels of continual tummy problems, runny noses, recurring ear infections, tonsillitis, bronchiolitis and asthma that we now see in the developed world.

What about all the Third World or Asian babies being fed rice and other starches? Why is it OK for them? It's an ironically simple answer: for thousands of years, mothers in these continents have always chewed their baby's food first, before feeding it to their infant — unknowingly, they coat the baby's food with the ptyalin enzyme from their own saliva.

But getting back to Western medicine and its history . . .

In the 1800s, renowned surgeon and obstetrician Pye Henry Chavasse wrote in one of his several books, 'I wish, then, to call your especial attention to the following facts, for they are facts — Farinaceous foods, of all kinds . . . are worse than useless — they are positively, injurious, they are, during the early period of infant life, perfectly indigestible . . . A babe's salivary glands . . . does not secrete its proper fluid — namely, ptyalin, and consequently the starch of the farinaceous food is not converted . . . and is, therefore, perfectly indigestible and useless — nay, injurious to an infant'.

Since then there have been numerous other respected doctors and professors all saying the same thing, over and over and over again, e.g. Prospiro Sonsino, Tilden, Routh, Huxley, Youmans, Dalton, Page, Densmore, to name but a few. However, in recent decades medicine seems to have 'forgotten' this knowledge.

Dr Page wrote, 'Milk is the food for babies and contains all the elements necessary to make teeth, and until they are made, it should continue to be the sole food. It is not enough that two or three or a half dozen teeth have come through, that they should be expected to do any part of a grown child's work . . . Upon no consideration should any of the farinaceous or starchy articles be added until the mouth bristles with teeth.'

Then, in the early- to mid-1900s, rebel health pioneer and prolific writer Dr Herbert Shelton focused on this when he wrote, 'The fact that Nature makes no provisions for the digestion of starches before full dentition [growing of teeth], should be sufficient evidence that she does not intend it to form any part of the infant's diet. Before the teeth are fully developed the saliva of the infant contains a mere trace of ptyalin, the digestive ferment or enzyme that converts starch into sugar . . . Certain it is that nature did not intend the baby to chew food until its teeth are sufficiently developed to perform this function . . . No starchy foods or cereals should be given under two years.' Dr T.C. Fry reiterated this later last century.

This is such important knowledge, I truly cannot begin to fathom why, with such massive indisputable scientific evidence, our society remains so obsessed with starchy baby foods — and the equally nonsensical belief that carbohydrate starches should be the main staple of all infants' ongoing diet.

It is all rubbish, utter lies and complete drivel! Is it some mad commercial greed for money? Who knows? In some ways it is reminiscent of how completely accepted cigarettes were half a century ago, when most people genuinely did not understand — simply because they were not told — that smoking was damaging to their health.

So OK, I hear you wondering, if you don't use baby rice, baby cereal, baby porridge, mashed potato, kumara, bread, pasta, noodles, crackers, biscuits and rusks — then what the heck do you feed a baby instead? It's such an easy answer: primarily vegetables and fruit — topped up with some protein (e.g. meat and dairy-food.)

> If Mother Nature had wanted her human babies to chew starchy foods at five months old, she would have provided the molar [grinding] teeth and saliva ptyalin enzyme to do it!

Month-by-month sample menu

Although Western culture has created a 'norm' of starting infants as young as four months old on solid food, the enlightened experts now view this as antiquated advice, because current research is proving that babies need preferably nothing but breastmilk (or formula) until six months of age.

Unless the baby can sit well unaided, has good head control, is starting to put things into his mouth, and is perhaps interested in watching other people eat, you can feel confident that your baby is probably not quite ready for eating solids.

Below is a sample menu to help you when the right time comes. Now, I *know* there could be *loads* of experts that might disagree with the menu below, so I suggest you don't just take my advice. Do your own research, and make your own choices!

At the end of the day, one thing all the nutrition experts will probably agree on is that there are opponents to almost every infant feeding theory that exists!

6 MONTHS:

4–6 milk feeds plus
- Puréed brunch or dinner (pumpkin, avocado, carrot, courgettes, beans, squash, beet).

7 MONTHS:

4–5 milk feeds plus
- Puréed brunch (add apricot, apple, peach, pear, mango, papaya, watermelon, honeydew melon and very ripe banana) plus
- Puréed early dinner (adding parsnip, cauliflower and broccoli)
- Finger food can start to be offered now such as thin strips of raw, peeled carrot, celery sticks, peas, apple wrapped in muslin, finger of grilled steak — all great stuff to gnaw and teethe on, rather than something they're fully consuming.

8 MONTHS:

3–4 milk feeds (say as first morning drink, morning tea, afternoon tea and supper), plus
- Textured breakfast (adding grapes, cherries, dates, figs, prunes, raisins and skinless plums) plus
- Textured lunch and dinner (adding spinach, Brussels sprouts, asparagus

and small amounts of herbs, garlic, onion, minced chicken, beef, lamb, pork, veal, liver, kidney and well-cooked egg yolks)
- Iron now becomes more important in babies' diet, as the iron stores they were born with are depleting.

Note: 'Textured' food is something lumpier than puréed, but not as coarse as mashed — I leave it to your imagination.

9–11 MONTHS:

3 milk feeds (upon waking, before day-sleep and before bedtime), plus
- Three mashed or finely chopped meals (adding mushrooms, cabbage, lettuce and small amounts of peas, yoghurt, fish, custards and cheese).
- Morning- and afternoon-tea snacks (soft ripe/canned fruit, steamed veggies, moderate amounts of cubed, sliced or grated cheese, and small pieces of soft meat).

12–15 MONTHS:

It is now optional to discontinue using any formula, and reduce milk to 2 bottles a day (say before day-sleep and at bedtime), with a maximum of about 600 ml milk a day — so it does not affect their appetite for solids. Or, be down to two breastfeeds a day.
- Add citrus fruits, berry fruits (strawberries and raspberries are particularly rich in iron), cooked egg white, honey, tomatoes, eggplant, corn and capsicums.
- Your toddler is now pretty much eating the same food as you at mealtimes, but just chopped up. Toddlers can also be useful consumers of adult leftovers the next day (or freeze leftovers in meal-sized lots for later).
- Encourage them to enjoy raw vegetables, e.g. carrot sticks and cherry tomatoes.
- Once walking, toddlers can want to increase their food intake — though they can also begin to display more prominent personal likes and dislikes!
- At about two years you can add in shellfish and all nuts — but go easy on the peanuts.

ONCE SOME MOLAR TEETH ARE THROUGH:

- In moderation, add wheat, potatoes, kumara, cereal, rice, crackers, bread, pasta, porridge, noodles, and couscous.

Feeding points to note

- It makes very good sense to add just one new food item every few days, to enable you to know if your infant has any kind of food allergy reaction (such as a mouth rash, nappy rash, itchy skin, hives, runny nose, colic, prolonged crying, diarrhoea, constipation, eczema, coughing, sneezing or wheezing).
- Always have a sipper-cup of water on the highchair tray at meal times so your baby can have a drink to slosh it all down. (I always used coloured sipper-cups for water/juice and clear bottles for milk — that way Bub had some predictability of what sort of liquid her tastebuds were about to receive.)
- There are many different theories regarding the timing and order of feeding milk and solids. My recommendation is to not offer a milk feed at the same time as a solid feed after the first month or so, because there is enough time in each 24-hour period to offer them separately. If you feel your baby is beginning to enjoy solids 'too much, too soon' in comparison to the milk feeds, offer more milk feeds and fewer solids. You are in the driver's seat.
- I always taught our children to get a taste for veggies first — before moving them on to the 'yummier' things like puréed fruit. It can be hard to get them onto veggies if you've introduced the sweet things first.
- A solids meal usually starts as just a few messy teaspoons, moving up to say an eighth of a cup, then within weeks moves up to more like half a cup. Eventually by about their first birthday they will be consuming around 1–1¹/2 cups of food for each full meal.
- The body is designed to absorb nutrients from the carbohydrates, proteins and lipids (fats) it ingests, which primarily occurs in the small intestines. The human body cannot digest roughage fibre (i.e. plant cellulose), but this bulk is important to assist the foodstuff being moved along the gastrointestinal tract. If residue food remains too long in the large intestine (where water is absorbed) then this can cause constipation and hard poos. A diet rich in veggies enables the colon to produce soft, easy-to-excrete poo.
- It is usually recommended to offer only clear juices to babies less than one year of age (e.g. grape, apple, cranberry, prune, fig and melon). Also, due to the sugar content and acidity of fruit, it is strongly recommended to water juices down 50–95 percent to protect tooth enamel. Some theorists say not to offer pulpy or citrus juices (e.g. orange) until around the first birthday — but others disagree, saying that the juice from sweet

oranges is 'wonderful' for infants. From the dental-health perspective, and the interests of not encouraging a fussy baby, 100 percent water can be best.

- Another drink option is vegetable juices such as tomato juice and carrot juice — or the cooled water left over from boiling vegetables, so long as there's been nothing added, such as salt.
- Leftover gravy and sauces (especially tomato-based) are great to add to baby mush for flavour variety.
- Generally speaking, the commercially prepared baby foods are of good quality — so don't feel slack or guilty if you're using them — you are not malnourishing your little cherub (but check the labels for their starch content — often listed as 'carbohydrates minus sugars').
- Canned fish (especially tuna and salmon) and canned vegies (e.g. tomatoes, peas and corn) are great pantry back-ups to help make up a nourishing toddler dinner.
- If your good feeder goes 'off' his food, just remember his gums could be aching from teething, so perhaps try giving food that doesn't require chewing.
- If your 8–9 month old starts wrestling you for the spoon — just chill out and give them one to practice with too. Yes it's messy . . . but that doesn't have to matter. The benefit is that later on you could have a one-year-old who can confidently feed himself, instead of a two-year-old who still needs to be spoon-fed.
- From one year old, when toddlers often convert from formula to cows' milk, ensure you feed them full-cream milk, as toddlers need that fat content to grow (every cell in the human body has a lipid-fat exterior plasma membrane).
- Carotene is a yellow-orange pigment found abundantly in carrots, squash, and other orange or deep yellow vegetables. When a human eats large amounts of carotene rich vegetables, it can harmlessly turn our skin a yellow-orange colour. So just be aware that your baby is not really getting jaundice if they adore carrot-and-pumpkin mash!
- It is possible for your infant to get complete nutrition on a dairy-free or vegetarian diet — but you'll need to be very well informed.
- Never feed infants hard, small pieces of food which could get stuck in their throats, such as round carrot slices, peanuts, popcorn, sausage skins or hard fruit pieces — and always buy boneless fillets of fish, and chop up pieces of dried fruit.
- Fresh fruit should be well ripened before being consumed, particularly bananas. With canned fruit and fruit-snack tubs, choose fruit in natural fruit juice rather than sugary syrup.

- Don't hesitate to get cunning with baby-food mixtures — you can always use up leftovers by adding cooked apple or custard to a bowl of vegetable-mush as a new meal 'category'. When they're little they don't seem to mind much at all!
- If your baby is experiencing asthma or eczema, then a reduction (or sometimes complete elimination) of dairy products can help enormously (especially cheese), though you will need to replace their calcium intake with other food sources (e.g. rice milk, soy milk, hummus, almond butter, broccoli, oranges, molasses, canned tuna and canned salmon).
- Losing the ability to smell significantly reduces one's ability to taste, so when infants have a cold with a blocked nose, it can be quite normal that they lose interest in their favourite foods. Keeping their fluids up can be all they need to recover.
- Sugary foods such as sugared breakfast cereals, jam, biscuits, cakes, desserts, jelly, ice-cream, chocolate, many commercial fruit-juices, soft drinks, ice blocks and lollies are all close to 'poison', biologically speaking, for all children — especially pre-schoolers: it rots their teeth, disturbs their digestion, plays havoc with their insulin balance, cultivates an undesirable sweet-tooth, wrecks their concentration, and crazies their mood. Salted snacks are also not recommended food for children. So do try hard to limit their sugar and salt intake to genuinely special treats — not part of their everyday diet.
- Don't be overly perturbed if your infant has a reduced appetite on hot summer days, and an increased appetite on chillier winter days. Do you remember skipping your own lunch on a summer's day, or simply desiring lighter types of food in warm weather? This is normal behaviour for the human species!

Sterilising, straws and toddler-poo

I find it helps to organise chores into categories:
Things I won't do now; Things I won't do later; Things I'll never do.
J. Wagner, *Maxine's Maxim*

When to stop sterilising

Once your baby is a few months old and is putting every object he gets his hands on into his mouth, you do start to wonder if sterilising his bottles and dummy is becoming rather futile.

There is a menagerie of opinions on this topic, but my personal recommendation (don't shoot me, please) is that by that stage the dishwasher is probably adequate, so long as you give the bottles and teats a scrub first with a bottle-brush to prevent build-up of milk in hidden crevices.

Remember, contrary to all the advertising of antibacterial products, children do need to be exposed to germs to build a robust immune system — so they don't later get sick just from playing in a sand-pit!

Drinking from a straw

I found that all our children could be successfully taught to drink from a straw at around 8–9 months. I always used fruit juice or flavoured milk to teach them, because it was a bigger incentive to succeed than plain water.

What goes in must come out

Once your baby starts on solids, expect the poo to radically change.

If, until now, your bub has been primarily breastfed, his poo will begin to reek of a more indelicate odour.

As your baby grows into a toddler and is eating less mushy food, be prepared too for the poo to sometimes contain food that doesn't even look like it has been digested! From my observations, this seems to occur particularly with carrot, corn, peas and raisins.

Also, beetroot can make poos look bloody and turn pee red; bananas can add black specks or black threads to the poos; and liquorice can turn poos greeny-black.

Oh, such a divine topic!

A baby is an alimentary canal with a loud voice at one end and no responsibility at the other.

Ronald Reagan

Chapter 14

Almost time to post first-birthday invitations

Giving birth is like taking your lower lip and forcing it over your head.

Carol Burnett, Comedian

What a transformational year and a half you've just experienced, from the nine months or so of pregnancy, and first nine months or so of motherhood! Can you even recall the person you had been before becoming a mother?

It has probably become difficult to remember what you used to do with all your spare time; what it felt like to *have* spare time; and there is the unanswered question, will you ever have spare time again? I like cartoonist Cathy Guisewite's definition, 'The story of a mother's life: Trapped between a scream and a hug.'

For some of you, this has been the most pleasurable and joyful year and a half of your life — and that is awesome. I am so happy for you, truly. For others of you, this has been the hardest and most difficult year and a half of your life — and I would like to be able to say that is unusual, but it's not.

People are probably already asking you when you will be thinking of having more children — or perhaps you're already pregnant again! Then come all those opinions about the best age gap between children:

With anything under 18 months, you'll really have two babies on your hands and two lots of nappy expenses, but the children can become good playmates for each other in the near-ish future. Gaps of 2–3 years are better on your body, but then you're fitting in baby day-sleeps around playcentre or kindy sessions. With gaps of 4–5 years your pre-schooler can be quite helpful with the baby, but then it will be some time, if ever, before the children become true playmates, and the mothering of pre-schoolers goes on for almost a whole decade.

There is no best or worst age gap between siblings — each has its own advantages and disadvantages. And there's always the possibility of being really radical (for these days) by having more than two children!

Do you know first aid?

Toddlers are independently mobile and quick on their feet — but have almost zero commonsense — and that can be a deadly combination.

So if you have never attended a first aid course, then as an investment in your parenting skills (especially for toddlerdom), it could be a very wise idea to learn how to deal with medical emergencies such as choking, severe bleeding, burns, poisoning and resuscitation. (I know of mothers who did not have the first aid knowledge to save their child, and it can be a hideous price they can pay.)

Remember, dads do it differently

No matter how calmly you try to referee, parenting will eventually produce bizarre behavior, and I'm not talking about the kids. Their behavior is always normal.

Bill Cosby — *Fatherhood*

If you are annoyed by the way your partner rarks up your child with much physical play (winding them up just before bedtime seems to be a globally popular activity for dads), then remember that what he is doing is inherently programmed into him, and part of his valuable parental contribution.

Just as most mums are naturally programmed to play with their baby in a steady and slow way . . . menfolk are wired for fast and furious, vigorous activities (must be the testosterone). So that is why dads all over the planet seem to enjoy 'rough play', touch, forceful tickling, loads of movement, making loud noises and throwing their toddlers in the air (whereas Mums can struggle to enjoy doing that).

So don't get too annoyed at your macho, he-man clown — he's fulfilling the role Nature intended. It's all part of a big, beautiful, balanced plan — babies get excited by their dads, and calmed by their mums.

Dad-play typically tends to have a clear start and clear end; it often uses play 'props' (e.g. toys); and dads can have a shorter play time-span. However, mums typically create games out of nothing that can go on for ages.

Fathers can also *naturally* take a back seat in the parenting until the baby is a full-blown toddler at around two years of age, when the dare-devil dad talents can be better used.

Omega 3

You are, by now, probably well aware of how important it is for a child to metabolise (digest) a mixture of carbohydrates, protein, fat, fibre, vitamins, minerals and water. At the end of the day, our bodies are anatomic 'vehicles' that require specific 'fuels' to operate smoothly.

The central nervous system, consisting of the brain and spinal cord (which is a continuation of the brain stem), is the control centre of the human body's many organ systems. So, it is important to focus on the brain's nutritional requirements. There is one nutrient, the EFA (essential fatty acid) called omega 3 — and more specifically the omega 3 EFAs known as EPA (eicosapentaenoic acid) and DHA (docosahexaenoic acid) — that demands attention.

Medical science has not yet grasped a full understanding of the beneficial physiological effects of omega 3 on the brain's neurons (nerve cells) and neuro-transmitters (chemical messages), but it is clearly understood that a generous dietary intake of omega 3 improves the brain's functions at the very simplest and most fundamental levels, i.e. its efficiency in sending electrical signals from one neuron to the next.

Unfortunately, the modern diet does not usually include very much omega 3. And the process that gives foods a long shelf life, called hydrogenation (which prevents fatty acids from turning rancid), removes omega 3.

Natural sources rich with omega 3 include oily fish (e.g. salmon, tuna, sardines, trout, anchovy, mackerel, herring), venison, canola oil, rapeseed oil, wheatgerm, walnuts and flaxseed (linseed). It is also possible to buy omega-3-enriched eggs (enhanced through hen-food) and omega-3-enriched breads (with milled flaxseeds). The best-known omega-3 nutritional supplements are fish oil and flaxseed oil.

But none of these usually make it on to an infant or toddler's list of favourite foods! So here are two more practical suggestions:

- Flavoured fish oil: health shops stock child-friendly fish oil that is flavoured (e.g. with citrus, peppermint, vanilla) to make it more palatable, and the dosage is just a teaspoon or two a day.
- Smoothie shakes: a blender mix of fruit (e.g. banana and berries); milk (e.g. cows' milk, soy milk, goats' milk, rice milk or yoghurt), one teaspoon vanilla essence; and one tablespoon flaxseed oil. Great optional extras for toddlers can include walnuts, spirulina and barley-grass powder. Or, another option is making a frozen yoghurt treat that has flaxseed oil included.

These long-chain fatty-acids are vital nutritional ingredients for about 20 percent of the structure of brain tissue (cell membranes): they are essential for healthy growth and development, vision, and brain functions (e.g. memory, learning and behaviour). When the brain doesn't receive enough omega 3, the body then substitutes it with the next best thing, the EFA omega 6, which is generously found in the Western diet (e.g. cereals, margarine, olive oil). However, this is known to be an 'inferior' nutrient for the neuron transmission functions in the brain.

Omega-3 supplements are also proving to be a particularly beneficial therapy for children with learning, memory and concentration disorders, such as dyspraxia (poor physical co-ordination), dyslexia (reading and writing disorder), ADD and ADHD.

Day-sleep changes

Children aren't always angels: You don't have to like your child all the time — you only have to love them. A parent's job is to parent their children — not primarily be their friend. Children can make plenty of friends, but they can't make parents.

My mum

By the time your baby is nine months old, hopefully you should be enjoying a fairly predictable baby with routine morning and afternoon sleeps at regular times. But at some stage, before Bub's first birthday, your baby will start to transform into a toddler. The morning sleep will probably commence later and later, and the afternoon sleep may become so late that it starts to conflict with dinner and getting ready for evening bedtime. This is when your baby is ready to move into one long day-sleep starting late-morning/middle-of-the-day.

Bubs may swing between one day-sleep and two day-sleeps for a few weeks before settling into a new routine of one long day-sleep. Or it may be a long late-morning sleep with afternoon catnap. Or you may make his evening bedtime earlier, to cope with the middle-of-the-day sleep. It may also mean an early lunch.

But you will find your own way of accommodating a middle-of-the-day sleep, and in the end it should become a piece of cake. Especially by a year old, toddlers thrive on their routines!

This last rearrangement of your daily schedule is usually the final significant change to a baby's routine for the next 1–2 years — until their middle-of-the-day sleep changes to an afternoon nap, before Bub eventually drops day-sleeps completely.

If your baby 'doesn't want' to have a morning or afternoon nap, she should still spend that time in her cot resting or playing, and getting used to her own company. You need a break, and she doesn't need you all the time. Toddlers need safe time alone to develop confident independence, and mothers need a little time out too every day to maintain sanity!

Also around this time an infant's sleeping can become even more active, getting into some strange sleeping positions, moving all around the cot during their sleep, kicking blankets off, getting limbs stuck through cot-bars, practising 'crawling' and 'standing' during their dreams. Then not long after, dependent on their personality, toddlers can begin pulling themselves up to standing and jumping in the cot, and pretty soon after that they're usually climbing over the bars and, potentially, falling to the floor head first! This is a very good time (if not earlier) to start using a BabyOK™ Babe-Sleeper infant cot sleep-secure (see page 227).

If your baby has never habitually slept through the night by this age, then realise that this is a problem you may have helped to create. Do not expect your baby to fix the problem on his own, as he quite obviously can't.

You will need to go back to the basics of *teaching* your baby (now your toddler) how to sleep (see page 205 or other infant sleep literature). Eradicate the problem now, before it gets even more ingrained and ends up going on for years! You deserve solid night sleeps, and your baby needs them!

Breastfeed weaning

There is no slave out of heaven like a loving woman; and, of all
loving women, there is no such slave as a mother.
    H.W. Beecher [1813–1887], American clergyman and writer

I'm just so glad to have my breasts back to myself,
I don't care where they've ended up!
                            My girlfriend Ali

Not all mothers choose to wean their babies; some prefer for their baby to self-wean when ready — no matter how long it takes. But for the majority of breastfeeding mothers, for whatever reasons, weaning often does take place — and usually around toddlerhood.

It is generally agreed that the most ideal way to wean a baby (for the mother and baby's sake) is gradually, over a 2–3 week period. It is a simple theory of replacing one breastfeed with a bottle-feed every 2–3 days; one feed at a time; so that your milk production can gradually reduce. Using the motto, 'Never offer, never refuse a breastfeed' can be helpful.

But, what if your baby is refusing formula? Then logically you have limited options!

Below are some suggestions. Now I am not advocating that *any* of these ideas are ideal. But mums often find themselves 'stuck between a rock and a hard place'. These are simply crowbars and levers that might help pry you out of the stuck place — though controversial they always are.

- Stick to breastfeeding until your baby is one year old and technically old enough to drink cows' milk — and hope the wee babe likes it.
- Try all the various formulas on the market to see if there is one your baby will accept — though that can turn into a rather expensive exercise.
- Add a little brown sugar to the formula milk to see if sweetening it will make it more appealing — if that works then try gradually reducing the amount of sugar over time until it is eliminated.
- Forget about traditional formula and use other foods to fulfil the dairy intake, e.g. yoghurt, cheese and rice milk (vanilla rice milk is especially yummy).
- Realise that there is nothing yucky about formula and all you're really dealing with is a case of stubborn willpower. When I was dealing with a stubborn toddler I'd say to myself, 'You might be stubborn baby, but I'm more stubborn than you, 'cause I'm your mum and I know best.' Then keep offering that bottle (and nothing else) until she's hungry enough to give in and accepts it. (You may think that's cruel — well I don't agree, but we are entitled to have differing opinions.)
- Introduce cows' milk *slightly* earlier than generally recommended — or perhaps to be gentler on a baby's tummy you could introduce goats' milk sweetened with a little brown sugar (or honey if over 12 months).

If your baby is nearing a year old, and you haven't introduced him to formula or breastmilk in a *bottle*, then there's not a lot of point in starting to use nipple-teats — you might as well start with the sipper-spout-style, non-spill cup that you're probably already using for water.

Babyless friends

Author Deborah McKinlay, in her book *Bosom Buddies*, makes the very true observation that when your baby is a newborn, to your babyless girlfriends it is either adorable, boring or mildly irritating (when crying). But . . . babies turn into toddlers, and then they are wilful, demanding, exhausting and *mobile*. As Deborah McKinlay so superbly describes, 'They grind biscuits into the carpet, demand juice to go with the biscuit, drop juice on the carpet, knock things over and break them, scream at the top of their lungs when this happens, pull hair (your girlfriend's), torment cats (your girlfriend's), and scream at the top of their lungs when the cat acts in self defence . . . Somehow, your child, who used to look so cute asleep in its Moses basket, is now completely devoid of charming likeableness. Babies might cry but they *do not* throw Lego!'

No matter how often babyless friends say 'Ooh, I don't mind . . . honestly', a mum is more relaxed sitting on a sofa already loaded down with toys. Mums of pre-schoolers tend to be more comfortable hanging out with other mums who are in the same boat-in-the-bathtub phase.

As those babyless girlfriends become new mothers themselves, impress them with the 'right' gift. As an old hand, you know what new mothers really need when they have newborns.

- A new-mummy pressie — let everyone else buy for the baby.
- A prepared dinner — a one-dish wonder of meat and vegies ready for re-heating.
- A 'voucher' for an afternoon's free babysitting that must be used within the first six weeks.
- When your friends are having second children, it's a great idea to include a little present for the older sibling — like a $2 colouring-book.

The uterosexual

There is a hidden history that few people know, a history that holds many interwoven truths — about women, about the earth, and about how Western civilisation lost its soul . . . and did tremendous damage to the status of women — laws were passed forbidding them to inherit, to own property, to receive an education, to divorce . . . Only men were allowed to be educated, and only men could be doctors . . . women have been locked within shuttered towers, hidden behind black veils, victimised by religion and endless social prohibitions, refused the right to vote, work, travel freely, own property, preach in churches, speak the wisdom of their hearts . . . [but] they are once again rising, not as singularly remarkable exceptions, but as a global community, to their rightful, equal, and vital places as creators.

Phyllis Curott — *Book of Shadows*

There is a collective force rising up on the earth today, an energy of the reborn feminine . . . She remembers our function on earth . . . This is a time of a monumental shift, from the male dominance of human consciousness back to a balanced relationship between masculine and feminine. The Goddess archetype doesn't replace God; she merely keeps him company. She expresses his feminine face.

Marianne Williamson — *A Woman's Worth*

Throughout the world, but most prominently in Westernised

countries, we are witnessing a reawakening of the feminine, a
profound upheaval within the conciousness of women . . . Slowly, but
irrevocably, this ferment inside women, and the reaction going on in
men is starting to affect every aspect of our lives and thinking . . .
If we look around, there are more than a few outer signs of this
emergence of new feminine awareness.

J.B. & R.J. Woolger — *The Goddess Within*

We all know the terms heterosexual, homosexual, bisexual and transsexual. And now society is inventing more terms, such as solosexual (you can work it out); and the epitome of affluent urban male lifestyle, the metrosexual: a trend-setting, image-conscious, fashion couture heterosexual (or 'closet gay' some say), with his manicured and pedicured nails, mono-brow plucked to estrangement, waxed-smooth hairless torso, and bathroom cabinet overflowing with chic-salon male skin-care regimes.

Let me introduce you to my term: the strictly female, lesbian or straight, *uterosexual!*

So what is a uterosexual?

Explained in simplistic terms, a uterosexual is a woman who is able to publicly acknowledge the precious and immense importance of the rewarding friendships she has with her close female friends.

This is a woman who probably greets girl friends with a kiss on the cheek, and farewells them with a hug. This is the woman who perhaps will grab a girlfriend's hand during a movie's saddest moment; and will always wipe a friend's tears during life's saddest moments. This is a woman who can engage in engrossingly honest and deeply personal conversations with a bunch of girl friends; or dance at a party with rapturous delight, in a coven-ish circle of women, to the likes of Shania Twain's 'Man! I Feel Like A Woman!'.

A uterosexual is a woman who is very proud to be female. And often, motherhood can be the trigger that allows a woman's uterosexuality to, as they say, come 'out of the closet'.

For Westernised women it has been (and still is for most Third World women) a long hard journey to reach today's levels of uterosexual freedom — and the journey is still far from over.

Thousands of years ago, before the patriarchal god(s) of most of today's religions, there had always co-existed reverent beliefs in the uniquely feminine 'jewel-of-the-lotus' powers of the goddess, such as Hinduism's shrines to the Yoni and their many goddesses; the Celt's goddesses Ana, Anu, Dana and Danu; the Greek's many goddesses such as Aphrodite, Artemis and Athena; the Roman's many goddesses such as Venus, Diana and

Aurora; Egypt's goddesses such as Isis; Moslem's Islamic mystic Sufi female spirit Fravahi; Buddhism's Tantric belief in the superior female energy; and Judaism's female soul of God Shakti.

But over thousands of years this slowly changed, to the point that nearly all of man's gods came to be depicted as male; and the status of women slowly and violently declined. Females were no longer sacred, mystical and powerful — no, they were impure, unclean and stigmatised. Eventually, most women around the world were seen to be part of their husbands' chattels, because their bodies were sinful and their intellects inferior. They were expected to 'love, honour and obey' their husbands.

Do you realise that each year many an African teenage daughter receives pharaonic circumcision, when the crudest of sharp implements removes her clitoris and inner pair of delicate labia, then her outer pair of labia is cut and sewn together to cover her vagina, with just a small opening for her urine and menstrual blood to pass through? Later, her husband will cut or rip open that skin for intercourse, and he will be able to insist on her being re-stitched shut and reopened for subsequent intercourse and childbirth. The situation is so diabolical to us in the West that it does not seem believable.

The first modern wave of the movement to vehemently oppose the long-held belief in women's second-class citizenship came with the suffragettes winning the right for women to vote; later, two world wars saw women doing the work of men.

The second wave came in the sixties and seventies, with women's liberation, the sexual revolution, widespread use of contraception, and economic equality. It was the prophesised 'dawning of the New Age of Aquarius' (which saw patriarchy being slowly forced to give way to matriarchy).

And now the third wave has started, with the uterosexual's visible pride in being female.

One particularly politically active ambassador for the ending of violence against women, with her iconic uterosexuality, is Eve Ensler, playwright of the provocatively titled and globally celebrated *Vagina Monologues*. She is a brave leader on the frontier of consciousness-raising in her fight to protect women, using candid bluntness, wit, compassion and wisdom. Her plays give voice to heartbreaking and real testimonials from women, on taboo subjects such as orgasm, menstruation, rape, birth and menopause.

What of *Sex In The City*? Can we guess at how many million women worldwide were glued to their TV sets as they watched the final episode? What an unforeseen phenomenon the series became. It was so crudely offensive, and yet so passionately caring; it was so lavishly unrealistic, and yet so bluntly realistic; and throughout the years the programme's foundation was the friendship forged between four very different girlfriends. And the world (well, a lot of it anyway) simply adored them!

All over the globe we girls could relate to those four women: Were we a sweet, prim and proper Charlotte, or a conservative, career-minded Miranda; a sexually uninhibited vixen Samantha, or an energetic, optimistic, vivacious Carrie? I remember saying to my hairdresser Melissa one day, 'Oh you're a Charlotte with a secret Samantha side', and millions of women all over the planet could have understood that conversation.

Perhaps a huge reason for the amazing success of that TV series was that it began to quench just a little of the huge thirst women have to receive respect for the almightiness of our femininity. At the core of womanhood's nature is the need to care and share with others, and that TV show was one of the first real times the modern generation's new style of open and frank girlfriend-to-girlfriend friendship was being shown through the media of television. From our own uterosexual friendships we could relate to their conversations — or we'd yearn for uterosexual friendships that good.

Some women live their entire life in denial of any uterosexual desires, by choosing not to invest time or effort in establishing friendships with other women — or they only do so with a cautiously selected one or two. Sometimes, this can be due to snobbery, or to a debilitating shyness. Sometimes, it can be due to an abrasively de-feminising level of exposure to the testosterone-driven corporate rat-race, a dutiful loyalty to the sanctity of marriage, or a fierce level of personal self-reliance and independence. There are a lot of potential reasons — it's a complicated subject.

Can you organise casually going out to a chick-flick on a Thursday night with a bunch of great girlfriends; or ring from a bad traffic-jam to ask a girlfriend to drop everything and pick your child up from daycare? If you can't you're missing out on something very special.

Many new mothers feel a little uneasy and uncomfortable about discovering their uterosexual side, because they've never been ones for having a lot of close girlfriends who they open up to, or perhaps they've always 'preferred the company of men'. But motherhood awakens their pride in being a woman, and they begin to discover the real benefits of female friendships. When they allow it, motherhood can enable women to become more open and receptive people, providing them with a developing talent and confidence to make new contacts.

Other mothers find it easy to have uterosexual relationships — they've probably always had loads of girlfriends, or an established group of very close girlfriends. For them, extending their social circle through motherhood can be relatively easy. They realise there are some mums they'll never get on with, just as there will be some mums they'll click with straight away. For them motherhood automatically broadens their circle of friends — there is no need to preach to these converts about the benefits of having great uterosexual friendships, they're already addicted.

As the adage says: 'Friendship isn't a big thing — it's a million little things' and we women can be so darned good at them. Girlfriend friendships can allow you to see each other at your worst, because it doesn't matter, we don't care — because we care.

When your girlfriend wipes your son's pooey butt and puts the stinky nappy in her own rubbish bin, or doesn't stress about your daughter power-chucking over her lounge suite; that's being with a true friend. When your girlfriend finds you unshowered in a bombsite house, spiking your 10 am coffee with Kahlua, and she hugs you closely as you release a good cry; that's being with a true friend. When a major devastating and unforeseen disaster occurs, and almost straight away you find a girlfriend right there by your side; that's being with a true friend. As one proverb says, 'A real friend is someone who walks in when the rest of the world walks out.'

Deepak Chopra writes in *The Seven Spiritual Laws of Success*: 'The universe operates through dynamic exchange . . . giving and receiving are different aspects of the flow of energy in the universe. And in our willingness to give that which we seek, we keep the abundance of the universe circulating in our lives.'

Uterosexuals naturally understand that, when a woman is feeling overwhelmed with anger, sadness, fear or sorrow, it is the little girl within her — the one with clouded vision, who is feeling vulnerable and aware of what she is missing. She has to go through a cathartic 'housekeeping' cycle of bottoming-out, before she can begin to get back up and feel fulfilled again with what she has. Uterosexuals intuitively know that while she's down, all she really needs is an empathetic non-judgemental and loving reassuring ear to listen to her. She needs to share her feelings of what she's going through to 'get it off her chest', so she can release, heal and purify her emotions. Uterosexuals instinctually know that with support, patience and understanding, their girlfriend's darkness will be temporary, and that she will eventually spontaneously rise up from the 'depths of her well'.

So I encourage you, as a woman and mother, to open your heart and free any inhibitions of your own uterosexuality — because developing a wide circle of close girlfriends can be marvellously enriching. As someone once said, 'The worst solitude is to be destitute of sincere friendship.'

Perhaps the greatest social service that can be rendered by anybody to the country and to mankind is to bring up a family. But here again, because there is nothing to sell, there is a very general disposition to regard a married woman's work as no work at all, and to take it as a matter of course that she should not be paid for it.

George Bernard Shaw [1856–1950],
Playwright and commentator

I think that I will spend about half my life feeling like I am not myself. If you count the week or so every month before my period, when I am less than efficient, then throw in pregnancy, nursing and recovery, and top it off with that whole perimenopause and menopause part, it really adds up. My question is — if I am not myself for so much of my life, who am I really?

Tracy W. Gaudet — *Consciously Female*

Chapter 15

My child is very bright ... definitely above average, I'm sure !

I discovered one of motherhood's oldest secrets: That infants offer a place to hide, a human skin not your own in which to retreat. Infants can single-handedly obscure outward reality, by acting as a kind of human roadblock to every outstanding problem and uncertainty in your life. In this way they keep fear at bay by placing their small bodies directly in your line of vision, blocking out everything else.

Susan Johnson — *A Better Woman*

Wow — this is the final chapter in my guide through the daunting and intrepid journey to become a new mother. But, you're not a *new* mother anymore!

Did you have any idea you would need to dig so deep within yourself to find the levels of courage required for childbirth? Could you ever have really comprehended the awesome responsibilities thrust upon your soul within minutes of birth? Could you have imagined the degree of personal loss required by the Old You, to become the New You? Did you know you could be such a heroine? *Well, you are!*

What of this child of yours? Is it not so amazing, and so rewarding, to be a mother? At first you gave your microscopic baby a few molecules of protein, lipids and glucose. Then you gave it your abdominal cavity and physical discomfort. Then after three-quarters of a year, like a sci-fi flick about an alien taking over Earth, this tiny human being completely took over your body, then took over your world! It became your world, your whole world — there was nothing else in your world except baby for a while.

But now, you're getting to know the New You, and hopefully you like her, quite a lot, because she's so much wiser than the Old You.

You really know you're a woman now — and it's good to be a woman. You're not a woman struggling in a 'man's world' — you're a woman who's proud to be a woman.

You are the Goddess! Oh yes, just like Aphrodite and Venus, you are a Goddess of Love to your child. For you are a Mother!

This last chapter contains final girlfriend-to-girlfriend hints and tips to help lead you into the pending crazy and non-sensible two years ahead of you — TODDLERDOM! This is when visiting non-childproofed environments becomes genuinely hazardous and tiring, as you constantly get up and down (and up and down), to control your virtually impossible-to-control but gorgeous and inquisitive 'monster'.

This is also when your coffee concession card may not get so much use at your favourite café, and when you'll probably discover the true value of the companionship and relaxed environment in the homes of other mothers with toddlers.

So chill, you have about two years ahead of you before your toddler will be redefined as a preschooler — they're the under-five-year-olds that have a little bit of common sense!

Eat something, please!
Just try it — you'll like it!

Every day I start out as Mary Poppins,
but I end up as Cruella De Vil.
                    Linda Carson et al — *Mum's The Word*

For the past few months you have probably been preparing, with loving dedication, wonderfully nutritious mush for your precious baby to consume. But at *around* a year (9–14 months) your infant's growth rate will slow down to about an ounce (28 g) in weight every four days or so (a quarter of the rate of a newborn) . . . so expect their food consumption to reduce a bit too. Additionally, one-year-olds can become fairly insistent that they feed themselves.

These two aspects do not always combine brilliantly, and often this is when mums assume their little gobblers have been mysteriously swapped with fussy eaters. *Welcome* to the fun, fun world of the FDTs (frustrating dinner-times)!

Some toddlers *love* nearly all food, and always will. That's their personality . . . they're a 'foodie'. Then other toddlers can seem to detest almost all vaguely healthy food, and would happily spend years eating canned spaghetti, fairy bread and ice-cream. So, it may (dependent on your child) become an ever-tedious search for the Holy Grail to find food your toddler will consume. Below is a list of ideas that you may not have thought of. There are also some excellent recipe books to help you further, such as *Babies and Toddlers Good Food* put out by the *Australian Women's Weekly*, and *Feeding Babies and Toddlers*, by Jacki Passmore.

BREAKFAST FOOD IDEAS:

(Apart from a bowl of fresh fruit, and instead of cereal or toast)
- Omelettes.
- Scrambled eggs with toast triangles.
- Egg in an eggcup with bread soldiers to dip.

LUNCH FOOD IDEAS:

(Apart from sandwiches, yoghurt and fruit)
- Milk and fruit smoothie drink (good for teething toddlers).
- Macaroni cheese.
- Tomato soup and toast soldiers.
- Creamed-corn fritters.
- Two-minute noodles.
- Pinwheel sandwiches (slice of bread with topping, crusts removed, then rolled into a 'log' and sliced).
- Mini pizza bases or halved pita breads — kids can design their own grilled pizzas with canned spaghetti, meat and cheese.

NIBBLE FOOD IDEAS:

- Frozen peas.
- Yoghurt-coated raisins.
- Little packets of raisins.
- Cheese slices.
- Luncheon/salami/meat slices.
- Baby corn.
- Baby carrots.
- Cherry tomatoes.

- Crunchy noodles.
- Scones and pikelets.
- Frozen fruit-juice or frozen yoghurt ice-blocks.
- Little muesli snack-bars and yoghurt-coated snack-bars.

DINNER FOOD IDEAS:

- Carrots and parsnips mashed together.
- Potatoes and pumpkin mashed together.
- Canned baby potatoes.
- Corn on the cob (using corn forks).
- Stuffed baked potatoes.
- Lasagne.
- Fresh filled pasta with Italian tomato sauce.
- Wiener schnitzel with mashed potatoes.
- Corned beef with mashed potatoes.
- Mild curry, basmati rice and pappadums. Kids like breaking up pappadums to scoop up the meat and rice.
- Mince patties with mashed potatoes — kids can help roll the patties.
- Beef meatballs with spaghetti pasta and Italian tomato sauce — kids can help roll the meatballs.
- Pork meatballs with jasmine rice and plum sauce — kids can help roll the meatballs.
- Falafels with yoghurt sauce, hummus and lettuce — kids can make their own pita pockets.
- Tacos or burritos — kids can make their own.
- Couscous sand castles — couscous pressed into a cup and turned upside down onto the plate.
- Boiled and skinned saveloy or polony sausages with mashed potatoes and tomato sauce.
- 'Daddy's shepherd's pie' (bottom layer can of spaghetti, middle layer cooked mince, top layer mashed potato).
- Lamb cutlets to hold and gnaw on and dip in redcurrant jelly and mint sauce.
- Sushi — store-bought or kids can help roll home-made sushi.
- Banana custard (warm custard with sliced banana).
- Egg custard (beaten egg added to custard and heated).
- Apple fritters.

At the end of the day, if you have serious diet and nutrition concerns for your toddler, there are an assortment of children's chewable multivitamins available to give you some peace of mind — though, due to the risk of choking, they are only recommended for three-year-olds and older. But, you can try crushing them and adding them into toddler food.

By the way, don't be naïve enough to believe that food marketed as having childhood health benefits, contains nothing of harm. Read the ingredients label well, remembering that ingredients are listed from the highest amount downwards . . . so, for example, when a 'natural fruit juice' lists sugar as its first ingredient — eeeeek!

The good news however, is that in about a year's time, when your two-year-old is understanding more of what you're saying, he/she can be bribed . . . 'Eat all your vegetables and you can have a scoop of ice-cream — and eat all your meat and you can have some chocolate sprinkles on top too'. So there is salvation at the end of the tunnel.

When do babies outgrow bottles and dummies?

I'm turning into my mother! My rebellion, tattoos and body-piercing have been for nothing!

Linda Carson et al — *Mum's the Word*

Most parents don't want their 3–5-year-old with the insecurity of being addicted to their baby bottle, and there are lots of possible ways you can deal with the need to wean your toddler off their bottle and nipple-teat.

With our first child we had no idea at what age toddlers should be finished with their bottles, but I noticed that the fast-flow teats only went up to 18 months old, and so I figured that somewhere in the months following the first birthday, teat-weaning was a task to have completed. Since then, I have learnt that it is easier to wean a baby from the bottle to a non-spill cup *before* they are 1½ years old, because by two years old toddlers can become emotionally attached to their bottles.

One method I can recommend is keeping the clear bottles with nipple-teats just for their milk, and the colourful sipper cups for water. Then a few months after their first birthday, over the course of a couple of weeks, replace all their standard clear milk-bottle nipple-teats with silicone toddler trainer-spouts. Generally, young toddlers have no difficulty accepting the new system, as it is still the same milk bottles they have grown used to, and they are already familiar with using sipper-spouts. And hey presto, the job is done

— no more baby nipple-teats.

Then, a little later, you can buy a new, large, see-through, sipper-spout drink bottle, to replace the 'baby' bottles.

But if you do end up with a 2–3-year-old who 'loves' his bottle, then you could always do what a few of my friends did, and that was create a little ceremony to 'post' their baby bottles (via your own letterbox works) to the new babies being born who now need bottles. Or, perhaps, help your little toddler wrap the bottles up as a present for another new baby.

As for pacifiers, my personal philosophy is that one- and two-year-olds should not have insecurities instilled already to the point of being unable to be without their dummy! Realise that the longer you avoid this parenting issue, the harder and more traumatic it will become for your child. So don't be mean — remove the dummy from his life while he's little, then he'll never remember. Don't wait until he's a 4½-year-old who needs to be separated from his dummy before he starts school!

If you have a dummy-addicted 2–3-year-old, you could try explaining that the 'dummy has died' (pierce the pacifier with a needle to release the vacuum so it isn't an enjoyable suck anymore) — then you could have a special 'burying-the-dead-dummy' ceremony! It sounds morbid, but it's worked really well for a couple of friends' toddlers.

Toddler tantrums and midget meltdowns

A one-year-old wants to be completely independent and she wants to be protected. A two-year-old wants to wear her red pyjamas and her blue ones. A three-year old wants a playmate and she wants all the toys to herself.

Dr Benjamin Spock — *Baby and Child Care*

Oh the fun, fun times of tantrums — when your toddler has enough self-awareness to know what she wants, and just enough language to loudly express it.

This book is not going to attempt to give lengthy advice on dealing with toddler temper tantrums, hissy-fits, midget meltdowns, tannies, paddies, or whatever you'll end up nicknaming them — there's way too many child psychologist-type experts with fiercely strong, yet differing opinions to contend with, and enough literature out there already. (However, I can particularly recommend the book *Of Course I Love You . . . Now Go to Your Room!* by Diane Levy.) I also have three observations:

• Tantrums are personality related — some toddlers are worse than others.

- Constitutional homeopathy can be particularly helpful, as can omega 3.
- Dr Robert Needlman wrote a very good explanation in his book *Dr Spock's Baby Basics:* 'Children have a natural, inborn need to feel connected to and protected by their parents. But now they also have powerful urges to explore and be on their own, in control and free — while also staying completely connected to you at the same time. So it is the pull and tug between their two needs of Dependence and Independence which fuels a lot of toddler tantrums.'

What's with your P.C. terminologies?

Always keep your words soft and sweet, just in case you have to eat them. And if you can't be kind, at least have the decency to be vague!

Unknown Author

Why do some parents insist on teaching very young children the 'proper' ('politically correct') names of their sexual body parts: penis and scrotum, or vulva and vagina? Oh please! Let them remain children for a little while longer. That's like teaching a child that they have an abdomen not a tummy; umbilical cord scar not a belly-button; or a minimums finger instead of their pinkie.

We decided 'willy' and 'fanny' were laid-back, easily pronounceable and utterly adequate for our kids as toddlers.

But you may prefer to go for more anatomically correct nouns . . . each to their own! (Please don't send me hate-mail on all the beneficial psychiatric reasons why anatomically correct terms are advantageous for toddlers, as it won't change my mind, sorry.)

P.S.: Definition of the Vulva
Even after childbirth many women are not really clear on what their vulva is. To quote Eve Ensler's *Vagina Monologues*, 'It's the package . . . It's the entire deal.' The vulva is all the external female genitalia, so it includes the labia majora (two outer folds), labia minora (two thin inner folds), vagina vestibule (vagina entrance) and of course we won't forget the clitoris (the erectile organ of sexual stimulation). So now it's finally clear!

Cot versus bed

I am a nobody, and nobody is perfect; therefore, I am perfect.
I live in my own little world. But it's OK. They know me here.

Unknown Author

What is the right age to be moving your toddler from her cot to a bed? Oh my goodness. That's almost like asking 'At what age should little girls get their ears pierced?' Probably the best answer is when *you* are ready.

This 'advancement' commonly occurs between $1^1/2$ and $2^1/2$ years, quite often because the cot is needed for a younger sibling. Some parents are very proud of promoting their 18-month-old to the bed, and some parents are very happy to have their three-year-old still sleeping in a cot. Here are a few ideas to help smooth the transfer:

- Initially, at least, transfer the familiar bedding of their BabyOK™ Babe-Sleeper to the bed until they're happy and settled — and it helps stop them falling out of the bed. (See chapter 5, page 227.)
- Remember, it is not logical to be toilet-training a child who is still in a cot — he needs the freedom to get up to go to the toilet.
- If you have produced a toddler who is not good at going to sleep, then save yourself the extra stress, leave him in the cot for longer and teach him to go down to sleep properly before promoting him to a bed. Maybe the bed could be the incentive reward . . . seven nights of going to bed properly, and he helps to choose the new pillow . . . seven more nights of going to bed properly, and he helps to choose the new linen . . . seven more nights of going to bed properly, and he helps to go and buy the bed . . . and once in the bed, being naughty means back to the cot that night, and being good means a lolly the next day . . . or something along those lines.

A clingy tyke

I try to take one day at a time, but sometimes several days attack me at once.

Author Unknown

The most effective form of birth control I know is spending the day with my kids.

Jill Bensley

For many toddlers there can be another clingy period that peaks at 15–24 months — so don't become surprised when your toddler who used to 'go to anyone' suddenly only wants you. They are growing up.

This can be particularly prevalent at about 20–24 months when most toddlers go through a stage of increased fearfulness, usually related to being separated from their parents. (We call this the ankle-biter attached-to-your-leg-with-superglue phase).

When your little toddler is in this clingy phase, it can make it particularly tricky when you need to leave them with someone else for a while. One system my sister used when her children were little was the 'I'm going for "this" long' strategy. How this works is that as you are telling your toddler that you're leaving them, you are also *showing* them with your hands (think along the lines of 'the fish was this big' and you should get the idea).

Then when you're at the petrol station and you're just going in to pay, you can show them you'll be away for only a *short* period of time (because 'back in a minute' means little to a toddler). Then too, when you're going for your all-day, full-body, luxury massage with deluxe facial at the spa *(we all can dream)*, you can show Bub you'll be away for a *long* period of time.

The terrible twos usually arrive before due date

Child-care experts (often males who've never had sole responsibility
for a child in their lives) list at length the needs of children which we
Wonder Mothers must fulfil. They also fill us with panic by telling us
such gems as 'a child's personality is fixed by the age of three.' An
extra dose of guilt for the mother who reads the article when her
child is four and acting like a little Hitler.

Jenny Phillips — *Mothers Matter Too*

'Oh what's happening to my innocent little sweet-pea? Are the "terrible twos" starting early? Surely not yet . . . but my little darling is . . . quite unmistakably being . . . oh-no . . . it can't really be happening . . . heck I hope not . . . he'll have a paddy if I stop him . . . oh blow . . . *my little tyke is intentionally being NAUGHTY!*'

There comes a time, usually somewhere between a toddler's first and second birthdays, that they stop being quite such a little 'darling'. Your little angel's wings seem to have disappeared and your angel is now being human!

It is now time for you, as parents, to consciously consider your discipline style and standards — as it is *essential* that both mum and dad, in front of their children at least, always have a *united front* of omnipotent leadership.

'Discipline' — what a *yuck* word, conjuring up cranky teachers and spankings. But it doesn't have to feel that way. You have already been providing your child with a disciplined lifestyle through the sleep routines, good diet and 'don't touch' habits you have instilled. And the word 'discipline' (remember Jesus' 'disciples') is historically interpreted as 'learning through loving example'. And that's what it can continue to mean.

Now I know I have a personal affinity towards wee babies — I am captivated by and besotted with them, newborns in particular. But I can offer you two specific tips relating to toddlers:

- Firstly, a golden rule I was told about, and continue to use, is to make a concerted effort to give 3–5 praises to every telling-off. As they get older, it can certainly be a struggle with some toddlers to find 3–5 compliments for every reprimand — but it is worth making the effort, as kids seem to turn into monsters when they are being constantly told that is what they are.
- And secondly, one favourite line I have discovered is — and it seems over time to have a miraculous impact — 'I'm so lucky to have you, you're my favourite x-year-old in the whole world.' Say it often. It's a goodie.

A kind of grieving sadness has always crept over me, with each of our children, the first time I have needed to *tell my wee child off* because they have been deliberately and undeniably *naughty*.

Vanished in that moment is your perfect, sinless babe — and staring back at you, with determined eyes and annoyed frown, is your new child . . . your toddler. Every day, from that split second on, what's left of your innocent angelic baby begins to 'disintegrate' before your eyes; for their purpose now is to discover every boundary they can, good and bad.

And you realise, then, that in some fashion you may be 'telling them off' for the next one-and-a-half decades. How daunting and tiring a task that can seem.

So enjoy every moment of your babies as babies — for they will be children for a much longer time indeed.

It's quite normal!

To reassure you that your 'dysfunctional toddler' is really functionally pretty normally, here are approximate figures from the New York 'Chamberlain Study'. From the parents' perspective, of normal two-year-olds:

42% talk back cheekily
44% hurt their younger sibling
43% resist sitting on the toilet
50% eat too little
52% wake in the night
54% get jealous
56% play with their sex organs
64% don't eat the right kind of foods
68% hit others or take things
70% resist going to bed
71% poo in their pants
72% fight or quarrel
73% are not toilet trained
75% pee in their pants
79% cling to mother
79% cry easily
82% pee in their bed
82% are disobedient
83% whine, whinge and nag
83% have temper outbursts
95% are stubborn
94% constantly seek attention
100% are (over)active and rarely still

Love is . . . a mother

Having lived for so long high up in the bickering romantic quarters
of love, it is as if I were suddenly cast down to its basement, its
foundations. Love is more respectable, more practical, more
hardworking than I had ever suspected . . . The storm of emotion, of
the new, that accompanied her arrival is over now.

I find that I am living in the knowledge of what I have, so that I
see happiness before it quite passes. It has taken me a year to achieve
this feat, this skill that has eluded me over a lifetime.

Rachel Cusk — *A Life's Work*

Perhaps the most profound side effect of becoming a mother is that of gaining a hugely enlarged understanding of the breadth and depth of what 'loving' someone really can mean. It's a new, compassionate, feminine wisdom that more deeply appreciates what lack of love means, how miraculous a baby truly is, how spectacular every child is — and even how precious every unborn baby is.

It is a deep inner knowing that in the big picture of life, the wellbeing of any fetus completely outweighs all a pregnant woman's other collective responsibilities, including her image, her career, her professional reputation, her workplace irreplaceability, her body, her social hierarchy, her home, her financial security, almost her everything . . . perhaps, probably, even her soul?

It creates a restorative realisation of just how much our society doesn't permit that understanding to fully transcend into a new mum-to-be's psyche, because there is such an absence of honouring the miracle called *pregnancy*: society's right hand obsessionally promotes the piously perfect pregnancy, while its left hand presumes the hardiness of the fetus, with modern life dictating and anticipating that the woman will maintain her normal unrelenting schedule. Mums-to-be slog at stressful careers and sweat beads of perspiration through addictive aerobic workouts, while their unborn baby grows, and all the while thinking, 'If I'm not bleeding, then my baby's doing just fine, thank you!'

But, after childbirth, a woman can be left with guilt that resides in the dark spaces between her brain's memory cells. Is her babe's inability to relax for successful breastfeeding caused by her adrenaline-pumped, career-stressed pregnancy? Is her toddler's need for spectacles caused from the forceps delivery, due to her resorting to an epidural from overly toned, inflexible pelvic-floor muscles?

We never know, we sometimes wonder, we always worry.

You see, with the utopian experience of knowing more about what love feels like, comes the slavery of being utterly responsible for supplying a defenceless person's life force of maternal love — retrospectively from the moment of conception.

Deep in all our mother-to-be hearts we always knew that the combination of a relaxed pregnancy and secondhand belongings was much better for our baby than a stressed pregnancy and all new belongings. However we weren't able to listen to *Her* then . . . *but we are listening to Her now!*

Motherhood teaches you to comprehend first-hand the unlimited human capacity to love (and the brittle human capacity to loathe).

Before children we experienced yearning for love and being *in* love — but after childbirth we experience being *with* love (and choking with love). We learn, usually for the first time in our life, that God (the Universe if you prefer) does not make junk! No junk, at all, ever.

Your baby is perfect, even with any imperfections: it is just the way it is meant to be.

On that one momentous day, (perhaps at childbirth, perhaps later), you know, beyond *any* doubt, that your child is *perfect*, and, more important to you than You . . . and afterwards you occasionally frolic in the sandpit of ideas wondering if perhaps you were always already perfect too.

Then, in a split magnanimous and pivotal millisecond, the gravity of that realisation can forever alleviate and elevate You from You, and from all those thoughts about your own vain imperfect self, because you are no longer your priority . . . and that is a great and delicate comforter, and an enormously freeing liberaliser!

You can be stunned as you realise how absorbed your old self was with her self-perfection and eternal quest for adrenaline-pumping mini-moments of euphoria. You may be flabbergasted at the revelation of how hard you looked in every nook and cranny of life to find happiness . . . yet now it sleeps peacefully before your eyes!

Some people fervently believe 'If it is to be, then it's up to me, and nobody else', which has some truthful aspects. Effort, conviction, dedication and determination *are* worthy and invaluable attributes. But, post new-parenthood, you also now realise that fate, destiny (and probably Karma) are also all involved — especially for the liberating of Oneself towards a spiritually maturing, enriched understanding.

You see, we learn little in the easy phases — they are like the smoko breaks between work shifts. We thought we were experiencing life — but that was the intermission between scenes.

Motherhood liberates us to finally strip away from ourselves (if we empower it to) *everything* we have built up as an intrinsic definition of our selves.

Let's not delude ourselves, it's not like some pleasant undressing behind an elegant privacy screen . . . *oh no!* In the easier times, it feels like a coarse emery board. But, in the tougher times (the really defining moments) it can feel like a chainsaw hacking away at precious pieces of your prized persona, chopping off parts of yourself you'd adored and never ever agreed to lose; while, at the same time, a fire is torching much of your previously held ideologies.

It's brutal, and even violently insensitive. Tougher than you'd ever imagined.

But afterwards you can reflect that this was the only way to meet her, the true genuine and beautiful, uncomplicated, uninhibited, goddess Self.

You now know, if it was all gone in a flash — the make-up, the hair, the nails, the body, the shoes, the clothes — you would handle it: heck, you've already been through that!

If you were ever to lose the job, the car, the house — you know you could get through that as well.

And, Heaven forbid, if you were to lose even more . . . the partner, the breasts, the womb, the eyes, the face . . . you would get through that too, you would survive, you would find the courage you need.

But losing a child?

From that you could never recover, not fully.

You are more than just You now, more than the individual person.

You are a *mother!*

Like mothers before us, and mothers after us, as life's elegant shroud is finally disrobed to reveal its beautiful yet scarred and imperfect raw nudity; you have profoundly realised, that you will never always be, *and are not meant to be,* **happy** all the time.

What a comforting relief! *What a deliverance from purgatory!*

Finally, the search is over.

God, that's so f**king reassuring.

Perhaps that is the ultimate gift that motherhood can bestow:

A knowing relief that happiness is always with us, and never with us always.

Your children are not your children.
They are the sons and daughters of Life's longing for itself.
They come through you but not from you,
And though they are with you yet they belong not to you.
You may give them your love but not your thoughts,
For they have their own thoughts.

You may house their bodies but not their souls,
For their souls dwell in the house of tomorrow,
which you cannot visit, not even in your dreams.
You may strive to be like them, but seek not to make them like you.
For life goes not backward nor tarries with yesterday.
You are the bows from which your children as living arrows are sent
  forth.
The Archer sees the mark upon the path of the infinite,
and He bends you with His might that His arrows may go swift and
  far.
Let your bending in the Archer's hand be for gladness;
For even as He loves the arrow that flies,
so He loves also the bow that is stable.

Kahlil Gibran — *The Prophet*

Conclusion and acknowledgements

My generation ... pretty much believed we had a right to anything and were in complete control of every damn thing.

These days, I am not so sure about inalienable rights and absolute control. These days, everything good in my life strikes me as a blessing, a fragile, happy gift held in trust. I have no idea how I came by these blessings, nor when or if they will be taken away again, but I certainly know that it is not my will alone which holds them. My swaggering days, you see, are well and truly over.

Susan Johnson — *A Better Woman*

You have reached the end of my book. My hope is that it was a worthwhile read for you. I have written it with love, and immense respect and admiration for you and your role as a mother ... You know we are the most important people in civilisation, for without us, there would be no civilisations.

In case you're curious, my primary motivations for writing this book were:

- As a personally cathartic experience of being able to speak my thoughts bluntly — to plain get things off my chest.
- To create a 'tool' to fill in the gaps of missing wise-woman wisdom that most of us no longer have access to in our modern, isolating lifestyles.
- To provide you with unbiased, informative and intelligent medical information.
- To endorse that the middle-of-the-road methodology of mothering can be just as wonderful as some of the idealistic parenting philosophies.
- And, as a way to spread the news as far and wide as possible, of how 'very normal' most of our experiences of motherhood really are!

As parents we are all so magnificently different, and you, my dear reader, are of course free to have attitudes and viewpoints that differ greatly from my own, and from those of every other person on the planet! For you are unique.

So please, take from this book only that which you see to be of benefit to *you*.

Do set aside the parts of this book that you feel aren't for you ... *on the condition* that in your heart you promise yourself to be happy and content with the decisions you make — for they are decisions only you can and *need* make, and you must have faith in and trust your judgements.

Please, only ever do what you believe is right for you, right for your baby and right for your family. (Whether or not it is the same as what was right for our family is irrelevant.) I honour the fact that every baby, and every mother, is unique — I celebrate nonconformity!

Listen attentively to your own feminine intuition, so you can gain total respect for and trust in your own inherent wisdom. For that is the Universe's extra special gift given only to mothers — the gift of infinite maternal wisdom.

My wish for you, precious mum, is utter elation, complete rapture and fantastic delight in your immeasurably valuable role — motherhood.

For you are all-encompassingly what life is ALL about.

I remember once reading a book acknowledgement where the author (to whom I sincerely apologise since I can't recall who it was) thanked her husband for 'indulging her endless ideas and flights of fancy'. She called him her 'Equilibrium'. For me, it is such a brilliant description that I have to say ... DITTO! Thank you, Mark, for being my Equilibrium too, for being such a cool and caring Dad, and for being such a fab best friend.

I have to thank my own soul for so wisely choosing my parents. I'm sure I must have had quarrels in Heaven with other souls, as we squabbled over who would get to have them. Thank you, Mum and Dad, especially for believing in my endeavours, no matter how fanciful. And, loving thanks to our family, for embracing me and all my eccentricities.

It is imperative I thank my literary agent Ray Richards and his daughter Nicki Richards Wallace, for believing in my book. And thank you to the patient team at publishers Random House for seeing the same vision.

Thanks to my midwife, Diana, for her friendship over the years. Thanks too, to our retired family homeopath, Jackie, for her faith in my ability.

Thanks to the outstanding team of medical specialists who so willingly assisted me with their infinite knowledge and endorsements, especially Simon Rowley, Nikki Turner, Yvonne LeFort, Cathy Hapgood, Jenny Kruger and Carolyn Young. I sincerely thank the New Zealand Obstetric and Gynaecology Society for their fantastic commitment to supporting my writing. And I gratefully thank the New Zealand College of Midwives, for their friendship and passion, especially Judith, Clare, Jacky and Dawn.

William Ferguson, my gentle and kind GP-obstetrician, who knows me intimately well — inside and out! Your unceasing encouragement and support throughout my pregnancies and at our babies' births were so gratefully appreciated. As has also been your wonderful encouragement and support through the gestation and birth of this book. Without having had you enter our lives, and guide me through empowering births, perhaps this book would never have been written.

Most essentially, I have to thank the girlfriends! You're a cool bunch of amazing ladies — and I'm a better person from making friends with each one of you. Thank you for teaching me so much.

Finally, I give eternal thanks to the Universe for my darlings, my sweet precious children. Without you in our lives, this book definitely would never have been written — but much more importantly, I would have missed out on the most enriching transformations of my life. You're only on loan to us as children, until you spread your wings and fly on your own adventurous journeys — and I'm honoured to be a guide during your odysseys.

It seems to me that since I gave birth to my sons my life in every way has become broader, deeper, richer. They have drawn from me my best self, and while physically I am not the woman I once was, I am a better woman.

I know for certain now that I am fully attached to life and love, and that life and love have fully attached themselves to me. My arms are full. I no longer have the sense that my true life is just out of reach, if only I could find my way to it.

I am fully here, at last.

Susan Johnson — *A Better Woman*

Bibliography / Recommended Reading

Acredolo, Linda and Goodwin, Susan, *Baby Signs*, New York, McGraw Hill, 2002.

Arms, Suzanne, *Immaculate Deception*, Boston, Houghton Mifflin, 1975.
——*Immaculate Deception II: Myth, Magic & Birth*, Berkeley, Celestial Arts, 1994.
——*Seasons of Change*, Colorado, Kivaki Press, 1994.

Australian Women's Weekly, *Babies and Toddlers: Good Food*, Sydney, ACP Books, 2003.

Banks, Maggie, *Home Birth Bound: Mending the Broken Weave*, Hamilton, Birthspirit Ltd, 2000.

Barbar, Carol, *The Birth Book*, Pymble NSW, Simon & Schuster, 2001.

Barker, Robin, *Baby Love*, Australia, Pan Macmillan, 1997.
——*Baby & Toddler Meals*, Australia, Pan Macmillan, 2004.
——*The Mighty Toddler*, Australia, Pan Macmillan, 2005.

Blum, Jeanne Elizabeth, *Woman Heal Thyself: An Ancient Healing System for Contemporary Women*, Boston, Tuttle Publishing, 1997.

Brown, Sylvia & Struck, Mary Dowd, *The Post-Pregnancy Handbook*, New York, St Martin's Press, 2003.

Buttrose, Ita & Adams, Dr. Penny, *Motherguilt*, Australia, Penguin, 2005.

Carroll, Lee & Tober, Jan, *The Indigo Children*, Australia, Hay House, 1999.

Carson, Linda; Daum, Jill; Kelly, Alison; Nicol, Robin; Pollard, Barbara & Williams, Deborah, *Mum's The Word*, Vancouver, Talonbooks Ltd, 2000.

Chopra, Deepak, *The Seven Spiritual Laws of Success*, California, Group West, 1994.

Cooke, Kaz, *Up The Duff*, Australia, Penguin Books, 1999.
——*Kid-Wrangling: The Real Guide to Caring for Babies, Toddlers and Preschoolers*, Australia, Penguin Books, 2003.

Cosby, Bill, *Fatherhood*, New York, Peter Pauper Berkley, 1986.

Curott, Phyllis, *Book of Shadows*, New York, Broadway, 1998.

Cusk, Rachel, *A Life's Work: On Becoming a Mother*, New York, Picador, 2001.

Davis, Elizabeth, *Women's Intuition*, New York, Celestial Arts, 1989.

Dunham, Carol & the Body Shop Team, *Mamatoto: A Celebration of Birth*, New York, Penguin Books, 1991.

Eisenberg, Arlene, *What to Expect When You're Expecting*, New York, Workman Publishing Company, 1996.

Enright, Anne, *Making Babies: Stumbling into Motherhood*, London, Jonathan Cape, 2004.

Ensler, Eve, *The Vagina Monologues*, New York, Villard Books, 1998.

Ezzo, Gary & Bucknam, Robert, *On Becoming Baby Wise*, Oregon, Multnomah, 1995.
——*On Becoming Baby Wise II: Parenting Your Pre-toddler Five to Fifteen Months*, Oregon, Multnomah, 1995.

Fancourt, Robin, *Brainy Babies*, Australia, Penguin Books, 2000.

Figes, Kate, *Life After Birth*, London, Penguin Books, 1998.

Flamm, Bruce, *Birth After Cesarean: The Medical Facts*, New Jersey, Prentice Hall, 1990.

Ford, Gina, *The New Contented Little Baby Book*, London, Vermilion, 1999.

Forna, Aminatta, *Mother of All Myths*, London, HarperCollins, 1998.

Garcia, Joseph, *Sign with Your Baby*, Seattle, Northlight Communications, 2002.

Garland, Dianne, *Waterbirth: An Attitude to Care*, Oxford, Butterworth-Heinemann, 1995.

Gaskin, Ina May, *Spiritual Midwifery*, Tennessee, Book Publishing Company, 1990 (1977).
——*Ina May's Guide to Childbirth*, New York, Bantam Doubleday Dell, 2003.

Gaudet, Tracy W., *Consciously Female: How to Listen to Your Body and Your Soul for a Lifetime of Healthier Living*, New York, Bantam Press, 2004.

Gibran, Kahlil, *The Prophet*, London, William Heinemann, 1991.

Gordon, Doris, *Backblocks Baby-Doctor*, London, Faber & Faber, 1955.

Gottman, John and Silver, Nan, *The Seven Principles of Making Marriage Work*, New York, Three Rivers Press, 1999.

Gray, John, *Men Are From Mars, Women Are From Venus*, New York, HarperCollins, 1993.
——*Children Are from Heaven*, Australia, Pan Macmillan, 1999.

Grayson, Sandra, *Childbirth: As it Really Is*, Auckland, HarperCollins, 1995.

Green, Christopher, *Babies!: A Parent's Guide to Enjoying Baby's First Year*, London, Simon & Schuster, 1989.
——*Toddler Taming: The Guide to Your Child from One to Four*, Australia, Doubleday, 1990.

Hale, Thomas, *Medications and Mothers Milk*, Texas, Pharmasoft Medical Publishing, 1999.

Hammer, Kathryn, *You're Pregnant!!: A Guide for the Longest Nine Months of Your Life*, New York, McGraw-Hill, 1995.

Heath, Alan & Bainbridge, Nicki, *Baby Massage*, London, Dorling Kindersley, 2004.

Hogg, Tracy, *Secrets of the Baby Whisperer*, London, Vermilion, 2001.
——*Secrets of the Baby Whisperer for Toddlers*, New York, Ballantine, 2002.
——*The Baby Whisperer Solves All Your Problems*, London, Vermilion, 2004.

Iovine, Vicki, *Girlfriend's Guide to Pregnancy*, New York, Pocket Books, 1995.
——*Girlfriend's Guide to Surviving the First Year of Motherhood*, New York, Perigee Books, 1997.
——*Girlfriend's Guide to Toddlers*, New York, Perigee Books, 1999.

Johnson, Susan, *A Better Woman*, Australia, Vintage, 1999.

Jolly, Hugh, *Book of Child Care*, London, Allen & Unwin, 1975.

Karmel, Annabel, *Feeding Your Baby & Toddler*, London, Dorling Kindersley, 2004.

Karp, Harvey, *The Happiest Baby on the Block*, New York, Bantam Press, 2003.

Kedgley, Sue, *Eating Safely in a Toxic World*, Auckland, Penguin, 1998.

Kitzinger, Sheila, *Breastfeeding Your Baby*, London, Dorling Kindersley, 1989.
——*The Year after Childbirth*, Oxford, Oxford University Press, 1994.
——*Birth Over Thirty-five*, London, Sheldon Press, 1994.
——*Pregnancy Day-by-Day*, London, Dorling Kindersley, 1998.
——*Rediscovering Birth*, London, Little Brown, 2000.
——*Birth Your Way*, London, Dorling Kindersley, 2002.
——*The New Pregnancy & Childbirth*, London, Dorling Kindersley, 2003
——*The New Experience of Childbirth*, London, Orion, 2004.

La Leche League International, *The Womanly Art of Breastfeeding*, New York, Plume, 2004.

Lamott, Anne, *Operating Instructions*, New York, Random House, 1993.

Lawrence Beach, Beverley, *Water Birth Unplugged*, Cheshire, Midwives Press, 1996.

Leach, Penelope, *Your Baby and Child*, Harmodsworth, Penguin, 1979.

LeBlanc, Wendy, *Naked Motherhood*, Australia, Random House, 1999.

Leboyer, Frederick, *Birth Without Violence*, Vermont, Inner Traditions, 1975.
——*Birth Without Violence: The Book that Revolutionized the Way We Bring Our Children into the World*, New York, Ballentine, 1990.

Lee, Mara, *Baby's First Year for Dummies*, Australia, Hungry Minds, 2002.
——*Staying Mum: The First Year*, Australia, John Wiley & Sons, 2003.

Levy, Diane, *Of Course I Love You . . . Now Go to Your Room!*, Auckland, Random House, 2002.

Lim, Robin, *After the Baby's Birth — A Woman's Way to Wellness*, New York, Celestial Arts, 2001.

McKenzie, Leanne and Thomas, Gail, *Doing Our Best*, Auckland, Exisle, 2003.

McKinlay, Deborah, *Bosom Buddies: Beyond Girls' Talk — What Women Do (and Men Don't)*, London, HarperCollins, 1996.

Mitchell, Karen, *Careers and Motherhood: Challenges and Choices*, North Ryde NSW, McGraw-Hill, 2004.

Naish, Francesca & Roberts, Janette, *The Natural Way to Better Babies*, Australia, Random House, 1996.
——*The Natural Way to Better Pregnancy*, Australia, Random House, 1999.
——*The Natural Way to Better Birth & Bonding*, Australia, Random House, 2000.
——*The Natural Way to Better Breastfeeding*, Australia, Random House, 2002.

Needleman, Robert, *Dr Spock's Baby Basics: Take Charge Parenting Guides for a New Generation*, New York, Pocket Books, 2003.

Nilsson, Lennart, *A Child Is Born*, New York, Dell Publishing, 2004.

Northrup, Christina, *Women's Bodies, Women's Wisdom*, London, Piatkus, 1995.

Odent, Michael, *Birth Reborn*, New York, Pantheon Books, 1984.

Oriah Mountain Dreamer, *The Invitation*, San Francisco, Harper Colins, 1995.

Passmore, Jacki, *Feeding Babies and Toddlers*, Ultimo NSW, Murdoch Books, 1998.

Phillips, Jenny, *Mothers Matter Too*, Middlesex, Penguin, 1985.

Redfield, James, *The Celestine Prophecy*, New York, Bantam Books, 1993.

Sears, William & Martha, *The Birth Book: Everything You Need to Know About Your Baby from Birth to Age Two*, London, Little Brown & Co, 1994.

Solter, Aletha, *Aware Baby*, Goleta California, Shining Star Press, 2001 (1984).

Spock, Benjamin, *Baby and Child Care*, New York, Pocket Books, 1945.

Stern, Daniel N. & Bruschweiler-Stern, Nadia, *The Birth of a Mother: How the Motherhood Experience Changes You Forever*, London, Bloomsbury, 1998.

Stoppard, Miriam, *Conception, Pregnancy & Birth: The Childbirth Bible for Today's Parents*, London, Dorling Kindersley, 2000.
——*Complete Baby & Child Healthcare: The Essential A–Z Home Reference to Children's Illnesses, Symptoms and Treatments*, London, Dorling Kindersley, 2001.
——*Baby First Aid*, London, Dorling Kindersley, 2003.
——*The New Pregnancy & Birth Book: The Complete Practical Guide for All Parents-to-be*, London, Dorling Kindersley, 2004.
——*Baby's First Skills*, London, Dorling Kindersley, 2005.

Thomas, Pat, *Every Woman's Birth Rights*, London, HarperCollins, 1996.

Tsiaras, Alexander, *From Conception to Birth*, London, Vermilion Press, 2002.

Van De Rijt, Hetty & Plooij, Frans, *Why They Cry: Understanding Child Development in Their First Year*, London, HarperCollins, 1992.

Virtue, Doreen, *The Crystal Children*, London, Hay House, 2000.

Ward, Sally, *Babytalk: Strengthen Your Child's Ability to Listen, Understand and Communicate*, New York, Ballantine Books, 2001.

Weissbluth, Marc, *Healthy Sleep Habits, Happy Child*, New York, Ballantine Books, 1999.

Westcott, Malcolm, *Toward a Contemporary Psychology in Intuition*, New York, Holt Rinehart Winston, 1968.

Williamson, Marianne, *A Return To Love*, New York, HarperCollins, 1992.
——*A Woman's Worth*, New York, Ballantine Books, 1993.

Wolf, Naomi, *Misconceptions*, New York, Doubleday, 2001.

Woolger, Jennifer B. & Roger J., *The Goddess Within*, New York, Ballantine Books, 1989.

Joy and sadness – the bi-polar world we live in.

Moi

Appendix A: General development guide

Based on due date — though every infant is different

Some believe in the super scientific view of childcare and that trusting your instincts is no longer good enough. One expert will tell us we should be playing classical music to the unborn baby . . . whilst another says the birth should be underwater with the lights out . . . another group implies that your baby is deprived unless massaged in oil each day . . . then there are those who want swimming by one year, reading by two and would like breastfeeding almost until high school . . .

There are many correct ways to bring up a baby, and it's best to latch on to the advice that feels right for you and your style.

Dr Christopher Green — *Babies*

Following is a dot-point guideline list of (very approximately) what you can *generally* expect babies and small children to be doing as they grow, along with some play ideas and other comments. To reiterate what is said elsewhere in this book, many infants will excel in certain areas and be slower in other areas. This is not a sign of their intelligence — but it is more likely to be a sign of their personality, interests and natural talents. Please do not be alarmed if your baby does not do all the things listed within each time-line — a genius often likes to focus more on certain things!

NEWBORN (full-term)
- Body curls (curved spine) and fingers curl inwards.
- Has fairly acute senses of taste, smell and hearing (though can abhor lots of noise).
- Soon recognises mum by her smell and can smell her breastmilk.
- Can see about 20–25 cm (8–10 inches) — about the distance to mum's face while breastfeeding. (Infants can go cross-eyed trying to see things closer though they can make out the darkened areola around the nipple. They are unable to see things further away.)
- Will look towards a light.
- Eyes will follow a slowly moving object

- Makes jerking random movements (no control of limbs).
- Needs neck supported as head is too big for underdeveloped neck muscles.
- Moves little during sleep.
- Enjoys skin-to-skin contact.
- Enjoys looking at expressive faces at about an arm's length away or closer.
- Enjoys listening to (and in fact prefers) mum's voice — without background noise.
- Enjoys listening to high-pitched voices (people speaking 'parentese').
- Communicates by crying, and responds to sounds by changing breathing.
- Startles easily (e.g. loud noises), so desires a soothing environment
- Grabs your finger.
- Very easily overstimulated, and very easily overtired.

3–4 WEEKS
- Recognises mum by sight — e.g. turns towards her in a room.
- Has, it is believed, a rudimentary level of emotional feelings (e.g. hungry, full, tired, overwhelmed, contented, uncomfortable).
- Coos and goos.
- Talks by poking out tongue and opening and closing mouth (experimenting with mimicking expressions).
- Lifts head for a few seconds during tummy time.
- Will raise head in small jerks when leaning on your shoulder.
- Enjoys listening to soft soothing music (e.g. lullabies, classical).
- Enjoys communicative interaction (e.g. 'chats' with pauses for the baby to 'respond').
- Enjoys gentle physical interaction (e.g. cuddles, baby massage).
- One interesting thing to look at is enough — favourites include black and white pictures and bold stripes and lines.
- Avoid stimulation-overload toys such as ones that shake, rattle, jiggle, wiggle, squeak or vibrate.
- Head circumference dramatically increases.

5 WEEKS
- A stormier period of more crying and clinginess.
- Easily overstimulated.

6–7 WEEKS
- A happier phase; baby will be particularly sunny at around 6 weeks.
- With vision improvement and brain growth, the first 'smiles' are seen — a crucial milestone in baby's development.
- Is less floppy with more head and neck control — can probably hold head up independently for about a minute when held under the arms.
- Plenty of tummy time starts to become beneficial (lying on his tummy instead of lying on his back) — though baby's individual personality can dictate how long he'll wish to endure tummy time.
- Has fixed gaze, focused stares at something (e.g. person, object).
- Pays closer attention — more aware of surroundings and people, starting to see

things to the side (not just straight in front).
- Smiling, babbling, chuckling, gurgling, early laughs.
- Communicating (coos, oohs, aahs).
- Cries real tears (tear ducts have started working), and cries at an angry voice.
- Socially responsive, stays awake for longer.
- Starting to discover his own hands.
- Black and white toys particularly appeal.
- Enjoys pictures of brightly coloured simple shapes like circles and wavy lines.
- Emotions can be fleeting — rapidly changing from inconsolably crying to happy gurgles.
- Gets physically excited when he sees you.

7–8 WEEKS
- Head circumference dramatically increases.
- Vision extended now to about 30 cm (12 inches).

8–9 WEEKS
- A stormier period of more crying, clinginess, boredom, shyness with strangers, less hungry, unsettled sleep — peaking at around 8 weeks.
- Will start to display more complex feelings (e.g. anger, sadness, assertiveness, joy).

10–11 WEEKS
- A happier phase, baby will be particularly sunny at around 10 weeks.
- Wiggles with delight when you enter the room.
- Makes responsive sounds and gestures — is learning early forms of emotional responses (e.g. the smile response).
- Makes stringed-together babbling sounds like 'dabadabadaba' — and likes you repeating sound back.
- Laughs.
- Can hold head upright for a while when alert.
- Initial discovery that his hands, feet and knees might actually belong to him — hands are still closed fists most of the time, and arms wave around rather uncontrollably.
- Consciously brings his hands to his face.
- Kicks.
- Hands starting to uncurl.
- Reaches and swipes unsuccessfully grabbing for toys.
- Holds a toy and moves it jerkily.
- Vision is sharpening, including peripherally (to the sides), and colours are more distinguished.
- Watches (e.g. faces, children, pets, TV, shapes, mum's movements and colours on supermarket shelves, loves bright primary colours), and eyes can follow an object with less jerky movements.
- Pictures of smiling faces can make him smile in response.
- Likes listening to voices.
- Loves having cosy conversational 'chats' — wants to make contact — loves your

lively enthusiastic responses (e.g. riveting amazement).
- Likes pull-up games and sitting-standing games.
- Enjoys rattles, cuddly toys, and moving musical mobiles (within about a foot).
- While lying on tummy can turn head to the side.
- Rocking from side-to-side when lying down maybe early attempts of rolling over.
- Head circumference dramatically increases.

12 WEEKS
- A stormier period of more crying, clinginess, boredom, shyness with strangers, less hungry, unsettled sleep, and quieter.
- Remember some babies are more easily overloaded by stimulation than others.

13–14 WEEKS (3+ MONTHS)
- A happier phase, particularly sunny at around 13 weeks.
- Laughing, giggling, more sociable, recognising familiar people.
- Responds more with smiles and gestures to people, noises, sounds, etc.
- Initiating interactions — sometimes by making funny sounds.
- Makes squeals, shrieks, chuckles and gurgle sounds when hearing others speak.
- Turns to the sound of mum's voice.
- Can watch things intently.
- Blows saliva bubbles, blows raspberries.
- Hands opening up to wave and hold things.
- Getting to know hands well (e.g. examining fingers) — knows they're his.
- Holds head up high during tummy-time, lifting shoulders and chest off the floor while leaning on forearms — like a push-up action. (Tummy-time is increasingly very important.)
- Rocking from side to side trying to roll over.
- Rolling side-to-back and/or side-to-front.
- Smooth head and eye movements.
- Sits with straight back when held or propped up.
- Puts everything into mouth for inspection, including perhaps toes (because mouth is the most sensitive part of baby's body).
- Maybe pushes lower lip out in protest, looking sorry for himself.
- Curious about things and people, making eye contact and grinning.
- Likes different textures and shapes (e.g. cubes, balls, triangles).
- Likes response toys (e.g. rattles), brightly coloured plastic toys, soft toys with texture (e.g. silky or furry), and colourful revolving musical mobiles.
- Grabs and clutches objects, shakes rattles, studies things.
- Loves cause-and-effect response toys like rattles, other noisy toys and wobble toys that bounce back.
- Likes dolls with realistic faces.
- Loves games involving movement (e.g. aeroplane, rocking chair, bouncing).
- Enjoys simple nursery-rhyme songs.
- Gets excited anticipating feedtime or bathtime.

15–19 WEEKS (4–5 MONTHS)
- A stormier period of more crying, crankiness, grumpy impatience, clinginess,

boredom, shyness with strangers, less hungry, unsettled sleep, and quieter — peaking at around 17 weeks.
- Laughs at things that amuse him.
- Improved head control.
- Attempting to roll over in one direction (front-to-back or back-to-front).
- Sits up propped with pillows.
- Reaches for things.
- Finds small things fascinating (e.g. the label tag on a soft toy).
- Develops hand–eye co-ordination by trying to grasp and reach for objects, will inspect objects briefly exploring their shapes and textures by putting them into drooling mouth, before dropping them.
- Recognises friends (e.g. other babies at Coffee Group).
- Head circumference dramatically increases.
- At four months of age, because their eyes are focusing better and they can see colours well, babies are more motivated to stay awake for longer during the daytime as the world becomes much more fascinating to them. It is common for their day-sleeps to reduce and their night-sleeps to lengthen.

20–22 WEEKS (5 MONTHS)
- A happier phase, particularly sunny at around 21 weeks.
- Holds head up well and smoothly moves it independently.
- Makes babble sounds starting with consonants.
- Stretches arms out to be picked up.
- Clearly looks forward to food/feeds and tells you when he's had enough.
- May sit well propped up with support (not normally properly sitting until their body has grown into their heavy head, at around six months of age).
- Probably rolling over from tummy to back — may attempt to crawl.
- Explores things with fingers and mouth, grabs things dangled in front, recognises things, shakes/bangs toys, studies details.
- Can get excited staring at faces — laughs when you pull a funny face.
- Displays clear facial expressions or pure emotion (too young to 'fake' their feelings). Such as delight and excitement for some things (e.g. music), and showing concern if situation is stressful (e.g. being within earshot of an argument).
- Likes looking in mirrors (particularly during tummy time).
- Likes naked time.
- Likes splashing water (e.g. bath-time, warm swimming pool).
- Likes peek-a-boo games, tickling games, nursery rhymes, children's songs, raspberries blown on their tummy, dancing in mum's arms to upbeat music (e.g. some Top-20 type songs).
- Likes bath toys, activity centres and picture books.
- Likes having hands held to 'help' to stand or walk. (Climate permitting, bare feet are developmentally beneficial.)
- Enjoys 'trampolining' (e.g. Jolly Jumper, Exersaucer).
- Good age for wrist and ankle bell rattles.

23–26 WEEKS (6–7 MONTHS)

- A stormier period of more crying, bad-tempered crankiness, whining, boredom, clinginess, shy wariness with strangers, less hungry, unsettled sleep, quieter, and wants cuddly toys — peaking at around 26 weeks.
- Incessant babbling and making long-vowel sounds.
- Perhaps sitting unsupported without prop cushions — probably hands forward.
- Can reach to grab a toy.
- Grasps, shakes and turns objects.
- Perhaps swapping objects from one hand to the other.
- Holding finger-food, feeding themselves finger-food.
- Tries to get from lying down to sitting up.
- Continues to attempt crawling.
- Sits unaided (unsupported) with a straight back somewhere between about 6 and 7 months — though may still topple over with a 'puff of wind'.
- May commando-crawl (wriggle-creep forward on their tummy).
- May roll over back-to-tummy and/or tummy-to-back.
- Stands when you hold his arms.
- May pull himself up on to furniture.
- Watches mouths to try to imitate new sounds by altering the shape of mouth.
- Likes noisy toys (e.g. saucepan lids).
- Loves 'I'm gonna getcha' games with your 'tickle finger'.

27–33 WEEKS (7–8 MONTHS)

- A couple of happier weeks, then a couple of clingy irritable weeks, then a few happier weeks, particularly sunny at around 31 weeks.
- Baby no longer seems like a fragile newborn, and can be appealingly engaging with development of more complex and responsive emotions.
- For brain development, baby becomes a 'new-experience junkie'.
- It's definitely time to ensure your home is safely toddler-proof (maybe get down on all fours to really see all the 'exciting' dangerous possibilities) and check out the baby shop for toddler-proofing safety gear.
- Sight is developing depth perception.
- Listens with great intensity, checks things out with solemn seriousness, uses focused, contented concentration on activities of interest.
- Makes lots of noise such as shouting, giggling, shrieking or yelling to get attention.
- Makes word sounds (but not actual first word).
- Echos sounds and mimics actions that others make.
- Perhaps understands words like 'no', 'Mummy's back', own name, and even waving 'bye-bye'.
- Has good control over upper body (arms, head and torso) but not legs yet.
- Stretches arms out to say 'Pick me up'; perhaps points to say 'I want that'.
- Has full head control and will turn head to locate a sound.
- May try to master the 'pincer' grip (thumb and first finger).
- Passes things between own hands, then into the mouth — not usually something in both hands at once.

- Plays with toes — toes probably going into the mouth.
- Points and gestures, perhaps starting to wave 'bye-bye', can be wary of strangers.
- Offers things to people, but can't make own hands let go at will.
- May sit up from lying down.
- May hold a bottle, or use sipper-cup with two hands, or self-feed finger-food, making a lot of mess.
- May pull self up to standing, cruise around furniture.
- Stands quite well with support (e.g. with someone holding their hands).
- Kneels, sways and rocks in crawling position (crawling forward in the next month or so).
- May start early crawling (e.g. backwards or bum-shuffling).
- Likes standing with hands held so can jump.
- Rolls balls, throws toys, pulls socks off, 'boogies' to music.
- Likes toys that they can make things happen through whacking or pressing a lever (e.g. jack-in-the-box and pop-up type toys).
- Likes peek-a-boo games to see things disappear and reappear.
- Likes swapping back and forth games, e.g. 'Mummy gives rattle to baby, now baby gives rattle to Mummy' — or rolling a ball back and forth.
- Enjoys movement like balancing games.
- Likes swimming.
- Likes looking at mirrors (starting to realise he is looking at himself).
- Likes 'own' cupboard or shelf in the kitchen.
- Likes throwing things onto floor from high-chair.
- Likes nesting/stacking cups, building blocks, large plastic trucks, photos, noisy toys, shape-sorter toys, and rhythmic music perhaps with musical instruments (e.g. wooden spoon and saucepan 'drum').
- Likes being outdoors with grass, clouds, butterflies, passers-by, children playing, swings, slides.
- May be time to introduce big crayons or pencils with paper.
- May be time to introduce a stand-and-push-along toy.
- Can really enjoy infant movement and music classes.
- Gets annoyed and irked (e.g. grizzling) at trying to make his body do what he wants it to do, e.g. trying to get to things. But don't feel you need to rescue him — he's just venting steam.
- A nice age to start bedtime storybook reading.

NOTE: Babies will focus their language skills development, on the language(s) they are routinely hearing from 6–10 months of age. So always 'bathe' them in your languages if you want them to be multi-lingual.

34–37 WEEKS (8–9 MONTHS)
- A stormier period with more crying, being bad-tempered, cranky, fretful, emotional, bored, clingy, tantrums, shyness around strangers, less hungry, unsettled sleep and nightmares, peaking at around 36 weeks.
- Babbling conversation beginning to sound more like words.
- Maybe starting to crawl.
- When you point to things, baby's eyes may follow.

- Can look for and find something.
- Points very deliberately at things.
- Sucks toes and may clap hands.
- Understands your voice has different tones.
- Waves hello and good-bye.
- Spends time day-dreaming.
- Likes filling up and emptying things (e.g. stacker cups in the bath, or plastic containers in the paddling pool).
- Likes toys on wheels that can be pushed or pulled.
- Enjoys cuddly toys.
- May interact with another child.
- Tries to imitate you (e.g. feeding himself, brushing his hair).
- At around eight months old, head circumference dramatically increases.

38–41 WEEKS (9–10 MONTHS)
- A happier phase, particularly sunny at around 39 weeks.
- Making pre-speech melodic double-syllable babble sounds, maybe says 'Ma-ma' or 'Da-da'.
- Understands names of some items, recognises lots of things, responds to name and other simple words, following simple instructions (e.g. 'Wave bye-bye').
- Starting to understand more of what you're saying, starting to know the meaning of simple explanations like 'All gone', instructions like 'Find Daddy', requests like 'Give Mummy the spoon please', or commands like 'Stop' (and may not agree).
- Seeing well to about three metres (10 feet).
- Becoming less mouthy (puts fewer things in mouth).
- Obviously trying to communicate with people, expressing more personality.
- Observes . . a lot.
- May create words for familiar objects, knows where objects belong, knows an object exists even when he can't see it.
- Shows jealousy when mother is with other children.
- Becomes more social (smiling, babbling, giggling).
- Acts 'extra' sweet, puts on acts, starts 'role-playing'.
- Can make choices (perhaps shows strong preferences).
- Develops a sense of humour.
- Probably using the 'pincer' grip (thumb and index finger) quite well now.
- Tries to feed self with a spoon or fork or sipper-cup.
- Demands to be picked up with arms outstretched.
- Claps hands.
- Pulls self up to standing, maybe cruising the furniture, perhaps standing unsupported.
- Probably crawling (usually starts 7–10 months), often starts with going backwards, or bottom shuffling.
- Once crawling, becomes a 'busy little bee'.
- Likes things to crawl over, under or into.
- Learning cause and effect (e.g. sharp yelling gets attention, dropping things makes you pick them up).

- Loves bright colours, likes toy cars, loves rolling, rattling and noisy toys.
- Likes knocking down brick towers, play-dough, mirrors and using crayons.
- Likes naming games with books, copy-cat imitation games, hide and seek, peek-a-boo games, and rhythmic rhymes like pat-a-cake.
- Likes noisy toys (e.g. bells, switches).
- Likes things that open and close (e.g. buttons, domes, clothes-pegs, containers).
- Likes paper for ripping, balls of all sizes, spinning tops, dolls, building blocks.
- Likes paddling pools, sandpits, swings.

42–46 WEEKS (10–11 MONTHS)

- A stormier period of more crying, being bad-tempered, cranky, fretful, emotional, bored, clingy, acts 'too' sweet, mischievous, tantrums, jealous, shy with strangers, less hungry, unsettled sleep, nightmares, quieter, day-dreams, reaches for cuddly toys, and is more 'babyish' — peaking at around 44 weeks.
- On the move exploring a lot and creating 'chaos' (e.g. pulling books off shelves, opening cupboards).
- May feed self.
- Imitates sounds or words or gestures.
- Starts to create more of own language for things.
- May talk (e.g. say 'all gone').
- Stands alone for a few seconds.
- May take first few steps.
- From sitting can swivel, turn and lean in almost any direction.
- Playtime consists of crawling to an object, examining it, discarding it, and crawling to the next item of interest.
- Masters using a sipper-cup.
- Grabs toys off other children.
- Responds to choices of interest (e.g. toy or book).
- Enjoys things that make them laugh (things that they think are funny).
- Particularly enjoys slides and swings.
- Enjoys music and movement (e.g. nursery-rhyme songs with actions).
- Enjoys pet stores and zoos.
- Changing nappies can become challenging with a squirming wriggler, try giving baby a distraction to play with. Another favourite tactic of mine was to sit on the floor and rest one of my legs over baby's tummy to hold them in place.
- Keeping toddler library books in the car can be of great interest to them while you're out doing all those 'boring' errands.

47–50 WEEKS (11–12 MONTHS)

- A happier phase, particularly sunny at around 49 weeks.
- Loves to be talked to, likes pointing-naming games.
- Says 'Yum', 'Yuck', and 'No, no'.
- Understands action directions such as 'Don't touch', 'Come here', 'Sit down', 'Come to Mummy' (remember toddlers learn much of their own language before they can speak it).
- Knows the meaning of familiar words (e.g. book, shoe, flower) — understands more than you think.

- Is adding gestures to familiar words (e.g. shakes head for 'Yes' and 'No').
- Points things out to you.
- First word(s) may be heard — their brain's speech centres are usually ready at around 12 months to say one or two words in the correct context.
- Vocalises gobbledy-gook 'sentences' which sound like questions or demands or objections (there are some scientists who believe that all toddlers actually speak the same 'primal' language — and the only reason they learn our language, is because we don't learn theirs).
- Can start to show inexplicable fears, can be easily startled or clingy.
- Has mastered the 'pincer grip'.
- Can use a spoon (messily), sticks things on fork prongs, blows steam off food.
- Stands alone unaided (maybe bends down to pick something up).
- Stands, cruising along furniture.
- Moves rapidly with fast crawling or crabwise bum-shuffling.
- Goes backwards down stairs (on tummy).
- Deliberately lets go of things while standing.
- May try to climb.
- Deliberately throws and drops things.
- Starts to 'get into' everything.
- Loves hide-and-seek games.
- May like pushing and pulling things (e.g. dolly pram, block trolley, toy shopping trundler).
- Likes copying games.
- Likes singing-movement games and children's songs.
- Likes helping out with household chores (e.g. dusting, holding peg basket).
- Likes dressing and grooming.
- Likes playing with different kinds of shapes and sizes.
- Likes wooden train sets, dolls with toy bottles, drums, pots and pans to beat.
- Likes sandpit, bucket and spade.
- Likes posting boxes, peg-posting, building bricks, balls.
- Likes boxes with lids to put things into and take them out again.
- Likes rolling toys, e.g. toy cars and trains.
- Likes ride-on to sit on and move about.
- Likes small plastic figures of people and animals.
- Likes imitating (e.g. toy phone).

51–56 WEEKS (12–13 MONTHS)
- A stormy period again, peaking at around 55 weeks.
- Understands very clearly first commands, 'Wave Bye-Bye', 'No', 'Stop'.
- Understands first words, e.g. cat, dog, bottle, more.
- Says 'No' while shaking head, nods for 'Yes' — clearly knows what he wants.
- Can use fingers efficiently.
- Cruises around furniture efficiently.
- May take first few steps — legs wide apart, arms outstretched.
- May attempt to 'help' with getting dressed.
- Feeds self with a spoon, drinks from a cup (messily), may begin to show right- or

left-hand dominance.

- Enjoys using a pushing toy (e.g. trolley) to support walking.
- Walks with support, e.g. holding hands.
- Uses thick pencil or crayon to make first scribbles.
- Can make a two-brick tower.
- Watches animals and socialises with people including children (e.g. playgroup, crèche, Playcentre).
- Explores, then comes back, then explores again.
- Likes throwing, dropping and banging objects.
- Likes singing and movement games (e.g. row your boat).
- Likes pulling things apart.
- Recognises self in a mirror.

13–14 MONTHS

- A happy, sunny phase again.
- Follows simple directions.
- Says small single words.
- Likes copying adults.
- Enjoys sandpits, mud and picking flowers.
- Enjoys containers in the bath.
- Enjoys stories, toy phone, toy broom, toy brush and shovel.
- Starts to walk somewhere between nine and eighteen months.

15 MONTHS

- A stormy period again — peaking at around 64 weeks.
- Due to nervous system development, baby is probably now aware of when he has urinated.

16 MONTHS

- A happy sunny phase.
- May join two words.
- Learning names of body parts.
- Starting to run stiffly, stoop, kick and perhaps climb.
- Scribbles with pencil or crayon.
- Likes to help with 'tidying up' toys.
- Likes to try to fit shapes into holes — e.g. shape-sorter toys.
- Enjoys dancing and singing to music.
- Likes push-along and ride-on toys.
- Likes basic jigsaws.
- Likes building blocks and stacking toys.
- Likes hammer and peg toys.
- Likes books.
- Likes dolls, prams, cars and trucks.
- Likes swings and water play.
- Good age for getting a little table and chair set.
- When baby begins walking, probably looks quite bow-legged — this is normal and resolves itself by about two years.

17 MONTHS

- A stormy period again, peaking at around 75 weeks.

18 MONTHS to 2 YEARS

- Vocabulary increasing almost daily: says 10 words at 18 months, and 20 words by 21 months, linking a couple of words by two years. (Words and language are the most important things a child will ever learn.)
- Will point to named body parts or animal pictures.
- Jumps (two feet off the ground) and likes running.
- Walks up stairs.
- Partially undresses self.
- Shows right- or left-handed preference.
- Enjoys same toys/activities as before, but also . . .
- Likes undoing lids and turning knobs (turning and screwing).
- Likes threading toys (e.g. large beads/cotton reels).
- Likes play-dough and painting.
- Stacks three blocks on top of each other.
- Likes musical instruments (e.g. drums, xylophones).
- Starts to like playhuts.
- Listens to simple stories.
- Toddler's sense of 'self' (personal identity) begins to emerge — begins to define experiences as being personally his.
- Toddler starts to become able to 'hold' urine in bladder, which can allow daytime toilet-training to begin — though many parents prefer to leave this until the toddler is older and more able to follow instructions. (Overnight bladder control may not occur until four years of age.)
- Nearing two years of age, an average girl has grown to about half her adult height.
- At a bit over two years of age, an average boy has grown to about half his adult height.

2–3 YEARS

- Knows own name well.
- Speaks little sentences with grammar starting to improve. (Some toddlers just suddenly start to talk with a speech explosion, others do it more gradually — dependent on what a chatterbox their personality is or isn't.)
- Toddler learns a staggering 10 new words a day.
- Starts to understand language tenses (e.g. past, present and future).
- Starts to understand numbers (can recite 1–10), knows colour names.
- Starts to understand that words can have different meanings depending on how they are put together with other words (the brain's built-in ability to learn multi-languages begins to wane by the age of four).
- Walks down stairs.
- Can stop when running, kicks a ball, throws a ball over-arm.
- Starts to learn how to ride a tricycle.
- Does quite well with dressing and undressing.

- Draws circles, maybe stick figures, may try copying a 'V' or 'O' with a pencil.
- Enjoys inventive, imaginative, pretend play (e.g. role-play).
- Likes to play around other children, but not necessarily with them.
- Enjoys same toys/activities as before, but also . . .
- Likes playhouses, tea-sets, dressing-up clothes.
- Likes hammering, sawing, pasting and playgrounds.
- Enjoys toddler dance and gymnastic classes.
- Understands gender identity (boys/girls) by around 2½ years.
- Bandy, bow-legs are being replaced with legs that have a knobbly set of knees.
- Nappy stays dry overnight (somewhere between 18 months and 8 years!).

For more information on infant development, great resources are available through the Brainwave Trust at www.brainwave.org.nz.

Appendix B: Baby weight conversion (pounds–kilos)

5lb	2.268kg	7lb	3.175kg	9lb	4.082kg
5lb 1oz	2.296kg	7lb 1oz	3.203kg	9lb 1oz	4.111kg
5lb 2oz	2.325kg	7lb 2oz	3.232kg	9lb 2oz	4.139kg
5lb 3oz	2.353kg	7lb 3oz	3.260kg	9lb 3oz	4.167kg
5lb 4oz	2.381kg	7lb 4oz	3.288kg	9lb 4oz	4.196kg
5lb 5oz	2.410kg	7lb 5oz	3.317kg	9lb 5oz	4.224kg
5lb 6oz	2.438kg	7lb 6oz	3.346kg	9lb 6oz	4.252kg
5lb 7oz	2.466kg	7lb 7oz	3.374kg	9lb 7oz	4.281kg
5lb 8oz	2.495kg	7lb 8oz	3.402kg	9lb 8oz	4.309kg
5lb 9oz	2.523kg	7lb 9oz	3.430kg	9lb 9oz	4.337kg
5lb 10oz	2.551kg	7lb 10oz	3.459kg	9lb 10oz	4.366kg
5lb 11oz	2.580kg	7lb 11oz	3.487kg	9lb 11oz	4.394kg
5lb 12oz	2.608kg	7lb 12oz	3.515kg	9lb 12oz	4.423kg
5lb 13oz	2.637kg	7lb 13oz	3.544kg	9lb 13oz	4.451kg
5lb 14oz	2.665kg	7lb 14oz	3.572kg	9lb 14oz	4.479kg
5lb 15oz	2.693kg	7lb 15oz	3.600kg	9lb 15oz	4.506kg
6lb	2.722kg	8lb	3.629kg	10lb	4.536kg
6lb 1oz	2.750kg	8lb 1oz	3.657kg	10lb 1oz	4.564kg
6lb 2oz	2.778kg	8lb 2oz	3.685kg	10lb 2oz	4.593kg
6lb 3oz	2.807kg	8lb 3oz	3.714kg	10lb 3oz	4.621kg
6lb 4oz	2.835kg	3lb 4oz	3.742kg	10lb 4oz	4.649kg
6lb 5oz	2.863kg	8lb 5oz	3.770kg	10lb 5oz	4.678kg
6lb 6oz	2.892kg	8lb 6oz	3.799kg	10lb 6oz	4.706kg
6lb 7oz	2.920kg	8lb 7oz	3.827kg	10lb 7oz	4.734kg
6lb 8oz	2.948kg	8lb 8oz	3.856kg	10lb 8oz	4.763kg
6lb 9oz	2.977kg	8lb 9oz	3.884kg	10lb 9oz	4.791kg
6lb 10oz	3.005kg	8lb 10oz	3.912kg	10lb 10oz	4.819kg
6lb 11oz	3.033kg	8lb 11oz	3.941kg	10lb 11oz	4.848kg
6lb 12oz	3.062kg	8lb 12oz	3.969kg	10lb 12oz	4.876kg
6lb 13oz	3.090kg	8lb 13oz	3.997kg	10lb 13oz	4.904kg
6lb 14oz	3.118kg	8lb 14oz	4.026kg	10lb 14oz	4.933kg
6lb 15oz	3.147kg	8lb 15oz	4.054kg	10lb 15oz	4.961kg

Appendix C: Maternity terms and abbreviations

ARM — artificial rupture of membranes (waters being intentionally broken)

BFI — baby-friendly initiative (hospital breastfeeding policy)

BP — blood pressure

BPM — heartbeats per minute

CCT — controlled cord traction (during third stage of active labour)

CDH — congenital dislocation of the hips (e.g. clicky hips)

CPD — cephalopelvic disproportion (fetus too big for mother's pelvis)

CTG — cardiotocogram (graph trace of fetal heart and uterine contraction)

D&C — dilatation and curettage (scraping of uterine wall under general anaesthetic)

D&V — diarrhoea and vomiting

DVT — deep venous thrombosis (blot clot obstructing vein, usually in calf)

EBL — estimated blood loss

EFM — electronic fetal monitoring

EPA — examination per abdomen (abdominal exam)

EPV — examination per vaginum (vaginal exam)

FHR — fetal heart rate

FSE — fetal scalp electrode

G — gravida (number of pregnancies)

GPH — gestational proteinurea and hypertension (protein in urine and high-blood pressure)

Grande Multigravida — pregnant woman who has had 4 or more previous pregnancies

IM — intramuscular (into muscle)

IV — intravenous (into a vein)

IUD/IUCD — intrauterine contraceptive device

IUGR — intrauterine growth retardation/restriction (fetus too small)

LBW — low birth weight

LFD — light for dates (baby is smaller than expected)

LMC — lead maternity carer

LMP — last menstrual period

MI — membranes intact

MSU — mid-stream urine (test)

Multigravida — pregnant woman who has previously had a pregnancy

Multipara (Multi p) — woman who has borne more than one live infant

NICU — neonatal intensive care unit

NVD — normal vaginal delivery

Obs — observations (vital signs such as blood pressure, temperature, pulse rate and respiration)

P — Parity (Live babies previously born by a woman)

PIH — pregnancy-induced hypertension (high blood-pressure)

PPH — post-partum haemorrhage (excessive bleeding after giving birth)

Primigravida — woman pregnant for the first time

Primipara (Primi p) — woman giving birth for the first time

PROM — prolonged rupture of membranes (more than 18 hours), or premature rupture of membranes (before 36 weeks)

RDS — respiratory distress syndrome

R/MW — registered midwife

RPOC — retained products of conception (increased risk of PPH and infection)

SCBU — special-care baby unit

SFD — small for dates (baby is smaller than expected)

S/MW — student midwife

SRM/SROM — spontaneous rupture of membranes

SVD — spontaneous vaginal delivery

TENS — transcutaneous electrical nerve stimulation

UTI — urinary tract infection

VE — vaginal examination

Appendix D:
Benefits of breastmilk

Below are some of the disputable (and controversial) potential benefits announced by researchers of an infant being required to digest nothing other than human breastmilk for at least the first six months (and ideally being breastfed until two years of age):

- Nil risk of infection from contaminated formula (rare in Westernised countries, but can occur).
- General improved infant morbidity (unwellness) and toddler health (fewer doctor's visits for infant illnesses such as coughs, vomiting and prolonged colds), due probably to breastmilk stimulation of immunoglobulin development in the immune system. Although most of a newborn's natural immunity is received during the last trimester in the womb — not primarily through the breastmilk — breastmilk certainly does continue to boost the baby's own defence mechanism, the immune system. For example, breastmilk is rich in lymphocytes (such as T-cells and B-cells that circulate antibodies); phagocytic macrophages (that engulf disease causing parasites); neutrophils (that ingest and kill bacteria); and lysosomes (that rid the body of potentially harmful foreign substances).
- 20–40 percent reduction in infant gastrointestinal infection medical problems, because the breastfed baby receives within the breastmilk immunoglobulins (antibodies), and bifiduslactobacilli (beneficial microflora bacteria) from the surface of the mother's nipples, which colonise the baby's intestines to protect the baby from the likes of gastroenteritis. (Gastroenteritis is the number-one reason for under-one-year-olds to visit a hospital A&E department.)
- 50–80 percent reduction in infant diarrhoea.
- 25–75 percent reduction in infant otitis media (middle ear infection).
- 50–70 percent reduction in childhood asthma and wheezing.
- 20–60 percent reduction in childhood atopy (as a result of an inherited predisposition to certain allergic reactions) e.g. eczema, asthma, food allergies and respiratory allergies. Breastfeeding delays the onset of symptoms, and when they first appear they're milder.
- 15–50 percent reduction in childhood acute and general respiratory diseases and respiratory-tract infections (e.g. haemophilus influenza pneumonia, pneumococcal

disease, respiratory syncytical virus and serious childhood bronchiolitis).

- 35–40 percent reduction in infant urinary-tract infections.
- 40 percent reduction in childhood coeliac disease (allergic disease where intestine lining is sensitive to gluten, preventing the small intestine from digesting fat).
- Reduction into adulthood of chronic inflammatory bowel diseases, such as Crohn's disease (inflammation and blocking of lower part of the small intestine), and ulcerative colitis (severe colon pain with diarrhoea).
- Reduction of neurological and cognitive side effects from environmental contaminants (e.g. dioxins).
- 5–8 percent higher IQ: educational, vocabulary and cognitive (mental processes) neuro-development of intelligence from childhood through to adulthood; including social development, movement co-ordination, reading comprehension, mathematical ability and scholastic academic achievement.
- 30–70 percent reduction in childhood obesity.
- 5–30 percent reduction of childhood type-I diabetes (when pancreatic insulin-producing beta cells are damaged and no longer produce insulin, with patient requiring regular insulin injections); and type-II diabetes (insulin resistance requiring oral medications to maintain correct insulin levels).
- Adulthood improvement of lipid (fat) metabolism, with reduced cholesterol from teenage years, lowering risk of cardiovascular disease.
- Improvement in childhood thymus-gland production of the immune system's lymphocyte T-cells.
- 20–30 percent reduction of childhood cancers such as leukaemia (blood leucocyte disorder) and lymphomas (lymphoid tissue tumours).
- Theoretically reduced chances of cot-death SIDS (sudden infant death syndrome).
- Human milk also carries biochemical hormonal messages (e.g. to stimulate red blood-cell production), and gonadal hormones.
- Research is also seeing correlations between breastfeeding and improved rates in auto-immune thyroid disease, cryptorchidism (undescended testicle), gastro-oesophageal reflux, pyloric stenosis (blockage between stomach and duodenum small intestine); low bone density; adult breast cancer; Hodgkin's disease (swollen lymph glands, attacking liver and spleen); nursing caries (baby-teeth decay); childhood haemophilus influenzae meningitis; JRA (juvenile rheumatoid arthritis); tonsillitis; transplant outcomes; and vaccine responses.
- 50 percent of breastmilk iron is absorbed, in comparison to only 10 percent of formula. This is due to a protein in breastmilk called lactoferrin, which binds iron and transports it across the intestinal tissue into the body, also then making the iron unavailable for bacterial consumption. (But by six months of age, infants need solids for increased iron requirements.)

Appendix E:
Maternal medications
during breastfeeding

To assist you as a lactating mother to be able to make judgements with some confidence as to what is OK for you to consume, below is a list of the more commonly prescribed and over-the-counter medications. (Some general information on pharmaceutical medicines can be found at www.medsafe.govt.nz.)

Disclaimer: This book is NOT confirming that use of any medication is 100 percent safe. It is ultimately the reader's responsibility to ensure they agree with this information before following it. The author can accept no liable responsibility.

General pain relief
- Aspro (aspirin)
- Disprin (aspirin)
- Panadeine (paracetamol and codeine phosphate)
- Panadol (paracetamol)

Summary:
Due to thinning of the blood, avoid aspirin while recovering from childbirth. Avoid codeine with an under-two-week-old, and be wary of its constipative side effect on mothers. Paracetamol is fine.

Sore throat
- Cepacol (cetylphyridinium chloride)
- Difflam (benzydamine hydrochloride and sometimes chlorhexidine gluconate; or cetylphyridinium chloride; or pholcodine)
- Lemsip Lozenges (cetylpyridinium chloride)
- Strepsils (amylmetacresol and sometimes lignocaine hydrochloride; or fluriprofen; or dextromethorphan hydrobromide)

Summary:
Safe.

Indigestion and heartburn
- All antacid lozenges
- Gavilast (ranitidine as hydrochloride)
- Gaviscon (sodium alginate and sodium bicarbonate and calcium carbonate)
- Mylanta Tablets (simethicone)
- Zantac (ranitidine as hydrochloride)

Summary:
Safe — used in paediatrics without concern.

Cough syrups
- Benedryl (various combinations of bromhexine hydrochloride, guaiphenesin, destromethorphan hydrobromide, diphenhydramine hydrochloride, ammonium chloride and sodium citrate)
- Dimetapp Liquid (brompheniramine maleate, phenylephrine hydrocholoride and perhaps dextromethorphan hydrobromide)
- Robitussin (guaiphenesin and sometimes bromhexine hydrochloride)

Summary:
Generally safe as also used in paediatric doses, but avoid cough syrups with sedative effects. (Guaiphenesin is an expectorant which is not necessarily all that effective. Its poor efficiency may not justify it being used in breastfeeding mothers.)

Antihistamines
- Beconase Hayfever (beclomethasone dipropionate BP)
- Claramax (desloratedine)
- Claratyne (loratadine)
- Demazin (chlorpheniramine maleate and phenylephrine hydrochloride)
- Flixonase Allergy (fluticasone propionate)
- Loratabs (loratadine)
- Telfast (fexofenadine hydrochloride)
- Zyrtec (cetirizine)

Summary:
The best antihistamines to use during lactation are Claratyne and Zyrtec (Beconase Hayfever and Flixonase Allergy are steroids, not antihistamines).

Decongestants
- Codral Cold and Flu (paracetamol, pseudoephedrine hydrochloride and codeine phosphate)
- Codral Day and Night (paracetamol, pseudoephedrine hydrocloride, destromethorphan hydrobromide and chlorpheniramine maleate)
- Nurofen Cold and Flu (ibuprophen and pseudoephedrine hydrochloride)
- Sinutab Allergy (paracetamol, pseudoephedrine hydrochloride and chlorpheniramine maleate)
- Sudafed Daytime (paracetamol and pseudoephedrine hydrochloride)

- Sudafed Daytime/Nightime (paracetamol, pseudoephedrine hydrochloride and triprolidine hydrochloride)

Summary:
Low levels of pseudoephedrine do enter the milk, and in paediatric use it can cause irritability in infants. Avoid decongestants that include a sedative.

Anti-inflammatories
- Cataflam (diclofenac)
- Nurofen Migraine (ibuprofen lysine)
- Nurofen (ibuprofen)
- Nurofen Plus (ibuprofen and codeine)
- Panafen (ibuprofen)
- Sonaflam (naproxen sodium)
- Voltaren (diclofenac potassium)

Summary:
Some anti-inflammatory medication has the potential to interfere with blood platelet clotting. Choose a shorter-acting lower-dose anti-inflammatory instead of a long-acting sustained-release variety. Studies have been done on short-acting ibuprofen that assures its safety during lactation.

Period pain medications
- Apo-Mefenamic (mefenamic acid)
- Naprogesic (naproxen sodium)
- Ponstan (mefenamic acid)

Summary:
These are anti-inflammatories — so the best choice instead is ibuprofen (e.g. Nurofen or Panofen).

Antibiotics
- Augmentin (amoxicillin and clavulanate)

Summary:
This is the preferred first choice for mastitis or wound infections, and controlled studies have demonstrated no adverse effects with infants — it is also commonly prescribed for infants.

- Flagyl (metronidazole) — oral or IV

Summary:
This is a strong antibiotic used in addition to penicillin, and is the preferred first choice for serious postnatal hospitalised infection such as puerperal sepsis uterine infection, or breast abscess — it is also prescribed to infants for the likes of Giardia.

- E-Mysin or ERA (erythromycin)

Summary:
Used if allergic to penicillin.

Antidepressants
- Aropax (paroxetine)

Summary:
This is the first-preferred post-natal depression SSRI antidepressant. It has been well studied for use by lactating mothers, with the levels in the infant bloodstream almost undetectable.

Sundry medications
- For **Acute Mucous Cough**: Broncelix (choline theophyllinate and guaiphenesin)

Summary:
Theophyllinate is a bronchodilator, which can cause nausea, vomiting or irritability when given to babies. Better to use Ventolin.

- For **Migraine** and **Nausea**: Paramax (paracetamol, metclopramide HCL BP equivalent to metoclopramide HCL anhydrous)

Summary:
May affect baby's alertness. Not recommended.

- For **Diarrhoea**: Imodium (loperamide hydrochloride, and sometimes simethicone)

Summary:
Minimal absorption through breastmilk, but generally not recommended in young children.

- For **Vaginal Thrush**: Diflucan oral capsule (fluconazole)

Summary:
Creams and suppositories are all safe. Oral capsule is safe, and is used in paediatrics — the breastfed dose is one percent of the maternal dose, which works out to only five percent of the normal paediatric dose.

- For **Travel Sickness**: Sea-Legs (meclozine hydrochloride BP)

Summary:
This is an antihistamine — so the best choice instead is cetirizine or loratidine (e.g. Claratyne, Loratab or Zyrtec).

Index